CLASSICAL AND CONTEMPORARY

METAPHYSICS

CLASSICAL AND CONTEMPORARY

METAPHYSICS

A SOURCE BOOK

Richard T. De George

University of Kansas

HOLT, RINEHART AND WINSTON / NEW YORK

PREFACE

There is no doubt in my mind that the best way to present the subject matter of metaphysics to the student as well as to the general reader is through the medium of original writings in the field. The problems dealt with are so basic that they deserve to be encountered in the words of original thinkers rather than in distillations or secondhand reports, and some of the answers given are so controversial that the only fair way to judge their validity is by examining them for oneself. The purpose of this volume is to make some of the outstanding material in this subject readily available.

I have drawn the contents of this book from a great variety of sources. The selections represent many points of view and are grouped around the topics with which they deal. The wealth of material from which to choose was so enormous that I have made numerous changes in the selections of readings in order to arrive at the present balance and scope. The Part headings indicate the nature of the articles grouped together. Each article is a clear statement of a position and is intelligible in itself, even when it has been excerpted from a book. The topics covered are the main topics being discussed in metaphysics today. The emphasis of the book is on contemporary or near-contemporary writings. Classical texts—both ancient and modern—have been included in each Part to give perspective to the contemporary discussions. In selecting classical texts, however, consideration was taken of contemporary statements of the same or of a very similar position, and where there was a choice, preference was given to the latter.

Since the purpose of this book is to let the authors speak for themselves, I have tinkered as little as possible with internal editing of the articles, and wherever feasible I have presented them *in toto*. As a result, the selections are sufficiently complete to allow the reader to enter into the spirit of the author's thought as well as to grasp the essential statements of each position.

Although the selections in each Part are interrelated, there is, of course, no necessity for a teacher to follow the order presented in the book. Many of the articles could have been included in any one of several of the Parts. The selection from Berkeley, for instance, might have been as appropriate to the Part on substance, or to that on God, as to the Part on idealism. In such cases the author is represented in only one of the Parts. There seemed to be little justification either for repetition or for trying to divide a text into smaller pieces for inclusion in several sections.

Each Part is preceded by an introduction, which serves mainly to locate the authors of that Part via biographical data and a concise statement of their positions. The introductions also interrelate the readings and place them briefly in the perspective of the basic problem with which they deal. Selected bibliographies are supplied at the end of each Part for additional reading and as supplementary suggestions for more advanced students.

I am indebted to many people—especially to my colleagues and students at the University of Kansas—for their many suggestions as to the choice of articles. I wish to express my gratitude to the authors who have made this volume possible and to the publishers, noted throughout the text, who have granted me permission to reproduce their material. I am grateful also to all those at the University of Kansas who have contributed to the production of this book. To my wife, who has helped in many ways, goes my sincerest appreciation.

R.D.G.

Lawrence, Kansas
February, 1962

TABLE OF CONTENTS

PART V
THE WORLD, EMERGENCE, AND GOD

CLASSICAL AND CONTEMPORARY

METAPHYSICS

PART I

THE NATURE AND FUNCTION

OF METAPHYSICS

INTRODUCTION

The term "metaphysics" is replete with connotations that have accrued to it over the past two thousand years. Its meaning has varied somewhat from century to century and from philosopher to philosopher. It has both been held in the highest esteem and been submitted to ridicule within the philosophical community as well as outside of it. The answer to the question "What is metaphysics?" is thus, historically speaking, by no means a simple one.

The term was first used (about 70 B.C.) by Andronicus of Rhodes in editing Aristotle's works. The word merely designated those treatises of Aristotle which came after (*meta*) a series of other treatises called the *Physics* (*physica*). In time the use of the word was extended to designate any philosophical work treating the same material as Aristotle did in these treatises. To the popular mind the subject matter of metaphysics was quite abstract and abtruse, and thus another notion of metaphysics arose: the prefix *meta* lost its original meaning and the term "metaphysics" was employed to refer to the study of those things—for example, God, the soul—which are "beyond" physics.

In the eighteenth century, a follower of Leibniz, Christian Wolff (1679–1754), a rationalist systematizer and an extremely influential pedagogue, divided the subject matter of speculative philosophy into general metaphysics (or ontology) —a transcendental science of all Being, real or possible—and special metaphysics, composed of theodicy (or natural theology), which deals with man's natural knowledge of God; cosmology (or the philosophy of nature), which deals with inanimate matter; and rational psychology, which deals with animate beings, especially man insofar as he is rational. This division of metaphysics, though once widely accepted and still referred to, is no longer generally followed. Nowadays even the distinction between metaphysics and ontology is not usually sharply drawn in Anglo-American philosophy, although it continues to be employed on the continent. There ontology refers to an analysis of structure, whereas metaphysics deals with existential propositions, that is, with propositions concerning the existence of what is.

Since metaphysics in its widest sense is concerned with the nature and structure of all reality, its concerns are both basic and general; thus historically it has been used by systematic philosophers as a basis for such other philosophical disciplines as ethics, esthetics, the philosophy of history, and philosophical anthropology. Yet although metaphysics is taken by some to be the heart of philosophy, it has not been without its critics. There have been many attacks on metaphysics —most recently by the logical positivists (see Part V)—for its being "other-worldly," imaginative unfounded speculation, or utterly meaningless. To some extent the attacks have been justified, and to that extent they have happily resulted in clarification of some of the issues involved and have served as periodic checks on unbridled speculation. The basic problems, however, though somewhat reformulated and reconceived, still remain to challenge the philosophers bold enough to face them.

For Aristotle (384–322 B.C.), a pupil of Plato and the teacher of Alexander the Great, and one of the most influential philosophers of all time, metaphysics is the "science which studies Being *qua* Being, and the properties inherent in it in virtue of its own nature." It arises from wonder and is a search for the first principles and ultimate causes of everything which is; and that which is, primarily, is substance. The Aristotelian view of metaphysics continues to exert an influence today (see Gilson, Part III).

With the rationalist approach to philosophy culminating in the systems of Leibniz (see Part V) and Wolff, metaphysics lost its empirical origin. It was concerned not only with what is but with all *possible* reality which was uncovered by "pure reason," proceeding deductively from certain clear and distinct ideas. This was the tradition in which Immanuel Kant (1724–1804) was educated. He was roused from his dogmatic slumbers by reading David Hume, however, and in his *Critique of Pure Reason* (1781) he both launched on rationalist metaphysics an attack from which it never recovered and outlined what seemed to him to be the limits of our possible experience and knowledge. His notion of metaphysics remains tinged with rationalism, however; he holds that since metaphysical knowledge lies beyond experience it cannot have an empirical source, and so its principles must be *a priori*. He acknowledges that the attempt to attain knoweldge of the World, the soul, and God is a natural disposition of human reason. But such knowledge is unattainable. Consequently, metaphysics cannot deal with these topics, and if it is to be established as a valid science, it must consist only of a critique of reason so that it will uncover the whole stock of *a priori* concepts contained therein. Metaphysics for Kant thus becomes not an analysis of being or reality as such, but rather an analysis of pure reason. He restates these views clearly in his *Prolegomena to Any Future Metaphysics* (1783), which he intended as an introduction to the critical standpoint for teachers of philosophy. In the hands of the nineteenth-century idealists who followed him, however, the dichotomy between an analysis of reality as such and an analysis of pure reason was overcome by the claim that the real is rational and the rational, real (see Part II).

In the twentieth century, Alfred North Whitehead (1861–1947) is probably the outstanding Anglo-Saxon philosopher. He was educated at Cambridge and taught mathematics there and at London University until 1924. Together with Bertrand Russell he wrote the monumental work in logic *Principia Mathematica* (1910). From 1924 until 1937, he was Professor of Philosophy at Harvard, and from this period issued his original philosophical synthesis, usually referred to as the philosophy of organism. His *Science and the Modern World* (1925), *Process and Reality: An Essay in Cosmology* (1929), and *Adventures of Ideas* (1933) are the best expressions of his position. For Whitehead, "speculative philosophy is the endeavor to frame a coherent, logical, necessary system of general ideas in terms of which every element of an experience can be interpreted." He has thus both an empirical and a rational side: his starting point is immediate experience, which thought is to elucidate. He views metaphysical categories as tentative formulations of the ultimate generalities and claims that the task of philosophy is to elaborate these categoreal schemes. Each system, then, is but a partial enunciation of truths about the universe, and each fails insofar as it is unable to account for some element of experience. "These general truths, involved in the meaning of every particular notion respecting the actions of things, are the subject matter for speculative philosophy."

In *The Nature of Metaphysics* (1957) H. P. Grice, Fellow of St. John's College, Oxford; D. F. Pears, Fellow of Corpus Christi College, Oxford; and P. F. Strawson, Fellow of University College, Oxford, attempt to present a neutral and dispassionate account of what metaphysics is. After looking briefly at a number of historical positions, they discuss in what sense metaphysical theories arise in response to certain difficulties or quandaries, and they conclude that "the enterprise of metaphysics emerges as, above all, an attempt to re-order or to reorganize the set of ideas with which we think about the world."

Frederick C. Copleston, S. J. (1907–   ), Professor of Metaphysics at Gregorian University, Rome, Professor of History of Philosophy at Heythrop College, Oxford, and author of a number of works including a six-volume history of philosophy, is considered by some to be the leading Catholic philosopher in the Anglo-Saxon world. In his article "The Function of Metaphysics" (1953), he points out that the origin of philosophy is the desire to understand the world, he argues for the necessity of clarity, and he emphasizes the importance of language. He defends the view that one of the functions of speculative metaphysics is to state and make explicit the implications of a prereflective awareness.

ARISTOTLE

THE METAPHYSICS: BOOK IV*

I. There is a science which studies Being *qua* Being, and the properties inherent in it in virtue of its own nature. This science is not the same as any of the so-called particular sciences, for none of the others contemplates Being generally *qua* Being; they divide off some portion of it and study the attribute of this portion, as do for example the mathematical sciences. But since it is for the first principles and the most ultimate causes that we are searching, clearly they must belong to something in virtue of its own nature. Hence if these principles were investigated by those also who investigated the elements of existing things, the elements must be elements of Being not incidentally, but *qua* Being. Therefore it is of Being *qua* Being that we too must grasp the first causes.

II. The term "being" is used in various senses, but with reference to one central idea and one definite characteristic, and not as merely a common epithet. Thus as the term "healthy" always relates to health (either as preserving it or as producing it or as indicating it or as receptive of it), and as "medical" relates to the art of medicine (either as possessing it or as naturally adapted for it or as being a function of medicine)—and we shall find other terms used similarly to these—so "being" is used in various senses, but always with reference to one principle. For some things are said to "be" because they are substances; others because they are modifications of substance; others because they are a process towards substance, or destructions or privations or qualities of substance, or productive or generative of substance or of terms relating to substance, or negations of certain

of these terms or of substance. (Hence we even say that not-being *is* not-being.) And so, just as there is one science of all healthy things, so it is true of everything else. For it is not only in the case of terms which express one common notion that the investigation belongs to one science, but also in the case of terms which relate to one particular characteristic; for the latter too, in a sense, express one common notion. Clearly then the study of things, which *are, qua* being, also belongs to one science. Now in every case knowledge is principally concerned with that which is primary, *i.e.* that upon which all other things depend, and from which they get their names. If, then, substance is this primary thing, it is of substances that the philosopher must grasp the first principles and causes.

Now of every single class of things, as there is one perception, so there is one science: *e.g.,* grammar, which is one science, studies all articulate sounds. Hence the study of all the species of Being *qua* Being belongs to a science which is generically one, and the study of the several species of Being belongs to the specific parts of that science.

Now if Being and Unity are the same, *i.e.* a single nature, in the sense that they are associated as principle and cause are, and not as being denoted by the same definition (although it makes no difference but rather helps our argument if we understand them in the same sense), since "one man" and "man" and "existent man" and "man" are the same thing, *i.e.* the duplication in the statement "he is a man and an *existent* man" gives no fresh meaning (clearly the concepts of humanity and existence are not dissociated in respect of either coming to be or ceasing to be), and similarly in the case of the term "one," so that obviously the additional term in these phrases has the same significance,

* Reprinted by permission of the publishers and The Loeb Classical Library, translated by Hugh Tredennick, ARISTOTLE: *The Metaphysics*, Cambridge, Mass.: Harvard University Press.

and Unity is nothing distinct from Being; and further if the substance of each thing is one in no accidental sense, and similarly is of its very nature something which *is*— then there are just as many species of Being as of Unity. And to study the essence of these species (I mean, *e.g.,* the study of Same and Other and all the other similar concepts —roughly speaking all the "contraries" are reducible to this first principle; but we may consider that they have been sufficiently studied in the "Selection of Contraries"[1]) is the province of a science which is generically one.

And there are just as many divisions of philosophy as there are kinds of substance; so that there must be among them a First Philosophy and one which follows upon it. For Being and Unity at once entail genera, and so the sciences will correspond to these genera. The term "philosopher" is like the term "mathematician" in its uses; for mathematics too has divisions—there is a primary and a secondary science, and others successively, in the realm of mathematics.

Now since it is the province of one science to study opposites, and the opposite of unity is plurality, and it is the province of one science to study the negation and privation of Unity, because in both cases we are studying Unity, to which the negation (or privation) refers, stated either in the simple form that Unity is not present, or in the form that it is not present in a particular class; in the latter case Unity is modified by the differentia, apart from the content of the negation (for the negation of Unity is its absence); but in privation there is a substrate of which the privation is predicated.—The opposite of Unity, then, is Plurality; and so the opposites of the above-mentioned concepts— Otherness, Dissimilarity, Inequality and everything else which is derived from these or from Plurality or Unity—fall under the cognizance of the aforesaid science. And one of them is Oppositeness; for this is a form of Difference, and Difference is a form of Otherness. Hence since the term "one" is used in various senses, so too will these terms be used; yet it pertains to one science to take cognizance of them all. For terms fall under different sciences, not if they are used in various senses, but if their definitions are neither identical nor referable to a common notion. And since everything is referred to that which is primary, *e.g.* all things which are called "one" are referred to the primary "One," we must admit that this is also true of Identity and Otherness and the Contraries. Thus we must first distinguish all the senses in which each term is used, and then attribute them to the primary in the case of each predicate, and see how they are related to it; for some will derive their name from possessing and others from producing it, and others for similar reasons.

Thus clearly it pertains to one science to give an account both of these concepts and of substance (this was one of the questions raised in the "Difficulties"[2]), and it is the function of the philosopher to be able to study all subjects. If this is not so, who is it who will investigate whether "Socrates" and "Socrates seated" are the same thing; or whether one thing has one contrary, or what the contrary is, or how many meanings it has?[3] and similarly with all other such questions. Thus since these are the essential modifications of Unity *qua* Unity and of Being *qua* Being, and not *qua* numbers or lines or fire, clearly it pertains to that science[4] to discover both the essence and the attributes of these concepts. And those who investigate them err, not in being unphilosophical, but because the substance, of which they have no real knowledge, is prior. For just as number *qua* number has its peculiar modifications, *e.g.* oddness and evenness, commensurability and equality, excess and defect, and these things are inherent in numbers both considered independently and in relation to other numbers; and as similarly other peculiar modifications are inherent in the solid and the immovable and the moving and the weight-

---

[1] It is uncertain to what treatise Aristotle refers; in any case it is not extant.

[2] See III. i. 8 10, ii. 18, 19.
[3] Cf. X. iv.
[4] *i.e.,* Philosophy or Metaphysics.

less and that which has weight; so Being *qua* Being has certain peculiar modifications, and it is about these that it is the philosopher's function to discover the truth. And here is evidence of this fact. Dialecticians and sophists wear the same appearance as the philosopher, for sophistry is Wisdom in appearance only, and dialecticians discuss all subjects, and Being is a subject common to them all; but clearly they discuss these concepts because they appertain to philosophy. For sophistry and dialectic are concerned with the same class of subjects as philosophy, but philosophy differs from the former in the nature of its capability and from the latter in its outlook on life. Dialectic treats as an exercise what philosophy tries to understand, and sophistry seems to be philosophy, but is not.

Further, the second column of contraries is privative, and everything is reducible to Being and Not-being, and Unity and Plurality; *e.g.* Rest falls under Unity and Motion under Plurality. And nearly everyone agrees that substance and existing things are composed of contraries; at any rate all speak of the first principles as contraries—some as Odd and Even,[5] some as Hot and Cold,[6] some as Limit and Unlimited,[7] some as Love and Strife.[8] And it is apparent that all other things also are reducible to Unity and Plurality (we may assume this reduction); and the principles adduced by other thinkers fall entirely under these as genera. It is clear, then, from these considerations also, that it pertains to a single science to study Being *qua* Being; for all things are either contraries or derived from contraries, and the first principles of the contraries are Unity and Plurality. And these belong to one science, whether they have reference to one common notion or not. Probably the truth is that they have not; but nevertheless even if the term "one" is used in various senses, the others will be related to the primary sense (and similarly with the contraries)—even if

---

[5] The Pythagoreans.
[6] Perhaps Parmenides.
[7] The Platonists.
[8] Empedocles.

Being or Unity is not a universal and the same in all cases, or is not separable from particulars (as it presumably is not; the unity is in some cases one of reference and in others one of succession). For this very reason it is not the function of the geometrician to inquire what is Contrariety or Completeness or Being or Unity or Identity or Otherness, but to proceed from the assumption of them.

Clearly, then, it pertains to one science to study Being *qua* Being, and the attributes inherent in it *qua* Being; and the same science investigates, besides the concepts mentioned above, Priority and Posteriority, Genus and Species, Whole and Part, and all other such concepts.

III. We must pronounce whether it pertains to the same science to study both the so-called axioms in mathematics and substance, or to different sciences. It is obvious that the investigation of these axioms too pertains to one science, namely the science of the philosopher; for they apply to all existing things, and not to a particular class separate and distinct from the rest. Moreover all thinkers employ them—because they are axioms of Being *qua* Being, and every genus possesses Being—but employ them only in so far as their purposes require; *i.e.* so far as the genus extends about which they are carrying out their proofs. Hence since these axioms apply to all things *qua* Being (for this is what is common to them), it is the function of him who studies Being *qua* Being to investigate them as well. For this reason no one who is pursuing a particular inquiry—neither a geometrician nor an arithmetician—attempts to state whether they are true or false; but some of the physicists did so, quite naturally; for they alone professed to investigate nature as a whole, and Being. But inasmuch as there is a more ultimate type of thinker than the natural philosopher (for nature is only a genus of Being), the investigation of these axioms too will belong to the universal thinker who studies the primary reality. Natural philosophy is a kind of Wisdom, but not the primary kind. As for the attempts of some of those who discuss how the truth should be received, they are due to lack of training in logic; for they should understand these things before they approach their task, and not investigate while they are still learning. Clearly then it is the function of the philosopher, *i.e.* the student of the whole of reality in its essential nature, to investigate also the principles of syllogistic reasoning. And it is proper for him who best understands each class of subject to be able to state the most certain principles of that subject; so that he who understands the modes of Being *qua* Being should be able to state the most certain principles of all things. Now this person is the philosopher, and the most certain principle of all is that about which one cannot be mistaken; for such a principle must be both the most familiar (for it is about the unfamiliar that errors are always made), and not based on hypothesis. For the principle which the student of any form of Being must grasp is no hypothesis; and that which a man must know if he knows anything he must bring with him to his task.

Clearly, then, it is a principle of this kind that is the most certain of all principles. Let us next state *what* this principle is. "It is im-

possible for the same attribute at once to belong and not to belong to the same thing and in the same relation"; and we must add any further qualifications that may be necessary to meet logical objections. This is the most certain of all principles, since it possesses the required definition; for it is impossible for anyone to suppose that the same thing is and is not, as some imagine that Heraclitus says [9]—for what a man says does not necessarily represent what he believes. And if it is impossible for contrary attributes to belong at the same time to the same subject (the usual qualifications must be added to this premise also), and an opinion which contradicts another is contrary to it, then clearly it is impossible for the same man to suppose at the same time that the same thing is and is not; for the man who made this error would entertain two contrary opinions at the same time. Hence all men who are demonstrating anything refer back to this as an ultimate belief; for it is by nature the starting point of all the other axioms as well.

---

[9] For examples of Heraclitus' paradoxes cf. fragments 36, 57, 59 (Bywater); and for their meaning see Burnet, *Early Greek Philosophy*, §80.

IMMANUEL KANT

PREAMBLE ON THE PECULIARITIES OF ALL METAPHYSICAL KNOWLEDGE*

1. Of the Sources of Metaphysics

If it becomes desirable to organize any knowledge as science, it will be necessary first to determine accurately those peculiar features which no other science has in common with it, constituting its peculiarity; otherwise the boundaries of all sciences become confused, and none of them can be treated thoroughly according to its nature.

The peculiar characteristic of a science may consist of a simple difference of object, or of the sources of knowledge, or of the kind of knowledge, or perhaps of all three conjointly. On these, therefore, depends the idea of a possible science and its territory.

First, as concerns the sources of meta-

* From Immanuel Kant: *Prolegomena to any Future Metaphysics*, translated by Lewis White Beck. New York, 1951 ("The Library of Liberal Arts" No. 27). Reprinted by permission of the publishers, The Bobbs-Merrill Company.

physical knowledge, its very concept implies that they cannot be empirical. Its principles (including not only its maxims but its basic notions) must never be derived from experience. It must not be physical but metaphysical knowledge, namely, knowledge lying beyond experience. It can therefore have for its basis neither external experience, which is the source of physics proper, nor internal, which is the basis of empirical psychology. It is therefore *a priori* knowledge, coming from pure understanding and pure reason.

But so far metaphysics would not be distinguishable from pure mathematics; it must therefore be called *pure philosophical* knowledge; and for the meaning of this term I refer to the *Critique of the Pure Reason,*[1] where the distinction between these two employments of reason is sufficiently explained. So far concerning the sources of metaphysical knowldege.

---

[1] *Critique of Pure Reason,* "Methodology," Ch. I, Sec. 2.

2. Concerning the Kind of Knowledge Which Can Alone Be Called Metaphysical

a. On the distinction between analytical and synthetical judgments in general. The peculiarity of its sources demands that metaphysical knowledge must consist of nothing but *a priori* judgments. But whatever be their origin or their logical form, there is a distinction in judgments, as to their content, according to which they are either merely *explicative,* adding nothing to the content of knowledge, or *expansive,* increasing the given knowledge. The former may be called *analytical,* the latter *synthetical,* judgments.

Analytical judgments express nothing in the predicate but what has been already actually thought in the concept of the subject, though not so distinctly or with the same (full) consciousness. When I say: "All bodies are extended," I have not amplified in the least my concept of body, but have only analyzed it, as extension was really thought to belong to that concept before the judgment was made, though it was not expressed. This judgment is therefore analytical. On the contrary, this judgment, "All bodies have weight," contains in its predicate something not actually thought in the universal concept of body; it amplifies my knowledge by adding something to my concept, and must therefore be called synthetical.

b. The common principle of all analytical judgments is the law of contradiction.

All analytical judgments depend wholly on the law of contradiction, and are in their nature *a priori* cognitions, whether the concepts that supply them with matter be empirical or not. For the predicate of an affirmative analytical judgment is already contained in the concept of the subject, of which it cannot be denied without contradiction. In the same way its opposite is necessarily denied of the subject in an analytical, but negative, judgment, by the same law of contradiction. Such is the nature of the judgments: "All bodies are extended," and "No bodies are unextended (that is, simple)."

For this very reason all analytical judgments are *a priori* even when the concepts are empirical, as, for example, "Gold is a yellow metal"; for to know this I require no experience beyond my concept of gold as a yellow metal. It is, in fact, the very concept, and I need only analyze it without looking beyond it.

c. Synthetical judgments require a different principle from the law of contradiction. There are synthetical *a posteriori* judgments of empirical origin; but there are also others which are certain *a priori,* and which spring from pure understanding and reason. Yet they both agree in this, that they cannot possibly spring from the principle of analysis, namely, the law of contradiction, alone. They require a quite different principle from which they may be deduced, subject, of course, always to the law of contradiction, which must never be violated, even though everything cannot be deduced from it. I shall first classify synthetical judgments.

1. Judgments of experience are always synthetical. For it would be absurd to base an analytical judgment on experience, as our concept suffices for the purpose without requiring any testimony from experience. That body is extended is a judgment established *a priori,* and not an empirical judgment. For before appealing to experience, we already have all the conditions of the judgment in the concept, from which we have but to elicit the predicate according to the law of contradiction, and thereby to become conscious of the necessity of the judgment, which experience could not in the least teach us.

2. Mathematical judgments are all synthetical. This fact seems hitherto to have altogether escaped the observation of those who have analyzed human reason; it even seems directly opposed to all their conjectures, though it is incontestably certain and most important in its consequences. For as it was found that the conclusions of mathematicians all proceed according to the law of contradiction (as is demanded by all apodictic certainty), men persuaded themselves that the fundamental principles were known from the same law. This was a great mistake, for a synthetical proposition can indeed be established by the law of contradiction, but only by presupposing another synthetical proposition from which it follows, but never by that law alone.

First of all, we must observe that all strictly mathematical judgments are *a priori,* and not empirical, because they carry with them necessity, which cannot be obtained from experience. But if this be not conceded to me, very good: I shall confine my assertion to *pure mathematics,* the very notion of which implies that it contains pure *a priori* and not empirical knowledge.

It must at first be thought that the proposition $7 + 5 = 12$ is a mere analytical judgment, following from the concept of the sum of seven and five, according to the law of contradiction. But on closer examination it appears that the concept of the sum of $7 + 5$ contains merely their union in a single number, without its being at all thought what the particular number is that unites them. The concept of twelve is by no means thought by merely thinking of the combination of seven and five; and, analyze this possible sum as we may, we shall not discover twelve in the concept. We must go beyond these concepts, by calling to our aid some intuition which corresponds to one of the concepts—that is, either our five fingers or five points (as Segner has it in his *Arithmetic*)—and we must add successively the units of the five given in the intuition to the concept of seven. Hence our concept is really amplified by the proposition $7 + 5 = 12$, and we add to the first concept a second concept not thought in it. Arithmetical judgments are therefore synthetical, and the more plainly according as we take larger numbers; for in such cases it is clear that, however closely we analyze our concepts without calling intuition to our aid, we can never find the sum by such mere dissection.

Just as little is any principle of geometry analytical. That a straight line is the shortest path between two points is a synthetical proposition. For my concept of straight contains nothing of quantity, but only a quality. The concept "shortest" is therefore altogether additional and cannot be obtained by any analysis of the concept "straight line." Here, too, intuition must come to aid us. It alone makes the synthesis possible. What usually makes us believe that the predicate of such apodictic judgments is already contained in our concept, and that the judgment is therefore analytical, is the duplicity of the expression. We must think a certain predicate as attached to a given concept, and necessity indeed belongs to the concepts. But the question is not what we must join in thought *to* the given concept, but what we actually think together with and in it, though obscurely; and so it appears that the predicate belongs to this concept necessarily indeed, yet not directly but indirectly by means of an intuition which must be present.

Some other principles, assumed by geometers, are indeed actually analytical, and depend on the law of contradiction; but they only serve, as identical propositions, as a method of concatenation, and not as principles—for example $a = a$, the whole is equal to itself, or $a + b > a$, the whole is greater than its part. And yet even these, though they are recognized as valid from mere concepts, are admitted in mathematics only because they can be represented in some intuition.

The essential and distinguishing feature of pure mathematical knowledge among all other *a priori* knowledge is that it cannot at all proceed from concepts, but only by means of the construction of concepts.[2] As therefore in its propositions it must proceed beyond the concept to that which is corresponding intuition contains, these propositions neither can, nor ought to, arise analytically, by dissection of the concept, but are all synthetical.

I cannot refrain from pointing out the disadvantage resulting to philosophy from the neglect of this easy and apparently insignificant observation. Hume being prompted to cast his eye over the whole field of *a priori* cognitions in which human understanding claims such mighty possessions (a calling he felt worthy of a philosopher) heedlessly severed from it a whole, and indeed its most valuable, province, namely, pure mathematics; for he imagined its nature or, so to speak, the state constitution of this empire depended on totally different principles, namely, on the law of contradiction alone; and although he did not divide judgments in this manner formally and universally as I have done here, what he said was equivalent to this; that mathematics contains only analytical, but metaphysics synthetical, *a priori* propositions. In this, however, he was greatly mistaken, and the mistake had a decidedly injurious effect upon his whole conception. But for this, he would have extended his question concerning the origin of our synthetical judgments far beyond the metaphysical concept of causality and included in it the pos-

sibility of mathematics *a priori* also, for this latter he must have assumed to be equally synthetical. And then he could not have based his metaphysical propositions on mere experience without subjecting the axioms of mathematics equally to experience, a thing which he was far too acute to do. The good company into which metaphysics would thus have been brought would have saved it from the danger of a contemptuous ill-treatment, for the thrust intended for it must have reached mathematics, which was not and could not have been Hume's intention. Thus that acute man would have been led into considerations which must needs be similar to those that now occupy us, but which would have gained inestimably by his inimitably elegant style.

3. Metaphysical judgments, properly so called, are all synthetical. We must distinguish judgments pertaining to metaphysics from metaphysical judgments properly so called. Many of the former are analytical, but they only afford the means for metaphysical judgments, which are the whole end of the science and which are always synthetical. For if there be concepts pertaining to metaphysics (as, for example, that of substance), the judgments springing from simple analysis of them also pertain to metaphysics, as, for example, substance is that which only exists as subject, etc.; and by means of several such analytical judgments we seek to approach the definition of the concepts. But as the analysis of a pure concept of the understanding (the kind of concept pertaining to metaphysics) does not proceed in any different manner from the dissection of any other, even empirical, concepts, not belonging to metaphysics (such as, air is an elastic fluid, the elasticity of which is not destroyed by any known degree of cold), it follows that the concept indeed, but not the analytical judgment, is properly metaphysical. This science has something peculiar in the production of its *a priori* cognitions, which must therefore be distinguished from the features it has in common with other rational knowledge. Thus the judgment that all the substance in things is

---

[2] *Critique of Pure Reason,* "Methodology," Ch. I, Sec. 1.

permanent is a synthetical and properly metaphysical judgment.

If the *a priori* concepts which constitute the materials and tools of metaphysics have first been collected according to fixed principles, then their analysis will be of great value; it might be taught as a particular part (as a *philosophia definitiva*), containing nothing but analytical judgments pertaining to metaphysics, and could be treated separately from the synthetical which constitute metaphysics proper. For indeed these analyses are not of much value except in metaphysics, that is, as regards the synthetical judgments which are to be generated by these previously analyzed concepts.

The conclusion drawn in this section then is that metaphysics is properly concerned with synthetical propositions *a priori,* and these alone constitute its end, for which it indeed requires various dissection of its concepts, namely, analytical judgments, but wherein the procedure is not different from that in every other kind of knowledge, in which we merely seek to render our concepts distinct by analysis. But the generation of *a priori* knowledge by intuition as well as by concepts, in fine, of synthetical propositions *a priori,* especially in philosophical knowledge, constitutes the essential subject of metaphysics. . . .

SOLUTION OF THE GENERAL QUESTION OF THE *PROLEGOMENA*

How Is Metaphysics Possible as Science?

Metaphysics, as a natural disposition of reason, is actual; but if considered by itself alone (as the analytical solution of the third principal question showed), dialectical and illusory. If we think of taking principles from it, and in using them follow the natural, but on that account not less false, illusion, we can never produce science, but only a vain dialectical art, in which one school may outdo another but none can ever acquire a just and lasting approbation.

In order that as a science metaphysics may be entitled to claim, not mere fallacious plausibility, but insight and conviction, a critique of reason itself must exhibit the whole stock of *a priori* concepts, their division according to their various sources (sensibility, understanding, and reason), together with a complete table of them, the analysis of all these concepts, with all their consequences, and especially the possibility of synthetical knowledge *a priori* by means of a deduction of these concepts, the principles and the bounds of their application, all in a complete system. Critique, therefore, and

critique alone contains in itself the whole well-proved and well-tested plan, and even all the means, required to establish metaphysics as a science; by other ways and means it is impossible. The question here, therefore, is not so much how this performance is possible as how to set it going and to induce men of clear heads to quit their hitherto perverted and fruitless cultivation for one that will not deceive, and how such a union for the common end may best be directed.

This much is certain, that whoever has once tasted critique will be ever after disgusted with all dogmatic twaddle which he formerly had to put up with because his reason had to have something and could find nothing better for its support.

Critique stands in the same relation to the common metaphysics of the schools as chemistry does to alchemy, or as astronomy to the astrology of the fortune teller. I pledge myself that nobody who has thought through and grasped the principles of critique, even in these *Prolegomena* only, will ever return to that old and sophistical pseudo-science; but will rather with a certain delight look forward to metaphysics, which is now indeed in his power, requiring no more preparatory discoveries and affording permanent satisfaction to reason at last. For here is an advantage upon which, of all possible sciences, metaphysics alone can with certainty reckon: that it can be brought to such completion and fixity as to be in need of no further change or be subject to any augmentation by new discoveries; because here reason has the sources of its knowledge in itself, not in objects and their observation,[3] by which its stock of knowledge could be further increased. When, therefore, it has exhibited the fundamental laws of its faculty completely and so definitely as to avoid all misunderstanding, there remains nothing further which pure reason could know *a priori;* nay, there is no ground even to raise further questions. The sure prospect of knowledge so definite and so compact has a peculiar charm, even though we should set aside all its advantages, of which I shall hereafter speak.

All false art, all vain wisdom, lasts its time but finally destroys itself, and its highest culture is also the epoch of its decay. That this time is come for metaphysics appears from the state into which it has fallen among all learned nations, despite all the zeal with which other sciences of every kind are prosecuted. The old arrangement of our university studies still preserves its shadow. Now and then an academy of science tempts men by offering prizes to write some essay on it, but it is no longer numbered among the rigorous sciences; and let anyone judge for himself how a sophisticated man, if he were called a great metaphysician, would receive the compliment, which may be well meant but is scarcely envied by anybody.

Yet, though the period of the downfall of all dogmatic metaphysics has undoubtedly arrived, we are yet far from being able to say that the period of its regeneration is come by means of a thorough and complete critique of reason. All transitions from a

tendency to its contrary pass through the stage of indifference, and this moment is the most dangerous for an author but, in my opinion, the most favorable for the science. For when party spirit has died out by a total dissolution of former connection, minds are in the best state to listen to several proposals for an organization according to a new plan.

When I say I hope these *Prolegomena* will excite investigation in the field of critique and afford a new and promising object to sustain the general spirit of philosophy, which seems on its speculative side to want sustenance, I can imagine beforehand that everyone whom the thorny paths of my *Critique* have tired and put out of humor will ask me upon what I found this hope. My answer is: upon the irresistible law of necessity.

That the human mind will ever give up metaphysical researches is as little to be expected as that we, to avoid inhaling impure air, should prefer to give up breathing altogether. There will, therefore, always be metaphysics in the world; nay, everyone, especially every reflective man, will have it and, for want of a recognized standard, will shape it for himself after his own pattern. What has hitherto been called metaphysics cannot satisfy any critical mind, but to forego it entirely is impossible; therefore a *Critique of Pure Reason* itself must now be attempted or, if one exists, investigated and brought to the full test, because there is no other means of supplying this pressing want which is something more than mere thirst for knowledge.

Ever since I have come to know critique, whenever I finish reading a book of metaphysical contents which, by the preciseness of its notions, by variety, order, and an easy style, was not only entertaining but also helpful, I cannot help asking, "Has this author indeed advanced metaphysics a single step?" The learned men whose works have been useful to me in other respects and always contributed to the culture of my mental powers will, I hope, forgive me for saying that I have never been able to find either their essays or my own less important ones (though self-love may recommend them to

---

[3] [*Anschauung.*]

me) to have advanced the science of metaphysics in the least.

There is a very obvious reason for this: metaphysics did not then exist as a science, nor can it be gathered piecemeal; but its germ must be fully preformed in critique. But, in order to prevent all misconception, we must remember what has been already said—that, by the analytical treatment of our concepts, the understanding gains indeed a great deal; but the science of metaphysics is thereby not in the least advanced, because these dissections of concepts are nothing but the materials from which the intention is to carpenter our science. Let the concepts of substance and of accident be ever so well dissected and determined; all this is very well as a preparation for some future use. But if we cannot prove that in all which exists the substance endures and only the accidents vary, our science is not the least advanced by all our analyses.

Metaphysics has hitherto never been able to prove *a priori* either this proposition or that of sufficient reason, still less any more complex theorem such as belongs to psychology or cosmology, or indeed any synthetical proposition. By all its analyzing, therefore, nothing is affected, nothing obtained or forwarded; and the science, after all this bustle and noise, still remains as it was in the days of Aristotle, though there were far better preparations for it than of old if only the clue to synthetical cognitions had been discovered.

If anyone thinks himself offended, he is at liberty to refute my charge by producing a single synthetical proposition belonging to metaphysics which he would prove dogmatically *a priori;* for until he has actually performed this feat I shall not grant that he has truly advanced the science, even if this proposition should be sufficiently confirmed by common experience. No demand can be more moderate or more equitable and, in the (inevitably certain) event of its nonperformance, no assertion more just than that hitherto metaphysics has never existed as a science.

But there are two things which, in case the challenge be accepted, I must deprecate: first, trifling about probability and conjecture, which are suited as little to metaphysics as to geometry; and secondly, a decision by means of the magic wand of so-called common sense, which does not convince everyone but accommodates itself to personal peculiarities.

For as to the former, nothing can be more absurd than in metaphysics, a philosophy from pure reason, to think of grounding our judgments upon probability and conjecture. Everything that is to be known *a priori* is thereby announced as apodictically certain, and must therefore be proved in this way. We might as well think of grounding geometry or arithmetic upon conjectures. As to the calculus of probabilities in the latter, it does not contain probable but perfectly certain judgments concerning the degree of the possibility of certain cases under given uniform conditions, which, in the sum of all possible cases, must infallibly happen according to the rule, though the rule is not sufficiently definite with respect to every single instance. Conjectures (by means of induction and of analogy) can be suffered in an empirical science of nature only, yet even there at least the possibility of what we assume must be quite certain.

The appeal to common sense is even more absurd—if anything more absurd can be imagined—when it is a question of concept and principles claimed as valid, not in so far as they hold with regard to experience, but beyond the conditions of experience. For what is common sense? It is normal good sense, so far it judges right. But what is normal good sense? It is the faculty of the knowledge and use of rules *in concreto,* as distinguished from the speculative understanding, which is a faculty of knowing rules *in abstracto.* Common sense can hardly understand the rule that every event is determined by means of its cause and can never comprehend it in its generality. It therefore demands an example from experience; and when it hears that this rule means nothing but what it always thought when a pane was broken or a kitchen utensil missing, it then understands the principle and grants it. Common sense, therefore, is only of use so far as it can see its rules (though they actually are *a priori*) confirmed by experience; consequently to comprehend them *a priori,* or independently of experience, belongs to the speculative understanding and lies quite beyond the horizon of common sense. But the province of metaphysics is entirely confined to the latter kind of knowledge, and it is certainly a bad sign of common sense to appeal to it as a witness, for it cannot here form any opinion whatever, and men look down upon it with contempt until they are in straits and can find in their speculation neither advice nor help.

It is a common subterfuge of those false friends of common sense (who occasionally prize it highly, but usually despise it) to say that there must surely be at all events some propositions which are immediately certain and of which there is no occasion to give any proof, or even any account at all, because we otherwise could never stop inquiring into the grounds of our judgments. But if we except the principle of contradiction, which is not sufficient to show the truth of synthetical judgments, they can never adduce, in proof of this privilege, anything else indubitable which they can immediately ascribe to common sense, except mathematical propositions, such as twice two make four, between two points there is but one straight line, etc. But these judgments are radically different from those of metaphysics. For in mathematics I can by thinking itself construct whatever I represent to myself as possible by a concept: I add to the first two the other two, one by one, and myself make the number four, or I draw in thought from one point to another all manner of lines, equal as well as unequal; yet I can draw one only which is like itself in all its parts. But I cannot, by all my power of thinking, extract

from the concept of a thing the concept of something else whose existence is necessarily connected with the former; for this I must call in experience. And though my understanding furnishes me *a priori* (yet only in reference to possible experience) with the concept of such a connection (that is causation), I cannot exhibit it, like the concepts of mathematics, by intuiting it *a priori,* and so show its possibility *a priori.* This concept, together with the principles of its application, always requires, if it shall hold *a priori* —as is requisite in metaphysics—a justification and deduction of its possibility, because we cannot otherwise know how far it holds good and whether it can be used in experience only or beyond it also.

Therefore in metaphysics, as a speculative science of pure reason, we can never appeal to common sense, but may do so only when we are forced to surrender it and to renounce all pure speculative knowledge which must always be theoretical cognition,[4] and thereby under some circumstances to forego metaphysics itself and its instruction for the sake of adopting a rational faith which alone may be possible for us, sufficient to our wants, and perhaps even more salutary than knowledge itself. For in this case the state of affairs is quite altered. Metaphysics must be science, not only as a whole, but in all its parts; otherwise it is nothing at all; because, as speculation of pure reason, it finds a hold only on common convictions. Beyond its field, however, probability and common sense may be used justly and with advantage, but on quite special principles, the importance of which always depends on their reference to practical life.

This is what I hold myself justified in requiring for the possibility of metaphysics as a science.

---

[4] [*Ein Wissen.*]

ALFRED NORTH WHITEHEAD

SPECULATIVE PHILOSOPHY*

Section I

This course of lectures is designed as an essay in Speculative Philosophy. Its first task must be to define "speculative philosophy," and to defend it as a method productive of important knowledge.

Speculative Philosophy is the endeavour to frame a coherent, logical, necessary system of general ideas in terms of which every element of our experience can be interpreted. By this notion of "interpretation" I mean that everything of which we are conscious, as enjoyed, perceived, willed, or thought, shall have the character of a particular instance of the general scheme. Thus the philosophical scheme should be coherent, logical, and, in respect to its interpretation, applicable and adequate. Here "applicable" means that some items of experience are thus interpretable, and "adequate" means that there are no items incapable of such interpretation.

"Coherence," as here employed, means that the fundamental ideas, in terms of which the scheme is developed, presuppose each other so that in isolation they are meaningless. This requirement does not mean that they are definable in terms of each other; it means that what is indefinable in one such notion cannot be abstracted from its relevance to the other notions. It is the ideal of speculative philosophy that its fundamental notions shall not seem capable of abstraction from each other. In other words, it is presupposed that no entity can be conceived in complete abstraction from the system of the universe, and that it is the business of speculative philosophy to exhibit this truth. This character is its coherence.

The term "logical" has its ordinary meaning, including "logical" consistency, or lack of contradiction, the definition of constructs in logical terms, the exemplification of general logical notions in specific instances, and the principles of inference. It will be observed that logical notions must themselves find their places in the scheme of philosophic notions.

It will also be noticed that this ideal of speculative philosophy has its rational side and its empirical side. The rational side is expressed by the terms "coherent" and "logical." The empirical side is expressed by the terms "applicable" and "adequate." But the two sides are bound together by clearing away an ambiguity which remains in the previous explanation of the term "adequate." The adequacy of the scheme over every item does not mean adequacy over such items as happen to have been considered. It means that the texture of observed experience, as illustrating the philosophic scheme, is such that all related experience must exhibit the same texture. Thus the philosophic scheme should be "necessary," in the sense of bearing in itself its own warrant of universality throughout all experience, provided that we confine ourselves to that which communicates with immediate matter of fact. But what does not so communicate is unknowable, and the unknowable is unknown;[1] and

---

* From *Process and Reality: An Essay in Cosmology* by Alfred North Whitehead. New York. The Macmillan Company, 1929. Part I, Chapter I. Reprinted by permission.

[1] This doctrine is a paradox. Indulging in a species of false modesty, "cautious" philosophers undertake its definition.

so this universality defined by "communication" can suffice.

This doctrine of necessity in universality means that there is an essence to the universe which forbids relationships beyond itself, as a violation of its rationality. Speculative philosophy seeks that essence.

Section II

Philosophers can never hope finally to formulate these metaphysical first principles. Weakness of insight and deficiencies of language stand in the way inexorably. Words and phrases must be stretched towards a generality foreign to their ordinary usage; and however such elements of language be stabilized as technicalities, they remain metaphors mutely appealing for an imaginative leap.

There is no first principle which is in itself unknowable, not to be captured by a flash of insight. But, putting aside the difficulties of language, deficiency in imaginative penetration forbids progress in any form other than that of an asymptotic approach to a scheme of principles, only definable in terms of the ideal which they should satisfy.

The difficulty has its seat in the empirical side of philosophy. Our datum is the actual world, including ourselves; and this actual world spreads itself for observation in the guise of the topic of our immediate experience. The educidation of immediate experience is the sole justification for any thought; and the starting point for thought is the analytic observation of components of this experience. But we are not conscious of any clear-cut complete analysis of immediate experience, in terms of the various details which comprise its definiteness. We habitually observe by the method of difference. Sometimes we see an elephant, and sometimes we do not. The result is that an elephant, when present, is noticed. Facility of observation depends on the fact that the object observed is important when present, and sometimes is absent.

The metaphysical first principles can never fail of exemplification. We can never catch the actual world taking a holiday from their sway. Thus, for the discovery of metaphysics, the method of pinning down thought to the strict systematization of detailed discrimination, already effected by antecedent observation, breaks down. This collapse of the method of rigid empiricism is not confined to metaphysics. It occurs whenever we seek the larger generalities. In natural science this rigid method is the Baconian method of induction, a method which, if consistently pursued, would have left science where it found it. What Bacon omitted was the play of a free imagination, controlled by the requirements of coherence and logic. The true method of discovery is like the flight of an aeroplane. It starts from the ground of particular observation; it makes a flight in the thin air of imaginative generalization; and it again lands for renewed observation rendered acute by rational interpretation. The reason for the success of this method of imaginative rationalization is that, when the method of difference fails, factors which are constantly present may yet be observed under the influence of imaginative thought. Such thought supplies the differences which the direct observation lacks. It can even play with inconsistency; and can thus throw light on the consistent, and persistent, elements in experience by comparison with what in imagination is inconstent with them. The negative judgment is the peak of mentality. But the conditions for the success of imaginative construction must be rigidly adhered to. In the first place, this construction must have its origin in the generalization of particular factors discerned in particular topics of human interest; for example, in physics, or in physiology, or in psychology, or in aesthetics, or in ethical beliefs, or in sociology, or in languages conceived as storehouses of human experience. In this way the prime requisite, that anyhow there shall be some important application, is secured. The success of the imaginative experiment is always to be tested by the applicability of its results beyond the restricted locus from which it originated. In default of such extended application, a generalization started from physics, for example, remains merely an alternative expression of notions applicable to physics. The partially successful philosophic generalization will, if derived from physics, find applications in fields of experience beyond physics. It will enlighten observation in those remote fields, so that general principles can be discerned as in process of illustration, which in the absence of the imaginative generalization are obscured by their persistent exemplification.

Thus the first requisite is to proceed by the method of generalization so that certainly there is some application; and the test of some success is application beyond the immediate origin. In other words, some synoptic vision has been gained.

In this description of philosophic method, the term "philosophic generalization" has meant "the utilization of specific notions, applying to a restricted group of facts, for the divination of the generic notions which apply to all facts."

In its use of this method natural science has shown a curious mixture of rationalism and irrationalism. Its prevalent tone of thought has been ardently rationalistic within its own borders, and dogmatically irrational beyond those borders. In practice such an attitude tends to become a dogmatic denial that there are any factors in the world not fully expressible in terms of its own primary notions devoid of further generalization. Such a denial is the self-denial of thought.

The second condition for the success of imaginative construction is unflinching pursuit of the two rationalistic ideals, coherence and logical perfection.

Logical perfection does not here require any detailed explanation. An example of its importance is afforded by the rôle of mathematics in the restricted field of natural science. The history of mathematics exhibits the generalization of special notions observed in particular instances. In any branches of mathematics, the notions presuppose each other. It is a remarkable characteristic of the history of thought that branches of mathematics developed under the pure imaginative impulse, thus controlled, finally receive their important application. Time may be wanted. Conic sections had to wait for eighteen hundred years. In more recent years, the theory of probability, the theory of tensors, the theory of matrices are cases in point.

The requirement of coherence is the great preservative of rationalistic sanity. But the validity of its criticism is not always admitted. If we consider philosophical controversies, we shall find that disputants tend to require coherence from their adversaries, and to grant dispensations to themselves. It has been remarked that a system of philosophy is never refuted; it is only abandoned. The reason is that logical contradictions, except as temporary slips of the mind—plentiful, though temporary—are the most gratuitous of errors; and usually they are trivial. Thus, after criticism, systems do not exhibit mere illogicalities. They suffer from inadequacy and incoherence. Failure to include some obvious elements of experience in the scope of the system is met by boldly denying the facts. Also while a philosophical system retains any charm of novelty, it enjoys a plenary indulgence for its failures in coherence. But after a system has acquired orthodoxy, and is taught with authority, it receives a sharper criticism. Its denials and its incoherences are found intolerable, and a reaction sets in.

Incoherence is the arbitrary disconnection of first principles. In modern philosophy Descartes' two kinds of substance, corporeal and mental, illustrate incoherence. There is, in Descartes' philosophy, no reason why there should not be a one-substance world, only corporeal, or a one-substance world, only mental. According to Descartes, a substantial individual "requires nothing but itself in order to exist." Thus this system makes a virtue of its incoherence. But on the other hand, the facts seem connected, while Descartes' system does not; for example, in the treatment of the body-mind problem. The Cartesian system obviously says something that is true. But its notions are too abstract to penetrate into the nature of things.

The attraction of Spinoza's philosophy lies in its modification of Descartes' position into greater coherence. He starts with one substance, *causa sui,* and considers its essential attributes and its individualized modes, i.e. the *"affectiones substantiae."* The gap in the system is the arbitrary introduction of the "modes." And yet, a multiplicity of modes is a fixed requisite, if the scheme is to retain any direct relevance to the many occasions in the experienced world.

The philosophy of organism is closely allied to Spinoza's scheme of thought. But it differs by the abandonment of the subject-predicate forms of thought, so far as concerns the presupposition that this form is a direct embodiment of the most ultimate characterization of fact. The result is that the "substance-quality" concept is avoided; and that morphological description is replaced by description of dynamic process. Also Spinoza's "modes" now become the sheer actualities; so that, though analysis of them increases

our understanding, it does not lead us to the discovery of any higher grade of reality. The coherence, which the system seeks to preserve, is the discovery that the process, or concrescence, of any one actual entity involves the other actual entities among its components. In this way the obvious solidarity of the world receives its explanation.

In all philosophic theory there is an ultimate which is actual in virtue of its accidents. It is only then capable of characterization through its accidental embodiments, and apart from these accidents is devoid of actuality. In the philosophy of organism this ultimate is termed "creativity"; and God is its primordial, nontemporal accident. In monistic philosophies, Spinoza's or absolute idealism, this ultimate is God, who is also equivalently termed "The Absolute." In such monistic schemes, the ultimate is illegitimately allowed a final, "eminent" reality, beyond that ascribed to any of its accidents. In this general position the philosophy of organism seems to approximate more to some strains of Indian, or Chinese, thought, than to western Asiatic, or European, thought. One side makes process ultimate; the other side makes fact ultimate.

Section III

In its turn every philosophy will suffer a deposition. But the bundle of philosophic systems expresses a variety of general truths about the universe, awaiting co-ordination and assignment of their various spheres of validity. Such progress in co-ordination is provided by the advance of philosophy; and in this sense philosophy has advanced from Plato onwards. According to this account of the achievement of rationalism, the chief error in philosophy is overstatement. The aim at generalization is sound, but the estimate of success is exaggerated. There are two main forms of such overstatement. One form is what I have termed elsewhere,[2] the "fallacy

of misplaced concreteness." This fallacy consists in neglecting the degree of abstraction involved when an actual entity is considered merely so far as it exemplifies certain categories of thought. There are aspects of actualities which are simply ignored so long as we restrict thought to these categories. Thus the success of a philosophy is to be measured by its comparative avoidance of this fallacy, when thought is restricted within its categories.

The other form of overstatement consists in a false estimate of logical procedure in respect to certainty, and in respect to premises. Philosophy has been haunted by the unfortunate notion that its method is dogmatically to indicate premises which are

---

[2] Cf. *Science and the Modern World,* Chap. III.

severally clear, distinct, and certain; and to erect upon those premises a deductive system of thought.

But the accurate expression of the final generalities is the goal of discussion and not its origin. Philosophy has been misled by the example of mathematics; and even in mathematics the statement of the ultimate logical principles is beset with difficulties, as yet insuperable.[3] The verification of a rationalistic scheme is to be sought in its general success, and not in the peculiar certainty, or initial clarity, of its first principles. In this connection the misuse of the *ex absurdo* argument has to be noted; much philosophical reasoning is vitiated by it. The only logical conclusion to be drawn, when a contradiction issues from a train of reasoning, is that at least one of the premises involved in the inference is false. It is rashly assumed without further question that the peccant premise can at once be located. In mathematics this assumption is often justified, and philosophers have been thereby misled. But in the absence of a well-defined categoreal scheme of entities, issuing in a satisfactory metaphysical system, every premise in a philosophical argument is under suspicion.

Philosophy will not regain its proper status until the gradual elaboration of categoreal schemes, definitely stated at each stage of progress, is recognized as its proper objective. There may be rival schemes, inconsistent among themselves; each with its own merits and its own failures. It will then be the purpose of research to conciliate the differences. Metaphysical categories are not dogmatic statements of the obvious; they are tentative formulations of the ultimate generalities.

If we consider any scheme of philosophic categories as one complex assertion, and apply to it the logician's alternative, true or false, the answer must be that the scheme is false. The same answer must be given to a like question respecting the existing formulated principles of any science.

The scheme is true with unformulated qualifications, exceptions, limitations, and new interpretations in terms of more general notions. We do not yet know how to recast the scheme into a logical truth. But the scheme is a matrix from which true propositions applicable to particular circumstances can be derived. We can at present only trust our trained instincts as to the discrimination of the circumstances in respect to which the scheme is valid.

The use of such a matrix is to argue from it boldly and with rigid logic. The scheme should therefore be stated with the utmost precision and definiteness, to allow of such argumentation. The conclusion of the argument should then be confronted with circumstances to which it should apply.

The primary advantage thus gained is that experience is not interrogated with the benumbing repression of common sense. The observation acquires an enhanced penetration by reason of the expectation evoked by the conclusion of the argument. The outcome from this procedure takes one of three forms: (i) the conclusion may agree with the observed facts; (ii) the conclusion may exhibit general agreement, with disagreement in detail; (iii) the conclusion may be in complete disagreement in the facts.

In the first case, the facts are known with more adequacy and the applicability of the system to the world has been elucidated. In the second case, criticisms of the observation of the facts and of the details of the scheme are both required. The history of thought shows that false interpretations of observed facts enter into the records of their observation. Thus both theory, and received notions as to fact, are in doubt. In the third case, a fundamental reorganization of theory is required either by way of limiting it to some special province, or by way of entire abandonment of its main categories of thought.

After the initial basis of a rational life, with a civilized language, has been laid, all productive thought has proceeded either by the poetic insight of artists, or by the imaginative elaboration of schemes of thought

---

[3] Cf. *Principia Mathematica*, by Bertrand Russell and A. N. Whitehead, Vol. I, Introduction and Introduction to the Second Edition. These introductory discussions are practically due to Russell, and in the second edition wholly so.

capable of utilization as logical premises. In some measure or other, progress is always a transcendence of what is obvious.

Rationalism never shakes off its status of an experimental adventure. The combined influences of mathematics and religion, which have so greatly contributed to the rise of philosophy, have also had the unfortunate effect of yoking it with static dogmatism. Rationalism is an adventure in the clarification thought, progressive and never final. But it is an adventure in which even partial success has importance.

Section IV

The field of a special science is confined to one genus of facts, in the sense that no statements are made respecting facts which lie outside that genus. The very circumstance that a science has naturally arisen concerning a set of facts secures that facts of that type have definite relations among themselves which are very obvious to all mankind. The common obviousness of things arises when their explicit apprehension carries immediate importance for purposes of survival, or of enjoyment—that is to say, for purposes of "being" and of "well-being." Elements in human experience, singled out in this way, are those elements concerning which language is copious and, within its limits, precise. The special sciences, therefore, deal with topics which lie open to easy inspection and are readily expressed by words.

The study of philosophy is a voyage towards the larger generalities. For this reason in the infancy of science, when the main stress lay in the discovery of the most general ideas usefully applicable to the subject-matter in question, philosophy was not sharply distinguished from science. To this day, a new science with any substantial novelty in its notions is considered to be in some way peculiarly philosophical. In their later stages, apart from occasional disturbances, most sciences accept without question the general notions in terms of which they develop. The main stress is laid on the adjustment and the direct verification of more special statements. In such periods scientists repudiate philosophy; Newton, justly satisfied with his physical principles, disclaimed metaphysics.

The fate of Newtonian physics warns us that there is a development in scientific first principles, and that their original forms can only be saved by interpretations of meaning and limitations of their field of application—interpretations and limitations unsuspected during the first period of successful employment. One chapter in the history of culture is concerned with the growth of generalities. In such a chapter it is seen that the older generalities, like the older hills, are worn down and diminished in height, surpassed by younger rivals.

Thus one aim of philosophy is to challenge the half-truths constituting the scientific first principles. The systematization of knowledge cannot be conducted in watertight compartments. All general truths condition each other; and the limits of their application cannot be adequately defined apart from their correlation by yet wider generalities. The criticism of principles must chiefly take the form of determining the proper meanings to be assigned to the fundamental notions of the various sciences, when these notions are considered in respect to their status relatively to each other. The determination of this status requires a generality transcending any special subject-matter.

If we may trust the Pythagorean tradition, the rise of European philosophy was largely promoted by the development of mathematics into a science of abstract generality. But in its subsequent development the method of philosophy has also been vitiated by the example of mathematics. The primary method of mathematics is deduction; the primary method of philosophy is descriptive generalization. Under the influence of mathematics, deduction has been foisted onto philosophy as its standard method, instead of taking its true place as an essential auxiliary mode of verification whereby to test the scope of generalities. This misapprehension of philosophic method has veiled the very considerable success of philosophy in providing generic notions which add lucidity to our apprehension of the facts of experience. The depositions of Plato, Aristotle, Thomas Aquinas, Descartes, Spinoza, Leibniz, Locke, Berkeley, Hume, Kant, Hegel, merely mean that ideas which these men introduced into the philosophic tradition must be construed with limitations, adaptations, and inversions, either unknown to them, or even explicitly repudiated by them. A new idea introduces a new alternative; and we are not less indebted to a thinker when we adopt the alternative which he discarded. Philosophy never reverts to its old position after the shock of a great philosopher.

Section V

Every science must devise its own instruments. The tool required for philosophy is language. Thus philosophy redesigns language in the same way that, in a physical science, pre-existing appliances are redesigned. It is exactly at this point that the appeal to facts is a difficult operation. This appeal is not solely to the expression of the facts in current verbal statements. The adequacy of such sentences is the main question at issue. It is true that the general agreement of mankind as to experienced facts is best expressed in language. But the language of literature breaks down precisely at the task of expressing in explicit form the larger generalities—the very generalities which metaphysics seeks to express.

The point is that every proposition refers to a universe exhibiting some general systematic metaphysical character. Apart from this background, the separate entities which go to form the proposition, and the proposition as a whole, are without determinate character. Nothing has been defined, because every definite entity requires a systematic universe to supply its requisite status. Thus every proposition proposing a fact must, in its complete analysis, propose the general character of the universe required for that fact. There are no self-sustained facts, floating in nonentity. This doctrine, of the impossibility of tearing a proposition from its systematic context in the actual world, is a direct consequence of the fourth and the twentieth of the fundamental categoreal explanations which we shall be engaged in expanding and illustrating. A proposition can embody partial truth because it only demands a certain type of systematic environment, which is presupposed in its meaning. It does not refer to the universe in all its detail.

One practical aim of metaphysics is the accurate analysis of propositions; not merely of metaphysical propositions, but of quite ordinary propositions such as "There is beef for dinner today," and "Socrates is mortal." The one genus of facts which constitutes the field of some special science requires some common metaphysical presupposition respecting the universe. It is merely credulous to accept verbal phrases as adequate statements of propositions. The distinction between verbal phrases and complete propositions is one of the reasons why the logicians' rigid alternative, "true or false," is so largely irrelevant for the pursuit of knowledge.

The excessive trust in linguistic phrases has been the well-known reason vitiating so much of the philosophy and physics among the Greeks and among the mediaeval thinkers who continued the Greek traditions. For example John Stuart Mill writes: "They (the Greeks) had great difficulty in distinguishing between things which their language confounded, or in putting mentally together things which it distinguished; and could hardly combine the objects in nature, into any classes but those which were made for them by the popular phrases of their own country; or at least could not help fancying those classes to be natural, and all others arbitrary and artificial. Accordingly, scientific investigation among the Greek schools of speculation and their followers in the Middle Ages, was little more than a mere sifting and analysing of the notions attached to common language. They thought that by determining the meaning of words they could become acquainted with facts."[4] Mill then proceeds to quote from Whewell[5] a paragraph illustrating the same weakness of Greek thought.

But neither Mill, nor Whewell, tracks this difficulty about language down to its sources. They both presuppose that language does enunciate well-defined propositions. This is quite untrue. Language is thoroughly indeterminate, by reason of the fact that every occurrence presupposes some systematic type of environment.

For example, the word "Socrates," referring to the philosopher, in one sentence may stand for an entity presupposing a more closely defined background than the word "Socrates," with the same reference, in another sentence. The word "mortal" affords an analogous possibility. A precise language must await a completed metaphysical knowledge.

The technical language of philosophy represents attempts of various schools of thought to obtain explicit expression of general ideas presupposed by the facts of experience. It follows that any novelty in metaphysical doctrines exhibits some measure of disagreement with statements of the facts to be found in current philosophical literature. The extent of disagreement measures the extent of metaphysical divergence. It is, therefore, no valid criticism on one metaphysical school to point out that its doctrines do not follow from the verbal expression of the facts accepted by another school. The whole contention is that the doctrines in question supply a closer approach to fully expressed propositions.

The truth itself is nothing else than how the composite natures of the organic actualities of the world obtain adequate representation in the divine nature. Such representations compose the "consequent nature" of God, which evolves in its relationship to the evolving world without derogation to the eternal completion of its primordial conceptual nature. In this way the "ontological principle" is maintained—since there can be no determinate truth, correlating impartially the partial experiences of many actual entities, apart from one actual entity to which it can be referred. The reaction of the temporal world on the nature of God is considered subsequently in Part V:* it is there termed "the consequent nature of God."

Whatever is found in "practice" must lie within the scope of the metaphysical description. When the description fails to include the "practice," the metaphysics is inadequate and requires revision. There can be no appeal to practice to supplement metaphysics, so long as we remain contended with our metaphysical doctrines. Metaphysics is nothing but the description of the generalities which apply to all the details of practice.

No metaphysical system can hope entirely to satisfy these pragmatic tests. At the best such a system will remain only an approximation to the general truths which are sought. In particular, there are no precisely stated axiomatic certainties from which to start. There is not even the language in which to frame them. The only possible procedure is to start from verbal expressions which, when taken by themselves with the current meaning of their words, are ill-defined and ambiguous. These are not premises to be immediately reasoned from apart from elucidation by further discussion; they are endeavours to state general principles which will be exemplified in the subsequent description of the facts of experience. This subsequent elaboration should elucidate the meanings to be assigned to the words and phrases employed. Such meanings are incapable of accurate apprehension apart from

---

[4] Cf. *Logic*, bk. V, chap. III.
[5] Cf. Whewell's *History of the Inductive Sciences*.

* [See Part V of this volume.]

a correspondingly accurate apprehension of the metaphysical background which the universe provides for them. But no language can be anything but elliptical, requiring a leap of the imagination to understand its meaning in its relevance to immediate experience. The position of metaphysics in the development of culture cannot be understood without remembering that no verbal statement is the adequate expression of a proposition.

An old established metaphysical system gains a false air of adequate precision from the fact that its words and phrases have passed into current literature. Thus propositions expressed in its language are more easily correlated to our flitting intuitions into metaphysical truth. When we trust these verbal statements and argue as though they adequately analysed meaning, we are led into difficulties which take the shape of negations of what in practice is presupposed. But when they are proposed as first principles they assume an unmerited air of sober obviousness. Their defect is that the true propositions which they do express lose their fundamental character when subjected to adequate expression. For example consider the type of propositions such as "The grass is green," and "The whale is big." This subject-predicate form of statement seems so simple, leading straight to a metaphysical first principle; and yet in these examples it conceals such complex, diverse meanings.

Section VI

It has been an objection to speculative philosophy that it is overambitious. Rationalism, it is admitted, is the method by which advance is made within the limits of particular sciences. It is, however, held that this limited success must not encourage attempts to frame ambitious schemes expressive of the general nature of things.

One alleged justification of this criticism is ill-success: European thought is represented as littered with metaphysical systems, abandoned and unreconciled.

Such an assertion tacitly fastens upon philosophy the old dogmatic test. The same criterion would fasten ill-success upon science. We no more retain the physics of the seventeenth century than we do the Cartesian philosophy of that century. Yet within limits, both systems express important truths. Also we are beginning to understand the wider categories which define their limits of correct application. Of course, in that century, dogmatic views held sway; so that the validity both of the physical notions, and of the Cartesian notions, was misconceived. Mankind never quite knows what it is after. When we survey the history of thought, and likewise the history of practice, we find that one idea after another is tried out, its limitations defined, and its core of truth elicited. In application to the instinct for the intellectual adventures demanded by particular epochs, there is much truth in Augustine's rhetorical phrase, *Securus judicat orbis terrarum.* At the very least, men do what they can in the way of systematization, and in the event achieve something. The proper test is not that of finality, but of progress.

But the main objection, dating from the sixteenth century and receiving final expression from Francis Bacon, is the uselessness of philosophic speculation. The position taken by this objection is that we ought to describe detailed matter of fact, and elicit the laws with a generality strictly limited to the systematization of these described details. General interpretation, it is held, has no bearing upon this procedure; and thus any system of general interpretation, be it true or false, remains intrinsically barren. Unfortunately for this objection, there are no brute, self-contained matters of fact, capable of being understood apart from interpretation as an element in a system. Whenever we attempt to express the matter of immediate experience, we find that its understanding leads us beyond itself, to its contemporaries, to its past, to its future, and to the universals in terms of which its definiteness is exhibited. But such universals, by their very character of universality, embody the potentiality of other facts with variant types of definiteness. Thus the understanding of the immediate brute fact requires its metaphysical interpretation as an item in a world with some systematic relation to it. When thought comes upon the scene, it finds the interpretations as matters of practice. Philosophy does not initiate interpretations. Its search for a rationalistic scheme is the search for more adequate criticism, and for more adequate justification, of the interpretations which we perforce employ. Our habitual experience is a complex of failure and success in the enterprise of interpretation. If we desire a record of uninterpreted experience, we must ask a stone to record its autobiography. Every scientific memoir in its record of the "facts" is shot through and through with interpretation. The methodology of rational interpretation is the product of the fitful vagueness of consciousness. Elements which shine with immediate distinctness, in some circumstances, retire into penumbral shadow in other circumstances, and into black darkness on other occasions. And yet all occasions proclaim themselves as actualities within the flux of a solid world, demanding a unity of interpretation.

Philosophy is the self-correction by consciousness of its own initial excess of subjectivity. Each actual occasion contributes to the circumstances of its origin additional formative elements deepening its own peculiar individuality. Consciousness is only the last and greatest of such elements by which the selective character of the individual obscures the external totality from which it originates and which it embodies. An actual individual, of such higher grade, has truck with the totality of things by reason of its sheer actuality; but it has attained its individual depth of being by a selective emphasis limited to its own purposes. The task of philosophy is to recover the totality obscured by the selection. It replaces in rational experience what has been submerged in the higher sensitive experience and has been sunk yet deeper by the initial operations of consciousness itself. The selectiveness of individual experience is moral so far as it conforms to the balance of importance disclosed in the rational vision; and conversely the conversion of the intellectual insight into an emotional force corrects the sensitive experience in the direction of morality. The correction is in proportion to the rationality of the insight.

Morality of outlook is inseparably conjoined with generality of outlook. The antithesis between the general good and the individual interest can be abolished only when the individual is such that its interest is the general good, thus exemplifying the loss of the minor intensities in order to find them again with finer composition in a wider sweep of interest.

Philosophy frees itself from the taint of ineffectiveness by its close relations with religion and with science, natural and sociological. It attains its chief importance by fusing the two, namely, religion and science, into one rational scheme of thought. Religion should connect the rational generality of philosophy with the emotions and purposes springing out of existence in a particular society, in a particular epoch, and conditioned by particular antecedents. Religion is the translation of general ideas into particular thoughts, particular emotions, and particular purposes; it is directed to the end of stretching individual interest beyond its self-defeating particularity. Philosophy finds religion, and modifies it; and conversely religion is among the data of experience which philosophy must weave into its own scheme. Religion is an ultimate craving to infuse into the insistent particularity of emotion that non-temporal generality which primarily belongs to conceptual thought alone. In the higher organisms the differences of tempo between the mere emotions and the conceptual experiences produce a life-tedium, unless this supreme fusion has been effected. The two sides of the organism require a reconciliation in which emotional experiences illustrate a conceptual justification, and conceptual experiences find an emotional illustration.

This demand for an intellectual justification of brute experience has also been the motive power in the advance of European science. In this sense scientific interest is only a variant form of religious interest. Any survey of the scientific devotion to "truth," as an ideal, will confirm this statement. There is, however, a grave divergence between science and religion in respect to the phases of individual experience with which they are concerned. Religion is centered upon the harmony of rational thought with the sensitive reaction to the percepta from which experience originates. Science is concerned with the harmony of rational thought with the percepta themselves. When science deals with emotions, the emotions in question are percepta and not immediate passions—other people's emotion and not our own; at least our own in recollection, and not in immediacy. Religion deals with the formation of the experiencing subject; whereas science deals with the objects, which are the data forming the primary phase in this experience. The subject originates from, and amid, given conditions; science conciliates thought with this primary matter of fact; and religion conciliates the thought involved in the process with the sensitive reaction involved in that same process. The process is nothing else than the experiencing subject itself. In this explanation it is presumed that an experiencing subject is one occasion of sensitive reaction to an actual world. Science finds religious experiences among its percepta; and religion finds scientific concepts among the conceptual experiences to be fused with particular sensitive reactions.

The conclusion of this discussion is, first, the assertion of the old doctrine that breadth of thought reacting with intensity of sensitive experience stands out as an ultimate claim of existence; secondly, the assertion that empirically the development of self-justifying thoughts has been achieved by the complex process of generalizing from particular topics, of imaginatively schematizing the generalizations, and finally by renewed comparison of the imagined scheme with the direct experience to which it should apply.

There is no justification for checking generalization at any particular stage. Each phase of generalization exhibits its own peculiar simplicities which stand out just at that stage, and at no other stage. There are simplicities connected with the motion of a bar of steel which are obscured if we refuse to abstract from the individual molecules; and there are certain simplicities concerning the behaviour of men which are obscured if we refuse to abstract from the individual peculiarities of particular specimens. In the same way, there are certain general truths, about the actual things in the common world of activity, which will be obscured when attention is confined to some particular detailed mode of considering them. These general truths, involved in the meaning of every particular notion respecting the actions of things, are the subject matter for speculative philosophy.

Philosophy destroys its usefulness when it indulges in brilliant feats of explaining away. It is then trespassing with the wrong equipment upon the field of particular sciences. Its ultimate appeal is to the general consciousness of what in practice we experience. Whatever thread of presupposition characterizes social expression throughout the various epochs of rational society, must find its place in philosophic theory. Speculative boldness must be balanced by complete humility before logic, and before fact. It is a disease of philosophy when it is neither bold nor humble, but merely a reflection of the temperamental presuppositions of exceptional personalities.

Analogously, we do not trust any recasting of scientific theory depending upon a single performance of an aberrant experiment, unrepeated. The ultimate test is always widespread, recurrent experience; and the more general the rationalistic scheme, the more important is this final appeal.

The useful function of philosophy is to promote the most general systematization of civilized thought. There is a constant reaction between specialism and common sense. It is the part of the special sciences to modify common sense. Philosophy is the welding of imagination and common sense into a restraint upon specialists, and also into an enlargement of their imaginations. By providing the generic notions philosophy should make it easier to conceive the infinite variety of specific instances which rest unrealized in the womb of nature.

H. P. GRICE, D. F. PEARS, and P. F. STRAWSON

METAPHYSICS*

We are to enquire what metaphysics is, what distinguishes metaphysics from the rest of philosophy. It seems likely that the question is one which it is particularly difficult to answer neutrally, dispassionately. Many people think that the essential task of philosophers is to provide metaphysical doctrines; some even say that this is the only justification for the existence of philosophers. But many people, including many philosophers, think that all metaphysical doctrines are spurious; some have even called them meaningless. Metaphysics has a unique power to attract or repel, to encourage an uncritical enthusiasm on the one hand, an impatient condemnation on the other. All the more reason for giving, if possible, a neutral and dispassionate account.

The name of the subject is the name given to a treatise by Aristotle. And Aristotle described the subject of his treatise as the science of Being as such, a supremely general study of existence or reality, distinct from any of the special sciences and more fundamental than they. He argued that there must be such a science; since each of the special sciences, besides having its own peculiar subject matter, made use in common with all the others of certain quite general notions, such as those of identity and difference, unity and plurality. Such common notions as these would provide the topics of the general science of being, while various different kinds of existence or reality, each with its own peculiar features provided the subject matter of the more departmental studies.

The conception of metaphysics as a supremely general study which is somehow presupposed by the special sciences, is a fairly enduring one. We find it, for example, though with variations, in Descartes, Leibniz and Kant. But some metaphysicians could have agreed with Aristotle about the comprehensive and general and ultimate nature of their subject without sharing Kant's or Descartes' concern with the foundations of science. Bradley is an example. He says: "We may agree, perhaps, to understand by metaphysics an attempt to know reality as against mere appearance, or the study of first principles or ultimate truths, or again the effort to comprehend the universe, not simply piecemeal or by fragments, but somehow as a whole." This agrees with Aristotle in contrasting metaphysics with departmental or, as Bradley would say, fragmentary studies. The "attempt to know reality" sounds something like "the study of being as such." And both would agree on the task of discovering "first principles." But Bradley would have ridiculed the idea that he was concerned to get at the presuppositions or foundations of science.

Some contemporary accounts of metaphysics sound, on the face of it at least, very different from either of these. Consider, for

* From *The Nature of Metaphysics*, edited by D. F. Pears. Macmillan & Company Ltd. and St. Martin's Press, Inc. Copyright 1957. Reprinted by permission of the publishers.

example, John Wisdom's description of a metaphysical statement. He says that a metaphysical proposition is, characteristically, a sort of illuminating falsehood, a pointed paradox, which uses language in a disturbing and even shocking way in order to make us aware of hidden differences and resemblances in things—differences and resemblances hidden by our ordinary ways of talking. Of course Wisdom does not claim this to be a complete characterisation, nor perhaps a literally correct one. Perhaps it should itself be seen as an illuminating paradox. In any case, its relation to Aristotle's, or Bradley's, account of the matter is not obvious.

But perhaps a relation can be established. Certainly not all metaphysical statements are paradoxes serving to call attention to usually unnoticed differences and resemblances. For many metaphysical statements are so obscure that it takes long training before their meaning can be grasped, whereas a paradox must operate with familiar concepts; for the essence of a paradox is that it administers a shock, and you cannot shock people when they are standing on such unfamiliar ground that they have no particular expectations. Nevertheless there is a connection between metaphysics and Wisdom's kind of paradox. Suppose we consider the paradox that everyone is really always alone. Considered by itself, it is no more than an epigram—rather a flat one—about the human condition. It might be said, at least, to minimize the differences between being by oneself and being with other people. But now consider it, not simply by itself, but surrounded and supported by a certain kind of argument: by argument to the effect that what passes for knowledge of each other's mental processes is, at best, unverifiable conjecture, since the mind and the body are totally distinct things, and the working of the mind is always withdrawn behind the screen of its bodily manifestations. When the solitude-affirming paradox is seen in the context of a general theory about minds and bodies and the possibilities and limits of knowledge, when it is seen as embodying such a theory, then indeed it is clearly a metaphysical statement. But the fact that the

statement is most clearly seen as metaphysical in such a setting does not mean that there is no metaphysics at all in it when it is deprived of the setting. "Everyone is *really* alone" invites us to change, for a moment at least and in one respect, our ordinary way of looking at things, and hints that the changed view we get is the truer, the profounder, view. And part of Bradley's characterization of metaphysics—"the attempt to know reality as against mere appearance" —seems to herald a general invitation to a general change of view, which will also be a change to a profounder view. We may surmise, perhaps, that the attempt to secure that comprehensiveness, which both Aristotle and Bradley find characteristic of their enquiry, leads often enough to those shifts of view, expressible in paradox, which Wisdom finds characteristically metaphysical.

But what exactly is the meaning of the requirement that metaphysics should yield a comprehensive system of reality? A theory about the nature of reality might be held to be comprehensive is so far as there were no elements of reality to which the theory did not apply; and might be held to be systematic if the propositions comprised in the theory were interdependent; that is to say, if the propositions of the theory were not divided into a number of independent groups. An extreme case of something systematic in the required sense would be a deductive system in which from a limited number of axioms one could derive, as logical consequences, the remaining propositions of the theory; and it is notable that some seventeenth-century rationalist metaphysicians thought of metaphysics as constituting a deductive system. It might be objected that if we are to understand in this way the idea of a comprehensive and systematic account of reality, then science as a whole, or even some particular science, would qualify as metaphysics; for example, physics, which is certainly systematic enough, might be said to deal with the whole of reality. But this objection has little force. For though physics might be said to be concerned with the whole of reality, it could not be said to be concerned with every aspect or feature of reality. Physical laws may govern, for example, part of the behaviour of living bodies; but if we wish to know about the way organisms develop, we have to go, not to the physicist, but to the biologist. So we can still regard physics as insufficiently comprehensive to qualify as metaphysics. And though science as a whole might be thought to be comprehensive, in that every aspect of reality falls under some particular science or other, nevertheless particular sciences are too independent of one another for science as a whole to count as a single system.

Nevertheless a difficulty remains in drawing a distinction between metaphysics and science. It is perhaps not inconceivable that the sciences might advance to a point at which it would be possible to recast the whole of science as a single system. For example, after enormous strides within biology itself, it might perhaps become possible to reinterpret the basic concepts of biology in terms of the concepts of physics, and so represent biological phenomena as obeying laws which were only special cases of physical laws. What is here envisaged is, roughly speaking, a very large-scale version of the unification effected by the Kinetic Theory of Gases, which brought certain seemingly independent laws concerning gases within a single wider system, by exhibiting them as special cases of dynamical laws. This result was achieved, roughly, by thinking of gases as being composed of particles, and redefining, in terms of the properties of the particles, certain concepts involved in the laws about gases. Such a unification and systematization of the whole of science is of course, at present, the wildest of dreams, and may even be logically impossible, though it has not been shown to be so. But suppose it were to occur; one would still surely refuse to call the resulting systematized science, or even the most general part of it, a metaphysical system.

This refusal would not be the result of mere prejudice. Just because the universal systematized science *was* science, it would not

be metaphysics. For even the most general and basic laws it contained would ultimately depend for their acceptability upon the results of observation and experiment in a way which is quite uncharacteristic of the principles of a metaphysical system. The *methods* of science, the tests for acceptability of scientific laws, remain quite different from the methods of metaphysics and the test for acceptability of metaphysical principles. So we have here a further question. For even though it is true that the most general laws or axioms of a unified science would not count as metaphysics, it is also true that many metaphysicians have thought it at least a part of their task to lay, or to lay bare, the foundations of science. We must ask, then, how we are to conceive, or how *they* conceived, of the relations between the metaphysical foundations and the scientific superstructure. That relation, it is clear, is not to be understood simply as the relation of the most general to less general laws of nature.

Many metaphysicians did not explicitly ask themselves this question, nor is it clear what answer they would have given if they had. But there are exceptions. One of them is Kant. He thought there were certain principles which had a quite special place in knowledge, in that they stated the conditions under which alone scientific knowledge of nature, considered as a spatio-temporal system, was possible. These principles were not themselves a part of science. Rather, they embodied the conditions of the possibility of science, and of ordinary everyday knowledge too, for that matter. It was an important part of the metaphysician's task to discover what fundamental ideas these principles involved, and what the principles themselves were; and also to *prove* that they had this peculiar character. For this was the only kind of proof of which they were susceptible. Whatever the shortcomings of Kant's doctrine, it at least gives a clear meaning to saying that metaphysics is concerned with the presuppositions of science, and not merely its most general part.

Yet the shortcomings were important. Kant's fundamental principles varied greatly in character; and very few would now agree that they embodied general presuppositions of the possibility of scientific knowledge. And most would now be very sceptical of the possibility of establishing any rival set of principles with just this status. A more acceptable notion might be that of a body of ideas or principles which were, in something like Kant's sense, the presuppositions, not of scientific knowledge in general, but of a particular *kind* of scientific enquiry, or of the science of a particular time. And this was in fact Collingwood's idea of the nature of metaphysics: the metaphysician exposed the presuppositions of the science of a particular epoch. Only we need not, like Collingwood, think of the metaphysician just as an archaeologist of thought. He might also be, as he has often intended to be and sometimes has been, a revolutionary, fostering new directions in scientific discovery rather than uncovering the foundations of scientific remains.

This line of thought about metaphysics is not peculiar to a relatively traditional thinker like Collingwood. There is at least some analogy between his views and those, for example, of Carnap, who was once a member of the philosophically radical Vienna Circle. Carnap draws a sharp distinction between questions which arise *within* a given system of concepts, or framework of ideas, and questions which are sometimes raised *about* that framework or system. Questions of the first sort belong to the field of some science or of everyday life, and are answered by the methods appropriate to those fields. Questions of the latter sort have traditionally appeared in metaphysics in the misleading form of questions about the reality or existence of some very general class of entities corresponding to the fundamental ideas of the system of concepts in question. Thus philosophers have asked whether there really existed such things as numbers, whether the space-time points of physics were real, and so on. But such questions can be significantly understood only as raising the *practical* issue of whether or not to embrace and use a given conceptual scheme or framework of ideas.

To answer affirmatively, according to Carnap, is simply to adopt such a framework for use, and hence to give shape or direction to a whole field of enquiry.

Carnap's view of the matter might seem to make it mysterious that there should be such things as metaphysical assertions, as opposed to metaphysical decisions. The mystery could be solved in principle by regarding metaphysicians as engaged in a kind of propaganda on behalf of some conceptual scheme, the acceptance of which is obscurely felt to be a presupposition of the development of science in a particular direction. Like all forms of propaganda, conceptual or metaphysical propaganda is liable to involve distortion and exaggeration. As Carnap's remarks suggest, one form which conceptual advocacy is liable to take is the entering of a strong claim for the status of *reality* on behalf of some general class of entities, together with a disposition to deny this status to other, less favoured things. At least from Aristotle's time till the end of the eighteenth century, the traditional honorific title for things declared to be real, or ultimately real, was that of *substance*. So we constantly find the entities favoured in any particular metaphysical system being accorded the rank of substances, while everything else is given some inferior, dependent status, or is even declared to be merely appearance. The types of entity favoured in this way have varied enormously. For Berkeley, it was minds or spirits; for Leibniz, some curious mind-like centers of conscious or unconscious experience. Hume was inclined to scoff at the whole notion; but in so far as anything deserved the title, he thought it was individual sense-impressions and images. For Spinoza, on the other hand, it was nothing less than everything: the single comprehensive system of reality, which he called God or Nature.

But the best example for the immediate purpose is provided by Descartes. He, unlike Berkeley and Hume, was a very scientifically-minded philosopher, with very clear ideas about the proper direction for science. He seems to have thought that mathematics, and in particular geometry, provided the model for scientific procedure. And this determined his thinking in two ways. First, he thought that the fundamental method in science was the deductive method of geometry, and this he conceived of as rigorous reasoning from self-evident axioms. Second, he thought that the subject-matter of all the physical sciences, from mechanics to medicine, must be fundamentally the same as the subject-matter geometry. The only characteristics that the objects studied by geometry possessed were spatial characteristics. So from the point of view of science in general, the only important features of things in the physical world were also their spatial characteristics. Physical science in general was a kind of dynamic geometry. Here we have an exclusive preference for a certain type of scientific method, and a certain type of scientific explanation: the method is deductive, the type of explanation mechanical. These beliefs about the right way to do science are exactly reflected in Descartes' ontology, in his doctrine, that is, about what really exists. Apart from God, the divine substance, he recognized just two kinds of substance, two types of real entity. First, there was material substance, or matter; and the belief that the only scientifically important characteristics of things in the physical world were their spatial characteristics goes over, in the language of metaphysics, into the doctrine that these are their only *real* characteristics. Second, Descartes recognized minds, or mental substances, of which the essential characteristic was thinking; and thinking itself, in its pure form at least, was conceived of as simply the intuitive grasping of self-evident axioms and their deductive consequences. These restrictive doctrines about reality and knowledge naturally called for adjustments elsewhere in our ordinary scheme of things. With the help of the divine substance, these were duly provided.

It is not always obvious that the metaphysician's scheme involves this kind of ontological preference, this tendency, that is, to promote one or two categories of entity to the rank of the real, or of the ultimately real, to the exclusion of others. Kant, as much concerned as Descartes with the foundations

of science, seems, in a sense, to show no such preference. He seems prepared to accord reality to all the general types of phenomena which we encounter in experience or, rather, to draw the distinction between the illusory and the real, as we normally do, within these types and not between them. Yet it is only a relative reality or, as he said, an empirical reality, that he was willing to grant in this liberal way to all the general classes of things we encounter. For the whole world of nature, studied by science, was declared by him to be ultimately only appearance, in contrast with the transcendent and unknowable reality which lay behind it. So, in a sense, he downgraded the whole of what we know in favour of what we do not and cannot know. But this thoroughgoing contrast between appearance and reality was perhaps of less importance to him in connection with science than in connection with morality. The transcendent reality was of interest to us, not as scientific enquirers, but as moral beings, not as creatures faced with problems of knowledge, but as creatures faced with problems of conduct. Kant was a very ambitious metaphysician, who sought to secure, at one stroke the foundations of science *and* the foundations of morality.

The last point is of importance. Though a concern with the foundations of science is, or has been, one impetus to the construction of metaphysical systems, it is only one among others. Concern with morality, with the right way to behave, has been scarcely less important. And other disciplines have contributed to the metaphysical drive. In the nineteenth century, for example, when history came of age and began to preoccupy philosophers as science had done in the seventeenth century, metaphysical systems started to grow out of historical studies. Thus the historically minded metaphysician searches for the true nature of historical explanation and concludes, perhaps, that the key concept is that of a certain mode of development of human institutions. Suppose he then extends this theory beyond the confines of history, maintaining that this same concept, which is, in a certain sense, a concept of mental development, provides the only true explanation of the whole universe. The result is a comprehensive system something like Hegel's. Hegel honoured one type of historical explanation by making it the foundation of his system; and it was this system that Marx turned upside down, making the whole process of development material instead of mental.

Systems like those of Marx and Hegel had, and were intended to have, implications regarding human behaviour. But concern with moral and emotional, even with aesthetic, requirements may take many different forms. It may take the form of a desire to provide some transcendental authority, some more than human backing, for a particular morality: moral conclusions about how we ought to behave are to follow from metaphysical premises about the nature of reality. It may take the more general form of a wish to supply transcendental backing for morality in general. Or it may take the form of a wish to demonstrate that there is some surpassing and unobvious excellence about the nature of things, an ultimate satisfactioness in the universe. Spinoza provides another example of the first of these. He claims to demonstrate, from the nature of reality, that the supreme satisfaction is also the supreme virtue, and that both consist of what he calls the intellectual love of God: which seems to mean, for him, a kind of acquiescent and admiring understanding of the workings of Nature. Kant is the supreme example of the second. The whole world of nature, including our ordinary human selves—the whole province of scientific knowledge, in fact—is declared to be mere appearance, in contrast with the world of transcendent reality, the world of things in themselves. Reality is set behind a curtain impenetrable to scientific enquiry, a removal which both guarantees its security and heightens its prestige. But communications are not wholly severed. From behind the curtain Reality speaks—giving us, indeed, not information, but commands, moral imperatives. In some admittedly unintelligible way, Reality is within

us, as rational beings; and, with unquestionable authority, it lays down the general form of the moral law which we ought, as ordinary human beings, to obey. Finally, Leibniz, who unites so many intellectual concerns in a brilliant, if precarious, harmony, provides a good example of the third form which this element in metaphysics may take. The celebrated optimism—"Everything is for the best in the best of all possible worlds"—is not, in the context of his system, at all as absurd as Voltaire made out. We may find it unsympathetic, which is another matter; for Leibniz's criteria of the highest excellence were peculiarly his own. He thought he could demonstrate that reality must exhibit a peculiarly satisfying combination of the maximum possible diversity and richness of phenomena, together with the greatest possible simplicity of natural laws. Sometimes the demonstration appears to be theological, sometimes purely logical. In any case it was this combination of richness and elegance which he found so admirable—worth, no doubt, a Lisbon earthquake or a Turkish war. It seems a taste that we might find unsympathetic, but could scarcely find ridiculous.

It is time, however, to enter a caveat. It would be misleading to suggest that the sources of metaphysics are always of the kinds we have so far described—such as the wish to get morality transcendentally underwritten, or the desire to give science the right direction, or the urge to show that some departmental study holds the key to the universe at large. Metaphysics may have a humbler origin. It often enough happens that philosophers, reflecting upon a particular matter, find themselves, or seem to find themselves, in a certain kind of quandary. We can best illustrate this by considering in a little detail one particular quandary of this kind. We select the problem of our knowledge of the material world, a problem —or apparent problem—which has long occupied the attention of philosophers. On the one hand, in their unphilosophical moments, they (like all the rest of us) have no hesitation in sometimes claiming to know on the evidence of the senses that this or that material object exists or is of such and such a character; they do, in practice, seem to have no difficulty (in many cases) in distinguishing between situations in which it is in order to claim to know, for example, that the milk is on the doorstep and situations in which such a claim would not be in order. Naturally, therefore, they have a strong antipathy to any suggestion that all such claims to knowledge should be rejected as false. Nevertheless, on reflection, they find themselves faced with philosophical considerations which seem to force them into just such a rejection. For (the argument runs) if we are to have perceptual knowledge of the material world, this knowledge must be based on the appearances which material things present to us, on our sense-impressions. But it is clear that our sense-impressions may be deceptive or even hallucinatory; the fact that it looks to me as if there were milk bottles on the doorstep does not guarantee that there really are milk bottles on the doorstep, or even that there is in fact *anything* on the doorstep. If we try to remove this doubt in a given case by further observation, all we are doing is providing ourselves with further sense-impressions, each of which is open to the same suspicion of deceptiveness as the sense-impressions with which we started; so we are no better off. Indeed (the argument may continue) so far from providing us with certain knowledge about the material world, our sense-impressions cannot even be justifiably regarded as more or less reliable clues to, or indications of, the character of the material world. For they could only properly function as clues if we could correlate particular kinds of sense-impression with particular kinds of material object, and to do this we should have to possess some kind of direct access to material objects, and not merely indirect access via sense-impressions. This direct access we do not have. This is an example of the kind of philosophical consideration which seems to lead to the conclusion that all claims to knowledge of the material world must be rejected. The result is a quandary of just the kind we are seeking to illustrate: that is to say, a conflict between a reluctance to discard some range of propositions with which in everyday life everyone is perfectly satisfied, and the pressure of a philosophical argument which seemingly leaves no alternative but to reject the propositions in question. The propositions in jeopardy often (though not always) state that we have knowledge of this or that kind, in which case the philosophical arguments which undermine them do so by setting up a barrier between appearance and reality, or between the evidence and that for which it is (supposedly) evidence.

Now, when is the response to such a quandary a metaphysical response? One kind of response, which would be generally admitted to be metaphysical is what one might call the Transcendentalist response. To respond in this way to the quandary about the material world, for example, would be to maintain that material objects may be known to exist, even though not observable, and to explain the possibility of such knowledge by invoking some transcendental hypothesis, some principle which is supposed to be acceptable independently of experience. For example, one might invoke the principle that God is not a deceiver, or that appearances must have causes; and then, by invoking the further principle that there must be some resemblance between cause and effect (and so between reality and appearance) one might guarantee some knowledge of the character, as well as of the existence, of material objects. In general, it is characteristic of the Transcendentalist to admit both unobservable entities and principles which are not empirically testable; by this means he may hope to reinstate, at least in part, the propositions which he was in danger of having to give up.

A very different type of response to the problem was Hume's. Put very baldly, his view was that all our everyday statements about material objects incorporate mistakes in a systematic way, and so none of them can, as they stand, be rationally accepted; hence, of course, claims to know them to be true must be false or absurd. He adds, however, that we are so constituted as human beings that we are incapable of ceasing to make and accept such statements in our everyday life, even though in our reflective moments we may see the error of our ways. We might perhaps confer the label of "rejector" upon one who, when it is asked how we are to preserve a particular range of everyday assertions from destruction by philosophical argument, replies that such preservation is not rationally possible. The rejector's response is not less metaphysical than the Transcendentalist's.

A more recently fashionable method of dealing with our kind of quandary is the method of reduction. For instance, some philosophers have tried to remove the barrier between sense-impressions and material objects by maintaining that material objects are just collections or families of sense-impressions; or to put the view in a more modern garb, they have suggested that sentences about material objects are translatable, in principle at least, into complicated sentences about the sense-impressions that people actually do have, or would have, in certain conditions. If so much is granted, it would be claimed, there remains no difficulty in the idea that facts about sense impressions constitute a legitimate evidential basis for statements about material objects; for to conclude that since certain sorts of sense-impressions have been obtained in certain sorts of conditions, therefore more or less similar sense-impressions would be obtained in more or less similar conditions, is not more objectionable in principle than to argue (say) from the character of a sample to the character of the population from which the sample is drawn. In general, the procedure of the reducer when faced with a question of the type "How can we legitimately claim to know about Xs when our only direct information is about Ys" is to reply that the difficulty disappears if we recognize that Xs are nothing over and above Ys, that to talk about Xs is to talk in a concealed way about Ys. Whether we are to count the reductive response as metaphysical or not depends on how seriously it is pressed. If the "reducer" maintains that his proposed reduction, or something like it, *must* be accepted as the

only way of avoiding on the one hand the introduction of transcendental hypotheses, and on the other hand wholesale rejection of a certain class of everyday statements, then he, too, is to be counted as a metaphysician; but if he is prepared to allow his proposed reduction to be treated purely on its merits, and does not regard its acceptance as being the only satisfactory way of meeting some threat to common sense, then he is not a metaphysician. But then, too, he cannot be taking the quandary very seriously: he must be thinking of it as an *apparent* quandary, the illusion of a quandary, which can be dispelled without recourse to any of these drastic measures.

The question arises: How is our characterization of these quandary-responses as metaphysical connected with what we have previously had to say about metaphysics? In more ways than one. In the first place, it is necessary, in order for the quandary to arise at all, and to appear as something requiring drastic measures, that some conceptual shift, some perhaps unnoticed change in our ordinary way of looking at things, should already be occurring. That change of view, on which Wisdom lays such emphasis, is already taking place. Second, behind the quandary and the change of view, we may sometimes glimpse the working of one of those preferences among the categories which we earlier mentioned. For example, it may be that Plato believed in the supreme reality of those eternal changeless entities, the Forms, partly at least because he wished to preserve the possibility of scientific knowledge and yet was threatened with having to reject it; for philosophical reflection made it appear that knowledge of perceptible things was impossible, since perceptible things were constantly in process of change. In order, then, to resolve his quandary, to find a subject-matter for scientific knowledge, Plato was led to introduce, and to exalt, the Forms. But the idea that knowledge of changeable things is impossible, which gives rise to the quandary, may itself arise from a preference: from the feeling that to be unchanging (and so permanent and stable) is so much better than to be changing (and so fleeting and insecure) that only knowledge of unchanging things is *worthy* of the name of knowledge.

We have spoken of some of the springs, and of some of the characteristic features, of metaphysics. Our survey is summary and incomplete. It will be supplemented by more detailed discussion of different aspects of the subject in the essays that follow. But even from a summary survey, a general picture emerges. The enterprise of metaphysics emerges as, above all, an attempt to re-order or to reorganize the set of ideas with which we think about the world; assimilating to one another some things which we customarily distinguish, distinguishing others which we normally assimilate; promoting some ideas to key positions, downgrading or dismissing others. It is supremely a kind of conceptual revision which the metaphysician undertakes, a re-drawing of the map of thought— or parts of it—on a new plan. Of course such revisions are often undertaken *within* particular departments of human thought, and are not then metaphysical ventures. But the revision which the metaphysician under-takes, although it may be undertaken in the interests—or supposed interests—of science, or in the light of history, or for the sake of some moral belief, is always of a different order from a merely departmental revision. For among the concepts he manipulates are always some—like those of knowledge, existence, identity, reality—which, as Aristotle said, are common to all the departmental studies. Partly for this reason, the metaphysical revision tends to comprehensiveness, tends to call for readjustments everywhere. Not that it inevitably issues in a comprehensive system, although it is never merely departmental. For though the notions to be revised are general, and not departmental, notions, they need not all be revised at once and to the limit. So we have those comparatively localized disturbances, where, from the interplay of quandary and preference, there emerges some minor metaphysical shift in the contours of thought. But the metaphysician *par excellence* will not stop short at this. With more or less of boldness, ingenuity and imagination, he re-draws the whole map.

FREDERICK C. COPLESTON

THE FUNCTION OF METAPHYSICS[1]*

I

Aristotle stated that philosophy began with "wonder" and that men continue to philosophize because and in so far as they continue to "wonder." Philosophy, in other words, is rooted in the desire to understand the world, in the desire to find an intelligible pattern in events and to answer problems which occur to the mind in connection with the world. By using the phrase "the world"

I do not mean to imply that the world is something finished and complete at any given moment: I use the phrase in the sense of the data of outer and inner experience with which any mind is confronted. One might say just as well that philosophy arises out of the desire to understand the "historical situation," meaning by the last phrase the external material environment in which a man finds himself, his physiological and psychological make-up and that of other people, and the historic past. One might discuss the question whether the desire to understand ought to be interpreted or analyzed in terms of another drive or other drives.

[1] This paper represents a lecture given at The Royal Institute of Philosophy in February, 1952.
* From *Philosophy*, XXVIII (January 1953), pp. 3–15. Reprinted by permission.

Nietzsche, for example, suggested in the notes which have been published under the title "The Will to Power" that the desire to understand is one of the forms taken by the will to power. Or it might be suggested by some that the desire to understand is subordinate to the life-impulse, in the sense that it is the necessity of acting in a given historical situation which drives us to attempt to attain clarity concerning this situation. But I do not propose to discuss these psychological questions. I am concerned at the moment to point out that philosophy—and I include metaphysical philosophy—has its origin on the consious level in the desire to understand the world. We are all familiar with children asking for explanations without any other obvious motive than that of resolving some perplexity, solving some difficulty or understanding some event or set of events; and I suggest that philosophy, as far as its original motive is concerned, is inspired by the same sort of desire which is observable in children.

What I have been saying may appear very obvious and trivial. But the original drive behind philosophical inquiry may possibly become obscured owing to the contention of some contemporary anti-metaphysicians that metaphysical problems are pseudo-problems which have their origin in linguistic confusion and error. Metaphysicians, it is said, were misled by language; they did not understand the proper use of terms; and they thus came to utter a lot of unintelligible sentences—or rather sentences which, though *prima facie* intelligible, can be shown by analysis to lack any definite meaning. That some metaphysical theories were due in part at least to linguistic confusion I should not attempt to deny, though I do not think that this can properly be said of metaphysics in general. But I am not now concerned with assessing the part played by linguistic confusion in the genesis of metaphysical theories. What I should like to point out is that we are not entitled to say of any question or theory that it is meaningless until it has been formulated. Otherwise we do not know what we are calling "meaningless." The questions

must first be raised before analysis of them is possible. And they were raised in the first place because the people who raised them wanted to understand something, because they wanted answers; and this fact remains true even if it could be shown that they were mistaken in thinking that there was anything to understand or that any answers to their questions were possible. I think that it is as well to have drawn attention to this point, even if it appears to be a trivial point. For acquaintance with detailed disputes between metaphysicians may give the impression that metaphysics is a mere verbal game and obscure the fact that in its origin metaphysics arises simply out of a natural desire to understand the world or the historical situation.

II

It is evident that science, too, owes its birth to the desire to understand. Francis Bacon emphasized the practical function of scientific knowledge, and living as we do in a highly technical civilization we are not likely to forget this aspect of science. We are also aware today of the part played by hypothesis in scientific theory, while the development of mathematical physics in particular has led thinkers like Eddington to lay great emphasis on the rôle of *a priori* mental construction in the framing of physical hypotheses. But though on the one hand technics obviously has a practical function while on the other hand we are now aware of the hypothetical character of scientific theory, it is not, I think, unreasonable to say that philosophy and science had a common origin in the natural desire to understand the world. However much any one may be inclined to stress the practical function of science, he can hardly maintain that astronomy proper, as distinct from astrology, had any other origin than the desire to understand.

Originally, of course, there was no clear distinction between philosophy and science. Nor, indeed, could there have been. The distinction could not be drawn until science had developed far enough for the distinction to be brought clearly before the mind. It is sometimes difficult to say, therefore, whether a particular theory of a Greek philosopher should be classed as a metaphysical theory or as a scientific hypothesis, a primitive scientific hypothesis, that is to say. In a state of affairs when philosophy and science are not yet distinguished, it is a tautology to say that contours are vague and outlines obscure. For example, any philosopher today who wishes to defend the Aristotelian hylomorphic theory must of necessity present it as a metaphysical theory; for it would be absurd to present it as a rival physical hypothesis to, say, the atomic theory. And he will probably also wish to maintain that it was propounded by Aristotle as a metaphysical theory. If he does not maintain this, he lays himself open to the charge of holding the theory merely out of respect for tradition. He is determined to keep the theory, it would be said, because it was Aristotle's theory; but since he sees that it cannot now be put forward as a rival physical hypothesis he changes what he admits to have been originally a physical hypothesis into a metaphysical theory in order to preserve it from attack on scientific grounds. A person, on the other hand, who does not wish to maintain the hylomorphic theory and who regards Aristotle's idea of "form," for example, as having been given definite content by the concepts of structure developed at a much later date by the various empirical sciences, may be inclined to speak of the Aristotelian theory as a primitive scientific hypothesis. And arguments could be adduced both for and against this way of speaking. One might say against it, for instance, that the theory involves mention of an entity, or rather of an essential constituent of entities, which is in principle unobservable. I refer to "first matter." On the other hand, an alchemist might say in favour of calling the theory a primitive scientific hypothesis that one could derive from it the testable conclusion that the so-called "baser" metals can ultimately be turned into gold. But it might also be claimed that the whole dispute is superfluous. It is only to be expected, it might be said, that at

a time when the sciences had not yet taken shape speculative theories should have been put forward which it is difficult to classify in terms of distinctions which were made at a later date; and one should not attempt to make any rigid classification of this sort. To do so serves no useful purpose. All that one can profitably do is to distinguish, or to attempt to distinguish, those early speculative theories which represent answers to questions which have proved to be or are thought to be answerable by some branch of science from those other theories which represent answers to questions which are not answerable, or which we cannot see to be answerable, by any branch of science. The latter type of theory is properly called a "metaphysical" theory. As for the former type of theory, it does not matter much whether one calls it a metaphysical theory which has been succeeded by scientific theories or a primitive scientific theory, though the latter way of speaking may involve a misuse of the term "scientific." The main point is to recognize that theories of this type have been succeeded in the course of time by fruitful scientific theories which have formed the basis for further research, hypothesis and experiment. It is a matter of minor importance whether we say that the movement was from metaphysics to science or from "primitive science" to science proper. On the whole, however, it is preferable to speak in the first way, since the development and progress of the sciences have involved their gradual purification from metaphysics.

I do not want to discuss the terminological question any further or to make any definite recommendation about the proper way of speaking. But it seems to me undeniable that at least some lines of inquiry were once pursued by philosophers in a speculative manner which are no longer pursued in this way. It is significant that when Aristotle stated that philosophy began with wonder he went on to state that people wondered first about the more obvious difficulties and that they then gradually advanced and stated difficulties about greater matters, like the phenomena of the moon and sun and stars and about the genesis of the universe. Astronomical inquiries were once regarded as pertaining to philosophy. But this is not so today. If we want information about the sun or the moon, we do not turn to philosophers for that information. Again, if we want information about the physical constitution of matter, we turn to the physicists. Questions about these matters are now classed as scientific questions, not as philosophical questions. And this is not simply an affair of terminology. The point is that we do not think that questions of this sort can be answered by means of the pure reason, that is, by armchair reflection alone. We see that another method, or other methods, are required. (I say "we see"; but as a matter of fact it was more or less clearly recognized in the late Middle Ages that if we want to learn empirical facts, *a priori* deduction will not enable us to do so.)

It seems to me, then, that it is undeniable that the empirical sciences have gradually taken over some tracts of the territory which was once supposed to belong to philosophy. And in this sense it is true to say that the field of philosophy has been narrowed. On the other hand, it is undeniable that philosophers have asked questions which cannot be answered by any particular science. Some might, perhaps, take exception to the use of the word "cannot" in an absolute sense. They might prefer to say of these questions that we do not see how they can be answered by any particular science. But I fail to see how a question about the origin of all finite beings, for example, could conceivably be answered by any empirical science. So I am content to say quite simply that philosophers have asked a number of questions which cannot be answered by any particular science. And if anyone chooses to say that these questions are the properly philosophical questions and that questions about the sun and moon were never proper philosophical questions, he can go on to say that philosophy proper has *not* in fact been narrowed.

I do not mean to imply that all questions which cannot be answered by the empirical sciences are "metaphysical" questions. For I think that there are moral questions which cannot be answered by empirical science but which one would not normally call "metaphysical" questions. But I confine my attention in this chapter to metaphysical questions. And I think that both metaphysicians and anti-metaphysicians would agree that as far as words are concerned a number of questions are properly called "metaphysical" questions. Some anti-metaphysicians would then go on to say that these questions cannot be answered scientifically because they are unanswerable and that they are unanswerable because no intelligible question has been asked. Speculative questions about the "Absolute" or about the "Cause" of "the world" or about the spiritual soul would be classified as questions of this sort. But I want to leave aside for the moment this type of difficulty and to ask whether there are any inquiries which the antimetaphysician would concede to be meaningful and which at the same time can sensibly be called "metaphysical."

III

A good deal of attention has been paid by modern philosophers to the analysis of statements about material things like chairs, tables and so on. And some have argued that objects like these are "logical constructions" out of sense-data or sense-contents. This might be taken to mean that a table, for example, is a fictitious entity, in the sense that there is no existent entity denoted by the word "table" but only a multiplicity of entities called "sense-data" or "sense-contents." We should then presumably have a form of idealistic phenomenalism, arrived at by philosophic reflection rather than by scientific hypothesis and verification. For it would be as difficult to prove scientifically that a table consists of sense-data as it would be to prove scientifically Berkeley's theory that material objects are "ideas" presented to us by God. In this case the theory might well be called a "metaphysical" theory. What other name could one give it?

But those analysts who maintain the truth of this theory refuse to allow that it means that a table, for example, is a fictitious entity. The statement that a table is a "logical construction" out of sense-data or sense-contents is a linguistic statement, not a statement about the constitution of material things. What it says is that sentences which name a material thing like a "table" can be translated into sentences which refer to sense-data or sense-contents but which do not contain the word "table." This interpretation of the theory of "logical constructions" as a purely linguistic theory is highly ingenious; but I feel some misgivings about it. A table is a "phenomenon" in the sense that it is an object appearing to us; and if we say that statements about this phenomenon can be translated into statements of equivalent meaning about sense-data, it is difficult to avoid the impression that what we are saying is that this phenomenon is a collection of sense-data. I am not concerned with the truth or falsity of the contention that a table is a collection of sense-data. What I want to remark is this. The contention is not a metaphysical contention in the sense that anything is said about a substance in Locke's sense of the word "substance"; but it seems to me to be metaphysical in another sense, namely in the sense that it is not the result of any physical or chemical analysis of the table. It is the result of a philosophical analysis of meaning, and in this sense it can be called "linguistic"; but it is not linguistic in the sense that it concerns words exclusively. Philosophical analysis is not the same thing as grammatical analysis. I suggest, then, that the theory of "logical constructions" can sensibly be called a "metaphysical" theory[2] and that what it does is to replace the metaphysic of substance by a phenomenalistic metaphysic. Possibly this is felt by those analysts who tend to exclude the sense-datum theory and the theory of "logical constructions" in the name of "ordinary language."

Perhaps one can apply the same line of reflection to the analysis of causality. This is often represented as an instance of linguistic analysis. So it is in a sense. But in what sense? If it is simply an analysis of the meaning of the term as used by scientists, or by a number of them, or if it is simply an analysis of the meaning of the term as used by certain social groups at certain periods, it is linguistic analysis in a strict sense. But if it is possible by means of this analysis to establish what people "ought" to mean by causality, the procedure involved does not seem to me to be radically different from the procedure followed by those philosophers who would have regarded the analysis of causality as an instance of metaphysical analysis.

It may be objected that metaphysicians have imagined that they could find out fresh information about the world by reflective analysis, whereas in point of fact we cannot do this. We can analyze the way in which people speak about the world, but any facts we learn in this way are linguistic facts. But I think that a distinction ought to be made. There is certainly a sense in which philosophical analysis gives no fresh knowledge of "facts." For example, by analyzing relation-sentences we do not obtain fresh knowledge of actual relations: that is obvious. Nor do we obtain knowledge that things stand in relation to one another in some sense. For this knowledge is presupposed by the ordinary use of language involving relation-sentences. But we can obtain information of what it "means" to say that one thing stands in relation to another thing. As this knowledge concerns "meaning" it can be said to concern linguistic usage; but it can also be called a knowledge of what relations "are"; it is not knowledge simply of what A or B thinks is the meaning of relation-sentences. And it seems to me that this kind of analysis can sensibly be called "metaphysical" analysis. It is certainly not physical or chemical analysis. It may be objected that it is precisely in order to distinguish it from physical and chemical analysis that it is called "linguistic analysis"; but what I am suggesting is

---

[2] It may be said that I am neglecting Carnap's distinction between the "formal" and "material" modes of speech. But I am not at all happy about the way in which this distinction is applied.

that what is called by philosophers "linguistic" analysis is not radically different from what in the past has been known as "metaphysical" analysis.[3]

There is, of course, an obvious comment which can be made about what I have been saying. An anti-metaphysician might reply as follows. "Leaving aside the question whether your account of analysis is correct or incorrect, I am quite prepared to admit that if you choose to call analysis 'metaphysics,' metaphysics is possible and has a useful function. But to call analysis 'metaphysics' does nothing at all towards justifying metaphysics in the sense in which I reject metaphysics. If an astronomer rejects astrology, it would be futile to select some part of astronomy and call it 'astrology' under the impression that astrology in the sense in which the astronomer rejects it was thus being justified."

There is obviously truth in this line of reply. I entirely agree that to call analysis as practised by the modern analyst "metaphysics" does little to justify metaphysics in the sense in which the anti-metaphysical analyst rejects metaphysics. At the same time I do not think that my line of argument is as futile as the analogy about astronomy and astrology might suggest. In the first place I have maintained that some at least of what passes for "analysis" bears a marked resemblance to what used to be called "metaphysics." The analyst might reply, of course, that he does not deny the resemblance but that the kind of inquiry referred to should be called "analysis" and not "metaphysics" whether it is practised by Plato or by Berkeley or by a modern analyst. The point is, however, that the phrase "linguistic analysis" may be misleading; and to draw attention to resemblances of the kind mentioned may help to show how it can be misleading. In the second place it is not, I think, futile to point out that the interpretation of the word "metaphysics" which is fairly common today, that is, as a study of or talk about transcendent

and unobservable entities, has not been the sense in which the word has been exclusively understood by metaphysicians themselves. If one analyzes, for example, the meaning of the word "thing," one is, I suggest, engaging in precisely one of those pursuits which metaphysicians have not infrequently engaged in and which they have regarded as pertaining to metaphysics. And it is just as well to realize this.

However, as I have said, the classification of analysis, or some of it, as "metaphysics," does little or nothing to rescue what the anti-metaphysical analysts call "metaphysics." And I want now to turn to this subject.

IV

1. If one looks at the history of metaphysical theories which involve reference to a being or to beings in some sense transcending empirical reality, one will see that in some of them the transcendent being is postulated in order to explain or to account for the world being in some respect like this rather than like that. In the myth of the *Timaeus* the divine craftsman is postulated (with what degree of seriousness it is unnecessary to discuss here) to account for the intelligible structure of the world, that is, for what Plato took to be the world's intelligible structure. Again, in Aristotle's *Metaphysics* the first unmoved mover is postulated as the ultimate explanation of "movement." In Whitehead's philosophy eternal objects and God seem to have the function of explaining how the pattern of the world comes to be what it is, while in Bergson's *Creative Evolution* the idea of the evolutionary process leads on to the idea of a creative power at work in the world. In the case of metaphysical theories of this kind their function seems to be that of explaining what may be called the *how* of the world rather than the *that* of the world. This distinction certainly cannot be rigidly applied to philosophies like those of Whitehead and Bergson; but it applies very well in the case of Aristotle, who did not postulate the first unmoved mover in order to explain the exist-

---

[3] One may note in passing that Carnap found himself compelled to distinguish "syntax" and "semantics."

ence of things, but rather in order to explain a feature of things, namely "movement" or becoming.

It is obvious, I think, that a metaphysical theory of this kind can claim to be taken seriously only if it is based on the conviction that any non-metaphysical explanation must be regarded as insufficient. An anti-metaphysician may think that all metaphysical theories are gratuitous hypotheses; but one could not expect him to give serious consideration to a metaphysical theory which even for its author was a gratuitous hypothesis. It is indeed unlikely that agreement will be reached in all cases whether a given feature of the world or a given set of empirical data can be adequately accounted for without the introduction of metaphysics. And I fail to see that the anti-metaphysician is entitled to issue a kind of advance prohibition against the introduction of metaphysics if he is unable to shake the conviction of another philosopher about the inadequacy of any non-metaphysical explanation. He is entitled, of course, to challenge the metaphysician to show that a metaphysical theory is required; for when any feature of the world can be adequately accounted for in terms of phenomenal causes, one should not drag in a metaphysical entity or theory to account for it. But, as I have said, agreement about the adequacy of non-metaphysical explanations is unlikely to be reached in all cases; and the metaphysician has as much right to his convictions on this matter as the anti-metaphysician has to his. In my opinion, there could be only one cogent ground for ruling out all metaphysical theories. This ground would obtain if it could be shown that the questions asked and theories propounded by metaphysicians are all meaningless, in the sense that to one or more of the terms no definite meaning can be assigned. But, as I said earlier in this paper, linguistic criticism of metaphysical questions and theories has to await their formulation. One has to allow the desire for understanding full play and permit it to lead to the formulation of questions and problems. Once a question has been asked, it is legitimate to ask what it

means; but one is hardly entitled to say in advance: "Be silent! For if you speak, you will utter nonsense." One does not know *a priori* that nonsense is going to be uttered.

2. Some metaphysicians might perhaps comment that I have misrepresented what they try to do. They do not take some isolated or selected feature of reality and build up a speculative theory on a narrow basis: they are more concerned with working out a general theoretical standpoint from which empirical data of various types can be seen as forming a coherent pattern. It is true that one type of metaphysician has tried to work out a system of philosophy, a comprehensive world-view, in a purely deductive manner, and that a procedure of this sort involves the application to empirical reality of a preconceived scheme, with the result that inconvenient data are slurred over or explained away. And it is true that some metaphysicians have emphasized one aspect of reality at the expense of other aspects. Schopenhauer is a case in point. But it is an exaggeration to suggest that metaphysicians in general attempt to force empirical data into a preconceived scheme or that they attend exclusively to one aspect of empirical reality. A philosopher like Bergson was not concerned with elaborating a "system." He considered problems separately, moving from one problem to another. And though his conclusions certainly converged on the formation of a unified world-view, this was the result, rather than a presupposition, of his reflections.

It is doubtless quite true that metaphysics does not stand or fall with the validity of Spinoza's method. And it is, I think, an exaggeration to depict all metaphysicians as endeavouring to prove a preconceived system. But a full understanding of reality has surely been the limiting goal of speculative metaphysics, even with those who have recognized from the start the practical unattainability of the goal. And though this does not involve the *a priori* assumption of any definite answers to questions, it does involve the assumption that reality is intelligible. But we should never attempt to understand anything unless we believed that there was something to understand. Whether subsequent confirmation of our initial belief is forthcoming is another question.

3. The attempt to understand empirical reality involves at the end, even if not at the beginning, an attempt to understand the *that* of finite beings. In the *Tractatus* Wittgenstein has said, "Not *how* the world is, is the mystical, but *that* it is." I should not care to use the word "mystical" here. But, provided that I am not understood as contradicting what I have said earlier about metaphysics and analysis, one might perhaps say, "Not *how* the world is, is the metaphysical, but *that* it is." I should be inclined to say at least that the more prominent this existential problem is in a philosophy, the more metaphysical the philosophy is. The attempt might be made to dress up some metaphysical theories in the guise of scientific hypotheses, but it would be difficult to pass off any answer which might be given to the problem of the existence of finite beings as a scientific hypothesis in the common understanding of the term.

What I am concerned with is the question why this problem constantly recurs. Its prominence in western philosophy may be connected in part with Judaeo-Christian theology; but it is not peculiar to western philosophy. It is, indeed, easy to say that the problem is a pseudo-problem, which has its origin in linguistic confusion. We should ask, it may be said, only precise questions. If we ask for the cause or the causes of a given phenomenon, we can be given, in principle at least, a definite answer in terms of other phenomena. If we do not ask precise questions, we shall find ourselves talking about "all phenomena" or "all finite things" or "all empirical reality" or about "finite being as such." And all these phrases give rise to logical difficulties. The metaphysician trades on linguistic confusion, vagueness and imprecision; he is able to impress other people only in so far as they are already involved in the same confusion as himself or in so far as he can involve them by the use of obscure and probably emotively-charged

language in this confusion. Yet the fact remains that the problem of which I am speaking continues to be raised. Indeed, if the more important metaphysical problems are excluded from academic philosophy in a given period or in a certain region, what happens is that they are raised and discussed outside the confines of academic philosophy. It may be said that this is largely due to the fact that human beings are prone to wishful thinking, and that there are always a large number of them who endeavour to find some rational or pseudo-rational justification for what they believe or want to believe on other grounds. But what is the origin of this "wishful thinking"? That metaphysical speculation, when it is indulged in, is the fulfilment of a desire of some sort is obvious enough: nobody would practise it otherwise. But more than this can be said on the subject. And I want to suggest what seems to me a possible origin of the problem of the existence of finite beings.

The primary datum is not, I think, either subject or object but the self as existing in an undefined and unarticulated situation. Man finds himself "there," within the area of Being. The consciousness of the self as a reflectively apprehended centre and of definite external objects, a consciousness which grows with experience, presupposes a pre-reflective awareness of existing in encompassing Being. As empirical knowledge grows and as definite objects are marked off within a general field, that is, as "my world" is gradually constructed, these objects are still conceived, perhaps in a very vague way, as existing against a background of Being or as within encompassing Being. And accompanying the building-up, as it were, of a definite empirical world there is an articulation, an expression to the self, of the nature of this background. By a great many people it is thought of as "the world" or "the universe." There are, I think, many people who, perhaps without clearly recognizing the fact, conceive themselves and other things as existing within "the world," as though all definite things were phenomena existing within an all-encompassing and metaphenomenal "world." In this sense there is an implicit metaphysic in the outlook of many people who are far from being metaphysicians. Again, the pre-reflective awareness (perhaps one might say the "felt" awareness) of things as standing in relation to an obscure Ground of existence may be expressed in the way in which we find it expressed in the writings of some poets. On the other hand, there may be an attempt to render explicit on the reflective level this pre-reflective awareness. And this attempt gives rise to various metaphysical systems. The attempt to state the "felt" dependence of finite things may give rise to a system like that of Spinoza or to a theistic philosophy or even to a philosophy like that of Sartre, with its conception of the *en-soi*. I do not want to argue here in favour of any particular philosophy or type of philosophy; but I do suggest that the question of the ultimate Ground of empirical existence would never be raised, were there not a primary implicit awareness of existing against a background of Being. To avoid misunderstanding I had better say that by using the word "Being" with a capital letter I do not mean to imply a direct awareness of God. A pre-reflective awareness of dependence or of what used to be called "contingency" is not the same thing as a direct awareness of God. If it were, there could hardly be those disputes between rival metaphysical systems of different types, to which we are accustomed in the history of philosophy.

It may be said that I have been putting forward a purely gratuitous hypothesis. I do not think that this is the case. I think that my hypothesis helps to explain a prominent feature of certain types of poetry, the origin, in part at least, of speculative metaphysics, a good deal of natural religion, and even the common though perhaps implicit conviction that things exist in "the world." I am perfectly well aware, of course, that what I have been saying is extremely vague: it could hardly be anything else when one attempts to discuss a matter of this sort within the limits of a few sentences. In any case, though one certainly ought to strive after clarity language can be used to draw attention to what lies on the pre-reflective level; and one function of speculative metaphysics is to make explicit the pre-reflective awareness of which I have been speaking and to state its implications. Once the attempt to do this is made linguistic difficulties arise, and the philosopher must consider them honestly. But one should not allow oneself to be paralysed by Wittgenstein's dictum that "what can be said at all can be said clearly." It is indeed obvious that "whereof one cannot speak, thereof one must be silent"; but one is not compelled to choose between absolute clarity on the one hand and silence on the other. Language can have various functions: it can be used to "draw attention to." And when one has drawn attention, one can then endeavour to express in clear language, so far as this is possible, what one has drawn attention to. This, I think, is what speculative metaphysics tries to do in regard to the primary awareness of Being. One cannot bypass linguistic analysis, but one must first strive to state. Otherwise there can be no analysis.

What I have been saying will be regarded by some as a relapse into "mysticism," as an exhibition of the inherent weakness of metaphysics, as confirmation of the theory that metaphysical propositions possess no more than emotive significance, and even perhaps as an indication that metaphysicians stand in need of psychoanalysis. But many quite ordinary people possess an implicit metaphysic; and the real reason why the central metaphysical problem constantly recurs in different forms in spite of critical analysis is, I think, that it springs from man's existential situation, accompanied by an awareness of dependence or "contingency," and not from linguistic confusion. It is open to anyone, of course, to deny this. But one might, perhaps, reverse Wittgenstein's saying "the limits of my language mean the limits of my world," and say, "the limits of my world mean the limits of my language," "my world" signifying here the experience which I am willing to acknowledge. Inability to find any value in metaphysics may very well be an indication of the limits of a man's "world."

SUGGESTED READINGS

Bergson, Henri. *Introduction to Metaphysics*. New York: The Liberal Arts Press, 1949.

Bradley, Francis H. *Appearance and Reality: A Metaphysical Essay*. Oxford: Clarendon Press, 1951, Introduction.

Collingwood, R. G. "The Reform of Metaphysics," *An Essay on Metaphysics*. Oxford: Clarendon Press, 1940.

Descartes, René. *Discourse on Method*. New York: Library of Liberal Arts, 1956.

Dewey, John. "The Subject Matter of Metaphysics," *Journal of Philosophy*, XII (1915), pp. 337–45.

Emmet, Dorothy. "Metaphysical Analogies," *The Nature of Metaphysical Thinking*. New York: St. Martin's Press, 1957, pp. 189–214.

Hartmann, Nicolai. *The New Ways of Ontology*. Chicago: Henry Regnery Co., 1953.

Henle, Robert J. *Method in Metaphysics*. Milwaukee: Marquette University Press, 1950.

Lazerowitz, Morris. "The Three Layer Structure of Metaphysics," *The Structure of Metaphysics*. London: Routledge and Kegan Paul, 1955, pp. 67–79.

Maritain, Jacques. *A Preface to Metaphysics*. London: Sheed and Ward, 1948, Lecture I, III.

Pepper, Stephen C. "The Root Metaphor Theory of Metaphysics," *The Journal of Philosophy*, XXXII (1935), pp. 365–74.

Russell, Bertrand. "Language and Metaphysics," *An Inquiry into Meaning and Truth*. London: Allen & Unwin, 1956.

Taylor, Alfred E. "Metaphysical Criterion and Metaphysical Method," *Elements of Metaphysics*. London: Methuen & Co., 1903, pp. 18–41.

Williams, B. A. O. "Metaphysical Arguments," *Nature of Metaphysics*, ed. D. F. Pears. New York: St. Martin's Press, 1957.

Wisdom, John. "Metaphysics and Verification," *Mind*, XLVII (1938), pp. 452–98.

PART II

REALITY: REALISM VERSUS IDEALISM

INTRODUCTION

Reality comprises everything there is. But the basic nature of reality—what it is composed of and its relation to our knowledge of it—has been and continues to be a controversial metaphysical issue. The two opposing views which have dominated the modern scene are idealism and realism. Neither position is simple or homogeneous, and each includes within it a number of different types or varieties. Moreover, both theories have epistemological conterparts with which they are closely, though not necessarily, related (it is possible, for instance, to be a metaphysical idealist and an epistemological realist) and from which they should be kept distinct.

If there is one tenet common to all types of metaphysical idealism, it is that reality is in some sense mind-dependent. The first of the modern idealists, whose position is often referred to as subjective idealism, was George Berkeley (1685–1753). Born in Kilkenny County, Ireland, he studied and taught in Trinity College, Dublin. He later became a bishop in the Church of England. His most important works are *Essay Toward a New Theory of Vision* (1709), *Principles of Human Knowledge* (1710), and *Three Dialogues Between Hylas and Philonous* (1713). Berkeley agrees with Locke that what we perceive and know, namely, the objects of human knowledge, are ideas and that what perceives them are minds. But if this is so, he continues, then what could one mean by saying that something exists, except that either it could be perceived or it is that which does the perceiving? He thus claims that *esse est percipi aut percipere* (to be is to be perceived or to perceive). The result is that what some philosophers call "material substance" is without meaning and that only spirit or mind or immaterial substance exists. This type of idealism is called subjective because it posits a plurality of subjects or knowers each of which exists, with God, the creator and sustainer of ideas, providing continuity to objects of the world when they are not being perceived by finite minds.

A more direct influence than Berkeley on twentieth-century philosophy was exerted by Hegel, and to his type of idealism—in which the philosophies of such men as Josiah Royce, T. H. Green, Francis Bradley, J. M. E. McTaggart, and Brand Blanshard are usually grouped—the name of absolute or objective idealism is given. For these idealists all reality is a rational system expressed in mind or spirit, and everything that is forms part of a single totality, Absolute Mind.

George Edward Moore (1873–1958), one of the founders of the British analytic movement, led the revolt against idealism and initiated the neo-realist movement with his essay "The Refutation of Idealism" (1903). An emeritus professor at Cambridge University and former editor of *Mind,* his works include *Principia Ethica* (1903), *Ethics* (1912), and *Philosophical Studies* (1922). In his "Refutation of Idealism," Moore does not deny that "reality is spiritual," but claims that one important argument for it is false. The alternative to idealism he suggests is that matter as well as spirit exists, and he argues that absolute skepticism is the only reasonable alternative to this latter position.

Realism, in general, maintains that objects exist independently of our knowing them and that they are essentially as they appear to us. Though realism as a metaphysical orientation goes back to the Greeks, modern realism, as we have seen, developed in the twentieth century in opposition to idealism. Some realists are naturalists, claiming that only nature, in the sense of what is studied by the natural sciences, exists. John Dewey and R. W. Sellars are realists of this type. Others are dualists, claiming that both mind and matter exist. Thomists (for example, see Gilson, Part III) are usually placed in this latter category, although they often call themselves critical realists. The neo-realist movement thus includes within its scope many different schools of philosophy, all of which are opposed to idealism.

The attack against idealism begun by Moore was continued in the United States as well as in England. *The New Realism* (1912) represented the united effort of six prominent American philosophers to state their common position concerning the relation between the knowing process and the thing known. E. B. Holt (1873–1946), Professor of Psychology at Harvard, and later at Princeton, and author of a number of books, including *The Concept of Consciousness* (1914); W. T. Marvin (1872–1944), author and Professor of Philosophy at Rutgers; W. P. Montague (1873–1953), Professor of Philosophy at Columbia University, lecturer at many universities in the United States and abroad, and author of *The Ways of Knowing* (1925), *The Ways of Things* (1940), and *Great Visions of Philosophy* (1950), among others; R. B. Perry (1876–1957), Professor of Philosophy at Harvard, Gifford Lecturer (1946–48), and Pulitzer Prize winner, noted for such works as *Present Philosophical Tendencies* (1912) and *Realms of Value* (1954); W. B. Pitkin (1878–1953), author and Professor of Journalism at Columbia University; and E. G. Spaulding (1873–1940), lecturer, author, and Professor of Philosophy at Princeton—all added their weight to the realistic movement in this joint endeavor. Their aim as stated in the Introduction to *The New Realism* is to return to an amended and critical version of naïve realism, which holds that "things *are* just what they *seem.*" They thus make no distinction between appearance and reality. Their position is developed in successive stages, first detailing their disagreements with idealism, next outlining their program of reform, and then discussing realism as a constructive philosophy. Together with all realists, they insist on the independence of things known and the knowing of them, and claim that "that which lies in or before the mind when knowledge takes place, is numerically identical with the thing known."

As Moore had attacked idealism, so some thirty years later Walter T. Stace (1888–   ), Emeritus Professor of Philosophy at Princeton University and author of such works as *The Philosophy of Hegel* (1924), *The Theory of Knowledge and Existence* (1932), *The Nature of the World* (1946), and *Time and Eternity* (1952), refuted what he took to be the main tenet of realism.

In his book *Beyond Realism and Idealism,* Wilbur M. Urban (1873–1952), Emeritus Professor of Philosophy at Yale University, holds that neither realists nor idealists can either prove their own position or refute the other. He claims that the great stream of European thought *(philosophia perennis)* is above the opposition of realism and idealism, and he attempts to go beyond the opposition by combining what he sees to be true in each view. Urban's solution, however, has not been widely accepted, and so the debate continues.

GEORGE BERKELEY

OF THE PRINCIPLES OF HUMAN KNOWLEDGE*

Part I

It is evident to anyone who takes a survey of the *objects* of human knowledge that they are either ideas actually imprinted on the senses, or else such as are perceived by attending to the passions and operations of the mind, or lastly, ideas formed by help of memory and imagination—either compounding, dividing, or barely representing those originally perceived in the aforesaid ways. By sight I have the ideas of light and colors, with their several degrees and variations. By touch I perceive, for example, hard and soft, heat and cold, motion and resistance, and of all these more and less either as to quantity or degree. Smelling furnishes me with odors, the palate with tastes, and hearing conveys sounds to the mind in all their variety of tone and composition. And as several of these are observed to accompany each other, they come to be marked by one name, and so to be reputed as one thing. Thus, for example, a certain color, taste, smell, figure, and consistence having been observed to go together, are accounted one distinct thing signified by the name *"apple";* other collections of ideas constitute a stone, a tree, a book, and the like sensible things—which as they are pleasing or disagreeable excite the passions of love, hatred, joy, grief, and so forth.

2. But, besides all that endless variety of ideas or objects of knowledge, there is like-

* From George Berkeley: *A Treatise Concerning the Principles of Human Knowledge*, edited by Colin M. Turbayne. New York, 1957 ("The Library of Liberal Arts" No. 53). Reprinted by permission of the publishers, The Bobbs-Merrill Company. Editor's footnotes omitted.

wise something which knows or perceives them and exercises divers operations, as willing, imagining, remembering about them. This perceiving, active being is what I call *mind, spirit, soul,* or *myself.* By which words I do not denote any one of my ideas, but a thing entirely distinct from them, wherein they exist or, which is the same thing, whereby they are perceived—for the existence of an idea consists in being perceived.

3. That neither our thoughts, nor passions, nor ideas formed by the imagination exist without the mind is what everybody will allow. And it seems no less evident that the various sensations or ideas imprinted on the sense, however blended or combined together (that is, whatever objects they compose), cannot exist otherwise than in a mind perceiving them.—I think an intuitive knowledge may be obtained of this by anyone that shall attend to what is meant by the term *exist* when applied to sensible things. The table I write on I say exists, that is, I see and feel it; and if I were out of my study I should say it existed—meaning thereby that if I was in my study I might perceive it, or that some other spirit actually does perceive it. There was an odor, that is, it was smelled, there was a sound, that is to say, it was heard; a color or figure, and it was perceived by sight or touch. This is all that I can understand by these and the like expressions. For as to what is said of the absolute existence of unthinking things without any relation to their being perceived, that seems perfectly unintelligible. Their *esse* is *percipi,* nor is it possible they should have any existence out of the minds or thinking things which perceive them.

4. It is indeed an opinion strangely prevailing amongst men that houses, mountains, rivers, and, in a word, all sensible objects have an existence, natural or real, distinct from their being perceived by the understanding. But with how great an assurance and acquiescence soever this principle may be entertained in the world, yet whoever shall find in his heart to call it in question may, if I mistake not, perceive it to involve a manifest contradiction. For what are the forementioned objects but the things we perceive by sense? And what do we perceive besides our own ideas or sensations? And is it not plainly repugnant that any one of these, or any combination of them, should exist unperceived?

5. If we thoroughly examine this tenet it will, perhaps, be found at bottom to depend on the doctrine of *abstract ideas.* For can there be a nicer strain of abstraction than to distinguish the existence of sensible objects from their being perceived, so as to conceive them existing unperceived? Light and colors, heat and cold, extension and figures—in a word, the things we see and feel —what are they but so many sensations, notions, ideas, or impressions on the sense? And is it possible to separate, even in thought, any of these from perception? For my part, I might as easily divide a thing from itself. I may, indeed, divide in my thoughts, or conceive apart from each other, those things which, perhaps, I never perceived by sense so divided. Thus I imagine the trunk of a human body without the limbs, or conceive the smell of a rose without thinking on the rose itself. So far, I will not deny, I can abstract—if that may properly be called *abstraction* which extends only to the conceiving separately such objects as it is possible may really exist or be actually perceived asunder. But my conceiving or imagining power does not extend beyond the possibility of real existence or perception. Hence, as it is impossible for me to see or feel anything without an actual sensation of that thing, so is it impossible for me to conceive in my thoughts any sensible thing or object distinct from the sensation or perception of it.

6. Some truths there are so near and obvious to the mind that a man need only open his eyes to see them. Such I take this important one to be, to wit, that all the choir of heaven and furniture of the earth, in a word, all those bodies which compose the mighty frame of the world, have not any subsistence without a mind—that their *being* is to be perceived or known, that, consequently, so long as they are not actually per-

ceived by me or do not exist in my mind or that of any other created spirit, they must either have no existence at all or else subsist in the mind of some eternal spirit—it being perfectly unintelligible, and involving all the absurdity of abstraction, to attribute to any single part of them an existence independent of a spirit. To be convinced of which, the reader need only reflect, and try to separate in his own thoughts, the *being* of a sensible thing from its *being perceived.*

7. From what has been said it follows there is not any other substance than *Spirit,* or that which perceives. But, for the fuller proof of this point, let it be considered the sensible qualities are color, figure, motion, smell, taste, and such like—that is, the ideas perceived by sense. Now, for an idea to exist in an unperceiving thing is a manifest contradiction, for to have an idea is all one as to perceive; that, therefore, wherein color, figure, and the like qualities exist must perceive them; hence it is clear there can be no unthinking substance or *substratum* of those ideas.

8. But, say you, though the ideas themselves do not exist without the mind, yet there may be things like them, whereof they are copies or resemblances, which things exist without the mind in an unthinking substance. I answer, an idea can be like nothing but an idea; a color or figure can be like nothing but another color or figure. If we look but ever so little into our thoughts, we shall find it impossible for us to conceive a likeness except only between our ideas. Again, I ask whether those supposed originals or external things, of which our ideas are the pictures or representations, be themselves perceivable or no? If they are, then they are ideas and we have gained our point; but if you say they are not, I appeal to anyone whether it be sense to assert a color is like something which is invisible; hard or soft, like something which is intangible; and so of the rest.

9. Some there are who make a distinction betwixt *primary* and *secondary* qualities. By the former they mean extension, figure, motion, rest, solidity or impenetrability, and

number; by the latter they denote all other sensible qualities, as colors, sounds, tastes, and so forth. The ideas we have of these they acknowledge not to be the resemblances of anything existing without the mind or unperceived, but they will have our ideas of the primary qualities to be patterns or images of things which exist without the mind, in an unthinking substance which they call "matter." By "matter," therefore, we are to understand an inert, senseless substance in which extension, figure, and motion do actually subsist. But it is evident from what we have already shown that extension, figure, and motion are only ideas existing in the mind, and that an idea can be like nothing but another idea, and that consequently neither they nor their archetypes can exist in an unperceiving substance. Hence it is plain that the very notion of what is called *matter* or *corporeal subsance* involves a contradiction in it.

10. They who assert that figure, motion, and the rest of the primary or original qualities do exist without the mind in unthinking substances do at the same time acknowledge that colors, sounds, heat, cold, and suchlike secondary qualities do not—which they tell us are sensations existing in the mind alone, that depend on and are occasioned by the different size, texture, and motion of the minute particles of matter. This they take for an undoubted truth which they can demonstrate beyond all exception. Now, if it be certain that those original qualities are inseparably united with the other sensible qualities, and not, even in thought, capable of being abstracted from them, it plainly follows that they exist only in the mind. But I desire anyone to reflect and try whether he can, by any abstraction of thought, conceive the extension and motion of a body without all other sensible qualities. For my own part, I see evidently that it is not in my power to frame an idea of a body extended and moved, but I must withal give it some color or other sensible quality which is acknowledged to exist only in the mind. In short, extension, figure, and motion, abstracted from all other qualities, are incon-

ceivable. Where therefore the other sensible qualities are, there must these be also, to wit, in the mind and nowhere else.

11. Again, *great* and *small, swift* and *slow* are allowed to exist nowhere without the mind, being entirely relative, and changing as the frame or position of the organs of sense varies. The extension, therefore, which exists without the mind is neither great nor small, the motion neither swift nor slow; that is, they are nothing at all. But, say you, they are extension in general, and motion in general: thus we see how much the tenet of extended movable substances existing without the mind depends on that strange doctrine of *abstract ideas.* And here I cannot but remark how nearly the vague and indeterminate description of matter or corporeal substance, which the modern philosophers are run into by their own principles, resembles that antiquated and so much ridiculed motion of *materia prima,* to be met with in Aristotle and his followers. Without extension, solidity cannot be conceived; since, therefore, it has been shown that extension exists not in an unthinking substance, the same must also be true of solidity.

12. That number is entirely the creature of the mind, even though the other qualities be allowed to exist without, will be evident to whoever considers that the same thing bears a different denomination of number as the mind views it with different respects. Thus the same extension is one, or three, or thirty-six, according as the mind considers it with reference to a yard, a foot, or an inch. Number is so visibly relative and dependent on men's understanding that it is strange to think how anyone should give it an absolute existence without the mind. We say one book, one page, one line; all these are equally units, though some contain several of the others. And in each instance it is plain the unit relates to some particular combination of ideas arbitrarily put together by the mind.

13. Unity I know some will have to be a simple or uncompounded idea accompanying all other ideas into the mind. That I have any such idea answering the word *unity* I do not find; and if I had, methinks I could not miss finding it; on the contrary, it should be the most familiar to my understanding, since it is said to accompany all other ideas and to be perceived by all the ways of sensation and reflection. To say no more, it is an *abstract idea.*

14. I shall further add that, after the same manner as modern philosophers prove certain sensible qualities to have no existence in matter, or without the mind, the same thing may be likewise proved of all other sensible qualities whatsoever. Thus, for instance, it is said that heat and cold are affections only of the mind, and not at all patterns of real beings existing in the corporeal substances which excite them, for that the same body which appears cold to one hand seems warm to another. Now, why may we not as well argue that figure and extension are not patterns or resemblances of qualities existing in matter, because to the same eye at different stations, or eyes of a different texture at the same station, they appear various and cannot, therefore, be the images of anything settled and determinate without the mind? Again, it is proved that sweetness is not really in the sapid thing, because, the thing remaining unaltered, the sweetness is changed into bitter, as in case of a fever or otherwise vitiated palate. Is it not as reasonable to say that motion is not without the mind, since if the succession of ideas in the mind become swifter, the motion, it is acknowledged, shall appear slower without any alteration in any external object?

15. In short, let anyone consider those arguments which are thought manifestly to prove that colors and taste exist only in the mind, and he shall find they may with equal force be brought to prove the same thing of extension, figure, and motion. Though it must be confessed this method of arguing does not so much prove that there is no extension or color in an outward object as that we do not know by sense which is the true extension or color of the object. But the arguments foregoing plainly show it to be impossible that any color or extension at all, or other sensible quality whatsoever, should

exist in an unthinking subject without the mind, or, in truth, that there should be any such thing as an outward object.

16. But let us examine a little the received opinion.—It is said extension is a mode or accident of matter, and that matter is the *substratum* that supports it. Now I desire that you would explain what is meant by matter's *supporting* extension. Say you, I have no idea of matter and, therefore, cannot explain it. I answer, though you have no positive, yet, if you have any meaning at all, you must at least have a relative idea of matter; though you know not what it is, yet you must be supposed to know what relation it bears to accidents, and what is meant by its supporting them. It is evident "support" cannot here be taken in its usual or literal sense—as when we say that pillars support a building; in what sense therefore must it be taken?

17. If we inquire into what the most accurate philosophers declare themselves to mean by *material substance,* we shall find them acknowledge they have no other meaning annexed to those sounds but the idea of being in general together with the relative notion of its supporting accidents. The general idea of being appears to me the most abstract and incomprehensible of all other: and as for its supporting accidents, this, as we have just now observed, cannot be understood in the common sense of those words; it must, therefore, be taken in some other sense, but what that is they do not explain. So that when I consider the two parts or branches which make the signification of the words *material substance,* I am convinced there is no distinct meaning annexed to them. But why should we trouble ourselves any further in discussing this material *substratum* or support of figure and motion and other sensible qualities? Does it not suppose they have an existence without the mind? And is not this a direct repugnance and altogether inconceivable?

18. But, though it were possible that solid, figured, movable substances may exist without the mind, corresponding to the ideas we have of bodies, yet how is it possible for us to know this? Either we must know it by sense or by reason. As for our senses, by them we have the knowledge only of our sensations, ideas, or those things that are immediately perceived by sense, call them what you will; but they do not inform us that things exist without the mind, or unperceived, like to those which are perceived. This the materialists themselves acknowledge. It remains therefore that if we have any knowledge at all of external things, it must be by reason, inferring their existence from what is immediately perceived by sense. But what reason can induce us to believe the existence of bodies without the mind, from what we perceive, since the very patrons of matter themselves do not pretend there is any necessary connection betwixt them and our ideas? I say it is granted on all hands (and what happens in dreams, frenzies, and the like, puts it beyond dispute) that it is possible we might be affected with all the ideas we have now, though no bodies existed without resembling them. Hence it is evident the supposition of external bodies is not necessary for the producing our ideas; since it is granted they are produced sometimes, and might possibly be produced always in the same order we see them in at present, without their concurrence.

19. But though we might possibly have all our sensations without them, yet perhaps it may be thought easier to conceive and explain the manner of their production by supposing external bodies in their likeness rather than otherwise; and so it might be at least probable there are such things as bodies that excite their ideas in our minds. But neither can this be said, for, though we give the materialists their external bodies, they by their own confession are never the nearer knowing how our ideas are produced, since they own themselves unable to comprehend in what manner body can act upon spirit, or how it is possible it should imprint any idea in the mind. Hence it is evident the production of ideas or sensations in our minds can be no reason why we should suppose matter or corporeal substances, since that is acknowledged to remain equally in-

explicable with or without this supposition. If therefore it were possible for bodies to exist without the mind, yet to hold they do so must needs be a very precarious opinion, since it is to suppose, without any reason at all, that God has created innumerable beings that are entirely useless and serve to no manner or purpose.

20. In short, if there were external bodies, it is impossible we should ever come to know it; and if there were not, we might have the very same reasons to think there were that we have now. Suppose—what no one can deny possible—an intelligence without the help of external bodies, to be affected with the same train of sensations or ideas that you are, imprinted in the same order and with like vividness in his mind. I ask whether that intelligence has not all the reason to believe the existence of corporeal substances, represented by his ideas and exciting them in his mind, that you can possibly have for believing the same thing? Of this there can be no question—which one consideration is enough to make any reasonable person suspect the strength of whatever arguments he may think himself to have for the existence of bodies without the mind.

21. Were it necessary to add any further proof against the existence of matter after what has been said, I could instance several of those errors and difficulties (not to mention impieties) which have sprung from that tenet. It has occasioned numberless controversies and disputes in philosophy, and not a few of far greater moment in religion. But I shall not enter into the detail of them in this place as well because I think arguments *a posteriori* are unnecessary for confirming what has been, if I mistake not, sufficiently demonstrated *a priori,* as because I shall hereafter find occasion to speak somewhat of them.

22. I am afraid I have given cause to think me needlessly prolix in handling this subject. For to what purpose is it to dilate on that which may be demonstrated with the utmost evidence in a line or two to anyone that is capable of the least reflection? It is but looking into your own thoughts, and so trying whether you can conceive it possible for a sound, or figure, or motion, or color to exist without the mind or unperceived. This easy trial may make you see that what you contend for is a downright contradiction. Insomuch that I am content to put the whole upon this issue: if you can but conceive it possible for one extended movable substance, or, in general, for any one idea, or anything like an idea, to exist otherwise than in a mind perceiving it, I shall readily give up the cause. And, as for all that compages of external bodies which you contend for, I shall grant you its existence, though you cannot either give me any reason why you believe it exists, or assign any use to it when it is supposed to exist. I say the bare possibility of your opinion's being true shall pass for an argument that it is so.

23. But, say you, surely there is nothing easier than to imagine trees, for instance, in a park, or books existing in a closet, and nobody by to perceive them. I answer you may so, there is no difficulty in it; but what is all this, I beseech you, more than framing in your mind certain ideas which you call books and trees, and at the same time omitting to frame the idea of anyone that may perceive them? But do not you yourself perceive or think of them all the while? This therefore is nothing to the purpose; it only shows you have the power of imagining or forming ideas in your mind; but it does not show that you can conceive it possible the objects of your thought may exist without the mind. To make out this, it is necessary that you conceive them existing unconceived or unthought of, which is a manifest repugnancy. When we do our utmost to conceive the existence of external bodies, we are all the while only contemplating our own ideas. But the mind, taking no notice of itself, is deluded to think it can and does conceive bodies existing unthought of or without the mind, though at the same time they are apprehended by or exist in itself. A little attention will discover to anyone the truth and evidence of what is here said, and make it unnecessary to insist on any other proofs against the existence of *material substance.*

24. It is very obvious, upon the least inquiry into our own thoughts, to know whether it be possible for us to understand what is meant by the *absolute existence of sensible objects in themselves, or without the mind.* To me it is evident those words mark out either a direct contradiction or else nothing at all. And to convince others of this, I know no readier or fairer way than to entreat they would calmly attend to their own thoughts; and if by this attention the emptiness or repugnance of those expressions does appear, surely nothing more is requisite for their conviction. It is on this, therefore, that I insist, to wit, that "the absolute existence of unthinking things" are words without a meaning, or which include a contradiction. This is what I repeat and inculcate, and earnestly recommend to the attentive thoughts of the reader.

25. All our ideas, sensations, or the things which we perceive, by whatsoever names they may be distinguished, are visibly inactive—there is nothing of power or agency included in them. So that one idea or object of thought cannot produce or make any alteration in another. To be satisfied of the truth of this, there is nothing else requisite but a bare observation of our ideas. For since they and every part of them exist only in the mind, it follows that there is nothing in them but what is perceived; but whoever shall attend to his ideas, whether of sense or reflection, will not perceive in them any power or activity; there is, therefore, no such thing contained in them. A little attention will discover to us that the very being of an idea implies passiveness and inertness in it, insomuch that it is impossible for an idea to do anything or, strictly speaking, to be the cause of anything; neither can it be the resemblance or pattern of any active being, as is evident from sect. 8. Whence it plainly follows that extension, figure, and motion cannot be the cause of our sensations. To say, therefore, that these are the effects of powers resulting from the configuration, number, motion, and size of corpuscles must certainly be false.

26. We perceive a continual succession of ideas, some are anew excited, others are changed or totally disappear. There is, therefore, some cause of these ideas, whereon they depend and which produces and changes them. That this cause cannot be any quality or idea or combination of ideas is clear from the preceding section. It must therefore be a substance; but it has been shown that there is no corporeal or material substance: it remains, therefore, that the cause of ideas is an incorporeal, active substance or spirit.

27. A spirit is one simple, undivided, active being—as it perceives ideas it is called the *understanding,* and as it produces or otherwise operates about them it is called the *will.* Hence there can be no *idea* formed of a soul or spirit; for all ideas whatever, being passive and inert (*vide* sect. 25), they cannot represent unto us, by way of image or likeness, that which acts. A little attention will make it plain to anyone that to have an idea which shall be like that active principle of motion and change of ideas is absolutely impossible. Such is the nature of *spirit,* or that which acts, that it cannot be of itself perceived, but only by the effects which it produces. If any man shall doubt of the truth of what is here delivered, let him but reflect and try if he can frame the idea of any power or active being, and whether he has ideas of two principal powers marked by the names *will* and *understanding,* distinct from each other as well as from a third idea of substance or being in general, with a relative notion of its supporting or being the subject of the aforesaid powers—which is signified by the name *soul* or *spirit.* This is what some hold; but, so far as I can see, the words *will, soul, spirit* do not stand for different ideas or, in truth, for any idea at all, but for something which is very different from ideas, and which, being an agent, cannot be like unto, or represented by, any idea whatsoever. Though it must be owned at the same time that we have some notion of soul, spirit, and the operations of the mind, such as willing, loving, hating—in as much as we know or understand the meaning of those words.

28. I find I can excite ideas in my mind at pleasure, and vary and shift the scene as oft as I think fit. It is no more than willing, and straightway this or that idea arises in my fancy; and by the same power it is obliterated and makes way for another. This making and unmaking of ideas does very properly denominate the mind active. Thus much is certain and grounded on experience; but when we talk of unthinking agents or of exciting ideas exclusive of volition, we only amuse ourselves with words.

29. But, whatever power I may have over my own thoughts, I find the ideas actually perceived by sense have not a like dependence on my will. When in broad daylight I open my eyes, it is not in my power to choose whether I shall see or no, or to determine what particular objects shall present themselves to my view; and so likewise as to the hearing and other senses; the ideas imprinted on them are not creatures of my will. There is therefore some *other* will or spirit that produces them.

30. The ideas of sense are more strong, lively, and distinct that those of the imagination; they have likewise a steadiness, order, and coherence, and are not excited at random, as those which are the effects of human wills often are, but in a regular train or series, the admirable connection whereof sufficiently testifies the wisdom and benevolence of its Author. Now the set rules or established methods wherein the mind we depend on excites in us the ideas of sense are called the *laws of nature;* and these we learn by experience, which teaches us that such and such ideas are attended with such and such other ideas in the ordinary course of things.

31. This gives us a sort of foresight which enables us to regulate our actions for the benefit of life. And without this we should be eternally at a loss; we could not know how to act anything that might procure us the least pleasure or remove the least pain of sense. That food nourishes, sleep refreshes, and fire warms us; that to sow in the seedtime is the way to reap in the harvest; and in general that to obtain such or such ends, such or such means are conducive— all this we know, not by discovering any necessary connection between our ideas, but only by the observation of the settled laws of nature, without which we should be all in uncertainty and confusion, and a grown man no more know how to manage himself in the affairs of life than an infant just born.

32. And yet this consistent, uniform working which so evidently displays the goodness and wisdom of that Governing Spirit whose Will constitutes the laws of nature, is so far from leading our thoughts to Him that it rather sends them awandering after second causes. For when we perceive certain ideas of sense constantly followed by other ideas, and we know this is not of our own doing, we forthwith attribute power and agency to the ideas themselves and make one the cause of another, than which nothing can be more absurd and unintelligible. Thus, for example, having observed that when we perceive by sight a certain round, luminous figure, we at the same time perceive by touch the idea or sensation called heat, we do from thence conclude the sun to be the cause of heat. And in like manner perceiving the motion and collision of bodies to be attended with sound, we are inclined to think the latter an effect of the former.

33. The ideas imprinted on the senses by the Author of Nature are called *real things;* and those excited in the imagination, being less regular, vivid, and constant, are more properly termed *ideas* or *images of things* which they copy and represent. But then our sensations, be they never so vivid and distinct, are nevertheless ideas, that is, they exist in the mind, or are perceived by it, as truly as the ideas of its own framing. The ideas of sense are allowed to have more reality in them, that is, to be more strong, orderly, and coherent than the creatures of the mind; but this is no argument that they exist without the mind. They are also less dependent on the spirit, or thinking substance which perceives them, in that they are excited by the will of another and more powerful spirit; yet still they are *ideas;* and certainly no idea,

whether faint or strong, can exist otherwise than in a mind perceiving it. . . .

135. Having dispatched what we intended to say concerning the knowledge of *ideas,* the method we proposed leads us in the next place to treat of *spirits*—with regard to which, perhaps, human knowledge is not so deficient as is vulgarly imagined. The great reason that is assigned for our being thought ignorant of the nature of spirits is our not having an *idea* of it. But surely it ought not to be looked on as a defect in a human understanding that it does not perceive the idea of spirit if it is manifestly impossible there should be any such idea. And this, if I mistake not, has been demonstrated in section 27; to which I shall here add that a spirit has been shown to be the only substance or support wherein the unthinking beings or ideas can exist; but that this *substance* which supports or perceives ideas should itself be an idea or like an idea is evidently absurd.

136. It will perhaps be said that we want a sense (as some have imagined) proper to know substances withal, which, if we had, we might know our own soul as we do a triangle. To this I answer, that, in case we had a new sense bestowed upon us, we could only receive thereby some new sensations or ideas of sense. But I believe nobody will say that what he means by the terms *soul* and *substance* is only some particular sort of idea or sensation. We may, therefore, infer that, all things duly considered, it is not more reasonable to think our faculties defective in that they do not furnish us with an idea of spirit or active thinking substance than it would be if we should blame them for not being able to comprehend a *round square.*

137. From the opinion that spirits are to be known after the manner of an idea or sensation have risen many absurd and heterodox tenets, and much skepticism about the nature of the soul. It is even probable that this opinion may have produced a doubt in some whether they had any soul at all distinct from their body, since upon inquiry they could not find they had an idea of it. That an *idea* which is inactive, and the existence whereof consists in being perceived, should be the image or likeness of an agent subsisting by itself seems to need no other refutation than barely attending to what is meant by those words. But perhaps you will say that though an idea cannot resemble a spirit in its thinking, acting, or subsisting by itself, yet it may in some other respects; and it is not necessary than an idea or image be in all respects like the original.

138. I answer, if it does not in those mentioned, it is impossible it should represent it in any other thing. Do but leave out the power of willing, thinking, and perceiving ideas, and there remains nothing else wherein the idea can be like a spirit. For by the word *spirit* we mean only that which thinks, wills, and perceives; this, and this alone, constitutes the signification of that term. If therefore it is impossible that any degree of those powers should be represented in an idea, it is evident there can be no idea of a spirit.

139. But it will be objected that, if there is no idea signified by the terms *soul, spirit,* and *substance,* they are wholly insignificant or have no meaning in them. I answer, those words do mean or signify a real thing, which is neither an idea nor like an idea, but that which perceives ideas, and wills, and reasons about them. What I am myself, that which I denote by the term *I,* is the same with what is meant by *soul* or *spiritual substance.* If it be said that this is only quarreling at a word, and that, since the immediate significations of other names are by common consent called *ideas,* no reason can be assigned why that which is signified by the name *spirit* or *soul* may not partake in the same appellation. I answer, all the unthinking objects of the mind agree in that they are entirely passive, and their existence consists only in being perceived; whereas a soul or spirit is an active being whose existence consists, not in being perceived, but in perceiving ideas and thinking. It is therefore necessary, in order to prevent equivocation and confounding na-

tures perfectly disagreeing and unlike, that we distinguish between *spirit* and *idea*. See sect. 27.

140. In a large sense, indeed, we may be said to have an idea or rather a notion of *spirit;* that is, we understand the meaning of the word, otherwise we could not affirm or deny anything of it. Moreover, as we conceive the ideas that are in the minds of other spirits by means of our own, which we suppose to be resemblances of them, so we know other spirits by means of our own soul— which in that sense is the image or idea of them; it having a like respect to other spirits that blueness or heat by me perceived has to those ideas perceived by another.

141. It must not be supposed that they who assert the natural immortality of the soul are of opinion that it is absolutely incapable of annihilation even by the infinite power of the Creator who first gave it being, but only that it is not liable to be broken or dissolved by the ordinary laws of nature or motion. They indeed who hold the soul of man to be only a thin vital flame, or system of animal spirits, make it perishing and corruptible as the body; since there is nothing more easily dissipated than such a being, which it is naturally impossible should survive the ruin of the tabernacle wherein it is enclosed. And this notion has been greedily embraced and cherished by the worst part of mankind, as the most effectual antidote against all impressions of virtue and religion. But it has been made evident that bodies, of what frame or texture soever, are barely passive ideas in the mind, which is more distant and heterogeneous from them than light is from darkness. We have shown that the soul is indivisible, incorporeal, unextended, and it is consequently incorruptible. Nothing can be plainer than that the motions, changes, decays, and dissolutions which we hourly see befall natural bodies (and which is what we mean by the *course of nature*) cannot possibly affect an active, simple, uncompounded substance; such a being therefore is indissoluble by the force of nature; that is to say, the soul of man is naturally immortal.

142. After what has been said, it is, I suppose, plain that our souls are not to be known in the same manner as senseless, inactive objects, or by way of *idea*. *Spirits* and *ideas* are things so wholly different that when we say "they exist," "they are known," or the like, these words must not be thought to signify anything common to both natures. There is nothing alike or common in them: and to expect that by any multiplication or enlargement of our faculties we may be enabled to know a spirit as we do a triangle seems as absurd as if we should hope to see a sound. This is inculcated because I imagine it may be of moment toward clearing several important questions and preventing some very dangerous errors concerning the nature of the soul. We may not, I think, strictly be said to have an *idea* of an active being, or of an action, although we may be said to have a *notion* of them. I have some knowledge or notion of my mind, and its acts about ideas, inasmuch as I know or understand what is meant by those words. What I know, that I have some notion of. I will not say that the terms *idea* and *notion* may not be used convertibly, if the world will have it so; but yet it conduces to clearness and propriety that we distinguish things very different by different names. It is also to be remarked that, all relations including an act of the mind, we cannot so properly be said to have an idea, but rather a notion of the relations or habitudes between things. But if, in the modern way, the word *idea* is extended to spirits, and relations, and acts, this is, after all, an affair of verbal concern.

143. It will not be amiss to add that the doctrine of *abstract ideas* has had no small share in rendering those sciences intricate and obscure which are particularly conversant about spiritual things. Men have imagined they could frame abstract notions of the powers and acts of the mind and consider them prescinded as well from the mind or spirit itself as from their respective objects and effects. Hence a great number of dark and ambiguous terms, presumed to stand for abstract notions, have been introduced into

metaphysics and morality, and from these have grown infinite distractions and disputes amongst the learned.

144. But nothing seems more to have contributed toward engaging men in controversies and mistakes with regard to the nature and operations of the mind than the being used to speak of those things in terms borrowed from sensible ideas. For example, the will is termed the *motion* of the soul: this infuses a belief that the mind of man is as a ball in motion, impelled and determined by the objects of sense, as necessarily as that is by the stroke of a racket. Hence arise endless scruples and errors of dangerous consequence in morality. All which, I doubt not, may be cleared, and truth appear plain, uniform, and consistent, could but philosophers be prevailed on to retire into themselves, and attentively consider their own meaning.

145. From what has been said it is plain that we cannot know the existence of other spirits otherwise than by their operations, or the ideas by them excited in us. I perceive several motions, changes, and combinations of ideas that inform me there are certain particular agents, like myself, which accompany them and concur in their production. Hence, the knowledge I have of other spirits is not immediate, as is the knowledge of my ideas, but depending on the intervention of ideas, by me referred to agents or spirits distinct from myself, as effects or concomitant signs.

146. But though there be some things which convince us human agents are concerned in producing them, yet it is evident to everyone that those things which are called "the works of nature," that is, the far greater part of the ideas or sensations perceived by us, are not produced by, or dependent on, the wills of men. There is therefore some other spirit that causes them; since it is repugnant that they should subsist by themselves. See sect. 29. But, if we attentively consider the constant regularity, order, and concatenation of natural things, the surprising magnificence, beauty, and perfection of the larger, and the exquisite contrivance of the smaller parts of the creation, together

with the exact harmony and correspondence of the whole, but above all the never-enough-admired laws of pain and pleasure, and the instincts or natural inclinations, appetites, and passions of animals; I say if we consider all these things, and at the same time attend to the meaning and import of the attributes: one, eternal, infinitely wise, good, and perfect, we shall clearly perceive that they belong to the aforesaid spirit, "who works all in all," and "by whom all things consist."

147. Hence it is evident that God is known as certainly and immediately as any other mind or spirit whatsoever distinct from ourselves. We may even assert that the existence of God is far more evidently perceived than the existence of men; because the effects of nature are infinitely more numerous and considerable than those ascribed to human agents. There is not any one mark that denotes a man, or effect produced by him, which does not more strongly evince the being of that spirit who is the Author of Nature. For it is evident that in affecting other persons the will of man has no other object than bearly the motion of the limbs of his body; but that such a motion should be attended by, or excite any idea in the mind of another, depends wholly on the will of the Creator. He alone it is who, "upholding all things by the word of his power," maintains that intercourse between spirits whereby they are able to perceive the existence of each other. And yet this pure and clear light which enlightens everyone is itself invisible.

148. It seems to be a general pretense of the unthinking herd that they cannot *see* God. Could we but see him, say they, as we see a man, we should believe that he is, and, believing, obey his commands. But alas, we need only open our eyes to see the sovereign Lord of all thing, with a more full and clear view than we do any one of our fellow creatures. Not that I imagine we see God (as some will have it) by a direct and immediate view; or see corporeal things, not by themselves, but by seeing that which represents them in the essence of God, which doctrine is, I must confess, to me incom-

prehensible. But I shall explain my meaning:—a human spirit or person is not perceived by sense, as not being an idea; when therefore we see the color, size, figure, and motions of a man, we perceive only certain sensations or ideas excited in our own minds; and these being exhibited to our view in sundry distinct collections, serve to mark out unto us the existence of finite and created spirits like ourselves. Hence it is plain we do not see a man—if by *man* is meant that which lives, moves, perceives, and thinks as we do—but only such a certain collection of ideas as directs us to think there is a distinct principle of thought and motion, like to ourselves, accompanying and represented by it. And after the same manner we see God; all the difference is that, whereas some one finite and narrow assemblage of ideas denotes a particular human mind, whithersoever we direct our view, we do at all times and in all places perceive manifest tokens of the divinity; everything we see, hear, feel, or anywise perceive by sense, being a sign or effect of the power of God; as is our perception of those very motions which are produced by men.

149. It is therefore plain that nothing can be more evident to anyone that is capable of the least reflection than the existence of God, or a spirit who is intimately present to our minds, producing in them all that variety of ideas or sensations which continually affect us, on whom we have an absolute and entire dependence, in short "in whom we live, and move, and have our being." That the discovery of this great truth, which lies so near and obvious to the mind, should be attained to by the reason of so very few, is a sad instance of the stupidity and inattention of men who, though they are surrounded with such clear manifestations of the Deity, are yet so little affected by them that they seem, as it were, blinded with excess of light. .

GEORGE EDWARD MOORE

THE REFUTATION OF IDEALISM*

Modern Idealism, if it asserts any general conclusion about the universe at all, asserts that it is *spiritual*. There are two points about this assertion to which I wish to call attention. These points are that, whatever be its exact meaning, it is certainly meant to assert (1) that the universe is very different indeed from what it seems, and (2) that it has quite a large number of properties which it does not seem to have. Chairs and tables and mountains *seem* to be very different from us; but, when the whole universe is declared to be spiritual, it is certainly meant to assert that they are far more like us than we think. The idealist means to assert that they are *in some sense* neither lifeless nor unconscious, as they certainly seem to be; and I do not think his language is so grossly deceptive, but that we may assume him to believe that they really are very different indeed from what they seem. And secondly when he declares that they are *spiritual,* he means to include in that term quite a large number of different properties. When the whole universe is declared to be spiritual, it is meant not only that it is in some sense *conscious*, but that it has what we recognise in ourselves as the *higher* forms of consciousness. That it is intelligent; that it is purposeful; that it is not mechanical; all these different things are commonly asserted of it. In general, it may be said, this phrase "reality is spiritual" excites and expresses the belief that the *whole* universe possesses

* From *Philosophical Studies* by G. E. Moore. London: Routledge & Kegan Paul Ltd., 1922. This essay first appeared in *Mind*, XII (October 1903), pp. 433-453. Reprinted by permission.

all the qualities the possession of which is held to make us so superior to things which seem to be inanimate: at least, if it does not possess exactly those which we possess, it possesses not one only, but several others, which, by the same ethical standard, would be judged equal to or better than our own. When we say it is *spiritual* we mean to say that it has quite a number of excellent qualities, different from any which we commonly attribute either to stars or planets or to cups and saucers.

Now why I mention these two points is that when engaged in the intricacies of philosophic discussion, we are apt to overlook the vastness of the difference between this idealistic view and the ordinary view of the world, and to overlook the number of *different* propositions which the idealist must prove. It is, I think, owing to the vastness of this difference and owing to the number of different excellences which Idealists attribute to the universe, that it seems such an interesting and important question whether Idealism be true or not. But, when we begin to argue about it, I think we are apt to forget what a vast number of arguments this interesting question must involve: we are apt to assume, that if one or two points be made on either side, the whole case is won. I say this lest it should be thought that any of the arguments which will be advanced in this paper would be sufficient to disprove, or any refutation of them sufficient to prove, the truly interesting and important proposition that reality is spiritual. For my own part I wish it to be clearly understood that I do not suppose that anything I shall say has the smallest tendency to prove that reality is not spiritual: I do not believe it possible to refute a single one of the many important propositions contained in the assertion that it is so. Reality may be spiritual, for all I know; and I devoutly hope it is. But I take "Idealism" to be a wide term and to include not only this interesting conclusion but a number of arguments which are supposed to be, if not sufficient, at least *necessary,* to prove it. Indeed I take it that modern Idealists are chiefly distinguished by certain argu-

ments which they have in common. That reality is spiritual has, I believe, been the tenet of many theologians; and yet, for believing that alone, they should hardly be called Idealists. There are besides, I believe, many persons, not improperly called Idealists, who hold certain characteristic propositions, without venturing to think them quite sufficient to prove so grand a conclusion. It is, therefore, only with Idealistic *arguments* that I am concerned; and if any Idealist holds that *no* argument is necessary to prove that reality is spiritual, I shall certainly not have refuted him. I shall, however, attack at least one argument, which, to the best of my belief, is considered necessary to their position by *all* Idealists. And I wish to point out a certain advantage which this procedure gives me—an advantage which justifies the assertion that, if my arguments are sound, they will have refuted Idealism. If I can refute a single proposition which is a necessary and essential step in all Idealistic arguments, then, no matter how good the rest of these arguments may be, I shall have proved that Idealists have *no reason whatever* for their conclusion.

Suppose we have a chain of argument which takes the form: Since A is B, and B is C, and C is D, it follows A is D. In such an argument, though "B is C" and "C is D" may both be perfectly true, yet if "A is B" be false, we have no more reason for asserting A is D than if all three were false. It does not, indeed, follow that A is D is false; nor does it follow that no other arguments would prove it to be true. But it does follow that, so far as this argument goes, it is the barest supposition, without the least bit of evidence. I propose to attack a proposition which seems to me to stand in this relation to the conclusion "Reality is spiritual." I do not propose to dispute that "Reality is spiritual"; I do not deny that there may be reasons for thinking that it is: but I do propose to show that one reason upon which, to the best of my judgment, all other arguments ever used by Idealists depend is *false.* These other arguments may, for all I shall say, be eminently ingenious and true;

they are very many and various, and different Idealists use the most different arguments to prove the same most important conclusions. Some of these *may* be sufficient to prove that B is C and C is D; but if, as I shall try to show, their "A is B" is false the conclusion A is D remains a pleasant supposition. I do not deny that to suggest pleasant and plausible suppositions may be the proper function of philosophy: but I am assuming that the name Idealism can only be properly applied where there is a certain amount of argument, intended to be cogent.

The subject of this paper is, therefore, quite uninteresting. Even if I prove my point, I shall have proved nothing about the Universe in general. Upon the important question whether Reality is or is not spiritual my argument will not have the remotest bearing. I shall only attempt to arrive at the truth about a matter, which is in itself quite trivial and insignificant, and from which, so far as I can see and certainly so far as I shall say, no conclusions can be drawn about any of the subjects about which we most want to know. The only importance I can claim for the subject I shall investigate is that it seems to me to be a matter upon which not Idealists only, but all philosophers and psychologists also, have been in error, and from their erroneous view of which they have inferred (validly or invalidly) their most striking and interesting conclusions. And that it has even this importance I cannot hope to prove. If it has this importance, it will indeed follow that all the most striking results of philosophy—Sensationalism, Agnosticism and Idealism alike—have, for all that has hitherto been urged in their favour, no more foundation than the supposition that a chimera lives in the moon. It will follow that, unless new reasons never urged hitherto can be found, all the most important philosophic doctrines have as little claim to assent as the most superstitious beliefs of the lowest savages. Upon the question what we have *reason* to believe in the most interesting matters, I do therefore think that my results will have an important bearing; but I cannot too clearly insist that upon the question

whether these beliefs are true they will have none whatever.

The trivial proposition which I propose to dispute is this: that *esse* is *percipi*. This is a very ambiguous proposition, but, in some sense or other, it has been very widely held. That it is, in some sense, essential to Idealism, I must for the present merely assume. What I propose to show is that, in all the senses ever given to it, it is false.

But, first of all, it may be useful to point out briefly in what relation I conceive it to stand to Idealistic arguments. That wherever you can truly predicate *esse* you can truly predicate *percipi,* in some sense or other, is, I take it, a necessary step in all arguments, properly to be called Idealistic, and, what is more, in all arguments hitherto offered for the Idealistic conclusion. If *esse* is *percipi,* this is at once equivalent to saying that whatever is, is experienced; and this, again, is equivalent, in a sense, to saying that whatever is, is something mental. But this is not the sense in which the Idealist *conclusion* must maintain that Reality is *mental.* The Idealist *conclusion* is that *esse* is *percipere;* and hence, whether *esse* be *percipi* or not, a further and different discussion is needed to show whether or not it is also *percipere.* And again, even if *esse* be *percipere,* we need a vast quantity of further argument to show that what has *esse* has also those higher mental qualities which are denoted by spiritual. This is why I said that the question I should discuss, namely, whether or not *esse* is *percipi,* must be utterly insufficient either to prove or to disprove that reality is spiritual. But, on the other hand, I believe that every argument ever used to show that reality is spiritual has inferred this (validly or invalidly) from "*esse* is *percipere*" as one of its premises; and that this again has never been pretended to be proved except by use of the premiss that *esse* is *percipi.* The type of argument used for the latter purpose is familiar enough. It is said that since whatever is, is experienced, and since some things are which are not experienced by the individual, these must at least form part of some experience. Or again that, since an object necessarily implies a subject, and since the whole world must be an object, we must conceive it to belong to some subject or subjects, in the same sense in which whatever is the object of our experience belongs to us. Or again, that, since thought enters into the essence of all reality, we must conceive behind it, in it, or as its essence, a spirit akin to ours, who thinks: that "spirit greets spirit" in its object. Into the validity of these inferences I do not propose to enter: they obviously require a great deal of discussion. I only desire to point out that, however correct they may be, yet if *esse* is not *percipi*, they leave us as far from a proof that reality is spiritual, as if they were all false too.

But now: Is *esse percipi?* There are three very ambiguous terms in this proposition, and I must begin by distinguishing the different things that may be meant by some of them.

And first with regard to *percipi.* This term need not trouble us long at present. It was, perhaps, originally used to mean "sensation" only; but I am not going to be so unfair to modern Idealists—the only Idealists to whom the term should now be applied without qualification—as to hold that, if they say *esse* is *percipi*, they mean by *percipi* sensation only. On the contrary I quite agree with them that, if *esse* be *percipi* at all, *percipi* must be understood to include not sensation only, but that other type of mental fact, which is called "thought"; and, whether *esse* be *percipi* or not, I consider it to be the main service of the philosophic school, to which modern Idealists belong, that they have insisted on distinguishing "sensation" and "thought" and on emphasising the importance of the latter. Against Sensationalism and Empiricism they have maintained the true view. But the distinction between sensation and thought need not detain us here. For, in whatever respects they differ, they have at least this in common, that they are both forms of consciousness or, to use a term that seems to be more in fashion just now, they are both ways of experiencing. Accordingly, whatever *esse* is *percipi* may mean, it does *at least* assert that whatever is,

is *experienced.* And since what I wish to maintain is, that even this is untrue, the question whether it be experienced by way of sensation or thought or both is for my purpose quite irrelevant. If it be not experienced at all, it cannot be either an object of thought or an object of sense. It is only if being involves "experience" that the question, whether it involves sensation or thought or both, becomes important. I beg, therefore, that *percipi* may be understood, in what follows, to refer merely to what is *common* to sensation and thought. A very recent article states the meaning of *esse* is *percipi* with all desirable clearness in so far as *percipi* is concerned. "I will undertake to show," says Mr. Taylor,[1] "that what makes [any piece of fact] real can be nothing but its presence as an inseparable aspect of *a sentient experience.*" I am glad to think that Mr. Taylor has been in time to supply me with so definite a statement that this is the ultimate premiss of Idealism. My paper will at least refute Mr. Taylor's Idealism, if it refutes anything at all: for I *shall* undertake to show that what makes a thing real cannot possibly be its presence as an inseparable aspect of a senient experience.

But Mr. Taylor's statement though clear, I think, with regard to the meaning of *percipi* is highly ambiguous in other respects. I will leave it for the present to consider the next ambiguity in the statement: *Esse* is *percipi.* What does the copula mean? What can be meant by saying that Esse *is* percipi? There are just three meanings, one or other of which such a statement *must* have, if it is to be true; and of these there is only one which it can have, if it is to be important. (1) The statement may be meant to assert that the word "esse" is used to signify nothing either more or less than the word "percipi": that the two words are precise synonyms: that they are merely different names for one and the same thing: that what is meant by *esse* is absolutely identical with what is meant by *percipi.* I think I need not prove that the principle *esse* is *percipi* is *not* thus intended

---

[1] *International Journal of Ethics*, October, 1902.

merely to define a word; nor yet that, if it were, it would be an extremely bad definition. But if it does *not* mean this, only two alternatives remain. The second is (2) that what is meant by *esse*, though not absolutely identical with what is meant by *percipi*, yet *includes* the latter as a *part* of its meaning. If this were the meaning of "esse is percipi," then to say that a thing was real would not be the same thing as to say that it was experienced. That it was *real* would mean that it was experienced and *something else besides*: "being experienced" would be *analytically essential* to reality, but would not be the whole meaning of the term. From the fact that a thing was real we should be able to infer, by the law of contradiction, that it was experienced; since the latter would be *part* of what is meant by the former. But, on the other hand, from the fact a thing was experienced we should *not* be able to infer that it was real; since it would not follow from the fact that it had one of the attributes essential to reality, that it *also* had the other or others. Now, if we understand *esse* is *percipi* in this second sense, we must distinguish *three* different things which it asserts. First of all, it gives a definition of the word "reality," asserting that word stands for a complex whole, of which what is meant by "percipi" forms a part. And secondly it asserts that "being experienced" forms a part of a certain whole. Both these propositions may be true, and at all events I do not wish to dispute them. I do not, indeed, think that the word "reality" is commonly used to include "percipi"; but I do not wish to argue about the meaning of words. And that many things which are experienced are also something else—that to be experienced forms part of certain wholes, is, of course, indisputable. But what I wish to point out is, that neither of these propositions is of any importance, unless we add to them a *third*. That "real" is a convenient name for a union of attributes which *sometimes* occurs, it could not be worth any one's while to assert: no inferences of any importance could be drawn from such an assertion. Our principle could only mean that when a thing happens to have

percipi as well as the other qualities included under *esse,* it has *percipi:* and we should never be able to *infer* that it was experienced, except from a proposition which already asserted that it was both experienced and something else. Accordingly, if the assertion that *percipi* forms part of the whole meant by reality is to have any importance, it must mean that the whole is organic, at least in this sense, that the other constituent or constituents of it *cannot* occur without percipi, even if percipi can occur without them. (Let us call these other constituents *x.*) The proposition that *esse* includes *percipi,* and that therefore from *esse percipi* can be inferred, can only be important if it is meant to assert that *percipi* can be inferred from *x.* The only importance of the question whether the whole *esse* includes the part *percipi* rests therefore on the question whether the part *x* is necessarily connected with the part *percipi.* And this is (3) the third possible meaning of the assertion *esse* is *percipi:* and, as we now see, the only important one. *Esse* is *percipi* asserts that wherever you have *x* you also have *percipi:* that whatever has the property *x* also has the property that it is *experienced.* And this being so, it will be convenient if, for the future, I may be allowed to use the term *"esse"* to denote *x alone.* I do not wish thereby to beg the question whether what we commonly mean by the word "real" does or does not include *percipi* as well as *x*. I am quite content that my definition of "esse" to denote *x*, should be regarded merely as an arbitrary verbal definition. Whether it is so or not, the only question of interest is whether from *x percipi* can be inferred, and I should prefer to be able to express this in the form: can *percipi* be inferred from *esse?* Only let it be understood that when I say *esse,* that term will not for the future *include percipi:* it denotes only that *x*, which Idealists, perhaps rightly, include *along with percipi* under *their* term *esse.* That there is such an *x* they must admit on pain of making the proposition an *absolute* tautology; and that from this *x percipi* can be inferred they must admit, on pain of making it a perfectly barren analytic proposition. Whether *x* alone should or should not be called *esse* is not worth a dispute: what is worth dispute is whether *percipi* is necessarily connected with *x*.

We have therefore discovered the ambiguity of the copula in *esse* is *percipi,* so far as to see that this principle asserts two distinct terms to be so related, that whatever has the *one,* which I call *esse,* has *also* the property that it is experienced. It asserts a necessary connexion between *esse* on the one hand and *percipi* on the other; these two words denoting each a distinct term, and *esse* denoting a term in which that denoted by *percipi* is not included. We have, then, in *esse* is *percipi,* a *necessary synthetic* proposition which I have undertaken to refute. And I may say at once that, understood as such, it cannot be refuted. If the Idealist chooses to assert that it is merely a self-evident truth, I have only to say that it does not appear to me to be so. But I believe that no Idealist ever has maintained it to be so. Although this—that two distinct terms are necessarily related—is the only sense which "esse is percipi" can have if it is to be true and important, it *can* have another sense, if it is to be an important falsehood. I believe that Idealists all hold this important falsehood. They do not perceive that *Esse* is *percipi* must, if true, be *merely* a self-evident synthetic truth: they either identify with it or give as a reason for it another proposition which must be false because it is self-contradictory. Unless they did so, they would have to admit that it was a perfectly unfounded assumption; and if they recognised that it was *unfounded,* I do not think they would maintain its truth to be evident. *Esse* is *percipi,* in the sense I have found for it, *may* indeed be true; I cannot refute it: but if this sense were clearly apprehended, no one, I think, would *believe* that it was true.

Idealists, we have seen, must assert that whatever is experienced, is *necessarily* so. And this doctrine they commonly express by saying that "the object of experience is inconceivable apart from the subject." I have hitherto been concerned with pointing out what meaning this assertion must have, if it

is to be an important truth. I now propose to show that it may have an important meaning, which must be false, because it is self-contradictory.

It is a well-known fact in the history of philosophy that *necessary* truths in general, but especially those of which it is said that the opposite is inconceivable, have been commonly supposed to be *analytic,* in the sense that the proposition denying them was self-contradictory. It was in this way, commonly supposed, before Kant, that many truths could be proved by the law of contradiction alone. This is, therefore, a mistake which it is plainly easy for the best philosophers to make. Even since Kant many have continued to assert it; but I am aware that among those Idealists, who most properly deserve the name, it has become more fashionable to assert that truths are *both* analytic and synthetic. Now with many of their reasons for asserting this I am not concerned: it is possible that in some connexions the assertion may bear a useful and true sense. But if we understand "analytic" in the sense just defined, namely, what is proved by the law of contradiction *alone,* it is plain that, if "synthetic" means what is *not* proved by this alone, no truth can be both analytic and synthetic. Now it seems to me that those who do maintain truths to be both, do nevertheless maintain that they are so in this as well as in other senses. It is, indeed, extremely unlikely that so essential a part of the historical meaning of "analytic" and "synthetic" should have been entirely discarded, especially since we find no express recognition that it is discarded. In that case it is fair to suppose that modern Idealists have been influenced by the view that certain truths can be proved by the law of contradiction alone. I admit they also expressly declare that they can *not:* but this is by no means sufficient to prove that they do not also think they are; since it is very easy to hold two mutually contradictory opinions. What I suggest then is that Idealists hold the particular doctrine in question, concerning the relation of subject and object in experience, because they think it is an analytic truth in this restricted sense that it is proved by the law of contradiction alone.

I am suggesting that the Idealist maintains that object and subject are necessarily connected, mainly because he fails to see that they are *distinct,* that they are *two,* at all. When he thinks of "yellow" and when he thinks of the "sensation of yellow," he fails to see that there is anything whatever in the latter which is not in the former. This being so, to deny that yellow can ever *be* apart from the sensation of yellow is merely to deny that yellow can ever be other than it is; since yellow and the sensation of yellow are absolutely identical. To assert that yellow is necessarily an object of experience is to assert that yellow is necessarily yellow—a purely identical proposition, and therefore proved by the law of contradiction alone. Of course, the proposition also implies that experience is, after all, something distinct from yellow—else there would be no reason for insisting that yellow is a sensation: and that the argument thus both affirms and denies that yellow and sensation of yellow are distinct, is what sufficiently refutes it. But this contradiction can easily be overlooked, because though we are convinced, in other connexions, that "experience" does mean something and something most important, yet we are never distinctly aware *what* it means, and thus in every particular case we do not notice its presence. The facts present themselves as a kind of antinomy: (1) Experience *is* something unique and different from anything else; (2) Experience of green is entirely indistinguishable from green; two propositions which cannot both be true. Idealists holding both, can only take refuge in arguing from the one in some connexions and from the other in others.

But I am well aware that there are many Idealists who would repel it as an utterly unfounded charge that they fail to distinguish between a sensation or idea and what I will call its object. And there are, I admit, many who not only imply, as we all do, that green is distinct from the sensation of green, but expressly insist upon the distinction as an important part of their system. They would

perhaps only assert that the two form an inseparable unity. But I wish to point out that many, who use this phrase, and who do admit the distinction, are not thereby absolved from the charge that they deny it. For there is a certain doctrine, very prevalent among philosophers nowadays, which by a very simple reduction may be seen to assert that two distinct things both are and are not distinct. A distinction is asserted; but it is *also* asserted that the things distinguished form an "organic unity." But, forming such a unity, it is held, each would not be what it is *apart from its relation to the other.* Hence to consider either by itself is to make an *illegitimate abstraction.* The recognition that there are "organic unities" and "illegitimate abstractions" in this sense is regarded as one of the chief conquests of modern philosophy. But what is the sense attached to these terms? An abstraction is illegitimate, when and only when we attempt to assert of *a part*—of something abstracted—that which is true only of the *whole* to which it belongs: and it may perhaps be useful to point out that this should not be done. But the application actually made of this principle, and what perhaps would be expressly acknowledged as its meaning, is something much the reverse of useful. The principle is used to assert that certain abstractions are *in all cases* illegitimate; that whenever you try to assert *anything whatever* of that which is *part* of an organic whole, what you assert can only be true of the whole. And this principle, so far from being a useful truth, is necessarily false. For if the whole can, nay *must,* be substituted for the part in all propositions and for all purposes, this can only be because the whole is absolutely identical with the part. When, therefore, we are told that green and the sensation of green are certainly distinct but yet are not separable, or that it is an illegitimate abstraction to consider the one apart from the other, what these provisos are used to assert is, that though the two things are distinct yet you not only can but must treat them as if they were not. Many philosophers, therefore, when they admit a distinction, yet (following the lead of

Hegel) boldly assert their right, in a slightly more obscure form of words, *also* to deny it. The principle of organic unities, like that of combined analysis and synthesis, is mainly used to defend the practice of holding *both* of two contradictory propositions, wherever this may seem convenient. In this, as in other matters, Hegel's main service to philosophy has consisted in giving a name to and erecting into a principle, a type of fallacy to which experience had shown philosophers, along with the rest of mankind, to be addicted. No wonder that he has followers and admirers.

I have shown then, so far, that when the Idealist asserts the important principle *"Esse is percipi"* he must, if it is to be true, mean by this that: Whatever is experienced also *must* be experienced. And I have also shown that he *may* identify with, or give as a reason for, this proposition, one which must be false, because it is self contradictory. But at this point I propose to make a complete break in my argument. *"Esse is percipi,"* we have seen, asserts of two terms, as distinct from one another as "green" and "sweet," that whatever has the one has also the other: it asserts that "being" and "being experienced" are necessarily connected: that whatever *is* is *also* experienced. And this, I admit, cannot be directly refuted. But I believe it to be false; and I have asserted that anybody who saw that *"esse* and *percipi"* were as distinct as "green" and "sweet" would be no more ready to believe that whatever *is* is *also* experienced, than to believe that whatever is green is also sweet. I have asserted that no one would believe that *"esse* is *percipi"* if they saw how different *esse* is from *percipi:* but *this* I shall not try to prove. I have asserted that all who do believe that *"esse* is *percipi"* identify with it or take as a reason for it a self-contradictory proposition: but this I shall not try to prove. I shall only try to show that certain propositions which I assert to be believed, are false. That they are believed, and that without this belief *"esse* is *percipi"* would not be believed either, I must leave without a proof.

I pass, then, from the uninteresting question "Is *'esse percipi'?"* to the still more un-

interesting and apparently irrelevant question "What is a sensation or idea?"

We all know that the sensation of blue differs from that of green. But it is plain that if both are *sensations* they also have some point in common. What is it that they have in common? And how is this common element related to the points in which they differ?

I will call the common element "consciousness" without yet attempting to say what the thing I so call *is*. We have then in every sensation two distinct terms, (1) "consciousness," in respect of which all sensations are alike; and (2) something else, in respect of which one sensation differs from another. It will be convenient if I may be allowed to call this second term the "object" of a sensation: this also without yet attempting to say what I mean by the word.

We have then in every sensation two distinct elements, one which I call consciousness, and another which I call the object of consciousness. This must be so if the sensation of blue and the sensation of green, though different in one respect, are alike in another: blue is one object of sensation and green is another, and consciousness, which both sensations have in common, is different from either.

But, further, sometimes the sensation of blue exists in my mind and sometimes it does not; and knowing, as we now do, that the sensation of blue includes two different elements, namely consciousness and blue, the question arises whether, when the sensation of blue exists, it is the consciousness which exists, or the blue which exists, or both. And one point at least is plain: namely that these three alternatives are all different from one another. So that, if any one tells us that to say "Blue exists" is the *same* thing as to say that "Both blue and consciousness exist," he makes a mistake and a self-contradictory mistake.

But another point is also plain, namely, that when the sensation exists, the consciousness, at least, certainly does exist; for when I say that the sensations of blue and of green both exist, I certainly mean that what is common to both and in virtue of which both are called sensations, exists in each case. The only alternative left, then, is that *either* both exist or the consciousness exists alone. If, therefore, any one tells us that the existence of blue is the same thing as the existence of the sensation of blue he makes a mistake and a self-contradictory mistake, for he asserts *either* that blue is the same thing as blue together with consciousness, *or* that it is the same thing as consciousness alone.

Accordingly to identify either "blue" or any other of what I have called *"objects"* of sensation, with the corresponding sensation is in every case, a self-contradictory error. It is to identify a part either with the whole of which it is a part or else with the other part of the same whole. If we are told that the assertion "Blue exists" is *meaningless* unless we mean by it that "The sensation of blue exists," we are told what is certainly false and self-contradictory. If we are told that the existence of blue is inconceivable apart from the existence of the sensation, the speaker *probably*, means to convey to us, by this ambiguous expression, what is a self-contradictory error. For we can and must conceive the existence of blue as something quite distinct from the existence of the sensation. We can and must conceive that blue might exist and yet the sensation of blue not exist. For my own part I not only conceive this, but conceive it to be true. Either therefore this terrific assertion of inconceivability means what is false and self-contradictory or else it means only that *as a matter of fact* blue never can exist unless the sensation of it exists also.

And at this point I need not conceal my opinion that no philosopher has ever yet succeeded in avoiding this self-contradictory error: that the most striking results both of Idealism and of Agnosticism are only obtained by identifying blue with the sensation of blue: that *esse* is held to be *percipi*, solely because *what is experienced* is held to be identical with *the experience of it*. That Berkeley and Mill committed this error will, perhaps, be granted: that modern Idealists make it will, I hope, appear more probable

later. But that my opinion is plausible, I will now offer two pieces of evidence. The first is that language offers us no means of referring to such objects as "blue" and "green" and "sweet," except by calling them sensations: it is an obvious violation of language to call them "things" or "objects" or "terms." And similarly we have no natural means of referring to such objects as "causality" or "likeness" or "identity," except by calling them "ideas" or "notions" or "conceptions." But it is hardly likely that if philosophers had clearly distinguished in the past between a sensation or idea and what I have called its object, there should have been no separate name for the latter. They have always used the same name for these two different "things" (if I may call them so): and hence there is some probability that they have supposed these "things" *not* to be two and different, but one and the same. And, secondly, there is a very good reason why they should have supposed so, in the fact that when we refer to introspection and try to discover what the sensation of blue is, it is very easy to suppose that we have before us only a single term. The term "blue" is easy enough to distinguish, but the other element which I have called "consciousness"—that which sensation of blue has in common with sensation of green—is extremely difficult to fix. That many people fail to distinguish it at all is sufficiently shown by the fact that there are materialists. And, in general, that which makes the sensation of blue a mental fact seems to escape us: it seems, if I may use a metaphor, to be transparent—we look through it and see nothing but the blue; we may be convinced that there *is something* but *what* it is no philosopher, I think, has yet clearly recognized.

But this was a digression. The point I had established so far was that in every sensation or idea we must distinguish two elements, (1) the "object," or that in which one differs from another; and (2) "consciousness," or that which all have in common—that which makes them sensations or mental facts. This being so, it followed that when a sensation or idea exists, we have to choose between the alternatives that either object alone, or consciousness alone, or both, exist; and I showed that of these alternatives one, namely that the object only exists, is excluded by the fact that what we mean to assert is certainly the existence of a mental fact. There remains the question: Do both exist? Or does the consciousness alone? And to this question one answer has hitherto been given universally: That both exist.

This answer follows from the analysis hitherto accepted of the relation of what I have called "object" to "consciousness" in any sensation or idea. It is held that what I call the object is merely the "content" of a sensation or idea. It is held that in each case we can distinguish two elements and two only, (1) the fact that there is feeling or experience, and (2) *what* is felt or experienced; the sensation or idea, it is said, forms a whole, in which we must distinguish two "inseparable aspects," "content" and "existence." I shall try to show that this analysis is false; and for that purpose I must ask what may seem an extraordinary question: namely what is meant by saying that one thing is "content" of another? It is not usual to ask this question; the term is used as if everybody must understand it. But since I am going to maintain that "blue" is *not* the content of the sensation of blue, and what is more important, that, even if it were this analysis would leave out the most important element in the sensation of blue, it is necessary that I should try to explain precisely what it is that I shall deny.

What then is meant by saying that one thing is the "content" of another? First of all I wish to point out that "blue" is rightly and properly said to be part of the content of a blue flower. If, therefore, we also assert that it is part of the content of the sensation of blue, we assert that it has to the other parts (if any) of this whole the same relation which it has to the other parts of a blue flower—and we assert only this: we cannot mean to assert that it has to the sensation of blue any relation which it does not have to the blue flower. And we have seen that the sensation of blue contains at least one

other element beside blue—namely, what I call "consciousness," which makes it a sensation. So far then as we assert that blue is the content of the sensation, we assert that it has to this "consciousness" the same relation which it has to the other parts of a blue flower: we do assert this, and we assert no more than this. Into the question what exactly the relation is between blue and a blue flower in virtue of which we call the former part of its "content" I do not propose to enter. It is sufficient for my purpose to point out that it is the general relation most commonly meant when we talk of a thing and its qualities; and that this relation is such that to say the thing exists implies that the qualities also exist. The *content* of the thing is *what* we assert to exist, when we assert *that* the thing exists.

When, therefore, blue is said to be part of the content of the "sensation of blue," the latter is treated as if it were a whole constituted in exactly the same way as any other "thing." The "sensation of blue," on this view, differs from a blue bead or a blue beard, in exactly the same way in which the two latter differ from one another: the blue bead differs from the blue beard, in that while the former contains glass, the latter contains hair; and the "sensation of blue" differs from both in that, instead of glass or hair, it contains consciousness. The relation of the blue to the consciousness is conceived to be exactly the same as that of the blue to the glass or hair: it is in all three cases the *quality* of a *thing*.

But I said just now that the sensation of blue was analysed into "content" and "existence," and that blue was said to be *the* content of the idea of blue. There is an ambiguity in this and a possible error, which I must note in passing. The term "content" may be used in two senses. If we use "content" as equivalent to what Mr. Bradley calls the *"what"*—if we mean by it the *whole* of what is said to exist, when the thing is said to exist, then blue is certainly not *the* content of the sensation of blue: part of the *content* of the sensation is, in this sense of the term, that other element which I have called consciousness. The analysis of this sensation into the "content" "blue," on the one hand, and mere existence on the other, is therefore certainly false; in it we have again the self-contradictory identification of "Blue exists" with "The sensation of blue exists." But there is another sense in which "blue" might properly be said to be *the* content of the sensation—namely, the sense in which "content," like ειδος, is opposed to "substance" or "matter." For the element "consciousness," being common to all sensations, may be and certainly is regarded as in some sense their "substance," and by the "content" of each is only meant that in respect of which one differs from another. In this sense then "blue" might be said to be *the* content of the sensation; but, in that case, the analysis into "content" and "existence" is, at least, misleading, since under existence must be included *"what* exists" in the sensation other than blue.

We have it, then, as a universally received opinion that blue is related to the sensation or idea of blue, as its *content,* and that this view, if it is to be true, must mean that blue is part of *what* is said to exist when we say that the sensation exists. To say that the sensation exists is to say both that blue exists and that "consciousness," whether we call it the substance of which blue is *the* content or call it another part of the content, exists too. Any sensation or idea is a *"thing,"* and what I have called its object is the quality of this thing. Such a "thing" is what we think of when we think of a *mental image.* A mental image is conceived as if it were related to that of which it is the image (if there be any such thing) in exactly the same way as the image in a looking-glass is related to that of which it is the reflection; in both cases there is identity of content, and the image in the looking-glass differs from that in the mind solely in respect of the fact that in the one case the other constituent of the image is "glass" and in the other case, it is consciousness. If the image is of blue, it is not conceived that this "content" has any relation to the consciousness but what it has to the glass: it is conceived *merely* to be its

content. And owing to the fact that sensations and ideas are all considered to be *wholes* of this description—things in the mind—the question: What do we know? is considered to be identical with the question: What reason have we for supposing that there are things outside the mind *corresponding* to these that are inside it?

What I wish to point out is (1) that we have no reason for supposing that there are such things as mental images at all—for supposing that blue *is* part of the content of the sensation of blue, and (2) that even if there are mental images, no mental image and no sensation or idea is *merely* a thing of this kind: that "blue," even if it is part of the content of the image or sensation or idea of blue, is always *also* related to it in quite another way, and that this other relation, omitted in the traditional analysis, is the *only* one which makes the sensation of blue a mental fact at all.

The true analysis of a sensation or idea is as follows. The element that is common to them all, and which I have called "consciousness," really *is* consciousness. A sensation is, in reality, a case of "knowing" or "being aware of" or "experiencing" something. When we know that the sensation of blue exists, the fact we know is that there exists an awareness of blue. And this awareness is not merely, as we have hitherto seen it must be, itself something distinct and unique, utterly different from blue: it also has a perfectly distinct and unique relation to blue, a relation which is *not* that of thing or substance to content, nor of one part of content to another part of content. This relation is just that which we mean in every case by "knowing." To have in your mind "knowledge" of blue, is *not* to have in your mind a "thing" or "image" of which blue is the content. To be aware of the sensation of blue is *not* to be aware of a mental image—of a "thing," of which "blue" and some other element are constituent parts in the same sense in which blue and glass are constituents of a blue bead. It is to be aware of an awareness of blue; awareness being used, in both cases, in exactly the same sense. This element, we have seen, is certainly neglected by the "content" theory: that theory entirely fails to express the fact that there is, in the sensation of blue, this unique relation between blue and the other constituent. And what I contend is that this omission is *not* mere negligence of expression, but is due to the fact that though philosophers have recognized that *something* distinct is meant by consciousness, they have never yet had a clear conception of *what* that something is. They have not been able to hold *it* and *blue* before their minds and to compare them, in the same way in which they can compare *blue* and *green*. And this for the reason I gave above: namely that the moment we try to fix our attention upon consciousness and to see *what,* distinctly, it is, it seems to vanish: it seems as if we had before us a mere emptiness. When we try to introspect the sensation of blue, all we can see is the blue: the other element is as if it were diaphanous. Yet it *can* be distinguished if we look attentively enough, and if we know that there is something to look for. My main object in this paragraph has been to try to make the reader *see* it; but I fear I shall have succeeded very ill.

It being the case, then, that the sensation of blue includes in its analysis, beside blue, *both* a unique element "awareness" *and* a unique relation of this element to blue, I can make plain what I meant by asserting, as two distinct propositions, (1) that blue is probably not part of the content of the sensation at all, and (2) that, even it were, the sensation would nevertheless not be the sensation *of* blue, if blue had only this relation to it. The first hypothesis may now be expressed by saying that, if it were true, then, when the sensation of blue exists, there exists a *blue awareness:* offence may be taken at the expression, but yet it expresses just what should be and is meant by saying that blue is, in this case, a *content* of consciousness or experience. Whether or not, when I have the sensation of blue, my consciousness or awareness is thus blue, my introspection does not enable me to decide with certainty: I only see no reason for thinking that it is.

But whether it is or not, the point is unimportant, for introspection *does* enable me to decide that something else is also true: namely that I am aware *of* blue, and by this I mean, that my awareness has to blue a quite different and distinct relation. It is possible, I admit, that my awareness is blue *as well* as being *of* blue: but what I am quite sure of is that it is *of* blue; that it has to blue the simple and unique relation the existence of which alone justifies us in distinguishing knowledge of a thing from the thing known, indeed in distinguishing mind from matter. And this result I may express by saying that what is called the *content* of a sensation is in very truth what I originally called it—the sensation's *object.*

But, if all this be true, what follows?

Idealists admit that some things really exist of which they are not aware: there are some things, they hold, which are not inseparable aspects of *their* experience, even if they be inseparable aspects of some experience. They further hold that some of the things of which they are sometimes aware do really exist, even when they are not aware of them: they hold for instance that they are sometimes aware of other minds, which continue to exist even when they are not aware of them. They are, therefore, sometimes aware of something which is *not* an inseparable aspect of their own experience. They do *know* some things which are *not* a mere part or content of their experience. And what my analysis of sensation has been designed to show is, that whenever I have a mere sensation or idea, the fact is that I am then aware of something which is equally and in the same sense *not* an inseparable aspect of my experience. The awareness which I have maintained to be included in sensation is the very same unique fact which constitutes every kind of knowledge: "blue" is as much an object, and as little a mere content, of my experience, when I experience it, as the most exalted and independent real thing of which I am ever aware. There is, therefore no question of how we are to "get outside the circle of our own ideas and sensations." Merely to have a sensation is already to *be* outside that circle. It is to know something which is as truly and really *not* a part of *my* experience, as anything which I can ever know.

Now I think I am not mistaken in asserting that the reason why Idealists suppose that everything which *is* must be an inseparable aspect of some experience, is that they suppose some things, at least, to be inseparable aspects of *their* experience. And there is certainly nothing which they are so firmly convinced to be an inseparable aspect of their experience as what they call the *content* of their ideas and sensations. If, therefore, *this* turns out in every case, whether it be also the content or not, to be at least *not* an inseparable aspect of the experience of it, it will be readily admitted that nothing else which *we* experience ever is such an inseparable aspect. But if we never experience anything but what is *not* an inseparable aspect of *that* experience, how can we infer that anything whatever, let alone *everything,* is an inseparable aspect of *any* experience? How utterly unfounded is the assumption that *"esse* is *percipi"* appears in the clearest light.

But further I think it may be seen that if the object of an Idealist's sensation were, as he supposes, *not* the object *but* merely the content of that sensation, if, that is to say, it really were an inseparable aspect of his experience, each Idealist could never be aware either of himself or of any other real thing. For the relation of a sensation to its object is certainly the same as that of any other instance of experience to its object; and this, I think, is generally admitted even by Idealists: they state as readily that *what* is judged or thought or perceived is the *content* of that judgment or thought or perception, as that blue is the content of the sensation of blue. But, if so, then when any Idealist thinks he is *aware* of himself or of any one else, this cannot really be the case. The fact is, on his own theory, that himself and that other person are in reality mere *contents* of an awareness, which is aware *of* nothing whatever. All that can be said is that there is an awareness in him, *with* a certain content: it can never be true that there is in him a consciousness *of anything.* And similarly he is never aware either of the fact that he exists or that reality is spiritual. The real fact, which he describes in those terms, is that his existence and the spirituality of reality are *contents* of an awareness, which is aware of nothing—certainly not, then, of its own content.

And further if everything, of which he thinks he is aware, is in reality merely a content of his own experience he has certainly no *reason* for holding that anything does exist except himself: it will, of course, be possible that other persons do exist; solipsism will not be necessarily true; but he cannot possibly infer from anything he holds that it is not true. That he himself exists will of course follow from his premiss that many things are contents of *his* experience. But since everything, of which he thinks himself aware, is in reality merely an inseparable aspect of that awareness; this premiss allows no inference that any of these contents, far less any other consciousness, exists at all except as an inseparable espect of his awareness, that is, as part of himself.

Such, and not those which he takes to follow from it, are the consequences which *do* follow from the Idealist's supposition that the object of an experience is in reality merely a content or inseparable aspect of that experience. If, on the other hand, we clearly recognize the nature of that peculiar relation which I have called "awareness of anything"; if we see that *this* is involved equally in the analysis of *every* experience—from the merest sensation to the most developed perception or reflection, and that *this* is in fact the only essential element in an experience— the only thing that is both common and peculiar to all experiences—the only thing which gives us reason to call any fact mental; if, further, we recognize that this awareness is and must be in all cases of such a nature that its object, when we are aware of it, is precisely what it would be, if we were not aware: then it becomes plain that the existence of a table in space is related to my experience of *it* in precisely the same way as the existence of my own experience is related to my experience of *that*. Of both we are merely aware: if we are aware that the one exists, we are aware in precisely the same sense that the other exists; and if it is true that my experience can exist, even when I do not happen to be aware of its existence, we have exactly the same reason for supposing that the table can do so also. When, therefore, Berkeley, supposed that the only thing of which I am directly aware is my own sensations and ideas, he supposed what was false; and when Kant supposed that the objectivity of things in space *consisted* in the fact that they were "Vorstellungen," having to one another different relations from those which the same "Vorstellungen" have to one another in subjective experience, he supposed what was equally false. I am as directly aware of the existence of material things in space as of my own sensations; and *what* I am aware of with regard to each is exactly the same—namely that in one case the material thing, and in the other case my sensa-

tion does really exist. The question requiring to be asked about material things is thus not: What reason have we for supposing that anything exists *corresponding* to our sensations? but: What reason have we for supposing that material things do *not* exist, since *their* existence has precisely the same evidence as that of our sensations? That either exist *may* be false; but if it is a reason for doubting the existence of matter, that it is an inseparable aspect of our experience, the same reasoning will prove conclusively that our experience does not exist either, since that must also be an inseparable aspect of our experience of *it*. The only *reasonable* alternative to the admission that matter exists *as well as* spirit, is absolute Scepticism— that, as likely as not *nothing* exists at all. All other suppositions—the Agnostic's, that something, at all events, does exist, as much as the Idealist's, that spirit does—are, if we have no reason for believing in matter, as baseless as the grossest superstitions.

EDWIN B. HOLT, WALTER T. MARVIN, WILLIAM PEPPERELL MONTAGUE, RALPH BARTON PERRY, WALTER B. PITKIN, and EDWARD GLEASON SPAULDING

INTRODUCTION TO THE NEW REALISM*[1]

The new realism may be said to be at the present moment something between a tend-

* From *The New Realism: Cooperative Studies in Philosophy* by Edwin B. Holt, Walter T. Marvin, William Pepperell Montague, Ralph Barton Perry, Walter B. Pitkin, and Edward Gleason Spaulding. New York: The Macmillan Company, 1912. Reprinted by permission.

[1] [This] introduction expresses opinions common to the several authors of this book; but it has proved convenient to make use of parts of the following articles which have already appeared in print: Montague, "The New Realism and the Old," *J. of Phil., Psychol., etc.,* 1912, Vol. IX, p. 39; Perry, "Realism as a Polemic and Program of Reform," *J. of Phil., Psychol., etc.,* 1910, Vol. VII, pp. 337, 365.

ency and a school. So long as it was recognized only by its enemies it was no more than a tendency. But war has developed a class-consciousness, and the time is near at hand, if indeed it is not already here, when one realist may recognize another. This dawning spirit of fellowship, accompanied by a desire for better understanding and a more effective co-operation, has prompted the present undertaking.

It is perhaps inevitable that the new realism should for a time remain polemical in tone. A new philosophical movement invariably arises as a protest against tradition, and bases its hope of constructive achievement on the correction of established habits of thought. Neo-realism is still in a phase in which this critical motive dominates, and is the chief source of its vigor and unanimity. Before, however, a philosophy can come of age, and play a major part in human thought, it must be a complete philosophy, or must at least show promise of completeness. If it is to assume the role, it must undertake to play the whole part. The authors of the present book thus entertain the hope that they may have succeeded not only in amplifying, clarifying, and fortifying the realistic critique, but also in exhibiting that critique as a basis for the solution of special philosophical problems, and for the procedure of the special sciences.

I. The Historical Significance of the New Realism

The new realism is not an accident, nor a *tour de force,* nor an isolated and curious speculative eruption. Whatever may be thought of its correctness or power to endure, it must at least be accorded a place in the main current of modern thought. It is a fundamental and typical doctrine—definable in terms of the broad play of intellectual forces, and peculiarly characteristic of their present conjunction.

The historical significance of the new realism appears most clearly in its relations with "naive realism," "dualism" and "subjectivism." The new realism is primarily a doctrine concerning the relation between the knowing process and the thing known; and as such it is the latest phase of a movement of thought which has already passed through the three phases just indicated. Neo-realism, in other words, seeks to deal with the same problem that has given rise to "naive realism," "dualism" and "subjectivism"; and to profit by the errors as well as the discoveries for which these doctrines have been responsible.

1. The theory of naive realism is the most primitive of these theories. It conceives of objects as directly presented to consciousness and being precisely what they appear to be. Nothing intervenes between the knower and the world external to him. Objects are not represented in consciousness by ideas; they are themselves directly presented. This theory makes no distinction between seeming and being; things *are* just what they *seem.* Consciousness is thought of as analogous to a light which shines out through the sense organs, illuminating the world outside the knower. There is in this naive view a complete disregard of the personal equation and of the elaborate mechanism underlying sense perception. In a world in which there was no such thing as error, this theory of the knowledge relation would remain unchallenged; but with the discovery of error and illusion comes perplexity. Dreams are perhaps the earliest phenomena of error to arouse the primitive mind from its dogmatic realism. How can a man lie asleep in his bed and at the same time travel to distant places and converse with those who are dead? How can the events of the dream be reconciled with the events of waking experience? The first method of dealing with this type of error is to divide the real world into two realms, equally objective and equally external, but the one visible, tangible, and regular, the other more or less invisible, mysterious, and capricious. The soul after death, and sometimes during sleep, can enter the second of these realms. The objectified dreamland of the child and the ghostland of the savage are the outcome of the first effort of natural realism to cope with the problem of error. It is easy to see, however, that this doubling up of the world of existing objects will only explain a very limited number of dream experiences, while to the errors of waking experience it is obviously inapplicable. Whenever, for example, the dream is concerned with the same events as those already experienced in waking life, there can be no question of appealing to a shadow world.

Unreal events that are in conflict with the experience of one's fellows, and even with one's own more inclusive experience, must be banished completely from the external world. Where, then, shall they be located? What is more natural than to locate them inside the person who experiences them? For it is only upon him that the unreal object produces any effect. The objects of our dreams and our fancies, and of illusions generally, are held to exist only "in the mind." They are like feelings and desires in being directly experienced only by a single mind. Thus the soul, already held to be the mysterious principle of life, and endowed with peculiar properties, transcending ordinary physical things, is further enriched by being made the habitat of the multitudinous hosts of non-existent objects. Still further reflection on the phenomena of error leads to the discovery of the element of relativity in all knowledge, and finally to the realization that no external happening can be perceived until after it has ceased to exist. The events we perceive as present are always past, for in order to perceive anything it must send energy of some kind to our sense organs, and by the time the energy reaches us the phase of existence which gave rise to it has passed away. To this universal and necessary temporal aberration of perceived objects is added an almost equally universal spatial aberration. For all objects that move relatively to the observer are perceived not where they are when perceived, but, at best, where they were when the stimulus issued from them. And in addition to these spatial and temporal aberrations of perception we know that what we perceive will depend not only upon the nature of the object but on the nature of the medium through which its energies have passed on their way to our organism; and also upon the condition of our sense organs and brain. Finally, we have every reason to believe that whenever the brain is stimulated in the same way in which it is normally stimulated by an object we shall experience that object even though it is in no sense existentially present. These many undeniable facts prove that error is no

trivial and exceptional phenomenon, but the normal, necessary, and universal taint from which every perceptual experience must suffer.

2. It is such considerations as these that have led to the abandonment of naive realism in favor of dualism, the second of the aforementioned theories. According to this second theory, which is exemplified in the philosophies of Descartes and Locke, the mind never perceives anything external to itself. It can perceive only its own ideas or states. But as it seems impossible to account for the order in which these ideas occur by appealing to the mind in which they occur, it is held to be permissible and even necessary to infer a world of external objects resembling to a greater or less extent the effects, or ideas, which they produce in us. What we perceive is now held to be only a picture of what really exists. Consciousness is no longer thought of as analogous to a light which directly illumines the extra-organic world, but rather as a painter's canvas or a photographic plate on which objects in themselves imperceptible are represented. The great advantage of the second or picture theory is that it fully accounts for error and illusion; the disadvantage of it is that it appears to account for nothing else. The only external world is one that we can never experience, the only world that we can have any experience of is the internal world of ideas. When we attempt to justify the situation by appealing to inference as the guarantee of this unexperienceable externality, we are met by the difficulty that the world we infer can only be made of the matter of experience, that is, can only be made up of mental pictures in new combinations. An inferred object is always a perceptible object, one that could be in some sense experience; and, as we have seen, the only things that according to this view can be experienced are our mental states. Moreover, the world in which all our interests are centered is the world of experienced objects. Even if, *per impossible*, we could justify the belief in a world beyond that which we could experience, it would be but a barren achievement, for such a world

would contain none of the things that we see and feel. Such a so-called real world would be more alien to us and more thoroughly queer than were the ghostland or dreamland which, as we remember, the primitive realist sought to use as a home for certain of the unrealities of life.

3. It seems very natural at such a juncture to try the experiment of leaving out this world of extra-mental objects, and contenting ourselves with a world in which there exist only minds and their states. This is the third theory, the theory of subjectivism. According to it, there can be no object without a subject, no existence without a consciousness of it. To be, is to be perceived. The world of objects capable of existing independently of a knower (the belief in which united the natural realist and the dualistic realist) is now rejected. This third theory agrees with the first theory in being epistemologically monistic, that is, in holding to the presentative rather than to the representative theory of perception; for, according to the first theory, whatever exists must be perceived. Naive realism subsumed the perceived as a species under the genus existent. Subjectivism subsumes the existent as a species under the genus perceived. But while the third theory has these affiliations with the first theory, it agrees with the second theory in regarding all perceived objects as mental states—ideas inhering in the mind that knows them and as inseparable from that mind as any accident is from the substance that owns it.

Subjectivism has many forms, or rather, many degrees. It occurs in its first and most conservative form in the philosophy of Berkeley. Descartes and Locke, and other upholders of the dualistic epistemology, had already gone beyond the requirements of the picture theory in respect to the secondary qualities of objects. Not content with the doctrine that these qualities as they existed in objects could only be inferred, they had denied them even the inferential status which they accorded to primary qualities. The secondary qualities that we perceive are not even copies of what exists externally. They are the cloudy effects produced in the mind by combinations of primary qualities, and they resemble unreal objects in that they are *merely* subjective. The chief ground for this element of subjectivism in the systems of dualistic realism immediately preceding Berkeley, was the belief that relativity to the percipient implied subjectivity. As the secondary qualities showed this relativity, they were condemned as subjective. Now it was the easiest thing in the world for Berkeley to show that an equal or even greater relativity pertained to the primary qualities. The perceived form, size, and solidity of an object depend quite as much upon the relation of the percipient to the object as do its color and temperature. If it be axiomatic that whatever is relative to the perceiver exists only as an idea, why, then, the primary qualities which were all that remained of the physical world could be reduced to mere ideas. But just here Berkeley brought his reasoning to an abrupt stop. He refused to recognize that (1) the *relations between* ideas or the order in which they are given to us, and (2) the *other minds* that are known, are quite as relative to the knower as are the primary and secondary qualities of the physical world. You can know other minds only in so far as you have experience of them, and to infer their independent existence involves just as much and just as little of the process of objectifying and hypostatizing your own ideas as to infer the independent existence of physical objects. Berkeley avoided this obvious result of his own logic by using the word "notion" to describe the knowledge of those things that did not depend for their existence on the fact that they were known. If you had an *idea* of a thing—say of your neighbor's body—then that thing existed only as a mental state. But if you had a *notion* of a thing—say of your neighbor's mind—then that thing was quite capable of existing independently of your knowing it. Considering the vigorous eloquence with which Berkeley inveighed against the tendency of philosophers to substitute words for thoughts, it is pathetic that he should himself have furnished such a striking example of that very fallacy. In later times Clifford and Pearson have not hesitated to avail themselves of a quite similar linguistic device for escaping the solipsistic conclusion of a consistent subjectivism. The distinction between the physical *objects* which as "constructs" exist only in the consciousness of the knower, and *other minds* which as "ejects" can be known without being in any way dependent on the knower, is essentially the same both in its meaning and in its futility as the Berkeleian distinction of idea and notion. For the issue between realism and subjectivism does not arise from a psychocentric predicament—a difficulty of conceiving objects apart from any consciousness—but rather from the much more radical "ego-centric predicament,"[2] the difficulty of conceiving known things to exist independently of my knowing them. And the poignancy of the predicament is quite independent of the nature of the object itself, whether that be a physical thing such as my neighbor's body, or a psychical thing such as my neighbor's mind.

Some part of this difficulty Hume saw and endeavored to meet in his proof that the spiritual substances of Berkeley were themselves mere ideas; but Hume's position is itself subject to two criticisms: First, it succeeds no better than Berkeley's in avoiding a complete relativism or solipsism—for it is as difficult to explain how one "bundle of perceptions" can have any knowledge of the other equally real "bundle of perceptions" as to explain how one "spirit" can have knowledge of other "spirits." Second, the Humean doctrine suffers from an additional difficulty peculiar to itself, in that by destroying the conception of the mind as a "substance," it made meaningless the quite correlative conception of perceived objects as mental "states." If there is no substance there cannot be any states or accidents, and there ceases to be any sense in regarding the things that are known as dependent upon or inseparable from a knower.

4. Passing on to that form of subjectivism

developed by Kant, we may note three points: (1) A step back toward dualism, in that he dallies with, even if he does not actually embrace, the dualistic notion of a "ding-an-sich," a reality outside and beyond the realm of experienced objects which serves as their cause or ground. (2) A step in advance of the subjectivism of Berkeley and Hume, in that Kant reduces to the subjective status not merely the *facts* of nature but also her *laws,* so far, at least, as they are based upon the forms of space and time and upon the categories. (3) There appears in the Kantian system a wholly new feature which is destined to figure prominently in later systems. This is the dualistic conception of the knower, as himself a twofold being, transcendental and empirical. It is the transcendental or noumenal self that gives laws to nature, and that owns the experienced objects as its states. The empirical or phenomenal self, on the other hand, is simply one object among others, and enjoys no special primacy, in its relation to the world of which it is a part.

The post-Kantian philosophies deal with the three points just mentioned in the following ways: (1) The retrograde feature of Kant's doctrine—the belief in the *ding-an-sich*—is abandoned. (2) The step in advance—the legislative power conferred by Kant upon the self as knower—is accepted and enlarged to the point of viewing consciousness as the source not only of the *a priori* forms of relation, but of all relations whatsoever. (3) The doctrine of the dual self is extended to the point of identifying in one absolute self the plurality of transcendental selves held to by Kant, with the result that our various empirical selves and the objects of their experience are all regarded as the manifestations or fragments of a single, perfect, all-inclusive, and eternal self. But it is not hard to see that this new dualism of the finite and the absolute selves involves the same difficulties as those which we found in the Cartesian dualism of conscious state and physical object. For either the experience of the fragment embraces the experiences of the

---

[2] Cf. below, pp. 76-77.

absolute, or it does not. If the former, then the absolute becomes knowable, to be sure, but only at the cost of losing its absoluteness and being reduced to a mere "state" of the alleged fragment. The existence of the absolute will then depend upon the fact that it is known by its own fragments, and each fragmentary self will have to assume that its own experience constitutes the entire universe—which is solipsism. If the other horn of the dilemma be chosen and the independent reality of the absolute be insisted upon, then it is at the cost of making the absolute unknowable, of reducing it to the status of the unexperienceable external world of the dualistic realist. The dilemma itself is the inevitable consequence of making knowledge an internal relation and hence constitutive of its objects. Indeed, a large part of the philosophical discussion of recent years has been concerned with the endeavor of the absolutists to defend their doctrine from the attacks of empiricists of the Berkeleian and Humean tradition in such a way as to avoid equally the Scylla of epistemological dualism and the Charybdis of solipsism. But, as we have seen, the more empirical subjectivists of the older and strictly British school are open to the same criticism as that which they urge upon the absolutists; for it is as difficult for the Berkeleian to justify his belief in the existence of other spirits, or the phenomenalistic follower of Hume his belief in bundles or streams of experience other than his own, as it is for the absolutist to justify those features of the absolute experience which lie beyond the experience of the finite fragments.

5. And now enter upon this troubled scene the new realists, offering to absolutists and phenomenalists impartially their new theory of the relation of knower to known.

From the standpoint of this new theory all subjectivists suffer from a common complaint. The ontological differences that separate such writers as Fichte and Berkeley, Mr. Bradley and Professor Karl Pearson, are, for a realist, overshadowed by the epistemological error that unites them. The escape from subjectivism and the formulation of an alternative that shall be both remedial and positively fruitful, constitutes the central preëminent issue for a realistic protagonist. It is prior to all other philosophical issues, such as monism and pluralism, eternalism and temporalism, materialism and spiritualism, or even pragmatism and intellectualism. This does not mean that the new realism shall not lead to a solution of these problems, but only that as a basis for their clear discussion it is first of all essential to get rid of subjectivism.

The new realists' relational theory is in essentials very old. To understand its meaning it is necessary to go back beyond Kant, beyond Berkeley, beyond even Locke and Descartes—far back to that primordial common sense which believes in a world that exists independently of the knowing of it, but believes also that that same independent world can be directly presented in consciousness and not merely represented or copied by "ideas." In short, the new realism is, broadly speaking, a return to that naive or natural realism which was the first of our three typical theories of the knowledge relations; and as such, it should be sharply distinguished from the dualistic or inferential realism of the Cartesians. But the cause of the abandonment of naive realism in favor of the dualistic or picture theory was the apparently hopeless disagreement of the world as presented in immediate experience with the true or corrected system of objects in whose reality we believe. So the first and most urgent problem for the new realists is to amend the realism of common sense in such wise as to make it compatible with the facts of relativity.

For this reason especial attention has been given in the present volume[3] to a discussion of those special phenomena, such as illusion and error, which are supposed to discredit

---

[3] Cf. below, Nos. IV, V, VI. [The titles of the essays of the *New Realism* referred to are: "A Realistic Theory of Truth and Error," by William Pepperrell Montague; "The Place of Illusory Experience in a Realistic World," by Edwin B. Holt; and "Some Realistic Implications of Biology," by Walter B. Pitkin.]

natural realism, and set going a train of thought that cannot be stopped short of subjectivism. It is necessary to inquire closely into the mechanism of perception, and into the logic of contradiction and falsity. And it is necessary to obtain a definition of the central thesis of realism, the thesis of independ-

ence, that shall not be so loose as to violate the facts, nor so vague and formal as to disregard them.[4]

---

[4] Cf. below, No. II. ["A Realistic Theory of Independence," by Ralph Barton Perry.]

II. The Realistic Polemic

Inasmuch as subjectivism, renewed and fortified under the name of "idealism," is the dominant philosophy of the day, it affords the chief resistance which an innovating philosophy such as realism has to overcome. The realistic polemic is therefore primarily a polemic against subjectivism; but the errors of which realism finds subjectivistic philosopies to be guilty, are not necessarily confined to such philosophies. They may be generalized; and in so far as they are generalized their discovery is of greater moment. The following are some of the traditional errors which neo-realism has thus far succeeded in generalizing.

1. *The fallacy of argument from the egocentric predicament.* The "ego-centric predicament" consists in the impossibility of finding anything that is not known.[5] This is a predicament rather than a discovery, because it refers to a difficulty of procedure, rather than to a character of things. It is impossible to eliminate the knower without interrupting observation; hence the peculiar difficulty of discovering what characters, if any, things possess when not known. When this situation is formulated as a proposition concerning things, the result is either the redundant inference that all known things are known, or the false inference that all things are known. The former is, on account of its redundancy, not a proposition at all; and its use results only in confusing it with the second proposition, which involves a "petitio principii." The falsity of the inference, in the case of the latter proposition, lies in its

being a use of the method of agreement unsupported by the method of difference. It is impossible to argue from the fact that everything one finds is known, to the conclusion that knowing is a universal condition of being, because it is impossible to find non-things which are not known. The use of the method of agreement without negative cases is a fallacy. It should be added that at best the method of agreement is a preliminary aid to exact thought, and can throw no light whatsoever on which can be meant by saying that knowing is a condition of being. Yet this method, misapplied, is the main proof, perhaps the only proof, that has been offered of the cardinal principle of idealistic philosophies—the definition of being in terms of consciousness. It is difficult, on account of their very lack of logical form, to obtain pure cases of philosophical fallacies. Then, too, this particular fallacy has so far become a commonplace as to be regarded as a self-evident truth. The step in which it is employed is omitted or obscured in many idealistic treatises. In others it is spread so thin, is so pervasive and insidious, that while it lends whatever support is offered for the cardinal idealistic principle, it is nowhere explicitly formulated. But the following will serve as a typical illustration. "Things exist," says Renouvier, "and all things have a common character, that of being represented, of appearing; for if there were no representation of things, how should I speak of them?"[6] It is clear that no more is proved by this argument than that things must be "represented" if one is to "speak of them." That

---

[5] In this connection, "known" means "given as an object of thought."

[6] Renouvier, *Mind*, II (1877), p. 378.

all things have the common character of being "spoken of," which is the fundamental thesis restated in a new form, is left without any proof whatsoever.

2. *The fallacy of pseudo-simplicity.* There is a disposition in philosophy as well as in common sense to assume the simplicity of that which is only familiar or stereotyped. This error has conspired with the error just examined to lend a certain plausibility to subjectivism. For one would scarcely assert with so much gravity that the world was his idea, or that the "I think" must accompany every judgment, unless he supposed that the first personal pronoun referred to something that did not require further elucidation. Self-consciousness could never have figured in idealistic philosophies as the immediate and primary certainty if it were understood to be a complex and problematic conception. Yet such it must be admitted to be, once its practical simplicity, based on habits of thought and speech, is discounted. Similarly the common dogma, to the effect that consciousness can be known only introspectively, is based on the assumption that it *is* known introspectively, and that thus approached it is a simple datum. Traditional spiritistic conceptions of will, activity, immediacy, and life, rest on the same fundamental misapprehension as does the materialistic acceptance of body as an irreducible entity. Thus what is really at stake here is nothing less than the method of analysis itself. In exact procedure it is not permitted to assert the simplicity of any concept until *after* analysis. That the concepts enumerated above are not analytically simple, is proved by the fact that when they are treated as simple, it is necessary to give them a complex existence also in order to account for what is known about them. It is customary to say that this is a "manifestation" or "transformation" of the simple and more fundamental reality; but this is to reverse the order which is proper to thought as the deliberate and systematic attempt to know. It is equivalent to asserting that the more pains we take to know, the less real is the object of our knowledge; a proportion which is never asserted without being contradicted, since it expresses the final critical analysis of the thinker who asserts it. The following is a characteristic example of the error of "pseudo-simplicity," as applied to the conception of activity.

"Every man," says Professor Ward, "knows the difference between feeling and doing, between idle reverie and intense thought, between impotent and aimless drifting and unswerving tenacity of purpose, being the slave of every passion or the master of himself. . . . It must surely ever remain futile, nay, even foolish, to attempt to explain either receptivity or activity; for what is there in experience more fundamental? And being thus fundamental, the prime staple of all experience, it is absurd to seek to prove them real, since in the first and foremost sense of reality the real and they are one." [7] Nevertheless, activity and passivity *are* capable of being analyzed in a variety of ways, logical, physical, and psychological, [8] and their nature can be regarded as a simple datum only in so far as such analysis is deliberately avoided. They are simples only in so far as they are *not yet analyzed.*

3. *The fallacy of exclusive particularity.* It is ordinarily assumed that a particular term of any system belongs to such system *exclusively.* That this is a false assumption is proved empirically. The point *b* of the class of points that constitutes the straight line *abc* may belong also to the class of points that constitutes the intersecting straight line *xby.* The man John Doe who belongs to the class *Republican Party* may belong also to the interesting class *captains of industry.* Unless this multiple classification of terms were possible, discourse would break down utterly. All the terms of discourse are general in the sense that they belong to several contexts. It is this fact that accounts for the origin and the usefulness of language. Without this generality of terms the world would possess no structure, not even motion or similarity; for there could be no motion if the same could not be in different places at

---

[7] J. Ward, *Naturalism and Agnosticism*, II, pp. 52-53.
[8] Cf. e.g., W. James, "The Experience of Activity," in *Essays in Radical Empiricism*, VI.

different times, and there could be no similarity if the same could not appear in different qualitative groupings. It is little wonder, then, that the virtual rejection of this principle by philosophy has led to a fundamental and perpetual difficulty. To this error may perhaps be traced the untenability of Platonic universalism, recognized apparently by Plato himself, and the untenability of modern particularism, attested by the desperate efforts which almost every modern philosopher has made to save himself from it.

The most familiar variety of particularism is found in naturalism. This may be traced to the naive bias for the space-time order, or that historical series of bodily changes which constitutes the course of nature. Naturalism asserts that this is the only system, and that its terms, the several bodily events, belong to it exclusively. That this theory is untenable is evident at once, since in order that bodily events shall possess the structure and connections necessary to them, being must contain other terms, such as places, times, numbers, etc., that are not bodily events. But historically, naturalism has been discredited mainly by its failure to provide for the system of ideas, a system without which the bodily system itself could not be known; and it is the exclusive particularity of the terms of this latter that has figured most prominently in philosophical discussions.

In dualism of the Cartesian type the terms of nature and the terms of knowledge are regarded as exclusive, but in order that knowledge shall mean anything at all, it is assumed that there is some sort of representative relation between them. Spinoza and Leibniz endeavored to bring them together through a third and neutral term. Among the English philosophers the impossibility of showing how the mind can know nature if each mind is a closed circle, possessing its content wholly within itself, leads finally to the abolition of nature as an independent system. Thus the pendulum swings from naturalism to subjectivism; and in the whole course of this dialectic the mistaken principle of exclusive particularity is assumed.

4. *The fallacy of definition by initial predi-cation.* This form of error is a natural sequel to the last. A subject of discourse is viewed initially under one of its aspects, or is taken initially as a term in some specific complex or relational manifold. Then, owing to the error of exclusive particularity, it is assumed that this subject of discourse can have no other aspect, or belong to no other rational manifold. Thus the initial characterization becomes definitive and final.

Subjectivism again, affords the most notable instances of the error. Any subject of discourse may be construed *as such;* that is, as a thing talked about or "taken account of," as an object of experience or knowledge. The vogue of the psychological, introspective, or reflective method in modern thought has given rise to the custom of construing things first according to their place in the context of consciousness. Similarly, the habit of self-consciousness among philosophers has emphasized the relation of things to self; and the prominence of epistemology in modern philosophy has tended to an initial characterization of things according to their places in the process of knowledge, just as the prominence of religious issues led early Christian ascetics to name things first after their part in the drama of the soul's salvation.

Thus, idealism, quite unconscious of having prejudged the main question from the outset, "seeks to interpret the universe after the analogy of conscious life, and regards experience as for us the great reality."[9] Or, as another writer expressed it, "we must *start* . . . from the whole of experience as such."[10] But all such initial characterizations must be regarded as accidental. Allowance must be duly made for alternative and complementary characterizations; and the question of the priority of the characterization to which any subject of discourse submits must be discussed quite independently of the order which is determined by habit or bias. In short, the very general disposition at the present time to begin with a psychological or

[9] J. Lindsay, *Studies in European Philosophy*, p. 207.
[10] J. B. Baillie, *Idealistic Construction of Experience*, p. 105.

epistemological version of things must not be allowed in the least to prejudice the question as to whether that version is definitive or important.

5. *The speculative dogma.* By the "speculative dogma" is meant the assumption for philosophical purposes that there is an all-sufficient, all-general principle, a single fundamental proposition that adequately determines or explains everything. This assumption has commonly taken one or the other of two forms. By many it has been assumed that such a principle constitutes the proper content or subject matter of philosophy. Thus Plato said: "And when I speak of the other division of the intelligible you will understand me to speak of that other sort of knowledge which reason herself attains by the power of dialectic, using the hypotheses not as first principles, but only as hypotheses—that is to say, as steps and points of departure into a region which is above hypotheses, in order that she may soar beyond them to the first principle of the whole; and clinging to this and then to that which depends on this, by successive steps she descends again without the aid of any sensible object, beginning and ending in ideas."[11] And Caird makes the same assumption when he says that "Philosophy professes to seek and to find the principle of unity which underlies all the manifold particular truths of the separate sciences."[12] But such an assumption is dogmatic, because it ignores the prior question as to whether there is such a principle or not. So far as the general task of philosophy is concerned, this must be treated as an open question. Philosophy does aim, it is true, to generalize as widely and comprehend as adequately as possible; but a loosely aggregated world, abounding in unmitigated variety, is a philosophical hypothesis. The discovery of a highly coherent system under which all the wealth of experience could be subsumed would be the most magnificent of philosophical achievements; but if there is no such system, philosophy

must be satisfied with something less—with whatever, in fact, there happens to be. By others, in the second place, it has been assumed that the idea of such a principle or system is the property of every thoughtful person, the existence of an object corresponding to it being alone doubtful. This assumption gave rise to the ontological proof of God, which carried conviction only so long as man did not question the definiteness and meaning of the idea; for the assumption obscured a problem, the problem, namely, as to whether there is any idea corresponding to the words *ens realissimum.* The possibility of defining, on general logical grounds, a maximum of being of truth, is, to say the least, highly questionable; and it is certain that this problem must properly precede any inferences from such a maximal idea.

The speculative dogma has been the most prolific cause of the verbal abuses which abound in philosophy, and which are to be considered separately. It is through this dogma that various words have been invested with a certain hyperbole and equivocation, in consequence of the attempt to stretch their meaning to fit the speculative demand. A further evil arising from the speculative dogma is the unjust and confusing disparagement of positive knowledge through invidious comparison with this Unknown God to which the philosopher has erected his altar.

6. *The error of verbal suggestion.* Words which do not possess a clear and unambiguous meaning, but which nevertheless have a rhetorical effect owing to their association, lend themselves to a specious discourse, having no cognitive value in itself, and standing in the way of the attainment of genuine knowledge. This is Bacon's famous idol of the forum. In philosophy this reliance on the suggestive, rather than the proper denotative or connotative function of words, is due not only to man's general and ineradicable tendency to verbalism, but also to the wide vogue of doctrines that are fundamentally inarticulate. We have already examined two errors which lead philosophers to accept such doctrines. The error of pseudo-simplicity in-

---

[11] Plato (Jowett, trans.), *Republic*, 511, B.
[12] E. Caird, *The Social Philosophy and Religion of Comte*, p. xii.

volves a reference to topics that cannot be analytically expressed; they cannot be identified and assigned an unequivocal name. The speculative dogma has, as we have seen, led to the use of words which shall somehow convey a sense of finality, or of limitless and exhausting application, where no specific object or exact concept possessing such characters is offered for inspection. This is what Berkeley calls the "method of growing in expression, and dwindling in notion." Ordinarily the words so used have a precise meaning also, and there results a double evil. On the one hand, the exact meaning of such terms as "force," "matter," "consciousness," "will," etc., is blurred and vitiated; and on the other hand, their speculative meaning borrows a content to which it is not entitled. The desire of philosophers to satisfy the religious demand for an object of worship or faith, doubtless one of the fundamental motives of the speculative dogma, leads to yet another variety of verbal suggestion, in which a technical philosophical conception is given a name that possesses eloquence and power of edification. Thus philosophers commonly prefer the term "eternal" to the term "nontemporal," and "infinite" to "series with no last term," or "class, a part of which can be put in one-to-one correspondence with the whole." Such terms as "significance," "supreme," "highest," "unity," have a similar value. Or the same end may be achieved by decorating almost any word with a capital letter, as is exemplified by the emotional difference between truth and Truth, or absolute and Absolute.

Finally, there is a verbal abuse which is worse, even, than equivocation; for it is possible to invent utterly fictitious concepts simply by combining words. In such cases, the constituent concepts, if the words happen to signify any, are not united. They may be positively repugnant, or simply irrelevant. At any rate, they have not been tested for consistency, and whether they do or not constitute a true system or complex concept remains wholly problematic. Such, for example, is the case with Eucken's "total activity, which by its own movement develops into

an independent reality and at the same time comprehends the opposition of subject and object, subjectivity and objectivity."[13] Such procedure is the principal source of the fallacy of *obscurum per obscurius* and affords an almost unlimited opportunity for error.

7. *The fallacy of illicit importance.* This is one of the most insidious errors which has ever been foisted upon mankind, and it is the idealist who has popularized it. It consists in inferring that, because a proposition is self-evident or unchallengeable, therefore it is important. There is a healthy animal instinct behind the fallacy. Men have early learned that the certain affords, on the whole, a safer basis for conduct than the uncertain. The merchant who is sure of his market grows rich faster than his ignorant competitor. The statesman who is sure of his constituents acts with directness and decision. So it is throughout all practical life. Now, the practical man never reflects upon his own mental processes, and thus he fails to note that the certainty he feels toward things is not an attribute of them, but only a certain precision in his attitude toward them. But the fact that the relations are unequivocal and clear is no proof that they happen to be of much significance. A may surely be C, and yet its being C may be the most trivial circumstance. A man, for instance, may be absolutely sure he likes cucumbers; but this does not prove that cucumbers are the true foundation of dietetics, nor that his liking of them reveals either his own nature or the nature of cucumbers.

Undeterred by such obvious cases, however, the idealist is wont to reason that all philosophy and all science must be built upon the one fact that nobody can make any unchallengeable assertion about anything except his having an immediate experience.

One might ask the idealist whether he is any more certain of being aware than he is of the presented object; whether, for example, in addition to saying: "I am certain that I am experiencing"—he cannot say with equal assurance: "There certainly is a tree

---

[13] Eucken (Pogson, trans.), *Life of the Spirit*, p. 320.

of some sort over yonder." But to take up this debate is to pass beyond the fallacy which he has committed. And no solution of the question alters the fact that he has erred logically in holding that, because *A* is undeniably *B*, therefore *B* is an important characteristic of *A*. There is no sure connection between the axiomatic and the significant. To think there is, is vicious intellectualism. The fallacy is curable only by the use of strict logic, but by this very easily. If one person is certain that a distant object is a tree, while his companion is equally certain that the same object is an automobile, is it not obvious that certainty is a negligible factor in the problem of deciding what the object really is.

III. The Realistic Program of Reform

Philosophy has repeatedly thrown off its bad habits, and aroused itself to critical vigilance. Furthermore, there is good ground for asserting that there has never before been so great an opportunity of reform. Logic and mathematics, the traditional models of procedure, are themselves being submitted to a searching revision that has already thrown a new light on the general priciples of exact thinking; and there is promise of more light to come, for science has for all time become reflectively conscious of its own method. The era of quarrelsome misunderstanding between criticism and positive knowledge is giving way to an era of united and complementary endeavor. It must not be forgotten that philosophy is peculiarly dependent on logic. Natural science in its empirical and experimental phase can safely be guided by instinct, because it operates in the field of objects defined by common sense. But the very objects of philosophy are the fruit of analysis. Its task is the correction of the categories of common sense, and all hopes of a profitable and valid result must be based on an expert critical judgment. The present situation, then, affords philosophy an opportunity of adopting a more rigorous procedure and assuming a more systematic form. It is with reference to this opportunity that it is worth while here to repeat the advice which is our common inheritance from the great philosophical reformers. None of these canons is original, but all are pertinent and timely.

1. *The scrupulous use of words.* This is a moral rather than a logical cannon. There is need in philosophy of a greater fastidiousness and nicety in the use of words. A regard for words is, in philosophy, the surest proof of a sensitive scientific conscience; for words are the instruments of philosophical procedure, and deserve the same care as the lancet of the surgeon or the balance of the chemist. A complacent and superior disregard of words is as fatuous as it is offensive. It is a healthier intellectual symptom to feel as MacIan felt in Chesterton's *The Ball and the Cross.* "Why shouldn't we quarrel about a word? What is the good of words if they aren't important enough to quarrel over? Why do we choose one word more than another if there isn't any difference between them? If you called a woman a chimpanzee instead of an angel, wouldn't there be a quarrel about a word? If you're not going to argue about words, what are you going to argue about? Are you going to convey your meaning to me by moving your ears? The church and the heresies always used to fight about words, because they are the only things worth fighting about."[14]

2. *Definition.* "The light of human minds," says Hobbes, "is perspicuous words, but by exact definitions first snuffed and purged from all ambiguities." Words are properly signs. They are serviceable in proportion as they are self-effacing. A skillful word will introduce the hearer or reader to his object, and then retire; only the awkward

---

[14] G. K. Chesterton, *The Ball and the Cross*, p. 96.

word will call attention to itself. It follows, then, that the only means of escaping quarrels about words is to use words with discrimination, with careful reference to their objective purport, or usefulness as means of access to ideas. Furthermore, a word is essentially a social instrument, whether used for record or communication, and requires that its relation to an object or idea shall be agreed on and conventionalized. This is the only means of bringing several minds together in a common topic of discourse. "Syllables," says John Toland, "though never so well put together, if they have not ideas fix'd to them, are but words spoken in the air, and cannot be the ground of a reasonable service."[15]

Philosophy is peculiarly dependent upon a clear definition of the reference of words because, as we have already seen, its objects are not those of common sense. It cannot rely on the ordinary denotation of words. This fact affords a perennial and abundant source of confusion, from which there is no escape save through the creation of a technical vocabulary. Bacon's observations on this matter are worthy of being quoted in full. "Now words," he says, "being commonly framed and applied according to the capacity of the vulgar, follow those lines of division which are most obvious to the vulgar understanding. And whenever an understanding of greater acuteness or a more diligent observation would alter those lines to suit the true divisions of nature, words stand in the way and resist the change. Whence it comes to pass that the high and formal discussions of learned men and oftentimes in disputes about words and names, with which (according to the use and wisdom of the mathematicians) it would be more prudent to begin, and so by means of definitions reduce them to order."[16]

Definition, then, means, in the first instance, the unequivocal and conventional reference of words. But there is a further question which arises from the use of single words to refer to complex objects. If such a reference is to be unequivocal, it is necessary that there should be a verbal complex mediating between the single word and the complex object. Thus if a circle is defined as "the class of points equidistant from a given point," this means that a circle is a complex object whose components are specified by the words in the given phrase. The single word is virtually an abbreviation of the phrase. The clarity of words depends in the end on their possessing a conventional reference to simple objects. But with the progress of analysis and the demonstration of the unsuspected or unexplored complexity of things, the single word which at first denoted the object in its pre-analytical simplicity, comes to stand for several words which denote the components of the object in their post-analytical simplicity. Definition, then, means two things: first, a convention regarding the substitution of a single word for a group of words; second, a convention regarding the reference of words to objects.[17]

3. *Analysis.* The term "analysis" properly refers not to the special method of any branch of knowledge, but to the method of exact knowledge in general, to that method of procedure in which the problematic is discovered to be a complex of simples. Such procedure may lead to the discovery of fine identities in the place of gross differences, or fine differences in the place of gross identities. Analysis in this sense means only the careful, systematic, and exhaustive examination of any topic of discourse. It cannot, then, be proper to assert that such procedure destroys its object. It does, it is true, require that naiveté and innocence of mind shall give place to sophistication; or that ignorance shall give place to some degree of explicitly formulated knowledge. But even the discovery that such psychological or moral values are lost is itself the result of analysis. Nor is there any difficulty in providing a place for such values within the psychological or moral systems to which they belong. In

---

[15] Toland, *Christianity Not Mysterious* (2d ed.), p. 30.
[16] Francis Bacon, *Novum Organum* (edition of Ellis and Spedding), IV, 61.

[17] The definition of things, rather than words, is apparently the same as knowledge in general.

the second place, it cannot be proper to assert that there is anything which necessarily escapes analysis, such as "real" change or "real" activity. The method of analysis does not require that change and activity shall be anything other than what any investigation shall discover them to be. Analysis may show either that they are unanalyzable or that they may be further reduced. If they turn out to be unanalyzable, it can only be because they exhibit no complexity of structure, no plurality of necessary factors. If they turn out to be reducible, then they must be identical with the totality of their components. If they appear to differ from such a totality, then they must appear so to differ in some respect, and this respect must at once be added to complete the totality. It is especially important not to forget the combining relations. A toy is not identical with the collection of the fragments into which it has been shattered, but it is identical with those fragments in that particular arrangement which has been destroyed. Similarly dynamics does not reduce motion to the occupancy of positions, but to the occupancy of positions *in a temporal order.* There is a perfectly clear difference between geometry or statics, on the one hand, and dynamics on the other. It is important also not to confuse analysis and synthesis with the physical operation that often accompanies them. For the purposes of knowledge it is not necessary to put Humpty Dumpty together again, but only to recognize that Humpty Dumpty is not himself unless the pieces are together.

The common prejudice against analysis is due in part to this false supposition that it is an attempt to substitute a *collection* of parts for an *arrangement* of parts. But it is due also to a more or less habitual confusion between things and words. Those who have employed the analytical method have been by no means guiltless in the matter. So soon as any word obtains currency it begins to pose as a thing in its own right, and discourse is constantly tending to take on the form of a logomachy. It has not unnaturally been supposed that analysis intended to ver-

balize reality, to give to its parts the artificial and stereotyped character of words, and to its processes the formal arrangement of grammar. But, as we have already seen, verbalism cannot be avoided by a deliberate carelessness in the use of words. If words are to be both useful and subordinate, it is necessary that they should be kept in working order, like signposts kept up to date, with their inscriptions legible and their pointing true.

4. *Regard for logical form.* Logic is at the present time in a state of extraordinary activity, and able both to stimulate and to enrich philosophy. The principal contribution which modern logic is prepared to make to philosophy concerns the form of exact knowledge. This problem is by no means wholly solved, and there is important work to be done which only philosophers can do. But the mathematical logicians have already broken and fertilized the ground. The theory of relations, the theory of "logical constants" or indefinables, the theory of infinity and continuity, and the theory of classes and systems, concern everything fundamental in philosophy. No philosopher can ignore these and like theories without playing the part of an amateur. The mathematical logicians may be quite mistaken, or they may have failed to go to the root of things; but in that case they must be overtaken in their error and corrected on their own grounds, if the field of scientific philosophy is not to be abandoned to them altogether. The present situation is certainly intolerable; for philosophy deals with the same topics as modern logic, but treats popularly and confusedly what modern logic treats with the painstaking thoroughness and exactness of the expert.

There is another respect in which modern logic should be of service to philosophy. In the course or a reconstruction of the foundations of mathematics, certain general canons of good thinking have come to light; and these are directly applicable to philosophical procedure.[18] We refer to such canons

---

[18] Cf. Schmidt, "Critique of Cognition and its Principles," *J. of Phil., Psychol.,* etc., 1909, Vol. VI, p. 281.

as "consistency" and "simplicity." These canons are new in the sense that they are now well enough defined to afford a means of testing any theory. A theory is consistent when its fundamental proportions actually generate terms, or when a class can be found which they define; and a theory satisfies the criterion of simplicity or parsimony when none of its fundamental propositions can be deduced from the rest. It behooves philosophy, then, both to ally itself with logic, in the investigation of the most ultimate concepts, such as relations, class, system, order, indefinable, etc., and also to apply to its own constructive procedure the most refined tests of scientific form. It is one of the major purposes of the new realism to justify and to extend the method of logic and of exact science in general. For this reason one of the essays in this volume[19] is especially devoted to defending the truthfulness of that method and giving it full ontological validity.

5. *Division of the question.* Although philosophy is especially charged with correcting the results obtained from other investigations, it is folly to ignore the necessity, humanly speaking, of dealing with one problem at a time. Not only is the attempt to raise and answer all questions together futile, but it prevents either definiteness of concepts or cogency of reasoning. Exact knowledge must be precisely limited in its application. A disposition in philosophy to employ terms in an unlimited sense, and to make unlimited assertions, is the principal reason why philosophy at the present time possesses no common body of theory. And for the same reason philosophy is today without any common plan of work to be done. English and American philosophers have been much exercised during the past decade over what is called "the problem of truth." It is assumed that the various parties to this discussion are referring to the same thing; but it is doubtful if this would ever the suspected, did they not specifically mention one another's names

and writings. These quarrels are perhaps due less to disagreement on the merits of any question, than to an irritable determination to be heard. If a sober and patient attempt were made to reduce the present differences of philosophical opinion to debatable propositions, the first result would be a division of the question at issue. It would certainly appear that the present-day problem of truth is one problem only so long as it is a symbol of factional dispute; discuss it, and it at once proves to be many problems, as independent of one another as any problems can be. If one undertakes to enumerate these problems, one readily finds as many as seven: (1) The problem of non-existence: What disposition is to be made of negated propositions, of non-temporal propositions, and of imaginary propositions? (2) The problem of the one and the many: How many elements belong to one system? (3) The problem of logical form: What are the ultimate categories? (4) The problem of methodology: How shall one best proceed in order to know? (5) The problem of universality: How can that which is known at a moment transcend that moment? (6) The problem of the values of knowledge: What are the criteria of right believing? (7) The problem of the relation between belief and its object: In what respect does belief directly or indirectly modify its object?

If agreement, or even intelligent disagreement, is to be obtained, philosophical issues must be sharpened. If any steady advance is to be made, special problems must be examined in order, and one at a time. There is a large group of such special problems that is by general consent assigned to philosophy. In addition to those already enumerated, there are such problems as consciousness, causality, matter, particularity and generality, individuality, teleology, all of them problems whose solution is of the first importance both for the special sciences and for religious belief. These problems are examined by the traditional philosophy; but they are not sufficiently isolated, nor examined with sufficient intensive application. They find their place in most philosophical

---

[19] No. III. ["A Defense of Analysis," by Edward Gleason Spaulding.]

treatises as application of a general system, and not as problems to be examined independently on their merits.

6. *Explicit agreement.* The recent discussion of the desirability and expediency of a "philosophical platform" has developed a difference of opinion as to whether agreement should be explicit or implicit.[20] Agreement of some sort is conceded to be a desideratum, but there are some who believe that a common tradition or historical background is all that is necessary. Now is it not evident that in theoretical or scientific procedure there *is* no agreement until it is explicitly formulated? The philosophical classics afford no basis for agreement, because they are open to interpretation. The difficulty is merely complicated through the necessity of first agreeing on the meaning of a text. To employ terms and propositions in their historical sense is to adopt precisely the course which is adopted by common sense. It means the introduction into what is supposed to be exact discourse of the indeterminate human values with which tradition is encrusted. In exact discourse the meaning of every term must be reviewed; no stone can be allowed to go into the building that has not been inspected and approved by the builder. Otherwise the individual philosopher is no more than an instrument in the hands of the *Weltgeist.* He must be possessed by a fatalistic confidence that the truth will take care of itself if he only repeats the formulas that he has learned in the schools or in the market place. But the most precious and cherished privilege of philosophy is the critical independence of each generation. Every philosophical reformer from the beginning of European thought has been moved by a distrust of tradition, and has proclaimed the need of a perpetual watchfulness lest the prestige of opinion be mistaken for the weight of evidence.

If agreement is to be based on tradition, then tradition, with all its ambiguity, its admixture of irrelevant associations, and its unlawful authority, is made the arbiter of philosophical disputes. That no theoretical difference is ever really judged in this way is abundantly proved from the present situation in philosophy. We sympathize, but we do not agree; we differ, but we do not disagree. It is of more importance in theoretical procedure that two or three should agree, than that all should sympathize. "If the trumpet gives an uncertain sound," says Toland, "who shall prepare himself to the battle?" Agreement and disagreement alike require the explicit formulation of theories in terms freshly defined. It is not to be supposed that those who insist on the necessity of explicit agreement have in mind any general unanimity. The principle would be satisfied if a single philosopher could be found to agree with himself—provided the agreement were explicit. For then it would be possible for others to disagree with him, and to disagree explicitly. We should then have before us a number of carefully formulated propositions, which could be tested and debated in the light of the evidence, propositions which would be the common property of philosophers and the material with which to construct an impersonal system of philosophical knowledge.

The first duty of philosophers, then, is not to agree, but to make their implicit agreements or disagreements explicit. Moreover it is not easy to see how this duty can be escaped without entirely abandoning philosophy's claim to be a theoretical discipline. If we cannot express our meaning in exact terms, in terms that we are willing should stand as final, if like the sophists of old we must make long speeches and employ the arts of rhetoric; then let us at least cultivate literature. At present we are bad scientists and worst poets. But philosophy is not necessarily ineffable.[21] The difficulties which some philosophies have in meeting the demands of exact discourse are gratuitous, and are due to a habit of mixing theory, on the one hand, with the history of theory, and,

---

[20] Cf. Schmidt, Creighton, and Leighton, *J. of. Phil., Psychol., etc.,* 1909, Vol. VI, pp. 141, 240, 519, 673.

[21] Cf. H. M. Sheffer, "Ineffable Philosophies," *J. of Phil., Psychol., etc.,* 1909, Vol. VI, p. 123.

on the other hand, with common belief. It is not necessary that philosophy should abandon its interest in either history or common belief, but it is necessary that it should isolate those interests, and not permit them to compromise its direct study of problems.

7. *The separation of philosophical research from the study of the history of philosophy.* A problem can be solved only by the attentive examination of that which the problem denotes. But a problem of historical exegesis, and an original philosophical problem, necessarily denote different things and direct the attention to different quarters. Thus the problem of *Hume's conception of causality* directs attention to a text, whereas the problem of *causality* directs attention to types of sequence or independence exhibited in nature. It is worth while to formulate this commonplace because there is a present-day habit of procedure that obscures it. It is customary to assume that it is the mark of rigorous scholarship in philosophy to confine oneself to commentaries on the classics. To raise the question of the importance of the history of philosophy is not necessary. That it has an indispensable place in human culture and in the discipline of every philosopher is not to be doubted; but that it has a higher dignity that a direct and independent analysis of special problems seems to be nothing more than a superstition. What dignity the history of philosophy possesses it derives from the originality of the individual philosophers whose achievements it records. If philosophy were to consist in the study of the history of philosophy, it would have no history. Doubtless the by-product of original-

ity is charlatanry and sophomoric conceit; but mankind is not less well served by this than by the complacent pedantry which is the by-product of erudition.

But whether the historical form of treatment does or does not lend dignity to philosophical discourse, it certainly adds complexity and difficulty. Ferrier, good Hegelian though he was at heart, confided to his readers the hopelessness of undertaking to show whether his conclusion agreed with Hegel's or not. "It is impossible to say to what extent this proposition coincides, or does not coincide, with his opinions; for whatever truth there may be in Hegel, it is certain that his meaning cannot be wrung from him by any amount of mere reading, any more than the whisky which is in bread . . . can be extracted by squeezing the loaf into a tumbler. He requires to be *distilled,* as all philosophers do more or less—but Hegel to an extent which is unparalleled. A much less intellectual effort would be required to find out the truth for oneself than to understand *his* exposition of it."[22] Ferrier does not exaggerate the difficulty of historical exegesis; for it is true not only that the great philosophies require to be distilled, but that they also require to be translated from the terms of their own traditional context to the terms of another. Moreover there must always be a large marginal error in any such interpretation. This being the case, it is not only gratuitous, but suicidal, to add the difficulties of this problem to the difficulties of each special philosophical problem.

---

[22] Ferrier, *Institutes of Metaphysics,* pp. 96-97.

IV. Realism as a Constructive Philosophy

As is almost universally the case with conscious and methodical criticism, realism finds itself committed to certain positive beliefs. The very act of criticism itself cannot but define, however broadly and tentatively, the outline of a general philosophy. Thus, the grounds on which realism rejects subjectivism

determine to some extent the superstructure which is to be reared in its place; while the very fact of the rejection of subjectivism excludes one of the leading metaphysical alternatives, and gives heightened emphasis to the alternatives that remain.

1. Perhaps the most notable feature of a

realistic philosophy is the emancipation of metaphysics from epistemology.[23] This means that the nature of things is not to be sought primarily in the nature of knowledge. It does not follow that a realist may not be brought in the end to conclude that moral or spiritual principles dominate the existent world, but only that this conclusion is not to be reached by arguing from the priority of knowledge over its objects. Moralism and spiritualism must take their chance among various hypotheses; and the question of their truth is to be determined by the place of such principles among the rest within the world. The general fact that whatever the world be judged to be, it is at any rate so judged, and therefore an object of cognition, is to be ignored; and one is left to decide only whether on empirical grounds one may fairly judge the world to be spiritual or moral in part only, or on the whole. It will be seen at once that the chief ground on which a spiritualistic or ethical metaphysics has latterly been urged is removed. But at the same time the metaphysical significance of life, consciousness, and morality as facts among facts is at once increased; and these may now be employed for the formulation of hypotheses that are at least pragmatic and veritable.

2. Again, in rejecting anti-intellectualism and espousing the analytical method, realism is committed to the rejection of all mystical philosophies. This holds of all philosophies that rely on immediacy for a knowledge of complexness; of all philosophies that regard the many in one as a mystery that can be resolved only by an ineffable insight. A neo-realist recognizes no ultimate immediacies nor non-relational nor indefinable entities, except the simples in which analysis terminates. The ultimate terms of knowledge are the terms that survive an analysis that has been carried as far as it is possible to carry it; and not the terms which possess simplicity only because analysis has not been applied them. Such a course of procedure is fatal, not only to a mystical universalism in which

the totality of things is resolved into a moment of ecstasy, but also to those more limited mysticisms in which complexes such as substance, will, activity, life, energy or power, are regarded despite the obvious manifoldness of their characters, as nevertheless fused and inarticulate. It follows that neo-realism rejects all philosophies in which metaphysics is sharply divorced from the special sciences, on the ground that while the latter must analyze, specify, and systematize, the former may enjoy a peculiar illumination of its own, in which the true heart of things is made apparent, and the facts and laws of science are reduced to dead abstractions, or mere instrumental artifacts.

3. For several reasons the new realism tends, at least in the present state of knowledge, to be metaphysically pluralistic rather than monistic. Most metaphysical monisms have been based on one or the other of two grounds. The first of these is the internality of relations; the supposition that the nature of terms contains their relations. It is easy to argue from this premise, that since all things are interrelated, the nature of each contains the nature of all. Realism rejects the premise that all relations are internal, because it is believed that it is contrary to the facts of existence, and to the facts of logic. The second ground of monism is the universality of cognition. The rejection of this is, as we have seen, the very starting-point of realism. Without one or the other of these grounds it is not possible to construct a monism dialectically or *a priori*. This question also becomes an empirical question, and in lieu of the discovery of a law, or set of postulates that shall explain everything, we must at least remain skeptical. The evidence at present available indicates that while all things may perhaps be related, many of these relations are not constitutive or determinative; that is, do not enter into the explanation of the nature or existence of their terms.

4. Again, the primary polemical contention of realism, its rejection of subjectivism, has its constructive implications. If cognition is not the universal condition of being, then

[23] Cf. below, No. I. ["The Emancipation of Metaphysics from Epistemology," by Walter T. Marvin.]

cognition must take its place within being, on the same plane as space, or number, or physical nature. Cognition, in other words, has its genesis and its environment. When knowledge takes place, there is a knower interacting with things. The knower, furthermore, since it cannot legitimately be saved from analysis, and referred to a unique mystical revelation, must take its place in one manifold with the things it knows. The difference between knower and known is like the difference between bodies, or states of consciousness, or societies, or colors, or any grouping of things whatsoever in the respect that they must be brought into one field of study, and observed in their mutual transactions.

In all this it is presupposed that if there is to be knowledge, there must be something there to be known, and something there to know; "there" meaning the field in which their relation obtains. Their correlation is not a basic and universal dichotomy, but only a special type of correlation, having no greater *prima facie* dignity than the many other correlations which the world exhibits. It is not to be taken in bare formal terms, but is to be observed concretely, and in its native habitat. The realist believes that he thus discovers that the interrelation in question is not responsible for the characters of the things known. In the first place being known is something that *happens* to a preëxisting thing. The characters of that preëxisting thing determine what happens when it *is known*. Then, in the second place, when the knowing takes place, these characters are at least for the most part undisturbed. If they are disturbed, or modified, then the modification itself has to be explained in terms of certain original characters, as conditions of the modification. So that even if it proved necessary to conclude that illusion and hallucination are due to modifications of the stimulus by the reacting organism, this very conclusion would imply the preëxisting and independent character of the body in which the stimulus originated.

5. In immediate and intimate connection with this doctrine of the independence of things known and the knowing of them, stands another special doctrine—to the effect that the content of knowledge, that which lies in or before the mind when knowledge takes place, is numerically identical with the thing known. Knowledge by intermediaries is not denied, but is made subordinate to direct or presentative knowledge. There is no special class of entities, qualitatively or substantively distinguished from all other entities, as the media of knowledge. In the end all things are known through being themselves brought directly into that relation in which they are said to be witnessed or apprehended. In other words, things when consciousness is had of them become themselves contents of consciousness; and the same things thus figure both in the so-called external world and in the manifold which introspection reveals.

6. Finally, because he regards analysis and conception as means of access to reality, and not as transformations or falsifications of it, and because he asserts the independence of reality in the knowing of it, the neo-realist is also a Platonic realist. He accords full ontological status to the things of thought as well as to the things of sense, to logical entities as well as physical entities, or to subsistents as well as existents.

7. In short, for realists, knowledge plays its part within an independent environment. When that environment is known it is brought into direct relations with some variety of agency or process, which is the knower. The knower however is homogeneous with the environment, belonging to one cosmos with it, as does an attracting mass, or physical organism, and may itself be known as are the things it knows. The world is of an articulate structure that is revealed by analysis, consisting of complexes, like bodies, persons, and societies, as well as of simples. The simple constituents of the world comprise both sensible qualities and logical constants. Both enter into the tissue of fact, and both possess an inherent and inalienable character of their own. There is no safe refuge from this conclusion in any abandonment of intellectual rigor. Hence all specula-

tive versions of the world that require the withholding of analysis, or that depend on the unique and preëminent status of the act of cognition, must be rejected, no matter how eagerly they may be desired for the justification of faith. They must be rejected in favor of such hypotheses as may be formulated in terms of the evident composition of the known world, and verified by its actual interrelations, history, and trend.

These conclusions in the aggregate can scarcely be said to be negative. It is true that they constitute neither a complete philosophy, nor, even so far as they go, an absolutely systematic philosophy. But that a philosophy should be absolutely systematic in the sense of being deducible from one principle is itself a philosophical doctrine that the realist is by no means prepared to adopt. Moreover that his philosophy should be as yet incomplete is, to the realist at least, a wholesome incentive, rather than a ground for uneasiness. There are endless special philosophical questions to which there is no inevitable realistic answer, such questions as mind and body, teleology, the good, and freedom; and there is verdict on the issues of religion. Nevertheless, the foundations and the scaffolding of the realistic universe are already built; and it is even possible for some to live in it and feel at home.

WALTER T. STACE

THE REFUTATION OF REALISM*

More than thirty years have now elapsed since Professor Moore published in *Mind* his famous article, "The Refutation of Idealism." Therewith the curtain rose upon the episode of contemporary British realism. After three decades perhaps the time is now ripe for the inauguration of another episode. And it is but fitting that "The Refutation of Realism" should appear on the same stage as its famous predecessor.

I shall not gird at realism because its exponents disagree among themselves as to what precisely their philosophy teaches. But disagreements certainly exist, and they make it difficult for a would-be refuter to know precisely what is the proposition which he ought to refute. It is far from certain that all idealists would agree that the idealism which Professor Moore purported to refute represented adequately, or even inadequately, their views. And it may be that a similar criticism will be urged by realists against

what I shall here have to say. But I must take my courage in my hands. Realists, it seems to me, agree in asserting that "some entities sometimes exist without being experienced by any finite mind." This, at any rate, is the proposition which I shall undertake to refute.

I insert the word "finite" in this formula because if I wrote "some entities exist without being experienced by any mind," it might be objected that the proposition so framed would imply that some entities exist of which God is ignorant, if there is such a being as God, and that it is not certain that all realists would wish to assert this. I think that we can very well leave God out of the discussion. In front of me is a piece of paper. I assume that the realist believes that this paper will continue to exist when it is put away in my desk for the night, and when no finite mind is experiencing it. He *may* also believe that it will continue to exist even if God is not experiencing it. But he must *at least* assert that it will exist when no finite mind is experiencing it. That, I think, is essential to

* From *Mind*, XLIII (April 1934), pp. 145-155. Reprinted by permission of the editor and the author.

his position. And therefore to refute that proposition will be to refute realism. In what follows, therefore, when I speak of minds I must be understood as referring to finite minds.

Possibly I shall be told that although realists probably do as a matter of fact believe that some entities exist unexperienced, yet this is not the essence of realism. Its essence, it may be said, is the belief that the relation between knowledge and its object is such that the knowledge makes no difference to the object, so that the object *might* exist without being known, whether as a matter of fact it does so exist or not.

But it would seem that there could be no point in asserting that entities *might* exist unexperienced, unless as a matter of fact they at least sometimes do so exist. To prove that the universe *might* have the property X, if as a matter of fact the universe has no such property, would seem to be a useless proceeding which no philosophy surely would take as its central contribution to truth. And I think that the only reason why realists are anxious to show that objects are such, and that the relation between knowledge and object is such, that objects might exist unexperienced, is that they think that this will lead on to the belief that objects actually do exist unexperienced. They have been anxious to prove that the existence of objects is not dependent on being experienced by minds because they wished to draw the conclusion that objects exist unexperienced. Hence I think that I am correct in saying that the essential proposition of realism, which has to be refuted, is that "some entities sometimes exist without being experienced by any finite mind."

Now, lest I should be misunderstood, I will state clearly at the outset that I cannot prove that no entities exist without being experienced by minds. For all I know completely unexperienced entities may exist, but what I shall assert is that we have not the slightest reason for believing that they do exist. And from this it will follow that the realistic position that they do exist is perfectly groundless and gratuitous, and one

which ought not to be believed. It will be in exactly the same position as the proposition "there is a unicorn on the planet Mars." I cannot prove that there is no unicorn on Mars. But since there is not the slightest reason to suppose that there is one, it is a proposition which ought not to be believed.

And still further to clarify the issue, I will say that I shall not be discussing in this paper whether sense-objects are "mental." My personal opinion is that this question is a pointless one, but that if I am forced to answer it with a "yes" or "no," I should do so by saying that they are not mental; just as, if I were forced to answer the pointless question whether the mind is an elephant, I should have to answer that it is not an elephant. I will, in fact, assume for the purposes of this paper that sense-objects, whether they be colour patches or other sense-data, or objects, are not mental. My position will then be as follows: There is absolutely no reason for asserting that these non-mental, or physical, entities ever exist except when they are being experienced, and the proposition that they do so exist is utterly groundless and gratuitous, and one which ought not to be believed.

[The refutation of realism will therefore be sufficiently accomplished if it can be shown that we do *not* know that any single entity exists unexperienced.] And that is what I shall in this paper endeavour to show. I shall inquire how we could possibly know that unexperienced entities exist, even if, as a matter of fact they do exist. And I shall show that there is no possible way in which we could know this, and that therefore we do *not* know it, and have no reason to believe it.

For the sake of clearness, let us take once again the concrete example of the piece of paper. I am at this moment experiencing it, and at this moment it exists, but how can I know that it existed last night in my desk when, so far as I know, no mind was experiencing it? How can I know that it will continue to exist tonight when there is no one in the room? The knowledge of these alleged facts is what the realists assert that they possess. And the question is, Whence could such knowledge have been obtained, and how can it be justified? What I assert is that it is absolutely impossible to have any such knowledge.

There are only two ways in which it could be asserted that the existence of any sense-object can be established. One is by sense-perception, the other by inference from sense-perception. I know of the existence of this paper *now* because I see it. I am supposed to know of the existence of the other side of the moon, which no one has ever seen, by inference from various actual astronomical observations, that is, by inference from things actually experienced. There are no other ways of proving the existence of a sense-object. Is either of them possible in the present case?

1. Sense-perception. I obviously cannot know by perception the existence of the paper when no one is experiencing it. For that would be self-contradictory. It would amount to asserting that I can experience the unexperienced.

2. Inference. Nor is it possible to prove by inference the existence of the paper when no mind is experiencing it. For how can I possibly pass by inference from the particular fact of the existence of the paper now, when I am experiencing it, to the quite different particular fact of the existence of the paper yesterday or tomorrow, when neither I nor any other mind is experiencing it? Strictly speaking, the onus of proving that such an inference is impossible is not on me. The onus of proving that it is possible is upon anyone who asserts it, and I am entitled to sit back and wait until someone comes forward with such an alleged proof. Many realists who know their business admit that no valid inference from an experienced to an unexperienced existence is possible. Thus Mr. Russell says, "Belief in the existence of things outside my own biography must, from the stand-point of theoretical logic, be regarded as a prejudice, not as a well-grounded theory"[1]

I might therefore adopt the strategy of masterly inaction. But I prefer to carry the war into the enemy's camp. (I propose to *prove* that no proof of the existence of unexperienced objects is possible.)

It is clear in the first place that any supposed reasoning could not be inductive. Inductive reasoning proceeds always upon the basis that what has been found in certain observed cases to be true will also be true in unobserved cases. But there is no single case in which it has been observed to be true that an experienced object continues to exist when it is not being experienced; for, by hypothesis, its existence when it is not being experienced cannot be observed. Induction is generalisation from observed facts, but there is not a single case of an unexperienced existence having been observed on which could be based the generalization that entities continue to exist when no one is experiencing them. And there is likewise not a single known instance of the existence of an unexperienced entity which could lead me to have even the slightest reason for supposing that this paper ever did exist, or will exist, when no one is experiencing it.

Since inductive reasoning is ruled out, the required inference, if there is to be an inference, must be of a formal nature. But deductive inference of all kinds depends upon the principle of consistency. If $P \supset Q$, then we can only prove Q, *if* P is admitted. From $P \supset Q$, therefore, all that can be deduced is that P and not-Q are inconsistent, and that we cannot hold both P and not-Q together, though we may hold either of them separately.

Hence, if it is alleged that a deductive inference can be drawn from the existence of the paper now, when I am experiencing it, to its existence when no one is experiencing it, this can only mean that to assert together the two propositions, (1) that it exists now, and (2) that it does not exist when no one is experiencing it, is an internally inconsistent position. But there is absolutely no inconsistency between these two propositions. If I believe that nothing whatever exists or ever did or will exist, except my own personal sense-data, this may be a view of the uni-

---

[1] *Analysis of Mind*, p. 133.

verse which no one would ever hold, but there is absolutely nothing internally inconsistent in it. Therefore, no deductive inference can prove the existence of an unexperienced entity. Therefore, by no reasoning at all, inductive or deductive, can the existence of such an entity be proved.

Nevertheless, arguments have been put forward from time to time by realists which are apparently intended to prove this conclusion. I will deal shortly with those with which I am acquainted. I am not bound to do this, since I have already proved that no proof of the realists' conclusion is possible. And for the same reason, if there are any arguments of this kind with which I am not acquainted, I am under no obligation to disprove them. But it will be better to meet at least the most well-known arguments.

a. It was Mr. Perry, I believe, who invented the phrase "egocentric predicament." The egocentric predicament was supposed to indicate where lay a fallacy committed by idealists. It consisted in arguing from the fact that it is impossible to discover anything which is not known to the conclusion that all things are known. That any competent idealist ever did use such an argument may well be doubted, but I will waive that point. Mr. Perry's comment was that the egocentric predicament, as employed by idealists, appeared to imply that from our ignorance of unexperienced entities we could conclude to their non-existence, and that to do so is a fallacy.

No doubt such a procedure would be a fallacy. But though Mr. Perry's argument may refute a supposed idealistic argument, *it does not prove anything whatever in favour of realism*. It would be a fallacy to argue that, because we have never observed a unicorn on Mars, therefore there is no unicorn there; but by pointing out this fallacy, one does not prove the existence of a unicorn there. And by pointing out that our ignorance of the existence of unexperienced entities does not prove their non-existence, one does nothing whatever towards proving that unexperienced entities do exist. As regards the unicorn on Mars, the correct position, as far as logic is concerned, is obviously that

if anyone asserts that there is a unicorn there, the onus is on him to prove it; and that until he does prove it, we ought not to believe it to be true. As regards the unexperienced entities, the correct position, as far as logic is concerned, is that if realists assert their existence, the onus is on them to prove it; and that until they do prove it, we ought not to believe that they exist. Mr. Perry's argument, therefore, proves nothing whatever in favour of realism.

Possibly all this is admitted and understood by realists. But there seems, nevertheless, to have been a tendency to think that the overthrow of the supposed idealistic argument was a very important matter in forwarding the interests of realism. To point out, therefore, that it actually accomplishes nothing seems desirable.

b. Mr. Lovejoy, in his recent book, *The Revolt Against Dualism*, argues that we can infer, or at least render probable, the existence of things during interperceptual intervals by means of the law of causation. He writes, "The same uniform causal sequences of natural events which may be observed within experience appear to go on in the same manner when not experienced. You build a fire in your grate of a certain quantity of coal, of a certain chemical composition. Whenever you remain in the room there occurs a typical succession of sensible phenomena according to an approximately regular schedule of clock-time; in, say, half an hour the coal is half consumed; at the end of the hour the grate contains only ashes. If you build a fire of the same quantity of the same material under the same conditions, leave the room, and return after any given time has elapsed, you get approximately the same sense-experiences as you would have had at the corresponding moment if you had remained in the room. You infer, therefore, that the fire has been burning as usual during your absence, and that being perceived is not a condition necessary for the occurrence of the process."[2]

This argument is simply a *petitio principii*.

[2] The Revolt Against Dualism, p. 268.

It assumes that we must believe that the law of causality continues to operate in the universe when no one is observing it. But the law of causality is one aspect of the universe, the unobserved existence of which is the very thing to be proved.

Why must we believe that causation continues to operate during interperceptual intervals? Obviously, the case as regards unexperienced processes and laws is in exactly the same position as the case regarding unexperienced *things*. Just as we cannot perceive unexperienced things, so we cannot perceive unexperienced processes and laws. Just as we cannot infer from anything which we experience the existence of unexperienced things, so we cannot infer from anything we experience the existence of unexperienced processes and laws. There is absolutely no evidence (sense-experience) to show that the fire went on burning during your absence, nor is any inference to that alleged fact possible. Any supposed inference will obviously be based upon our belief that the law of causation operates continuously through time whether observed or unobserved. But this is one of the very things which has to be proved. Nor is there the slightest logical inconsistency in believing that, when you first observed the phenomena, unburnt coal existed, that there followed an interval in which nothing existed, not even a law, and that at the end of the interval ashes began to exist.

No doubt this sounds very absurd and contrary to what we usually believe, but that is nothing to the point. We usually believe that things go on existing when no one is aware of them. But if we are enquiring how this can be *proved*, we must, of course, begin from the position that we do not know it, and therefore that it might not be true.

c. The distinction between sense-data and our awareness of them, which was first emphasized, so far as I know, by Professor Moore, has been made the basis of an argument in favour of realism. Green, it is said, is not the same thing as awareness of green. For if we compare a green sense-datum with a blue sense-datum, we find a common element, namely awareness. The awareness must be different from the green because awareness also exists in the case of awareness of blue, and *that* awareness, at any rate, is not green. Therefore, since green is not the same thing as awareness of green, green might exist without awareness. Connected with this argument, too, is the assertion of a special kind of relationship between the awareness and the green.

Possibly this argument proves that green is not "mental." I do not know whether it proves this or not, but the point is unimportant, since I have already admitted that sense-data are not "mental." But whatever the argument proves, it certainly does *not* prove that unexperienced entities exist. For suppose that it proves that green has the predicate x (which may be "non-mental" or "independent of mind," or anything else you please), it still can only prove that green has the predicate x during the period when green is related to the awareness in the alleged manner, that is, when some mind is aware of the green. It cannot possibly prove anything about green when no mind is aware of it. Therefore, it cannot prove that green exists when no mind is aware of it.

For the sake of clearness, I will put the same point in another way. Suppose we admit that green and awareness of green are two quite different things, and suppose we admit that the relation between them is r—which may stand for the special relation asserted in the argument. Now it is not in any way inconsistent with these admissions to hold that green begins to exist only when awareness of green begins to exist, and that when awareness of green ceases to exist, green ceases to exist. It may be the case that these two quite different things always co-exist, always accompany each other, and are co-terminous in the sense that they always begin and end simultaneously, and that while they co-exist, they have the relation r. And this will be so *whatever* the relation r may be. And not only is this supposition that they always co-exist not at all absurd or arbitrary. It is on the contrary precisely the conclusion to which such evidence as we possess points. For we never have evidence that green exists except when some mind is aware of green. And it will not be asserted that awareness of green exists when green does not exist.

The argument from the distinction between green and the awareness of it, therefore, does nothing whatever towards proving the realist conclusion that some entities exist unexperienced.

d. It has also been argued that if we identify a green or a square sense-datum with our awareness of it, then, since awareness is admittedly a state of mind, we shall have to admit that there exist green and square states of mind.

This argument is merely intended to support the previous argument that a sense-datum is different from our awareness of it. And as it has already been shown that this proposition, even if admitted, proves nothing in favour of realism, it is not necessary to say anything further about the present argument.

I will, however, add the following. It is not by any means certain, as is here assumed, that awareness is a state of mind, or indeed that such a thing as a *state* of mind exists. For the mind is not static. It is active. And what exists in it are *acts* of mind. Now the *attention* involved in being aware of a sense-datum is certainly an act of mind. But it is certainly arguable that *bare* awareness of a sense-datum (if there is such a thing as *bare* awareness) would be identical with the sense-datum and would not be an act of mind. For such bare awareness would be purely passive. In that case, the conclusion that there must exist green or square states of mind would not follow.

Moreover, even if we admit that there exist green and square states of mind, what then? I can see no reason why we should not admit it, except that (1) it is an unusual and unexplored view, and (2) it seems to smack of materialism, although I do not believe that it does really involve materialism. This shows that the whole argument is not really a logical argument at all. It is merely an attempt to throw dust in our eyes by appealing to the popular prejudices against

(1) unfamiliar views, and (2) materialism.

It is not possible in the brief space at my disposal to make plausible the suggestions contained in the last two paragraphs. A full discussion of them would be necessary and this I have endeavoured to give elsewhere. In the present place, therefore, I must rely upon the strict logical position, which is, that this argument, since it is merely intended to support argument (c) above, and since argument (c) has already been refuted, proves nothing in favour of realism.

By the preceding discussion, I claim to have proved (1) that the existence of an unexperienced entity cannot be known by perception, (2) that it cannot be known by reasoning, and (3) that the arguments commonly relied upon by realists to prove it are all fallacies.

I think it is not worth while to discuss the possible suggestion that the arguments in favour of realism, although not proving their conclusion rigorously, render that conclusion probable. For what has been shown is that no valid reasoning of *any* kind can possibly exist in favour of this conclusion. Any conceivable reasoning intended to prove that unexperienced entities exist must, it has been shown, be *totally* fallacious. It cannot, therefore, lead even to a probable conclusion. The position, therefore, is that we have not even the faintest reason for believing in the existence of unexperienced entities.

That this is the correct logical position seems to be dimly perceived by many realists themselves, for it is common among them to assert that our belief in unexperienced existences is a "primitive belief," or is founded upon "instinctive belief," or upon "animal faith." This suggestion is obviously based upon the realization that we cannot obtain a knowledge of unexperienced existences either from perception or from reasoning. Since this is so, realists are compelled to appeal to instinctive beliefs.

Such a weak position seems hardly to require discussion. A "primitive belief" is merely a belief which we have held for a long time, and may well be false. An "instinctive belief" is in much the same case. An "instinct," so far as I know, is some kind of urge to *action,* not an urge to believe a proposition. And it is therefore questionable whether there are such things as instinctive beliefs in any strict sense, although, of course, no one will deny that we have beliefs the grounds of which are only dimly, or not at all, perceived. Certainly the psychology of such alleged instinctive beliefs has not been adequately investigated. And certainly we have no good ground for supposing that an instinctive belief (if any such exists) might not be false.

And if we have such an instinctive or primitive belief in unexperienced existences, the question must obviously be asked How, When, and Why such a belief arose in the course of our mental evolution. Will it be alleged that the amoeba has this belief? And if not, why and when did it come into existence? Or did it at some arbitrarily determined stage in our evolution descend suddenly upon us out of the blue sky, like the immortal soul itself?

Is it not obvious that to base our belief in unexperienced existences on such grounds is a mere gesture of despair, an admission of the bankruptcy of realism in its attempt to find a rational ground for our beliefs?

Strictly speaking, I have here come to the end of my argument. I have refuted realism by showing that we have absolutely no good reason for believing in its fundamental proposition that entities exist unexperienced. Nothing I have said, of course, goes any distance towards proving that entities do *not* exist unexperienced. That, in my opinion, cannot be proved. The logically correct position is as follows. We have no reason whatever to believe that unexperienced entities exist. We cannot prove that they do not

exist. The onus of proof is on those who assert that they do. Therefore, as such proof is impossible, the belief ought not to be entertained, any more than the belief that there is a unicorn on Mars ought to be entertained.

It is no part of the purpose of this essay to do more than arrive at this negative result. But lest it should be thought that this thinking necessarily leads to nothing but a negative result, or to a pure scepticism, I will indicate in no more than a dozen sentences that there is the possibility of a positive and constructive philosophy arising from it. That positive philosophy I have attempted to work out in detail in another place. Here, I will say no more than the following. Since our belief in unexperienced existences is not to be explained as either (1) a perception, or (2) an inference, or (3) an "instinctive belief," how is it to be explained? I believe that it can only be explained as a mental construction or fiction, a pure assumption which has been adopted, not because there is the slightest evidence for it, but solely because it simplifies our view of the universe. How it simplifies our view of the universe, and by what detailed steps it has arisen, I cannot discuss in this place. But the resulting conception is that, in the last analysis, nothing exists except minds and their sense-data (which are not "mental"), and that human minds have, out of these sense-data, slowly and laboriously constructed the rest of the solid universe of our knowledge. Unexperienced entities can only be said to exist in the sense that minds have chosen by means of a fiction to project them into the void of interperceptual intervals, and thus to construct or create their existence in imagination.

WILBUR MARSHALL URBAN

REALISM, IDEALISM AND PHILOSOPHIA PERENNIS: EPILOGUE*

I — A

The theme, Beyond Realism and Idealism, has now been developed through the various stages of the argument as outlined in our introductory statement of the problem. Whether the general argument is convincing or the more specific attempt at a conciliation of realism and idealism of the preceding chapter is found tenable must be left for the reader to decide. In any case, nothing more can be added to the argument itself. There is, however, still a question that may significantly be raised. Granted that the case has been made out with some degree of convincingness, what is its meaning for philosophy and for the general culture of which philosophy is always the epitome?

That significance, I am bold enough to believe, would be very great. In the first place, if this position could be maintained, it would, as I have already suggested, free philosophy from many of the inhibitions from which it is now suffering and release its energies for the genuine problems of speculative thought which it has so long suppressed. In the second place, it would re-unite philosophy with the great stream of *philosophia perennis* from which it has been so long estranged. Since I believe both of these to be fundamental *desiderata* of our present culture this epilogue becomes an important part of our general study.

B

The arrest of spiritual initiative is an outstanding fact of our modern culture. The sources of our inhibitions are many and varied, but underlying them all is, I believe,

---

* From *Beyond Realism and Idealism* by Wilbur Marshall Urban. London: George Allen & Unwin Ltd., 1949. Reprinted by permission of the publisher.

the deep-seated feeling that there is no answer to the demand—as fundamental as life itself—we must know! Positivism in its various forms has sought to meet this depression by telling us that the problems generated by this demand are not genuine problems at all, but the human mind knows that this is not true. If these problems are meaningless, so also is life itself, for science as a human enterprise demands a valour which science as a negation of ultimate meaning cannot give.

Not the least of these problems is this recurrent opposition of idealism and realism which, as I have maintained, has, for a long time arrested the energies of metaphysical thought. Is it strange that many have deprecated the constant revolving of our thought around this "fruitless issue" and have sought to find a way out of the *impasse* by calling the whole problem meaningless. So far as the technical aspect of this issue is concerned all that is necessary has already been said. Still less is the problem meaningless from the standpoint of the cultural life of man. It represents, as we have seen, two irrefutable tendencies of life—two "life forms" of thought, both of which are equally necessary. Denial of either can result only in arrest of the life of reason and ultimately in a fundamental dissociation of life and thought. Recognition of mere necessity, either psychological or social, is, however, as depressing as scepticism. It is only when they are seen to be reconcilable, not only in life but in thought and reason also, that the issue becomes significant; and with the recognition of its significance the energies of men can be turned to the fundamental problems—the very problems which not only interest philosophers but are profoundly significant for all thinking men.

C

The freeing of philosophy's energies for the genuine problems of speculative thought is, then, the first result which might legitimately be expected to follow from the transcendence of this opposition. But there is a second result, equally significant for modern culture, namely, the reuniting of our thought with the great stream of traditional philosophy from which we have long been estranged.

That this estrangement is the source of much of our present social and political ill is felt by many, and a return is advocated in many quarters. The doubtful wisdom of some forms of this reaction need not be denied, but the feeling that has motivated them is wholly sound. It is gradually coming home to many minds that our cultural and spiritual values are indeed bound up with a fundamental metaphysical structure and that estrangement from these ways of thinking means estrangement from the values themselves. It is increasingly realized that the foundations of our culture are Hellenism and Christianity, and it is this, more than anything else, that has led men to rethink the more ancient ways of thought.

The more general conditions of such a return to *philosophia perennis* I have discussed elsewhere,[1] but certainly among them is the solution of the epistemological problems which the modern conceptions of the physiology of knowledge have generated. I have no wish to exaggerate the importance in culture, either of the problem of knowledge itself or of the specific problem with which our discussion has been engaged, but he would be blind indeed who did not recognize that scepticism regarding human reason and knowledge is the root, acknowledged or unacknowledged, of scepticism in morals and religion. The conditions which created the modern epistemological problem are the same which have cut us off from traditional philosophy, and the confusions which this problem has engendered have led to a deep-seated confusion regarding the fundamental issues of philosophy. It is above all the senseless opposition of realism and idealism which has closed our eyes to the more fundamental issues which have made *philosophia perennis* what it is. It is only when we shall have freed ourselves from this senseless conflict that our eyes will again be opened to what these ultimate issues really are. That the rapidly changing cultural and intellectual *mileu* is itself relegating this conflict to the background is fortunately true, but it is still a disease of philosophy which philosophy itself alone can ultimately cure.

With this we are brought to the final stage of our argument, namely, the demonstration of the thesis, propounded in the introduction, that this entire European tradition in philosophy, with which our culture is bound up, is beyond the issue of epistemological realism and idealism; or, in terms of the preceding chapter, constitutes a synthesis of the cognitive values of both, and contains elements of both positions as necessary parts of its structure.

The development of this phase of the argument involves three stages: (*a*) the justification of the idea of a *philosophia perennis;* (*b*) the development of the cognitive presuppositions of this philosophy; (*c*) the relating of these presuppositions to the modern epistemological contrast of idealism and realism.

---

[1] "The Return to Perennial Philosophy," *The Intelligible World*, chap. v.

II

THE IDEA OF A PHILOSOPHIA PERENNIS:
"THE UNITY OF PHILOSOPHICAL EXPERIENCE"

A

The idea of a *philosophia perennis,* so long the object of neglect, and even of contempt, is again coming into prominence. So long as men lived in the afterglow of the Renaissance called the Enlightenment it seemed only natural to think that precisely this glow—and still more the colder light of reason which followed—marked a complete break with the "dark ages" in which the natural light of reason was obscured by the clouds of superstition and obscurantism. Nothing, we now know, is further from the truth. The break with this philosophy did not occur in the Renaissance. The great stream of European rationalism not only continues this tradition, but carries along, in new forms, all the basal presuppositions of this philosophy.

We are now seeing European philosophy in a new perspective, and it is chiefly the experiences of modern Darwinian naturalism which have changed the point of view. We now see that the real break came with Locke's "physiology of knowledge," a naturalization of the intelligence which found its culmination and final form in the evolutionary naturalism which followed upon Darwin. In contrast with this naturalism, and its corresponding naturalization of the entire spirit of man, all that precedes takes on a significant unity and continuity, both of intention and of fundamental presuppositions.

The unity and continuity of the entire European tradition is the outstanding insight of the history of philosophy of the present. The continuance of this tradition with its *corpus philosophicum*—not the least part of which was the rational proofs for the exist-

ence of God—is the outstanding fact of the entire rationalistic movement from Descartes to Kant and Hegel. This continuity in one of its important aspects has already been made clear in earlier chapters. The significant point here is that it constituted the one "comprehensive and magnificent scheme of thought which dominated European culture for a thousand years," and with which all its values were bound up. This is the outward aspect of the tradition, but if one looks below the surface it becomes clear that that which determined both the unity and the continuity of this *philosophia perennis* were certain common presuppositions of intelligibility and intelligible thought which dominated the entire period, and which were first seriously challenged by modern sensationalism and naturalism. It is these, rather than the particular content of the *corpus philosophicum,* which determined both its character and its form. It is these that made it the perennial philosophy which it is.

B

It is true that the character of this *philosophia perennis* is often more narrowly conceived, namely, as identical with scholasticism. They are, however, far from identical. Scholasticism, as a unitary closed system, has never existed. True, there was a philosophy of the scholastics, but this philosophy appears quite different in the early scholasticism, the classical period and late scholasticism. The philosophy of an Erigina is another from that of an Anselm and an Abelard. St. Thomas carries on his battle on two fronts—against Augustinianism and Platonism, on the one side, and the Aristoteleanism of Averroes on the other. The basal question of the relation of knowledge to faith is differently solved in the early scholasticism of Anselm in the classical period by Albert and Thomas, and in the late scholasticism by Duns Scotus and William of Occam. At one point in particular the differences within the general movement of scholasticism become especially significant for our present purpose. The idealistic motive, with its so-called ontologism, to which perhaps St. Thomas himself made significant concessions, is as much a part of this perennial philosophy as the Aristotelean realistic motive. But while scholasticism has never existed as a closed system, it has existed as a form of thought determined by certain universally accepted presuppositions, which we shall examine presently. In this sense it represents not only a necessary part of *philosophia perennis,* but a part which is in a sense symptomatic of the whole.

St. Thomas was himself far removed from identifying his own system with the *philosophia perennis,* or conceiving it as a final stage of philosophy. He valued rightly the limited contributions of the individual to this stream of philosophy. The knowledge of truth is not a matter of the individual, but a common enterprise. As the present stands on the shoulders of the past and its tradition, so is it also the basis for progress in the future. Above all, St. Thomas knew that knowledge of a thing does not mean complete knowledge. This is a root principle of his thought. His thesis concerning the knowledge of being, namely, that our understanding is by nature directed to being, is meant only in the sense of an ideal programme. As he did not exclude from *philosophia perennis* his predecessors and compatriots, no more would he have excluded his philosophical successors who should carry on in the spirit of the Great Tradition. In this general movement St. Thomas is, however, an all-important figure. He was not only the great architect and systematizer of philosophy, raising it to a self-sufficient and independent

"science," but he, more than anyone else, became fully conscious of the presuppositions of this philosophy. In this respect he is the outstanding figure and it is, accordingly, about his thought that much of the succeeding discussion must revolve.

C

This idea of a *philosophia perennis* underlies Étienne Gilson's recent book, *The Unity of Philosophical Experience.* Philosophy is perennial in the sense, first of all, that, as he says, "it always buries its undertakers." But it is perennial in a second and more fundamental sense; it exhibits a unity and continuity which is essentially dialectical, although, for understandable reasons, he does not use the term.

It is dialetical in the sense that while philosophizing depends for its activity, in the first instance, upon individual philosophers, and is never found separate from them, it has in a certain sense its own independent life. Philosophy consists in "the concepts of philosophy taken in the naked impersonal necessity of their own content and relations." "The constant recurrence of definite philosophical attitudes should suggest to the mind," he holds, "the presence of an abstract philosophical necessity. Granted that there is no such thing as historical determinism, it still remains true that history contains a metaphysical determinism. In each instance of philosophical thinking, both the philosopher and his particular doctrine are ruled from above by an impersonal necessity. Philosophers are free to lay down their own set of principles, but once this is done, they no longer think as they wish—they think as they can." In the second place, it seems to result from the facts under discussion that any attempt on the part of the philosopher to shun the consequences of his own position is doomed to failure. "What he declines to say will be said by his disciples, if he has any; if he has none, it will remain eternally unsaid, but it is there, and anyone going back to the same principles, be it several centuries later, will have to face the same conclusions."[2]

The unity and continuity of philosophical experience is thus dialectical in character, and it is this which constitutes *philosophia perennis* in the second and more fundamental sense. *"Philosophia perennis"* is thus for Gilson, as he rightly says, "not an honorary title for any particular form of philosophical thinking, but a necessary designation of philosophy itself, almost a tautology. That which is philosophical is also perennial in its own right."[3] With this, one must in the main agree. *Philosophia perennis* should not be applied as an honorary title to scholasticism, however important in the history of thought the scholastic movement may be. But we cannot agree that it is merely a necessary designation for philosophy itself—almost a tautology. In fact, it is this expression, "almost," that we find significant. If it is not a complete tautology, then there must be elements in *philosophia perennis* which are not characteristic of all philosophizing; there must be some types of philosophizing which are not in the movement of *philosophia perennis* and are contrary to its very spirit. In fact, it is only in a very limited sense that philosophers are free to lay down their own set of set principles. Even in philosophy there is a difference between freedom and license, and an uncharted freedom—one

which violates the conditions of intelligibility and intelligible expression—not only tires us but very properly serves only to call out our indifference if not contempt.

There is, then, a narrower sense in which the term *philosophia perennis* has been and, as I believe, must be used. As ordinarily used, the term has been employed to characterize certain elements in philosophical thinking that have persisted amid all the changes which have been brought about by historical and social conditions. These elements may be described as the necessary presuppositions of intelligible thought. Philosophy not only buries its undertakers: it also, by its own inherent logic or dialectic, refutes and reduces to futility those forms of philosophizing which violate the conditions of philosophical intelligibility as such. Philosophy also buries some of its own practitioners. In other contexts, I have developed both the conditions of philosophic intelligibility and the form of an intelligible world which have been developed and established in the dialectic of European thought.[4] In the present context we are concerned with only one aspect—namely, the presuppositions of *philosophia perennis* as they concern the problem of knowledge—those presuppositions without which an intelligible theory of knowledge is impossible. This study involves the relation of these presuppositions to the issue set by realism and idealism.

III

THE COGNITIVE PRESUPPOSITIONS OF PHILOSOPHIA PERENNIS:

THEIR RELATION TO IDEALISM AND REALISM

A

The unity of philosophical experience in the sense in which we have defined it, is very real and is, indeed, the outstanding fact

of the entire Greek and Christian tradition. This unity is determined not so much by continuity of specific philosophical beliefs— although such continuity is there—as by the fundamental presuppositions that underlie the

---

[2] *Op. cit.*, p. 302.
[3] *Op. cit.*, p. 318.

[4] *The Intelligible World*, chaps. v and vi; *Language and Reality*, chap. xiv.

movement. It is these, rather than specific metaphysical beliefs, that distinguish it fundamentally from what I have called modernism in philosophy.

The presuppositions of such a *philosophia perennis* are twofold. On the one hand, there is the assumption of antecedent being; being is uniformly and necessarily a first principle of this philosophy. On the other hand, there is an equally fundamental assumption or first principle, namely, that *ratio est capabilis,* in other words, that there is such a relation between mind or reason and being that being can be known. This we may describe as the double cognitive presupposition underlying traditional philosophy. Without either an intelligible theory of knowledge is impossible.

The first of these presuppositions, as the scholastics have always rightly seen, is the *sine qua non* of philosophy as such; the first metaphysical principle is being. This presupposition or postulate is quite independent of distinctions of idealism and realism within the European tradition, and was never denied prior to modern naturalism and pragmatism. This principle of antecedent being is itself not provable. It is, in Fichte's terms, an underivable first principle. The only sense in which it may be said to have any ground or reason is that with its denial the peculiar significance of knowledge is lost, or, as Maritain says, the denial of this first principle "strikes at the very roots of the intelligence itself."

The second of these necessary presuppositions is that *ratio est capabilis,* the assumption, namely, that the human spirit possesses the power to apprehend or understand being in ever-increasing measure. The rationality of being (the meaningfulness of the given) and the possibility of translating this rationality into the categories of human experience and knowldege, are the necessary presuppositions of the whole of traditional philosophy. They represent the idealistic ingredient in perennial philosophy. This second principle is no more provable than the first. The validity of the intellect—and of its primary ideas and principles—cannot, as for instance

St. Thomas admits, be directly proven. We can only show that the denial of this validity leads to self-contradiction and unintelligibility. Its denial also strikes at the very roots of intelligence, and with such denial also the peculiar significance of knowledge is lost. The transcendence of mind, in this sense, is as much a presupposition of this philosophy as the transcendence of being.

This is the double epistemological presupposition underlying perennial philosophy, and its presence may be used as a touch-stone to differentiate traditional from modernistic forms of thought. But there is a third element or presupposition, closely related to these primary principles and without which they themselves would scarcely be understandable, namely, the inseparability of value and being. This is the axiom of intelligibility which constitutes the underlying presupposition, and ultimately the driving force, of the entire Greco-Christian tradition. In so far as this is true, the driving force of this tradition is idealistic in the more fundamental and metaphysical sense, although, as we shall see, the position is beyond idealism and realism in the epistemological sense.

This characteristic presupposition of all traditional philosophy is a fact which Dewey also recognizes in his account of traditional European philosophy. An essential part of that philosophy, as he rightly sees, is its conception of the relation of values to antecedent reality.[5] In this tradition "idealist" and "realist" alike agree that ultimately being and value are inseparable—that the validity of our values rests upon the fact that they are grounded in being, while the significance of being rests upon the fact that being includes values as part of its nature.

This was technically expressed in the famous doctrine of the "transcendentals." Whatever is, in so far as it is or has being, is at the same time, and for this very reason, also true, good and beautiful. "The humblest form of existence exhibits the inseparable privileges of being, which are truth, goodness and beauty." These transcen-

---

[5] John Dewey, *The Quest for Certainty.*

dentals are not predicates in the ordinary sense that being might have them or have them not; rather are they inseparable from being as such. This is the axiom of intelligibility—the inseparability of being and value—which underlies *philosophia perennis* in all its forms and expressions.

In this third, and basal, presupposition is included already the double presupposition of which we have spoken. By this very doctrine it has already placed itself beyond realism and idealism in the narrow modern sense, for it includes in it the motives of both. It is true that in the Thomistic version of *philosophia perennis* substance is first in the order of knowledge, but this does not mean that it is first in the order of being. From this more ultimate point of view being and value are equally primal. These "modes," as St. Thomas calls them, do not add anything to being. They are aspects of being as such. All reality, therefore, has meaning, is intelligible. It is this basal assumption which, while beyond realism and idealism in the epistemological sense, is the very essence of metaphysical idealism as we have come to understand it."[6]

B

These, then, are the necessary presupposition of *philosophia perennis* in the sense in which we have used the term. The universal acknowledgment of these underivable first principles, whether merely tacit or explicit, constitutes the unity and continuity of philosophical experience which is the outstanding character of European thought. It is now necessary to examine the relations of these presuppositions to idealism and realism in the epistemological sense.

As the character of *philosophia perennis* itself is often too narrowly conceived, so also are its epistemological presuppositions. Scholastics frequently identify it with the Aristotelean and Thomistic strain in traditional philosophy and characterize this philosophy as realistic in the modern sense. I agree, however, with Hans Meyer that "realistic epistemology in the sense of the idealism-realism controversy, is wholly secondary to the concept of *philosophia perennis*."[7] This I shall attempt to show and, in so showing, shall hope to make good the thesis that *philosophia perennis* is above realism and idealism in the epistemological sense.

I consider it one of the fatalities of modern thought that so frequently the issues are confused by this identification of the realism of the scholastics with realism in the modern sense. One might almost speak of a "modern perversion" of the notion of realism, for realism in the sense of the postulate of antecedent being is as much a part of historic idealism as of realism. Certainly, as our historical sketch has shown, realism for scholasticism had almost an opposite meaning from that which it has today.

Realism, as understood in the scholastic philosophy, has as its opposite not idealism but nominalism. Realism, whether extreme or moderate, presupposes that the ultimate object of knowledge is the *idea* or *essence,* whether that idea is *ante rem* or *in re.* Knowledge is ultimately of the idea; only that which is ideal is intelligible. The ground of truth lies in its being independent of the knower, but only because reality itself is the realization of a spiritual content or idea. Only so do things possess a meaning and a sense; only so are they knowable. Further, the *logos* or idea in the real is understandable only because of the highest logos or divine spirit. It is true that there is an element in scholasticism—at least in the Thomistic version—which seems to justify to an extent the identification of this realism with modern naturalistic realism. For St. Thomas the only objects immediately known are physical objects. Knowledge of mind, both of the self and the other, and knowledge of God are possible only by inference. The physical object thus becomes the starting point and the norm of all knowledge, and in this sense

[6] See on this question of the "transcendentals," Fulton J. Sheen, *The Philosophy of Science,* pp. 137 ff.

[7] Hans Meyer, *Die Philosophie,* 1936, p. 179.

constitutes a common ground for modern and mediaeval realism. It is probably true that this notion of the physical object as the object of knowledge *par excellence* has, through a long period of time, sufficed to give this object a privileged position in modern thought. But granted this, it still remains true that the Aristotelean epistemology is not a necessary part of *philosophia perennis*. It is not necessarily involved in the primary principle of antecedent being and is at least secondary in this philosophy. Moreover, even in the realism of St. Thomas, the physical object is not the physical object as understood by modern naturalistic realism; for him realism does not in the least imply naturalism. For whatever is, is, by its very being, also good, true and beautiful. This not only separates it completely from the naturalism bound up with modern realism, but embodies the very essence of all metaphysical idealism, namely, the cosmic significance of values.

Philosophia perennis is of course realistic —in the sense that any sane philosophy is realistic. For it every truth is *veritas ontologica*. The ground of truth lies in an antecedent reality; but only—and this is a most important *but*—because reality itself is the realization of a spiritual content or "idea." Only so do things possess a meaning and a sense. Further, the *logos* or idea in the real is understandable only because of the highest *logos* or divine spirit. A realistic epistemology, in the sense of the reality of ideas, is, of course, a necessary presupposition of this philosophy—as it is of its teleological world view, and of the absoluteness of our knowledge as well as of our values and norms. But realism in the narrow sense of modern epistemological discussion is not a necessary presupposition. I do not mean that many of the representatives of this tradition have not been realistic in this modern sense also, or at least may be made to appear so, That is, of course, a fact. What I do mean is that many have not. Thus realism in this second sense is, I repeat, not a primary presupposition of *philosophia perennis*, but at best a secondary character of some aspects of it.

C

The necessary presuppositions of traditional European philosophy are then, when examined, seen to be beyond realism and idealism in the modern epistemological sense. But more than this is true. Both realistic and idealistic presuppositions, as we have defined them, are necessary and complementary parts of this philosophy; it really represents a genuine synthesis of the two—of the driving force of idealism and the resistance of realism. This we shall now attempt to show.

"The most tempting of all the false first principles," writes Gilson, "is that thought, not being, is involved in all my representations. Here lies the initial option between realism and idealism which will settle once and for all the future course of our philosophy and make it a failure or success. Are we to encompass being with thought, or thought with being? In other words, are we to include the whole in one of its parts or one of the parts in its whole? If intellectual evidence is not enough to dictate our choice, history is there to remind us that no one ever regains the whole of reality after locking himself up in one of its parts. Man is not a mind that thinks, but a being who knows other beings as true, who loves them as good and who enjoys them as beautiful. For all that which is, down to the humblest form of existence, exhibits the inseparable privileges of being, which are truth, goodness or beauty."[8]

With much of this we can fully sympathize—especially with the last sentences which, as we have maintained, contain the very essence of the Great Tradition. But so far as the problem of realism and idealism is concerned, it represents, I believe, a serious misunderstanding and states the issue falsely.

First of all, I should maintain, the initial option of philosophy is itself wrongly stated. There *is* an initial option but it is found elsewhere. It is an option which lies far deeper than any choice between being and thought; it is the option between the insep-

---

[8] *Op. cit.*, p. 316.

arability of being and value, which is the underlying principle or presupposition of *philosophia perennis* in all its forms, and the divorce of being and value which is the root principle of modern naturalistic realism. If this ultimate principle is rejected, if the cosmic significance of values is denied, then, as we have already seen, there is no significant difference between epistemological realism and idealism so far at least as fundamental issues are concerned.[9] The initial option which determines our entire philosophy is embodied in the doctrine of the "transcendentals." In comparison with this the option between "thought and being" is wholly secondary. This cannot, I think, be too much emphasized. So far as the major issues of philosophy are concerned, a metaphysical idealism based upon this principle is closer to traditional philosophy than a realism which denies it.

In the second place, the principle of being is not the initial option in the sense that its choice *excludes* the second primary and underivable principle. A large part of our study has been devoted to showing that the realistic and idealistic presuppositions are not contradictory but mutually supplement each other. But since Gilson makes so much of the exclusive primacy of the principle of being we must examine the issue again.

Now that antecedent being is a fundamental notion of all philosophy or metaphysics is beyond question. Anyone who denies it (as for instance Dewey, if he really does) really abandons the philosophical enterprise as it has been understood. For, as Gilson says, "Our mind is so made that it cannot formulate a single proposition without relating it to some being. We cannot speak about that which is not." This is the primary element in all analyses of knowledge, realistic and idealistic alike. "But if it is true," Gilson continues, "that human thought is always about being, it follows that the understanding of being is the first to be attained, the last into which all knowledge is ultimately resolved and *the only one* to be included in all

our apprehensions. What is first, last and always in human knowledge is its first principle, and its constant point of reference. . . . We can safely conclude that since being is the first principle of all human knowledge it is *a fortiori,* the first principle of metaphysics."[10]

Now I do not, for a moment, deny that being *is* an underivable first principle and that this principle is first, last and always in human knowledge. I merely deny that it is the *only* first principle. From the fact that we cannot formulate a single proposition without relating it to being, it does not at all follow that we can formulate it wholly by this relation. It does not follow that being is the only principle to be included in our apprehensions. As a matter of fact it is neither true that any metaphysics can be developed from this first principle alone nor that traditional philosophy has ever worked with this as its sole initial principle.

The classical objection to Gilson's position is, as he recognizes, that from such a vague idea as that of being alone, no distinct knowledge can be developed or deduced . . . (This is the basal argument of all those who, from Hegel on, have insisted that in order that knowledge should be possible, not only must mind be organic to being, but being must be organic to mind.) It is true, Gilson holds, that from the mere idea of being no knowledge can be deduced, but he also holds that it is not really an objection. "To describe being as the principle of knowledge does not mean that all subsequent knowledge can be analytically deduced from it, but rather that being is the first knowledge, through which all subsequent knowledge can be progressively acquired. As soon as it comes into touch with sensible experience, the human intellect elicits the immediate intuition of being, X is, or exists; but from the intuition that something is, the knowledge of what it is, beyond the fact that it is something, cannot be deduced, nor is it the task of the intellect to deduce it. The intellect does not deduce, it intuits, it sees, and in

---

[9] Chap. ix.

[10] *Op. cit.,* p. 312.

the light of the intellectual intuition, the discursive power of reason slowly builds up from experience a determinate knowledge of concrete reality." [11]

I do not think that the notion of an immediate intuition of being constitutes an answer to this classical objection. First of all, it seems clear to me that the belief in the mind-independent character of being is not part of the sense intuition itself. That much modern epistemological analysis, from Locke on, has made clear. It is doubtless an "assurance that deserves the name of knowledge," but it is itself not knowledge in the sense of intuition. It is a faith, a postulate, what you will, but not sense experience. But perhaps this intuition of antecedent being is an "intellectual" intuition. If it is so conceived, the difficulty is increased rather than diminished. For an intellectual intuition can be only of ideas or essences, and this is the very heart of idealism in the traditional sense; only an ideal world is ultimately intelligible. But Gilson's answer to this classical objection contains still another difficulty. This lies in the fact that "the discursive power of reason," which, according to him, "builds up from experience a determinate kind of concrete reality" is itself wholly unintelligible unless this very reason is in some way organic to a principle of mind or reason in the world itself. For knowledge to be possible, not only must mind be organic to the world, but the world must be organic to mind.

Actually, as I have already maintained, traditional philosophy has never worked with the principle of being alone. It has always had a second equally fundamental and underivable principle, namely, the rationality of being, the meaningfulness of the given and the possibility of translating this rationality or ideality into the categories of human experience and knowledge. This is just as much an underivable principle as the first; no more provable than the first and no less certain. Indeed, these two principles mutually imply each other. For without the second

the first is empty—the emptiest notion the mind can conceive—in itself it contains by no means all the flower and fruit of knowledge which Gilson supposes. Without the first principle the second is not less empty—can indeed be nothing more than the spinning of empty ideas in the inane. Each requires the other—as much as the notion of a valley requires the notion of a mountain, or the inside of a curve requires the outside. Any theory of knowledge which works with either, alone, is not sane in the meaning of the term given to it by Alexander, and *philosophia perennis* is, above all things, sane.

D

Philosophia perennis, as we have come to understand it, constitutes, then, a genuine synthesis of the two primary motives of first principles which we have characterized as realism and idealism. It is for this reason that it is equally possible to describe it as idealism or realism, according to the perspective in which it is viewed. It is possible to say with Willmann in his *Geschichte des Idealismus,* that this is the true idealism in contrast to the false which arose from starting exclusively from the subject. In contrast to this false idealism, it is possible to say that it is realism and to emphasize the realistic elements in the position. *But in the actual life of European philosophy they are held together in a genuine synthesis.* I call it a genuine synthesis for it is not merely an arbitrary union, attempting by some merely logical formula to combine cognitive values which are themselves metalogical, but a natural synthesis deeply grounded in the life of reason itself.

Philosophia perennis is the natural metaphysic of the human mind, and therefore, pre-eminently a sane philosophy—close to earth with all the furniture of earth, and close to Heaven with its celestial choirs. Arising out of life in all its fullness, it shares the fundamental initiatives of life itself, and, therefore, quite naturally presents in theory a reconciliation of these two tendencies which

---

[11] *Op. cit.,* p. 313.

are equally indigenous to life. But the synthesis is really ultimately genuine because it takes as its initial option the axiom of all intelligibility—namely, the inseparability of value and being—an axiom incapable of "proof," to be sure, but for that reason no less part of the natural light of reason itself. In this initial option is presupposed from the beginning the transcendence of realism and idealism.

IV

THE RETURN TO PERENNIAL PHILOSOPHY:

THE MODERN ERA IN A NEW PERSPECTIVE

A

So much then for the main thesis—that the great stream of European thought is above the opposition of realism and idealism in the modern epistemological sense. Recognition of that fact should enable us to transcend the opposition in our own thought and thus again make connections with those more fundamental ways of thought from which we have been long estranged.

Whether such a return is either desirable or possible, is of course, a debatable question and much in the forefront of philosophy today. It may not be desirable. It may be that not only an irreligion of the future, but also a purely positivistic and anti-metaphysical culture is the ultimate ideal of man. But even if a return were desirable, it might now be no longer possible. It may be that Western civilization, having passed through the stages of creative religious faith and the philosophical culture that developed from it, has now reached the stage of mere civilization, with its techniques—a stage in which only positivism and anti-metaphysical attitudes are possible. These are, indeed, debatable questions, answers to which can ultimately be little more than expressions of philosophic faith. Nevertheless, a word on these points may be in place.

Of the desirability—even imperative necessity—enough has perhaps been said. The pathetic attempts of modern man to retain his values without the rational structure with which they have been bound up, and to graft them upon an evolutionary naturalism with which they are wholly incompatible, constitutes the intellectual scandal of modern thought. A case could, indeed, be made out for the abandonment of these ideals themselves. I am myself not insensible to the force of the Nietzschean argument which, starting with the assumption that this structure is gone, and proceeding from the premises of evolutionary naturalism, concludes that all our values, moral, cognitive and metaphysical, must be transvalued. That seems to me to be perfectly logical and coherent. It is possible that our attempts to retain them, despite their absurdity in the light of the reigning naturalistic premises, is itself a weakness; that these very ideals themselves are "ghosts" which in the light of a more scientific day will vanish away.

The possibility of such a return is even more a matter of doubt. There is a certain sense in which it is impossible to turn back the clock, even if it were desirable. For better or for worse, modern man has gone through certain experiences which have made him what he is and he cannot be other. Perhaps a positivistic and wholly anti-metaphysical culture is, even if not desirable, at least inevitable.

Signs are not wanting that this may be so. One need not accept the metaphysics of Spengler's philosophy of history in order to admit to an unhappy feeling that our culture is going very much the way that he describes.

One need not bow to such notions as fate and destiny in order to recognize that the tide in the affairs of men has set in this direction, and to recognize also that there is little that can be done until the tide turns. It may be that it will never turn, or it may be that it is turning now; who shall say? But unless—and until—it does turn, all argument will be of little avail.

Whether then such a return is possible or desirable is a question which turns on such large issues, both cultural and philosophical, that answers to it, whether positive or negative, can be little more than matters of philosophic faith. Into this region I shall not seek to press further. Instead, I shall attempt to illuminate my main thesis by giving an account of what seems to me the present situation in philosophy as seen against the background of traditional thought. I shall characterize it as "the modern era seen in a new perspective."

B

I cannot escape the conviction that we have been viewing the modern era in large part in a false perspective. It is ordinarily assumed, almost without question, that "the break with traditional philosophy" began with Descartes. This I believe to be a fundamental misunderstanding. Despite his method of doubt and his *cogito ergo sum,* which is thought by many to contain the germs of subjectivism, actually he continued the main motives of *philosophia perennis,* as indeed did the entire rationalistic movement of the continent. In the *corpus philosophicum* of this movement was included not only the entire theistic argument but the conception of reason upon which that argument was based. The break began rather with Locke's physiology of knowledge which Kant recognized for what it was. It implied already a naturalization of the intelligence which needed only to be confirmed by Darwinism, to be extended to the entire spirit of man. The key to the understanding of the nineteenth and twentieth centuries is then the fight of idealism with naturalism or, in its epistemological form, of transcendentalism with sensationalism. Modernism, as distinguished from the modern era in philosophy, is the story of the triumph of naturalism and positivism in every form of human life and culture.

Assuming the truth of this thesis recent European philosophy first becomes understandable. The story of this philosophy really concerns the nature and significance of the modern idealistic movement for it is about it that all the issues of recent philosophy centre. As an inveterate enemy of naturalism, it alone, I shall maintain, has attempted to keep the faith of perennial philosophy and, however unsuccessful the attempt, to state its essential elements in a new form. It is opposition to this movement that has generated modernistic forms of philosophy, and this opposition has logically led to the "destruction" of traditional philosophy itself.

Seen in this perspective, Kant's critical philosophy, despite its negative elements, takes on a positive form. His understanding of man as more than empirical and natural, and as linked with supernatural values, is a reaffirmation, in opposition to sensationalistic naturalism, of the driving force of the entire European tradition. It is true, he denied the mediaeval doctrine of the transcendentals with his lips, but he accepted it fully in his heart. Kant attempted valiantly to stem the tide of naturalism, already implied in Locke's physiology of knowledge, and thus the epistemological problem becomes central. For Kant knowledge is not possible, *i.e.* intelligible, except on the basis of the presupposition of transcendental mind: and values are not possible (or intelligible) except on the assumption of a transcendental free subject. Indeed, knowledge itself, including the distinction between truth and falsity, is possible only on the presupposition and postulate of freedom, for reason in all its forms is oriented towards the good.[12] It is, however, his position regarding realism

---

[12] For a fuller development of this interpretation of Kant, see my article entitled "Kant and Modern Axiology," published in *The Heritage of Kant*, The Princeton University Press, 1939.

and idealism which is from this point of view most significant. The ambiguity of Kant on this point, his attempt to combine an empirical realism with a transcendental idealism, is really his way of expressing the double presupposition of *philosophia perennis*. That it does not express it satisfactorily, either for the realists of that tradition, or for the still more exclusive naturalistic realists of the modern era, does not in the least affect either its intention or its significance. It is precisely because of this attempt at combination, however unsatisfactorily he may have expressed it, that he is still the philosopher that has most to say, not only to the critical philosopher, but to the critical scientist also.[13]

The objective idealism, following upon Kant, is a continuation of the attempt to restore traditional philosophy in a new form. It may almost be said (*pace* the Neo-scholastics) to restore the scholasticism of the middle ages. It takes God, not man, as its starting point, being, not sensation, as its initial option. God or the absolute reason, becomes again the centre of the world and the subjectivism which followed from starting with man, and the physiology of his knowledge, was transcended in a conception which again connected the human and the divine *logos*. This is the essential of the movement and in any attempt to evaluate it, it must be given first place.

In so far as the particular epistemological opposition is concerned, this too was an attempt to express the double presupposition of *philosophia perennis* in a new form. For the "either—or" of the exclusive realist or idealist, Hegel is constantly saying "both—and." That he does not express it satisfactorily, either for the exclusive realists of that tradition or the still more exclusive realists of modern naturalism, does not, again affect either his intention or its significance. His attempted synthesis of the two may fail to convince, but Royce is wholly right in maintaining that objective idealism is an attempt to effect just such a synthesis.[14]

---

[13] Chap. vi, p. 168.
[14] Chap. iv, pp. 112 f.

It was, I suppose, recognition of the general truth of this interpretation which, partly at least, led Whitehead to hope that his own philosophy would be viewed as a transformation of the main ideas of objective idealism unto a realistic basis. That these ideas, expressed in the idiom of objective idealism failed to convince, is a matter of history. The reasons for this failure are many and varied. Internal logical weaknesses of its own, doubtless contribute to this downfall, weaknesses too well known to require mention here. Failure to recognize the relative autonomy of science and rightly to evaluate the empirical element in knowledge—above all, a certain over-intellectualization of the hands of narrow logicians led to a far-reaching reaction to the pragmatic or "life" philosophies. A progressive subjectification of its originally objective character, especially on the part of the English idealists, led to a justified revolt which gave rise to modern forms of logical realism. Doubtless, too, idealism in the main "tended to overreach itself" and weakened the force of its more fundamental arguments by attempting to prove too much. All this may be admitted, but these internal weaknesses would in themselves not have been sufficient. It was evolutionary naturalism which gave it its final *coup de grâce*. It was one of those cases in which the Time-Spirit did not change its mind but woke up to find its mind changed.

Seen in this larger perspective, the meaning of typical movements in present-day philosophy first really becomes clear. The essential irrationalism which characterizes them all, whether that of pragmatism or that of the still more fundamental existential philosophy of the continent, all stem from the reaction against objective idealism. But as the movement proceeded it became ever clearer that it is not merely this idealism which is attacked, but the entire rationalistic European tradition. Kierkegaard, the father of much of this irrationalism in Europe, was the first, so we are told, "to break with the philosophy of essence which continued from the Greeks to Hegel," and in a sense this is doubtless true. For this reason Heidegger, influenced by Kierkegaard, proposes in his *Sein and Zeit* the "destruction" of all philosophy (meaning thereby the Greco-Christian tradition) as the propaedeutic to his own modern philosophy of existentialism. John Dewey's attack on this tradition is part of the same movement. In all this we have, however, a confirmation of our main thesis, that this idealism is a continuation of the essentials of that tradition and that modern naturalism is the common enemy of both. It is little wonder that this same existential philosophy has already become in many quarters an expression of post-war disillusionment and irrationalism, and still less that Catholic philosophers find it more inimical than the scientific rationalism and positivism of preceding decades.

C

This interpretation of modern philosophy does not mean that I am arguing for a return to this idealism. The preceding account recognizes not only its internal weaknesses but also the fact that this particular formulation of perennial philosophy was conditioned by cultural and scientific factors which belong to the past also. It does mean, however, that I am arguing for a truer and saner evaluation of the movement in the entire story of European philosophy. In saying this I do not have in mind those childish attacks on Kant and Hegel arising out of the passions and prejudices of war, which would charge them with responsibility for all the ideas which we dislike in our enemies—with such things no really responsible or critical philosopher is for a moment concerned. What I have in mind is something much more fundamental, namely, the recognition of the fact that, however disguised at times, the "main" ideas" of this idealism constitute a continuation of the European tradition—and that which is more important in this context, when once modern naturalism with its physiology of knowledge and its naturalization of the intelligence, was inaugurated, these same main ideas could be expressed only in

the form of this transcendentalism, and that therefore, seen in this perspective, this idealism has a permanently significant place in European thought.

If, however, I am not arguing for a return to objective idealism, just as little am I arguing for a return to *philosophi perennis* in any of its specific ancient forms. It is doubtless tempting to try to reinstate such ancient forms literally—and there are those who have yielded to the temptation—but this is surely to try to turn back the clock. Even in scholasticism, as we have seen, a *philosophia perennis* as a unitary and closed system never existed, and St. Thomas himself was far from identifying his own system with such a philosophy. These ancient formulations, magnificent as they are, had their local conditioning also, and this makes it necessary to separate the spirit from the letter. What then, it may properly be asked, perhaps impatiently, do you really mean by traditional philosophy and by advocating a return to its principles?

Tradition in philosophy, no more than in any other sphere of culture, is a literal repetition of dead concepts; it is life, movement and perpetual reinterpretation. But the reinterpretation which is necessary for life and movement, is always limited by the bounds of certain necessary presuppositions within which life and thought themselves must move if they are to be meaningful and intelligible. There are certain conditions of intelligibility and it is the recognition and acknowledgment of these presuppositions which alone makes philosophy perennial.

First of all, it is my contention that philosophers are really not free to lay down their own first principles. This is true of individuals and epochs alike. Even in thought, free as it must necessarily be, there is a difference between freedom and license. Philosophy is sometimes defined as thinking without prejudices or presuppositions, but this is true only in a limited sense. The philosopher does, indeed, seek to free himself from certain prejudices—of temperament, of time and of race—but precisely in that he does so he brings to light certain hidden presuppositions and postulates from which he cannot free himself and remain a philosopher. In fact, it is only in the light of these more fundamental presuppositions that he is able to recognize and eliminate his particular prejudices. These more ultimate presuppositions he cannot transcend. To do so is to court the irony of self-refutation, either in his own time or later. For there are conditions of philosophical intelligibility which cannot be gainsaid. It is my contention also that it is the acknowledgment, either explicitly or implicitly, of these necessary presuppositions, rather than the presence of particular doctrines, which constitutes the essence of *philosophia perennis*.

It is of the utmost importance that this position should not be misunderstood. To contend that there is a philosophy, however perennial, that remains unchanged and unchangeable despite the development of knowledge in the sciences, is precisely the dogmatism which it is the task of critical philosophy in all stages of its history to expose and transcend. Again, to maintain that this philosophy, however perennial, is final in the sense that it is completely coherent and intelligible, is to claim for it the status of a divine revelation rather than the product of fallible human thought. But neither of these impossible positions would any philosopher in his right senses for a moment maintain. Far reaching changes, not only in our knowledge of facts but in our categories of knowledge, such as our notions of space, time and causality, affect the form of statement of a metaphysical position. But no such changes, however vast, can affect in the slightest degree the ultimate demands of rationality and intelligibility. This is what I mean by *philosophia perennis* whatever elements in this traditional philosophy time, and the knowledge of things in time, may change, there is that in its basal presuppositions, its initial options, which is, I believe, timeless and in principle irrefutable. What particular forms this philosophy may take in the future we cannot know. But of one thing we may be assured—if one form is refuted, it will immediately take another.

These general reflections apply with special force to the specific problem which constitutes the theme of this book. Here too, in the problem of human knowledge, the philosopher is not free to lay down his first principles. He is not free to choose to be either an exclusive idealist or an exclusive realist. Both realistic and idealistic postulates are necessary to an intelligible theory of knowledge; both realism and idealism are necessary parts of the natural metaphysic of the human mind and, therefore, of *philosophia perennis*. Both have undergone endless transmutations; but both are in the end irrefutable. It is for this reason that no sane philosopher has ever been exclusively realistic or idealistic and that every philosophy that has endured has really been beyond the opposition, at least in spirit if not in the letter. When we penetrate beneath the letter, with which naïve and literal minds ever seek to fetter the human spirit, we shall find that on the supreme issues, the great minds, whether we call them realists or idealists, are really one. Thus it is that, not only in their understanding of the issues but in the main ideas in which they have expressed their solutions, they are beyond realism and idealism.

SUGGESTED READINGS

Blanshard, Brand. *The Nature of Thought.* 2 vols. New York: The Macmillan Co., 1955, Chap. 26.

Bosanquet, Bernard. *The Meeting of Extremes in Contemporary Philosophy.* London: The Macmillan Co., 1925.

Bradley, Francis H. *Appearance and Reality: A Metaphysical Essay.* Oxford: Clarendon Press, 1951.

Broad, Charlie D. *Examination of McTaggart's Philosophy.* Cambridge, England: Cambridge University Press, 1933.

Creighton, James E. "Two Types of Idealism," *Philosophical Review,* XVI (1917), pp. 514–36.

Dewey, John. "Brief Studies in Realism," *Journal of Philosophy,* VIII (1911), pp. 393–400, 546–54.

Ewing, Alfred C. *The Idealist Tradition.* Glencoe, Illinois: The Free Press, 1957.

Feibleman, James. *The Revival of Realism: Critical Studies in Contemporary Philosophy.* Chapel Hill: University of North Carolina Press, 1946.

Hegel, Georg W. *The Phenomenology of Mind.* New York: The Macmillan Co., 1931.

Hocking, William E. *Types of Philosophy.* New York: C. Scribner's Sons, 1959, Part III.

Lovejoy, Arthur O. *The Revolt Against Dualism.* London: G. Allen & Unwin, Ltd., 1930.

McTaggart, J. M. Ellis. *The Nature of Existence.* 2 vols. Cambridge, England: The University Press, 1921–27.

———— "An Ontological Idealism," *Contemporary British Philosophy,* First Series, (1924).

Perry, Ralph Barton. "The Egocentric Predicament," *Journal of Philosophy, Psychology and Scientific Method,* VII (1910), pp. 5–14.

Royce, Josiah. *Lectures in Modern Idealism.* New Haven: Yale University Press, 1923.

———— *The Spirit of Modern Philosophy.* Rev. ed. New York: George Braziller, Inc., 1955.

Sellars, Wilfrid. "Realism and the New Way of Words," *Philosophy and Phenomenological Research,* VIII (1948).

PART III

BEING AND SUBSTANCE

INTRODUCTION

The question of Being, central to metaphysics, is basically ambiguous. It has consequently been interpreted in a number of different ways. As a noun, "being" can designate either *a* being or substance; or it can designate some property common to everything that is, in which everything participates. As a verb, a present participle of the verb "to be," it designates the act by which any reality exists. A consequent problem arises from taking both meanings together. If something exists it must be, and therefore it must be a part of Being. But philosophers (and ordinary men) do speak of *possible* beings which do not exist. A tension thus arises between essence and existence, some philosophers giving precedence to one or the other of them. From the relation of beings to each other and to Being as such arises also the problem of the One and the Many, that is, the problem of explaining both the unity of everything that is (Being) and the multiplicity of beings.

Aristotle, we saw (Part I), considered metaphysics to be the study of Being qua Being. In Book VII of the *Metaphysics* Aristotle tells us that the primary sense of being is substance, which he defines both as that which alone can exist separately and as that of which other things are predicated. After examining the claims that the essence, the universal, the genus, and the substratum of a given particular are substantial, he tells us that each individual thing is one with its essence, that their formula is the same. Since neither form nor essence is generated, however, whereas the concrete whole is, this latter must be more than form alone. Aristotle's analysis of concrete material substances leads him to his hylomorphic doctrine that such substances are composed of matter and substantial form. Substance is thus the form or cause which determines the material element of all composite individuals.

Etienne Gilson (1884–   ), a distinguished historian of medieval philosophy, Professor at the Collège de France, and Director of Studies at the Pontifical Institute of Mediaeval Studies in Toronto, is widely known for his extensive writings, which include *The Spirit of Mediaeval Philosophy* (1932), *The Unity of Philosophical Experience* (1937), and *Being and Some Philosophers* (1952). In the chapter "Being and Existence" of this latter work, Gilson presents Saint

Thomas Aquinas' metaphysical interpretation of being. Although Aquinas accepts much of the Aristotelian doctrine of substance, he goes beyond Aristotle to deal with existence as well as with essence. For Aquinas the world is created and contingent: existence is *in* the world, but the world never is its existence. After clarifying the meaning of this doctrine, Gilson explains Aquinas' view of the real distinction between essence and existence, and his dissociation of the two Aristotelian notions of form and act.

The notion of substance changed somewhat in the hands of some modern philosophers. For John Locke, who held that what we know directly are sensible qualities capable of producing simple ideas in us, substance became a term referring to an unknown something which supported the sensible qualities. We do not know what it is, but we know what it does. From Locke's starting point, Berkeley (see Part II) argues that material substance is meaningless, although he defends the notion of spiritual substance. David Hume extended Berkeley's arguments to do away with all substance—material as well as spiritual. In his article "Substratum" Morris Lazerowitz (1907–   ), Professor of Philosophy at Smith College and author of *The Structure of Metaphysics,* carries the discussion one step further. He argues that there is no way of deciding whether the substratum theory (which holds that a thing is composed of a substance that supports a variety of attributes said to inhere in it) is merely the semblance of an empirical hypothesis into which we have been tricked by the subject-predicate structure of language, or whether it is an actual hypothesis about the structure of things which determines a form of language about them. After analyzing Locke's view of substance, he presents a Humean argument against it, concluding that this substance theory produces the illusion of its being a theory about things because it is based on a concealed revision of ordinary subject-predicate sentences.

Bertrand Russell (1872–   ) was educated at Trinity College, Cambridge. He has taught at Cambridge, has lectured throughout the world, and has written a large number of books and articles containing important contributions in logic, theory of knowledge, metaphysics, and almost every other branch of philosophy. His works include *Principia Mathematica* (with A. N. Whitehead, 1910–12), *Mysticism and Logic* (1918), *Analysis of Mind* (1921), *Analysis of Matter* (1927), and *A History of Western Philosophy* (1944). In the chapter "The World of Universals" from his book *The Problems of Philosophy* (1912), he presents a modified version of Plato's world of ideas or essences or forms. These do not exist in the world of sense; each is one, eternal, immutable, and indestructible. Since a universal is anything which may be shared by particulars, Russell argues from resemblance as a universal to the world of universals. The being proper to them is neither material nor mental, although when known they are objects of thought. For Russell the world of universals is the world of being, where "being" is opposed to existence.

Paul Weiss (1901–   ), Professor of Philosophy at Yale University, founder and editor of *The Review of Metaphysics,* founder and first president of the Metaphysical Society of America, and author of such books as *Reality* (1938) and *Modes of Being* (1958), discusses the problem of the One and the Many in his article "On Being Together." He presents and analyzes five typical answers previously given to this problem, to which he assigns the identifying names "Synthesis," "Concurrence," "Self-Diremption," "Dualism," and "Identity in Difference." Each, he claims, provides some answer to the problem. But each is faced with certain embarrassments, thus forcing him to take up a sixth and new approach.

Martin Heidegger (1889–   ) is a philosopher usually linked with the existentialist movement, though he himself repudiates this characterization of his work. A student of Edmund Husserl, he succeeded to his chair at Freiburg (Germany) in 1929 and occupied it until his retirement in 1945. His works include *Being and Time* (1927) and *Kant and the Problem of Metaphysics* (1929). His essay "What is Metaphysics?" was his inaugural address to his fellow professors upon acceding to his chair at Freiburg. The "Postscript" was added in 1943. In this essay, in which Heidegger takes as his theme the problem of Nothing, he presents a new and critical approach to the problem of metaphysics. His originality consists in his claim that a proper analysis of Being necessarily involves an analysis of Nothing as well, for "Being and Nothing hang together," and "Nothing, conceived as the pure 'Other' than what-is, is the veil of Being." Just as boredom or joy reveals to us what-is in its totality, so dread reveals Nothing. For Heidegger Nothingness is the source of negation as well as of wonder, and it is revealed as ingredient in the very basis of what we are, as well as of what-is.

ARISTOTLE

THE METAPHYSICS: BOOK VII*

I. The term "being" has several senses, which we have classified in our discussion[1] of the number of senses in which terms are used. It denotes first the *"what"* of a thing, *i.e.* the individuality; and then the quality or quantity or any other such category. Now of all these senses which "being" has, the primary sense is clearly the "what," which denotes the *substance* (because when we describe the quality of a particular thing we say that it is "good" or "bad," and not "five feet high" or "a man"; but when we describe *what* it is, we say not that it is "white" or "hot" or "five feet high," but that it is "a man" or "a god"), and all other things are said to "be" because they are either quantities or qualities or affections or some other such thing.

Hence one might raise the question wheth-

* Reprinted by permission of the publishers and The Loeb Classical Library, translated by Hugh Tredennick, ARISTOTLE: *The Metaphysics*, Cambridge, Mass.: Harvard University Press.
[1] V. vii.

er the terms "to walk" and "to be well" and "to sit" signify each of these things as "being," or not; and similarly in the case of any other such terms; for not one of them by nature has an independent existence or can be separated from its substance. Rather, if anything it is the *thing* which walks or sits or is well that is existent. The reason why these things are more truly existent is because their subject is something definite; *i.e.* the substance and the individual, which is clearly implied in a designation of this kind, since apart from it we cannot speak of "the good" or "the sitting." Clearly then it is by reason of the substance that each of the things referred to exists. Hence that which *is* primarily, not in a qualified sense but absolutely, will be substance.

Now "primary" has several meanings; but nevertheless substance is primary in all senses, both in definition and in knowledge and in time. For none of the other categories can exist separately, but substance alone; and it is primary also in definition, because in the formula of each thing the formula of substance must be inherent; and we assume that we know each particular thing most truly when we know *what* "man" or "fire" is—rather than its quality or quantity or position; because we know each of these points too when we know *what* the quantity or quality is. Indeed, the question which was raised long ago, is still and always will be, and which always baffles us—"What is Being?"—is in other words "What is substance?" Some say that it is one;[2] others, more than one; some, finite;[3] others, infinite.[4] And so for us too our chief and primary and practically our only concern is to investigate the nature of "being" in the sense of substance.

II. Substance is thought to be present most obviously in bodies. Hence we call animals and plants and their parts substances, and also natural bodies, such as fire, water, earth, etc., and all things which are parts of these

or composed of these, either of parts of them or of their totality; *e.g.* the visible universe and its parts, the stars and moon and sun. We must consider whether (*a*) these are the only substances, or (*b*) these and some others, or (*c*) some of these, or (*d*) some of these and some others, or (*e*) none of these, but certain others. Some[5] hold that the bounds of body—*i.e.* the surface, line, point and unit—are substances, and in a truer sense than body or the solid. Again, some[6] believe that there is nothing of this kind besides sensible things, while others believe in eternal entities more numerous and more real than sensible things. Thus Plato posited the Forms and the objects of mathematics as two kinds of substance, and as a third the substance of sensible bodies; and Speusippus[7] assumed still more kinds of substances, starting with "the One," and positing principles for each kind: one for numbers, another for magnitudes, and then another for the soul. In this way he multiplies the kinds of substance. Some[8] again hold that the Forms and numbers have the same nature, and that other things—lines and planes—are dependent upon them; and so on back to the substance of the visible universe and sensible things. We must consider, then, with regard to these matters, which of the views expressed is right and which wrong; and what things are substances; and whether there are any substances besides the sensible substances, or not; and how sensible substances exist; and whether there is any separable substance (and if so, why and how) or no substance besides the sensible ones. We must first give a rough sketch of what substance is.

III. The term "substance" is used, if not in more, at least in four principal cases; for both the essence and the universal and the genus are held to be the substance of the particular, and fourthly the substrate. The substrate is that of which the rest are

---

[2] The Milesians and Eleatics.
[3] The Pythagoreans and Empedocles.
[4] Anaxagoras and the Atomists.

[5] The Pythagoreans.
[6] The pre-Socratics.
[7] Plato's nephew and successor as head of the academy.
[8] The followers of Xenocrates, successor to Speusippus.

predicated, while it is not itself predicated of anything else. Hence we must first determine its nature, for the primary substrate is considered to be in the truest sense substance.

Now in one sense we call the *matter* the substrate; in another, the *shape;* and in a third, the combination of the two. By matter I mean, for instance, bronze; by shape, the arrangement of the form; and by the combination of the two, the concrete thing: the statue. Thus if the form is prior to the matter and more truly existent, by the same argument it will also be prior to the combination.

We have now stated in outline the nature of substance—that it is not that which is predicated of a subject, but that of which the other things are predicated. But we must not merely define it so, for it is not enough. Not only is the statement itself obscure, but also it makes matter substance; for if matter is not substance, it is beyond our power to say what else is. For when everything else is removed, clearly nothing but matter remains; because all the other things are affections, products and potencies of bodies, and length, breadth and depth are kinds of quantity, and not substances. For quantity is not a substance; rather the substance is that to which these affections primarily belong. But when we take away length and breadth and depth we can see nothing remaining, unless it be the something bounded by them; so that on this view matter must appear to be the only substance. By matter I mean that which in itself is neither a particular thing nor a quantity nor designated by any of the categories which define Being. For there is something of which each of these is predicated, whose being is different from that of each one of the categories; because all other things are predicated of substance, but this is predicated of matter. Thus the ultimate substrate is in itself neither a particular thing nor a quantity nor anything else. Nor indeed is it the negations of these; for the negations too will only apply to it accidentally.

If we hold this view, it follows that matter is substance. But this is impossible; for it is accepted that separability and individuality belong especially to substance. Hence it would seem that the form and the combination of form and matter are more truly substance than matter is. The substance, then, which consists of both—I mean of matter and form—may be dismissed, since it is posterior and obvious. Matter too is in a sense evident. We must consider the third type, for this is the most perplexing.

Now it is agreed that some sensible things are substances, and so we should begin our inquiry in connexion with these. IV. It is convenient to advance to the more intelligible[9]; for learning is always acquired in this way, by advancing through what is less intelligible by nature to what is more so. And just as in actions it is our task to start from the good of the individual and make absolute good good for the individual,[10] so it is our task to start from what is more intelligible to oneself and make what is by nature intelligible intelligible to oneself. Now that which is intelligible and primary to individuals is often but slightly intelligible, and contains but little reality; but nevertheless, starting from that which is imperfectly intelligible but intelligible to oneself, we must try to understand the absolutely intelligible; advancing, as we have said, by means of these very things which are intelligible to us.

Since we distinguished at the beginning[11] the number of ways in which substance is defined, and since one of these appeared to be essence, we must investigate this. First, let us make certain linguistic statements about it.

The essence of each thing is that which it is said to be *per se*. "To be you" is not "to be cultured," because you are not of your own nature cultured. Your essence, then, is that which you are said to be of your

---

[9] *sc.* by nature. All learning proceeds by induction from that which is intelligible to *us* (*i.e.,* the complex facts and objects of our experience, which are bound up with sensation and therefore less intelligible in themselves), to that which is intelligible in itself (*i.e.,* the simple universal principles of scientific knowledge).

[10] Cf. *Ethics* 1129 b 5.

[11] c. iii. 1.

own nature. But not even all of this is the essence; for the essence is not that which is said to be *per se* in the sense that whiteness is said to belong to a surface,[12] because "being a surface" is not "being white." Nor is the essence the combination of both, "being a white surface." Why? Because the word itself is repeated. Hence the formula of the essence of each thing is that which defines the term but does not contain it. Thus if "being a white surface" is the same as "being a smooth surface," "white" and "smooth" are one and the same.[13]

But since in the other categories too there are compounds with substance (because there is a substrate for each category, *e.g.* quality, quantity, time, place and motion), we must inquire whether there is a formula of the essence of each one of them; whether these compounds, *e.g.* "white man," also have an essence. Let the compound be denoted by X.[14] What is the essence of X?

"But this is not even a *per se* expression." We reply that there are two ways in which a definition can be not *per se* true of its subject: (*a*) by an addition, and (*b*) by an omission. In one case the definition is not *per se* true because the term which is being defined is combined with something else; as if, *e.g.*, in defining whiteness one were to state the definition of a white man. In the other, because something else (which is not in the definition) is combined with the subject; as if, *e.g.*, X were to denote "white man," and X were defined as "white." "White man" is white, but its essence is not "to be white." But is "to be X" an essence at all? Surely not. The essence is an individual type; but when a subject has something distinct from it predicated of it, it is not an individual type. *E.g.*, "white man" is

not an individual type; that is, assuming that individuality belongs only to substances. Hence essence belongs to all things the account of which is a definition. We have a definition, not if the name and the account signify the same (for then all accounts would be definitions; because any account can have a name, so that even "the *Iliad*" will be a definition), but if the account is of something primary. Such are all statements which do not involve the prediction of one thing of another. Hence essence will belong to nothing except species of a genus, but to these only; for in these the predicate is not considered to be related to the subject by participation or affection, nor as an accident. But of everything else as well, if it has a name, there will be a formula of *what it means*—that X belongs to Y; or instead of a simple formula one more exact—but no definition, nor essence.

Or perhaps "definition," like the "what," has more than one sense. For the "what" in one sense means the substance and the individual, and in another each one of the categories: quantity, quality, etc. Just as "is" applies to everything, although not in the same way, but primarily to one thing and secondarily to others; so "what it is" applies in an unqualified sense to substance, and to other things in a qualified sense. For we might ask also what quality "is," so that quality also is a "what it is"; not however without qualification, but just as in the case of not-being some say by a verbal quibble that not-being "is"—not in an unqualified sense, but "is" not-being—so too with quality.

Now although we must also consider how we should express ourselves in each particular case, it is still more important to consider what the facts are. Hence now, since the language which we are using is clear, similarly essence also will belong primarily and simply to substance, and secondarily to other things as well; just as the "what it is" is not essence simply, but the essence of a quality or quantity. For it must be either by equivocation that we say that these things *are,* or by adding and subtracting qualifications, as we say that the unknowable

---

12 Cf. V. xviii. 3, 4.
13 The statement that "to be a white surface" is the same as "to be a smooth surface" tells us nothing fresh about surface; it simply identifies "white" with "smooth." Aristotle has in mind Democritus's theory of colour (that it is an impression conveyed to our eyes from the superficial texture of the object; Theophrastus, *De Sensu* 73-75); *cf. De Sensu* 442 b 11, *De Gen. et Corr.* 316 a 1.
14 Literally "cloak," but the word is chosen quite arbitrarily. Cf. VIII. vi. 4.

is known;[15] since the truth is that we use the terms neither equivocally nor in the same sense, but just as we use the term "medical" in *relation* to one and the same thing; but not *of* one and the same thing, nor yet equivocally. The term "medical" is applied to a body and a function and an instrument, neither equivocally nor in one sense, but in relation to one thing.[16]

However, in whichever way one chooses to speak of these things, it matters nothing; but this point is clear: that the primary and unqualified definition, and the essence, belong to substances. It is true that they belong equally to other things too, but not *primarily*. For if we assume this, it does not necessarily follow that there is a definition of anything which means the same as any formula; it must mean the same as a particular kind of formula, *i.e.* the formula of one thing —one not by continuity, like the *Iliad,* or things which are arbitrarily combined, but in one of the proper senses of "one." And "one" has the same variety of senses as "being." "Being" means sometimes the individual thing, sometimes the quantity, sometimes the quality. Hence even "white man" will have a formula and definition; but in a different sense from the definition of "whiteness" and "substance."

V. The question arises: If one denies that a formula involving an added determinant is a definition, how can there be a definition of terms which are not simple but coupled? Because they can only be explained by adding a determinant. I mean, *e.g.,* there is "nose" and "concavity" and "snubness," the term compounded of the two, because the one is present in the other. Neither "concavity" nor "snubness" is an accidental, but a *per se* affection of the nose.[17] Nor are they attributes in the sense that "white" is of Callias or a man, because Callias is white

and is by accident a man; but in the sense that "male" is an attribute of animal, and equality of quantity, and all other attributes which we say belong *per se.* That is, all things which involve the formula or name of the subject of the affection, and cannot be explained apart from it. Thus "white" can be explained apart from "man," but not "female" apart from "animal." Thus either these terms have no essence or definition, or else they have it in a different sense, as we have said.

But there is also another difficulty about them. If "snub nose" is the same as "concave nose," "snub" will be the same as "concave." But if not, since it is impossible to speak of "snub" apart from the thing of which it is a *per se* affection (because "snub" means a concavity in the nose), either it is impossible to call the nose snub, or it will be a tautology, "concave-nose nose" because "snub nose" will equal "concave-nose nose." Hence it is absurd that such terms as these should have an essence. Otherwise there will be an infinite regression; for in "snub-nose nose" there will be yet another nose.

Clearly, then, there is definition of substance alone. If there were definition of the other categories also, it would have to involve an added determinant, as in the case of the qualitative; and of the odd, for this cannot be defined apart from number; nor can "female" apart from "animal." By "involving an added determinant" I mean descriptions which involve a tautology, as in the above examples. Now if this is true, there will be no definition of compound expressions either; *e.g.,* "odd number." We fail to realize this because our terms are not used accurately. If on the other hand there are definitions of these too, either they are defined in a different way, or, as we have said, "definition" and "essence" must be used in more than one sense; thus in one sense there will be no definition of anything, and nothing will have an essence, except substances; and in another those other things will have a definition and essence. It is obvious, then, that the definition is the formula of

---

15 *sc.* to be unknowable.
16 Cf. IV. ii. 2.
17 Snubness is a *per se* affection of the nose, because it applies only to the nose and cannot be explained apart from it, but the same can hardly be said of concavity. Aristotle himself uses the word (κοιλότης) elsewhere in other connexions.

the essence, and that the essence belongs either *only* to substances, or especially and primarily and simply.

VI. We must inquire whether the essence is the same as the particular thing, or different. This is useful for our inquiry about substance; because a particular thing is considered to be nothing other than its own substance, and the essence is called the substance of the thing. In accidental predications, indeed, the thing itself would seem to be different from its essence; *e.g.*, "white man" is different from "essence of white man." If it were the same, "essence of man" and "essence of white man" would be the same. For "man" and "white man" are the same, they say, and therefore "essence of white man" is the same as "essence of man." But perhaps it is not necessarily true that the essence of accidental combinations is the same as that of the simple terms; because the extremes of the syllogism are not identical with the middle term in the same way.[18] Perhaps it might be thought to follow that the accidental extremes are identical; *e.g.* "essence of white" and "essence of cultured"; but this is not admitted.[19]

But in *per se* expressions, is the thing necessarily the same as its essence, *e.g.*, if there are substances which have no other substances or entities prior to them, such as some hold the Ideas to be? For if the Ideal Good is to be different from the essence of good, and the Ideal Animal and Being from the essence of animal and being, there will be other substances and entities and Ideas besides the ones which they describe; and prior to them, if essence is substance. And if they are separate from each other, there will be no knowledge of the Ideas, and the essences will not exist (by "being separate" I mean if neither the essence of good is present in the Ideal Good, nor "being good" in the essence of good); for it is when we know the essence of it that we have knowledge of a thing. And it is the same with other essences as with the essence of good; so that if the essence of good is not good, neither will the essence of being "be," nor the essence of one be one. Either all essences exist alike, or none of them; and so if not even the essence of being "is," neither will any other essence exist. Again that to which "essentially good" does not apply cannot be good. Hence "the good" must be one with the essence of good, "the beautiful" with the essence of beauty, and so with all terms which are not dependent upon something else, but self-subsistent and primary.[20] For it is enough if this is so, even if they are not Forms; or perhaps rather even if they are. (At the same time it is clear also that if the Ideas are such as some hold, the substrate will not be substance; for the Ideas must be substances, but not involving a substrate, because if they did involve one they would exist in virtue of its participation in them.)[21]

That each individual thing is one and the same with its essence, and not merely accidentally so, is apparent, not only from the foregoing considerations, but because to have knowledge of the individual is to have knowledge of its essence; so that by setting out examples it is evident that both must be identical. But as for the accidental term, *e.g.* "cultured" or "white," since it has two meanings, it is not true to say that the term itself is the same as its essence; for both

---

[18] The argument consists of two syllogisms:
  White man = essence of white man.
  Man = white man.
  △ man = essence of white man.
  But essence of man = man.
  △ essence of man = essence of white man.
The conclusion is faulty because whereas the first identity is assumed to be absolute, the second is accidental.

[19] Aristotle seems to mean that both "essence of white man" and "essence of cultured man" might be proved by the former syllogism to be identical in the same way with the middle term "man," in which case it would seem that "essence of white" and "essence of cultured" are the same. There is, however, the same fallacy as before.

[20] The example of the Ideas as *per se* terms is used by Aristotle to show incidentally the fallacy of the Ideal theory: there can be no self-subsistent entity apart from the essence.

[21] This criticism is irrelevant to the point under discussion. It simply points out that the Ideal theory conflicts with received opinion (cf. iii. 1).

the accidental term and that of which it is an accident are "white," so that in one sense the essence and the term itself are the same, and in another they are not, because the essence is not the same as "the man" or "the white man," but it is the same as the affection.

The absurdity ‹of separating a thing from its essence› will be apparent also if one supplies a name for each essence; for then there will be another essence besides the original one, *e.g.* the essence of "horse" will have a further essence. Yet why should not some things be identified with their essence from the outset,[22] if essence is substance? Indeed not only are the thing and its essence one, but their formula is the same, as is clear from what we have just stated; for it is not by accident that the essence of "one," and "the one," are one. Moreover, if they are different, there will be an infinite series; for the essence of "one" and "the one" will both exist; so that in that case too the same principle will apply.[23] Clearly, then, in the case of primary and self-subsistent terms, the individual thing and its essence are one and the same.

It is obvious that the sophistical objections to this thesis are met in the same way as the question whether Socrates is the same as the essence of Socrates; for there is no difference either in the grounds for asking the question or in the means of meeting it successfully. We have now explained in what sense the essence is, and in what sense it is not, the same as the individual thing.

VII. Of things which are generated, some are generated naturally, others artificially, and others spontaneously; but everything which is generated is generated by something and from something and becomes something. When I say "becomes something" I mean in any of the categories; it may come to be either a particular thing or of some quantity or quality or in some place.

Natural generation is the generation of things whose generation is by nature. That from which they are generated is what we call matter; that by which, is something which exists naturally; and that which they become is a man or a plant or something else of this kind, which we call substance in the highest degree. All things which are generated naturally or artificially have matter; for it is possible for each one of them both to be and not to be, and this possibility is the matter in each individual thing. And in general both that from which and that in accordance with which they are generated, is nature; for the thing generated, *e.g.* plant or animal, has a nature. And that by which they are generated is the so-called "formal" nature, which has the same form as the thing generated (although it is in something else); for man begets man.

Such is the generation of things which are naturally generated; the other kinds of generation are called productions. All productions proceed from either art or potency or thought. Some of them are also generated spontaneously and by chance in much the same way as things which are naturally generated; for sometimes even in the sphere of nature the same things are generated both from seed and without it.[24] We shall consider cases of this kind later.[25]

Things are generated artificially whose form is contained in the soul (by "form" I mean the essence of each thing, and its primary substance); for even contraries have in a sense the same form.[26] For the substance of the privation is the opposite substance; *e.g.*, health is the substance of disease; for disease is the absence of health, and health is the formula and knowledge in the soul. Now the healthy subject is produced as the result of this reasoning: since health is so-and-so, if the subject is to be healthy,

---

22 *i.e.* to avoid the infinite series implied in the last sentence.
23 *i.e.* since there is a distinct term "essence of one" besides "one," there will be a third distinct term "essence of essence of one"; and so on as in the case of "horse" above.

24 *e.g.* fish (*Hist. An.* 569 a 11) and insects (*ibid.* 539 a 24).
25 In c. ix.
26 The logical connexion is: It is sufficient to say that the form of objects which are artificially produced is contained in the soul; for although artificial production can produce contrary effects, the form of the positive effect is the absence of the form of the negative effect, so that in a sense they have the same form.

it must have such-and-such a quality, *e.g.* homogeneity; and if so, it must have heat. And the physician continues reasoning until he arrives at what he himself finally can do; then the process from this point onwards, *i.e.* the process towards health, is called "production." Therefore it follows in a sense that health comes from health and a house from a house; that which has matter from that which has not (for the art of medicine or of building is the *form* of health or the house). By substance without matter I mean the essence.

In generations and motions part of the process is called cogitation, and part production—that which proceeds from the starting-point and the form is cogitation, and that which proceeds from the conclusion of the cogitation is production. Each of the other intermediate measures is carried out in the same way. I mean, *e.g.*, that if A is to be healthy, his physical condition will have to be made uniform. What, then, does being made uniform entail? So-and-so; and this will be achieved if he is made hot. What does this entail? So-and-so; now this is potentially present, and the thing is now in his power.

The thing which produces, and from which the process of recovering health begins, is the form in the soul, if the process is artificial; if spontaneous, it is whatever is the starting-point of the production for the artificial producer; as in medical treatment the starting-point is, perhaps, the heating of the patient; and this the doctor produces by friction. Heat in the body, then, is either a part of health, or is followed (directly or through several intermediaries) by something similar which is a part of health. This is the ultimate thing, namely that produces, and in this sense is a part of, health—or of the house (in the form of stones)[27] or of other things. Therefore, as we say, generation would be impossible if nothing were already existent. It is clear, then, that some part must neces- sarily pre-exist; because the matter is a part, since it is matter which pre-exists in the product and becomes something. But then is matter part of the formula? Well, we define bronze circles in both ways; we describe the matter as bronze, and the form as such-and-such a shape; and this shape is the proximate genus in which the circle is placed. The bronze circle, then, has its matter in its formula. Now as for that from which, as matter, things are generated, some things when they are generated are called not "so-and-so," but "made of so-and-so"; *e.g.*, a statue is not called stone, but made of stone. But the man who becomes healthy is not called after that from which he becomes healthy. This is because the generation proceeds from the privation and the substrate, which we call matter (*e.g.*, both "the man" and "the in- valid" become healthy), but it is more prop- erly said to proceed from the privation; *e.g.*, a man becomes healthy from being an invalid rather than from being a man. Hence a healthy person is not called an invalid, but a man, and a healthy man. But where the privation is obscure and has no name—*e.g.* in bronze the privation of any given shape, or in bricks and wood the privation of the shape of a house—the generation is con- sidered to proceed from these materials, as in the former case from the invalid. Hence just as in the former case the subject is not called that from which it is generated, so in this case the statue is not called wood, but is called by a verbal change not wood, but wooden; not bronze, but made of bronze; not stone, but made of stone; and the house is called not bricks, but made of bricks. For if we consider the matter carefully, we should not even say without qualification that a statue is generated from wood, or a house from bricks; because that from which a thing is generated should not persist, but be changed. This, then, is why we speak in this way.

VIII. Now since that which is generated is generated *by* something (by which I mean the starting-point of the process of genera- tion), and *from* something (by which let us understand not the privation but the matter;

---

[27] There is no real analogy between the causal relation- ship of heat to health and of stones to a house. The former is both material and efficient; the latter only material. Cf. ix. 1.

for we have already distinguished the meanings of these), and *becomes* something (*i.e.* a sphere or circle or whatever else it may be); just as the craftsman does not produce the substrate, *i.e.* the bronze, so neither does he produce the sphere; except accidentally, inasmuch as the bronze sphere is a sphere, and he makes the former. For to make an individual thing is to make it out of the substrate in the fullest sense. I mean that to make the bronze round is not to make the round or the sphere, but something else; *i.e.* to produce this form in another medium. For if we make the form, we must make it out of something else; for this has been assumed.[28] *E.g.*, we make a bronze sphere; we do this in the sense that from A, *i.e.* bronze, we make B, *i.e.* a sphere. If, then, we make the spherical form itself, clearly we shall have to make it in the same way; and the processes of generation will continue to infinity.

It is therefore obvious that the form (or whatever we should call the shape in the sensible thing) is not generated—generation does not apply to it—nor is the essence generated; for this is that which is induced in something else either by art or by nature or by potency. But we do cause a bronze sphere to be, for we produce it from bronze and a sphere; we induce the form into this particular matter, and the result is a bronze sphere. But if the essence of sphere in general is generated, something must be generated from something; for that which is generated will always have to be divisible, and be partly one thing and partly another; I mean partly matter and partly form. If then a sphere is the figure whose circumference is everywhere equidistant from the centre, part of this will be the medium in which that which we produce will be contained, and part will be in that medium; and the whole will be the thing generated, as in the case of the bronze sphere. It is obvious, then, from what we have said, that the thing in the sense of form or essence is not generated, whereas the concrete whole which is called after it is gen-

erated; and that in everything that is generated matter is present, and one part is matter and the other form.

Is there then some sphere besides the particular spheres, or some house besides the bricks? Surely no individual thing would ever have been generated if form had existed thus independently.[29] Form means "of such a kind"; it is not a definite individual, but we produce or generate from the individual something "of such a kind"; and when it is generated it is an individual "of such a kind." The whole individual, Callias or Socrates, corresponds to "this bronze sphere," but "man" and "animal" correspond to bronze sphere in general.

Obviously therefore the cause which consists of the Forms (in the sense in which some speak of them, assuming that there are certain entities besides particulars), in respect at least of generation and destruction, is useless; nor, for this reason at any rate, should they be regarded as self-subsistent substances. Indeed in some cases it is even obvious that that which generates is of the same kind as that which is generated—not however identical with it, nor numerically one with it, but formally one—*e.g.* in natural productions (for man begets man), unless something happens contrary to nature, as when a horse sires a mule. And even these cases are similar; for that which would be common to both horse and ass, the genus immediately above them, has no name; but it would probably be both, just as the mule is both.[30]

Thus obviously there is no need to set up a form as a pattern (for we should have looked for Forms in these cases especially, since living things are in a special sense sub-

---

[29] If forms are self-subsistent substances, individual substances cannot be generated from them; for the individual contains the form, but one substance cannot contain another actually existing substance (chap. xiii. 8). Form, however, is not a substance but a characteristic.

[30] Normally the sire communicates his form to the offspring. In the case of a mule, the material element contributed by the dam, which is an ass, limits the effect of the formal element contributed by the sire, which is a horse; but even so the form of the sire is generically the same as that of the offspring.

stances); the thing which generates is suffi-cient to produce, and to be the cause of the form in the matter. The completed whole, such-and-such a form induced in this flesh and these bones, is Callias or Socrates. And it is different from that which generated it, because the matter is different; but identical in form, because the form is indivisible.

IX. The question might be raised why some things are generated both artificially and spontaneously—*e.g.* health—and others not; *e.g.* a house. The reason is that in some cases the matter—which is the starting-point of the process in the production and genera-tion of artificial things, and in which some part of the result is already existent—is such that it can initiate its own motion, and in other cases it is not; and of the former kind some can initiate motion in a particular way, and some cannot. For many things can move themselves, but not in a particular way, *e.g.* so as to dance. It is impossible, then, for any things whose matter is of this kind (*e.g.* stones) to be moved in *this* par-ticular way except by something else; but in *that* particular way it is possible. And it is so with fire.[31] For this reason some things cannot exist apart from the possessor of the art, and others can; because the motion can be initiated by those things which do not indeed possess the art, but can themselves be moved either by other things which do not possess the art, or by the motion from the part of the product which pre-exists in them.[32]

It is clear also from what we have said that in a sense all artificial things are gen-erated either from something which bears the same name (as is the case with natural objects) or from a part of themselves which bears the same name as themselves (*e.g.* a house from a house, inasmuch as it is gener-ated by mind; for the art is the form), or from something which contains some part; that is if the generation is not accidental;

for the direct and independent cause of the production is a part of the product. Heat in the motion produces heat in the body; and either this is health or a part of health, or a part of health or health accompanies it. And this is why heat is said to produce health, because it produces that of which health is a concomitant and consequence. Therefore as essence is the starting-point of everything in syllogisms (because syllogisms start from the "what" of a thing), so too generation pro-ceeds from it.

And it is the same with natural formations as it is with the products of art. For the seed produces just as do those things which function by art. It contains the form poten-tially, and that from which the seed comes has in some sense the same name as the product (for we must not expect that all should have the same name in the sense that "man" is produced by "man"—since woman is also produced by man); unless the product is a freak. This is why a mule is not pro-duced by a mule.

Those natural objects which are produced, like artificial objects, spontaneously, are those whose matter can also initiate for itself that motion which the seed initiates. Those whose matter cannot do this cannot be generated otherwise than by their proper parents.

It is not only with reference to substance that our argument shows that the form is not generated; the same argument is common in its application to all the primary divisions, *i.e.* quantity, quality and the other categories. For just as the bronze sphere is generated, but not the sphere nor the bronze; and as in the case of bronze, if it is generated the form and matter are not (because they must always pre-exist), so it is too with the "what" and the quality and quantity and the other categories similarly; for it is not the quality that is generated, but the wood of that qual-ity; nor is it the size, but the wood or animal of that size. But a peculiarity of substance may be gathered from this: that some other substance must pre-exist in actuality which produces it; *e.g.* an animal, if an animal is being generated; but a quality or quantity need not pre-exist otherwise than potentially.

---

[31] Stones can fall by themselves, but cannot by them-selves build a house; fire can rise by itself, but cannot boil a kettle.
[32] *e.g.*, health can be produced as the result of the activ-ity set up by heat in the body.

X. Since a definition is a formula, and every formula has parts; and since the formula is related to the thing in the same way as the part of the formula to the part of the thing, the question[33] now arises: Must the formula of the parts be contained in the formula of the whole, or not? It seems clear that it is so in some cases, but not in others. The formula of the circle does not include that of the segments, but the formula of the syllable includes that of the letters. And yet the circle is divisible into its segments in just the same way as the syllable into its letters.

Again, if the parts are prior to the whole, and the acute angle is part of the right angle, and the finger part of the animal, the acute angle will be prior to the right angle, and the finger to the man. But it is considered that the latter are prior; for in the formula the parts are explained from them; and the wholes are prior also in virtue of their ability to exist independently. The truth probably is that "part" has several meanings, one of which is "that which measures in respect of quantity." However, let us dismiss this question and consider of what, in the sense of parts, substance consists.

If then matter, form, and the combination of the two are distinct, and if both matter and form and their combination are substance, there is one sense in which even matter may be called "part" of a thing; and another in which it is not, but the only parts are those elements of which the formula of the form consists. *E.g.*, flesh is not a part of concavity, because flesh is the matter in which concavity is induced; but it is a part of snubness. And bronze is part of the statue as a concrete whole, but not of the statue in the sense of form. We may speak of the form (or the thing as having a form) as an individual thing, but we may never so speak of that which is material by itself. This is why the formula of the circle does not contain that of the segments, whereas the formula of the syllable does contain that of the

letters; for the letters are parts of the formula of the form; they are not matter; but the segments are parts in the sense of matter in which the form is induced. They approximate, however, more closely to the form than does the bronze when roundness is engendered in bronze. But there is a sense in which not even all the letters will be contained in the formula of the syllable; *e.g.* particular letters on wax[34] or sounds in the air; for these too are part of the syllable in the sense that they are its sensible matter. For even if the line is divided and resolved into its halves, or if the man is resolved into bones and muscles and flesh, it does not follow that they are composed of these as parts of their essence, but as their matter; and these are parts of the concrete whole, but not of the form, or that to which the formula refers. Hence they are not in the formulae. Accordingly in some cases the formula will include the formula of such parts as the above, but in others it need not necessarily contain their formula, unless it is the formula of the concrete object. It is for this reason that some things are composed of parts in the sense of principles into which they can be resolved, while others are not. All things which are concrete combinations of form and matter (*e.g.* "the snub" or the bronze circle) can be resolved into form and matter, and the matter is a part of them; but such as are not concrete combinations with matter, but are without matter—whose formulae refer to the form only—cannot be resolved; either not at all, or at least not in this way. Thus these material components are principles and parts of the concrete objects, but they are neither parts nor principles of the form. For this reason the clay statue can be resolved into clay, and the sphere into bronze, and Callias into flesh and bones, and the circle too into segments, because it is something which is combined with matter. For we use the same name for the absolute circle and for the particular circle, since there is no special name for the particular circles.

---

[33] The questions discussed in chaps. x.-xii. arise out of the consideration of essence as definition.

[34] *i.e.* written on a waxed tablet.

We have now stated the truth; nevertheless let us recapitulate and state it more clearly. All constituents which are parts of the formula, and into which the formula can be divided, are prior to their wholes—either all or some of them. But the formula of the right angle is not divisible into the formula of an acute angle, but *vice versa;* since in defining the acute angle we use the right angle, because "the acute angle is less than a right angle." It is the same with the circle and the semicircle; for the semicircle is defined by means of the circle. And the finger is defined by means of the whole body; for a finger is a particular kind of part of a man. Thus such parts as are material, and into which the whole is resolved as into matter, are posterior to the whole; but such as are parts in the sense of parts of the formula and of the essence as expressed in the formula, are prior; either all or some of them. And since the soul of animals (which is the substance of the living creature) is their substance in accordance with the formula, and the form and essence of that particular kind of body (at least each part, if it is to be properly defined, will not be defined apart from its function; and this will not belong to it apart from perception[35]); therefore the parts of the soul are prior, either all or some of them, to the concrete animal; and similarly in other individual cases. But the body and its parts are posterior to this substance, and it is not the substance, but the concrete whole, which is resolved into these parts as into matter. Therefore in one sense these parts are prior to the concrete whole, and in another not; for they cannot exist in separation. A finger cannot in every state be a part of a living animal; for the dead finger has only the name in common with the living one. Some parts are contemporary with the whole: such as are indispensable and in which the formula and the essence are primarily present; *e.g.* the heart or perhaps the brain,[36] for it does not matter which of them is of this nature. But "man" and "horse" and terms which are

applied in this way to individuals, but universally, are not substance, but a kind of concrete whole composed of *this* particular formula and *this* particular matter regarded as universal. But individually Socrates is already composed of ultimate matter; and similarly in all other cases.

A part, then, may be part of the form (by form I mean essence), or of the concrete whole composed of form and matter, or of the matter itself. But only the parts of the form are parts of the formula, and the formula refers to the universal; for "circle" is the same as "essence of circle," and "soul" the same as "essence of soul." But when we come to the concrete thing, *e.g. this* circle—which is a particular individual, either sensible or intelligible (by intelligible circles I mean those of mathematics,[37] and by sensible those which are of bronze or wood)—of these individuals there is no definition; we apprehend them by intelligence or perception; and when they have passed from the sphere of actuality it is uncertain whether they exist or not, but they are always spoken of and apprehended by the universal formula. But the matter is in itself unknowable. Some matter is sensible and some intelligible; sensible, such as bronze and wood and all movable matter; intelligible, that which is present in sensible things not *qua* sensible, *e.g.* the objects of mathematics.[38]

We have now discussed the case of the whole and part, and of prior and posterior. But we must answer the question, when we are asked which is prior—the right angle and circle and animal, or that into which they are resolved and of which they are composed, *i.e.* their parts—by saying that neither is *absolutely* prior. For if the soul also *is* the animal or living thing, or the soul of the individual *is* the individual, and "being a circle" *is* the circle, and "being a right angle" or the essence of the right angle *is* the right angle, then we must admit that the whole in one sense is posterior to the part in one sense: *e.g.* to the parts in the formula and

35 Which implies soul.
36 Cf. V. i. 1.
37 *i.e.*, something very similar to the Platonic "intermediates."
38 See XIII. ii., iii.

the parts of a particular right angle (since both the material right angle of bronze and the right angle included by individual lines are posterior to their parts), but the immaterial angle is posterior to the parts in the formula, but prior to the parts in the individual. We must not give an unqualified answer. And if the soul is not the animal but something else, even so we must say that some wholes are prior and some are not, as has been stated.

XI. The question naturally presents itself, what sort of parts belong to the form and what sort belong not to it but to the concrete object. Yet if this is not plain it is impossible to define the particular; because the definition refers to the universal and the form. Therefore if it is not clear what kind of parts are material and what kind are not, the formula of the thing will not be clear either. In the case of things which can be seen to be induced in specifically different materials, as, *e.g.*, a circle is in bronze and stone and wood, it seems clear that these things, the bronze and the stone, are in no sense part of the essential substance of the circle, because it is separable from them. As for things which are not visibly separable, there is no reason why the same should not apply to them; *e.g.*, if all the circles that had ever been seen were bronze; for the bronze would be none the less no part of the form, but it is difficult to separate it in thought. For example, the form of "man" is always manifested in flesh and bones and elements of this kind; then are these actually parts of the form and formula, or are they not so, but matter, though since the form is not induced in other materials, we cannot separate it. Now since this seems to be possible, but it is not clear *when*, some thinkers[39] are doubtful even in the case of the circle and the triangle, considering that it is not proper to define them by lines and continuous space, but that all these are to the circle or triangle as flesh or bone is to man, and bronze or stone to the statue; and they reduce every-

thing to numbers, and say that the formula of "line" is the formula of 2. And of the exponents of the Forms, some make 2 the Ideal line, and some the form of the line;[40] for they say that in some cases the form and that of which it is the form, *e.g.* 2 and the form of 2, are the same; but in the case of "line" this is no longer so. It follows, then, that there is one form of many things whose form is clearly different (a consequence which confronted the Pythagoreans too[41]), and that it is possible to make one supreme Form of everything, and not to regard the rest as forms. In this way, however, all things would be one.

Now we have stated that the question of definitions involves some difficulty, and have shown why this so.[42] Hence to reduce everything in this way and to dispose of the matter is going too far; for some things are presumably a particular form in particular matter, or particular things in a particular state. And the analogy in the case of the living thing which the younger Socrates[43] used to state is not a good one; for it leads one away from the truth, and makes one suppose that it is possible for a man to exist without his parts, as a circle does without the bronze. But the case is not similar; for the animal is sensible and cannot be defined without motion, and hence not unless its parts are in some definite condition; for it is not the hand in *any* condition that is a part of a man, but only when it can perform its function, and so has life in it. Without life in it it is not a part.

And with respect to mathematical objects, why are the formulae of the parts not parts of the formulae of the whole; *e.g.*, why are the formulae of the semicircles not parts of the formula of the circle? for they are not sensible. Probably this makes no difference;

---

[39] The Pythagoreans.

[40] The distinction seems to be that given in VIII. iii. 1. Some held that the line, considered absolutely, is simply "twoness"; others that it is "twoness in length."
[41] Cf. I. v. 17.
[42] In chap. v.
[43] A "disciple" of the great Socrates; one of the speakers in the *Politicus* and referred to in *Theaetetus* 147 c, *Sophist* 218 B.

because there will be matter even of some things which are not sensible. Indeed there will be matter in some sense in everything which is not essence or form considered independently, but a particular thing. Thus the semicircles will be parts not of the universal circle but of the particular circles, as we said before [44]—for some matter is sensible, and some intelligible. It is clear also that the soul is the primary substance, and the body matter; and "man" or "animal" is the combination of both taken universally. And "Socrates" or "Coriscus" has a double sense, that is if the soul too can be called Socrates (for by Socrates some mean the soul and some the concrete person); but if Socrates means simply *this* soul and *this* body, the individual is composed similarly to the universal.

Whether there is some other material component of these substances besides their matter, and whether we should look for some further substance in them, such as numbers or something of that kind, must be considered later.[45] It is with a view to this that we are trying to determine the nature of sensible substances, since in a sense the study of sensible substances belongs to physics or secondary philosophy; for the physicist must know not only about the matter, but also about the substance according to the formula; this is even more essential. And in the case of definitions, in what sense the elements in the formula are parts of the definition, and why the definition is one formula (for the thing is clearly one, but in virtue of what is it one, seeing that it has parts?); this must be considered later.[46]

We have stated, then, in a general account which covers all cases, what essence is, and how it is independent;[47] and why the formula of the essence of some things contains the parts of the thing defined, while that of others does not; and we have shown that the material parts of a thing cannot be present

in the formula of the substance (since they are not even parts of the substance in that sense, but of the concrete substance; and of this in one sense there is a formula, and in another sense there is not. There is no formula involving the matter, for this is indeterminate; but there is a formula in accordance with the primary substance, *e.g.,* in the case of a man, the formula of the soul; because the substance is the indwelling form, of which and of the matter the so-called concrete substance is composed. *E.g.,* concavity is such a form, since from this and "nose" is derived "snub nose" and "snubness"—for "nose" will be present twice over in these expressions); but in the concrete substance, *e.g.* snub nose or Callias, matter will be present too.[48] We have stated also that the essence and the individual are in some cases the same, as in the case of the primary substances; *e.g.* crookedness and "essence of crookedness," if this is primary. By primary I mean that which does not imply the presence of something in something else as a material substrate. But such things as are material or are compounded with matter are not the same as their essence; not even if they are accidentally one, *e.g.* Socrates and "cultured"; for these are only accidentally the same.[49]

XII. Now let us first deal with definition, in so far as it has not been dealt with in the *Analytics;* for the problem stated there[50] has a bearing upon our discussion of substance. The problem I mean is this: what constitutes the unity of the thing of which we say that the formula is a definition? *E.g.,* in the case of man, "two-footed animal"; for let us take this as the formula of "man." Why, then, is this a unity and not a plurality, "animal" and "two-footed"? For in the case of "man" and "white" we have a plurality when the latter does not refer to the former, but a unity when it does refer to it, and the subject, "man," has an attribute; for then they become a unity and we have "the white

44 Chap. x. 17.
45 In bks. XIII. and XIV.
46 VIII. vi.
47 Chap. iv.

48 Chaps. x. xi.; and cf. chap. v.
49 Chap. vi.
50 *An. Post.* 92 a 29.

man." But in the case before us one term does not partake of the other; the genus is not considered to partake of its differentiae, for then the same thing would be partaking simultaneously of contraries, since the differentiae by which the genus is distinguished are contrary. And even if it does partake of them, the same argument applies, since the differentiae are many; *e.g.* terrestrial, two-footed, wingless. Why is it that these are a unity and not a plurality? Not because they are present in one genus, for in that case all the differentiae of the genus will form a unity. But all the elements in the definition must form a unity, because the definition is a kind of formula which is one and defines substance, so that it must be a formula of one particular thing; because the substance denotes one thing and an individual, as we say.

We must first[51] examine definitions which are reached by the process of division. For there is nothing else in the definition but the primary genus and the differentiae; the other genera consist of the primary genus together with the differentiae which are taken with it. *E.g.*, the primary genus is "animal"; the next below it, "two-footed animal"; and again, "two-footed wingless animal"; and similarly also if the expression contains more terms still. In general it does not matter whether it contains many or few terms, nor, therefore, whether it contains few or two. Of the two one is differentia and the other genus; *e.g.*, in "two-footed animal" "animal" is genus, and the other term differentia. If, then, the genus absolutely does not exist apart from the species which it includes, or if it exists, but only as matter (for speech is genus and matter, and the differentiae make the species, *i.e.* the letters, out of it), obviously the definition is the formula composed of the differentiae.

But further we must also divide by the differentia of the differentia. *E.g.,* "having feet" is a differentia of "animal"; then in turn we must discover the differentia of "animal

having feet" *qua* "having feet." Accordingly we should not say that of "that which has feet" one kind is winged and another wingless, (that is if we are to speak correctly; if we say this it will be through incapability), but only that one kind is cloven-footed and another not; because these are differentiae of "foot," since cloven-footedness is a kind of footedness. And thus we tend always to progress until we come to the species which contain no differentiae. At this point there will be just as many species of foot as there are differentiae, and the kinds of animals having feet will be equal in number to the differentiae. Then, if this is so, obviously the ultimate differentia will be the substance and definition of the thing, since we need not state the same things more than once in definitions, because this is superfluous. However, it does happen; for when we say "footed two-footed animal" we have simply said "animal having feet, having two feet." And if we divide this by its proper division, we shall be stating the same thing several times, as many times as there are differentiae.

If, then, we keep on taking a differentia of a differentia, one of them, the last, will be the form and the substance. But if we proceed with reference to accidental qualities—*e.g.* if we divide "that which has feet" into white and black—there will be as many differentiae as there are divisions. It is therefore obvious that the definition is the formula derived from the differentiae, and strictly speaking from the last of them. This will be clear if we change the order of such definitions, *e.g.* that of man, saying "two-footed footed animal"; for "footed" is superfluous when we have already said "two-footed." But there is no question of order in the substance; for how are we to think of one part as posterior and the other prior?

With regard, then, to definitions by division, let this suffice as a preliminary statement of their nature.

XIII. Since the subject of our inquiry is substance, let us return to it. Just as the substrate and the essence and the combination of these are called substance, so too is the universal. With two of these we have

---

[51] The other type of definition, that which states the constituent parts of a thing, is not discussed here.

already dealt, *i.e.* with the essence[52] and the substrate;[53] of the latter we have said that it underlies in two senses—either being an individual thing (as the animal underlies its attributes), or as matter underlies the actuality. The universal also is thought by some[54] to be in the truest sense a cause and a principle. Let us therefore proceed to discuss this question too; for it seems impossible that any universal term can be substance.

First, the substance of an individual is the substance which is peculiar to it and belongs to nothing else; whereas the universal is common; for by universal we mean that which by nature appertains to several things. Of what particular, then, will the universal be the substance? Either of all or of none. But it cannot be the substance of all; while, if it is to be the substance of one, the rest also will be that one; because things whose substance is one have also one essence and are themselves one.

Again, substance means that which is not predicated of a subject, whereas the universal is always predicated of some subject.

But perhaps although the universal cannot be substance in the sense that essence is, it can be present in the essence, as "animal" can be present in "man" and "horse." Then clearly there is in some sense a formula of the universal. It makes no difference even if there is not a formula of everything that is in the substance; for the universal will be none the less the substance of something; *e.g.*, "man" will be the substance of the man in whom it is present. Thus the same thing will happen again;[55] *e.g.* "animal" will be the substance of that in which it is present as peculiar to it.

Again, it is impossible and absurd that the individual or substance, if it is composed of anything, should be composed not of substances nor of the individual, but of a quality; for then non-substance or quality will be prior to substance or the individual. Which is impossible; for neither in formula nor in time nor in generation can the affections of substance be prior to the substance, since then they would be separable.

Again, a substance will be present in "Socrates," who is a substance; so that it will be the substance of two things. And in general it follows that if "man" and all terms used in this way are substance, none of the elements in the formula is the substance of anything, nor can it exist apart from the species or in anything else; I mean, *e.g.*, that neither "animal" nor any other element of the formula can exist apart from the particular species.

If we look at the question from this standpoint it is obvious that no universal attribute is substance; and it is also clear from the fact that none of the common predicates means "so-and-so," but "such-and-such." Otherwise amongst many other awkward consequences we have the "third man."[56]

Again, it is clear in this way too. Substance cannot consist of substances actually present in it; for that which is actually two can never be actually one, whereas if it is potentially two it can be one. E. g., the double consists of two halves—that is, potentially; for the actualization separates the halves. Thus if substance is one, it cannot consist of substances present in it even in this sense, as Democritus rightly observes; he says that it is impossible for two to come from one, or one from two, because he identifies substance with the atoms.[57] Clearly then the same will also hold good in the case of number (assuming that number is a composition of units, as it is said to be by some); because either 2 is not 1, or there is not *actually* a unit in it.

The consequence involves a difficulty; for if no substance can consist of universals, because they mean "of such a kind," and not a particular thing; and if no substance can be actually composed of substances, every substance will be incomposite, and so there will be no formula of any substance. But in point of fact it is universally held, and has

---

[52] Chaps. iv.-vi., x.-xii.
[53] Chap. iii.
[54] The Platonists.
[55] *i.e.*, the argument in §3 will apply to this case also.
[56] See note on I. ix. 3.
[57] Cf. *De Caelo* 303 a 6, *De Gen. et Corr.* 325 a 35.

been previously stated,[58] that substance is the only or chief subject of definition; but on this showing there is no definition even of substance. Then there can be no definition of anything; or rather in a sense there can, and in a sense cannot. What this means will be clearer from what follows later.[59]

XIV. From these same considerations it is clear also what consequence follows for those who maintain that the Forms are substances and separable, and who at the same time make the species consist of the genus and the differentiae. If there are Forms, and if "animal" is present in the man and the horse, it is either numerically one and the same with them, or not. (In formula they are clearly one; for in each case the speaker will enunciate the same formula.) If, then, there is in some sense an Absolute Man, who is an individual and exists separately, then the constituents, *e.g.* "animal" and "two-footed," must have an individual meaning and be separable and substances. Hence there must be an Absolute Animal too.

(i) Then if the "animal" which is in the horse and the man is one and the same, as you are one and the same with yourself, how can the one which in things that exist separately be one, and why should not this "animal" also be separated from itself? Again, if it is to partake of "two-footed" and of "many-footed," an impossibility follows; for contrary attributes will belong to it although it is one and individual. But if it does not, in what sense is it that one calls an animal "two-footed" or "terrestrial"? Perhaps the terms are "combined" and "in contact" or "mixed." But all these expressions are absurd.

(ii) "But there is a different 'animal' in each species." Then there will be practically an infinity of things of which "animal" is the substance, since it is not in an accidental sense that "man" is derived from "animal." Again, the Absolute Animal will be a plurality. For (*a*) the "animal" in each species will be the substance of that species, since the species is called after it and no other thing. Otherwise "man" would be derived from that other thing, which would be the genus of "man." (*b*) Further, all the constituents of "man" will be Ideas. Then, since nothing can be the Idea of one thing and the substance of another (for this is impossible), each and every "animal" in the various species will be the Absolute Animal.

Further, from what will these Forms be derived, and how can they be derived from the Absolute Animal? Or how can "the animal," whose very essence is "animal," exist apart from the Absolute Animal? And further, in the case of sensible things both these and still more absurd consequences follow. If, then, these consequences are impossible, clearly there are not Forms of sensible things in the sense in which some hold that there are.

XV. Since substance is of two kinds, the concrete thing and the formula (I mean that one kind of substance is the formula in combination with the matter, and the other is the formula in its full sense), substances in the former sense admit of destruction, for they also admit of generation. But the formula does not admit of destruction[60] in the sense that it is ever *being* destroyed, since neither does it so admit of generation (for the essence of house is not generated, but only the essence of *this* house); formulae *are,* and *are not,* independently of generation and destruction; for it has been shown[61] that no one either generates or creates them. For this reason also there is no definition or demonstration of particular sensible substances, because they contain matter whose nature is such that it can both exist and not exist. Hence all the individual instances of them are perishable. If, then, the demonstration and definition of necessary truths requires scientific knowledge, and if, just as knowledge cannot be sometimes knowledge and sometimes ignorance (it is opinion that is of this nature), so too demonstration and definition cannot vary (it is opinion that is con-

---

[58] Chap. v. 5-7.
[59] Chap. xv., VIII. vi.

[60] Cf. chap. viii. 3.
[61] Cf. chap. viii. 3.

cerned with that which can be otherwise than it is)—then clearly there can be neither definition nor demonstration of individual sensible substances. For (*a*) things which perish are obscure to those who have knowledge of them when they are removed from the sphere of their perception, and (*b*) even though their formulae are preserved in the soul, there will no longer be either definition or demonstration of them. Therefore in cases relating to definition, when we are trying to define any individual, we must not fail to realize that our definition may always be upset; because it is impossible to define these things.

Nor, indeed, can any Idea be defined; for the Idea is an individual, as they say, and separable; and the formula must consist of words, and the man who is defining must not coin a word, because it would not be comprehensible. But the words which are in use are common to all the things which they denote; and so they must necessarily apply to something else as well. *E.g.,* if a man were to define you, he would say that you are an animal which is lean or white or has some other attribute, which will apply to something else as well. And if it should be said that there is no reason why all the attributes separately should not belong to several things, and yet in combination belong to this alone, we must reply, (i.) that they also belong to both the elements; *e.g.,* "two-footed animal" belong both to "animal" and to "two-footed" (and in the case of eternal elements this is even necessarily so; since they are prior to the compound, and parts of it. Indeed they are also separable, if the term "man" is separable—for either neither can be separable, or both are so. If neither, the genus will not exist apart from the species, or if it is so to exist, so will the differentia); (ii.) that "animal" and "two-footed" are prior in being to "two-footed animal," and that which is prior to something else is not destroyed together with it.

Again, if the Ideas are composed of Ideas (for constituents are less composite than that which they compose), still the elements of which the Idea is composed (*e.g.* "animal"

and "two-footed") will have to be predicated of many particulars. Otherwise, how can they be known? For there would be an Idea which cannot be predicated of more than one thing. But this is not considered possible; every Idea is thought to admit of participation.

Thus, as we have said,[62] the impossibility of defining individuals is hard to realize when we are dealing with eternal entities, especially in the case of such as are unique, *e.g.* the sun and moon. For people go wrong not only by including in the definition attributes on whose removal it will still be sun—*e.g.,* "that which goes round the earth," or "night-hidden" (for they suppose that if it stops or becomes visible[63] it will no longer be sun; but it is absurd that this should be so, since "the sun" denotes a definite substance)—they also mention attributes which may apply to something else; *e.g.,* if another thing with those attributes comes into being, clearly it will be a sun. The formula, then, is general; but the sun was supposed to be an individual, like Cleon or Socrates. Why does not one of the exponents of the Ideas produce a definition of them? If they were to try, it would become obvious that what we have just said is true.

XVI. It is obvious that even of those things which are thought to be substances the majority are potentialities; both the parts of living things (for none of them has a separate substantial existence; and when they are separated, although they still exist, they exist as matter), and earth, fire and air; for none of these is one *thing*—they are a mere aggregate before they are digested and some one thing is generated from them. It might be supposed very reasonably that the parts of living things and the corresponding parts of their vital principle are both, *i.e.* exist both actually and potentially, because they contain principles of motion derived from something in their joints; and hence some animals[64] live even when they are divided.

---

[62] The statement has only been implied in the preceding arguments.
[63] *sc.* in the night.
[64] *e.g.* wasps, bees, tortoises (*P. Nat.* 467 a 18, 468 a 25).

Nevertheless it is only potentially that all of them will exist when they are one and continuous by nature and not by force or concretion; for this sort of thing is malformation.[65]

And since "unity" has the same variety of senses as "being," and the substance of Unity is one, and things whose substance is numerically one are numerically one, evidently neither Unity nor Being can be the substance of things, just as neither "being an element" or "principle" can be the substance; but we ask what the principle is so that we may refer to something more intelligible.[66] Now of these concepts Being and Unity are more nearly substance than are principle, element and cause; but not even the former are quite substance, since nothing else that is common is substance; for substance belongs to nothing except itself and that which contains it and of which it is the substance. Again, Unity cannot exist in many places at the same time, but that which is common is present in many things at the same time. Hence it is clear that no universal exists in separation apart from its particulars. The exponents of the Forms are partly right in their account when they make the Forms separate; that is, if the Forms are substances, but they are also partly wrong, since by "Form" they mean the "one-over-many."[67] The reason for this is that they cannot explain what are the imperishable substances of this kind which exist besides particular sensible substances; so they make them the same in kind as perishable things (for these we know); *i.e.,* they make "Ideal Man" and "Ideal Horse," adding the word "Ideal" to the names of sensible things. However, I presume that even if we had never seen the stars, none the less there would be eternal substances besides those which we knew; and so in the present case even if we cannot apprehend what they are, still there must be eternal substances of some kind.

It is clear, then, both that no universal term is substance and that no substance is composed of substances.

XVII. As for what and what sort of thing we mean by substance, let us explain this by making, as it were, another fresh start. Perhaps in this way we shall also obtain some light upon that kind of substance which exists in separation from sensible substances. Since, then, substance is a kind of principle and cause, we had better pursue our inquiry from this point.

Now when we ask why a thing is, it is always in the sense "why does A belong to B?" To ask why the cultured man is a cultured man is to ask either, as we have said, why the man is cultured, or something else. Now to ask why a thing is itself is no question; because when we ask the reason of a thing the fact must first be evident; *e.g.,* that the moon suffers eclipse; and "because it is itself" is the one explanation and reason which applies to all questions such as "why is man man?" or "why is the cultured person cultured?" (unless one were to say that each thing is indivisible from itself, and that this is what "being one" really means); but this, besides being a general answer, is a summary one.[68] We may, however, ask why a man is an animal of such-and-such a kind. It is clear, then, that we are not asking why he who is a man is a man; therefore we are asking why A, which is predicated of B, belongs to B. (The fact that A does belong to B must be evident, for if this is not so, the question is pointless.) *E.g.,* "Why does it thunder?" means "why is a noise produced in the clouds?" for the true form of the question is one thing predicated in this way

---

[65] *i.e.,* it is only when they do not properly constitute a unity that parts can be said to exist actually.
[66] *i.e.,* a thing is a principle in relation to something else which it explains; therefore a principle is less substantial than unity or being, which belong to a thing in itself.
[67] *i.e.* universal; cf. I. ix. 1.

[68] The argument is: The question "Why is the cultured man a cultured man?" if it does *not* mean "Why is the man cultured?" can only mean "Why is a thing itself?" But when we ask a question the fact must be obvious; and since it is obvious that a thing is itself, "because it is itself" (or "because each thing is indivisible from itself") is the one and only complete answer to all questions of this type. Since this answer (in either form) is clearly unsatisfactory, the question which it answers cannot be a proper question.

of another. Or again, "why are these things, *e.g.* bricks and stones, a house?" Clearly then we are inquiring for the cause (*i.e.*, to speak abstractly, the essence); which is in the case of some things, *e.g.* house or bed, the *end,* and in others the prime mover—for this also is a cause. We look for the latter kind of cause in the case of generation and destruction, but for the former also in the case of existence.

What we are now looking for is most obscure when one term is not predicated of another; *e.g.* when we inquire what man is; because the expression is a simple one not analysed into subject and attributes. We must make the question articulate before we ask it; otherwise we get something which shares the nature of a pointless and of a definite question. Now since we must know that the fact actually exists, it is surely clear that the question is "why is the *matter* so-and so?" *e.g.* "why are these materials a house?" Because the essence of house is present in them. And this matter, or the body containing this particular form, is man. Thus what we are seeking is the cause (*i.e.* the form) in virtue of which the matter is a definite thing; and this is the substance of the thing.

Clearly then in the case of simple entities[69] inquiry and explanation are impossible; in such cases there is a different mode of inquiry.

Now since that which is composed of something in such a way that the whole is a unity; not as an aggregate is a unity, but as

a syllable is[70]—the syllable is not the letters, nor is BA the same as B and A; nor is flesh fire and earth; because after dissolution the compounds, *e.g.* flesh or the syllable, no longer exist; but the letters exist, and so do fire and earth. Therefore the syllable is some particular thing; not merely the letters, vowel and consonant, but something else besides. And flesh is not merely fire and earth, or hot and cold, but something else besides. Since then this something else must be either an element or composed of elements, (*a*) if it is an element, the same argument applies again; for flesh will be composed of *this* and fire and earth, and again of another element, so that there will be an infinite regression. And (*b*) if it is composed of elements, clearly it is composed not of one (otherwise it will itself be that element) but of several; so that we shall use the same argument in this case as about the flesh or the syllable. It would seem, however, that this "something else" is something that is not an element, but is the cause that *this* matter is flesh and *that* matter a syllable, and similarly in other cases. And this is the substance of each thing, for it is the primary cause of its existence. And since, although some things are not substances, all substances are constituted in accordance with and by nature, substance would seem to be this "nature," which is not an element but a principle.[71] An element is that which is present as matter in a thing, and into which the thing is divided; *e.g.*, A and B are the elements of the syllable.

---

[69] Pure forms which contain no matter; in their case the method just described obviously will not apply. They can only be apprehended intuitively (cf. IX. x.).

[70] This sentence is not finished; the parenthesis which follows lasts until the end of the chapter.
[71] *i.e.* the formal cause. Cf. V. iv. 4-6.

ETIENNE GILSON

BEING AND EXISTENCE*

It may seem strange, and almost preposterous, to look back to the thirteenth century for a complete metaphysical interpretation of being, according to which neither essence nor existence is considered as irrelevant to it. Yet, such a return is unavoidable, since all other philosophies have advocated either a metaphysics of being minus existence, or a phenomenology of existence minus being. On the other hand, at least in the present state of historical knowledge, it would be vain for us to go farther back into the past than the time of Thomas Aquinas, because nobody that we know of has cared to posit existence *in* being, as a constituent element *of* being. And it would be no less vain to look in the more immediate past for a more modern expression of the same truth, because, paradoxically enough, what was perhaps deepest in the philosophical message of Thomas Aquinas seems to have remained practically forgotten since the very time of his death.

The better to recapture his message, we must first consider the essential transformation which the Aristotelian notion of metaphysics underwent in Thomas Aquinas' own doctrine.

For Aristotle, metaphysics was that science whose proper subject was being *qua* being.[1] Now, to know being as such may mean three somewhat different things: first, the abstract notion of being, conceived both in itself and with its inherent properties, such as, for instance, self-identity and resistance

to contradiction. Thus understood, being would be what will be called by later Aristotelians the formal object of metaphysics. Next, metaphysics may deal with those beings which can truly be said to be because their being actually answers to the true definition of being. Such is, for instance, the First Act, as well as the other Pure Acts which we call gods. In this second sense, the science of being is Divinity, that is, theology.[2] In a third sense, inasmuch as it is a science, metaphysics has to know its subject through its cause, and, since the subject at hand, namely, being, is the first of all subjects, metaphysics has to know everything that is through its first causes. As a commentator of Aristotle, Thomas Aquinas does little more than repeat Aristotle on this point, except that he clears up what was obscure in his text and puts some order into this complex problem.[3] True enough, the very order which he puts into it is not without significance from the point of view of his own thought; yet, had we nothing else to rely on than his Commentary on the *Metaphysics* of Aristotle, we would be reduced to conjectures concerning his own position on the question.[4]

The problem here is to know if those various determinations of the subject of metaphysics can be reduced to unity. And it is a very important problem indeed, for, if metaphysics is concerned with three different subjects, it is not a science, but a name for

---

* From *Being and Some Philosophers* by Etienne Gilson. Toronto, Canada: Pontifical Institute of Mediaeval Studies, 1952. Chapter V. Reprinted by permission of the publisher.
[1] Aristotle, *Metaphysics*, K, 3, 1060 b 31, and Γ, 1, 1003 a 21-31.

[2] Aristotle, *Metaphysics*, E, 1, 1026 a 6-32; as such, metaphysics is the science of the οὐσία ἀκίνητος, *op. cit.*, E, 1, 1026 a 29-30. Cf. *op. cit.*, K, 7, 1064 b 6-14.
[3] Thomas Aquinas, *In Metaph. Arist.*, Prooemium, ed. Cathala, p. 2.
[4] *Ibid.*

three distinct sciences, each of which has to deal with a different subject. True enough, those three subjects are all related to being and, to the whole extent to which they are, they are one. But to what extent are they?

In order to simplify the problem, let us leave aside the consideration of being in general as the "formal object" of a possible metaphysics. Although many things which have been said by Aristotle may bear such an interpretation of his thought, he himself has certainly not reduced the highest of all sciences to the abstract knowledge of a merely formal object. Nor, for that matter, has Thomas Aquinas himself ever done anything like it. We then find ourselves confronted with two possible points of view on being, that of the supreme beings, and that of the first causes of being. Obviously, if the supreme beings are the first causes of all that is, there is no problem. In such a case, the knowledge of the absolutely first being is one with that of the absolutely first cause. But it is not so in the metaphysics of Aristotle. It is not so and it cannot be, for the decisive reason which follows.

It is true that Aristotle himself had called metaphysics a "divine science,"[5] because, if there is a science which deals with things divine, it is metaphysics. It is also true that Aristotle has said that supreme beatitude lies for man in the contemplation of divine things,[6] but he does not seem to have inferred from these two propositions what anybody would hold as their necessary consequence, namely, that, as a science of being *qua* being, metaphysics is wholly ordered to the knowledge of the first cause of being. And he could not well say it, because the very notion of a cause which is absolutely first in all the departments of being was lacking in his doctrine, or, at any rate, was absent from it.

In one of the very texts quoted by Thomas Aquinas in support of his own position, Aristotle had said this: "It is therefore manifest that the science here to be gained [namely, metaphysics] is that of the first causes, since we say of each thing that we know it only when we think that we know its first cause." Whereupon, Aristotle immediately proceeds to add: "Now, causes are said to be in a fourfold way."[7] And, indeed, among the celebrated four Aristotelian causes, there is at least one, namely, the material cause, which cannot possibly be reduced to the other three. That which is a "formal" cause can also be a "final" cause and, in its capacity as "final" cause, it can likewise be held as a "moving" cause, but it cannot well be that and, at the same time, be matter. Whence it follows that, in its own way, matter itself is a first cause in the metaphysics of Aristotle. It is so because it enters the structure of material substances as one of their irreducible constituent elements. Now, if it is so, you cannot say that metaphysics is both the science of true beings and the science of all beings through their causes, for there is at least one cause, that is, matter, which does not truly deserve the title of being. In short, because the God of Aristotle is one of the causes and one of the principles of all things,[8] but not *the* cause nor *the* principle of all things, there remains in the Aristotelian domain of being something which the God of Aristotle does not account for, which is matter, and for this reason the metaphysics of Aristotle cannot be reduced to unqualified unity.

The answer is quite clear in the doctrine of Thomas Aquinas, in which God is the cause of all that is, including even matter. The doctrine of creation is bound to modify the notion of metaphysics itself, in that it introduces into the realm of being a first cause to whose causality everything is strictly subjected. This is why, in his *Contra Gentiles,* in which he does not speak as a commentator of Aristotle, but in his own name, Thomas Aquinas can take over the very formulas of Aristotle, yet give them a distinctly

[5] Aristotle, *Metaphysics,* A, 2, 983 a 6-11.
[6] Aristotle, *Eth. Nic.,* X., 10.

[7] Aristotle, *Metaphysics,* A, 3, 983 a 24-27.
[8] *Ibid.,* A, 2, 983, a 8-9.

new turn. For it still remains true to say that perfect knowledge is knowledge through causes, but metaphysical knowledge no longer is sufficiently defined as the science of being through its first causes; what metaphysics really is, is the science of being through its first "cause."

This is why, in Thomas Aquinas' own doctrine, inasmuch as he wants to know reality through its first cause, since God is that first cause, man naturally desires, as his ultimate end, to know God. Aristotle therefore was speaking better than he knew, when he said that metaphysics truly deserves the name of "divine science," for what it ultimately aims to achieve is to know God: the ultimate end of metaphysics is the same as the ultimate end of man. What deeply alters the Aristotelian notion of metaphysics in the doctrine of Thomas Aquinas is the presence, above natural theology, of a higher theology, which is the science of God as known through revelation. The very fact that the absolutely highest of all human sciences, namely, revealed theology, is in itself a knowledge of God, makes it impossible for us to define metaphysics as the science of being *qua* being, *and* the science of beings as known through their first causes, *and* the knowledge which man may have of the gods. Metaphysics, then, necessarily becomes that science which is the science of being both in itself and in its first cause, because it is the science of God as knowable to natural reason. This inner reordering of metaphysics by the final causality of its ultimate object confers upon the diversity of its aspects an organic unity. The science of being *qua* being passes into the science of the first causes, which itself passes into the science of the first cause, because God is, at one and the same time, both the First Cause and being *qua* being. This inner ordering is what Thomas Aquinas suggests when he says: "Prime philosophy itself is wholly directed towards the knowledge of God as towards its ultimate end; wherefore it is called divine science: *Ipsaque prima philosophia tota ordinatur ad Dei cognitionem sicut ad ultimum*

finem, unde et scientia divina nominatur." [9] By tearing ontology apart from natural theology Wolff was later to wreck that organic unity of metaphysics, and, if there is any consistency in the thought of both Thomas Aquinas and Wolff, this radical difference between their two notions of metaphysics should be to us a safe indication that there is a radical difference between their two conceptions of being.

What is being, according to Thomas Aquinas? In a first sense, it is what Aristotle had said it was, namely, substance. For, indeed, it is true that being is substance, although it may also be true that being entails something more, over and above mere substantiality. In other words, it may be that Aristotle has left something out while describing being, but what he has seen there, is there. The presence, in Thomism, of an Aristotelian level on which being is conceived as identical with οὐσία, is beyond doubt, and, because Aristotle is in Thomas Aquinas, there always is for his readers a temptation to reduce him to Aristotle. Texts without number could be quoted in support of such an interpretation, and there is no need to distort them in order to support it. All there is to do is to leave out all the other texts, a process, which, in fact has never ceased among generation after generation of his interpreters.

For those who identify what Thomas calls being with what is commonly called substance, there can be no distinction between essence and existence, since being and οὐσία are one and the same thing. Each time Thomas Aquinas himself is looking at being as at a substance, he thereby reoccupies the position of Aristotle, and it is no wonder that, in such cases, the distinction between essence and existence does not occur to his own mind.

---

[9] *Ibid.* On the distinction between natural theology, in which God is considered as cause of the subject of metaphysics (viz., being), and revealed theology (viz., Scripture), in which God Himself is the very subject of that science, see *In Boethium de Trinitate*, V, 4, Resp., ed. by P. Wyser (Fribourg, 1948), p. 48, ll. 28-33.

Such is eminently the case of a famous text which can be read in Thomas Aquinas' commentary on the *Metaphysics* of Aristotle, and nothing could be more natural. If there is a moment when the thought of Thomas Aquinas is bound almost to coincide with pure Aristotelianism, it normally should be while he is explaining Aristotle's own thought.

The text at stake is a passage of *Metaphysics,* Book IV, Chapter 2, which we have already met with, while dealing with Aristotle himself. In the short Chapter 1, Aristotle has just said that there is a science which deals with being *qua* being (τὸ ὂν ἧ ὄν) as well as with what belongs to it inasmuch as it is being. In Chapter 2, he will inquire into the meaning of the word "being." According to him, being is said in several different ways, but always in relation to one and the same fundamental reality, which is οὐσία. Certain things are called "beings" because they themselves are "substances" or (realities = οὐσίαι); others, because they are properties of some substance, and others because they beget some substance or else destroy it. If, therefore, there is a science of all that which deserves the title of "being," it is because all that which receives that name, receives it because of its relation to reality (οὐσία). Reality, then, along with οὐσία. its principles and its causes, is the proper object of the science of being. Moreover, since it deals with being, that science must deal with all its aspects, especially with "oneness," for, "to be" and to be "one" are one and the same thing (ταῦτὸ καὶ μία φύσις); which leads us to the conclusion that οὐσία (reality or substance), *being* and *one* are equivalent terms. Hence the oft-quoted formula which we have already mentioned: "A man," "being man," and "man" are the same thing. For, indeed, the reality signified by those various formulas is the same: "Just as the reality (or substance = οὐσία) of each thing is one, and is not so by accident, so also it is some being (ὅπερ ὄν τι)." The intention of Aristotle in this passage is therefore clear: Metaphysics shall deal with "oneness," as it deals with "being," because oneness and be-

ing are simply two other names for reality (οὐσία) which both *is,* and is one in its own right. If there is a docrine of the identity of being and substance, this is one, and Averroes was well founded in thinking that he was vindicating the authentic thought of Aristotle when he criticized Avicenna for teaching that existence was to the essence of reality, if not exactly an accident, at least a happening.

Confronted with such a text, what is Thomas Aquinas going to do? Under the circumstances a commentator, he will just say what that text means, and he will do it with the less scruple as, within its Aristotelian limits, that text is absolutely right. First of all, what it says about "being" and "oneness" is true from the point of view of Thomas Aquinas himself: *"One and being signify a single nature as known in different ways."* It is also true concerning the relation of essence (οὐσία) to existence itself, for, indeed, to beget a man is to beget an existing man, and for an existing man to die is precisely to lose his actual existence. Now, things that are begotten or destroyed together are one. Essence then is one with its own existence. These various words, "man," "thing," "being" (*ens*) and "one" designate various ways of looking at determinations of reality which always appear or disappear together. The same reality, therefore, is a "thing" because of the fact that it has a quiddity or essence; it is a "man" because of the fact that the essence it has is that of man; it is "one" because of its inner undividedness; last but not least, it is a "being" in virtue of the act whereby it exists (*nomen ens imponitur ab actu essendi*). To conclude, these three terms, *thing, being* and *one,* signify absolutely the same thing, but they signify it through different notions.[10]

The solid block of Aristotle's substance is here to be found in its perfect integrity, and Thomas Aquinas will never attempt to break it up. Yet, it would be a serious mistake to infer from such a text that, even while com-

---

[10] Aristotle, *Metaphysics,* Γ, 2, 1003 a 33-1004 a 9, and Thomas Aquinas, *In Metaph.,* lib. IV, lect. 2.

menting upon Aristotle, he had forgotten his own distinction between essence and existence. At any rate, his own notion of existence is there, and it makes itself felt at the very moment when Thomas reminds us that the noun "being" is derived from the verb "to be," which means the very act of existing. But that was not the occasion for him to apply the distinction of essence and existence, because, if, in a being, its "to be" is other than its "essence," the very thing which arises from the composition of its "to be" with its essence is in no way distinct from its intrinsic oneness or from its being. In other words, the Aristotelian substance remains intact in the doctrine of Thomas Aquinas.

Yet, the Aristotelian substance cannot enter the world of St. Thomas Aquinas without at the same time entering a Christian world; and this means that it will have to undergo many inner transformations in order to become a created substance. In the world of Aristotle, the existence of substances is no problem. To be and to be a substance are one and the same thing, so much so that no question can be asked as to the origin of the world, any more than any question can be asked about its end. In short, Aristotelian substances exist in their own right. Not so in the Christian world of Thomas Aquinas, in which substances do not exist in their own right. And this difference between these two worlds should be understood as both radical and total. The world of Aristotle is not a world which its philosopher has neglected to conceive as a created one. Because the acme of reality is substance and, in substance itself, essence, Aristotelian being is one with its own necessity. Such as its philosopher has conceived it, *it cannot possibly not exist.* On the contrary, the created world of Thomistic substances is radically contingent in its very existence, because it might never have existed. And it is not only radically contingent, but it is totally so. Even while it is actually existing in virtue of its first cause, it remains true to say that it might at any time cease to exist. But we are not yet saying enough, for, even though it were demonstratively proven that this

created world is destined always to exist, it still would remain a permanently contingent world. Unless one understands this, one will never understand why the problem of the eternity of the world appeared to Thomas Aquinas as philosophically indifferent. I do not think I am betraying him if I say that, had he not learned to the contrary from divine revelation, Thomas Aquinas would have found it quite natural to think of the world as being now as it always was and always will be, world forever, because, were it so, such an absolutely eternal world would still remain an eternally contingent world whose actual existence still would remain an eternal gratuity.

In his *Summa Theologica,* Thomas Aquinas has expressed his view on this fundamental point by means of an example which, though it is itself out of date, says it as forcefully as possible. In the physics of Aristotle, the diaphanous media, such as air or water, for instance, are the receiving subjects of light. Now, while light permeates such subjects completely, it never mixes with them. Light is in them, but it does not belong to them, and this is so true that, as soon as light ceases to shine, diaphanous subjects at once fall back into that nothingness of light which we call darkness. It is not so with all physical energies. For instance, when fire warms a certain quantity of water, that water actually assimilates warmth, so that it keeps warm, at least for some time, after being withdrawn from fire. On the contrary, that same water does not assimilate light as it does warmth, nor, for that matter, does air. Air may become bright, but it never shines as does the sun, which is the source of light, and this is why, as soon as the sun is hidden, everything grows dark. Now, it is in such guise that God is cause of existence. Just as the sun is not cause of light in *fieri,* but in *esse,* so God does not render things able to be; He makes them be. In other words, God does not grant things an existence which they could keep, be it only for one moment, if He suddenly ceased to give it. "Because," Thomas says, "[light] is not rooted in air, it ceases with the action of the sun: *quia non habet radicem in aere, statim cessat lumen, cessante actione solis;"* and "All creatures are to God as air is to the sun which makes it bright: *sic autem se habet omnis creatura ad Deum, sicut aer ad solem illuminantem."*[11] It would be difficult indeed to find stronger expressions: existence has no root in even actually existing things. In short, whereas the substance of Aristotle exists *qua* substance, existence never is of the essence of any substance in the created world of Thomas Aquinas.

Nothing looks more precarious than a thus-conceived world, in which no essence can ever *be* its own act of existing, yet the world of Thomas Aquinas is made by God to wear as long as that of Aristotle, that is, never to wear away. Why is it so? This is, I think, one of the most difficult points to grasp in the whole metaphysics of Thomas Aquinas, because we are here invited to conceive creatures as being, at one and the same time, indestructible in themselves, yet wholly contingent in their relation to God.

If we look at the world of creatures from the point of view of its existence, then it is true to say that it has no existence of its own. Existence is *in* it, just as light is in the air at noon, but the existence of the world never is *its* existence; so that, in so far, at least, as the world itself is concerned, it can lose existence at a moment's notice, or, rather, without previous notice. On the other hand, if we look at this existing world from the point of view of its substance, there are aspects in it that tally with such a view, but there are others that do not. We all are but too familiar with the sight of death, and, because we know that there is at least one death that lies in store for each of us, we easily realize the precariousness of existence in existing things. All is vanity and vexation of spirit. Yet, at the very same time, poets, at least, are fully aware of the scandalous indifference of Nature to the precariousness of human existence—a too easily explainable indifference indeed, since men pass away

while nature itself does not pass away. And science is here of one mind with poetry, just as science itself is of one mind with Aristotle's metaphysics in so far, at least, as existence is concerned. For this world is, if not *such as* it was, at least *as* it was, and now is and ever will be a world forever. And the created world of Thomas Aquinas is just like that, because it is a world of Aristotelian substances which *are* in their own right. It is both a substantially eternal and an existentially contingent world.

What makes it hard for us to reconcile both points of view is but an illusion. Exactly, it is the common illusion that corruptibility is of the essence of temporal beings. In fact, it is not so. Corruptibility is of the essence of substantially composite beings, because their very composition entails a possibility of decomposition and thus makes them to be corruptible. Such, for instance, is the union of form and matter in plants, in animals, in man. But, even in such composite beings, their constituent elements themselves are simple, and consequently they are indestructible. When a man dies, his "body" at once begins to decay and soon becomes that "I know not what," for which, as Bossuet says, there is no name in any language. Yes, indeed, the "body" passes away, but the very matter of that body does not pass away, because, as a first principle, matter is both simple and incorruptible. And, for the very same reason, the soul of that body does not pass away, because, inasmuch as it is a spiritual substance, it also is both simple and incorruptible. This is the very reason why, in Thomas Aquinas' philosophy, the immortality of the human soul is an immediate evidence. It stands in no need of being proven. If anything had to be proven about it, it would rather be that the human soul is *not* immortal, and one does not see how such a proof could possibly be formulated. Inasmuch as it is pure form, the human soul *is* in its own right. It is as any subsisting form is, since, in order to cease being, it would have to cease being a form.[12] In other words, if

---

[11] Thomas Aquinas, *Summa Theologica*, I, 104, 1, Resp. Cf. *In II de Anima*, lib. II, lect. 14, ed. by Pirotta, n. 403-421.

[12] Thomas Aquinas, *Qu. disp. de Anima*, art. 14, Resp.

God creates a circle, He has to make it round, and the roundness of that circle is inseparable from it. So, also, if God creates a human soul, He creates a "being," and, since it is a simple spiritual form, there is in it no occasion for decomposition to creep in. In so far, at least, as its *substance* is concerned, such a soul cannot lose its existence.[13] True enough, existence could be taken away from it, but of itself it cannot lose it. Man can kill himself, because he can separate his soul from his body, but there are two things he cannot kill, the matter of his body and his soul.

This sharp contrast between the point of view of existence and that of substance is thrown into relief by the very order of demonstration in the *Contra Gentiles,* in which, after proving, in II, 54, that "the composition of substance and existence is not the same as that of matter and form," Thomas Aquinas at once proceeds to prove, in the very next chapter, that "intellectual substances are incorruptible." And both statements are true, for even simple substances could be existentially destroyed, but they cannot become substantially corrupted.

To be sure, readers of Thomas Aquinas sometimes wonder how this can be. How is it that those very substances in which existence never takes root can nevertheless be everlasting in their own right? If, from moment to moment, they may cease to be, why should we say that they never will cease to be? But this is the very illusion we should get rid of if we want to understand the meaning of this doctrine. Even simple forms are engaged in time, if they are forms of a matter which they do not fully actualize. The more fully to actualize it, they operate, they change and they endure in time. Such is their life, made up of so much give and take that they require a lot of endurance to endure, and, when they have no more, they die. Man is not everlasting, precisely because to be is for him to last, but there are two things in him that are everlasting, precisely because,

taken in themselves, they do not *last,* they *are:* the matter of his body and his soul. Engaged in time through its operation, the human soul transcends time by the very simplicity of its being. The soul does not enjoy being a moment at a time. Its duration is not a chain of instantaneous acts of existing, each of which has to bridge an infinitesimal gap of nothingness. The being of true substance is whole, and, because it is such out of its own nature, it is not such a gift as stands in need of being renewed from moment to moment. God is not eternally busy retailing existence to beings, nor are substances applying for it from moment to moment. The gift of existence is irrevocable, when it is granted to beings which, as regards themselves, are unable to lose it.

Thus, God is perfectly free not to create substances, and He remains perfectly free to annihilate them after creating them, but that is God's own business; and if we look at substances themselves, or at least at simple substances, there is in them no reason why they should perish. On the contrary, no special act is required on the part of God to keep them in existence; God has not to re-create from moment to moment what has, out of itself, no moments; one and the same continued act of creation, that is, a non-lasting act of creation, is enough to keep them existing. As Thomas Aquinas himself forcefully says, concerning immaterial substances, since they are immaterial: "There is in them no potency towards non-being: *in eis non est potentia ad non esse.*" But, you will say, God still can destroy them, and, since their own existence has no roots in those substances, nothing can be more precarious than their very being. Not so in the mind of Thomas Aquinas, because, if you look at simple substances such as they actually are, it is obvious that they are made to endure. There is no more potency to non-being in a substance than there is potency to non-roundness in a circle, which entails for us the obligation literally to accept Thomas Aquinas' astounding statement about created beings in general: "The natures of creatures point out the fact that none of

---

[13] Thomas Aquinas, *Sum. Theol.*, I, 50, 5, Resp., and I, 75, 6, Resp.

them shall be reduced into nothingness: *creaturarum naturae hoc demonstravit ut nulla earum in nihilum redigatur."*[14] And indeed men do die, but they are not reduced to nothingness, for the very matter of their bodies still remains, already entering the composition of some new substance, and, as to their souls, they go on subsisting in themselves, and will go on doing it indefinitely.

We now find ourselves in a position accurately and technically to describe the relation of actual existence to God in the world of Thomas Aquinas. There is, *for* all creatures, a possibility not to be or, as Thomas himself says it, a potency to non-being (*potentia ad non esse*), but that possibility is not *in* them. At least there is no such thing in simple substances. In composite substances, yes; in simple substances, no. A composite substance, precisely in as much as it is composite, is indeed corruptible, but it is not so because God could annihilate it; it is so because, out of itself, any composition entails the possibility of its own decomposition.[15] On the contrary, when taken in itself, form as such is fully entitled to its own being, or, should we prefer to say it the other way around, being, of its very nature, belongs to form: *esse secundum se competit formae.*[16] All that we now have to do is to bring both aspects of created being together, that of its efficient cause, which is God, and that of its formal or material causes, which are matter and form. To do so will be nothing else than to bring together the two orders of existence and of substance. Existence is not what makes things to be either corruptible or incorruptible; it is what makes them to be corruptible or incorruptible existents; on the other hand, substance is not what makes things to exist, it is what makes them to exist either incorruptibly (if it is simple) or else corruptibly (if it is composite). Consequently, the efficient cause for actual existence is and always remains outside actually existing substances, either corruptible or incorruptible; but the formal

cause whereby this substance exists in an incorruptible way while that substance exists in a corruptible way rests with the substance itself, as being bound up with the definite nature of its substantiality. Thus, since the power which God has to annihilate anything is not what makes corruptible things to be corruptible, it does not, either, deprive incorruptible things of their corruptibility. "Corruptible" and "incorruptible" are *essential* predicates, because they follow essence itself taken as a formal or as a material principle,[17] and this is why the world of Thomas Aquinas can be both incorruptible like the world of Aristotle, yet, absolutely speaking, destructible by the will of God. True enough, the annihilation of the world remains in itself possible, but for it to happen would take just as ineffable a marvel as its creation once was. And an almost scandalous marvel to boot, since it would mean that *incorruptible* substances have been created in order to be, not at all corrupted, for, indeed, corrupted they cannot be, but annihilated. This is exactly what Thomas Aquinas meant when we heard him say that the natures of creatures *demonstrant,* that is, point out, that no one of them shall ever be reduced to nothingness. To conclude: "To be" belongs by itself to the forms of creatures, supposing, however, the influx of God. Hence, potency to non-being (that is, the possibility not to exist), in spiritual creatures as well as in heavenly bodies, lies more in God, Who can subtract His influx, than it is in the form or in the matter of such creatures: "*Esse per se consequitur formam creaturae, supposito tamen influxu Dei, sicut lumen sequitur diaphanum aëris, supposito influxu solis. Unde potentia ad non esse in spiritualibus creaturis et corporibus caelestibus magis est in Deo, qui potest subtrahere suum influxum, quam in forma vel materia talium creaturarum."*[18]

Such is the way the world of Aristotle can enter the Christian world of Thomas Aquinas, but there remains now for us to see that, while it enters it whole, it also becomes

---

[14] *Ibid.,* I, 104, 4, Resp. and ad 1^m.
[15] *Ibid.,* I, 50, 5, ad 3^m.
[16] *Ibid.,* Resp.

[17] *Qu. disp. de Anima,* art. 14, ad 5^m.
[18] *Sum. Theol.,* I, 104, 1 ad 1^m. Cf. *De Potentia,* q. 5, art. 1.

wholly different. The world of Aristotle is there whole in so far as reality is substance. It is the world of science, eternal, self-subsistent and such that no problem concerning existence needs nor can be asked about it. It is one and the same thing for a man in it to be "man," to be "one" and "to be." But, while keeping whole the world of Aristotle, Thomas Aquinas realizes that such a world cannot possibly be "metaphysical." Quite the reverse, it is the straight "physical" world of natural science, in which "natures" necessarily entail their own existence; and, even though such natures may happen to be gods, or even the supreme God, they still remain natures. Physics is that very order of substantial reality in which existence is taken for granted. As soon as existence no longer is taken for granted, metaphysics begins. In other words, Thomas Aquinas is here moving the whole body of metaphysics to an entirely new ground. In the philosophy of Aristotle, physics was in charge of dealing with all "natures," that is, with those beings that have in themselves the principle of their own change and of their own operations; as to those true beings which are unchangeable, they make up the order of metaphysics, in virtue of their own unchangeability. In the new philosophy of Thomas Aquinas, even unchangeable beings still remain natures, so that their handling falls within the scope of the philosophy of nature. Some of his readers sometimes wonder at the constant readiness of the "Angelic Doctor" to thrust angels into the very middle of his discussions concerning man or any other natural beings. Then they say that, of course, it helps him, because angels provide such convenient examples and means of comparison. In point of fact, if Thomas Aquinas is so familiar with angels, it is because to him they are just as "natural" beings as men themselves are, only they are better natural beings. With Thomas Aquinas, the supernatural does not begin with a certain class of substances. Precisely because composite substances are natures, only that which is beyond such substances can be said to be *supernatural*. But, even within these composite substances, where the physical ends, the metaphysical

begins, and, since there is nothing else beyond nature than its own existence, metaphysics begins with the consideration of existence. In short, Thomistic metaphysics is existential in its own right.

Yet, Thomistic philosophy is no existentialism, at least as the word is now understood, unless one prefers to say that it is existentialism as it should be understood. The crucial problem which has always worried the mind of Kirkegaard (how is it that, in man, existence is to be seen side by side with eternity?) is here meeting at last the sole principle which can lead to its solution. The error of Kirkegaard, as well as of all his modern followers, has been to mistake existence in time for existence as such. For, to endure in time is indeed to exist, and temporal existence is for us the more manifest mode of existence, but man does not exist in time only, he also transcends time inasmuch, at least, as he is, right now, communicating with his own eternity. He does so inasmuch as he is an intellectual substance which, as such, transcends both matter and mortality. And this is why there is nothing scandalous, or even paradoxical, in the fact that, although he is engaged in temporal existence, man naturally deals with eternal things, such as objective truth, objective goodness and objective beauty. For, indeed, such objects owe their very eternity to that of forever enduring subjects, of which man himself is one. Not eternity, but time, is the problem, since time is what ceaselessly interrupts man's own eternity. And here, at least, many of the great philosophers we could consult would be of one mind: from Plato to Aristotle, and to Kirkegaard himself, man's main business in life is to see to it that there be no such thing as lost time, and to use passing time itself as a means to achieve one's own eternity. That end is in sight for each of us, not at all when we wish, with Faust, for one exceptionally beautiful moment to stop, but when we can say with Rimbaud, be it for a split second: "Elle est arrivée. Quoi? L'éternité." [19]

---

[19] "It is come. What? Eternity," in A. Rimbaud, *Eternite*, and quoted later in *Une saison en Enfer.*

But why should we quote modern poets? Thomas Aquinas himself used to resort to another and much older poetry which still remains the most beautiful there ever was, that of Scripture. For it is written in *Ecclesiastes*, III, 14: "I have learned that all the works which God hath made, continue foreever." If it is true that all the works of God are there to stay, then each of us is already in the very midst of his eternity, surrounded on all sides by beings no less eternal than he himself is. The current view of the world as of a realm of progressively decaying and wearing away beings expresses just the reverse of what reality actually is. It betrays reality at least in so far as actual being entails actual existence, for, indeed, not to pass away, but to be for ever and ever, that is what it is to exist.

The technical result of the Thomistic reformation of metaphysics has been a twofold one. First, it has brought about a clear realization of the specific nature of efficient causality. It is not easy to find a clear-cut notion of the efficient cause in Aristotle's philosophy, save only where he deals with problems related to the making of objects by human artisans. He knows very well what it is "to make" artificial things, but he does not seem to think that their very being stands in need of being either produced or made. Such beings appear to him as so many terms of certain motions, whose final causes they are. Of course, there is a cause for each motion, and it is one of the four kinds of natural causes, but Aristotle does not consider it as the cause of the existence of that motion. Indeed, how could he, since motion never begins nor ceases? He merely sees it as the "origin" of this and that particular motion. Universal motion is, so to speak, constantly relayed from being to being, so that each particular nature becomes the starting point of particular motions which, in their turn, result in particular beings.[20] On the contrary, in Thomas Aquinas' aetiology, the Aristotelian "moving causes" (τὰ κινοῦντα αἴτια) become so many "efficient causes," so that, even when that which a cause produces is motion, it actually makes it to be. In such cases, to move truly is to display an efficient causality, whose effect is motion.

The second consequence of the Thomistic reform of metaphysics has been to introduce a clear-cut distinction between the two orders of formal causality and of efficient causality. Formal causality is that which makes things to be *what* they are, and, in a way, it also makes them to be, since, in order to be, each and every being has to be a *what*. But formal causality dominates the whole realm of substance, and its proper effect is substantiality, whereas efficient causality is something quite different. It does not make beings to be what they are, it makes them "to be." Now the relations of these two distinct types of causality are as follows. First, they cannot be deduced from each other: from the fact that a thing is, no conclusion can be drawn as to what it is, just as, conversely, from our knowledge of what a thing is, no inference as to its actual existence can be correctly deduced. Any such attempts are bound to result in so many failures, even if they are made on the notion of God; whence it appears that they must still more necessarily fail, if they are tried on the notion of any contingent being. On the other hand, Thomas Aquinas maintains the Aristotelian principle that causes which belong in distinct orders of causality can exert reciprocal causality. In this case, efficient causality can give existential being to substance, just as, conversely, formal causality can impart substantial being to actual existence. Where there is no existence, there is no substance, but, where there is no substance, there is no existence. It is then literally true to say that existence is a consequence which follows from the form of essence, but not as an effect follows from the efficient cause.[21] Let us here return to an example which Thomas Aquinas has already used. No one doubts that light is the cause of brightness in air, yet, in its turn, the diaphaneity of air causes

---

[20] Aristotle, *Metaphysics*, Λ, 3, 1070 a 21. Cf. B, 2, 996 b 22-23, and Z, 7, 1032 b 21-22.

[21] Thomas Aquinas, *Qu. disp. de Anima*, art. 14, ad 4ᵐ. Cf. ad 5ᵐ; and *In Boethium de Trinitate*, q. V, art. 4, ad 4ᵐ, ed. P. Wyser, p. 50, l. 19—p. 51, l. 11.

the existence of that very light in air (*causa essendi*), since it enables light to be there by enabling air to receive light. So, also, by constituting substances, the forms give rise to the receiving subjects of existence, and, to that extent, they are causes of existence itself.[22] In short, forms are "formal" causes of existence, to the whole extent to which they contribute to the establishment of substances which are capable of existing.

This is a cardinal point in the doctrine of Thomas Aquinas. To posit substance as the proper receiver of existence (*proprium susceptivum ejus quod est esse*)[23] is not to posit it as a "container" into which existence has but to flow in order to make it be. So long as there is no existence, there is no receptacle to receive it. Existence is here fulfilling an entirely different function. As we have already described it, the substance is "that which" exists, and it is *id quod est* in virtue of its form. Form then is ultimate act in the order of subtantiality. In other words, there is no form of the form. Consequently, should we have to ascribe "to be" or "is" to a form, it could not be considered as a form of that form. No point could be more clearly stated than is this one in the metaphysics of Thomas Aquinas. The form truly is "cause of being" for that subject in which it is, and it is not such owing to another form (*forma non habet sic esse per aliam formam*). To repeat, forms have not to be posited in their acts of forms by another form; quite the reverse: form reigns supreme within the order of substance, in its own being of form and in its own formal actuality. If form still requires and still has to receive a complement of actuality, that complementary actuality cannot belong in the order of formal actuality, but it belongs in an altogether different order, that of existential actuality. What substance can and must receive over and above what makes it to be "that which it is," is existence, which is imparted to it by some efficient cause:

habet tamen causam influentem ei esse. Thus, the act through which substance actually exists can and even must be added to that other act in virtue of which its form makes it to be a substance. It can be added to it because, though all forms are acts, not all acts are forms. And it must be added to it, in order that substance *be*. In case we find good reason to posit it, the composition of essence with existence shall have to be that of an act, which is not itself a form, with the form of a subsisting being.[24]

It is therefore somewhat surprising to read such statements as this: "Thomists always presuppose that existence is a form properly so called and that it should be handled as such: which is the very point at stake, and the one which Suarez perseveringly denies, but which his adversaries always take for granted, yet never prove."[25] Leaving aside the philosophical debate between Thomists and Suarezians, this at least can be said, that it will never end, if the doctrine ascribed by Suarezians to Thomists is not that of Thomas Aquinas. To those, at least among the Thomists, who agree with Thomas Aquinas, existence is emphatically *not* a form, and, to the best of my knowledge, he himself has never said that it was. What he has said, and more than once, is that existence is "formal" with respect to all that which is in the existing thing.[26] What he means in such cases is that, analogically speaking, existence is to form as form itself is to matter. In both cases, the relation is that of "the received to the receiver (*receptum ad recipiens*)." It is therefore true that, to the extent to which act stands on the side of actuality and not of potency, existence behaves formally, not materially, with respect to essence. And why did not Thomas Aquinas say "actual" instead of "formal"? Simply because, as has just been seen, though existence is the supreme

---

[22] Thomas Aquinas, *Contra Gentiles*, II, 54 ("*Deinde quia . . .*").
[23] *Ibid.*, II, 55.

[24] Thomas Aquinas, *De Spiritualibus creaturis*, art. 1, ad 5ᵐ.
[25] P. Descoqs, *Le Suarezisme*, in *Archives de Philosophie*, Vol. II, 2 (Paris, Beauchesne, 1924), p. 205.
[26] Thomas Aquinas, *Sum. Theol.*, I, 8, 1, Resp. Cf. I, 4, 1, ad 3ᵐ.

actuality of any existing substance, it is not act with respect to all that there is in that substance. If form is supreme in its own order, existence cannot be the act of essence *qua* essence. In other words, existence does not monopolize the whole actuality of existing substance. Rather, just as essence is in potency to the act of its own existence, so also is the act of existence in potency to the formal act of its own essence. If existential actuality is higher than formal actuality, the reason for it is that the very core of reality is existence. Thus, existence may well be said to be "formal," but it is not a form. Were it a form, it would be an essence, which it is not. For, indeed, there is no essence of existence, although there is essence in each and every existent.

A composition of essence with existence which is so conceived, then, is not inconsistent in itself, but has it been posited by Thomas Aquinas, and, if so, in what terms?

In at least one text, Thomas Aquinas has spoken of a "real composition" (*realis composito*); but most of the time he has simply said that they differ "in reality" (*re*). These and other similar expressions sufficiently account for the fact that his position is today designated by such denominations as the "real distinction" or the "real composition" of essence and existence.

What such formulas mean is, first of all, that each actually existing individual is, *qua* existing, a thing distinct from its own essence. This thesis should be understood as the properly Thomistic answer to the classic problem of universals. The question was: "How can the essence of the species be both one in itself and many in the plurality of individuals?" And philosophers had vainly looked at the essence of the species for an answer. What is new in Thomas Aquinas' answer is that he finds the answer in the order of existence. Actually existing individual beings are "beings" because of their own existing (*esse*). In other words, they are "beings" because of their own "to be," and this is why, within one species, whose quiddity is the same for all, each "being"

is a distinct individuality. It is distinct, first, from any other being that belongs in the same species, and next it is distinct from its own quiddity, since its own being belongs to itself alone, while its quiddity is the same for all the members of the same species. Thus, the composition is "real," because its result is a *res* (a thing), and the distinction also is "real" because its act of existing is what makes that thing to be, not a mere quiddity, but an actually real "being." [27] In short, what "real" composition or distinction seems to mean in the texts in which Thomas Aquinas himself uses such expressions, is that the existential actuality which a subsisting being owes to its own "to be" is radically other than what, in the substance itself, makes it to be "such a thing."

Justifiable as they are, we should not allow such formulas to mislead us into thinking that "to be" (*esse*) is itself a thing. "To be" (*esse*) is what makes an essence to be "a being," and, since the essence itself needs to receive it in order that it be, even while it has its own act of existence, it remains distinct from it. True enough, and the opponents of Thomas Aquinas are not yet weary of repeating it, unless it had already received actual existence, the essence of the substance could not be distinct from its own existence, since, were it otherwise, the essence would be nothing. Yet it is true that essence is really other than its own existence in virtue of its very act of existing, for, indeed, its act of existing is what enables essence to act as a formal cause, and to make actual being to be such a being. The very common mistake about this fundamental thesis of Thomism is due always to the same overlooking of the reciprocal character of efficient causality and of formal causality. [28] "To be" is not a thing distinct in itself from "essence" as from another thing. It is not, for the simple reason that, taken in themselves, "to be" and es-

[27] Thomas Aquinas, *Qu. disp. de Veritate*, q. 27, a. 1, ad 8[m] (*realis compositio*). Cf. *In I Sent.*, d. 19, q. 2, a. 2, Solutio (*differt . . . re quidem*).
[28] "*Causae ad invicem sunt causae, sed in diverso genere,*" Thomas Aquinas, *In Metaph.*, Bk. V, ch. 2, lect. 2.

sence are not "things." Their composition alone is what makes up a thing, but they both become, so to speak, "real" because "to be" then is to be a "being," just as "to be such" is to be "such a being." Actual existence, then, is the efficient cause by which essence in its turn is the formal cause which makes an actual existence to be "such an existence." Since they represent irreducibly distinct modes of causality, essence and existence are irreducibly distinct, but the reality of their distinction presupposes their composition, that is, it presupposes the actual reality of the thing. Existence is not distinct from essence as one being from another being; yet, in any given being, that whereby a being both is and actually subsists is really "other than" that whereby it is definable as such a being in the order of substantiality.

This fundamental thesis entails far-reaching consequences. For, although it was not posited by Thomas Aquinas as a means of distinguishing finite beings from God, once it was posited, it at once settled the whole question. *If* there is a distinction between essence and existence in each and every being, then any being is distinct from God in virtue of the composition which makes it to be "a being." In purely spiritual substances, such as angels, for instance, there is at least one composition, namely, that of its essence with its act of existing. In corporeal substances, such, for instance, as men, there are compositions: that of form with matter, which makes up substance, and that of the thus-constituted substance with its own act of existing. Thus, in a purely spiritual substance, in which substance is pure form, the composition of form with existence is enough to make up an actual being, but in a corporeal substance the composition of matter and form enjoys a metaphysical (not temporal) priority over the composition of the thus-constituted substance with its own act of existing. It should not be forgotten, however, that we are not here describing two different moments of the same composition, but two different *orders* of composition. For, indeed, in a corporeal being the substance *is* not in virtue of either its matter or its form; in other words, the act whereby the

substance exists is neither its matter nor its form, but it is received by that substance through its form.[29]

Let us investigate more closely the respective natures of these two orders of composition. Both of them are compositions of potency and act. On the one hand, form is to matter as act is to potency; on the other hand, "to be" is to substance as act is to potency. But, since we already know that these two compositions do not belong in the same order, the act whereby a substance *is* must belong in another order than does the act whereby a substance "is a substance." Thomas Aquinas himself says: "The composition of matter and form is not of the same nature as that of substance and existence [*esse,* to be], although both of them are compositions of potency and act."[30] What makes it hard for us to realize the difference is precisely that they both result in one and the same effect, namely, a "being." This is why, as has already been said, the form of a substance is, *in its own order,* a cause of existence; it is, as Boethius used to say, a *quo est,*[31] a "thing whereby a being is." Form is formal cause of existence, inasmuch as it is the supreme constituent of the substance which exists in virtue of its *esse,* or act of existing. To go back to Thomas Aquinas' pet example, form is cause of existence, just as its diaphaneity is the cause why air shines and why there is light. To get light, it takes both the sun and the air's diaphaneity, just as, in order to get actual being, it takes both to be and substantiality. In short, form is the cause of actual existence, inasmuch as it is the formal cause of the substance which receives its own act of existing.[32] This is why, as Thomas Aquinas so often says, *esse consequitur formam:* to be follows upon

---

[29] Thomas Aquinas, *De Substantiis separatis*, cap. VI.
[30] "*Nec est autem ejusdem rationis compositio ex materia et forma et ex substantia et esse, quamvis utraque sit ex potentia et actu,*" Thomas Aquinas, *Contra Gentiles,* II, 54.
[31] "*Forma . . . potest dici* quo est, *secundum quod est essendi principium,*" loc. cit.
[32] "*Per hoc enim in compositis ex materia et forma, dicitur forma esse principium essendi, quia est complementum* (i.e., the perfecting act) *substantiae, cujus actus est ipsum esse; sicut diaphanum est aeri principium lucendi, quia facit eum proprium subjectum lucis,*" Thomas Aquinas, *Contra Gentiles,* II, 54.

form. It does, indeed, because, where there is no form, there is nothing that can be. And the same reason accounts for the formula so sharply criticized by Siger of Brabant, namely, that "to be" is *quasi* constituted by the principles of an actual essence.[33] In point of fact, Thomas Aquinas has sometimes been even more positive about it, since, as he has said at least once: "To be is always to be found in a thing, and it is the act of a being, which results from the principles of that thing, just as to light is the act of a lighting thing: *esse in re est, et est actus entis, resultans ex principiis rei, sicut lucere est actus lucentis.*"[34] If "to be" always belongs to a being, it certainly results from the constituent principles of that being.

Yet, it is also true that any being results primarily from its act of existing as from one of its primary constituents, for, if the form is what makes it to be such a being, "to be" is what makes it to be a "being." Precisely because existence reaches substance *in* and *through* its form, forms have to receive existence in order that they become "beings." But Thomas Aquinas could not posit existence (*esse*) as the act of a substance itself actualized by its form, without making a decision which, with respect to the metaphysics of Aristotle, was nothing less than a revolution. He had precisely to achieve the dissociation of the two notions of form and act. This is precisely what he has done and what probably remains, even today, the greatest contribution ever made by any single man to the science of being. Supreme in their own order, substantial forms remain the prime acts of their substances, but, though there be no form of the form, there is an act of the form. In other words, the form is such an act as still remains in potency to another act, namely, existence. This notion of an act which is itself in potency was very difficult to express in the language of Aristotle. Yet, it had to be expressed, since even "those subsisting forms which, because they themselves are forms, do not require a formal cause for both being one and being,

do nevertheless require an external acting cause, which gives them to be."[35] In order to receive its to be, a form must needs be in potency to it. "To be," then, is the act of the form, not *qua* form, but *qua* being.

This is to say that "to be," or to exist, is the supreme act of all that is. And the reason for it is clear, since, before being anything else, that is, this or that substance, any substance *is*, or is a "being." The form of a horse makes it "to be a horse"; it does not make it to be, nor consequently, does it make it to be a being. And so, if being comes first in reality, then the existential act which causes it should come first among the constituent acts of concrete reality. But this is not an easy thing to say. Using the terminology of Boethius, to which he gives an entirely new meaning, Thomas Aquinas will say, for instance, that "to be is the ultimate act, which is participable by all, yet itself participates in nothing; hence, if there is such a thing as a self-subsisting *to be,* which we say that God is, we also say that it participates in nothing. But the case of other subsisting forms is not the same, because they must participate in existence itself (*esse, to be*) and, consequently, be related to it as potency to act. Thus, because in a way (*quodammodo*) they are in potency, they can participate in something else."[36] Forms are in potency, at least in a way, precisely because, although fully actual in their own formal order, they are not so with respect to existence. Hence the manifold formulas used by Thomas Aquinas in order to express the primacy of "to be" in the order of being: "*To be* is the act of the subsisting forms: *Ipsum esse est actus formae subsistentis.*"[37] Again: "*To be* is the actuality of all acts, and that is why it is the perfection of all perfections: *esse est actualitas omnium actuum, et propter hoc est perfectio omnium perfectionum.*"[38] And again: "*To be* is the actuality of all things, and even of forms themselves: *ipsum esse est actualitas omnium rerum et etiam formarum.*"[39] Where he is

---

[33] Cf. Thomas Aquinas, *In IV Metaph.*, lect. 2, ed Cathala, n. 558.

[34] Thomas Aquinas, *In III Sent.*, d. 6, q. 2, a. 2, Resp.

[35] Thomas Aquinas, *Qu. disp. de Anima*, art. 6, ad 9m.

[36] *Ibid.*, art. 6, ad 2m.

[37] *Ibid.*, art. 6, Resp.

[38] *Ibid.*, q. 7, art. 2, ad 9m.

[39] Thomas Aquinas, *Sum. Theol.*, I, 8, 1, ad 4m.

merely following his pen, Thomas Aquinas is liable to go still farther and to say, as he once did: "Each and every created being shares, so to speak, in the nature of existence: *quodcumque ens creatum participat, ut ita dixerim, naturam essendi,"*[40] which of course does not mean that "to be" is itself a nature, and still less that it *has* a nature, but that, as Saint Anselm had already said, God is the very *natura essendi* in which each and every being, so to speak, participates.

When correctly understood, the Thomistic metaphysics of being appears as established on a ground whose very nature its opponents do not even seem to suspect. How, they ask with persistence, can essence enter into composition with existence, if, apart from existence, essence in itself is nothing?[41] As so formulated, the objection is irrefutable, and this is probably why its authors obstinately refuse to move to another ground; but the reason why they triumph so easily is that their adversary is not there. Thomas Aquinas himself stands on an entirely different ground. He is not composing an essence which is not with an existence which is not a thing, and he does not do it because he does not make the mistake which his opponents reproach him with making, namely, to consider existence as an essence. They themselves are making that radical and decisive mistake, because their own essentialism makes it impossible for them to think of anything otherwise than as of an essence. Hence their faultless argumentation: all that which is real is essence; existence is not an essence; hence existence is nothing. And, since each and every essence is an object of both concept and definition, the very fact that there is no concept of existence as such is to them a sure sign that existence itself is nothing. "Existence," they say, *"existentia, id quo formaliter ens constituitur actu,* that is, that whereby being is constituted in act, is not

a concept, but a pseudo-concept." In short, as opposed to essence, it remains a "perfectly empty logical form," the only actual existence there is being that of individual, perceivable or conceivable reality.[42]

In a way, this is to raise as an objection to Thomas Aquinas what has always been his own doctrine, namely, that there is indeed no existence outside perceivable or conceivable things, that is, outside actually existing beings. In another way, this is to show complete blindness with respect to the very problem at stake. For the whole argumentation rests upon the fundamental assumption that there can be no real distinction where there is no distinct conceptual representation. God Himself, essentialism boldly says, cannot think of finite existence except in so far as it really identifies itself with that which it actualizes, and wherein it is but the "relation to the cause whence it proceeds."[43] But the whole problem is precisely to know if existence can be nothing else than either an empty logical concept in the mind or a relation in the thing. It cannot be, if to be an act is to be a form, but it can be, if there can be such an act of the form as is not itself a form; and, since it is not a form, such an act has no essence distinct from itself, and hence can be neither perceived nor even conceived apart through any kind of conceptual representation. God *knows* essences, but he *says* existences, and He does not say all that He knows.

What is here at stake is not mere formal correctness in logical reasoning; it is an option between two radically different metaphysics of being. In fact, what is at stake is the metaphysical realization of the autonomous character of the order of existence, and this is a realization which is impossible to anyone who approaches being only by way of conceptual representation. As a concept, "to be" is indeed a pseudo-concept, but "to be" might well escape representation in virtue of its very transcendence. When we say that God is only *to be (Deus est esse tantum),*

---

[40] *Ibid.,* I, 45, 5, ad 1ᵐ. Cf. Anselm, *Monologium,* III; *PL,* Vol. 158, col. 147. Cf. also *Qu. disp de Potentia,* q. 7, a. 2, ad 9ᵐ.
[41] P. Descoqs, *Thomisme et scolastique,* in *Archives de Philosophie,* Vol. V, 1 (Paris, G. Beauchesne, 1926), p. 103. Cf. *Archives de Philosophie,* Vol. X, 4 (1929), p. 589.

[42] *Ibid.,* Vol. I, p. 112.
[43] *Ibid.,* pp. 121-22. Cf. pp. 111-12.

we are not falling into the error of those who said that God was that universal being (that is, *being* taken as a mere universal) owing to which each and every thing should be said to be as through its form. Quite the reverse: the only instance in which "to be" is absolutely pure of any addition or determination is also the only instance in which being is absolutely distinct from all the rest. God does not owe His *esse* to His own individuality; rather, supreme and unique individuality necessarily belongs to Him, and He *is* He, precisely because He alone is "to be" in its absolute purity: *"Unde per ipsam suam puritatem est esse distinctum ab omni esse."* [44] It should not be said then that "to be" cannot truly be act because, out of itself, it is not an act but the emptiest of universals; rather, it should be said that, because pure "to be" is in itself the supreme and absolute act, it cannot be a universal. And, if this be true of God, it should also hold true in the case of finite beings. For "to be" is, in things, the very act by which they are actual beings whose essences can be conceived as universals by way of conceptual abstraction. Matter is non-being apart from its form; form itself is non-being apart from its own to be; but substances are not nothing; they are acts, namely, they are forms which themselves participate in their ultimate act of existing. [45]

As understood by Thomas Aquinas, being appears therefore as both radically contingent and literally indestructible in virtue of its composition of essence and existence. It is radically contingent because, with the exception of God Himself, Who is the pure act of existing, everything else hangs on some act which it cannot have unless it first receive it. At the lowest level of reality is matter, which cannot itself directly receive existence, or, in other words, cannot even be created alone. Matter is always the matter of a form; it can be but "concreated" with a form, so that existence reaches it only through the form with which it is concreated. But the very nature which is thus constituted of form and matter still needs to receive existence in order to be a "being." Just as matter is in potency to form, the nature to which that matter belongs is itself in potency with respect to the act of existing which makes it to be a "being." [46]

On the other hand, this radically contingent being is also indestructible, and what makes the combination of these two characters look paradoxical is a mere illusion. It is the same ever-recurring illusion, namely, the pseudo-primacy of essence over existence. We naturally begin by imagining some essence, which we conceive as the very core of some future being. It seems to us that, when such a being will finally be, it will be, before anything else, the very essence which, now a mere possible, will then have become real. If a metaphysician tells us that such a being receives its existence from an external cause and never ceases to receive it, its essential caducity is but too manifest, and we can then only wonder in what sense it could enjoy any degree of ontological stability.

Things will, however, appear quite different if we remember that reality is not essence, but being. Essence itself is primarily form, and form is what existence makes to be a being which, if it has a matter, makes its matter to be. What the contingency of existence means is, that all actual beings are contingent with respect to their cause, and this is but another way of saying that they might not exist; but, if they are actually produced by their cause, they do exist, and what they are in themselves is being. The primacy of existence means precisely that the radical contingency of finite beings has been overcome, and, once it has been overcome, we should no longer worry about it. Such is the true Thomistic meaning of the neopla-

---

[44] Thomas Aquinas, *De ente et essentia*, cap. VI (IV).

[45] *"Si igitur per hoc quod dico* non ens, *removeatur solum esse in actu, ipsa forma secundum se considerata est* non ens, *sed esse participans. Si autem* non ens *removeat non solum ipsum esse in actu, sed etiam actum seu formam per quam aliquid participat esse, sic materia est non ens; forma vero subsistens non est non ens, sed est actus, qui est forma participativa ultimi actus, qui est esse,"* Thomas Aquinas, *De Substantiis separatis*, cap. VI; in *Opuscula*, ed. by P. Mandonnet, Vol. I, p. 97.

[46] Thomas Aquinas, *De Spiritualibus creaturis*, art. 1, Resp. Cf. *Qu. disp. de Potentia*, q. III, a. 4, Resp.

tonic formula borrowed from Plotinus himself through the *Liber de Causis,* that the first created thing is actual being: *"Prima rerum creatarum est esse."* In Thomas Aquinas, the formula no longer means that actual being is the first effect of some higher principle which itself *is* not; on the contrary, it means that the very first effect of the Pure Act of existing is the very existence of what it causes. In other words, the very first thing that can be said of its effects is that they *are.* Of course, if they are, they are something, perhaps a pure form, or maybe a nature composited of both matter and form, but, before being anything else, each of them is a "being," because it *is.* "The first effect of their cause, then, is to make them to be, an effect which is presupposed by all the others and which itself presupposes no other: *Primus autem effectus est ipsum esse, quod omnibus aliis effectibus praesupponitur et ipsum non praesupponit aliquem alium effectum."* [47] And to be is not only what comes first in everything; for, since it is what makes it to be a "being," it is, so to speak, involved in all that any being actually is. But we should perhaps rather say that the whole being is involved in its own to be, since it is owing to it that it is a being. "To be" thus permeates the innermost recesses of each and every being. In Thomas Aquinas' own words, "Being is the most common of all effects [since it is presupposed by all others], the first effect, and the innermost of all effects: *Ipsum enim esse est communissimus effectus, primus, et interior omnibus aliis effectibus."* [48] Thus, contingent as it may be with respect to its cause, reality is "being," and it is so to the core, as appears from its very name. In the very formula, "that which is," there is the "that which," that is, the substance which is the proper receiver of existence, and there is the "is," which that substance receives.[49] In other words, being is that which is "*be*-ing" in virtue of the very "to be" which

it exercises. The noun *ens* (being) means *esse habens* (having *esse,* to be), so that it is derived from the very verb *esse* (*to be*): *"Hoc nomen ens . . . imponitur ab ipso esse."* [50] In such a doctrine, the word "being" can never be used without meaning both the thing which a certain being is and the existential act which makes it to be a "being." [51] Taken in itself, existential being is solidly full, totally blended together, as it were, by the very act in virtue of which it actually is.

A second character of existential being immediately follows from the first one. It is that the relation of its essence to its existence, instead of being the irreducible paradox which it is in the doctrine of Kirkegaard, appears as perfectly normal. More generally speaking, the classical antinomy between being and existence here simply disappears.

Being, philosophers are accustomed to say, is just what it is: it is its own essence, and it must therefore exhibit the characters of essence, which are essential selfhood and essential immutability. On the other hand, actual existence is perpetual otherness, because it is perpetual becoming. Whether it be asked in the terms once used by Plato: "What is it which always is and never becomes, and what is it which is always becoming but never is?" or whether it be raised in the terms used by Kirkegaard and modern existentialism: "If *x* is, *x* does not exist," the problem remains the same. It always rests upon the assumption that essence and becoming are incompatible, whereas, the very reverse is true. Far from being incompatible with becoming, essence is both the final cause of becoming and the formal condition of its possibility.

Where existence is alone, as is the case in God, Whose essence is one with His existence, there is no becoming. God is, and, because He is no particular essence, but the pure act of existence, there is nothing which He can become, and all that can be said about Him is *He Is.* On the contrary, as

---

[47] Thomas Aquinas, *Qu. disp. de Potentia,* q. III, a, 4, Resp.
[48] *Ibid.,* q. III, art. 7, Resp. Cf. *Compendium theologiae,* Pars. I, ch. 68.
[49] Thomas Aquinas, *Cont. Gentiles,* II, 55.

[50] Thomas Aquinas, *In IV Metaph.* lect. 2, ed. Cathala, n. 558. Cf. *In XII Metaph.,* lect. 1, n. 2419.
[51] Thomas Aquinas, *In I Perihermeneias,* lect. 5, n. 20.

soon as essence appears, there also appears some otherness, namely, the very otherness which distinguishes it from its own possible existence and, with it, the possibility of be-coming. This is particularly clear in the case of man, with which modern existentialism is almost exclusively, or, at any rate, chiefly concerned. It is of the essence of man to belong in the order of corporeal beings. This does not mean that intellectual souls, which are the forms of human beings, are fallen into their bodies and struggling to get out of them; rather, it means that they stand in need of such bodies in order both to subsist and to act. The cause of such a need on the part of souls is a certain incompleteness in actuality. Were they able to stand alone and to perform by themselves their own operations, they would be fully actual in themselves, that is, they would be pure subsisting forms, and no material element would enter their definition. On the contrary, since the essence of a human soul entails its relation to body (or else it would be a pure spirit, not a soul), it seems clear that, out of itself, such a form as a human soul is an act that stands in need of some further actualization. It does not need to be confirmed in its own nature: as has been said several times, there is no form of the form nor any act of the form *qua* form, but it still does need to become more fully that which it is. "Become what thou art" is for such a form an imperative order, because it is inscribed as a law in its very nature. And this is a purely existential problem, since the question never is for a soul to become *what* it is (it is such *qua* form) but *to become that which it is*. In other words, a human soul has more and more to actualize its very definition.

It thus appears that no form engaged in matter can simply and solely *be*. For it, "to be" is to become, and its "being" *is* "becoming." Always in existential potency to the absolute fullness of its own being, such a form is bound to exert manifold operations in order to fill the privation of actuality which it suffers: not a privation of essence, but that of a substance which still fails com-pletely *to be* its own essence, and which, in order more fully to be, must achieve its own being by exerting a series of operations, each of which shall ultimately bring it a step nearer its own completion. To do so is to move, to change, to "be-come," that is, progressively to arrive at its own being. Such is the law wherever there is matter. For, since to need matter points out a certain privation of being in the form, wherever there is matter, there also is in the form a potency to a more complete existential actualization. Hence the very motion or change which is required to achieve it. In short, since matter is there in view of its form, it is one and the same thing for a form to actualize its matter more completely and for itself more completely *to be*.[52]

To get rid of the current notion of essence is here an absolute necessity. Unless we do so, such a metaphysics of being as that of Thomas Aquinas cannot be understood at all. Essences are commonly conceived as abstract entities, which cannot suffer any change because their very nature is to be just what they are. First conceived by Plato as comparatively simple, they have become infinitely complex since the time of Leibniz, when the new resources provided by the infinitesimal calculus made it possible to include within their unity an infinite number of determinations. Yet, even after Leibniz, essences have always remained the fully achieved and purely static unities of possible subjects taken with the totality of all their determinations. In Julius Caesar's essence, Leibniz says, the crossing of the Rubicon is eternally included, just as, according to Kant, were there such an essence as that of the Wandering Jew, it should include each and every time and place of his endless peregrinations.

Now, it may be true that, in God's eternal cognition, essences are just like that, but the common mistake of both essentialists and existentialists is to think that the eternal essence of a being subject to becoming does not include the knowledge of its actual exist-

---

[52] Thomas Aquinas, *Cont. Gentiles*, III, 20.

ence as cause of its becoming. The ideas of all possible essences are to be found in God, and they include determinately all the determinations which would belong to the corresponding beings, if only they were created. But only some among those possibles are actually created, and their choice rests with the divine will. This further determination to actual existence is what turns the corresponding essences into so many divine ideas, in the full sense of the term. When thus conceived, ideas represent possible beings, including both their actual existence and their becoming. In other words, if *esse* (to be) is the supreme act of creatures, their idea must needs include it as the active energy through which the corresponding essence shall progressively receive all its determinations.

Essences are often conceived as *possible* beings, whose reality coincides with their very possibility. But we should be careful to distinguish between essential possibility and existential possibility. For, indeed, they belong in two distinct metaphysical orders, so much so that there is no way for us to reach the second one through the first one. An essence is possible, *qua* essence, when all its determining predicates are compossible. If they are, the existence of the corresponding being is possible; if they are not, it is not. And this is true, but it is true only in the order of essential possibility, not all in the order of existential possibility. Many metaphysicians seem to imagine that an essence cannot exist, so long as it has not received all its determinations, that, as soon as it has received them, it is bound either to burst into existence or, at least, to receive it. Now, a twofold error is responsible for such an illusion. The first one is not to see that to be fully completed in the order of essentiality does not bring an essence one inch nearer actual existence. A completely perfected possibility still remains a pure possibility. The second error is to forget that the essence of a possible being necessarily includes the possible existence through which alone it can achieve its essential determination. To repeat, essential possibility is no sufficient reason for existential possibility, and, since its

essence is what a being is going to become, if it exists, existence itself necessarily enters the calculation of its essential possibility. Thus, Julius Caesar does not cross the Rubicon because that is eternally included in his essence; it is eternally included in his essence because his essence is that of a Rubicon-crossing man. Such determinations have eternally to be known as existential, if they are to be known at all. Essences may well represent the balance sheets of so many already fulfilled essential possibilities, but actual existences are their very fulfilling, and this is why essences are actually becoming in time, despite the fact that a time-transcending knowledge eternally sees them as already fulfilled.

Actual and individual essences then are not static, because their own becoming is presupposed by their very definitions. Their progressive self-determination through acting and operating, that is, through the change of which time is but the numbering, is not extraneous to their eternal ideas; rather, it is eternally included in them. God is an immobile knowledge of becoming *qua* becoming. But, if it is so, there is no antinomy between eternity and existence in time. For Him Who Is there is no time, because He is to Himself His own essence, so that His own "now" is identically His own *is*. In short, because He Is, there is nothing that He can become, so that He is eternity.

To posit essence or supreme essentiality as the supreme degree of reality is therefore the most disastrous of all metaphysical mistakes, because it is to substitute *essentia* for *esse* as the ultimate root of all being. The whole of metaphysics is here at stake. If God is *esse,* He is He Whose own "to be" constitutes His own essence. Hence both His unicity and His singularity. Fully posited by its "to be," essence here entails neither limitation nor determination. On the contrary, finite essences always entail both limitation and determination, because each of them is the formal delimitation of a possible being. Yet, if such a possible essence actually receives existence, it is a being, owing to its own act of existing, so that, even in the order of finite being, the primacy of existence still obtains. Its act of existing is what insures the unity of the thing. Matter, form, substance, accidents, operations, everything in it directly or indirectly shares in one and the same act of existing. And this is why the thing is both being and one. Existence is not what keeps elements apart, it is what blends them together as constituent elements of the same being. For the same reason, temporal existence is neither the ceaseless breaking up of eternity nor the perpetual parceling out of being; it is rather their progressive achievement through becoming. Thus, becoming through *esse* is the road to fully determined being, just as time is the road to eternity. Man is not struggling in time not to lose eternity, since, like all true spiritual substances, he is eternal in his own right; but, if he must become in order the more fully to be, it is of the essence of man to be, in time, a self-achieving and self-eternalizing being.

The full import of this conclusion will perhaps appear more clearly if we consider a third characteristic of existential being, namely, its intrinsic dynamism. Because abstract essence is static, while existence is dynamic, such a metaphysics of being must needs be a dynamic one. The very existence of finite essence is the first and immediate effect of the first and absolute existential Act. To repeat, *prima rerum creatarum est esse.*[53] Born of an existential act, "to be" is itself an existential act, and, just as it is effect, so also it is cause. Even finite being is, in its own way, cause of being. This is why, in a chapter of his *Summa Contra Gentiles* (III, 69), Thomas Aquinas puts so much speculative passion into refuting the error of "those who deprive natural things of their own actions." He goes at it tooth and nail, because the very nature of being is here at stake. Not: to be, then to act, but: to be is to act.

And the very first thing which "to be" does, is to make its own essence to be, that is, "to be a being." This is done at once, completely and definitely, for, between to be or not to be, there is no intermediate position. But the next thing which "to be" does, is to begin bringing its own individual essence somewhat nearer its completion. It begins doing it at once, but the work will take time and, in the case of such corporeal beings as men, for instance, it is bound to be a slow process. It takes each of us a lifetime to achieve his own temporal individuality. True enough, essence itself is there from the very beginning, and, in a way, it is whole, but its wholeness is not that of a thing. The essence of the symphony is in the mind of the composer, and, since it is its essence to be a symphony, it will have to be it, but it will not exist until the last bar of its score has been orchestrated, and even that will not be the end of its becoming. So also with natural essences. Each of them is the progressive becoming of its own end. In short, the actual perfecting of essences is the final cause of their existences, and it takes many operations to achieve it.

Existence can perform those operations. Because *to be* is to *be act,* it also is to be able to act. Now, as an act is, so will be its operation. If a being acts *qua* being, it will be cause of being. Because God is pure act of existence, His first effect is existence, and He is the first cause why everything else exists.[54] But those existing things which God creates, are His images precisely inasmuch as they exist. If, therefore, God has made them like unto Himself by giving them existence, He has consequently made them like unto Himself by giving them causal efficacy, that is to say, by granting them the power to exert causal actions of their own.[55] Such is the reason why, although no finite being can create existence, each of them can at least impart it. In any relation of efficient causality, something of the *esse* (to be) of the cause is somehow imparted to its effect. Such a relation then is an existential one, and it is no wonder that all attempts to reduce it to some analytical relation have been

[53] Cf. above, p. 179.

[54] Thomas Aquinas, *Cont. Gentiles*, I, 10; I, 13; II, 15.
[55] *Ibid.*, III, 69.

unsuccessful. Hume was perfectly right in refusing to consider causal relations as deducible from the essences of the causes, and Kant was simply dodging the difficulty by transferring to a category of the understanding the synthetic nature of a relation which is grounded in things. From no essence will there ever spring any causal efficacy; as to the *a priori* synthetic judgment of Kant, it is nothing more than the mental dummy of being's existential causality. *Esse* (to be) is the ceaselessly overflowing source of its effects, and, if the relation of such effects to their causes is unintelligible in a world of abstract essences, it is quite intelligible in a world in which to be is to act, because beings themselves are acts.

This intrinsic dynamism of being necessarily entails a radical transformation of the Aristotelian conception of essences. True enough, Aristotle's metaphysics was already a thorough dynamism, but it was a dynamism of the form. The form of the being-still-to-be was there, acting as both the formal law of its development and as the end to be reached by that development. Aristotelian beings were self-realizing formal types, and the only cause for their individual variations rested with the accidental failures of various matters completely to imbibe the forms. Individuals then were little more than abortive attempts to be their own forms; none of them could add anything to its species; rather, there was infinitely more in the species than there was in the whole collection of its individuals. Because Aristotelianism had been a dynamism, Thomas Aquinas has seen his way to including it within his own metaphysics of being, but, because it had been a dynamism of the form, he has had to deepen it into a dynamism of *esse* (to be). When he did it, the whole philosophical outlook on reality at once became different. Each and every individual, even among corporeal beings, was henceforward to enjoy its own *to be*, that is, a to be of its own; and this is why, in such a doctrine, to be is not univocal, but analogical in its own right. True enough, corporeal individuals still remain individuated by matter, but if they owe mat-

ter their individuation, they are indebted to their to be for their individuality. For, indeed, "all that which is has its to be: *Omne quod est, esse habet.*"[56] "and that to be is its own: *Unumquodque est per suum esse.*"[57] It is also true that such individuals still are determined by their forms, but they no longer are the automatic self-realizations of forms merely hampered by the natural indocility of matter; they are individualities in the making, each of which is being actively built up by its own *esse*. And this, of course, is eminently true in the case of man, whose soul is itself an intellectual substance. There still is formal causality in such a doctrine, and it remains whole, but it has been metamorphosed by its subordination to efficient existential causality. Instead of a self-achieving end, form becomes an end to be achieved by its own *esse*, which progressively makes it an actual being. To be (*esse*) is to act (*agere*), and act is to tend (*tendere*) to an end wherein achieved being may ultimately rest.[58] But there is no rest for being in this life, where to be is to become. And this is why aetiology is here part and parcel of the metaphysics of being. "To be" is to be cause, that is, both immanent cause of its own being and transitive cause of other beings through efficient causality. Matter itself is no longer here as a mere obstacle, blindly aspiring to form; it is also a help. Actively engaged in it, the soul is giving itself the body which it needs; it progressively builds it up through physiological operations which pave the way for intellectual operations. Hence, in the end, the infinite variety of human minds, all human in the same measure and in the same way, yet all different, as though each of them were less the stereotyped copy of their common species than a monotype endowed with singular originality.

"To be" does it, and it can be done by nothing else. Saints, philosophers, scientists, artists, craftsmen—no two men are the same,

---

[56] Thomas Aquinas, *Qu. disp. de Potentia*, q. VII, art. 2, ad 9m.
[57] Thomas Aquinas, *Contra Gentiles*, I, 22. See E. Gilson, *Le Thomisme*, p. 134, note.
[58] Thomas Aquinas, *Qu. disp. de Veritate*, q. 21, art. 2, Resp.

because even the humblest among them ultimately is his own "to be"; yet none of them is really alone. To be is not to be a solitude. Each and every man can share in the common good of his species, and nothing that is human remains foreign to him. Nay, nothing that *is,* is foreign to him. A member of the universal brotherhood of being, he can experience in himself that being is "tending to," and he can see that everything else is acting to some purpose, a purpose which is indeed everywhere the same, namely, to be. His end, then, is in his beginning, and what is true of him holds true of everything else. All beings, from the most exalted to the humblest ones, are just as really distinct and as ultimately alike as the children of the same father; for, indeed, they all have the same Father, and He has made them all in His image or resemblance. They act because they are, and they are because His name is *He Who Is.*

Just as aetiology hangs on ontology, so also does epistemology. If to know is to know things as they are—for otherwise they are not known at all—to know them is to reach, not only their forms, but their very "to be." Unless it penetrates reality up to its innermost core, knowledge is bound to miss what is the very core of its object. There was a deep truth in Kirkegaard's statement, that any general knowledge about existing beings entails reducing them to the abstract condition of mere possibles. It was true, because, since being minus actual existence is, at best, possibility, the abstract knowledge of existence itself still remains knowledge of its possibility. But this is true only of abstract essences; it is not true of the essence of actual existence. To know existential being is not to know its essence only; it is not to know that it enjoys existence in a general way; it is not even to know existences; precisely, it is to know existents, which is but another word to designate in its fullness this ever-new notion of "being."

If this be true, real knowledge necessarily includes essence, since to know a thing is to know what it is, and this is why the first operation of the mind is to form such concepts as express what things are. Such is the situation with the very notion of being, the most common of all, which expresses all that "which has existence" (*ens: esse habens*). The truthfulness of such a concept fully appears when it is related to its object by a judgment; for then we see that it correctly expresses what the essence of a being truly is. In such cases, truth is correctly grounded in the very essence or quiddity of its object. Yet, such an object still remains an abstract and general one, so that its truth also remains an abstract and general one, applying to possible being as well as to actual beings. In short, it is not yet the knowledge of a "thing."

In order to go further, another class of judgments is required, namely, those by which we state that what the thing is, actually is, or exists. Such is the composite operation which we call a judgment of existence. By saying that *x is,* we mean to say that *x* is a certain *esse* (to be), and our judgment must needs be a composite operation precisely because, in such cases, reality itself is composite. Existence is synthetically united with essence in reality, owing to the efficient causality of its cause, and the synthetic nature of their actual relation entails the synthetic nature of the mental act whereby we express it. If our existential judgment is true, however, it is so because that to which we ascribe existence actually is, or exists. In short, it is true when the data of abstract, intellectual knowledge and those of sensible intuition fully agree. When they do, there still is no *objective* knowledge of a *subjective* existence, which Kirkegaard has quite rightly described as an intrinsic impossibility, but I have objective knowledge of a subjectively existing being. And this is what true knowledge should be, if for it to be true means to reach its object such as it is. For, indeed, to identify subjectivity with existence, as Kirkegaard always did, was but to turn existence into one more essence, namely, that whose very essence it is to preclude objectivity. If, on the contrary, actual being is the existential actualization of an objective essence, knowledge not only can, but must, be at one and the same time both objective and existential. It is directly objective through abstract concepts; it is directly existential through a certain class of judgments. If such judgments ultimately aim to reach actual beings, including their very "to be," then their truth must ultimately rest upon the actual "to be" of the thing. "Since," Thomas Aquinas says, "a thing includes both its quiddity and its existence (*esse:* to be), truth is more grounded on the existence (*esse*) of the thing than on its quiddity itself. For, indeed, the noun *ens* (being) is derived from *esse* (to be) so that the adequation in which truth consists is achieved by a kind of assimilation of the intellect to the existence (*esse*) of the thing, through the very operation whereby it accepts it such as it is."[59] Existential judgment expresses that assimilation.

These words are exceptionally meaningful, even in a philosophy which seldom indulges in wasting words. Because things are, true judgments are true inasmuch as they accept them as actual beings, and, because to be a "being" is primarily to be, *veritas fundatur in esse rei magis quam in ipsa quidditate:* truth is more principally grounded in the existence (*esse*) of the thing than it is in its essence. And this, I think, is undoubtedly true, because no other description of knowledge can do complete justice to the twofold nature of both actual reality and true knowledge. Both reality and our knowledge of it entail the subjective actualization by existence of an essential objectivity. Being *qua* being is their very unity. Unless such knowledge of reality be possible, no knowledge will ever grasp reality such as it is. The last word of Thomistic epistemology, then, is that our knowledge of being is more than an abstract concept; it is, or it should be, the living and organic unity of a concept and of a judgment. But is such knowledge of reality possible? The question is in itself so important that it requires to be submitted to detailed consideration.

---

[59] Thomas Aquinas, *In I Sent.*, d. 19, q. 5, a. 1, Solutio, ed. by P. Mandonnet, Vol. I, p. 486. Cf. *In Boethium de Trinitate*, V, 3, Resp., from "*Ad evidentiam . . .* to "*ut in substantiis simplicibus*" ed P. Wyser, p. 38, ll. 1–13

MORRIS LAZEROWITZ

SUBSTRATUM*

One of the most troublesome problems in the literature of philosophy concerns "the ancient and honourable notion of substance." As is well known, the metaphysical problem about the nature of material things, the question, that is to say, as to the *ultimate* constitution and structure of such objects as books and pennies and soap bubbles, has given rise to different theories none of which has, in essentials, turned out to be universally acceptable to professional philosophers. It has to be pointed out in this connexion that each theory has its convinced adherents and that the arguments for each theory, though not convincing to some philosophers, are accepted as conclusive by others. This is a bewildering state of affairs and we may well wonder what has happened to create it: we may well be curious to discover what it is about some demonstrations that makes it possible for one group of able philosophers who have studied the problem to reject them and another group to accept them. In this paper the main object is to examine the theory which Aristotle expressed by saying that "matter is unknowable in itself." And I wish to examine it in connexion with only one of the sources from which it derives. The theory has one source in the conception

---

* From *Philosophical Analysis*, edited by Max Black, pp. 176–194. Ithaca, N.Y.: Cornell University Press, 1950. Reprinted by permission of the publisher.

of a thing as being the invariant subject of change: "The thing, to be at all, must be the same after a change, and the change must, to some extent, be predicated of the thing."[1] It has another source in the distinction between a thing and its appearances, and still a further one, which is perhaps the basic source, in the distinction between a thing and its attributes. Only the last source will be of concern to us here.

According to what we may call the substratum theory, a thing such as an apple or a pebble is composed of a substance in which a variety of attributes inhere, or which supports them or is their bearer or their owner. The substance itself is held to be something distinct from the sum of its properties. It is also held that our "experience" of a thing is confined to its qualities, so that it is possible for us to know what attributes the thing has; but what the possessor of the attributes, the substratum itself, is, remains hidden from us. Substratum lies beyond the bounds of possible experience: "We cannot say anything at all about its nature."[2] When a philosopher says "We do not know what things really are,"[3] one cannot help feeling that he utters these words with deep regret. It is not too much to imagine that some people feel themselves to be living in a world of impenetrable mystery and have the intolerable thought, though it may also give them a certain amount of pleasure, that their curiosity about the world can never be satisfied.

Not all philosophers have been able to accept this theory. Instead, some have been attracted to a different view about the composition of physical things, one from which it follows that there are no unknowable substances. This view is to the effect that a thing is composed of nothing more than the properties which, in ordinary language, "it" is said to have: "What would commonly be called a 'thing' is nothing but a bundle of coexisting qualities such as hardness, redness, etc."[4] On this theory we can know what things really are, because there are no substances distinct from the experienceable qualities. There is nothing behind the barrier of knowable attributes, nothing to be an inner mystery which forever frustrates our curiosity.

Philosophers who adopt the view that a thing is just a bundle of properties sometimes reject the substratum theory in a way which throws it into an unexpected light. We quite naturally take the theory that a thing is made up of a substance together with a collection of attributes inhering in it to be a hypothesis with regard to the material facts about such things as tables and inkwells. And undoubtedly most philosophers, regardless of whether they hold the theory or reject it, conceive it to be about "the structure of reality." Some philosophers, however, appear to view it in a different light, which, if that is the right way to view it, makes it out to be utterly different from what we take it to be. Thus, one philosopher has written: "The introduction of an unknowable can generally, perhaps always, be avoided by suitable technical devices, and clearly it should be avoided whenever possible."[5] The sort of device by the use of which unknowables are to be avoided or "got rid of" consists of making up a new form of speech, one not found in the language of ordinary conversation, and substituting it for the familiar, common form of speech which, it is claimed, introduces unknowables:—

Common sense regards a "thing" as having qualities, but not as defined by them; it is defined by spatio-temporal position. I wish to suggest that, wherever there is, for common sense, a "thing" having the quality C, we should say, instead, that C itself exists in that place, and that the "thing" is to be replaced by the collection of qualities existing in the place in question. Thus "C" becomes a name, not a predicate.[6]

Our interest in the question as to what

[1] F. H. Bradley, *Appearance and Reality* (1925), p. 72.
[2] G. Watts Cunningham, *Problems of Philosophy* (1924), p. 167. It is not to be supposed that this is Prof. Cunningham's view.
[3] A. E. Taylor, *Elements of Metaphysics* (1912), p. 131.
[4] Bertrand Russell, *An inquiry into Meaning and Truth* (1940), p. 120.
[5] *Ibid.*, p. 122.
[6] *Ibid.*, pp. 121–2.

the metaphysical theory actually comes to, what its *nature* is, is justifiably aroused when we learn that some philosophers think it to be of a kind that can relevantly be dealt with by the use of a linguistic device, which consists in altering a current mode of speech. If the introduction of new way of speaking will "get rid" of the unknowables claimed to exist by the theory, then the theory is only apparently about things, not actually about them at all. For no sort of change in language could, by itself alone, alter the inaccessibility to us of facts about material things, just as no tinkering with our language will make accessible to us information about the topography of the dark side of the moon. The idea that behind the experienceable attributes we meet with in our everyday perception of things there exist unknowable substrata could only be got rid of by linguistic means if the idea of such substrata were produced by the language we used, not by the things we perceived. An appropriate change in language may very well destroy an illusion produced by the use of words, but it will not remove an idea genuinely connected with the perception of things. Thus, the ordinary sentence "This is red," which seems to ascribe an attribute to something referred to by the subject word "this," creates, according to some philosophers, the misconception that the substantive stands for an unknowable something, a bare particular behind the attribute "red": "One is tempted to regard 'this is red' as a subject-predicate proposition; but if one does so, one finds that 'this' becomes a substance, an unknowable something in which properties inhere, but which, nevertheless, is not identical with the sum of its properties." [7] The way to dispel this unreal notion, which has no relation to the facts about the "structure of reality," is to replace expressions like "this is red" by expressions of the form "redness is here" and treat adjectives like "red" as names, not as predicates.

According to this conception of the source and nature of the theory, many thinkers have been deceived by language into holding a *Scheintheorie;* while labouring under the notion that they were advocating a deep hypothesis about the constitution of things, they were taking a verbal shadow for an actual theory about the ultimate nature of material objects. What has happened has been summed up in the following way: "It happens to be the case that we cannot, in our language, refer to the sensible properties of a thing without introducing a word or phrase which appears to stand for the thing itself as opposed to anything which may be said about it. And, as a result of this, those who are infected by the primitive superstition that to every name a single real entity must correspond assume that it is necessary to distinguish logically between the thing itself and any, or all, of its sensible properties." [8] Another philosopher has put it in this way: " 'Substance,' in a word, is a metaphysical mistake, due to transference to the world-structure of the structure of sentences composed of a subject and a predicate." [9] Like a chronic psychological obsession which cannot be removed by confrontation with fact, the transference persists despite our familiarity with chairs and the like. And the explanation of the stubbornness with which the delusive idea persists is, apparently, that the source of the idea does not lie in the perception of things or in experiments conducted on them. The conception of substratum is a *metaphysical* mistake, not a scientific one, and is not correctable by scientific means. [10] It would seem that the technique designed to destroy the transference and cure the linguistic delusion consists of reframing language in such a way that it will no longer offer the temptation to make the transference. One is reminded of Freud's comments about some neurotic people who become well

---

[7] Bertrand Russell, *An Inquiry into Meaning and Truth* (1940), p. 120.

[8] A. J. Ayer, *Language, Truth and Logic* (1936), p. 32.
[9] Bertrand Russell, *A History of Western Philosophy* (1945), p. 202.
[10] 'If science keeps to its own sphere, it cannot clash with any metaphysical theory'. J. McT. E. McTaggart, *Some Dogmas of Religion* (1906), p. 91.

only after changing their environment. The linguistic neurosis, so to speak, is also to be cured by changing the linguistic environment, by making part of the language aseptic, to use John Wisdom's expression.

By no means, of course, are all or even most philosophers in agreement with this version of what the substratum theory of the nature of material things comes to. Where it is maintained that the substance theory is an illusion caused by the subject-predicate structure of language, many other philosophers make the claim that the established language, in everyday use is itself the natural result of an antecedent belief about the composition of material things. They, instead, explain the fact that language has a subject-predicate structure by reference to a prior hypothesis about reality. Thus: "When we ask how, if a 'thing' is merely the series or sum of its attributes, and possesses no underlying unity to which the attributes belong, the whole of our ordinary language about things comes to be constructed on the contrary assumption, how it is that we always talk and think as if every 'bundle' of attributes were owned by something of which we can say that it *has* the quality. . . ."[11]

Some philosophers maintain that the substratum theory is only the semblance of an empirical hypothesis into which we are tricked by language; others maintain that the theory is an actual hypothesis about the structure of things and that it determined the form of our language about things. How is one to decide between these two versions of what it comes to? What sort of observation or experiment or purely intellectual consideration will show that the words "Material things are constituted by substances in which attributes inhere" express a theory about material objects or that they are a verbal fraud which successfully masquerades as a theory? A little thought leads to the disconcerting conclusion that perhaps there is no way of definitely and conclusively deciding between the two versions. For those who

insist that it is a theory about things are in no better position to make relevant observations than those who deny this: the disagreement does not arise because of any difference in observation or from different results of experimentation. And those who maintain it is a verbal counterfeit know no more facts about grammar and the accepted usages of words than those who hold the opposite view; there is no linguistic fact about ordinary discourse they can point to of which the others are not aware, and such that their acquaintance with it would compel them to give up their view. Neither knowledge of actual language nor sense-observation of things seems adequate to settling the matter, and it would consequently seem that there is no way of settling it. For what else is there to turn to?

Where different hypotheses have been proposed without agreed success, it is certainly permissible to try out still another hypothesis. The worst thing that can happen is that we shall again fail to arrive at an acceptable solution, which is something we are all hardened against in philosophy. I propose to take the view, in partial agreement with one of the two contending versions, that the substance "theory" is only the verbal imitation of a theory and entirely different from what we are inclined to think it is. But I shall argue that it is not ordinary, everyday language that causes us to think this. Instead, I shall try to show that the illusion of its being a theory about things is produced by a concealed *revision* of ordinary subject-predicate sentences, by a manoeuvre with language, and not by the subject-predicate form of discourse itself. It is what *metaphysicians* have done with words, their metaphysical artistry, that creates the appearance of a theory about the structure of things; but what they have done is hidden from our conscious awareness, as well as their own. The theory may be compared to a dream; indeed, in this case, the metaphysician may be said to dream with words. As in the case of an ordinary dream, the linguistic metaphysical dream is consciously enjoyed or

---

[11] Taylor, *op. cit.*, p. 133.

disliked but only secretly understood. And in order to see how the illusory effect of a theory about the nature of things is produced, the language of the metaphysical fantasy has to be interpreted.

It is important, first of all, to see that the theory is not factual; i.e., it is important to see that it is not a theory about the constitution of material objects. Consider what Locke said:—

It is the ordinary qualities observable in iron or a diamond, put together, that make the true complex idea of those substances, which a smith or a jeweller commonly knows better than a philosopher; who, whatever substantial forms he may talk of, has no other idea of those substances than what is framed by a collection of those simple ideas which are to be found in them. Only we must take notice, that our complex ideas of substances, besides all these simple ideas they are made up of, have always the confused idea of something to which they belong and in which they subsist. And therefore, when we speak of any sort of substance, we say it is a thing having such or such qualities. . . . These and the like fashions of speaking intimate that the substance is supposed always something besides the extension, figure, solidity, motion, thinking, or other observable ideas, though we know not what it is.[12]

Not imagining how these simple ideas can subsist by themselves, we accustom ourselves to suppose some *substratum* wherein they do subsist, and from which they do result, which therefore we call *substance*.[13]

So that if any one will examine himself concerning his notion of pure substance in general, he will find he has no other idea of it at all, but only a supposition of he knows not what support of such qualities which are capable of producing simple ideas in us; which qualities are commonly called accidents. If any one should be asked, what is the subject wherein colour or weight inheres, he would have nothing to say, but the solid extended parts; and if he were demanded, what is it that that solidity and extension inhere in, he would not be in a much better case than the Indian before mentioned. . . .[14]

Hume's challenge, which seems based, in a soundly empirical manner, on the sense-observation of things, is well known:—

I would fain ask those philosophers, who found so much of their reasonings on the distinction of substance and accident, and imagine we have clear ideas of each, whether the idea of *substance* be derived from the impressions of sensation or reflection? If it be conveyed to us by our senses, I ask, which of them, and after what manner? If it be perceived by the eyes, it must be a colour; if by the ears, a sound; if by the palate, a taste; and so of the other senses. But I believe none will assert, that substance is either a colour, or sound, or a taste. The idea of substance must, therefore, be derived from an impression of reflection, if it really exist. But the impressions of reflection resolve themselves into our passions and emotions; none of which can possibly represent a substance.[15]

At first glance, Hume appears to have rejected the idea of substance as a "fiction" on the basis of observation. He seems to have come to his conclusion as the result of a closer, more careful, examination of things, a process comparable to inspecting a box to see whether it has a secret compartment. It looks as if he has made a thorough inventory of his sense-experiences of such a thing, say, as a table, experiences we should express by saying "This table is brown," "This table feels smooth," and the like, and discovered that he actually experienced *only* brownness and rectangularity, smoothness and hardness, etc. He never, in connexion with any of his senses, perceived the *thing* that is brown and smooth and rectangular, the substance in which the perceived attributes inhere. His description of what happened is the description of a person who in no instance of the sense-perception of objects comes upon anything over and above and in addition to attributes, a further something which owns them, and who in consequence rejects the notion that any such entities as substances exist. The impression his words give is that they describe the rejection of an empirical claim on empirical grounds, a rejection based on reasons similar to those which finally make us give up the belief in ghosts; we have never come upon one, not even its shadow. But this impression is erroneous.

It may first be noted that if the substratum hypothesis regarding the constitution of

[12] *An Essay Concerning Human Understanding*, Bk. II, Chap. XXIII, Sec. 3.
[13] *Ibid.*, Sec. 1.
[14] *Ibid.*, Sec. 2.

[15] *A Treatise of Human Nature*, Bk. I, Pt. I, Sec. 6.

material objects is empirical and if what Hume did, to test it, was really to make a series of observations, then his rejection of the theory was quite unwarranted. For if this was his procedure, we have to suppose that he looked for what he should have realized, if the theory were correct, he would not be able to find and, after looking for substance and not finding it, that he concluded that it did not exist. Those who hold the theory claim that we "experience qualities but not the substance in which they inhere." How, then, could his failure to perceive substance have led Hume to make the claim of having demonstrated the notion of substance to be a fiction? How can one refute a hypothesis by not finding what the hypothesis states one cannot find? No scientist would think of rejecting the atomic theory because he failed to see an atom through the microscope, and it is hard to believe that it was something like this that Hume was actually doing. It is hard, in spite of the empirical descriptive language he used, to think that his claim is empirical and that he based it on processes of looking at things, feeling them, tasting them, and so on.

Locke would certainly not have found his consideration impressive. For he *agrees* with Hume about what we discover from an examination and inventory of our experiences of things. In his own words:—

> Everyone upon inquiry into his own thoughts will find, that he has no other idea of any substance but what he has barely of those sensible qualities, which he supposes to inhere, with a supposition of such a substratum, as gives, as it were, a support to those qualities of simple ideas, which he has observed to exist united together. Thus the idea of the sun, what is it but an aggregate of those several simple ideas, bright, hot, roundish, having a constant regular motion, at a certain distance from us, and perhaps some other?[16]

How, then, is the difference of opinion between the two philosophers to be explained? Is it to be explained as resulting from the fact that not all information relevant to the refutation or establishment of the substratum

hypothesis is available, so that the lack of complete information leaves room for a divergence of beliefs? Is it to be hoped that examinations through future supermicroscopes, refined experiments, etc., will ever bring the metaphysical problem of substratum to an end? It is not difficult to see that laboratory science holds out no hope for its solution in the future. If physicists and chemists had satisfied themselves that at last they had reached the end of their quest and knew everything about matter, philosophers could show that the *metaphysical* problem of substance still remained unsolved. Nor would more ways of sensing things than the usual five be of the slightest help. A new and yet further way of perceiving a thing like an orange would only reveal new *qualities* of the thing; we still would not be able to perceive the substance itself, and the controversy over its existence would remain.

Consider again what Hume appears to have done, namely, to have looked for something by means of a series of careful observations. In the case of an actual search for anything we always have *some* idea of what it is we are looking for. We know, for example, what it would be like to look for and discover (or fail to discover) the unknown cause of a disease. But if we had no idea whatever, however rough, no inkling, of what it is we were trying to discover, we should not know where to begin nor where to turn, nor should we be able to recognize the thing as answering to what we want. The experiment Hume invites us to make is utterly different in this respect from an ordinary instance of looking for something. In this case, not finding what we are looking for implies that we had, to begin with, no idea whatever of what we were trying to discover. And it implies, moreover, that no process of looking had been resorted to. The search was only a sham. For when Hume points out that the supposed idea of substance derives neither from sensation nor reflection, which both he and Locke are agreed are the only sources of our ideas, he in effect tells us, not that it, like the idea of a centaur, is *fictitious,* but that there is

---

[16] *Op cit.*, Bk. II, Chap. XXIII, Sec. 6.

no such idea. He tells us that the phrases "substance in which attributes inhere," "owner of attributes," "support of qualities" describe nothing actual or imaginable and are literally empty phrases to which no application has been given. Of course, then, there can be no looking for a bearer of properties, no examination of anything for the purpose of trying to discover a substratum, any more than there can be a search for binomial scarlet or for a slithy tove.

When it is claimed that none of our senses acquaints us with substance, that they all fail to reveal to us a support of such experienced qualities as shape, colour, and taste, what this claim has to be construed as coming to is that it is *logically impossible* to perceive in any way the subject of attributes. When it is said "We experience qualities but not the subject in which they are supposed to inhere," what these words must be taken to be stating is that under no conceivable circumstances could we ever experience substance, that this is a logical impossibility, however much they look to be asserting an empirical fact about what we fail to perceive. No one could seriously be supposed to be maintaining that we do not perceive substratum because as a matter of fact it does not exist or that we are prevented from experiencing it by a physical obstacle or some sort of physiological inadequacy. Nothing can be said to be a goal if we cannot describe what it would be like to attain it, and nothing can be said to be a barrier preventing us from attaining a goal unless we can describe overcoming it and reaching the goal. And what makes it certain that the inaccessibility of substance is not to be explained on physical or physiological grounds is that there are no descriptions in philosophy of what it would be like to perceive substance or of what it is that prevents our experiencing it.

A familiar argument, which is substantially Hume's, helps make clear what it is that stands in the way of our experiencing the substratum support of attributes. It goes as follows. If, in our imagination, we take away the various properties of a thing, for exam-

ple, the shape, size, and other attributes of an orange, we find that there is nothing left; there is no residue, which is the owner of properties and distinct from them, for us to imagine. There is no difficulty about imagining Voltaire deprived of all his possessions, his garments, his money, books, and snuff box: bare Voltaire remains after his process. But when Voltaire's attributes are taken away from the substance in which they inhere, nothing whatever, no bare something, is left. This shows that the seemingly descriptive expression "substance in which properties inhere but which is distinct from them" is not used to describe anything. The impossibility of imagining substratum is a logical impossibility, which has its source in the linguistic fact that the word "substratum," in the sense of something "in which properties inhere but which is distinct from them," has been given no application. It might, of course, be urged that "substratum" does denote something, though what it denotes eludes us; but then we should have to accept the absurd consequence that the word has an application which it has never been given and is not known to have. It is clear, then, that we cannot perceive substratum for the same reason that we cannot see binomial scarlet: "perceives substratum," like "sees binomial scarlet," is a literally senseless expression. Hence, when a metaphysician says, "We do not know what things really are," his plaint would seem to be against language, namely, that to say such a thing as "*A* knows what it is, the substratum, that attributes ϕ_1, ϕ_2, ϕ_3 . . . inhere in" is not to say anything. And when another metaphysician states that "we cannot say anything about its nature," he seems to be remarking that there do not exist words for describing substratum, which is to say that the word "substratum" is connected with no descriptive phrases.

It would appear now that the explanation of the substance hypothesis which construes it to be the distorted recognition of a linguistic fact, the recognition of such a fact displaced, so to speak, on to the world of things, is correct. The idea that the theory is a mistake due to the transfer to the world-structure of the structure of subject-predicate sentences needs, apparently, to be qualified in the following way: it is this sentence structure take in conjunction with the linguistic fact that it makes no sense to speak of knowing what it is that is the subject of attribution which is responsible for the mistake. Can this explanation be the right one, however? It is sufficiently plain that the theory is not an account of the nature of things and that its appearing to be such is an illusion due to the form of words used to express it. But is the source of the theory to be found, as is claimed, in the language we use in everyday conversation, the language of ordinary discourse?

The claim would be correct if in ordinary language it made sense to speak of perceiving colours, shapes, etc., but did not make sense to speak of perceiving things. But this is not the case at all; and it must be a mistake to think that the metaphysical idea of unknowable substance could be produced by the subject-predicate structure of *ordinary* sentences like "The dog is barking" or "This table is heavy." For it makes perfectly good sense to speak not only of hearing the barking of the dog and feeling the weight of the table but also of seeing the dog and of seeing the table, i.e., of perceiving the *thing* that is barking and the *thing* that is heavy. Moore has said: "Some people may no doubt think that it is very unphilosophical in me to say that we *ever* can perceive such things [as doors and fingers]. But it seems to me that we do, in ordinary life, constantly talk of *seeing* such things, and that, when we do so, we are neither using language incorrectly, nor making any mistake about the facts— supposing something to occur which never does in fact occur."[17] Ordinary, *unphilosophical* people who speak in subject-predicate sentences do not have the idea that things, as opposed to attributes, are unknowable. How then could it possibly produce such an idea in the minds of metaphysicians? It seems plain that ordinary

language could not have produced the idea; the source has to be discovered elsewhere. When a person who maintains that we do perceive things and that to say that we do is not a misuse of language is condemned as being unphilosophical, then we have to think that being *philosophical* consists in doing something unusual with words, not mistakenly, but with purpose, whether or not with awareness. It becomes highly plausible to think that metaphysicians have, if not consciously then with unconscious skill, *introduced* "linguistic unknowables." If substratum is unknowable, then the word "substratum" does not mean what is ordinarily meant by the phrase "subject of attribution." In some way that is obscure to us, language has been altered; and it is this altered language which is responsible for the theory that things are unknowable substrata in which attributes inhere.

What has happened? How has the metaphysical dream been produced? Fortunately, there are statements to be found in the literature which give us insight into what has taken place. Consider the following statement:—

Those who maintain that there is an ultimate plurality of substances, and yet hold that characters are, as such, universals, seem logically bound to deny that a substance is the complex unity of all its qualities and relations. Thus Mr. McTaggart, who occupies this position, asserts in his *Nature of Existence,* Ch. V, that the complex unity is itself only a complex adjective, and therefore presupposes a subject ultimately distinct from itself.[18]

And also this statement:—

If we . . . suppose that his kind and all his particular attributes as well *belong* to the individual, the individual, to which they all belong, becomes a mere uncharacterized *something.* For in saying *what* it is, we should merely assign to it a fresh predicate; whereas we want to get not at its predicates but at that which "has" them. Thus we should reach a new way of considering the subject of predication. Originally it was the concrete individual, Socrates or Plato; but of what he is, one part was distinguished as what he is essentially, and the rest reduced to attributes

---

[17] G. E. Moore, *Philosophical Studies* (1922), p. 226. Moore said this in a different connexion.

[18] G. F. Stout, *Studies in Philosophy and Psychology* (1930), p. 394.

or "accidents" of him, not necessary to his being, and not to be included in an account of his essence. Now, what he is essentially is also reduced to the position of attribute and mere predicate, and the subject becomes a mere subject of which as such nothing more can be said except that it exists and is unique in each individual.[19]

What these quotations, on careful reading, can be seen to tell us is that the substratum theory expresses the linguistic result of juggling with words. The illusion that things are unknowable in themselves has its source in a linguistic creation. In almost so many words, these quotations explain the mechanics of the illusion as consisting of the change brought about in language by *reducing* general names to the status of "mere adjectives," that is to say, the change brought about by reclassifying general substantives as "complex adjectives" while retaining the subject-predicate form of sentence.

It appears that some metaphysicians wish to recompose language, for some reason or other. Ordinary grammar does not satisfy them; and they wish to change it by depriving general substantives of their grammatical noun function and give them the status of adjectives without, however, giving up the subject-predicate form of sentence. In order to do this, it is quite plain that linguistic reparations will have to be made. If the substantive "penny" is counted as a "complex adjective" which "presupposes a subject ultimately distinct from itself," then, since in English there is no term distinct from it which it presupposes as a subject term, a new term will have to be invented to supply the need. If we wish to deprive "penny" of its noun place in the sentence "The penny is round" and at the same time wish to keep the grammatical structure of the sentence intact, without replacing the noun by a synonym, then our only resort is to find a structural replacement for the deleted term. For obviously there cannot be a sentence which has a subject-predicate structure but fails to have some sort of subject term, if

only one which plays the rôle of subject in purely formal respects. A subject-predicate sentence *must* have a subject; this is the "necessity of thought" of which Locke speaks.

The introduction of a term which is only a formal, and not a material, substitute for a general noun is made possible by the fact that general names have two distinct functions. A word like "mouse" has, for one thing, a literal meaning; in this respect it has a semantic function which enables us to say *what* a thing is, e.g., that a thing is a mouse, or that a thing is a ball or a penny. In addition to this, it also has the formal syntactical function of serving as the subject of predication in sentences. If, now, general names are deprived of the syntactical use to which they are at present put, and given adjectival classification under parts of speech, the subject-predicate form of sentence in which they occur as subjects can nevertheless be preserved by introducing a term that will do part of the work of a general name, i.e., do its syntactical work without doing its semantic work. It will be sufficient if the new term is made to behave syntactically like an ordinary subject term and is otherwise a pseudo term, having no application to phenomena. Thus, to revert to the former example, the *structure* of the sentence "The penny is round" can be kept intact after its noun has been deleted, by letting the mark "x" occupy the place of "penny." We then have the new subject-predicate sentence "The x is round,"[20] where "x" differs from ordinary subject terms in respect of having been given no application. It is the failure to give "x" a meaning that makes it a "mere subject" or, to use Bertrand Russell's word, a *hook* on which to hang adjectives.

One philosopher seems to have divined what has happened when he observed that "Our idea of a substance, in fact, turns out to be no more than an unknown x, to which we refer the contents of experience."[21] The new subject term *is* an unknown x, which is to say it is a symbol that has no known

---

[19] H. W. B. Joseph, *An Introduction to Logic* (1931), p. 54.

[20] 'x' is not to be taken as representing a variable.
[21] James Gibson, *Locke's Theory of Knowledge and its Historical Relations* (1917), p. 95.

meaning assigned to it; it has no semantic use, though it has the appearance of having such a use. It is a term by means of which we cannot say *what* a thing is, although, in the subject-predicate sentences of the substratum language invented by metaphysicians, it supplants words with which we can, and in ordinary language do, say what things are. It is this new form of subject-predicate language that causes the idea of unknowable substratum: the new term is a "linguistic unknowable." The complaint that we cannot say anything about the nature of substance about what things really are, is not the factual complaint about things it may at first have seemed to be, nor is it about our everyday language, which, of course, contains general names. It is the expression of dissatisfaction with the substratum language of metaphysics and is of the same order as complaining that we cannot say what a "tove" is. The term "*x*" tells us nothing, conveys no information, about the thing described by the adjectives of a sentence in which it occurs as subject. Nor, of course, can we explain its meaning, in the way in which we can explain the meaning of a general name. If we are asked what a kangaroo is we can answer the question by describing the animal to which the word "kangaroo" applies, which is to say, by giving roughly the meaning of the word. This is impossible in the case of the metaphysical subject, which has no application; there is no explaining what an *x* is. The observation that on the substratum theory "the individual . . . becomes a mere uncharacterized *something*. For in saying *what* it is, we should merely assign to it a fresh predicate; whereas we want to get not at its predicates but at that which 'has' them"[22] comes to the same thing as the above complaint. It is easy to see why we cannot "get at" substance with a language in which general names have been reduced to adjectival status and have had their former position taken over by a term which does only their syntactical work. We can state what attributes a thing has but we cannot

say what it is in which they inhere, except that it is an *x*, and "uncharacterized something." We can "get at" some animals with the word "kangaroo," but we get at nothing with the term "*x*."

The idea of substance as being that which remains after a thing has been stripped bare of its qualities—the idea, in other words, of "bare substance" or the "bare particular"— turns out to be a disguised expression of a linguistic fact. That which remains, after a general name has been deprived of its application to things by depriving it of the meaning it has in common with an indeterminate set of adjectives, is a term which has only a syntactical use, an equivalent of the formal subject term of substratum metaphysics. "Bare substance" is nothing more that a "bare" substantive word, the metaphysical ghost of a general name. This is the conception of substratum as something *distinct* from its properties and in which they inhere. And this conception is nothing more than the conception of a subject-symbol which is *completely* distinct from its predicates by virtue of the fact that it has no meaning of its own, a fact which also makes impossible our saying, by means of it, what things are. It is possible in this language to say what properties a thing has, but not what it is. This fact, it may be noted, rids philosophers of the need of trying to distinguish the essence of a thing from its accidents. For without the ordinary distinction between general substantive words like "penny" and "horse" and adjectives like "round" and "roan"—a distinction which can be destroyed either by eliminating general nouns or by changing them into adjectives—there is no distinction between the essence and accidents of a thing. There is left only the distinction between a term which is a "pure" subject term (the pure abstract being of medieval metaphysics) and adjectives.

Consider, again, the familiar argument used to demonstrate the unknowability of substance, the argument, namely, that we cannot envisage the entity that is left after a thing has been stripped of its attributes,

---

[22] Joseph, *loc. cit.*

or, what amounts to the same thing, Hume's argument that in addition to the perceived qualities of colour, shape, odour, taste, and the like we never experience the thing which has them. This argument rests on and, indeed, is a distorted way of calling attention to actual points of difference and similarity between general names and adjectives. General names differ in their formal, syntactical use from adjectives, but also they are like them in important respects. For one thing, like adjectives, they have multiple applicability; or, to express this fact in metaphysical language, the universals for which they stand are capable of having a number of instances or of being possessed in common by a number of things. Thus, we can say that many things are grey and we can say that there are many mice. Also, and what is more specifically relevant in connexion with the argument, the application of a general noun is determined by a variable set of adjectives, not sharply defined or specified. To put it roughly, as regards their meaning, general names are "complex adjectives." This is what Locke was pointing out when he remarked that "everyone upon inquiry into his own thoughts will find, that he has no other idea of any substance but what he has barely of those sensible qualities, which he supposes to inhere. . . . Thus the idea of the sun, what is it but an aggregate of those several simple ideas, bright, hot, roundish . . . ?" Hence, to speak of an experiment, conducted in the imagination, of stripping a thing of its attributes is a disguised and more colourful way of expressing the linguistic fact that the meaning of a general noun like "mouse" is the same as that possessed by a complicated set of adjectives, so that by "stripping away" its adjectives, i.e., by depriving the noun of its adjectival meaning, we deprive it of its application to things. Noticing the impressive similarity between general nouns and adjectives makes some people wish to assimilate them to the class of adjectives. It is much as if, by their argument, they were to

say: "See, the difference between general nouns and adjectives is mainly a difference in the way they function syntactically in sentences. By comparison with their semantic similarity, this difference is trivial, but it hides their similarity." And to correct this state of affairs and bring out what is hidden by the structure of subject-predicate language, general nouns are reduced to adjectival status. The syntactical function of nouns is turned over to a new symbol, and in this way the structure of subject-predicate sentences using general names as subjects is preserved and also the mystifying illusion of a deep theory about the structure of reality is created. Undoubtedly, the motivation for the change goes deeper than the linguistic considerations; we may well think that psychological needs play an important rôle in the production of the illusion.

Metaphysicians who find the substratum theory unacceptable also feel the importance of the semantic similarity that grammar tends to conceal, and are dissatisfied with the grammar that conceals it. What impresses these philosophers seems mainly to be the fact that both sorts of words, adjectives and nouns, have multiple applicability, that, e.g., "white" and "snow" are each applicable to a number of things. They see, however, the possibility of a different reconstruction, to which they are attracted. They see the possibility of assimilating adjectives to the class of substantive words. Instead of reducing general names to complex adjectives they change adjectives into abstract nouns, "red" into "redness," "round" into "roundness," and so on, and dispense altogether with the subject-predicate form of sentence. In this way they get rid, not of linguistic unknowables in ordinary language (which has none), but of the pseudo unknowables, the introduced metaphysical subjects of the substratum language. Instead of having philosophical sentences like "The x is white," they have philosophical sentences like "Whiteness is here," or "Whiteness, here, now."

BERTRAND RUSSELL

THE WORLD OF UNIVERSALS*

At the end of the preceding chapter we saw that such entities as relations appear to have a being which is in some way different from that of physical objects, and also different from that of minds and from that of sense-data. In the present chapter we have to consider what is the nature of this kind of being, and also what objects there are that have this kind of being. We will begin with the latter question.

The problem with which we are now concerned is a very old one, since it was brought into philosophy by Plato. Plato's "theory of ideas" is an attempt to solve this very problem, and in my opinion it is one of the most successful attempts hitherto made. The theory to be advocated in what follows is largely Plato's, with merely such modifications as time has shown to be necessary.

The way the problem arose for Plato was more or less as follows. Let us consider, say, such a notion as *justice*. If we ask ourselves what justice is, it is natural to proceed by considering this, that, and the other just act, with a view to discovering what they have in common. They must all, in some sense, partake of a common nature, which will be found in whatever is just and in nothing else. This common nature, in virtue of which they are all just, will be justice itself, the pure essence the admixture of which with facts of ordinary life produces the multiplicity of just acts. Similarly with any other word which may be applicable to common facts, such as "whiteness" for example. The word will be applicable to a number of particular things because they all

participate in a common nature or essence. This pure essence is what Plato calls an "idea" or "form." (It must not be supposed that "ideas," in his sense, exist in minds, though they may be apprehended by minds.) The "idea" *justice* is not identical with anything that is just: it is something other than particular things, which particular things partake of. Not being particular, it cannot itself exist in the world of sense. Moreover it is not fleeting or changeable like the things of sense: it is eternally itself, immutable and indestructible.

Thus Plato is led to a supra-sensible world, more real than the common world of sense, the unchangeable world of ideas, which alone gives to the world of sense whatever pale reflection of reality may belong to it. The truly real world, for Plato, is the world of ideas; for whatever we may attempt to say about things in the world of sense, we can only succeed in saying that they participate in such and such ideas, which, therefore, constitute all their character. Hence it is easy to pass on into a mysticism. We may hope, in a mystic illumination, to *see* the ideas as we see objects of sense; and we may imagine that the ideas exist in heaven. These mystical developments are very natural, but the basis of the theory is in logic, and it is as based in logic that we have to consider it.

The word "idea" has acquired, in the course of time, many associations which are quite misleading when applied to Plato's "ideas." We shall therefore use the word "universal" instead of the word "idea," to describe what Plato meant. The essence of the sort of entity that Plato meant is that it is opposed to the particular things that are given in sensation. We speak of whatever is given in sensation, or is of the same nature as things given in sensation, as a *particular;* by opposition to this, a *universal* will be anything which may be shared by many particulars, and has those characteristics which, as we saw, distinguish justice and whiteness from just acts and white things.

When we examine common words, we find that, broadly speaking, proper names stand for particulars, while other substantives, adjectives, prepositions, and verbs stand for universals. Pronouns stand for particulars, but are ambiguous: it is only by the context or the circumstances that we know what particulars they stand for. The word "now" stands for a particular, namely the present moment; but like pronouns, it stands for an ambiguous particular, because the present is always changing.

It will be seen that no sentence can be made up without at least one word which denotes a universal. The nearest approach would be some such statement as "I like this." But even here the word "like" denotes a universal, for I may like other things, and other people may like things. Thus all truths involve universals, and all knowledge of truths involves acquaintance with universals.

Seeing that nearly all the words to be found in the dictionary stand for universals, it is strange that hardly anybody except students of philosophy ever realizes that there are such entities as universals. We do not naturally dwell upon those words in a sentence which do not stand for particulars; and if we are forced to dwell upon a word which stands for a universal, we naturally think of it as standing for some one of the particulars that come under the universal. When, for example, we hear the sentence, "Charles I's head was cut off," we may naturally enough think of Charles I, of Charles I's head, and of the operation of cutting off *his* head, which are all particulars; but we do not naturally dwell upon what is meant by the word "head" or the word "cut," which is a universal. We feel such words to be incomplete and insubstantial; they seem to demand a context before anything can be done with them. Hence we

succeed in avoiding all notice of universals as such, until the study of philosophy forces them upon our attention.

Even among philosophers, we may say, broadly, that only those universals which are named by adjectives or substantives have been much or often recognized, while those named by verbs and prepositions have been usually overlooked. This omission has had a very great effect upon philosophy; it is hardly too much to say that most metaphysics, since Spinoza, has been largely determined by it. The way this has occurred is, in outline, as follows: Speaking generally, adjectives and common nouns express qualities or properties of single things, whereas prepositions and verbs tend to express relations between two or more things. Thus the neglect of prepositions and verbs led to the belief that every proposition can be regarded as attributing a property to a single thing, rather than as expressing a relation between two or more things. Hence it was supposed that, ultimately, there can be no such entities as relations between things. Hence either there can be only one thing in the universe, or if there are many things, they cannot possibly interact in any way, since any interaction would be a relation, and relations are impossible.

The first of these views, advocated by Spinoza and held in our own day by Bradley and many other philosophers, is called *monism;* the second, advocated by Leibniz but not very common nowadays, is called *monadism,* because each of the isolated things is called a *monad.* Both these opposing philosophies, interesting as they are, result, in my opinion, from an undue attention to one sort of universals, namely the sort represented by adjectives and substantives rather than by verbs and prepositions.

As a matter of fact, if any one were anxious to deny altogether that there are such things as universals, we should find that we cannot strictly prove that there are such entities as *qualities,* i.e. the universals represented by adjectives and substantives, whereas we can prove that there must be *relations,* i.e.

the sort of universals generally represented by verbs and prepositions. Let us take in illustration the universal *whiteness*. If we believe that there is such a universal, we shall say that things are white because they have the quality of whiteness. This view, however, was strenuously denied by Berkeley and Hume, who have been followed in this by later empiricists. The form which their denial took was to deny that there are such things as "abstract ideas." When we want to think of whiteness, they said, we form an image of some particular white thing, and reason concerning this particular, taking care not to deduce anything concerning it which we cannot see to be equally true of any other white thing. As an account of our actual mental processes, this is no doubt largely true. In geometry, for example, when we wish to prove something about all triangles, we draw a particular triangle and reason about it, taking care not to use any characteristic which it does not share with other triangles. The beginner, in order to avoid error, often finds it useful to draw several triangles, as unlike each other as possible, in order to make sure that his reasoning is equally applicable to all of them. But a difficulty emerges as soon as we ask ourselves how we know that a thing is white or a triangle. If we wish to avoid the universals *whiteness* and *triangularity*, we shall choose some particular patch of white or some particular triangle, and say that anything is white or a triangle if it has the right sort of resemblance to our chosen particular. But then the resemblance required will have to be a universal. Since there are many white things, the resemblance must hold between many pairs of particular white things; and this is the characteristic of a universal. It will be useless to say that there is a different resemblance for each pair, for then we shall have to say that these resemblances resemble each other, and thus at last we shall be forced to admit resemblance as a universal. The relation of resemblance, therefore, must be a true universal. And having been forced to admit this universal, we find that it is no longer

worth while to invent difficult and unplausible theories to avoid the admission of such universals as whiteness and triangularity.

Berkeley and Hume failed to perceive this refutation of their rejection of "abstract ideas," because, like their adversaries, they only thought of *qualities,* and altogether ignored *relations* as universals. We have therefore here another respect in which the rationalists appear to have been in the right as against the empiricists, although, owing to the neglect or denial of relations, the deductions made by rationalists were, if anything, more apt to be mistaken than those made by empiricists.

Having now seen that there must be such entities as universals, the next point to be proved is that their being is not merely mental. By this is meant that whatever being belongs to them is independent of their being thought of or in any way apprehended by minds. We have already touched on this subject at the end of the preceding chapter, but we must now consider more fully what sort of being it is that belongs to universals.

Consider such a proposition as "Edinburgh is north of London." Here we have a relation between two places, and it seems plain that the relation subsists independently of our knowledge of it. When we come to know that Edinburgh is north of London, we come to know something which has to do only with Edinburgh and London: we do not cause the truth of the proposition by coming to know it, on the contrary we merely apprehend a fact which was there before we knew it. The part of the earth's surface where Edinburgh stands would be north of the part where London stands, even if there were no human being to know about north and south, and even if there were no minds at all in the universe. This is, of course, denied by many philosophers, either by Berkeley's reasons or for Kant's. But we have already considered these reasons, and decided that they are inadequate. We may therefore now assume it to be true that nothing mental is presupposed in the fact that Edinburgh is north of London. But this fact involves the relation "north of," which is a universal; and it would be impossible for the whole fact to involve nothing mental if the relation "north of," which is a constituent part of the fact, did involve anything mental. Hence we must admit that the relation, like the terms it relates, is not dependent upon thought, but belongs to the independent world which thought apprehends but does not create.

This conclusion, however, is met by the difficulty that the relation "north of" does not seem to *exist* in the same sense in which Edinburgh and London exist. If we ask "Where and when does this relation exist?" the answer must be "Nowhere and nowhen." There is no place or time where we can find the relation "north of." It does not exist in Edinburgh any more than in London, for it relates the two and is neutral as between them. Nor can we say that it exists at any particular time. Now everything that can be apprehended by the senses or by introspection exists at some particular time. Hence the relation "north of" is radically different from such things. It is neither in space nor in time, neither material nor mental; yet it is something.

It is largely the very peculiar kind of being that belongs to universals which has led many people to suppose that they are really mental. We can think *of* a universal, and our thinking then exists in a perfectly ordinary sense, like any other mental act. Suppose, for example, that we are thinking of whiteness. Then *in one sense* it may be said that whiteness is "in our mind." We have here the same ambiguity as we noted in discussing Berkeley in Chapter IV. In the strict sense, it is not whiteness that is in our mind, but the act of thinking of whiteness. The connected ambiguity in the word "idea," which we noted at the same time, also causes confusion here. In one sense of this word, namely the sense in which it denotes the *object* of an act of thought, whiteness is an "idea." Hence, if the ambiguity is not guarded against, we may come to think that whiteness is an "idea" in the other sense, i.e. an act of thought; and thus we come to

think that whiteness is mental. But in so thinking, we rob it of its essential quality of universality. One man's act of thought is necessarily a different thing from another man's; one man's act of thought at one time is necessarily a different thing from the same man's act of thought at another time. Hence, if whiteness were the thought as opposed to its object, no two different men could think of it, and no one man could think of it twice. That which many different thoughts of whiteness have in common is their *object*, and this object is different from all of them. Thus universals are not thoughts, though when known they are the objects of thoughts.

We shall find it convenient only to speak of things *existing* when they are in time, that is to say, when we can point to some time *at* which they exist (not excluding the possibility of their existing at all times). Thus thoughts and fellings, minds and physical objects *exist*. But universals do not exist in this sense; we shall say that they *subsist* or *have being*, where "being" is opposed to "existence" as being timeless. The world of universals, therefore, may also be described as the world of being. The world of being is unchangeable, rigid, exact, delightful to the mathematician, the logician, the builder of metaphysical systems, and all who love perfection more than life. The world of existence is fleeting, vague, without sharp boundaries, without any clear plan or arrangement, but it contains all thoughts and feelings, all the data of sense, and all physical objects, everything that can do either good or harm, everything that makes any difference to the value of life and the world. According to our temperaments, we shall prefer the contemplation of the one or of the other. The one we do not prefer will probably seem to us a pale shadow of the one we prefer, and hardly worthy to be regarded as in any sense real. But the truth is that both have the same claim on our impartial attention, both are real, and both are important to the metaphysician. Indeed no sooner have we distinguished the two worlds than it becomes necessary to consider their relations.

PAUL WEISS

ON BEING TOGETHER*

1. The Problem and Some Answers

He who would like to affirm that there is no more than one entity is faced with serious difficulties. To say nothing more than "One" is not yet, as Plato long ago observed, to say anything significant. Yet to say "One is" is already to have said two things, and in fact to have made a distinction between Unity and Being. An intelligible acknowledgment of a One involves an encounter with a Many.

Yet if there be a Many there must be a number of units somehow together. Were items entirely separate from one another, related in no way at all, they could not add up, make a plurality. A radical atomism offers not a Many but just a One, and then a One, and then a One, and so on, and thus has no way of ever knowing that there is more than one entity. To know that there are Many it is necessary to have them all brought together under the aegis of a common or comprehensive One.

The problem of the One and the Many is not simply a problem of knowing or saying that there is a One or a Many without somehow knowing or saying the other as well. It is also a problem of how a plurality of entities can be together without that very fact of their togetherness adding another member to the totality of things, which in turn must be brought together with the original set, and so on. This problem haunts every view, for every view acknowledges Many entities, if not in the shape of realities, then in the shape of illusions, elements, conditions, words or beliefs.

* From *The Review of Metaphysics*, IX (March 1956), 391–403. Reprinted by permission of the author and editor.

To this problem five grand answers have been offered in the past. They may be conveniently characterized as a) Synthesis, b) Concurrence, c) Self-Diremption, d) Dualism, e) Identity in Difference. Each does, I think, provide some answer to the problem. But each is also faced with embarrassments which cannot, I believe, be avoided unless we take up a new, sixth approach to the problem of the One and the Many.

a. *Synthesis.* Synthesis is a process (of being or of knowing) of forging disparate elements into a unity in such a way that each of the elements completes the others, offering them whatever additions they need in order to be as excellent as possible. It is thus a process by which a One for a Many is brought into existence, and the Many is thereby enriched. Taken at its thickest, as maximally engulfing the elements, leaving out either none or little of them so as to constitute a new being which is richer and more substantial than they are, synthesis is a source of novelty in thought or in being, the cause of the emergence of new values and new events in the universe of discourse or fact. Taken at its thinnest, as merely joining the elements without any or little affect on their being or natures, synthesis is a mode of sheer addition, of tying things together in an external way. Thick or thin, synthesis starts with entities which are unstable, incomplete and inadequate taken severally, to bring about a One of them all in which they all achieve supplementation from one another. There are of course many different theories of the nature and need for synthesis, but perhaps all can be treated as variations on Kant's brilliant attempt to explain how what is in fact diverse can be understood and exist in a single irreducible unitary whole. Hegel more resolutely and systematically exploited the idea of synthesis, but the principles and the problems involved in it do not seem to be for him really much different from what they were for Kant. I find four difficulties with the idea.

1. The doctrine of synthesis holds that the Many are brought together through some act. But then it is evident that synthesis presupposes someone or something to do the synthesizing. And since synthesizing is a real occurrence, it also presupposes, in addition to its Many, an activity affecting that Many. Whatever number of entities there be, if synthesis is the agency by which they are together, there will always be one more entity than those which are synthesized, since the synthesizer is another, and there will always be one other fact to take account of— the synthesizing, since this encompasses and is therefore not included in the original Many. Synthesis thus precludes us from saying that such and such make up the Many of the universe of thought or being, since no matter how few or how many entities are acknowledged to begin with, the synthesizer and the synthesizing must be added to them to make a larger Many.

2. Synthesis produces a One out of a Many. That One is a function of the Many, and of the method by which they are united. Such a One is only a One *from* a Many; it is not yet a One *for* the Many. A One for a Many must have a Many over against it, which it somehow relates. But a One which is merely produced out of the Many has as yet no significance for that Many. A synthesis somehow must cut back on itself, push aside the very items which it is bringing together, in order to have a Many for the One which it produces.

3. Synthesis operates on a Many. But before it can operate, the various items in the Many must somehow constitute a single Many. If they are entirely cut off from one another, there would be no Many to be synthesized. But if synthesis is the only agency by which a Many is to be brought together, every synthesis must presuppose a prior synthesis. Only because a Many already has a One for it, enabling it to be a single Many, is it possible to have a synthesis. But then the synthesis is no longer necessary.

4. A successful synthesis finally yields a new entity. That new entity must be related to the original Many. It must be a One among a Many, make up with the original Many a larger Many consisting of that original Many and itself. It will then require a further synthesis to bring it together with that Many. Every synthesis thus requires a subsequent synthesis to relate its outcome to the material with which it began. No synthesis can ever be more than partial, incomplete, requiring ever more syntheses to deal with the problems raised by earlier ones. But unless the problem of the togetherness of the Many were solved to begin with, these subsequent syntheses could not take place.

b. *Concurrence.* Some of the difficulties that beset the theory of synthesis are avoided in the theory of concurrence. On this view too we start with a Many. But instead of invoking a synthesizer and ending with a One which must apparently be synthesized with the original Many, the Many are acknowledged to produce a One by the mere concurrence of the Many outside themselves at some common point. To my knowledge, no one has urged this as the account of how there can be a One and a Many, though perhaps this is the idea at the root of Hobbes's theory of the origin of a state and his justification of sovereignty. In any case the One is here a derivative, which does not add an additional element to the totality of entities with which one starts and which were assumed to exhaust the furniture of the universe. It takes the Many seriously, seems to account for the One in a way that is intelligible and plausible, and does not, as synthesis seems to do, both require and make unnecessary prior and subsequent acts of bringing the Many together. I find three difficulties with the idea.

1. A concurrence happens either by chance

or by necessity. If by chance, there can be no guarantee that the various items in the Many will have a common convergence. A chance production of a One is a production which could conceivably fail. A One is necessary to the Many; the presence of the One cannot therefore be the outcome of chance; it is impossible for there to be a Many without a One. Yet if the One comes about through a necessary convergence of the Many, the Many must act in concert, and in order to do this they must make up a singular totality, presuppose a One. Thus, if a convergence does not presuppose a One it may never attain it, and cannot in any case take place without a miracle, for the Many has to be together from the very start. Yet if a One is presupposed, the need for the convergence disappears.

2. The One at which the Many is supposed to converge is part of that Many, or stands apart from it. It is the former if it is produced by the Many through their convergence; it is the latter if it makes the convergence possible. But if it is the former it is not yet a One for that Many; if it is the latter it is presupposed by and is not the product of the convergence.

3. A One which is produced through a convergence, and which somehow manages to stand apart from the Many, must dominate, encompass, bring the Many together. The Many out of which it issued through convergence must lose something of their original separateness or freedom, to constitute that One which dominates them, for otherwise the One would be a new entity adding to the original Many. The Many must engage in an act of self-diremption, self-denial in order that the One be, and yet not be something added to the Many. But self-diremption is a different solution to the problem of the One and the Many—it is, in fact, the third of the solutions we have listed.

c. *Self-Diremption.* Instead of starting with a Many, out of which a One is to be generated, it might be thought desirable to start instead with a One, and generate a Many out of it by a process of self-alienation, ex-foliation, or exteriorization. This is the alternative to which monists eventually resort to account for their acknowledged plurality of appearances, errors or subordinate realities. The most persistent effort in this direction has perhaps been made by Plotinus, although it would be difficult to term him a monist, since he takes seriously the reality of the generated items, granting them a status apart from the generating One. Both his view and the view of the monists, east and west, who minimize the reality of the Many, have the great merit of recognizing the ultimacy and power of the One, and the fact that in some sense the Many is subordinate to and depends on it for its being and its intelligibility. I find six difficulties with this idea.

1. The One by itself is unintelligible. What is without division, without complexity, allowing no distinction—in short, containing no Many—cannot be thought or known. The theory of self-diremption must begin with what it cannot understand, proceed by principles it cannot grasp, and end with what it affirms is not altogether true or real.

2. To produce a Many the One must act. It and its act are distinct, and constitute a Many. The production of a Many thus already presupposes a Many, at least in the shape of the pair of the One and its act of diversification. A One which does not act remains undivided, but on the other hand it does not engage in self-diremption.

3. The One allows the Many to be over against it, or it fails to produce a Many. But then it either generates new realities or minimizes itself, reduces itself in order to give some being or meaning to the Many. In the latter case it must presuppose not merely a prior One but a One which is more real than its self-dirempted being and the Many with which it is together.

4. The One engages in a single act or in many. If the latter, we have a radical plurality to begin with, before we have generated our Many. If the former, there will be only two things in the universe unless the product of that first act of generation generates a subordinate one, and so on, for a series of steps. This second alternative has no

beings on the same level of reality or excellence, but only beings of many orders. These orders must somehow be brought together, and, so far as they are, are on a level, each offering a unit to be united with other units. A self-diremptive One must not only be a source of a Many but must continue to engulf it, and thus must have two roles, be a Many from the very start.

5. The One before it gives rise to a Many is distinct from the One as originating a Many. But then before the Many has been produced we have Many Ones. The generating of the Many would have to be of the very essence of the One and instantly produce its Many; but then there would be no act of self-diremption. A One which was always faced with a Many could be said to require that Many, but not to have generated it, and surely not by first being a mere One and then becoming a generating source of whatever else there be.

6. A generated Many is thrust away from the One or is confined within it. If the former, the Many and the One constitute a larger Many and need a more inclusive One to encompass it. If the latter, there is no real Many, a Many collected or connected by means of a One. There is only a One. This pair of alternatives touches the core of the doctrine of creation in classical theology. If God creates a universe he gives it its own existence and the universe no longer needs God in order to be; if the universe does not really stand apart, over against God, there is in fact no universe that he creates.

The problem of the One and the Many cannot hope for solution in any account which starts with one side and tries to get the other out of it; each side has some standing, some being, some meaning apart from and over against the other.

d. *Dualism*. The dualist says flatly and finally, there is a One and a Many, and that is the end of the matter. Neither generates the other, neither grounds the other, neither owns the other. In the end most thinkers are perhaps pluralists; they end their thinking or their writing, with more than one item which they tacitly or explicitly grant to be separate, irreducible, merely over against one another. The dualist is a pluralist restricting himself to but two items, one of which may, as in the case of the problem of the One and the Many, be itself a plurality. There is strength in the doctrine, since it refuses to minimize the value or meaning of either side of such a basic issue as that of the One and the Many. Although it was one of his primary objectives to overcome dualisms of every type, perhaps Aristotle ought to be seen as a persistent dualist, particularly when account is taken of his contrasting views of God and nature, the active and the human reason, form and matter, substance and accident. Those who like Descartes deliberately set themselves to oppose the Aristotelian outlook usually do so without overcoming the basic dualism which defines the Aristotelian view. I find four difficulties with this idea.

1. A One *and* a Many is a Many. Dualism seems to side with one of the positions—that which starts and ends with a Many. And yet it confesses that a One is needed, for the One is the necessary correlate of the Many, never to be reduced to it or placed alongside it.

2. A One and a Many form a pair. They must be together in some way, and thus be under the aegis of a One. That One is and must be distinct from the One which is paired with the Many. A dualism thus proliferates endlessly, pairing opposites only by turning the result into a single item to be paired with a One in terms of which the original pairing occurred.

3. To form a pair the One and the Many must be related. That relation is neither the One nor the Many with which one begins. It is a third item which somehow must be paired with the supposedly original and exhausting pair. Once again a dualism proliferates without end, since it must pair ever new items which were produced in the course of a previous pairing.

4. A dualism has two final items on a level. If it is to avoid an infinite production of new items to pair, it must refuse to acknowledge anything more than the items with

which it begins. These must be thought of as irreducible, final, unrelated. But then to know or grasp or become acquainted with one of them is to be cut off from the other. How then, knowing or having one half of the duality, can it be possible to know the other? And if we do not know or have the other, what warrant is there for supposing there is anything more than the original side with which one begins? A dualist, to know his two items, must somehow be over and above or in both, and in any case force the acknowledgment of something other than the items with which he originally tried to remain content.

e. *Identity in Difference.* Identity in difference is the doctrine that the final items are in a sense the same: the One is the Many, the Many is the One. Each of the two components is seen to need the other, before it can have the status of a full reality. That other is in fact itself from another side, the two sides as together, as one despite their being two, alone constituting a reality. Starting with the Many it acknowledges a One, but not as another item to be added to the Many; starting with the One it acknowledges a Many, but not as a further reality somehow generated out of and standing over against the One. The doctrine is subtle, perhaps too subtle for a non-initiate to grasp, perpetually seeming to disappear as it does into self-contradiction. This is true even in the case of the master of this view, that resolute dialectician and rationalist, Hegel.

No one of the Hegelian school seems to have taken the One and the Many with equal seriousness. All tend to favor the One over the Many. They remark that the One exteriorizes itself as and yet continues to possess the Many, differentiating itself from while identifying itself with that Many. There are similar statements to be found faintly urging somewhat similar feats on the part of the Many, but on the whole the Many is thought of as a product of the One, subordinate to it in reality and in meaning.

But only a view which takes the Many as seriously as it does the One does justice to the thesis of identity in difference, though such justice will perhaps preclude the desire of the school to move from a world of heterogeneous items to a single absolute within which whatever Many there be is found reconciled and somehow absorbed. Taken this boldly the thesis of the identity in difference of the One and the Many seems to accommodate the contentions of the dualists without falling into the characteristic embarrassments of that view. It grants the One and the Many equal status, but does not cut them off from one another. The other is held on to while it stands apart. To be with either the One or the Many, it holds, is not to be cut off but instead is to have the Many or the One as well. I find three difficulties with this idea.

1. It is not clear whether the Identity is supposed to be identical with or different from the Difference. If it is identical with it, we have nothing more than sheer Identity; if it is different from it, we have a radical dualism right inside the initial Identity in Difference.

2. Each basic reality is supposed to have its other with which it is identifiable. But then Identity in Difference should have an other. The basic reality will, as a consequence, not be expressed as an Identity in Difference but rather as an Identity in Difference connecting an Identity in Difference with an other. This last in turn will need an other of its own, and so on, infinitely.

3. If the One is in any sense an other of the Many it must have features which the Many does not have, or lack features which the Many has. If this were not the case we would have nothing more than just a One, or just a Many. Yet if the One and the Many are genuinely distinct, the acknowledgement of a Many inevitably leads to the acknowledgement of one more entity, the One, which with the original Many will need a still further One, and so on.

2. On Being Together

Each of these five answers has considerable power, and no solution to the problem of the One and the Many which neglects their insights will eventually do. A satisfactory account must, like the theory of synthesis, recognize that if we start with a Many, a One must be an emergent of some sort and yet not add to the total number of entities in the universe. It must recognize, with the theory of concurrence, that the various members of the Many must have a common One, but must avoid thereby compromising the status of that One as a One for that Many. With the theory of self-diremption it must acknowledge that One is presupposed by the Many as that which allows the Many to be together and thus be a Many, at the same time that it recognizes this Many to be an inevitable referent of that One, without compromise to the fact that the Many is as basic and as real as the One. With the dualist it must affirm that the One and the Many are on a par, each irreducible and final, but related in such a way as to make possible a knowledge of them both. And finally it must, with the defenders of the doctrine of Identity in Difference recognize the fact that despite their diversity the One and the Many are not alien to one another in meaning or in being; but this recognition must not lead to the abrogation of the law of contradiction, nor prompt the forging of irresponsible paradoxes. This is a formidable array of demands; yet one cannot avoid trying to meet them except by giving up a claim to be self-critical and systematic beyond any pre-assignable limit.

For simplicity's sake let us begin with a consideration of only two entities, x and y, making up a Many. Let these exhaust the universe; let them be viewed as irreducible, final realities, one of two independent basic dimensions or modes of being. As simply over against one another, as apart from a One, let us symbolize them as "x,y." They cannot be in this state unless there is a One for them. Let us symbolize that One as " . ".

There will be an "x,y" only so far as they together constitute the " . ". The " . " is x and y as merged, as terminating in each other; the merging of x and y is what constitutes the togetherness of them both. Like a point which is the outcome of the intersection of two lines, a border which is the limit of two figures, a standing erect which is the outcome of opposite stresses, the " . " exists only as something constituted by the very items it serves to sustain. The togetherness of x and y is x and y as no longer distinct; it can have a nature of its own only so far as they continue to stand over against it as distinct, as "x,y."

Each of the elements, x and y, acts on and is blocked by the equal counter-thrust of the other. The " . " is not an entity additional to the x and y, since it is their togetherness, the being and meaning of them so far as they are intermingled, in no way distinct. But for each of the elements, x and y, the " . " which it constitutes with the help of the other is something over and against it. The " . " as partly constituted by x belongs to that x, and the x, in order that the part of its being which it contributes to make the " . " should not be in the control of y, is driven to try to possess the entire " . ". It tries to make the entire togetherness part of itself. Could it succeed it would then possess the y by virtue of its possession of that part of the " . " which is continuous with the y. It never wholly possesses the " . "; it can never manage to do more than to deal with it from its own angle. It does not possess it as a neutral fact—or what is the same thing, it gets the fact of togetherness only in the abstract and never in the concrete. As a consequence it never gets to the y entirely, but ends only with an abstract of it, what y is when approached by x through the agency or a biased mastery of the " . ".

No matter how much of x is comprehended by y, or how much of y is comprehended by x, the x and the y will continue to be as they were. The mastery of the other by each occurs within the area defined by "*x,y*" and " . ", the one expressing the fact that there are two entities, the other the fact that they are together, each saying what the other does, but in a different way. The " . " has the *x* and *y* together but at the price of their distinctness; "*x,y*" has the two so far apart that there is no relation to be found between them. We can say, if we like, that "*x,y*" is one mode of togetherness of which " . " is the other, the one having a minimum of the being of a togetherness, the other a maximum. Or we can say with equal justification the " . " is *x* and *y* in one guise, of which "*x,y*" offers a complementary other, the first distinguishing them to a minimum degree, the second to a maximum. In either way of speaking the *x* and *y* are recognized to constitute their own togetherness, and the togetherness is recognized to be distinct from the *x* and the *y* just so far as they are distinct from one another.

There is always a difference between the " . " and "*x,y*." That difference we can describe in a " . " way or in a "*x,y*" way, the one stressing the togetherness of the " . " and the "*x,y*," the other their distinctness. And these two descriptions can themselves be described in two ways and so on without end. This is a harmless progression, for it is a progression in analysis and not one towards presuppositions which have to be settled before there can be the situation with which we in fact began. We always possess both a " . " and an "*x,y*." And when we try to say how they are one we must continue to keep them distinct as a many. From the standpoint of " . " the " , " in "*x,y*" is a whole set of " . " which never make a single whole; from the standpoint of "*x,y*," the " . " is the unreachable limit of more and more intimate relations between *x* and *y*. Each standpoint expresses what the other is. If we wish to avoid either standpoint, we but take the standpoint of a neutral but abstract mind. We then assume something like the position of the " . " and see that which is before us as a manifold in which the various parts are conjoined, but never enough to make the kind of unity which we have in mind.

The One and the Many then are related by a kind of identity in difference, for the " . " and the "*x,y*" articulate one another, re-state one another in different terms. The one presents in a united way what the other has as separate. But the relation of the two parts is not a paradoxical self-sameness which is different; each is the continuation of the other, the extreme limit of what the other exhibits. They can be said to form a duality, but not as a pair of items characterizable in the same terms. The "*x,y*" are distinct and determinate, the " . " is indeterminate, with the *x* and the *y* hopelessly merged. The being of the " . " requires the distinguishing of its items; the being of "*x,y*" requires their merging. Both the distinguishing and the merging must occur, but the occurrence of the one is not a fact over against the occurrence of the other. The existence of *x* and *y* does not involve the production of another entity " . ", which together with them make a new Many. The *x* and *y* exist as " . " and as "*x,y*." These are one and the same, and if we start with either, we express ourselves through the use of the other. They can be had as distinct, but only by our standing over against them in a neutral position. But then it is evident that their status as distinct is but a way of articulating the fact that we have them together in an abstract rather than in a concrete way. Starting with "*x,y*," the " . " is the product of a convergence; starting with " . ", the "*x,y*" is a product of a self-diremption. But in neither case do we get a being separated from its origin, a genuine other adding another fact to the universe, additional to that with which we began. And finally the " . " can be viewed as a product of a synthesis of the *x* and the *y*, but a synthesis which never had to be performed. The synthesis of "*x,y*" is completed in the " . ", and this " . " exists when and as "*x,y*" does.

We started with *x* and *y*, a Many. That Many makes a unity by virtue of a togetherness which is distinct from the items that are together. But that togetherness is not a third substance; it is the very items which are together. The togetherness of beings is the being of them together.

MARTIN HEIDEGGER

WHAT IS METAPHYSICS?*

"What is metaphysics?" The question leads one to expect a discussion about metaphysics. Such is not our intention. Instead, we shall discuss a definite metaphysical question, thus, as it will appear, landing ourselves straight into metaphysics. Only in this way can we make it really possible for metaphysics to speak for itself.

Our project begins with the presentation of a metaphysical question, then goes on to its development and ends with its answer.

The Presentation of a Metaphysical Question

Seen from the point of view of sound common sense, Philosophy, according to Hegel, is the "world stood on its head." Hence the peculiar nature of our task calls for some preliminary definition. This arises out of the dual nature of metaphysical questioning.

Firstly, every metaphysical question always covers the whole range of metaphysical problems. In every case it is itself the whole. Secondly, every metaphysical question can only be put in such a way that the questioner as such is by his very questioning involved in the question.

From this we derive the following pointer: metaphysical questioning has to be put as a whole and has always to be based on the essential situation of existence, which puts the question. We question here and now, on our own account. Our existence—a community of scientists, teachers and students—is ruled by science. What essential things are happening to us in the foundations of our existence, now that science has become our passion?

The fields of the sciences lie far apart. Their methodologies are fundamentally different. This disrupted multiplicity of disciplines is today only held together by the technical organization of the Universities and their faculties, and maintained as a unit of meaning by the practical aims of those faculties. As against this, however, the root of the sciences in their essential ground has atrophied.

And yet—insofar as we follow their most specific intentions—in all the sciences we are related to what-is. Precisely from the point of view of the sciences no field takes precedence over another, neither Nature over History nor vice versa. No one methodology is superior to another. Mathematical knowledge is no stricter than philological or historical knowledge. It has merely the characteristic of "exactness," which is not to be identified with strictness. To demand exactitude of history would be to offend against the idea of the kind of strictness that pertains to the humanistic sciences. The world-relationship which runs through all the sciences as such constrains them to seek what-is *in itself*, with a view to rendering it, according to its quiddity (*Wasgehalt*) and its modality (*Seinsart*), an object of investigation and basic definition. What the sciences accomplish, ideally speaking, is an approximation to the essential nature of all things.

This distinct world-relationship to what-is in itself is sustained and guided by a freely chosen attitude on the part of our human

* Translated by R. F. C. Hull and Alan Crick. From *Existence and Being* by Martin Heidegger, edited with an introduction by Werner Brock. London: Vision Press Ltd., 1949. Reprinted by permission of the publisher.

existence. It is true that the pre-scientific and extra-scientific activities of man also relate to what-is. But the distinction of science lies in the fact that, in an altogether specific manner, it and it alone explicitly allows the object itself the first and last word. In this objectivity of questioning, definition and proof there is a certain limited submission to what-is, so that this may reveal itself. This submissive attitude taken up by scientific theory becomes the basis of a possibility: the possibility of science acquiring a leadership of its own, albeit limited, in the whole field of human existence. The world-relationship of science and the attitude of man responsible for it can, of course, only be fully understood when we see and understand what is going on in the world-relationship so maintained. Man—one entity (*Seiendes*) among others—"pursues" science. In this "pursuit" what is happening is nothing less than the irruption of a particular entity called "Man" into the whole of what-is, in such a way that in and through this irruption what-is manifests itself *as* and *how* it is. The manner in which the revelatory irruption occurs is the chief thing that helps what-is to become what it is.

This triple process of world-relationship, attitude, and irruption—a radical unity—introduces something of the inspiring simplicity and intensity of *Da-sein* into scientific existence. If we now explicitly take possession of scientific *Da-sein* as clarified by us, we must necessarily say:

That to which the world-relationship refers is what-is—and nothing else.

That by which every attitude is moulded is what-is—and nothing more.

That with which scientific exposition effects its "irruption" is what-is—and beyond that, nothing.

But it is not remarkable that precisely at that point where scientific man makes sure of his surest possesion he should speak of something else? What is to be investigated is what-is—and nothing else; only what-is—and nothing more; simply and solely what-is—and beyond that, nothing.

But what about this "nothing"? Is it only an accident that we speak like that quite naturally? Is it only a manner of speaking—and nothing more?

But why worry about this Nothing? "Nothing" is absolutely rejected by science and abandoned as null and void (*das Nichtige*). But if we abandon Nothing in this way are we not, by that act, really admitting it? Can we, though, speak of an admission when we admit Nothing? But perhaps this sort of crosstalk is already degenerating into an empty wrangling about words.

Science, on the other hand, has to assert its soberness and seriousness afresh and declare that it is concerned solely with what-is. Nothing—how can it be for science anything other than a horror and a phantasm? If science is right then one thing stands firm: science wishes to know nothing of Nothing. Such is after all the strictly scientific approach to Nothing. We know it by wishing to know nothing of Nothing.

Science wishes to know nothing of Nothing. Even so the fact remains that at the very point where science tries to put its own essence in words it invokes the aid of Nothing. It has recourse to the very thing it rejects. What sort of schizophrenia is this?

A consideration of our momentary existence as one ruled by science has landed us in the thick of an argument. In the course of this argument a question has already presented itself. The question only requires putting specifically: What about Nothing?

The Development of the Question

The development of our enquiry into Nothing is bound to lead us to a position where either the answer will prove possible or the impossibility of an answer will become evident. "Nothing" is admitted. Science, by adopting an attitude of superior indifference, abandons it as that which "is not."

All the same we shall endeavor to enquire into Nothing. What is Nothing? Even the initial approach to this question shows us something out of the ordinary. So questioning, we postulate Nothing as something that somehow or other "is"—as an entity (*Seiendes*). But it is nothing of the sort. The question as to the what and wherefore of Nothing turns the thing questioned into its opposite. The question deprives itself of its own object.

Accordingly, every answer to this question is impossible from the start. For it necessarily moves in the form that Nothing "is" this, that or the other. Question and answer are equally nonsensical in themselves where Nothing is concerned.

Hence even the rejection by science is superfluous. The commonly cited basic rule of all thinking—the proposition that contradiction must be avoided—and common "logic" rule out the question. For thinking, which is essentially always thinking about something, would, in thinking of Nothing, be forced to act against its own nature.

Because we continually meet with failure as soon as we try to turn Nothing into a subject, our enquiry into Nothing is already at an end—always assuming, of course, that in this enquiry "logic" is the highest court of appeal, that reason is the means and thinking the way to an original comprehension of Nothing and its possible revelation.

But, it may be asked, can the law of "logic" be assailed? Is not reason indeed the master in this enquiry into Nothing? It is in fact only with reason's help that we can define Nothing in the first place and postulate it as a problem—though a problem that consumes only itself. For Nothing is the negation (*Verneinung*) of the totality of what-is: that which is absolutely not. But at this point we bring Nothing into the higher category of the Negative (*Nichthaftes*) and therefore of what is negated. But according to the overriding and unassailable teachings of "logic" negation is a specific act of reason. How, then, in our enquiry into Nothing and into the very possibility of holding such

an equiry can we dismiss reason? Yet is it so sure just what we are postulating? Does the Not (*das Nicht*), the state of being negated (*die Verneintheit*) and hence negation itself (*Verneinung*), in fact represent that higher category under which Nothing takes its place as a special kind of thing negated? Does Nothing "exist" only because the Not, i.e. negation exists? Or is it the other way about? Does negation and the Not exist only because Nothing exists? This has not been decided—indeed, it has not even been explicitly asked. We assert: "Nothing" is more original than the Not and negation.

If this thesis is correct then the very possibility of negation as an act of reason, and consequently reason itself, are somehow dependent on Nothing. How, then, can reason attempt to decide this issue? May not the apparent nonsensicality of the question and answer where Nothing is concerned only rest, perhaps, on the blind obstinacy of the roving intellect?

If, however, we refuse to be led astray by the formal impossibility of an equiry into Nothing and still continue to enquire in the face of it, we must at least satisfy what remains the fundamental pre-requisite for the full pursuit of any enquiry. If Nothing as such is still to be enquired into, it follows that it must be "given" in advance. We must be able to encounter it.

Where shall we seek Nothing? Where shall we find Nothing? In order to find something must we not know beforehand that it is there? Indeed we must! First and foremost we can only look if we have presupposed the presence of a thing to be looked for. But here the thing we are looking for is Nothing. Is there after all a seeking without pre-supposition, a seeking complemented by a pure finding?

However that may be, we do know "Nothing" if only as a term we bandy about every day. This ordinary hackneyed Nothing, so completely taken for granted and rolling off our tongue so casually—we can even give an off-hand "definition" of it:

Nothing is the complete negation of the totality of what-is.

Does not this characteristic of Nothing

point, after all, in the direction from which alone it may meet us?

The totality of what-is must be given beforehand so as to succumb as such to the negation from which Nothing is then bound to emerge.

But, even apart from the questionableness of this relationship between negation and Nothing, how are we, as finite beings, to render the whole of what-is in its totality accessible *in itself*—let alone to ourselves? We can, at a pinch, think of the whole of what-is as an "idea" and then negate what we have thus imagined in our thoughts and "think" it negated. In this way we arrive at the formal concept of an imaginary Nothing, but never Nothing itself. But Nothing is nothing, and between the imaginary and the "authentic" (*eigentlich*) Nothing no difference can obtain, if Nothing represents complete lack of differentiation. But the "authentic" Nothing—is this not once again that latent and nonsensical idea of a Nothing that "is"? Once again and for the last time rational objections have tried to hold up our search, whose legitimacy can only be attested by a searching experience of Nothing.

As certainly as we shall never comprehend absolutely the totality of what-is, it is equally certain that we find ourselves placed in the midst of what-is and that this is somehow revealed in totality. Ultimately there is an essential difference between comprehending the totality of what-is and finding ourselves in the midst of what-is-in-totality. The former is absolutely impossible. The latter is going on in existence all the time.

Naturally enough it looks as if, in our everyday activities, we were always holding on to this or that actuality (*Seiendes*), as if we were lost in this or that region of what-is. However fragmentary the daily round may appear it still maintains what-is, in however shadowy a fashion, within the unity of a "whole." Even when, or rather, precisely when we are not absorbed in things or in our own selves, this "wholeness" comes over us—for example, in real boredom. Real boredom is still far off when this book or that play, this activity or that stretch of idleness merely bores us. Real boredom

comes when "one is bored." This profound boredom, drifting hither and thither in the abysses of existence like a mute fog, draws all things, all men and oneself along with them, together in a queer kind of indifference. This boredom reveals what-is in totality.

There is another possibility of such revelation, and this is in the joy we feel in the presence of the being—not merely the person —of someone we love.

Because of these moods in which, as we say, we "are" this or that (i.e. bored, happy, etc.) we find ourselves (*befinden uns*) in the midst of what-is-in-totality, wholly pervaded by it. The affective state in which we find ourselves not only discloses, according to the mood we are in, what-is-in-totality, but this disclosure is at the same time far from being a mere chance occurrence and is the ground-phenomenon of our *Da-sein*.

Our "feelings," as we call them, are not just the fleeting concomitant of our mental or volitional behaviour, nor are they simply the cause and occasion of such behavior, nor yet a state that is merely "there" and in which we come to some kind of understanding with ourselves.

Yet, at the very moment when our moods thus bring us face to face with what-is-in-totality they hide the Nothing we are seeking. We are now less than ever of the opinion that mere negation of what-is-in-totality as revealed by these moods of ours can in fact lead us to Nothing. This could only happen in the first place in a mood so peculiarly revelatory in its import as to reveal Nothing itself.

Does there ever occur in human existence a mood of this kind, through which we are brought face to face with Nothing itself?

This may and actually does occur, albeit rather seldom and for moments only, in the key-mood of dread (*Angst*). By "dread" we do not mean "anxiety" (*Aengstlichkeit*), which is common enough and is akin to nervousness (*Furchtsamkeit*)—a mood that comes over us only too easily. Dread differs absolutely from fear (*Furcht*). We are always *afraid* of this or that definite thing, which threatens us in this or that definite way. "Fear of" is generally "fear about" something. Since fear has this characteristic limitation—"of" and "about"—the man who is afraid, the nervous man, is always bound by the thing he is afraid of or by the state in which he finds himself. In his efforts to save himself from this "something" he becomes uncertain in relation to other things; in fact, he "loses his bearings" generally.

In dread no such confusion can occur. It would be truer to say that dread is pervaded by a peculiar kind of peace. And although dread is always "dread of," it is not dread of this or that. "Dread of" is always a dreadful feeling "about"—but not about this or that. The indefiniteness of *what* we dread is not just lack of definition: it represents the essential impossibility of defining the "what." The indefiniteness is brought out in an illustration familiar to everybody.

In dread, as we say, "one feels something uncanny."[1] What is this "something" (*es*) and this "one"? We are unable to say what gives "one" that uncanny feeling. "One" just feels it generally (*im Ganzen*). All things, and we with them, sink into a sort of indifference. But not in the sense that everything simply disappears; rather, in the very act of drawing away from us everything turns towards us. This withdrawal of what-is-in-totality, which then crowds round us in dread, this is what oppresses us. There is

nothing to hold on to. The only thing that remains and overwhelms us whilst what-is slips away, is this "nothing."

Dread reveals Nothing.

In dread we are "in suspense" (*wir schweben*). Or, to put it more precisely, dread holds us in suspense because it makes what-is-in-totality slip away from us. Hence we too, as existents in the midst of what-is, slip away from ourselves along with it. For this reason it is not "you" or "I" that has the uncanny feeling, but "one." In the trepidation of this suspense where there is nothing to hold on to, pure *Da-sein* is all that remains.

Dread strikes us dumb. Because what-is-in-totality slips away and thus forces Nothing to the fore, all affirmation (lit. "Is"-saying: *"Ist"-Sagen*) fails in the face of it. The fact that when we are caught in the uncanniness of dread we often try to break the empty silence by words spoken at random, only proves the presence of Nothing. We ourselves confirm that dread reveals Nothing —when we have got over our dread. In the lucid vision which supervenes while yet the experience is fresh in our memory we must needs say that what we were afraid of was "actually" (*eigentlich:* also "authentic") Nothing. And indeed Nothing itself, Nothing as such, was there.

With this key-mood of dread, therefore, we have reached that event in our *Da-sein* which reveals Nothing, and which must therefore be the starting-point of our enquiry.

What about Nothing?

---

[1] *ist es einem unheimlich.* Literally, "it is uncanny to one."

The Answer to the Question

The answer which alone is important for our purpose has already been found if we take care to ensure that we really do keep to the problem of Nothing. This necessitates changing man into his *Da-sein*—a change always occasioned in us by dread—so that we may apprehend Nothing as and how it reveals itself in dread. At the same time we have finally to dismiss those characteristics of

Nothing which have not emerged as a result of our enquiry.

"Nothing" is revealed in dread, but not as something that "is." Neither can be taken as an object. Dread is not an apprehension of Nothing. All the same, Nothing is revealed in and through dread, yet not, again, in the sense that Nothing appears as if detached and apart from what-is-in-totality when we have that "uncanny" feeling. We would say rather: in dread Nothing functions as if *at one with* what-is-in-totality. What do we mean by "at one with"?

In dread what-is-in-totality becomes untenable (*hinfällig*). How? What-is is not annihilated (*vernichtet*) by dread, so as to leave Nothing over. How could it, seeing that dread finds itself completely powerless in face of what-is-in-totality! What rather happens is that Nothing shows itself as essentially belonging to what-is while this is slipping away in totality.

In dread there is no annihilation of the whole of what-is in itself; but equally we cannot negate what-is-in-totality in order to reach Nothing. Apart from the fact that the explicitness of a negative statement is foreign to the nature of dread as such, we would always come too late with any such negation intended to demonstrate Nothing. For Nothing is anterior to it. As we said, Nothing is "at one with" what-is as this slips away in totality.

In dread there is a retreat from something, though it is not so much a flight as a spellbound (*gebannt*) peace. This "retreat from" has its source in Nothing. The latter does not attract: its nature is to repel. This "repelling from itself" is essentially an "expelling into": a conscious gradual relegation to the vanishing what-is-in-totality (*das entgleitenlassende Verweisen auf das versinkende Seiende im Ganzen*). And this total relegation to the vanishing what-is-in-totality—such being the form in which Nothing crowds round us in dread—is the essence of Nothing: nihilation.[2] Nihilation is neither an annihilation (*Vernichtung*) of what-is,

nor does it spring from negation (*Verneinung*). Nihilation cannot be reckoned in terms of annihilation or negation at all. Nothing "nihilates" (*nichtet*) of itself.

Nihilation is not a fortuitous event; but, understood as the relegation to the vanishing what-is-in-totality, it reveals the latter in all its till now undisclosed strangeness as the pure "Other"—contrasted with Nothing.

Only in the clear night of dread's Nothingness is what-is as such revealed in all its original overtness (*Offenheit*): that it "is" and is not Nothing. This verbal appendix "and not Nothing" is, however, not an *a posteriori* explanation but an *a priori* which alone makes possible any revelation of what-is. The essence of Nothing as original nihilation lies in this: that it alone brings *Da-sein* face to face with what-is as such.

Only on the basis of the original manifestness of Nothing can our human *Da-sein* advance towards and enter into what-is. But insofar as *Da-sein* naturally relates to what-is, as that which it is not and which itself is, Da-sein *qua Da-sein* always proceeds from Nothing as manifest.[3]

Da-sein means *being projected into* Nothing (*Hineingehaltenheit in das Nichts*).

Projecting into Nothing, *Da-sein* is already beyond what-is-in-totality. This "being beyond" (*Hinaussein*) what-is we call Transcendence. Were *Da-sein* not, in its essential basis, transcendent, that is to say, were it not projected from the start into Nothing, it could never relate to what-is, hence could have no self-relationship.

Without the original manifest character of Nothing there is no self-hood and no freedom.

Here we have the answer to our question about Nothing. Nothing is neither an object nor anything that "is" at all. Nothing occurs neither by itself nor "apart from" what-is as a sort of adjunct. Nothing is that which makes the revelation of what-is as such possible for our human existence. Nothing not merely provides the conceptual opposite of

---

[2] *Nichtung.* The word "nihilation" has been coined in the hope of conveying Heidegger's meaning. His thought, which is also expressed in the verb *nichten* at the end of this paragraph and elsewhere, is very difficult to reproduce in the negative terms of its German formulation. *Nichtung* is a causative process, and *nichten* a causative and intransitive verb. Ordinarily we would express the process in positive terms and would speak, for instance, of the "becoming" of Nothing or the "debecoming" of something, as would be clear in a term like *Nichtswerdung* or the *Entwerdung* of Meister Eckhart. A concept as important to philosophy as was the acceptance by psychology of an independent dynamic death-instinct (*Todestrieb*).

[3] Cf. "Tao Te Ching" XL: for though all creatures under heaven are the products of Being, Being itself is the product of Not-being. [Trans.]

what-is but is also an original part of essence (*Wesen*). It is in the Being (*Sein*) of what-is that the nihilation of Nothing (*das Nichten des Nichts*) occurs.

But now we must voice a suspicion which has been withheld far too long already. If it is only through "projecting into Nothing" that our *Da-sein* relates to what-is, in other words, has any existence, and if Nothing is only made manifest originally in dread, should we not have to be in a continual suspense of dread in order to exist at all? Have we not, however, ourselves admitted that this original dread is a rare thing? But above all, we all exist and are related to actualities which we ourselves are not and which we ourselves are—without this dread. Is not this dread, therefore, an arbitrary invention and the Nothing attributed to it an exaggeration?

Yet what do we mean when we say that this original dread only occurs in rare moments? Nothing but this: that as far as we are concerned and, indeed, generally speaking, Nothing is always distorted out of its original state. By what? By the fact that in one way or another we completely lose ourselves in what-is. The more we turn to what-is in our dealings the less we allow it to slip away, and the more we turn aside from Nothing. But all the more certainly do we thrust ourselves into the open superficies of existence.

And yet this perpetual if ambiguous aversion from Nothing accords, within certain limits, with the essential meaning of Nothing. It—Nothing in the sense of nihilation—relegates us to what-is. Nothing "nihilates" unceasingly, without our really knowing what is happening—at least, not with our everyday knowledge.

What could provide more telling evidence of the perpetual, far-reaching and yet ever-dissimulated overtness of Nothing in our existence, than negation? This is supposed to belong to the very nature of human thought. But negation cannot by any stretch of imagination produce the Not out of itself as a means of distinguishing and contrasting given things, thrusting this Not between them, as it were. How indeed could nega-

tion produce the Not out of itself, seeing that it can only negate when something is there to be negated? But how can a thing that is or ought to be negated be seen as something negative (*nichthaft*) unless all thinking as such is on the look-out for the Not? But the Not can only manifest itself when its source—the nihilation of Nothing and hence Nothing itself—is drawn out of concealment. The Not does not come into being through negation, but negation is based on the Not, which derives from the nihilation of Nothing. Nor is negation only a mode of nihilating behaviour, i.e. behaviour based *a priori* on the nihilation of Nothing.

Herewith we have proved the above thesis in all essentials: Nothing is the source of negation, not the other way about. If this breaks the sovereignty of reason in the field of enquiry into Nothing and Being, then the fate of the rule of "logic" in philosophy is also decided. The very idea of "logic" disintegrates in the vortex of a more original questioning.

However often and however various negation—whether explicit or not—permeates all thinking, it cannot *of itself* be a completely valid witness to the manifestation of Nothing as an essential part of *Da-sein*. For negation cannot be cited either as the sole or even the chief mode of nihilation, with which, because of the nihilation of Nothing, *Da-sein* is saturated. More abysmal than the mere propriety of rational negation is the harshness of opposition and the violence of loathing. More responsible the pain of refusal and the mercilessness of an interdict. More oppressive the bitterness of renunciation.

These possible modes of nihilating behaviour, through which our *Da-sein* endures, even if it does not master, the fact of our being thrown upon the world[4] are not modes of negation merely. That does not prevent them from expressing themselves in and through negation. Indeed, it is only then that

---

[4] *Geworfenheit.* Literally "thrownness." M. Corbin in his French version of this essay, renders the term by *déréliction.* The underlying thought would appear to be that in *Da-sein* we are "thrown there" and left derelict, like a thing cast up by the waves on the seashore

he empty expanse of negation is really revealed. The permeation of *Da-sein* by annihilating modes of behavior points to the perpetual, ever-dissimulated manifestness of Nothing, which only dread reveals in all its originality. Here, of course, we have the reason why original dread is generally repressed in *Da-sein*. Dread is there, but sleeping. All *Da-sein* quivers with its breathing: the pulsation is slightest in beings that are timorous, and is imperceptible in the "Yea, yea!" and "Nay, nay!" of busy people; it is readiest in the reserved, and surest of all in the courageous. But this last pulsation only occurs for the sake of that for which it expends itself, so as to safeguard the supreme greatness of *Da-sein*.

The dread felt by the courageous cannot be contrasted with the joy or even the comfortable enjoyment of a peaceable life. It stands—on the hither side of all such contrasts—in secret union with the serenity and gentleness of creative longing.

Original dread can be awakened in *Da-sein* at any time. It need not be awakened by any unusual occurrence. Its action corresponds in depth to the shallowness of its possible cause. It is always on the brink, yet only seldom does it take the leap and drag us with it into the state of suspense.

Because our *Da-sein* projects into Nothing on this basis of hidden dread, man becomes the "stand-in" (*Platzhalter*) for Nothing. So finite are we that we cannot, of our own resolution and will, bring ourselves originally face to face with Nothing. So bottomlessly does finalisation (*Verendlichung*) dig into existence that our freedom's peculiar and profoundest finality fails.

This projection into Nothing on the basis of hidden dread is the overcoming of what-is-in-totality: Transcendence.

Our enquiry into Nothing will, we said, lead us straight to metaphysics. The name "metaphysics" derives from the Greek τὰ μετὰ τὰ φυσικά. This quaint title was later interpreted as characterising the sort of enquiry which goes μετὰ—trans, beyond—what-is as such.

Metaphysics is an enquiry over and above what-is, with a view to winning it back again as such and in totality for our understanding.

In our quest for Nothing there is similar "going beyond" what-is, conceived as what-is-in-totality. It therefore turns out to be a "metaphysical" question. We said in the beginning that such questioning had a double characteristic: every metaphysical question at once embraces the whole of metaphysics, and in every question the being (*Da-sein*) that questions is himself caught up in the question.

To what extent does the question about Nothing span and pervade the whole of metaphysics?

Since ancient times metaphysics has expressed itself on the subject of Nothing in the highly ambiguous proposition: *ex nihilo nihil fit*—nothing comes from nothing. Even though the proposition as argued never made Nothing itself the real problem, it nevertheless brought out very explicitly, from the prevailing notions about Nothing, the overriding fundamental concept of what-is.

Classical metaphysics conceives Nothing as signifying Not-being (*Nichtseiendes*), that is to say, unformed matter which is powerless to form itself into "being"[5] and cannot therefore present an appearance (εἶδος). What has "being" is the self-creating product (*Gebilde*) which presents itself as such in an image (*Bild*), i.e. something seen (*Anblick*). The origin, law and limits of this ontological concept are discussed as little as Nothing itself.

Christian dogma, on the other hand, denies the truth of the proposition *ex nihilo nihil fit* and gives a twist to the meaning of Nothing, so that it now comes to mean the absolute absence of all "being"[6] outside God: *ex nihilo fit—ens creatum*: the created being is made out of nothing. "Nothing" is now the conceptual opposite of what truly and authentically (*eigentlich*) "is"; it becomes the *summum ens*, God as *ens increatum*. Here, too, the interpretation of Nothing points to the fundamental concept of what-is. Meta-

---

[5] Here *Seiendes* has been translated by "being," with the proviso that it be understood as "being" in simple contrast to "not-being." Heidegger's *Sein* is always rendered as "Being" with a capital B.

[6] See note 5.

physical discussion of what-is, however, moves on the same plane as the enquiry into Nothing. In both cases the questions concerning Being (*Sein*) and Nothing as such remain unasked. Hence we need not be worried by the difficulty that if God creates "out of nothing" he above all must be able to relate himself to Nothing. But if God is God he cannot know Nothing, assuming that the "Absolute" excludes from itself all nullity (*Nichtigkeit*).

This crude historical reminder shows Nothing as the conceptual opposite of what truly and authentically "is," i.e. as the negation of it. But once Nothing is somehow made a problem this contrast not only undergoes clearer definition but also arouses the true and authentic metaphysical question regarding the Being of what-is. Nothing ceases to be the vague opposite of what-is: it now reveals itself as integral to the Being of what-is.

"Pure Being and pure Nothing are thus one and the same." This proposition of Hegel's ("The Science of Logic," I, WW III, p. 74) is correct. Being and Nothing hang together, but not because the two things—from the point of view of the Hegelian concept of thought—are one in their indefiniteness and immediateness, but because Being itself is finite in essence and is only revealed in the Transcendence of *Da-sein* as projected into Nothing.

If indeed the question of Being as such is the all-embracing question of metaphysics, then the question of Nothing proves to be such as to span the whole metaphysical field. But at the same time the question of Nothing pervades the whole of metaphysics only because it forces us to face the problem of the origin of negation, that is to say, forces a decision about the legitimacy of the rule of "logic" in metaphysics.

The old proposition *ex nihilo nihil fit* will then acquire a different meaning, and one appropriate to the problem of Being itself, so as to run: *ex nihilo omne ens qua ens fit*: every being, so far as it is a being, is made out of nothing. Only in the Nothingness of *Da-sein* can what-is-in-totality—and this in

accordance with its peculiar possibilities, i.e. in a finite manner—come to itself. To what extent, then, has the enquiry into Nothing, i indeed it be a metaphysical one, included our own questing *Da-sein?*

Our *Da-sein* as experienced here and now is, we said, ruled by science. If our *Da-sein* so ruled, is put into this question concerning Nothing, then it follows that it must itself have been put in question by this question.

The simplicity and intensity of scientific *Da-sein* consist in this: that it relates in a special manner to what-is and to this alone. Science would like to abandon Nothing with a superior gesture. But now, in this question of Nothing, it becomes evident that scientific *Da-sein* is only possible when projected into Nothing at the outset. Science can only come to terms with itself when it does not abandon Nothing. The alleged soberness and superiority of science becomes ridiculous if it fails to take Nothing seriously. Only because Nothing is obvious can science turn what-is into an object of investigation. Only when science proceeds from metaphysics can it conquer its essential task ever afresh, which consists not in the accumulation and classification of knowledge but in the perpetual discovery of the whole realm of truth, whether of Nature or of History.

Only because Nothing is revealed in the very basis of our *Da-sein* is it possible for the utter strangeness of what-is to dawn on us. Only when the strangeness of what-is forces itself upon us does it awaken and invite our wonder. Only because of wonder, that is to say, the revelation of Nothing, does the "Why?" spring to our lips. Only because this "Why?" is possible as such can we seek for reasons and proofs in a definite way. Only because we can ask and prove are we fated to become enquirers in this life.

The enquiry into Nothing puts us, the enquirers, ourselves in question. It is a metaphysical one.

Man's *Da-sein* can only relate to what-is by projecting into Nothing. Going beyond what-is is of the essence of *Da-sein*. But this "going beyond" is metaphysics itself. That is why metaphysics belongs to the nature of man. It is neither a department of scholastic philosophy nor a field of chance ideas. Metaphysics is the ground-phenomenon of *Da-sein*. It is *Da-sein* itself. Because the truth of metaphysics is so unfathomable there is always the lurking danger of profoundest error. Hence no scientific discipline can hope to equal the seriousness of metaphysics. Philosophy can never be measured with the yard-stick of the idea of science.

Once the question we have developed as to the nature of Nothing is really asked by and among our own selves, then we are not bringing in metaphysics from the outside. Nor are we simply "transporting" ourselves into it. It is completely out of our power to transport ourselves into metaphysics because, in so far as we exist, we are already there. Φύσει γὰρ, ὦ φίλει, ἔνεστί τις φιλοσοφία τῇ τοῦ ἀνδρὸς διανοία (Plato: Phaedrus 279a).

While man exists there will be philosophising of some sort. Philosophy, as we call it, is the setting in motion of metaphysics; and in metaphysics philosophy comes to itself and sets about its explicit tasks. Philosophy is only set in motion by leaping with all its being, as only it can, into the ground-possibilities of being as a whole. For this leap the following things are of crucial importance: firstly, leaving room for what-is-in-totality; secondly, letting oneself go into Nothing, that is to say, freeing oneself from the idols we all have and to which we are wont to go cringing; lastly, letting this "suspense" range where it will, so that it may continually swing back again to the ground-question of metaphysics, which is wrested from Nothing itself:

Why is there any Being at all—why not far rather Nothing?

SUGGESTED READINGS

Aristotle. *Metaphysics*. New York: Columbia University Press, 1952, Book Delta, Chaps. VII, VIII; Books Eta, Theta, Lambda.

Bradley, Francis H. *Appearance and Reality: A Metaphysical Essay*. Oxford: Clarendon Press, 1951, Chaps. 2 and 8.

Feibleman, James. "On Substance," *Review of Metaphysics,* VIII (1954-55), pp. 373–78.

Hume, David. *Treatise of Human Nature*. Oxford: Clarendon Press, 1951, Part I, Sec. 6; Part IV, Sec. 5, 6.

James, William. *Pragmatism and Four Essays from The Meaning of Truth*. New York: Meridian Books, Inc., 1958, Chaps. 3 and 4.

Kant, Immanuel. *Critique of Pure Reason*. New York: St. Martin's Press, 1956, "Transcendental Analytic," Bk. II, Chap. 2, Sec. 3, 3a.

Leibniz, Gottfried W. *Monadology*. La Salle, Illinois: The Open Court Publishing Co., 1957.

Locke, John. *Essay Concerning Human Understanding*. Chicago: Henry Regnery, 1956, Book II, Chap. 23.

Lovejoy, Arthur O. *The Great Chain of Being*. Cambridge, Massachusetts: Harvard University Press, 1957.

Nelson, Everett J. "A Defense of Substance," *The Philosophical Review*, LVI (1947), pp. 491–509.

Pap, Arthur. *Elements of Analytic Philosophy*. New York: The Macmillan Company, 1949, Chap. 7.

Russell, Bertrand. *Analysis of Matter*. London: K. Paul, Trench, Trubner & Co., Ltd., 1927, Chap. 23.

Santayana, George. *The Realms of Being*. New York: Charles Scribner's Sons, 1937, Book I, Chaps. II-V.

Sellars, Roy W. "Causality and Substance," *Philosophical Review,* LII (1943), pp. 1–27.

Spinoza, Benedict de. *Ethics*. New York: St. Martin's Press, 1956, Props. 1–15.

PART IV

MIND, BODY, AND THE PERSON

INTRODUCTION

Few men would deny that they had bodies. But is man merely a body or is he something more? To a great many ordinary men as well as a large number of philosophers, there seems to be good reason to hold the latter. The attempt to determine what this "more" consists of, however, has led to a number of perplexing problems which continue to divide the philosophical world. In modern philosophy, Descartes perceived clearly and distinctly that he was essentially a mind, although he also admitted that he was or had a body. If man either is or has both a mind and a body, what is the interrelation between them? If they mutually interact, how can such activity be explained? Is man a single entity, a substance enduring through his various experiences, or is he some sort of a loosely-connected, functional unity? When he says "I" or speaks of "self," what, if anything, does he refer to by these words? These—together with the concept of "person" and the question of the possibility of personal immortality—are a few of the major problems involved in the mind-body controversy.

Charlie Dunbar Broad (1887–   ), Professor of Philosophy at Cambridge University from 1933 until his retirement in 1953, has greatly influenced Anglo-American philosophy by such works as *Scientific Thought* (1923), *The Mind and Its Place in Nature* (1925), and *Five Types of Ethical Theory* (1930). In his chapter "The Traditional Problem of Body and Mind," he raises the question of whether minds act on the organisms they animate and vice-versa and analyzes some of the answers given. He finds the arguments against "two-sided interaction" inconclusive and claims that some of the arguments in favor of it lend strong support to the theory. On the other hand, although the theory of "Psycho-neural Parallelism" may be true, he holds there is inadequate empirical evidence to support it.

In the first chapter of his book *The Concept of Mind* (1949), Gilbert Ryle (1900–   ), Professor of Metaphysical Philosophy at Oxford University and editor of *Mind,* attacks what he calls "Descartes's myth." His claim, which he defends via an analysis of ordinary language, is that Descartes's division of man into mind and body is a category mistake. He does not deny that mental processes occur, but argues that this is not equivalent to saying that physical processes occur, and therefore it is senseless either to disjoin or conjoin them. It should be noted that a myth is not a fairy story. He tells us consequently that "To explode a myth is . . . not to deny the facts but to re-allocate them."

David Hume (1711–76), a famous empiricist and skeptic, whose works include *An Inquiry Concerning Human Understanding* (1748) and *Dialogues Concerning Natural Religion* (1779), argues in his major work, *Treatise of Human Nature* (1739), that we have no idea of the self as ordinarily assumed. "For my part," he tells us, "when I enter most intimately into what I call *myself,* I always stumble on some particular perception or other. . . ." His empirical conclusion is that the self is a bundle or collection of different perceptions. His skeptical conclusion is that he cannot decide questions concerning personal identity.

Hume's denial of a substance view of the self is adhered to by many, but by no means all, contemporary philosophers. Charles A. Campbell (1897–   ), Professor at the University of Glasgow, defended the substance view of the self in his Gifford Lectures (1954 and 1955), entitled *On Selfhood and Godhood.* He claims that there is no valid argument against substantial theories as such, and that no alternative is acceptable. His view of substance is not that of Locke or Kant, however. He argues that the self is at least a spiritual substance and that although self-identity is a wider conception than personal identity, they are two aspects of one ontological entity.

Peter F. Strawson (1919–   ), a Fellow of University College, Oxford, is author of *Introduction to Logical Theory* (1952) and *Individuals: An Essay in Descriptive Metaphysics* (1959). In "Persons" he shows how it is impossible to hold either the "no subject" view or the dualistic view of the self. The problem of the principle of unity is seen to be no problem, for there is no such principle, he claims, once one sees the primitiveness of the concept of a "person" and the unique logical character of certain predicates.

CHARLIE DUNBAR BROAD

THE TRADITIONAL PROBLEM OF BODY AND MIND*

In the last Chapter we considered organisms simply as complicated material systems which behave in certain characteristic ways. We did

* From *The Mind and Its Place in Nature* by C. D. Broad, Chapter III. London: Routledge & Kegan Paul Ltd., 1925. Reprinted by permission of the publisher.

not consider the fact that some organisms are animated by minds, and that all the minds of whose existence we are certain animate organisms. And we did not deal with those features in the behaviour of certain organisms which are commonly supposed to be due to the mind which animates the organism. It is such facts as these, and certain problems to which they have given rise, which I mean to discuss in the present Chapter. There is a question which has been argued about for some centuries now under the name of "Interaction"; this is the question whether minds really do act on the organisms which they animate, and whether organisms really do act on the minds which animate them. (I must point out at once that I imply no particular theory of mind or body by the word "to animate." I use it as a perfectly neutral name to express the fact that a certain mind is connected in some peculiarly intimate way with a certain body, and, under normal conditions with no other body.) This is a fact even on a purely behaviouristic theory of mind; on such a view to say that the mind M animates the body B would mean that the body B, in so far as it behaves in certain ways, *is* the mind M. A body which did not act in these ways would be said not to be animated by a mind. And a different Body B', which acted in the same general way as B, would be said to be animated by a different mind M'.)

The problem of Interaction is generally discussed at the level of enlightened common-sense; where it is assumed that we know pretty well what we mean by "mind," by "matter" and by "causation." Obviously no solution which is reached at that level can claim to be ultimate. If what we call "matter" should turn out to be a collection of spirits of low intelligence, as Leibniz thought, the argument that mind and body are so unlike that their interaction is impossible would become irrelevant. Again, if causation be nothing but regular sequence and concomitance, as some philosophers have held, it is ridiculous to regard psychoneural parallelism, and interaction as mutually exclusive alternatives. For interaction will mean no more than parallelism, and parallelism will mean to less than interaction. Nevertheless I am going to discuss the arguments here at the common-sense level, because they are so incredibly bad and yet have imposed upon so many learned men.

We start then by assuming a developed mind and a developed organism as two distinct things, and by admitting that the two are now intimately connected in some way or other which I express by saying that "this mind *animates* this organism." We assume that bodies are very much as enlightened common-sense believes them to be; and that, even if we cannot define "causation," we have some means of recognizing when it is present and when it is absent. The question then is: "Does a mind ever act on the body which it animates, and does a body ever act on the mind which animates it?" The answer which common-sense would give to both questions is: "Yes, certainly." On the face of it my body acts on my mind whenever a pin is stuck into the former and a painful sensation thereupon arises in the latter. And, on the face of it, my mind acts on my body whenever a desire to move my arm arises in the former and is followed by this movement in the latter. Let us call this common-sense view "Two-sided Interaction." Although it seems so obvious it has been denied by probably a majority of philosophers and a majority of physiologists. So the question is: "Why should so many distinguished men, who have studied the subject, have denied the apparently obvious fact of Two-sided Interaction?"

The arguments against Two-sided Interaction fall into two sets:—Philosophical and Scientific. We will take the philosophical arguments first; for we shall find that the professedly scientific arguments come back in the end to the principles or prejudices which are made explicit in the philosophical arguments.

Philosophical Arguments against Two-sided Interaction

No one can deny that there is a close correlation between certain bodily events and certain mental events, and conversely. Therefore anyone who denies that there is action of mind on body and of body on mind must presumably hold (*a*) that concomitant variation is not an adequate criterion of causal connexion, and (*b*) that the other feature which is essential for causal connection is absent in the case of body and mind. Now the common philosophical argument is that minds and mental states are so extremely unlike bodies and bodily states that it is inconceivable that the two should be causally connected. It is certainly true that, if minds and mental events are just what they seem to be to introspection and nothing more, and if bodies and bodily events are just what enlightened common-sense thinks them to be and nothing more, the two *are* extremely unlike. And this fact is supposed to show that, however closely correlated certain pairs of events in mind and body respectively may be, they cannot be causally connected.

Evidently the assumption at the back of this argument is that concomitant variation, together with a high enough degree of likeness, is an adequate test for causation; but that no amount of concomitant variation can establish causation in the absence of a high enough degree of likeness. Now I am inclined to admit part of this assumption. I think it is practically certain that causation does not simply *mean* concomitant variation. (And, if it did, *cadit quaestio.*) Hence the existence of the latter is not *ipso facto* a proof of the presence of the former. Again, I think it is almost certain that concomitant variation between A and B is not in fact a sufficient sign of the presence of a *direct* causal relation between the two. (I think it may perhaps be a sufficient sign of *either* a direct causal relation between A and B *or* of several causal relations which indirectly unite A and B through the medium of other terms C, D, etc.) So far I agree with the assumptions of the argument. But I cannot see the least reason to think that the other characteristic, which must be added to concomitant variation before we can be sure that A and B are causally connected, is a high degree of likeness between the two. One would like to know just how unlike two events may be before it becomes impossible to admit the existence of a causal relation between them. No one hesitates to hold that draughts and colds in the head are causally connected, although the two are extremely unlike each other. If the unlikeness of draughts and colds in the head does not prevent one from admitting a causal connexion between the two, why should the unlikeness of volitions and voluntary movements prevent one from holding that they are causally connected? To sum up. I am willing to admit that an adequate criterion of causal connexion needs some other relation between a pair of events beside concomitant variation; but I do not believe for a moment that this other relation is that of qualitative likeness.

This brings us to a rather more refined form of the argument against Interaction. It is said that, whenever we admit the existence of a causal relation between two events, these two events (to put it crudely) must also form parts of a single substantial whole. *E.g.,* all physical events are spatially related and form one great extended whole. And the mental events which would commonly be admitted to be causally connected are always events in a single mind. A mind is a substantial whole of a peculiar kind too. Now it is said that between bodily events and mental events there are no relations such as those which unite physical events in different parts of the same Space or mental events in the history of the same mind. In the absence of such relations, binding mind and body into a single substantial whole, we cannot admit that bodily and mental events can be causally connected with each other, no matter how closely correlated their variations may be.

This is a much better argument than the argument about qualitative likeness and unlikeness. If we accept the premise that causal relations can subsist only between terms which form parts of a single substantial whole must we deny that mental and bodily events can be causally connected? I do not think that we need. (i) It is of course perfectly true that an organism and the mind which animates it do not form a physical whole, and that they do not form a mental whole; and these, no doubt, are the two kinds of substantial whole with which we are most familiar. But it does not follow that a mind and its organism do not form a substantial whole of *some* kind. There, plainly, is the extraordinary intimate union between the two which I have called "animation" of the one by the other. Even if the mind be just what it seems to introspection, and the body be just what it seems to perception aided by the more precise methods of science, this seems to me to be enough to make a mind and its body a substantial whole. Even so extreme a dualist about Mind and Matter as Descartes occasionally suggests that a mind and its body together form a quasi-substance; and, although we may quarrel with the language of the very numerous philosophers who have said that the mind is "the form" of its body, we must admit that such language would never have seemed plausible unless a mind and its body together had formed something very much like a single substantial whole.

(ii) We must, moreover, admit the possibility that minds and mental events have properties and relations which do not reveal themselves to introspection, and that bodies and bodily events may have properties and relations which do not reveal themselves to perception or to physical and chemical experiment. In virtue of these properties and relations the two together may well form a single substantial whole of the kind which is alleged to be needed for causal interaction. Thus, if we accept the premise of the argument, we have no right to assert that mind and body *cannot* interact; but only the much

more modest proposition that introspection and perception do not suffice to assure us that mind and body are so interrelated that they *can* interact.

(iii) We must further remember that the Two-sided Interactionist is under no obligation to hold that the *complete* conditions of any mental event are bodily or that the complete conditions of any bodily event are mental. He needs only to assert that some mental events include certain bodily events among their necessary conditions, and that some bodily events include certain mental events among their necessary conditions. If I am paralysed my volition may not move my arm; and, if I am hypnotised or intensely interested or frightened, a wound may not produce a painful sensation. Now, if the complete cause and the complete effect in all interaction include both a bodily and a mental factor, the two wholes will be related by the fact that the mental constituents belong to a single mind, that the bodily constituents belong to a single body, and that this mind animates this body. This amount of connexion should surely be enough to allow of causal interaction.

This will be the most appropriate place to deal with the contention that, in voluntary action, and there only, we are immediately acquainted with an instance of causal connexion. If this be true the controversy is of course settled at once in favour of the Interactionist. It is generally supposed that this view was refuted once and for all by Mr. Hume in his *Enquiry concerning Human Understanding* (Sect. VII, Part I). I should not care to assert that the doctrine in question is true; but I do think that it is plausible, and I am quite sure that Mr. Hume's arguments do not refute it. Mr. Hume uses three closely connected arguments. (1) The connexion between a successful volition and the resulting bodily movement is as mysterious and as little self-evident as the connexion between any other event and its effect. (2) We have to learn from experience which of our volitions will be effective and which will not. *E.g.*, we do not know, until we have tried, that we can voluntarily move our arms and cannot voluntarily move our livers.

And again, if a man were suddenly paralysed, he would still expect to be able to move his arm voluntarily, and would be surprised when he found that it kept still in spite of his volition. (3) We have discovered that the immediate consequence of a volition is a change in our nerves and muscles, which most people know nothing about; and is not the movement of a limb, which most people believe to be its immediate and necessary consequence.

The second and third arguments are valid only against the contention that we know immediately that a volition to make a certain movement is the *sufficient* condition for the happening of that movement. They are quite irrelevant to the contention that we know immediately that the volition is a *necessary* condition for the happening of just that movement at just that time. No doubt many other conditions are also necessary, *e.g.,* that our nerves and muscles shall be in the right state; and these other necessary conditions can be discovered only by special investigation. Since our volitions to move our limbs are in fact followed in the vast majority of cases by the willed movement, and since the other necessary conditions are not very obvious, it is natural enough that we should think that we know immediately that our volition is the *sufficient* condition of the movement of our limbs. If we think so, we are certainly wrong; and Mr. Hume's arguments prove that we are. But they prove nothing else. It does not follow that we are wrong in thinking that we know, without having to wait for the result, that the volition is a *necessary* condition of the movement.

It remains to consider the first argument. Is the connexion between cause and effect as mysterious and as little self-evident in the case of the voluntary production of bodily movement as in all other cases? If so, we must hold that the first time a baby wills to move its hand it is just as much surprised to find its hand moving as it would be to find its leg moving or its nurse bursting into flames. I do not profess to know anything about the infant mind; but it seems to me that this is a wildly paradoxical consequence, for which there is no evidence or likelihood.

But there is no need to leave the matter there. It is perfectly plain that, in the case of volition and voluntary movement, there *is* a connexion between the cause and the effect which is not present in other cases of causation, and which does make it plausible to hold that in this one case the nature of the effect can be foreseen by merely reflecting on the nature of the cause. The peculiarity of a volition as a cause-factor is that it involves as an essential part of it the idea of the effect. To say that a person has a volition to move his arm involves saying that he has an idea of his arm (and not of his leg or his liver) and an idea of the position in which he wants his arm to be. It is simply silly in view of this fact to say that there is no closer connexion between the desire to move my arm and the movement of my arm than there is between this desire and the movement of my leg or my liver. We cannot detect any analogous connexion between cause and effect in causal transaction which we view wholly from outside, such as the movement of a billiard-ball by a cue. It is therefore by no means unreasonable to suggest that, in the one case of our own voluntary movements, we can see without waiting for the result that such and such a volition is a necessary condition of such and such a bodily movement.

It seems to me then that Mr. Hume's arguments on this point are absolutely irrelevant, and that it may very well be true that in volition we positively know that our desire for such and such a bodily movement is a necessary (though not a sufficient) condition of the happening of just that movement at just that time. On the whole then I conclude that the philosophical arguments certainly do not disprove Two-sided Interaction, and that they do not even raise any strong presumption against it. And, while I am not prepared definitely to commit myself to the view that, in voluntary movement, we positively *know* that the mind acts on the body, I do think that this opinion is quite plausible when properly stated and that the arguments which have been brought against it are worthless. I pass therefore to the scientific arguments.

Scientific Arguments against Two-sided Interaction

There are, so far as I know, two of these. One is supposed to be based on the physical principle of the Conservation of Energy, and on certain experiments which have been made on human bodies. The other is based on the close analogy which is said to exist between the structures of the physiological mechanism of reflex action and that of voluntary action. I will take them in turn.

1. *The Argument from energy.* It will first be needful to state clearly what is asserted by the principle of the Conservation of Energy. It is found that, if we take certain material systems, *e.g.,* a gun, a cartridge, and a bullet, there is a certain magnitude which keeps approximately constant throughout all their changes. This is called "Energy." When the gun has not been fired it and the bullet have no motion, but the explosive in the cartridge has great chemical energy. When it has been fired the bullet is moving very fast and has great energy of movement. The gun, though not moving fast in its recoil, has also great energy of movement because it is very massive. The gases produced by the explosion have some energy of movement and some heat-energy, but much less chemical energy than the unexploded charge had. These various kinds of energy can be measured in common units according to certain conventions. To an innocent mind there seems to be a good deal of "cooking" at this stage, *i.e.,* the conventions seem to be chosen and various kinds and amounts of concealed energy seem to be postulated in order to make the principle come out right at the end. I do not propose to go into this in detail, for two reasons. In the first place, I think that the conventions adopted and the postulates made, though somewhat suggestive of the fraudulent company-promoter, can be justified by their coherence with certain experimental facts, and that they are not simply made *ad hoc.* Secondly, I shall show that the Conservation of Energy is absolutely irrelevant to the question at issue, so that it

would be waste of time to treat it too seriously in the present connexion. Now it is found that the total energy of all kinds in this system, when measured according to these conventions, is aproximately the same in amount though very differently distributed after the explosion and before it. If we had confined our attention to a part of this system and *its* energy this would not have been true. The bullet, *e.g.,* had no energy at all before the explosion and a great deal afterwards. A system like the bullet, the gun, and the charge, is called a "Conservative System"; the bullet alone, or the gun and the charge, would be called "Non-conservative Systems." A conservative system might therefore be defined as one whose total energy is redistributed, but not altered in amount, by changes that happen within it. Of course a given system might be conservative for some kinds of change and not for others.

So far we have merely defined a "Conservative System," and admitted that there are systems which, for some kinds of change at any rate, answer approximately to our definition. We can now state the Principle of the Conservation of Energy in terms of the conceptions just defined. The principle asserts that every material system is either itself conservative, or, if not, is part of a larger material system which is conservative. We may take it that there is good inductive evidence for this proposition.

The next thing to consider is the experiments on the human body. These tend to prove that a living body, with the air that it breathes and the food that it eats, forms a conservative system to a high degree of approximation. We can measure the chemical energy of the food given to a man, and that which enters his body in the form of Oxygen breathed in. We can also, with suitable apparatus, collect, measure and analyse the air breathed out, and thus find its chemical energy. Similarly, we can find the energy given out in bodily movement, in heat, and in excretion. It is alleged that, on the average, whatever the man may do, the energy of his bodily movements is exactly accounted for by the energy given to him in the form of food and of Oxygen. If you take the energy put in in food and Oxygen, and subtract the energy given out in waste-products, the balance is almost exactly equal to the energy put out in bodily movements. Such slight differences as are found are as often on one side as on the other, and are therefore probably due to unavoidable experimental errors. I do not propose to criticise the interpretation of these experiments in detail, because, as I shall show soon, they are completely irrelevant to the problem of whether mind and body interact. But there is just one point that I will make before passing on. It is perfectly clear that such experiments can tell us only what happens on the average over a long time. To know whether the balance was accurately kept at every moment we should have to kill the patient at each moment and analyse his body so as to find out the energy present then in the form of stored-up products. Obviously we cannot keep on killing the patient in order to analyse him, and then reviving him in order to go on with the experiment. Thus it would seem that the results of the experiment are perfectly compatible with the presence of quite large excesses or defects in the total bodily energy at certain moments, provided that these average out over longer periods. However, I do not want to press this criticism; I am quite ready to accept for our present purpose the traditional interpretation which has been put on the experiments.

We now understand the physical principle and the experimental facts. The two together are generally supposed to prove that mind and body cannot interact. What precisely is the argument, and is it valid? I imagine that the argument, when fully stated, would run somewhat as follows: "I will to move my arm, and it moves. If the volition has anything to do with causing the movement we might expect energy to flow from my mind to my body. Thus the energy of my body ought to receive a measurable in-

crease, not accounted for by the food that I eat and the Oxygen that I breathe. But no such physically unaccountable increases of bodily energy are found. Again, I tread on a tin-tack, and a painful sensation arises in my mind. If treading on the tack has anything to do with causing the sensation we might expect energy to flow from my body to my mind. Such energy would cease to be measurable. Thus there ought to be a noticeable decrease in my bodily energy, not balanced by increases anywhere in the physical system. But such unbalanced decreases of bodily energy are not found." So it is concluded that the volition has nothing to do with causing my arm to move, and that treading on the tack has nothing to do with causing the painful sensation.

Is this argument valid? In the first place it is important to notice that the conclusion does not follow from the Conservation of Energy and the experimental facts alone. The real premise is a tacitly assumed proposition about causation; viz., that, if a change in A has anything to do with causing a change in B, energy must leave A and flow into B. This is neither asserted nor entailed by the Conservation of Energy. What *it* says is that, *if* energy leaves A, it must appear in something else, say B; so that A and B together form a conservative system. Since the Conservation of Energy is not itself the premise for the argument against Interaction, and since it does not entail that premise, the evidence for the Conservation of Energy is not evidence against Interaction. Is there any independent evidence for the premise? We may admit that it *is* true of many, though not of all, transactions within the physical realm. But there are cases where it is not true even of purely physical transactions; and, even if it were always true in the physical realm, it would not follow that it must also be true of trans-physical causation. Take the case of a weight swinging at the end of a string hung from a fixed point. The total energy of the weight is the same at all positions in its course. It is thus a conservative system. But at every moment the direction and velocity of the weight's motion are different, and the proportion between its kinetic and its potential energy is constantly changing. These changes are caused by the pull of the string, which acts in a different direction at each different moment. The string makes no difference to the total energy of the weight; but it makes all the difference in the world to the particular way in which the weight moves and the particular way in which the energy is distributed between the potential and the kinetic forms. This is evident when we remember that the weight would begin to move in an utterly different course if at any moment the string were cut.

Here, then, we have a clear case even in the physical realm where a system is conservative but is continually acted on by something which affects its movement and the distribution of its total energy. Why should not the mind act on the body in this way? If you say that you can see how a string can affect the movement of a weight, but cannot see how a volition could affect the movement of a material particle, you have deserted the scientific argument and have gone back to one of the philosophical arguments. Your real difficulty is either that volitions are so very unlike movements, or that the volition is in your mind whilst the movement belongs to the physical realm. And we have seen how little weight can be attached to these objections.

The fact is that, even in purely physical systems, the Conservation of Energy does not explain what changes will happen or when they will happen. It merely imposes a very general limiting condition on the changes that are possible. The fact that the system composed of bullet, charge, and gun, in our earlier example, is conservative does not tell us that the gun ever will be fired, or when it will be fired if at all, or what will cause it to go off, or what forms of energy will appear if and when it does go off. The change in this case is determined by pulling the trigger. Likewise the mere fact that the human body and its neighborhood form a conservative system does not explain any particular bodily movement; it does not ex-

plain why I ever move at all, or why I sometimes write, sometimes walk, and sometimes swim. To explain the happening of these particular movements at certain times it seems to be essential to take into account the volitions which happen from time to time in my mind; just as it is essential to take the string into account to explain the particular behaviour of the weight, and to take the trigger into account to explain the going off of the gun at a certain moment. The difference between the gun-system and the body-system is that a little energy does flow into the former when the trigger is pulled, whilst it is alleged that none does so when a volition starts a bodily movement. But there is not even this amount of difference between the body-system and the swinging weight.

Thus the argument from energy has no tendency to disprove Two-sided Interaction. It has gained a spurious authority from the august name of the Conservation of Energy. But this impressive principle proves to have nothing to do with the case. And the real premise of the argument is not self-evident, and is not universally true even in purely intra-physical transactions. In the end this scientific argument has to lean on the old philosophic arguments; and we have seen that these are but bruised reeds. Nevertheless, the facts brought forward by the argument from energy do throw some light on the *nature* of the interaction between mind and body, assuming this to happen. They do suggest that all the energy of our bodily actions comes out of and goes back into the physical world, and that minds neither add energy to nor abstract it from the latter. What they do, if they do anything, is to determine that at a given moment so much energy shall change from the chemical form to the form of bodily movement; and they determine this, so far as we can see, without altering the total amount of energy in the physical world.

2. *The Argument from the Structure of the Nervous System.* There are purely reflex actions, like sneezing and blinking, in which there is no reason to suppose that the mind

plays any essential part. Now we know the nervous structure which is used in such acts as these. A stimulus is given to the outer end of an efferent nerve; some change or other runs up this nerve, crosses a synapsis between this and an afferent nerve, travels down the latter to a muscle, causes the muscle to contract, and so produces a bodily movement. There seems no reason to believe that the mind plays any essential part in this process. The process may be irreducibly vital, and not merely physico-chemical; but there seems no need to assume anything more than this. Now it is said that the whole nervous system is simply an immense complication of interconnected nervous arcs. The result is that a change which travels inwards has an immense number of alternative paths by which it may travel outwards. Thus the reaction to a given stimulus is no longer one definite movement, as in the simple reflex. Almost any movement may follow any stimulus according to the path which the afferent disturbance happens to take. This path will depend on the relative resistance of the various synapses at the time. Now a variable response to the same stimulus is characteristic of deliberate as opposed to reflex action.

These are the facts. The argument based on them runs as follows. It is admitted that the mind has nothing to do with the causation of purely reflex actions. But the nervous structure and the nervous processes involved in deliberate action do not differ in kind from those involved in reflex action; they differ only in degree of complexity. The variability which characterises deliberate action is fully explained by the variety of alternative paths and the variable resistances of the synapses. So it is unreasonable to suppose that the mind has any more to do with causing deliberate actions than it has to do with causing reflex actions.

I think that this argument is invalid. In the first place I am pretty sure that the persons who use it have before their imagination a kind of picture of how mind and body must interact if they interact at all. They find that the facts do not answer to this picture, and so they conclude that there is no interaction. The picture is of the following kind. They think of the mind as sitting somewhere in a hole in the brain, surrounded by telephones. And they think of the efferent disturbance as coming to an end at one of these telephones and there affecting the mind. The mind is then supposed to respond by sending an efferent impulse down another of these telephones. As no such hole, with efferent nerves stopping at its walls and afferent nerves starting from them, can be found, they conclude that the mind can play no part in the transaction. But another alternative is that this picture of how the mind must act if it acts at all is wrong. To put it shortly, the mistake is to confuse a gap in an explanation with a spatio-temporal gap, and to argue from the absence of the latter to the absence of the former.

The Interactionist's contention is simply that there is a gap in any purely physiological explanation of deliberate action; *i.e.*, that all such explanations fail to account completely for the facts because they leave out one necessary condition. It does not follow in the least that there must be a spatio-temporal breach of continuity in the physiological conditions, and that the missing condition must fill this gap in the way in which the movement of a wire fills the spatio-temporal interval between the pulling of a bell-handle and the ringing of a distant bell. To assume this is to make the mind a kind of physical object, and to make its action a kind of mechanical action. Really, the mind and its actions are not literally in Space at all, and the time which is occupied by the mental event is no doubt *also* occupied by some part of the physiological process. Thus I am inclined to think that much of the force which this argument actually exercises on many people is simply due to the presupposition about the *modus operandi* of interaction, and that it is greatly weakened when this presupposition is shown to be a mere prejudice due to our limited power of envisaging unfamiliar alternative possibilities.

We can, however, make more detailed

objections to the argument than this. There is a clear introspective difference between the mental accompaniment of voluntary action and that of reflex action. What goes on in our minds when we decide with difficulty to get out of a hot bath on a cold morning is obviously extremely different from what goes on in our minds when we sniff pepper and sneeze. And the difference is qualitative; it is not a mere difference of complexity. This difference has to be explained somehow; and the theory under discussion gives no plausible explanation of it. The ordinary view that, in the latter case, the mind is not acting on the body at all; whilst, in the former, it is acting on the body in a specific way, does at least make the introspective difference between the two intelligible.

Again, whilst it is true that deliberate action differs from reflex action in its greater variability of response to the same stimulus, this is certainly not the whole or the most important part of the difference between them. The really important difference is that, in deliberate action, the response is varied *appropriately* to meet the special circumstances which are supposed to exist at the time or are expected to arise later; whilst reflex action is not varied in this way, but is blind and almost mechanical. The complexity of the nervous system explains the *possibility* of variation; it does not in the least explain why the alternative which actually takes place should as a rule be appropriate and not merely haphazard. And so again it seems as if some factor were in operation in deliberate action which is not present in reflex action; and it is reasonable to suppose that this factor is the volition in the mind.

It seems to me that this second scientific argument has no tendency to disprove interaction; but that the facts which it brings forward do tend to suggest the particular form which interaction probably takes if it happens at all. They suggest that what the mind does to the body in voluntary action, if it does anything, is to lower the resistance of certain synapses and to raise that of others. The result is that the nervous current follows such a course as to produce the particular movement which the mind judges to be appropriate at the time. On such a view the difference between reflex, habitual, and deliberate actions for the present purpose becomes fairly plain. In pure reflexes the mind cannot voluntarily affect the resistance of the synapses concerned, and so the action takes place in spite of it. In habitual action it deliberately refrains from interfering with the resistance of the synapses, and so the action goes on like a complicated reflex. But it *can* affect these resistances if it wishes, though often only with difficulty; and it is ready to do so if it judges this to be expedient. Finally, it may lose the power altogether. This would be what happens when a person becomes a slave to some habit, such as drug-taking.

I conclude that, at the level of enlightened common-sense at which the ordinary discussion of Interaction moves, no good reason has been produced for doubting that the mind acts on the body in volition, and that the body acts on the mind in sensation. The philosophic arguments are quite inconclusive; and the scientific arguments, when properly understood, are quite compatible with Two-sided Interaction. At most they suggest certain conclusions as to the form which interaction probably takes if it happens at all.

Difficulties in the Denial of Interaction

I propose now to consider some of the difficulties which would attend the denial of Interaction, still keeping the discussion at the same common-sense level. If a man denies the action of body on mind he is at once in trouble over the causation of new sensations. Suppose that I suddenly tread on an unsuspected tin-tack. A new sensation suddenly comes into my mind. This is an event, and it presumably has some cause. Now, however carefully I introspect and retrospect, I can find no other mental event which is adequate to account for the fact that just that sensation has arisen at just that moment. If I reject the common-sense view that treading on the tack is an essential part of the cause of the sensation, I must suppose either that it is uncaused, or that it is caused by other events in my mind which I cannot discover by introspection or retrospection, or that it is caused telepathically by other finite minds or by God. Now enquiry of my neighbours would show that it is not caused telephathically by any event in their minds which they can introspect or remember. Thus anyone who denies the action of body on mind, and admits that sensations have causes, must postulate either (*a*) immense numbers of unobservable states in his own mind; or (*b*) as many unobservable states in his neighbours' minds, together with telepathic action; or (*c*) some non-human spirit together with telepathic action. I must confess that the difficulties which have been alleged against the action of body on mind seem to be mild compared with those of the alternative hypotheses which are involved in the denial of such action.

The difficulties which are involved in the denial of the action of mind on body are at first sight equally great; but I do not think that they turn out to be so serious as those which are involved in denying the action of body on mind. The *prima facie* difficulty is this. The world contains many obviously artificial objects, such as books, bridges, clothes, etc. We know that, if we go far enough back in the history of their production, we always do in fact come on the actions of some human body. And the minds connected with these bodies did design the objects in question, did will to produce them, and did believe that they were initiating and guiding the physical process by means of these designs and volitions. If it be true that the mind does not act on the body, it follows that the designs and volitions in the agents' minds did not in fact play any part

in the production of books, bridges, clothes, etc. This appears highly paradoxical. And it is an easy step from it to say that anyone who denies the action of mind on body must admit that books, bridges, and other such objects *could* have been produced even though there had been no minds, no thought of these objects and no desire for them. This consequence seems manifestly absurd to common-sense, and it might be argued that it reflects its absurdity back on the theory which entails it.

The man who denies that mind can act on body might deal with this difficulty in two ways: 1. He might deny that the conclusion *is* intrinsically absurd. He might say that human bodies are extraordinarily complex physical objects, which probably obey irreducible laws of their own, and that we really do not know enough about them to set limits to what their unaided powers could accomplish. This is the line which Spinosa took. The conclusion, it would be argued, *seems* absurd only because the state of affairs which it contemplates is so very unfamiliar. We find it difficult to imagine a body like ours without a mind like ours; but, if we could get over this defect in our powers of imagination, we might have no difficulty in admitting that such a body could do all the things which our bodies do. I think it must be admitted that the difficulty is not so great as that which is involved in denying the action of body on mind. There we had to postulate *ad hoc* utterly unfamiliar entities and modes of action; here it is not certain that we should have to do this.

2. The other line of argument would be to say that the alleged consequence does not necessarily follow from denying the action of mind on body. I assume that both parties admit that causation is something more than mere *de facto* regularity of sequence and concomitance. If they do not, of course the whole controversy between them becomes futile; for there will certainly be causation between mind and body and between body and mind, in the only sense in which there is causation anywhere. This being presupposed, the following kind of answer is logi-

cally possible. When I say that B could not have happened unless A had happened, there are two alternative possibilities. (*a*) A may itself be an indispensable link in any chain of causes which ends up with B. (*b*) A may not itself be a link in any chain of causation which ends up with B. But there may be an indispensable link α in any such chain of causation, and A may be a necessary accompaniment or sequent of α. These two possibilities may be illustrated by diagrams. (*a*) is represented by the figure below:—

$$A_0 \quad\quad A \quad\quad A_1 \quad\quad A_2 \quad\quad B$$
$$\bullet \longrightarrow \bullet \longrightarrow \bullet \longrightarrow \bullet \longrightarrow \bullet$$

The two forms of (*b*) are represented by the two figures below:—

$$\begin{array}{ccccc} & A & & & \\ A_0 & \uparrow & A_1 & A_2 & B \\ \bullet \longrightarrow & \bullet \longrightarrow & \bullet \longrightarrow & \bullet \longrightarrow & \bullet \\ & \alpha & & & \end{array}$$

$$\text{and} \quad \begin{array}{ccccc} & & \nearrow \bullet A & & \\ A_0 & & A_1 & A_2 & B \\ \bullet \longrightarrow & \bullet \longrightarrow & \bullet \longrightarrow & \bullet \longrightarrow & \bullet \\ & \alpha & & & \end{array}$$

Evidently, if B cannot happen unless α precedes, and if α cannot happen without A accompanying or immediately following it, B will not be able to happen unless A precedes it. And yet A will have had no part in causing B. It will be noticed that, on this view, α has a complex effect AA_1, of which a certain part, viz., A_1 is sufficient by itself to produce A_2 and ultimately B. Let us apply this abstract possibility to our present problem. Suppose that B is some artificial object, like a book or a bridge. If we admit that this could not have come into existence unless a certain design and volition had existed in a certain mind, we could interpret the facts in two ways. (*a*) We could hold that the design and volition are themselves an indispensable link in the chain of causation which ends in the production of a bridge or a book. This is the common view, and it requires us to admit the action of mind

on body. (*b*) We might hold that the design and the volition are not themselves a link in the chain of causation which ends in the production of the artificial object; but that they are a necessary accompaniment or sequent of something which *is* an indispensable link in this chain of causation. On this view the chain consists wholly of physical events; but one of these physical events (viz., some event in the brain) has a complex consequent. One part of this consequent is purely physical, and leads by purely physical causation to the ultimate production of a bridge or a book. The other is purely mental, and consists of a certain design and volition in the mind which animates the human body concerned. If this has any consequences they are purely mental. Each part of this complex consequent follows with equal necessity; this particular brain-state could no more have existed without such and such a mental state accompanying or following it than it could have existed without such and such a bodily movement following it. If we are willing to take some such view as this, we can admit that certain objects could not have existed unless there had been designs of them and desires for them; and yet we could consistently deny that these desires and designs have any effect on the movements of our bodies.

It seems to me then that the doctrine which I will call "One-sided Action of Body on Mind" is logically possible; i.e., a theory which accepts the action of body on mind but denies the action of mind on body. But I do not see the least reason to accept it, since I see no reason to deny that mind acts on body in volition. One-sided Action has, I think, generally been held in the special form called "Epiphenomenalism." I take this doctrine to consist of the following four propositions: (1) Certain bodily events cause certain mental events. (2) No mental event plays any part in the causation of any bodily event. (3) No mental event plays any part in the causation of any other mental event. Consequently (4) all mental events are caused by bodily events and by them only. Thus Epiphenomenalism is just One-sided

Action of Body on Mind, together with a special theory about the nature and structure of mind. This special theory does not call for discussion here, where I am dealing only with the relations between minds and bodies, and am not concerned with a detailed analysis of mind. In a later chapter we shall have to consider the special features of Epiphenomenalism.

Arguments in Favour of Interaction

The only arguments *for* One-sided Action of Body on Mind or for Parallelism are the arguments *against* Two-sided Interaction; and these, as we have seen, are worthless. Are there any arguments in favour of Two-sided Interaction? I have incidentally given two which seem to me to have considerable weight. In favour of the action of mind on body is the fact that we seem to be immediately aware of a causal relation when we voluntarily try to produce a bodily movement, and that the arguments to show that this cannot be true are invalid. In favour of the action of body on mind are the insuperable difficulties which I have pointed out in accounting for the happening of new sensations on any other hypothesis. There are, however, two other arguments which have often been thought to prove the action of mind on body. These are (1) an evolutionary argument, first used, I believe, by William James; and (2) the famous "telegram argument." They both seem to me to be quite obviously invalid.

1. The evolutionary argument runs as follows: It is a fact, which is admitted by persons who deny Two-sided Interaction, that minds increase in complexity and power with the growth in complexity of the brain and nervous system. Now, if the mind makes no difference to the actions of the body, this development on the mental side is quite unintelligible from the point of view of natural selection. Let us imagine two animals whose brains and nervous systems were of the same degree of complexity; and suppose, if possible, that one had a mind and the other had none. If the mind makes no difference to the behaviour of the body the chance of survival and of leaving descendants will clearly be the same for the two animals. Therefore natural selection will have no tendency to favour the evolution of mind which has actually taken place. I do not think that there is anything in this argument. Natural selection is a purely negative process; it simply tends to eliminate individuals and species which have variations unfavourable to survival. Now, by hypothesis, the possession of a mind is not *unfavourable* to survival; it simply makes no difference. Now it may be that the existence of a mind of such and such a kind is an inevitable consequence of the existence of a brain and nervous system of such and such a degree of complexity. Indeed we have seen that some such view is essential if the opponent of Two-sided Interaction is to answer the common-sense objection that artificial objects could not have existed unless there had been a mind which designed and desired them. On this hypothesis there is no need to invoke natural selection twice over, once to explain the evolution of the brain and nervous system, and once to explain the evolution of the mind. If natural selection will account for the evolution of the brain and nervous system, the evolution of the mind will follow inevitably, even though it adds nothing to the survival-value of the organism. The plain fact is that natural selection does not account for the origin or for the growth in complexity of anything whatever; and therefore it is no objection to any particular theory of the relations of mind and body that, if it were true, natural selection would not explain the origin and development of mind.

2. The "telegram argument" is as follows: Suppose there were two telegrams, one saying "Our son has been killed," and the other

saying: "Your son has been killed." And suppose that one or other of them was delivered to a parent whose son was away from home. As physical stimuli they are obviously extremely alike, since they differ only in the fact that the letter "*Y*" is present in one and absent in the other. Yet we know that the reaction of the person who received the telegram might be very different according to which one he received. This is supposed to show that the reaction of the body cannot be wholly accounted for by bodily causes, and that the mind must intervene causally in some cases. Now I have very little doubt that the mind does play a part in determining the action of the recipient of the telegram; but I do not see why this argument should prove it to a person who doubted or denied it. If two very similar stimuli are followed by two very different results, we are no doubt, justified in concluding that these stimuli are not the complete causes of the reactions which follow them. But of course it would be admitted by every one that the receipt of the telegram is not the complete cause of the recipient's reaction. We all know that his brain and nervous system play an essential part in any reaction that he may make to the stimulus. The question then is whether the minute structure of his brain and nervous system, including in this the supposed traces left by past stimuli and past reactions, is not enough to account for the great difference in his behaviour on receiving two very similar stimuli. Two keys may be very much alike, but one may fit a certain lock and the other may not. And, if the lock be connected with the trigger of a loaded gun, the results of "stimulating" the system with one or other of the two keys will be extremely different. We know that the brain and nervous system are very complex, and we commonly suppose that they contain more or less permanent traces and linkages due to past stimuli and reactions. If this be granted, it is obvious that two very similar stimuli may produce very different results, simply because one fits in with the internal structure of the brain and nervous system whilst the other does not. And I do not see how we can be sure that anything more is needed to account for the mere difference of reaction adduced by the "telegram argument."

The Positive Theory of Parallelism

The doctrine of Psycho-physical Parallelism, or, as I prefer to call it, "Psycho-neural Parallelism," has two sides to it. One is negative; it is the denial that mind acts on body and the denial that body acts on mind. With this side of it I have now dealt to the best of my ability, and have argued that there is no reason to believe it and tolerably good reason to disbelieve it. But Psychoneural Parallelism has also a positive side, which might be accepted by one who rejected its negative side. The positive assertion of Parallelism is that there is a one-one correlation between events in a mind and events in the brain and nervous system of the body which it animates. Is there any reason to believe this on empirical grounds?

I think we must say that it *may* be true, but that it is a perfectly enormous assumption unless there be some general metaphysical ground for it; and that the empirical evidence for it is, and will always remain, quite inadequate. The assertion is that to every particular change in the mind there corresponds a certain change in the brain which this mind animates, and that to every change in the brain there corresponds a certain change in the mind which animates this brain. What kind of empirical evidence *could* there be for such an assertion? At best the evidence would be of the following kind: "I have observed a number of brains and the minds which animate them; and I have never found a change in either which was not correlated with a specific change in the other. And all other people who have made similar observations have found the same thing." *If* we had evidence of this sort the positive side of Parallelism would be a straightforward inductive generalisation of it; *i.e.,* an argument from "A has never been observed to happen without B" to "A never does happen without B." But actually we have *no* evidence whatever of this kind. No one person in the world ever has observed, or probably ever will observe, a brain and *its* mind. The only mind that he can observe is his own and the only brains that he can observe are those of others. Nor is this the worst. We can very rarely observe other men's brains at all, and never when they are alive and in a state of normal consciousness. Thus the actual empirical data for the positive side of Parallelism consist of observations on brains which are no longer animated by minds at all or whose animating minds are in abeyance. And these minds could not be directly observed by us even if they were present and functioning normally.

It will therefore be worth while to consider carefully what amount of parallelism we really are justified on empirical grounds in assuming. 1. We have fairly good reasons for thinking that the existence and general integrity of a brain and nervous system is a necessary condition for the manifestation of a mind to itself and to other minds. We do not positively know that it is a sufficient condition; and the question whether it be so or not will have to be discussed later in this book. Our evidence is all of the following kind: (i) In the absence of a brain and nervous system we see none of those external actions which we know in our own case to be accompanied by consciousness. (ii) The brain and nervous system are known to increase in complexity up to a certain age, and we have observed in ourselves and can infer from the behaviour of others a corresponding growth in mental complexity. (iii) Soon after men have ceased to show signs of consciousness by their external behaviour their brains and nervous systems break up. It must be admitted that it might be maintained with almost equal

plausibility that these last facts show that the integrity of the brain and nervous system is dependent on the presence of the mind. We might just as well argue that the brain begins to break up because the mind has ceased to animate it, as that the mind has ceased to manifest itself because the brain has begun to break up. In fact, seeing the order in which we actually get our knowledge of the two facts, the former is *prima facie* the more plausible interpretation. (iv) In many cases where men's behaviour has been so odd as to suggest that their minds are abnormal, it is known that their brains have been injured or it has been found after their death that their brains were in an abnormal state. On the other hand, it must be admitted that the brains of some lunatics on dissection show no systematic differences from those of normal people. It would obviously be absurd to talk of "Parallelism" in reference to this very general relation between the integrity and complexity of the brain and nervous system, on the one hand, and the manifestation of a human mind, on the other.

2. There is, however, empirical evidence which goes rather further than this. It is found that wounds in certain parts of the brain make specific differences to the mind. *E.g.,* a wound in one part may be followed by a loss of memory for spoken words, and so on. Unfortunately, similar results can often be produced by causes like hypnotism or like those which psycho-analysts discuss. And here there is no positive empirical evidence that these specific areas of the brain are affected. Again, there seems to be some evidence that, after a time and within certain limits, another part of the brain can take over the functions of a part that has been injured. Thus the most that we can say is that the general integrity of certain parts of the brain seems to be at least a temporarily necessary condition for the manifestation of certain specific kinds of mental activity. It remains doubtful how far any given area is indispensable for a given kind of mental activity, and whether there may not be some kinds of activity which, though dependent

like all others on the general integrity of the brain, are not specially correlated with any particular area. We might sum up these facts by saying that there is good evidence for a considerable amount of "Departmental Parallelism" between mind and brain.

3. The orthodox Parallelist, however, goes much further than this, and much beyond the most rigid departmental parallelism. He would hold, not merely that there is a strict correlation between each distinguishable *department* of mental life and some specific *area* of the brain, but also that there is a strict parallelism of *events*. *E.g.*, he holds, not merely that I could not remember at all unless a certain area of my brain were intact, but also that if I now remember eating my breakfast there is a certain event in this area uniquely correlated with this particular mental event. And by "unique correlation" he means that if some other mental state had happened now instead of this particular memory there would necessarily have been a different brain-event, and conversely. So far as I know there is not, and could not possibly be, any empirical evidence for this "Parallelism of Events," as I will call it. For (i), while a man is conscious and can observe events in his own mind, his brain is not open to inspection by himself or by anyone else. And, when his brain is open to inspection, he is not likely to be in a position to introspect or to tell others what is going on in his mind, even if something is happening there at the time. (ii) In any case the events in the brain which are supposed to correspond to particular events in the mind would be admitted to be too minute to be observable even under the most favourable circumstances. They are as purely hypothetical as the motions of electrons, without the advantage that the assumption of them enables us to predict better than we could otherwise do what states of mind a man will probably have under given circumstances.

It seems to me then that there is no empirical evidence at all for a Parallelism of Events between mind and brain. If this doctrine is to be held, the grounds for it

must be general. *E.g. psycho-neural* parallelism might be plausible if, on other grounds, we saw reason to accept psycho-*physical* parallelism, *i.e.*, the doctrine that *every* physical event is correlated with a specific mental event, and conversely. And the wider doctrine might be defended as helping to explain the apparent origin of life and mind from apparently non-living and non-conscious matter. This is a question which we shall have to discuss later; all that I am concerned to argue at present is that, at the level of enlightened common-sense and apart from some general metaphysical theory of the nature of matter and mind, there is no adequate evidence for a psycho-neural parallelism of events. And, as parallelism has commonly been defended on the ground that it is established by empirical scientific investigation of the brain and nervous system, this fact is worth pointing out.

If there is no reason *for* psycho-neural parallelism of events, is there any positive reason *against* it? Some philosophers have held that there is. They have held that, while it is possible and even probable that *some* mental events are correlated with specific neural events, it is impossible that this should be true of *all* mental events. Those who take this view generally hold that there probably is psycho-neural parallelism of events for sensations, but that there certainly cannot be such parallelism for comparison, introspection, attentive inspection, and so on. This view is taken by Mr. Johnson in his *Logic* (Part III); and it will be worth while to consider his arguments. They are contained in Chapter VII, § 6 of that work. Mr. Johnson's argument, if I rightly understand it, comes to this: We must distinguish, *e.g.*, between the *fact* that I am having two sensations, one of which is light red and the other dark red, and my *recognition* that both are red and that one is darker than the other. We must likewise distinguish, *e.g.*, between the *fact* that the dark one started before the light one, and my recognition of this fact; and between the *fact* that the dark one is to the left of the light one in my visual field and my recognition of this fact. Finally, we must notice that we have to distinguish different degrees of clearness and determinateness with which a perfectly determinate fact may be recognized. We may merely judge that one sensum is separate from another or we may judge that one is to the left of the other, or we may judge that the first is as much to the left of the second as the second is to the right of a third, and so on. Now Mr. Johnson contends that the sensations themselves have neural correlates, and that the determinate qualities and relations which the sensations actually have are determined by the qualities and relations of these neural correlates. But he holds that there is then nothing left on the neural side for the *recognition* of these qualities and relations to be correlated with. Still less is there anything left on the neural side to be correlated with the infinitely numerous different degrees of determinateness with which the qualities and relations of the sensations may be apprehended. Hence he concludes that mental events above the level of sensations *cannot* be correlated one to one with specific neural events. He does not explicitly draw the distinction which I have done between Departmental Parallelism and Parallelism of Events; but I think it is plain that his argument is meant only to deny the latter. He would probably admit that, if certain specific areas of our brains were injured, we should lose altogether the power of making judgments of comparison and of recognising spatio-temporal relations; but he would hold that, given the general integrity of those areas, there is not some one specific event within them corresponding to each particular judgment of comparison or of spatio-temporal relation.

Before criticising this argument we must notice that Mr. Johnson does not explicitly distinguish sensations and sensa. By a "sensation" I think he means what I should call a "sensed sensum." And he thinks that, from the nature of the case, there can be no unsensed sensa. Thus a sensation for him is a sensum, regarded as existentially mind-dependent; and, in virtue of its supposed existential mind-dependence, it counts as a mental event belonging to the mind on which its existence depends. If we like to distinguish between mental *states* and mental *acts* we can say that a sensation, for Mr. Johnson, is apparently a mental *state* having certain sensible qualities, such as colour, position in the visual field, and so on. To recognise that one is having a sensation, that it is of such and such a kind, and that it stands in such and such spatio-temporal relations to other sensations, would be to perform a cognitive mental *act*. And his contention is that, whilst there is a parallelism of events for mental states, there cannot for this very reason be also a parallelism of events for mental acts. This at least is how I understand him.

Now I must confess that Mr. Johnson's argument seems to me to be so extremely weak that (knowing Mr. Johnson) I hesitate to believe that I can have properly understood it. Let us suppose that the actual relative position of two sensa s_1 and s_2 in a visual sense-field is determined by the relative position of two excited areas in the brain, b_1 and b_2. Let us suppose that the actual relative date of the two sensa in the sense-history of the experient is determined by the relative date of the excitement of these areas. And let us suppose that the determinate sensible qualities of the two sensa (*e.g.*, the particular shade of the particular colour possessed by each) is determined by the particular kind of movement which is going on in the microscopic particles within these two areas. Mr. Johnson's contention seems to be that, when we have mentioned the positions of the excited areas, the dates at which they begin to be excited, and the particular kind of movement which is going on within them, we have said all that can be said about the neural events. There is nothing left on the neural side to be correlated with our acts of recognition, of qualitative comparison, and of spatio-temporal judgment; and therefore these events can have no special neural correlate. To this there are two answers which seem so obvious that I am almost ashamed to make them.

1. At the very utmost the argument would

show only that there is nothing left *within the two areas b_1 and b_2* to be correlated with any judgments which we happen to make about the sensations s_1 and s_2. But these two areas do not exhaust the whole of the brain and nervous system. Why our acts of judgment about these two sensations should not have neural correlates in some other part of the brain I cannot imagine. The situation on the mental side is that we may, but need not, make these judgments if we do have the sensations; and that we cannot make them unless we have the sensations. This is exactly what we might expect if the neural correlates of the acts of judgment were in a different part of the brain from the neural correlates of the sensations themselves: and if a certain kind of disturbance in the latter were a necessary but insufficient condition of a certain kind of disturbance in the former.

2. But we could answer the argument without needing even to assume that the neural correlates of judgments about sensations are in a different area of the brain from the neural correlates of the sensations themselves. We have to remember that the same area may contain at the same time microscopic events of different scales of magnitude. Let us take a purely physical analogy. The same piece of metal may be at once hot and glowing. We have extremely good reasons to believe that *both* these apparent characteristics are correlated with microscopic motions which are going on throughout the whole volume occupied by the bit of metal. The heat is supposed to be correlated with the random movements of molecules and the light with the jumps of electrons from one stable orbit to another. The large-scale events can go on without the small-scale events (a body may be hot without glowing); but the more violent the large-scale events the more frequent will be the small-scale events (a body begins to glow if it be heated enough). Now I cannot imagine why the same thing might not be true of the neural correlates of sensations and the neural correlates of our judgments about our sensations. Suppose that the neural correlates of

sensations were large-scale events in a certain area of the brain; and suppose that the neural correlates of our judgments about these sensations were small-scale events in the same area. Then I should expect to find that sensations could happen without our making judgments about them; that we could not make the judgments unless we had the sensations; and that it would be more difficult not to make the judgments as the sensations became more intense, other things being equal. And this is exactly what I do find. It seems to me then, either that I have altogether misunderstood Mr. Johnson's argument, or that there is nothing whatever in it.

There remains one other point to be discussed before leaving the subject. It is true, as Mr. Johnson points out, that we make judgments of various degrees of determinateness about the same perfectly determinate fact. Does this raise any particular difficulty against the view that every act of judgment has a specific neural correlate? I do not think that it does, if we avoid certain confusions into which it is very easy to fall. I suppose that the difficulty that is felt is this: "Every neural event is perfectly determinate; how can an indeterminate judgment have a determinate neural correlate; and how can there be different determinate neural correlates for all the different degrees of determinateness in judgments?" To this I should answer (i) that of course the differences on the neural side which would correspond to different degrees of determinateness in the judgment are not themselves differences of determinateness. But why should they be? The differences on the neural side which correspond to differences of shade in sensations of colour are not themselves differences of shade. If, *e.g.*, the area which is correlated with judgments about our sensations be different from the area which is correlated with the sensations themselves, we might suppose that differences in the determinateness of the judgment were correlated with differences in the extent or the intensity of the disturbance within this area. If, on the other hand, we supposed that our sensations were correlated with large-scale events, and our judgments about these sensations with small-scale events in the same region of the brain, we might suppose that differences in the determinateness of the judgment are correlated with differences in the frequency of these small-scale events. There is thus no difficulty, so far as I can see, in providing neural correlates to every different degree of determinateness in our judgments. (ii) It is perhaps necessary to point out that what is called an "indeterminate judgment" is not an indeterminate event; every event, whether mental or physical, is no doubt perfectly determinate of its kind. *E.g.,* whether I merely judge that *some one* has been in the room or make the more determinate judgment that *John Smith* has been in the room, either judgment as a physical event has perfectly determinate forms of all the psychical determinables under which it falls. The indefiniteness is in what is asserted, not in the act of asserting as such. Hence the problem is not, as it might seem to a careless observer, to find a determinate neural correlate to an indeterminate psychical event; the problem is merely to find a determinate neural correlate to a determinate psychical event which consists in the asserting of a relatively indeterminate characteristic.

I conclude then that no adequate reason has been produced by Mr. Johnson to prove that there *cannot* be specific neural correlates to mental *acts* as well as to mental *states.* I have also tried to show that there neither is nor is likely to be any empirical evidence *for* the doctrine that all mental events have specific neural events as their correlates. Hence the positive doctrine of Psycho-neural Parallelism of Events seems to me to be a perfectly open question. This is not perhaps a wildly exciting result. But it is not altogether to be despised, since it leaves us with a perfectly free hand when we try to construct a speculative theory of the relations of matter and mind which shall do justice to all the known facts. For the known facts neither require nor preclude complete Psycho-neural Parallelism of Events.

Summary and Conclusions

I wish to make quite clear what I do and what I do not claim to have done in this chapter. I have definitely assumed that the body and the mind are two distinct entities, which are now in a very intimate union, which I express by saying that the former is "animated by" the latter. I have raised no question about the exact nature or origin of this relation of "animation"; and I have not considered the apparent growth of mind in the individual or the apparent development of consciousness from the non-conscious in the course of the earth's history. Again, I have taken the body to be very much as common-sense, enlightened by physical science, but not by philosophical criticism, takes it to be; I have supposed that we know pretty well what a mind is; and I have assumed that causation *is* not simply regular sequence and concomitant variation, though these are more or less trustworthy *signs* of the presence of a causal relation. These are the assumptions on which the question of Interaction has commonly been discussed by philosophers and by scientists; and it would be idle for me to conceal my opinion that it has been discussed extraordinarily badly. The problem seems to have exercised a most unfortunate effect on those who have treated it; for I have rarely met with a collection of worse arguments on all sides. I can only hope that I have not provided yet another instance in support of this generalisation.

My conclusion is that, subject to the assumptions just mentioned, no argument has been produced which should make any reasonable person doubt that mind acts on body in volition and that body acts on mind in sensation. I have tried to show the extreme difficulties which are involved in attempting to deny that body acts on mind. And I have tried to show that the apparently equal difficulties which seem to be involved in attempting to deny that mind acts on body could be evaded with a little ingenuity. Thus One-sided Action of Body on Mind is a possible theory. But there seems to me to be no positive reason for accepting it, and at least one reason for doubting it, viz., the conviction which many men have (and which Mr. Hume's arguments fail altogether to refute) that we *know* directly that our volitions are necessary conditions for the occurrence of our voluntary movements.

If these conclusions be sound, Parallelism, considered as an *alternative* which excludes Interaction, has no leg left to stand upon. But Parallelism has a positive side to it which is perfectly compatible with Interaction, and is therefore worth discussing for its own sake. I distinguished between the metaphysical doctrine of Psycho-*physical* Parallelism and the more restricted doctrine of Psycho-*neural* Parallelism. And I divided the latter into Departmental Parallelism and Parallelism of Events. It seemed to me that there was good empirical evidence for a considerable amount of Departmental Parallelism, but that there was not and is not likely to be adequate

empirical evidence for Parallelism of Events. On the other hand, I came to the conclusion that Mr. Johnson's arguments to prove that complete parallelism between mental and neural events is *impossible* were quite unsound.

This, I think, is as far as the discussion can be carried at this level. One thing seems to me to emerge clearly even at this point. If interaction has to be denied at a later stage it can only be because the relation between mind and body turns out to be so intimate that "interaction" is an unsuitable expression for the connection between a particular mental event and its correlated bodily event. This would be so if, *e.g.*, Materialism were true, so that the mind was just some part of the body. It might be so on a double-aspect Theory, or on a theory of Neutral Monism. But we cannot decide between such general theories until we know more about the true nature of Mind and of Matter, and have taken into consideration questions about origin and development of minds which we have hitherto explicitly left out of account. Thus the final discussion of the question can come only near the end of the book.

GILBERT RYLE

DESCARTES' MYTH*

1. The Official Doctrine

There is a doctrine about the nature and place of minds which is so prevalent among theorists and even among laymen that it deserves to be described as the official theory. Most philosophers, psychologists and religious teachers subscribe, with minor reservations, to its main articles and, although they

admit certain theoretical difficulties in it, they tend to assume that these can be overcome without serious modifications being made to the architecture of the theory. It will be argued here that the central principles of the doctrine are unsound and conflict with the whole body of what we know about minds when we are not speculating about them.

The official doctrine, which hails chiefly

* From *The Concept of Mind* by Gilbert Ryle, 1949, Chapter I. By permission of Hutchinson & Co. (Publishers) Ltd., London.

from Descartes, is something like this. With the doubtful exceptions of idiots and infants in arms every human being has both a body and a mind. Some would prefer to say that every human being is both a body and a mind. His body and his mind are ordinarily harnessed together, but after the death of the body his mind may continue to exist and function.

Human bodies are in space and are subject to the mechanical laws which govern all other bodies in space. Bodily processes and states can be inspected by external observers. So a man's bodily life is as much a public affair as are the lives of animals and reptiles and even as the careers of trees, crystals and planets.

But minds are not in space, nor are their operations subject to mechanical laws. The workings of one mind are not witnessable by other observers; its career is private. Only I can take direct cognisance of the states and processes of my own mind. A person therefore lives through two collateral histories, one consisting of what happens in and to his body, the other consisting of what happens in and to his mind. The first is public, the second private. The events in the first history are events in the physical world, those in the second are events in the mental world.

It has been disputed whether a person does or can directly monitor all or only some of the episodes of his own private history; but, according to the official doctrine, of at least some of these episodes he has direct and unchallengeable cognisance. In consciousness, self-consciousness and introspection he is directly and authentically apprised of the present states and operations of his mind. He may have great or small uncertainties about concurrent and adjacent episodes in the physical world, but he can have none about at least part of what is momentarily occupying his mind.

It is customary to express this bifurcation of his two lives and of his two worlds by saying that the things and events which belong to the physical world, including his own body, are external, while the workings of his own mind are internal. This antithesis of outer and inner is of course meant to be construed as a metaphor, since minds, not being in space, could not be described as being spatially inside anything else, or as having things going on spatially inside themselves. But relapses from this good intention are common and theorists are found speculating how stimuli, the physical sources of which are yards or miles outside a person's skin, can generate mental responses inside his skull, or how decisions framed inside his cranium can set going movements of his extremities.

Even when "inner" and "outer" are construed as metaphors, the problem how a person's mind and body influence one another is notoriously charged with theoretical difficulties. What the mind wills, the legs, arms and the tongue execute; what affects the ear and the eye has something to do with what the mind perceives; grimaces and smiles betray the mind's moods and bodily castigations lead, it is hoped, to moral improvement. But the actual transactions between the episodes of the private history and those of the public history remain mysterious, since by definition they can belong to neither series. They could not be reported among the happenings described in a person's autobiography of his inner life, but nor could they be reported among those described in some one else's biography of that person's overt career. They can be inspected neither by introspection nor by laboratory experiment. They are theoretical shuttlecocks which are forever being bandied from the physiologist back to the psychologist and from the psychologist back to the physiologist.

Underlying this partly metaphorical representation of the bifurcation of a person's two lives there is a seemingly more profound and philosophical assumption. It is assumed that there are two different kinds of existence or status. What exists or happens may have the status of physical existence, or it may have the status of mental existence. Somewhat as the faces of coins are either heads or tails, or somewhat as living creatures are either male or female, so, it is supposed some existing is physical existing, other existing is mental existing. It is a necessary feature of what has physical existence that it is in space and time, it is a necessary feature of what has mental existence that it is in time but not in space. What has physical existence is composed of matter, or else is a function of matter; what has mental existence consists of consciousness, or else is a function of consciousness.

There is thus a polar opposition between mind and matter, an opposition which is often brought out as follows. Material objects are situated in a common field, known as "space," and what happens to one body in one part of space is mechanically connected with what happens to other bodies in other parts of space. But mental happenings occur in insulated fields, known as "minds," and there is, apart maybe from telepathy, no direct causal connection between what happens in one mind and what happens in another. Only through the medium of the public physical world can the mind of one person make a difference to the mind of another. The mind is its own place and in his inner life each of us lives the life of a ghostly Robinson Cruso. People can see, hear and jolt one another's bodies, but they are irremediably blind and deaf to the workings of one another's minds and inoperative upon them.

What sort of knowledge can be secured of the workings of a mind? On the one side, according to the official theory, a person has direct knowledge of the best imaginable kind of the workings of his own mind. Mental states and processes are (or are normally) conscious states and processes, and the consciousness which irradiates them can engender no illusions and leaves the door open for no doubts. A person's present thinkings, feelings and willings, his perceivings, rememberings and imaginings are intrinsically "phosphorescent"; their existence and their nature are inevitably betrayed to their owner. The inner life is a stream of consciousness of such a sort that it would be absurd to suggest that the mind whose life is that stream might be unaware of what is passing down it.

True, the evidence adduced recently by Freud seems to show that there exist channels tributary to this stream, which run hidden from their owner. People are actuated by impulses the existence of which they vigorously disavow; some of their thoughts differ from the thoughts which they acknowledge; and some of the actions which they think they will to perform they do not really will. They are thoroughly gulled by some of their own hypocrisies and they successfully ignore facts about their mental lives which on the official theory ought to be patent to them. Holders of the official theory tend, however, to maintain that anyhow in normal circumstances a person must be directly and authentically seized of the present state and workings of his own mind.

Besides being currently supplied with these alleged immediate data of consciousness, a person is also generally supposed to be able to exercise from time to time a special kind of perception, namely inner perception, or introspection. He can take a (non-optical) "look" at what is passing in his mind. Not only can he view and scrutinize a flower through his sense of sight and listen to and discriminate the notes of a bell through his sense of hearing; he can also reflectively or introspectively watch, without any bodily organ of sense, the current episodes of his inner life. This self-observation is also commonly supposed to be immune from illusion, confusion or doubt. A mind's reports of its own affairs have a certainty superior to the best that is possessed by its reports of matters in the physical world. Sense-perceptions can, but consciousness and introspection cannot, be mistaken or confused.

On the other side, one person has no direct access of any sort to the events of the inner life of another. He cannot do better than make problematic inferences from the observed behaviour of the other person's body to the states of mind which, by analogy from his own conduct, he supposes to be signalised by that behaviour. Direct access to the workings of a mind is the privilege of that mind itself; in default of such privileged access, the workings of one mind are inevitably occult to everyone else. For the supposed arguments from bodily movements similar to their own to mental workings similar to their own would lack any possibility of observational corroboration. Not unnaturally, therefore, an adherent of the official theory finds it difficult to resist this consequence of his premises, that he has no good reason to believe that there do exist minds other than his own. Even if he prefers to believe that to other human bodies there are harnessed minds not unlike his own, he cannot claim to be able to discover their individual characteristics, or the particular things that they undergo and do. Absolute solitude is on this showing the ineluctable destiny of the soul. Only our bodies can meet.

As a necessary corollary of this general scheme there is implicitly prescribed a special way of construing our ordinary concepts of mental powers and operations. The verbs, nouns and adjectives, with which in ordinary life we describe the wits, characters and higher-grade performances of the people with whom we have do, are required to be construed as signifying special episodes in their secret histories, or else as signifying tendencies for such episodes to occur. When someone is described as knowing, believing or guessing something, as hoping, dreading, intending or shirking something, as designing this or being amused at that, these verbs are supposed to denote the occurrence of specific modifications in his (to us) occult stream of consciousness. Only his own privileged access to this stream in direct awareness and introspection could provide authentic testimony that these mental-conduct verbs were correctly or incorrectly applied. The onlooker, be he teacher, critic, biographer or friend, can never assure himself that his comments have any vestige of truth. Yet it was just because we do in fact all know how to make such comments, make them with general correctness and correct them when they turn out to be confused or mistaken, that philosophers found it necessary to construct their theories of the nature and place of minds. Finding mental-conduct concepts being regularly and effectively used, they properly sought to fix their logical geography. But the logical geography officially recommended would entail that there could be no regular or effective use of these mental-conduct concepts in our descriptions of, and prescriptions for, other people's minds.

2. The Absurdity of the Official Doctrine

Such in outline is the official theory. I shall often speak of it, with deliberate abusiveness, as "the dogma of the Ghost in the Machine." I hope to prove that it is entirely false, and false not in detail but in principle. It is not merely an assemblage of particular mistakes. It is one big mistake and a mistake of a special kind. It is, namely, a category-mistake. It represents the facts of mental life as if they belonged to one logical type or category (or range of types or categories), when they actually belong to another. The dogma is therefore a philosopher's myth. In attempting to explode the myth I shall probably be taken to be denying well-known facts about the mental life of human beings, and my plea that I aim at doing nothing more than rectify the logic of mental-conduct concepts will probably be disallowed as mere subterfuge.

I must first indicate what is meant by the phrase "category-mistake." This I do in a series of illustrations.

A foreigner visiting Oxford or Cambridge for the first time is shown a number of colleges, libraries, playing fields, museums, scientific departments and administrative offices. He then asks "But where is the University? I have seen where the members of the Colleges live, where the Registrar works, where the scientists experiment and the rest. But I have not yet seen the University in which reside and work the members of your University." It has then to be explained to him that the University is not another collateral institution, some ulterior counterpart to the colleges, laboratories and offices which he has seen. The University is just the way in which all that he has already seen is organized. When they are seen and when their co-ordination is understood, the University has been seen. His mistake lay in his innocent assumption that it was correct to speak of Christ Church, the Bodleian Library, the Ashmolean Museum *and* the University, to speak, that is, as if "the University" stood for an extra member of the class of which these other units are members. He was mistakenly allocating the University to the same category as that to which the other institutions belong.

The same mistake would be made by a child witnessing the march-past of a division, who, having had pointed out to him such and such battalions, batteries, squadrons, etc., asked when the division was going to appear. He would be supposing that a division was a counterpart to the units already seen, partly similar to them and partly unlike them. He would be shown his mistake by being told that in watching the battalions, batteries and squadrons marching past he had been watching the division marching past. The march-past was not a parade of battalions, batteries, squadrons *and* a division: it was a parade of the battalions, batteries and squadrons *of* a division.

One more illustration. A foreigner watching his first game of cricket learns what are the functions of the bowlers, the batsmen, and fielders, the umpires and the scorers. He then says "But there is no one left on the field to contribute the famous element of team-spirit. I see who does the bowling, the batting and the wicketkeeping; but I do not see whose role it is to exercise *esprit de corps.*" Once more, it would have to be explained that he was looking for the wrong type of thing. Team-spirit is not another cricketing-operation supplementary to all of the other special tasks. It is, roughly, the keenness with which each of the special tasks

is performed, and performing a task keenly is not performing two tasks. Certainly exhibiting team-spirit is not the same thing as bowling or catching, but nor is it a third thing such that we can say that the bowler first bowls *and* then exhibits team-spirit or that a fielder is at a given moment *either* catching *or* displaying *esprit de corps.*

These illustrations of category-mistakes have a common feature which must be noticed. The mistakes were made by people who did not know how to wield the concepts *University, division* and *team-spirit.* Their puzzles arose from inability to use certain items in the English vocabulary.

The theoretically interesting category-mistakes are those made by people who are perfectly competent to apply concepts, at least in the situations with which they are familiar, but are still liable in their abstract thinking to allocate those concepts to logical types to which they do not belong. An instance of a mistake of this sort would be the following story. A student of politics has learned the main differences between the British, the French and the American Constitutions, and has learned also the differences and connections between the Cabinet, Parliament, the various Ministries, the Judicature and the Church of England. But he still becomes embarrassed when asked questions about the connections between the Church of England, the Home Office and the British Constitution. For while the Church and the Home Office are institutions, the British Constitution is not another institution in the same sense of that noun. So inter-institutional relations which can be asserted or denied to hold between the Church and the Home Office cannot be asserted or denied to hold between either of them and the British Constitution. "The British Constitution" is not a term of the same logical type as "the Home Office" and "the Church of England." In a partially similar way, John Doe may be a relative, a friend, an enemy or a stranger to Richard Roe; but he cannot be any of these things to the Average Taxpayer. He knows how to talk sense in certain sorts of discussions about the Average Taxpayer, but he is baffled to say why he could not come across him in the street as he can come across Richard Roe,

It is pertinent to our main subject to notice that, so long as the student of politics continues to think of the British Constitution as a counterpart to the other institutions, he will tend to describe it as a mysteriously occult institution; and so long as John Doe continues to think of the Average Taxpayer as a fellow-citizen, he will tend to think of him as an elusive insubstantial man, a ghost who is everywhere yet nowhere.

My destructive purpose is to show that a family of radical category-mistakes is the source of the double-life theory. The representation of a person as a ghost mysteriously ensconced in a machine derives from this argument. Because, as is true, a person's thinking, feeling and purposive doing cannot be described solely in the idioms of physics, chemistry and physiology, therefore they must be described in counterpart idioms. As the human body is a complex organized unit, so the human mind must be another complex organized unit, though one made of a different sort of stuff and with a different sort of structure. Or, again, as the human body, like any other parcel of matter, is a field of causes and effects, so the mind must be another field of causes and effects, though not (Heaven be praised) mechanical causes and effects.

3. The Origin of the Category-mistake

One of the chief intellectual origins of what I have yet to prove to be the Cartesian category-mistake seems to be this. When Galileo showed that his methods of scientific discovery were competent to provide a mechanical theory which should cover every occupant of space, Descartes found in himself two conflicting motives. As a man of scientific genius he could not but endorse the claims of mechanics, yet as a religious and moral man he could not accept, as Hobbes accepted, the discouraging rider to those claims, namely that human nature differs only in degree of complexity from clockwork. The mental could not be just a variety of the mechanical.

He and subsequent philosophers naturally but erroneously availed themselves of the following escape-route. Since mental-conduct words are not to be construed as signifying the occurrence of mechanical processes, they must be construed as signifying the occurrence of non-mechanical processes; since mechanical laws explain movements in space as the effects of other movements in space, other laws must explain some of the non-spatial workings of minds as the effects of other non-spatial workings of minds. The difference between the human behaviours which we describe as intelligent and those which we describe as unintelligent must be a difference in their causation; so, while some movements of human tongues and limbs are the effects of mechanical causes, others must be the effects of non-mechanical causes, i.e. some issue from movements of particles of matter, others from workings of the mind.

The differences between the physical and the mental were thus represented as differences inside the common framework of the categories of "thing," "stuff," "attribute," "state," "process," "change," "cause" and "effect." Minds are things, but different sorts of things from bodies; mental processes are causes and effects, but different sorts of causes and effects from bodily movements. And so on. Somewhat as the foreigner expected the University to be an extra edifice, rather like a college but also considerably different, so the repudiators of mechanism represented minds as extra centers of causal processes, rather like machines but also considerably different from them. Their theory was a para-mechanical hypothesis.

That this assumption was at the heart of the doctrine is shown by the fact that there was from the beginning felt to be a major theoretical difficulty in explaining how minds can influence and be influenced by bodies. How can a mental process, such as willing, cause spatial movements like the movements of the tongue? How can a physical change in the optic nerve have among its effects a minds perception of a flash of light? This notorious crux by itself shows the logical mould into which Descartes pressed his theory of the mind. It was the self-same mould into which he and Galileo set their mechanics. Still unwittingly adhering to the grammar of mechanics, he tried to avert disaster by describing minds in what was merely an obverse vocabulary. The workings of minds had to be described by the mere negatives of the specific descriptions given to bodies; they are not in space, they are not motions, they are not modifications of matter, they are not accessible to public observation. Minds are not bits of clockwork, they are just bits of not-clockwork.

As thus represented, minds are not merely ghosts harnessed to machines, they are themselves just spectral machines. Though the human body is an engine, it is not quite an ordinary engine, since some of its workings are governed by another engine inside it—this interior governor-engine being one of a very special sort. It is invisible, inaudible and it has no size or weight. It cannot be taken to bits and the laws it obeys are not those known to ordinary engineers. Nothing is known of how it governs the bodily engine.

A second major crux points the same moral. Since, according to the doctrine, minds belong to the same category as bodies and since bodies are rigidly governed by mechanical laws, it seemed to many theorists to follow that minds must be similarly governed by rigid non-mechanical laws. The physical world is a deterministic system, so the mental world must be a deterministic system. Bodies cannot help the modifications that they undergo, so minds cannot help pursuing the careers fixed for them. *Responsibility, choice, merit* and *demerit* are therefore inapplicable concepts—unless the compromise solution is adopted of saying

that the laws governing mental processes, unlike those governing physical processes, have the congenial attribute of being only rather rigid. The problem of the Freedom of the Will was the problem how to reconcile the hypothesis that minds are to be described in terms drawn from the categories of mechanics with the knowledge that higher-grade human conduct is not of a piece with the behaviour of machines.

It is an historical curiosity that it was not noticed that the entire argument was broken-backed. Theorists correctly assumed that any sane man could already recognize the differences between, say, rational and non-rational utterances or between purposive and automatic behaviour. Else there would have been nothing requiring to be salved from mechanism. Yet the explanation given presupposed that one person could in principle never recognize the difference between the rational and the irrational utterances issuing from other human bodies, since he could never get access to the postulated immaterial causes of some of their utterances. Save for the doubtful exception of himself, he could never tell the difference between a man and a Robot. It would have to be conceded, for example, that, for all that we can tell, the inner lives of persons who are classed as idiots or lunatics are as rational as those of anyone else. Perhaps only their overt behaviour is disappointing; that is to say, perhaps "idiots" are not really idiotic, or "lunatics" lunatic. Perhaps, too, some of those who are classed as sane are really idiots. According to the theory, external observers could never know how the overt behaviour of others is correlated with their mental powers and processes and so they could never know or even plausibly conjecture whether their applications of mental-conduct concepts to these other people were correct or incorrect. It would then be hazardous or impossible for a man to claim sanity or logical consistency even for himself, since he would be debarred from comparing his own performances with those of others. In short, our characterisations of persons and their performances as intelligent, prudent and virtuous or as stupid, hypocritical and cowardly could never have been made, so the problem of providing a special causal hypothesis to serve as the basis of such diagnoses would never have arisen. The question "How do persons differ from machines?" arose just because everyone already knew how to apply mental-conduct concepts before the new causal hypothesis was introduced. This causal hypothesis could not therefore be the source of the criteria used in those applications. Nor, of course, has the causal hypothesis in any degree improved our handling of those criteria. We still distinguish good from bad arithmetic, politic from impolitic conduct and fertile from infertile imaginations in the ways in which Descartes himself distinguished them before and after he speculated how the applicability of these criteria was compatible with the principle of mechanical causation.

He had mistaken the logic of his problem. Instead of asking by what criteria intelligent behaviour is actually distinguished from non-intelligent behaviour, he asked "Given that the principle of mechanical causation does not tell us the difference, what other causal principle will tell it us?" He realised that the problem was not one of mechanics and assumed that it must therefore be one of some counterpart to mechanics. Not unnaturally psychology is often cast for just this role.

When two terms belong to the same category, it is proper to construct conjunctive propositions embodying them. Thus a purchaser may say that he bought a left-hand glove and a right-hand glove, but not that he bought a left-hand glove, a right-hand glove and a pair of gloves. "She came home in a flood of tears and a sedan-chair" is a well-known joke based on the absurdity of conjoining terms of different types. It would have been equally ridiculous to construct the disjunction "She came home either in a flood of tears or else in a sedan-chair." Now the dogma of the Ghost in the Machine does just this. It maintains that there exist both bodies and minds; that there occur physical processes and mental processes; that there are mechanical causes of corporeal movements

and mental causes of corporeal movements. I shall argue that these and other analogous conjunctions are absurd; but, it must be noticed, the argument will not show that either of the illegitimately conjoined propositions is absurd in itself. I am not, for example, denying that there occur mental processes. Doing long division is a mental process and so is making a joke. But I am saying that the phrase "there occur mental processes" does not mean the same sort of thing as "there occur physical processes," and, therefore, that it makes no sense to conjoin or disjoin the two.

If my argument is successful, there will follow some interesting consequences. First, the hallowed contrast between Mind and Matter will be dissipated, but dissipated not by either of the equally hallowed absorptions of Mind by Matter or of Matter by Mind, but in quite a different way. For the seeming contrast of the two will be shown to be as illegitimate as would be the contrast of "she came home in a flood of tears" and "she came home in a sedan-chair." The belief that there is a polar opposition between Mind and Matter is the belief that they are terms of the same logical type.

It will also follow that both Idealism and Materialism are answers to an improper question. The "reduction" of the material world to mental states and processes, as well as the "reduction" of mental states and processes to physical states and processes, presuppose the legitimacy of the disjunction "Either there exist minds or there exist bodies (but not both)." It would be like saying, "Either she bought a left-hand and a right-hand glove or she bought a pair of gloves (but not both)."

It is perfectly proper to say, in one logical tone of voice, that there exist minds and to say, in another logical tone of voice, that there exist bodies. But these expressions do not indicate two different species of existence, for "existence" is not a generic word like "coloured" or "sexed." They indicate two different senses of "exist," somewhat as "rising" has different senses in "the tide is rising," "hopes are rsing," and "the average

age of death is rising." A man would be thought to be making a poor joke who said that three things are now rising, namely the tide, hopes and the average age of death. It would be just as good or bad a joke to say that there exist prime numbers and Wednesdays and public opinions and navies; or that there exist both minds and bodies. In the succeeding, chapters I try to prove that the official theory does rest on a batch of category-mistakes by showing that logically absurd corollaries follow from it. The exhibition of these absurdities will have the constructive effect of bringing out part of the correct logic of mental-conduct concepts.

4. Historical Note

It would not be true to say that the official theory derives solely from Descartes' theories, or even from a more widespread anxiety about the implications of seventeenth century mechanics. Scholastic and Reformation theology had schooled the intellects of the scientists as well as of the laymen, philosophers and clerics of that age. Stoic-Augustinian theories of the will were embedded in the Calvinist doctrines of sin and grace; Platonic and Aristotelian theories of the intellect shaped the orthodox doctrines of the immortality of the soul. Descartes was reformulating already prevalent theological doctrines of the soul in the new syntax of Galileo. The theologian's privacy of conscience became the philosopher's privacy of consciousness, and what had been the bogy of Predestination reappeared as the bogy of Determinism.

It would also not be true to say that the two-worlds myth did no theoretical good. Myths often do a lot of theoretical good, while they are still new. One benefit bestowed by the para-mechanical myth was that it partly superannuated the then prevalent para-political myth. Minds and their Faculties had previously been described by analogies with political superiors and political subordinates. The idioms used were those of ruling, obeying, collaborating and rebelling. They survived and still survive in many ethical and some epistemological discussions. As, in physics, the new myth of occult Forces was a scientific improvement on the old myth of Final Causes, so, in anthropological and psychological theory, the new myth of hidden operations, impulses and agencies was an improvement on the old myth of dictations, deferences and disobediences.

DAVID HUME

OF PERSONAL IDENTITY*

There are some philosophers who imagine we are every moment intimately conscious of what we call our *self;* that we feel its existence and its continuance in existence; and are certain, beyond the evidence of a demonstration, both of its perfect identity and simplicity. The strongest sensation, the most violent passion, say they, instead of distracting us from this view, only fix it the more intensely, and make us consider their influence on *self* either by their pain or pleasure. To attempt a further proof of this were to weaken its evidence; since no proof can be derived

---

* From *A Treatise of Human Nature* by David Hume. Book I, Part IV, Section VI. First printed in 1739.

from any fact of which we are so intimately conscious nor is there anything of which we can be certain if we doubt of this.

Unluckily all these positive assertions are contrary to that very experience which is pleaded for them; nor have we any idea of *self,* after the manner it is here explained. For, from what impression could this idea be derived? This question it is impossible to answer without a manifest contradiction and absurdity; and yet it is a question which must necessarily be answered, if we would have the idea of self pass for clear and intelligible. It must be some one impression that gives rise to every real idea. But self or person is not any one impression, but that to which our several impressions and ideas are supposed to have a reference. If any impression gives rise to the idea of self, that impression must continue invariably the same, through the whole course of our lives; since self is supposed to exist after that manner. But there is no impression constant and invariable. Pain and pleasure, grief and joy, passions and sensations succeed each other, and never all exist at the same time. It cannot therefore be from any of these impressions, or from any other, that the idea of self is derived; and consequently there is no such idea.

But further, what must become of all our particular perceptions upon this hypothesis? All these are different, and distinguishable, and separable from each other, and may be separately considered, and may exist separately, and have no need of anything to support their existence. After what manner therefore do they belong to self, and how are they connected with it? For my part, when I enter most intimately into what I call *myself,* I always stumble on some particular perception or other, of heat or cold, light or shade, love or hatred, pain or pleasure. I never can catch *myself* at any time without a perception, and never can observe anything but the perception. When my perceptions are removed for any time, as by sound sleep, so long am I insensible of *myself,* and may truly be said not to exist. And were all my perceptions removed by death, and could I neither think, nor feel, nor see, nor love, nor hate, after the dissolution of my body, I should be entirely annihilated, nor do I conceive what is further requisite to make me a perfect nonentity. If any one, upon serious and unprejudiced reflection, thinks he has a different notion of *himself,* I must confess I can reason no longer with him. All I can allow him is, that he may be in the right as well as I, and that we are essentially different in this particular. He may, perhaps, perceive something simple and continued, which he calls *himself;* though I am certain there is no such principle in me.

But setting aside some metaphysicians of this kind, I may venture to affirm of the rest of mankind, that they are nothing but a bundle or collection of different perceptions, which succeed each other with an inconceivable rapidity, and are in a perpetual flux and movement. Our eyes cannot turn in their sockets without varying our perceptions. Our thought is still more variable than our sight; and all our other senses and faculties contribute to this change; nor is there any single power of the soul, which remains unalterably the same, perhaps for one moment. The mind is a kind of theatre, where several perceptions successively make their appearance; pass, repass, glide away, and mingle in an infinite variety of postures and situations. There is properly no *simplicity* in it at one time, nor *identity* in different, whatever natural propension we may have to imagine that simplicity and identity. The comparison of the theatre must not mislead us. They are the successive perceptions only, that constitute the mind; nor have we the most distant notion of the place where these scenes are represented, or of the materials of which it is composed.

What then gives us so great a propension to ascribe an identity to these successive perceptions, and to suppose ourselves possessed of an invariable and uninterrupted existence through the whole course of our lives? In order to answer this question we must distinguish betwixt personal identity, as it regards our thought or imagination, and as it regards our passions or the concern we take in ourselves. The first is our present subject; and to explain it perfectly we must take the matter pretty deep, and account for that identity, which we attribute to plants and animals; there being a great analogy betwixt it and the identity of a self or person.

We have a distinct idea of an object that remains invariable and uninterrupted through a supposed variation of time; and this idea we call that of *identity* or *sameness*. We have also a distinct idea of several different objects existing in succession, and connected together by a close relation; and this to an accurate view affords as perfect a notion of *diversity* as if there was no manner of relation among the objects. But though these two ideas of identity, and a succession of related objects, be in themselves perfectly distinct, and even contrary, yet it is certain that, in our common way of thinking, they are generally confounded with each other. That action of the imagination, by which we consider the uninterrupted and invariable object, and that by which we reflect on the succession of related objects, are almost the same to the feeling; nor is there much more effort of thought required in the latter case than in the former. The relation facilitates the transition of the mind from one object to another, and renders its passage as smooth as if it contemplated one continued object. This resemblance is the cause of the confusion and mistake, and makes us substitute the notion of identity, instead of that of related objects. However at one instant we may consider the related succession as variable or interrupted, we are sure the next to ascribe to it a perfect identity, and regard it as invariable and uninterrupted. Our propensity to this mistake is so great from the resemblance above mentioned, that we fall into it before we are aware; and though we incessantly correct ourselves by reflection, and return to a more accurate method of thinking, yet we cannot long sustain our philosophy, or take off this bias from the imagination. Our last resource is to yield to it, and boldly assert that these different related objects are in effect the same, however interrupted and variable. In order to justify to ourselves this absurdity, we often feign some new and unintelligible principle, that connects the objects together, and prevents their interruption or variation. Thus we feign

the continued existence of the perceptions of our senses, to remove the interruptoin; and run into the notion of a *soul,* and *self,* and *substance,* to disguise the variation. But, we may further observe, that where we do not give rise to such a fiction, our propension to confound identity with relation is so great, that we are apt to imagine something unknown and mysterious,[1] connecting the parts, beside their relation; and this I take to be the case with regard to the identity we ascribe to plants and vegetables. And even when this does not take place, we still feel a propensity to confound these ideas, though we are not able fully to satisfy ourselves in that particular, nor find anything invariable and uninterrupted to justify our notion of identity.

Thus the controversy concerning identity is not merely a dispute of words. For when we attribute identity, in an improper sense, to variable or interrupted objects, our mistake is not confined to the expression, but is commonly attended with a fiction, either of something invariable and uninterrupted, or of something mysterious and inexplicable, or at least with a propensity to such fictions. What will suffice to prove this hypothesis to the satisfaction of every fair inquirer, is to show, from daily experience and observation, that the objects which are variable or interrupted, and yet are supposed to continue the same, are such only as consist of a succession of parts, connected together by resemblance, contiguity, or causation. For as such a succession answers evidently to our notion of diversity, it can only be by mistake we ascribe to it an identity; and the relation of parts, which leads us into this mistake, is really nothing but a quality, which produces an association of ideas, and an easy transition of the imagination from one to another, it can only be from the resemblance, which this act of the mind bears to that by which we contemplate one continued object, that the error arises. Our

---

[1] If the reader is desirous to see how a great genius may be influenced by these seemingly trivial principles of the imagination, as well as the mere vulgar, let him read my Lord Shaftesbury's reasonings concerning the uniting principle of the universe, and the identity of plants and animals. See his *Moralists,* or *Philosophical Rhapsody.*

chief business, then, must be to prove, that all objects, to which we ascribe identity, without observing their invariableness and uninterruptedness, are such as consist of a succession of related objects.

In order to this, suppose any mass of matter, of which the parts are contiguous and connected, to be placed before us; it is plain we must attribute a perfect identity to this mass, provided all the parts continue uninterruptedly and invariably the same, whatever motion or change of place we may observe either in the whole or in any of the parts. But supposing some very *small* or *inconsiderable* part to be added to the mass, or subtracted from it; though this absolutely destroys the identity of the whole, strictly speaking, yet as we seldom think so accurately, we scruple not to pronounce a mass of matter the same, where we find so trivial an alteration. The passage of the thought from the object before the change to the object after it, is so smooth and easy, that we scarce perceive the transition, and are apt to imagine, that it is nothing but a continued survey of the same object.

There is a very remarkable circumstance that attends this experiment; which is, that though the change of any considerable part in a mass of matter destroys the identity of the whole, yet we must measure the greatness of the part, not absolutely, but by its *proportion* to the whole. The addition or diminution of a mountain would not be sufficient to produce a diversity in a planet; though the change of a very few inches would be able to destroy the identity of some bodies. It will be impossible to account for this, but by reflecting that objects operate upon the mind, and break or interrupt the continuity of its actions, not according to their real greatness, but according to their proportion to each other; and therefore, since this interruption makes an object cease to appear the same, it must be the uninterrupted progress of the thought which constitutes the imperfect identity.

This may be confirmed by another phenomenon. A change in any considerable part of a body destroys its identity; but it is remarkable, that where the change is produced

gradually and *insensibly,* we are less apt to ascribe to it the same effect. The reason can plainly be no other, than that the mind, in following the successive changes of the body, feels an easy passage from the surveying its condition in one moment, to the viewing of it in another, and in no particular time perceives any interruption in its actions. From which continued perception, it ascribes a continued existence and identity to the object.

But whatever precaution we may use in introducing the changes gradually, and making them proportionable to the whole, it is certain, that where the changes are at last observed to become considerable, we make a scruple of ascribing identity to such different objects. There is, however, another artifice, by which we may induce the imagination to advance a step further; and that is, by producing a reference of the parts to each other, and a combination to some *common end* or purpose. A ship, of which a considerable part has been changed by frequent reparations, is still considered as the same; nor does the difference of the materials hinder us from ascribing an identity to it. The common end, in which the parts conspire, is the same under all their variations, and affords an easy transition of the imagination from one situation of the body to another.

But this is still more remarkable, when we add a *sympathy* of part to their *common end,* and suppose that they bear to each other the reciprocal relation of cause and effect in all their actions and operations. This is the case with all animals and vegetables; where not only the several parts have a reference to some general purpose, but also a mutual dependence on, and connection with, each other. The effect of so strong a relation is, that though every one must allow, that in a very few years both vegetables and animals endure a *total* change, yet we still attribute identity to them, while their form, size, and substance, are entirely altered. An oak that grows from a small plant to a large tree is still the same oak, though there be not one particle of matter or figure of its parts the same. An infant becomes a man, and is sometimes fat, sometimes lean, without any change in his identity.

We may also consider the two following phenomena, which are remarkable in their kind. The first is, that though we commonly be able to distinguish pretty exactly betwixt numerical and specific identity, yet it sometimes happens that we confound them, and in our thinking and reasoning employ the one for the other. Thus, a man who hears a noise that is frequently interrupted and renewed, says it is still the same noise, though it is evident the sounds have only a specific identity or resemblance, and there is nothing numerically the same but the cause which produced them. In like manner it may be said, without breach of the propriety of language, that such a church, which was formerly of brick, fell to ruin, and that the parish rebuilt the same church of freestone, and according to modern architecture. Here neither the form nor materials are the same, nor is there anything common to the two objects but their relation to the inhabitants of the parish; and yet this alone is sufficient to make us denominate them the same. But we must, observe that in these cases the first object is in a manner annihilated before the second comes into existence; by which means, we are never presented, in any one point of time, with the idea of difference and multiplicity; and for that reason are less scrupulous in calling them the same.

Secondly, we may remark, that though, in a succession of related objects, it be in a manner requisite that the change of parts be not sudden nor entire, in order to preserve the identity, yet where the objects are in their nature changeable and inconstant, we admit of a more sudden transition than would otherwise be consistent with that relation. Thus, as the nature of a river consists in the motion and change of parts, though in less than four-and-twenty hours these be totally altered, this hinders not the river from continuing the same during several ages. What is natural and essential to anything is, in a manner, expected; and what is expected makes less impression, and appears of less moment than what is unusual and extraordinary. A considerable change of the former kind seems really less to the imagination than the most trivial alteration of the latter; and by breaking less the continuity of the thought, has less influence in destroying the identity.

We now proceed to explain the nature of *personal identity*, which has become so great a question in philosophy, especially of late years, in England, where all the abstruser sciences are studied with a peculiar ardour and application. And here it is evident the same method of reasoning must be continued which has so successfully explained the identity of plants, and animals, and ships, and houses, and of all compounded and changeable productions either of art or nature. The identity which we ascribe to the mind of man is only a fictitious one, and of a like kind with that which we ascribe to vegetable and animal bodies. It cannot therefore have a different origin, but must proceed from a like operation of the imagination upon like objects.

But lest this argument should not convince the reader, though in my opinion perfectly decisive, let him weigh the following reasoning, which is still closer and more immediate. It is evident that the identity which we attribute to the human mind, however perfect we may imagine it to be, is not able to run the several different perceptions into one, and make them lose their characters of distinction and difference, which are essential to them. It is still true that every distinct perception which enters into the composition of the mind, is a distinct existence, and is different, and distinguishable, and separable from every other perception, either contemporary or successive. But as, notwithstanding this distinction and separability, we suppose the whole train of perceptions to be united by identity, a question naturally arises concerning this relation of identity, whether it be something that really binds our several perceptions together, or only associates their ideas in the imagination; that is, in other words, whether, in pronouncing concerning the identity of a person, we observe some real bond among his perceptions, or only feel one among the ideas we form of them. This question we might easily decide, if we would recollect what has been already proved at large, that the understanding never observes any real connection among objects, and that even the union of cause and effect, when strictly examined, resolves itself into a customary association of ideas. For from thence it evidently follows, that identity is nothing really belonging to these different perceptions, and uniting them together, but is merely a quality which we attribute to them, because of the union of their ideas in the imagination when we reflect upon them. Now, the only qualities which can give ideas a union in the imagination, are these three relations above mentioned. These are the uniting principles in the ideal world, and without them every distinct object is separable by the mind, and may be separately considered, and appears not to have any more connection with any other object than if disjoined by the greatest difference and remoteness. It is therefore on some of these three relations of resemblance, contiguity, and causation, that identity depends; and as the very essence of these relations consists in their producing an easy transition of ideas, it follows that our notions of personal identity proceed entirely from the smooth and uninterrupted progress of the thought along a train of connected ideas, according to the principles above explained.

The only question, therefore, which remains is, by what relations this uninterrupted progress of our thought is produced, when we consider the successive existence of a mind or thinking person. And here it is evident we must confine ourselves to resemblance and causation, and must drop contiguity, which has little or no influence in the present case.

To begin with *resemblance;* suppose we could see clearly into the breast of another, and observe that succession of perceptions which constitutes his mind or thinking principle, and suppose that he always preserves the memory of a considerable part of past perceptions, it is evident that nothing could more contribute to the bestowing a relation on this succession amidst all its variations. For what is the memory but a faculty, by which we raise up the images of past perceptions? And as an image necessarily resembles its object, must not the frequent placing of

these resembling perceptions in the chain of thought, convey the imagination more easily from one link to another, and make the whole seem like the continuance of one object? In this particular, then, the memory not only discovers the identity, but also contributes to its production, by producing the relation of resemblance among the perceptions. The case is the same, whether we consider ourselves or others.

As to *causation;* we may observe that the true idea of the human mind, is to consider it as a system of different perceptions or different existences, which are linked together by the relation of cause and effect, and mutually produce, destroy, influence, and modify each other. Our impressions give rise to their correspondent ideas; and these ideas, in their turn, produce other impressions. One thought chases another, and draws after it a third, by which it is expelled in its turn. In this respect, I cannot compare the soul more properly to anything than to a republic or commonwealth, in which the several members are united by the reciprocal ties of government and subordination, and give rise to other persons who propagate the same republic in the incessant changes of its parts. And as the same individual republic may not only change its members, but also its laws and constitutions; in like manner the same person may vary his character and disposition, as well as his impressions and ideas, without losing his identity. Whatever changes he endures, his several parts are still connected by the relation of causation. And in this view our identity with regard to the passions serves to corroborate that with regard to the imagination, by the making our distant perceptions influence each other, and by giving us a present concern for our past or future pains or pleasures.

As memory alone acquaints us with the continuance and extent of this succession of perceptions, it is to be considered, upon that account chiefly, as the source of personal identity. Had we no memory, we never should have any notion of causation, nor consequently of that chain of causes and effects, which constitute our self or person. But having once acquired this notion of causation from the memory, we can extend the same chain of causes, and consequently the identity of our persons beyond our memory, and can comprehend times, and circumstances, and actions, which we have entirely forgot, but suppose in general to have existed. For how few of our past actions are there, of which we have any memory? Who can tell me, for instance, what were his thoughts and actions on the first of January 1715, the eleventh of March 1719, and the third of August 1733? Or will he affirm, because he has entirely forgot the incidents of these days, that the present self is not the same person with the self of that time; and by that means overturn all the most established notions of personal identity? In this view, therefore, memory does not so much *produce* as *discover* personal identity, by showing us the relation of cause and effect among our different perceptions. It will be incumbent on those who affirm that memory produces entirely our personal identity, to give a reason why we can thus extend our identity beyond our memory.

The whole of this doctrine leads us to a conclusion, which is of great importance in the present affair, viz. that all the nice and subtile questions concerning personal identity can never possibly be decided, and are to be regarded rather as grammatical than as philo-sophical difficulties. Identity depends on the relations of ideas; and these relations produce identity, by means of that easy transition they occasion. But as the relations, and the easiness of the transition may diminish by insensible degrees, we have no just standard by which we can decide any dispute concerning the time when they acquire or lose a title to the name of identity. All the disputes concerning the identity of connected objects are merely verbal, except so far as the relation of parts gives rise to some fiction or imaginary principle of union, as we have already observed.

What I have said concerning the first origin and uncertainty of our notion of identity, as applied to the human mind, may be extended with little or no variation to that of *simplicity*. An object, whose different coexistent parts are bound together by a close relation, operates upon the imagination after much the same manner as one perfectly simple and indivisible, and requires not a much greater stretch of thought in order to its conception. From this similarity of operation we attribute a simplicity to it, and feign a principle of union as the support of this simplicity, and the centre of all the different parts and qualities of the object.

Appendix

I had entertained some hopes, that however deficient our theory of the intellectual world might be, it would be free from those contradictions and absurdities which seem to attend every explication that human reason can give of the material world. But upon a more strict review of the section concerning *personal identity,* I find myself involved in such a labyrinth that, I must confess, I neither know how to correct my former opinions, nor how to render them consistent. If this be not a good *general* reason for scepticism, it is at least a sufficient one (if I were not already abundantly supplied) for me to entertain a diffidence and modesty in all my decisions. I shall propose the arguments on both sides, beginning with those that induced me to deny the strict and proper identity and simplicity of a self or thinking being.

When we talk of *self* or *subsistence,* we must have an idea annexed to these terms, otherwise they are altogether unintelligible. Every idea is derived from preceding impressions; and we have no impression of self or substance, as something simple and individual. We have, therefore, no idea of them in that sense.

Whatever is distinct is distinguishable, and whatever is distinguishable is separable by the thought or imagination. All perceptions are distinct. They are, therefore, distinguishable, and separable, and may be conceived as separately existent, and may exist separately, without any contradiction or absurdity.

When I view this table and that chimney, nothing is present to me but particular perceptions, which are of a like nature with all the other perceptions. This is the doctrine of philosophers. But this table, which is present to me, and that chimney, may, and do exist separately. This is the doctrine of the vulgar, and implies no contradiction. There is no contradiction, therefore, in extending the same doctrine to all the perceptions.

In general, the following reasoning seems satisfactory. All ideas are borrowed from preceding perceptions. Our ideas of objects, therefore, are derived from that source. Consequently no proposition can be intelligible or consistent with regard to objects, which is not so with regard to perceptions. But it is intelligible and consistent to say, that objects exist distinct and independent, without any common *simple* substance or subject of inhesion. This proposition, therefore, can never be absurd with regard to perceptions.

When I turn my reflection on *myself*, I never can perceive this *self* without some one or more perceptions; nor can I ever perceive anything but the perceptions. It is the composition of these, therefore, which forms the self.

We can conceive a thinking being to have either many or few perceptions. Suppose the mind to be reduced even below the life of an oyster. Suppose it to have only one perception, as of thirst or hunger. Consider it in that situation. Do you conceive anything but merely that perception? Have you any notion of *self* or *substance*? If not, the addition of other perceptions can never give you that notion.

The annihilation which some people suppose to follow upon death, and which entirely destroys this self, is nothing but an extinction of all particular perceptions; love and hatred, pain and pleasure, thought and sensation. These, therefore, must be the same with self, since the one cannot survive the other.

Is *self* the same with *substance*? If it be, how can that question have place, concerning the substance of self, under a change of substance? If they be distinct, what is the difference betwixt them? For my part, I have a notion of neither, when conceived distinct from particular perceptions.

Philosophers begin to be reconciled to the principle, *that we have no idea of external substance, distinct from the ideas of particular qualities.* This must pave the way for a like principle with regard to the mind, *that we have no notion of it, distinct from the particular perception.*

So far I seem to be attended with sufficient evidence. But having thus loosened all our particular perceptions, when I proceed to explain the principle of connection, which binds them together, and makes us attribute to them a real simplicity and identity, I am sensible that my account is very defective, and that nothing but the seeming evidence of the precedent reasonings could have induced me to receive it. If perceptions are distinct existences, they form a whole only by being connected together. But no connections among distinct existences are ever discoverable by human understanding. We only *feel* a connection or determination of the thought to pass from one object to another. It follows, therefore, that the thought alone feels personal identity, when reflecting on the train of past perceptions that compose a mind, the ideas of them are felt to be connected together, and naturally introduce each other. However extraordinary this conclusion may seem, it need not surprise us. Most philosophers seem inclined to think, that personal identity *arises* from consciousness, and consciousness is nothing but a reflected thought or perception. The present philosophy, therefore, has so far a promising aspect. But all my hopes vanish when I come to explain the principles that unite our successive perceptions in our thought or consciousness. I cannot discover any theory which gives me satisfaction on this head.

In short, there are two principles which I cannot render consistent, nor is it in my power to renounce either of them, viz. *that all our distinct perceptions are distinct existences,* and *that the mind never perceives any real connection among distinct existences.* Did our perceptions either inhere in something simple and individual, or did the mind perceive some real connection among them, there would be no difficulty in the case. For my part, I must plead the privilege of a sceptic, and confess that this difficulty is too hard for my understanding. I pretend not, however, to pronounce it absolutely insuperable. Others, perhaps, or myself, upon more mature reflections, may discover some hypothesis that will reconcile those contradictions.

CHARLES ARTHUR CAMPBELL

SELF-CONSCIOUSNESS, SELF-IDENTITY AND PERSONAL IDENTITY*

1. In the closing stages of my last lecture I argued that the judgment-theory of cognition throws into relief the hopelessness of trying to dispense with a distinguishable cognising subject. Today I want to begin consideration of the nature of this "subject." The fundamental difficulty we have to deal with is very well known. There seem to be respectable reasons for describing the cognising subject as a "substantival" entity in *some* sense of that term: and there seem to be equally respectable reasons for rejecting the "substantival" description in *any* sense of the term.

It is reasons of the latter order which, as one would expect, have received much the greater prominence in recent philosophy. But finding objections to the substantival theory has proved a great deal easier than fiding a plausible alternative to it. My own view is that, while there are certainly forms of the substantival theory that are indefensible, the objections taken to the substantival theory as such, or in general, are invalid; whereas against any alternative to the substantival theory which has so far been offered there seem to me to be objections of a completely conclusive character. That will be the main thesis to be argued in the present lecture; but I must introduce it somewhat gradually.

2. Let us begin with a proposition the truth of which seems to me easily demonstrable within the context of our recent discussions; the proposition that the cognising subject is always in some degree aware of itself, or "self-conscious."

This, I think, can be seen to be yet another implication of the judgment-theory of cognition. All cognition involves judgment. All judgment involves reference to an "objective" reality which the judging mind is seeking to know. But an essential part of the meaning which "objective reality" carries for the judging mind is its independence of that mind. Hence a mind that is aware of objective reality is always also in some degree aware of itself as subject. It follows that all cognition implies in the cognising subject some degree of self-awareness.

It goes without saying that in very many cognitions the degree of self-awareness present is exceedingly small. But so, for that matter, in many cognitions, is the degree of awareness of an independent objective reality; and yet, as we saw earlier, there are cogent reasons for presuming it present, in however inexplicit a fashion, wherever anything which can strictly be called a cognition occurs. Hence if it be the case that "objectivity" defines itself, for the cognising mind, at least in part, by contrast with "subjectivity," we must, I think, conclude that cognition always involves some awareness, however, inexplicit, of the subject as subject.

3. But now what kind of a being is this "subject" of which there is consciousness in all cognition? Its most important, and at the

* From *On Selfhood and Godhood* by C. A. Campbell. London: George Allen & Unwin Ltd. New York: The Macmillan Company, 1957. Lecture V. Reprinted by permission of the publishers.

same time its most perplexing, characteristic is that it is, for itself, somehow the *self-same* being throughout its different experiences; and the self-same being not merely in contemporaneous experiences, but in experiences far removed from one another in time. Thus I am conscious that I who am now thinking about a peculiarly intractable philosophical problem am the same being as I who am now feeling the room to be slightly on the warm side, and am *also* the same being as I who (as I remember) saw a rainbow yesterday. Indeed, "remembering" brings out in an especially striking manner the self's identity in difference. When we say "*I* remember that *I* saw a rainbow yesterday," we imply that the being who now remembers is identical with the being who saw the rainbow. The claim of the memory situation, a claim in the absence of which the situation ceases to be one of memory at all, is that the remember*ing* subject and the remember*ed* subject are somehow the *same* being in experiences that are different both temporally and qualitatively.

The difficulties in the way of attaching a clear meaning to the self-sameness of the subject in different apprehensions will engage us shortly. But we must first of all support by more formal argument the thesis that cognition of *any* kind—not merely in remembering—implies a subject conscious of its own identity in its different apprehensions.

4. The standard argument for this doctrine is so exceedingly well-worn as almost to require apology for its repetition, and I shall expound it in very summary fashion. It derives, of course, from Kant. What follows will perhaps serve as a sufficient reminder of its general character.

Cognition is never of an atomic simple. It is always of a related plurality *as* a related plurality. This is self-evident if all cognition involves judgment, for in all judgment there must be at least the differences of subject and predicate and the affirmation or denial of their union. But we need not invoke the judgment theory to establish our point. It is clear enough, on reflection, that an "object" which stands in no apprehended relation to other objects of our experience—"an atomic simple"—can have no significance for us, and is thus not an object of cognition at all. Even a "this" is, for cognition, a "this-not-that"; apart from its apprehended distinction from, and therefore relation to, a "that" it could not be cognised as "this." But it seems gratuitous to pursue further a point which has so often received classic expression in post-Kantian philosophy. The critic may be challenged to produce a single instance of cognition, or "meaningful apprehension," where the object does *not* consist in a related plurality.

What is cognised, then, is never bare A, but always A in some sort of relationship to B (C, D, etc.). But unless the subject to which B (C, D, etc.) is present in the same subject as that to which A is present, no relationship, obviously, could be apprehended between B (C, D, etc.) and A. To take the very familiar example of our cognition of succession in time, perhaps the most basic of all cognitions. If event B is cognised as sequent upon event A, clearly A must, in some form, be present to the same subject as that to which B is present. Otherwise A and B would simply fall apart into separate worlds of experience, and no discerned relationship—not even that of apartness, let alone that of temporal sequence—would be possible.

Does cognition imply not merely a subject identical in different cognitions, but a subject *conscious* of its identity in different cognitions? Some philosophers who are firmly persuaded of the subject's self-identity show a certain diffidence about pressing for the subject's consciousness of that identity. Nevertheless I would suggest that this must be pressed. For let us suppose that the subject, though in *fact* identical in two different apprehensions, is in no wise aware of its own identity in them. This subject, let us further suppose, has an apprehension of A, and then an apprehension of B. Now for an outside observer appraised, if that were possible, of the two apprehensions, A and B could be seen to be related, inasmuch as they could be seen both to be objects to the same subject. But for the *subject himself*, unaware (according to our supposition) that the self to whom B is present is the same being as the self to whom A was formerly present, the two apprehensions must fall apart into separate "worlds" just as surely and completely as though he, the self-same subject, were in fact *two different* subjects; and the discernment by him of any *relationship* between A and B (such as that of temporal sequence) must then become impossible. The *prius* of any discernment by the subject of a specific relation between A and B is surely that the subject is aware of A and B as having at least that general relationship to one another which consists in their both being objects for *him,* the one self. He must, in other words, be conscious of his own identity in the different apprehensions.

The point is apt to be as elusive as it is certainly important, and a further illustration may be helpful.

Suppose I hear Big Ben striking. A moment later I—the same subject—hear it striking again. Now is my being "the same subject" sufficient in itself to enable me to apprehend the second stroke *as* the second stroke, as *sequent upon* the first? Not, surely, unless by "the same subject" we *mean* a subject conscious of its self-sameness. I may be in so advanced a state of senility that my memory-span is no longer adequate to bridge the gulf between the two strokes, so that, having forgotten the first when I hear the second, I cannot relate the two to one another. It is a precondition of my apprehending the second stroke *as* the second stroke that I remember having heard the first. But then I do not "remember" having heard the first (and here is the crucial point) unless I am aware that it was *I*, the being who now hears the second stroke, who heard the first stroke; unless, in other words, I am not merely the same subject, but also conscious of my self-sameness, in the two experiences.

It seems to me, therefore, that while the identity of the cognising subject is a necessary, it is not, without consciousness of that identity, a sufficient, condition of cognitive awareness.

5. The point we have now reached (retracing, for the most part, familiar lines of argument) is that all cognition implies a subject that is conscious of itself, and that this self of which we are conscious in cognition is a being which is identical with itself throughout—and in despite of—the diversity of its cognitions. But now our troubles begin. We are led by the argument, apparently, to posit a self which is something "over and above" its particular experiences; something that *has,* rather than *is,* its experiences, since its experiences are all different, while *it* somehow remains the same. It is, in short, what would usually be called a "substance," in some sense of that term, and as such it provokes in the modern mind an hostility which, to say truth, the history of philosophy has done much to justify. What, it will be asked, *is* this "I" that is supposed to remain the same, and in what does its sameness consist? By universal admission we never have any acquaintance with it by itself, but only as manifested in particular changing experiences. What possible meaning can we attach to an "I" as an identical "something" over and above these experiences? And our perplexities, it will be urged, by no means end there. If we try to conceive the self as an identical substance, how are we to reconcile with this all the phenomena of radical disunity made familiar to us by abnormal psychology, such as sudden drastic transformations of a self-personal character, not to speak of these strange cases of "multiple personality" in which the "one" self seems to divide up into two or more separate selves?

The difficulty of returning satisfactory answers to such questions has proved so formidable that the strong trend of philosophic opinion today is in the direction of relinquishing the notion of a "substantival" self altogether. The notion of a self of *some* sort, it is conceded, must be retained. We do mean something by the word "I"; and we do mean something when we refer to a variety of different experiences as all "my" experiences. But an interpretation must be found, it is urged, in terms of the particular knowable experiences themselves, not in terms of an "unknowable" something beyond them. Hence it has appeared to many to be the most promising procedure to search *within* the different experiences for some identical quality or, more hopefully, some common relationship, in virtue of which they come to be regarded as all experiences of "one self."

6. What then *is* this quality or relationship? That is just the trouble. I think it is fair to say that, while the great body of contemporary philosophical opinion favours the view that this is where the meaning of self-identity must be sought, there is no manner of agreement as to what the quality or relationship can be. Indeed, no one seems to have much confidence even in the theory he himself proposes, but rather to be putting it forward tentatively as an hypothesis that is not wholly incredible, and is at any rate more credible than any form of substantival theory. As already hinted, some kind of common relationship, rather than some kind of identical quality, has been very generally taken to be the most hopeful thing to look for. But all the types of relationship between different experiences that are known to us in other contexts—similarity, causality, and the rest—seem open to obvious and crushing objections if we try to regard them as the basis of the mind's self-identity. Any one of them can exist between particular experiences without our having the slightest tendency to take these particular experiences to be all experiences of a single self.[1] It is, I think, not easy to

dissent from the conclusion reached by Dr. Ewing after a critical survey of the several types of relationship that have been, or conceivably might be, suggested, viz. that "if we adopt a view of the self according to which its identity is constituted . . . by a relation between its experiences, it is probably best just to say that the relation is unique and indefinable."[2]

I do not, however, propose to take up time rehearsing the various relational theories *seriatim,* for the following reason. It seems to me that the whole project of seeking for the identity of the self in a relation of *whatever* kind, definable *or* indefinable, between members of a series or group of experiences, is fundamentally futile; indeed self-contradictory. For consider. What we are trying to account for is the identity of a self *not* for some *external observer,* but for the *self itself;* the identity of the self as *subject,* not its identity as an *object*—which the self, *qua* self, just is *not.* Now as a result of cognition of particular events and their inter-relationships we might come to regard as belonging to "one and the same" *object* events which exhibited a certain form of inter-relationship. Applied to mental events, there is some sense in saying that we might thereby arrive at the notion of an object-mind as an identical *it.* But it is the *subject*-mind, the identical "I" of *self*-consciousness, which we are trying to account for; and by the route suggested this is plainly impossible. For, as we have already seen, cognition of relationships, and indeed cognition of any kind whatsoever, *presupposes* an identical subject conscious of its own identity. It follows that the "relational" way of explaining self-identity can only be in terms which presuppose the very thing it is purporting to explain.

I suggest, then, that the attempt to find a form of relationship between different experiences which is sufficient to account for my regarding these experiences as "mine" is doomed to failure from the outset. There *is,* indeed, an apprehended relationship in virtue of which I call experiences "mine," but it is

---

[1] Mr. D. G. C. McNabb, in what is otherwise a most penetrating discussion of Hume's treatment of personal identity, seems to think that while such relations as similarity, causality, and spatial and temporal conjunction of perceptions will obviously not account for the kind of identity that belongs to a self, the relational theory may perhaps still be saved if we supplement these relations by another "empirically given relation which we may call co-presentation, which holds between any two or more perceptions which I am in a position to compare with one another". He confesses himself, indeed, not too happy about this solution, since "it looks very much as if it were an empirical fact that this relation is at least a three-term relation, involving at least two perceptions and something else, the mind to which they are presented and which is able to compare them". I suggest that "looks very much as if" is, to put it mildly, an understatement. If "co-presentation" is really "co-*presentation*", it is surely an analytic proposition that there is this "third term"; while if "co-presentation" means something else (which it has no right to mean), like "co-occurrence" of perceptions, it is plainly useless for the purpose in hand. It may be that the "third term" is, in Mr. McNabb's words, "a very curious kind of entity"; but this hardly seems adequate ground for denying an analytic proposition. (*David Hume, His Theory of Knowledge amd Morality,* pp. 149–50.)

[2] *The Fundamental Questions of Philosophy,* p. 115. (Italics not in text.)

not a relationship of experiences to one another. It can, I think, only be stated as a relationship of experiences to *me*, an identical subject conscious of having or owning them; a relationship of "belonging to" which is unique and indefinable, but the apprehension of which is ingredient in all self-conscious experience. It is clear, however, that this relationship presupposes, and in no way constitutes, the identity of the self.

Still, the problem remains on our hands, "In what does self-identity consist?" The relational theory may be, and I think is, open to fatal objections; but so far nothing explicit has been said to show that the substantival account, the difficulties in which gave rise to the relational theory, is in any better case. Let us now look back, therefore, at the notion of the self as a substantival entity, distinguishable from its experiences, and, a little fortified by the apparent bankruptcy of the rival relational theory, consider whether it cannot be formulated in a way that escapes the objections usually thought to be conclusive against it.

7. Two preliminary points are worth making briefly. Critics of the substantival self seem to me a great deal too ready to assimilate it either to Locke's "unknowable substratum" of material things, or to Kant's "noumenal ego." This is, I think, unfortunate. It is by no means the case that the doctrine of the substantival self need take a form that lays it open to the objections to which Locke's and Kant's doctrines are notoriously exposed.

To take first the assimilation to Locke's unknowable substratum of material things, Berkeley has said perhaps all that needs to be said on the ineptitude of supposing that spiritual substance and material substance must stand or fall together. When Philonous in the Third Dialogue points out to Hylas that whereas I have no apprehension whatsoever of material substance, I yet "am conscious of my own being, and that I myself am not my ideas, but somewhat else, a thinking, active principle that perceives, knows, wills, and operates about ideas," he is indicating a *prima facie* difference in the epistemological status of spiritual substance and

material substance respectively that is fundamental. Self-consciousness, it must be insisted, is a *fact,* a datum from which we have to *start.* And in self-consciousness the subject of which we are conscious is a subject which in some sense has, not is, its different experiences, and is identical with itself in its different experiences. Even if it were possible for self-consciousness to be illusory, its mere occurrence is enough to refute those who take the view that the notion of a substantival self is as "meaningless" as the notion of an unknowable substratum of material things. It is idle to deny that the former of these notions has any meaning for us if that *is* in fact what the self is for itself in self-conscious experience.

Very little more reflection is needed to see that the substantival self cannot be straightway identified with Kant's noumenal ego.

For Kant, it will be remembered, the subject self has its reality beyond the space-time world of mere phenomena; and while we can know in self-consciousness *that* it is, we can say nothing at all about *what* it is. Cognition of the character, the "what," of the self through introspection is not, for Kant, discernment of the nature of the self as *subject*— i.e. of its real nature *qua* self—but only of the self as *object,* which is a mere appearance in time of the timeless "real" self. Kant's noumenal ego is, from the point of view of theoretical cogition at any rate, as characterless as Locke's substratum of material things.

But the defender of the substantival self is under no obligation to accept Kant's views either about time or about what introspection can and cannot reveal to us. One may perfectly well agree with the argument from self-conscious experience to a distinguishable subject-self without being committed to any of the special arguments which led Kant to assert that we can have no theoretical knowledge of that self as it really is. I shall in a later lecture have to give some attention to the problem of the nature and status of introspection as a mode of knowledge, and I shall try to show there that it is a mistake to suppose that introspection cannot reveal real characteristics of the self *qua* self, that is to say, of the self in its functioning as a *subject*. Meantime I would merely point to the direct testimony of self-consciousness. When I am conscious that I who think *A* am the I who desires *B* and the I who feels the emotion *C*, I regard my "I" as manifesting *itself* in these operations of thinking, desiring and feeling: and as thus, so far, "characterised" by these operations. The subject self as apprehended in self-consciousness is in that sense always a determinate or characterised self. To deny that the self is *reducible to* its experiences is by no means to deny that the self manifests its real character (in whole or in part) *in and through* these experiences. The onus of proof lies upon those who wish to maintain that to the self as subject we can assign no determinate characters at all.

I attach a fair amount of importance to these two points; for there is nothing to be gained by making the problem of justifying a substantival self still more difficult than it already is through pejorative misconceptions as to what belief in a substantival self in fact entails. But the puzzle about this self's identity remains baffling enough and must now be directly confronted.

8. I propose to work towards the view which seems to me in the end the most acceptable by raising in turn, and trying to answer, four distinct but closely related questions.

1. Can a *meaning* be given to the substantival description of the self; i.e. to the description of it as a being which is distinct from the states in which it manifests itself and is identical with itself throughout these manifestations?

2. Granted that the description is not "meaningless," is there good reason to believe that beings answering to that description actually *exist*?

3. Given an identical self as so described, of *what* is it an identity? Is it an identity of spiritual being, of material being, of both, or of something else?

4. How is the identity of the self, so understood, related to what is called *"personal identity"*?

Now so far as the first question is concerned, the answer has already been given in principle in the reference we made to Berkeley. Self-consciousness is a fact of experience; and the self of which we are conscious in self-consciousness *is* a subject which in some sense has, rather than is, its different experiences, and is identical with itself throughout them. It must be a strangely doctrinaire theory of meaning that would oblige us to denounce as meaningless a description which describes what the self is for itself in all self-conscious experience.

It is sometimes said that the substantival self is meaningless because openly self-contradictory. If "I" change with my changing experience—as I surely do, and as the substantival theory must allow if its ego is not to be something quite apart from the self which interests us, the self of our actual experience—how can it be said, as the substantival theory says, that "I" remain the same?

But this charge of self-contradiction rests on the assumption that sameness totally excludes difference; and this is an assumption to which all self-conscious experience gives the lie direct. I as a self-conscious subject cannot doubt that I who now hear the clock strike a second time am the same being who a moment ago also heard the clock strike, even though I must have become different in some respects in the interval. It can hardly be accepted as an irrefutable principle of philosophic criticism that sameness excludes all difference, when it is a datum of self-conscious experience that it does not.

It may be desirable to add, in order to avert possible misapprehensions, that to be meaningful is by no means the same thing as to be intelligible, where "intelligible" is a synonym for "capable of being understood." The self as we have described it would be intelligible (in this sense) only if it were possible to understand *how* it remains one amid the plurality of its changing experiences. No claim is made here that the self is, even in principle, capable of being "understood"; and no such claim will be made at any point in these lectures. We are aware of our self *as* of such and such a nature, not of *how* it is what it is. But awareness of the former is all that is necessary for it to have "meaning" for us.

9. The answer to the second question can again be given very briefly. Yes, there are excellent reasons for believing that selves so characterised do actually exist. And the evidence again comes from self-conscious experience. In self-conscious experience it is surely just not possible to doubt the self's existence. The consciousness of self in self-conscious experience is the consciousness not of something as having hypothetical existence, but of something as having actual existence. As I write these words I am conscious that I am casting about in thought for a suitable illustration, and conscious also that I am hearing "noises without" of a somewhat distracting character. Now, try as I will, I find that I cannot doubt, in the first place, that I am the same being in each of these different experiences and distinct from either of them. But I find it equally impossible to doubt, in the second place, that this I, this identical subject of the different experiences, does actually exist. And if the reader is (as of course he ought to be) unprepared to accept this report at second-hand, let him make a similar experiment for himself. If it be made without preconceptions, I do not fear for the result.

Conceivably it will be said "But the witness of self-consciousness may, after all, be false witness, generating mere illusion." I must confess, however, that I cannot see how this hypothesis can even be formulated without self-contradiction. It involves us in saying "Though I am certain whenever I am aware of my self that I do exist, nevertheless perhaps I don't." But what can "Perhaps *I* don't" mean if I am not aware of my*self* when I say it? But if I *am* aware of myself when I say it, I must, according to the *first* clause, be *certain* that I exist; and I am therefore contradicting myself when I say "Perhaps I don't."

The real source of most of the scepticism about the existence of the substantival self is, I suspect, doubts about its meaningfulness. But with these doubts we have already dealt. It may very well, we have agreed, not be

intelligible, in the sense of understandable; but that is irrelevant to the question of its meaningfulness.

10. Let us move on to our third question, "Of *what* is self-identity an identity?" The testimony of self-conscious experience (in any form, at any rate, in which we have so far considered it) is to the identity of the self as a *conscious* subject. I who *think* of A am aware of my identity with I who *feel* B and *desire* C—i.e. an I who has other *conscious* experiences. It is true that I who think of A may be aware of my identity with I who am walking about the room. But the second "I" here is, and must be, an "I" which has the *conscious experience* of "walking about the room." If it happened that, while thinking of A, I was so deeply absorbed in that thought as to be totally unconscious that I was walking about the room, then I clearly could not be conscious of identity between the I who thinks of A and the owner of this walking body. This consideration, of course, has no tendency to rule out the possibility that in fact "I" *am* a body as well as a mind. It is common ground to all theories of the self that recognise minds and bodies at all that there is some kind of extremely intimate relationship between the self as mind and a particular animal body: and those philosophers may be right who declare that the relationship in question is not merely intimate but *integral*. That, however, is a problem which must be treated at length if it is to be treated at all, and we shall postpone its discussion. Meantime, we are in a position to say only that the identity of the self, as revealed in self-conscious experience, is *at least* an identity of mind or spirit, though it may turn out to be more than that. "I" am *at least* a "spiritual substance."

11. How is the identity of the self, as above understood, related to *personal* identity? That was our fourth question, and the attempt to answer it will involve us in a long and somewhat complicated discussion. But it seems to me of particular moment that a clear answer to it should be reached. Not a few of the perplexities to which discussion of the self and its identity commonly gives

rise have their source, in my opinion, in a failure to appreciate that "self" and "person" cannot conveniently be treated as interchangeable expressions. An important distinction has got to be drawn within the general conception of selfhood; and if it be not drawn firmly, and marked by an appropriate and consistently employed nomenclature, serious confusion is well-nigh inevitable.

The general nature of the distinction I have in mind can perhaps be most clearly brought out by considering what is implied in such relatively common expressions as "I was not myself when I did that." Let us take the case of a man making this statement after being told of some violent act he has committed (and of which he has perhaps no recollection) during an epileptic seizure, or some other species of brain-storm. The term "I" in the statement is certainly intended by the speaker to designate his "self" in some sense of that term. Yet in saying "I was not myself" he seems by implication to be denying that the term "I" as used does designate his self. Presumably he must be regarding his self, when he makes the statement, in two different aspects.

Now as regards one of these aspects, that in which the self's participation in the violent deed is denied, there is, I think, no great difficulty in seeing what, in general, the self is taken by itself to be. The self here is being thought of as essentially the bearer of a specific "character." Every man comes in the course of experience to acquire a set of relatively stable dispositions to feel, think, and behave in more or less well-marked ways. He comes to regard himself, accordingly, and to be regarded by others, as the kind of man who, in such and such a sort of situation, can be depended upon to respond in such and such a sort of way. Naturally enough he will be moved to repudiate, as incapable of really issuing from his self, acts which he not merely may have no recollection of having performed, but which he simply cannot conceive himself, *qua* bearer of his specific character, as ever having performed. He does (in certain circumstances) feel constrained to admit that in *some* sense it was "he" who acted

—"I was not myself" he says "when *I* did that." But while thus allowing that in some sense his self-identity was retained in the act, he will vigorously dispute that it was his self-identity as a "person." For "personal identity" seems to him to lose its essential meaning if there be not preserved the salient features of that relatively stable set of dispositions which constitutes a man's character and marks him off as a distinct individual. (The term "person" has, admittedly, had a long and fluctuating history, and is even now of highly ambiguous import; but to associate it in this manner with the possession of a relatively definite character is a practice that has plenty of confirmation from ordinary linguistic usage. Thus we do not regard the young infant as having yet become a "person." Only later on, when it shows signs of "characteristic" interests and likes and dislikes and modes of response, do we come to speak of it as "now quite a little *person*.")

But what, now, is the self taken by itself to be in the *other* aspect, the aspect in which the self's engagement in the act is acknowledged even though its engagement as a *person* is denied? Why is it that in spite of the strong tendency to identify one's self with the "personal" bearer of a specific character—a tendency so strong that a not uncommon form of words for repudiating an act in one's personal authorship of which one cannot believe is "I was not my *real* self when I did that"—why is it that one does nevertheless refer to the author of the "contra-personal" act as *I*?

The reason is apparent enough, I think, in those cases where, as sometimes happens, one remembers, or even *thinks* one remembers, having committed the act. For the ontological identity of the subject of the remember*ing* experience—the I who remembers—with the subject of the remember*ed* experience is part of the very meaning of what we call "remembering." Remembering may be an illusion; but for the man who even thinks he remembers, that ontological identity is implied, and finds its natural expression in the verbal form "I remember that *I* did that." Thus in the case of my remembering having performed a "contra-personal" act, I cannot avoid regarding the author of it as "I"—the being that now remembers—at the same time as I may indignantly reject any suggestion that the remembered "I" and the remembering "I" are the same *person*.

The implication is, I think, that the "other aspect" in which the self is being regarded in the case before us is that of its *ontological* character. It is the same self "ontologically," but not "personally," that is acknowledged to have committed the contra-personal act. When a man says "I was not myself when I did that," the self-identity that is being *accepted* is identity of the self as what, in the light of our earlier argument, we may perhaps venture to call the same spiritual entity; whereas the self-identity that is being *denied* is the identity of that same spiritual entity considered *only in respect of its manifestations as a "person."*

A distinction in such terms may be said to be virtually forced upon us in cases like the above, where we "remember" having committed the contra-personal act. Where, as is probably more common, no recollection of the act remains, we may not be prepared to acknowledge that our self was engaged in it in any legitimate sense of the term "self." We may insist that the testimony of witnesses is only to the behaviour of our body, which we decline to accept as our self, however closely the two may be related. In that event we shall, of course, decline to use such words as "I was not myself when I did that," but shall rather say something like "It was not I, but only my body, that so acted." And in many instances we may be well justified in taking this line. There are many instances falling within the general class of actions we are discussing which offer no good evidence that anything save one's bodily processes are concerned. But on the other hand, there are also many instances in which, despite the absence of recollection, it is a reasonable inference that the self—even if not the self as "person"—was in fact engaged; and the individual concerned may himself be brought to acknowledge that the evidence is strong enough to compel this conclusion. For while the evidence can be directly only of bodily behaviour, it may well be of modes of bodily behaviour that strikingly suggest conscious purpose (e.g. "intelligible" speech), and which it is consequently hard not to interpret as betokening a directing "mind" of some sort. Where that is the case (and assuming, of course, adequate testimony by reliable witnesses), our choice would seem to lie between ascribing the "directing mind" to some intruding spirit that has in some mysterious manner obtained temporary control of our body, or, on the other hand, ascribing it to one's *self*, and recognising that the self does, under certain conditions, function in an abnormal way discontinuously with its "character." If only in view of the unique intimacy of the union which every man feels to exist between himself and "his" body, an intimacy so close that it is usual for a man to regard his body as virtually or actually a part of himself, the latter would seem much the more credible hypothesis.

The view to which we are being led, then, is that *self*-identity is a much wider conception than *personal* identity. But though "self" and "person" must be quite sharply distinguished, it is vital to bear in mind that they do not designate two different beings. They designate one and the same ontological entity in two different aspects. The self may function when the person does not, but the person cannot function when the self does not. The person *is* the self, *qua* functioning in terms of its definitive and normal character. Indeed the person, so far from being an entity different from the self, may be said to be something which the self tends gradually to become. The self starts upon its career with a variety of native instincts, impulses and capacities closely dependent upon its association with a particular animal body. Through the self's actions upon and reaction to its physical and social environment on the basis of these given propensities and powers, the relatively stable system of dispositions we call its "character" is gradually built up, and the self grows into what we call a "person."

But the self's energies, even when the self becomes a person, are not (as it were) poured without remainder into its functioning as a person. As we have seen, even "contra-personal" functioning must on occasion be attributed to the self; self-identity being retained though personal identity is interrupted. We have conceded, it is true, that it is not logically impossible to suppose that the contra-personal act is the work of some intruding spirit, some alien "self"; but it seems a far-fetched and extravagant hypothesis.

Moreover, our preferred hypothesis that it is the same self that functions in the contra-personal act as functions in the normal personal act is not so very mysterious once we accept the primal mystery that the spiritual substance in man functions only through the medium of, and under the limitations imposed by, a particular animal body. That the state of this body, and in particular the state of its brain and nervous system, conditions most and perhaps all mental functioning, is more or less agreed by everyone; though the advocate of spiritual substance would certainly want to insist (with many other philosophers) that the causal relation between mind and brain is not unilateral but mutual. Now if the brain in its normal state conditions the way in which the mind functions, it will presumably continue to condition it, but with very different effects, when in an abnormal state. More or less violent disturbances of the normal physical organisation of the brain, temporary or permanent, may be brought about by disease, by external injury, or by the chemical action of certain drugs; and where this occurs it is only to be expected that the mental functioning of the self will be abnormal. The degree and kind of abnormality it evinces, which may or may not entail a sharp discontinuity with its "characteristic" functioning, will depend upon the degree and kind and location of the physical disturbance—a matter upon which the researches of physiological psychologists throw great and constantly increasing light. The fundamental point, however, is that once we admit (and how can we deny?) that the self as mind, the spiritual substance in man, is at least partly in thrall to an animal body and functions subject to the conditions which that imposes, there is in principle no mystery about the *same* self functioning abnormally,

and perhaps "out of character" (with consequent loss of "personal identity"), where the bodily conditions have undergone sudden and drastic modifications with which the self has nothing to do.

It is not to be supposed, however, that the circumstances which give rise to loss or interruption of personal identity are by any means always purely physical (though it may well be the case that there is always associated with that loss or interruption some disturbance of the central nervous system). The well-known phenomena of "dissociation of personality" are, as a rule, more amenable to explanation in psychological than in physiological terms. It is worth while to say a word or two about this, though it must be with a brevity which will, I fear, make an appearance of dogmatism inevitable.

The key principle I take to be that, in an important sense, the developed human mind can be described as a system of sub-systems; each of these sub-systems being an organised group of tendencies oriented towards some specific interest in the life of the self. These sub-systems, in as much as it is the interests of the one self to which they minister, are developed in relatively close integration with one another—only on that account can the mind be described as a *system* of sub-systems—and normally they are maintained in relatively close integration. This integration is of two distinct kinds. In the first place, the different sub-systems are in substantial harmony with one another; they do not excite to mutually contradictory ways of behaving. In the second place, there is ease of transition from one sub-system to another; so that the self, when for the time being functioning in terms of one sub-system, is not debarred thereby from responding readily to stimuli appropriate to the evocation of other sub-systems. Integration, however, is never perfect in either of these forms, and the degree of *dis*integration may be great. It is disintegration with respect to the second form which in our present context most closely concerns us, but a chief factor in bringing it about is disintegration with respect to the first. Just because the self is one, incompatibility between its sub-systems engenders a distressing sense of conflict, and one of the many ways in which the self seeks relief from this conflict is "dissociation." We have, say, a group of sub-systems X in keenly felt conflict with another group of sub-systems Y. Each is able to be retained and indulged, and the inner tension nevertheless resolved, *if* the two can be so completely detached from one another that the self's conscious life in relation to X totally excludes its conscious life in relation to Y, and vice versa. Where that is successfully accomplished—we need not here consider the mechanisms—the conscious life of the self becomes broken into two mutually exclusive phases; one of them, very often, representing the dominant trend of the self's character, the other some group of sub-systems that is in sharp conflict with, perhaps, major ethical dispositions in the self's character. In extreme pathological cases, where a comprehensive group of sub-systems is maintained in complete detachment from the "main-stream" over a long period, it is understandable that the self-functioning in the detached group should gradually acquire a new, "secondary" personality which may differ in startling respects from the "primary" personality manifested in the dominant phase of conscious life (from which the group of sub-systems characteristic of the secondary phase has been totally excluded). Thus we get the phenomenon of dual (or it may be multiple) personality.

Now in the light of this general account of the processes involved it would seem really rather absurb to suggest that, because two "persons" have emerged, we must posit two *selves*—two ontologically different spiritual entities. For the self which, by its actions upon and reactions to its environment on the basis of its native endowment of powers and propensities, built up the specific group of sub-systems that have now become detached, was the *same* self that built up the group of sub-systems that persist in the main stream. It is surely gratuitous to suppose that the self which *now* functions in the detached group is a different being from the self which functioned prior to their detachment, and which

is still functioning in the "main-stream"? The natural interpretation is surely that it is the *same* self that functions throughout, and that it is its functioning over a prolonged period in a detached group of sub-systems that accounts for the emergence of a personality distinct from the primary personality. This interpretation, it should be added, finds strong confirmation in the frequent success of a psycho-therapy aimed at "restoring" integration of personality by breaking down the barriers that have been subconsciously erected to separate the detached groups from one another. It is certainly very hard to see how two personalities can be integrated if they belong to two independent spiritual entities! The successful therapy seems to presuppose that the "two persons" are different manifestations of a single entity, the "one self."

12. The main thesis I have been trying to establish in this somewhat prolonged consideration of our fourth question is that the conception of self-identity is a much wider one than that of personal identity. The self is a spiritual substance which can, and normally does, function in accordance with its personal character. But on occasion, for reasons not entirely obscure, it may function in a *contra-personal* way; and, on still rarer occasions, in a *secondary-personal* way. Nor do these two latter ways exhaust the self's modes of "non-personal" functioning. If the self's "personal" functioning is its functioning in terms of its character or personality, what are we to say, for example, of the self's functioning *prior to* the establishment of anything that can be called a "character" or a "personality"? It is no more contra-personal, *or* secondary-personal, than it is personal; and yet it is hard to say that it is not the "self" that is engaged in the building up of its own character. This is a case in which it would seem that the self as something *less* than personal is engaged. Furthermore, I shall suggest later, when I come to deal with the practical life of the self, that there is also a very important group of cases in which the self as something *more* than personal is engaged—that it can function in, as it were, a *supra-*personal as well as an *infra*-personal way. But

this must wait. It is unfortunately not practicable to say everything at once, though it would obviate many difficulties if we could.

Let me now sum up this long discussion by stating in formal terms the answers arrived at to the four questions that were propounded.

1. The answer to the first question is that certainly a meaning can be given to the substantival description of the self; for self-conscious experience is a fact, and the self of which we are conscious in self-conscious experience *is* a self to which this description applies.

2. The answer to the second question is that there is very good reason for believing in the actual existence of such selves; for in self-conscious experience one finds it just not possible to doubt the existence of the self of which one is conscious; and the hypothesis that what is thus indubitable for self-conscious experience may yet be mistaken is incapable of being formulated without an implicit self-contradiction.

3. The answer to the third question is that the self's identity is *at least* an identity of spiritual being, but that this does not rule out the possibility, to be considered at length later, that the relationship between the self and a particular animal body may be intrinsic to self-hood, part of its very essence.

4. The answer to the fourth question is that self-identity is a much wider conception than that of personal identity. The "person" is the self only in so far forth as the latter manifests itself in general accord with the relatively stable set of dispositions which it acquires in the course of its experience and which constitutes what is commonly called its "character." The

functioning of the self cannot be exhaustively described in terms of its "personal" functioning. We must recognize "contra-personal" and "secondary-personal" functioning of the same self, and also—we briefly suggested at the end—"infra-personal" and "supra-personal" functioning as well.

13. I have no serious objection if it be said that what I have been doing, in answering the fourth question, is to make a verbal recommendation, to the effect that the words "self" and "person" be used in a particular way. Certainly I have been doing that. I would only add that the recommendation is made, for what it is worth, on the basis of an analysis of the facts of self-experience which seems to disclose the need of a distinction within selfhood which is widely, but very vaguely, recognised, and whose nature is most clearly indicated by using the terms "self" and "person" in the way proposed. The proposal involves no revolution in established linguistic usage—that would only make confusion worse confounded. There is *no* established usage of these terms. Ordinary usage is confused and inconsistent, with the inevitable consequence of blurring a distinction that is of the utmost theoretical importance. But the usage here proposed has, for both terms, very considerable support from ordinary usage; and that (I suggest) is as much as anyone has a right to demand of the philosopher's use of language when—as is the rule rather than the exception in the discussion of major philosophical problems—distinctions emerge within the subject-matter which are not, and for the practical purposes of ordinary life need not be, clearly and consistently grasped by the layman.

PETER FREDERICK STRAWSON

PERSONS*

1. Each of us distinguishes between himself and states of himself on the one hand, and what is not himself or a state of himself on the other. What are the conditions of our making this distinction, and how are they fulfilled? In what way do we make it, and why do we make it in the way we do? It might appear a misnomer to refer to this group of questions as the issue of solipsism. But I have no qualms about appropriating the name: for that which customarily bears it is not, as we shall see, a genuine issue at all.

In the discussion of this topic, the notion of identification of particulars is once more crucial: primarily in the sense of distinguishing one particular from others in thought, or observation; but also in the original speaker-hearer senses.

Let me recall some of the steps which led to this issue of solipsism. I had argued that, in our actual conceptual scheme, material bodies, in a broad sense of the expression, were basic particulars: that is to say, that material bodies could be identified and reidentified without reference to particulars of other types or categories than their own, whereas the identification and reidentification of particulars of other categories rested ultimately on the identification of material bodies. I then inquired whether we could make intelligible to ourselves the idea of a conceptual scheme which provided for a system of objective particulars, but in which material bodies were not basic. This led to the construction of a model No-Space world, in which all the sensory items were auditory, but in which it did seem possible to find a place for the idea

of a reidentifiable particular, by exploiting certain auditory analogues of the idea of spatial distance. The requirement, however, was for a scheme in which a distinction was made between oneself and what is not oneself. Though it seemed possible that the conditions for this distinction could be fulfilled in such a world, it was not obvious *how* they were to be fulfilled. The introduction of the idea of agency—of a distinction between changes which were deliberately initiated, and those that just occurred—seemed inadequate to compel this crucial distinction; and a final attempt to produce in the auditory world the conditions of a non-solipsistic consciousness seemed just an attempt to copy indiscriminately the features of our ordinary human experience in the very restricted sensory terms available. So, to try to get clearer about what in general those conditions are, it seemed advisable to inquire how in fact they are fulfilled in ordinary human experience.

But though I want to ask this question in relation to our ordinary human experience, yet there is a certain advantage in keeping before our minds the picture of the purely auditory world, the picture of an experience very much more restricted than that which we in fact have. For it may help to sharpen for us the question we are concerned with; it may help to give us a continuing sense of the strangeness of what we in fact do; and this sense of strangeness we want to keep alive in order to see that we really meet it and remove it, and do not just lose or smother it. It helps in this way. We drew a picture of a purely auditory experience, and elaborated it to a point at which it seemed that the being whose experience it was—if any such being were possible at all—might recognize sound-universals and reidentify sound-particulars and in general form for himself an idea of

* From *Individuals: An Essay in Descriptive Metaphysics* by P. F. Strawson. London: Methuen & Co. Ltd., 1959. Chapter 3. Reprinted by permission of the publisher.

his auditory world; but still, it seemed, he would have no place for the idea of himself as the subject of this experience, would make no distinction between a special item in his world, namely himself, and the other items in it. Would it not seem utterly strange to suggest that he might distinguish himself as one item among others in his auditory world, that is, as a sound or sequence of sounds? For how could such a thing—a sound—be also what *had* all those experiences? Yet to have the idea of himself, must he not have the idea of the subject of the experiences, of that which has them? So it might begin to look impossible that he should have the idea of himself—or at any rate the right idea. For to have the idea at all, it seems that it must be an idea of some particular thing of which he has experience, and which is set over against or contrasted with other things of which he has experience, but which are not himself. But if it is just an item *within* his experience of which he has this idea, how can it be the idea of that which *has* all of his experiences? And now we seem to have come upon a form of problem which is completely general, which applies as much to the ordinary as to the auditory world. It must, it seems, be soluble for the ordinary world.

Let us now think of some of the ways in which we ordinarily talk of ourselves, of some of the things which we do ordinarily ascribe to ourselves. They are of many kinds. We ascribe to ourselves *actions* and *intentions* (I am doing, did, shall do this); *sensations* (I am warm, in pain); *thoughts* and *feelings* (I think, wonder, want this, am angry, disappointed, contented); *perceptions* and *memories* (I see this, hear the other, remember that). We ascribe to ourselves, in two senses, position: *location* (I am on the sofa) and *attitude* (I am lying down). And of course we ascribe to ourselves not only temporary conditions, states, and situations, like these, but also relatively enduring characteristics, including such physical characteristics like height, coloring, shape, and weight. That is to say, among the things we ascribe to ourselves are things of a kind that we also ascribe to material bodies to which we should

not dream of ascribing others of the things that we ascribe to ourselves. Now there seems nothing needing explanation in the fact that the particular height, coloring, physical position which we ascribe to ourselves, should be ascribed to *something or other;* for that which one calls one's body is, at least, a body, a material thing. It can be picked out from others, identified by ordinary physical criteria and described in ordinary physical terms. But, so long as we keep that for the present indispensable sense of strangeness, it can and must seem to need explanation that one's states of consciousness, one's thoughts and sensations, are ascribed *to the very same thing* to which these physical characteristics, this physical situation, is ascribed. That is, we have not only the question: *Why are one's states of consciousness ascribed to anything at all?* We have also the question: *Why are they ascribed to the very same thing as certain corporeal characteristics, a certain physical situation, &c.?* It is not to be supposed that the answers to these questions will be independent of one another.

2. It might indeed be thought that an answer to both of them could be found in the unique role which each person's body plays in his experience, particularly his perceptual experience. All philosophers who have concerned themselves with these questions have referred to the uniqueness of this role. Descartes was well aware of its uniqueness: "I am *not* lodged in my body like a pilot in a vessel." In what does this uniqueness consist? It consists, of course, in a great many things. Consider merely some of the ways in which the character of a person's *perceptual experience* is dependent on facts about his own body. Let us take his visual experience. The dependence is more complicated and many-sided than may at first be obvious. First, there is that group of empirical facts of which the most familiar is that if the eyelids of that body are closed, the person sees nothing. To this group belong all the facts known to ophthalmic surgeons. Second, there is the fact that what falls within his field of vision at any moment depends in part on the *orientation* of his eyes, i.e. on the direction

his head is turned in, and on the *orientation* of his eyeballs in their sockets. And, third, there is the fact that *where he sees from*—or what his possible field of vision at any moment is—depends on where his body, and in particular his head, is located. I divide these facts into three groups because I want to emphasize that the fact that visual experience is, in all three ways, dependent on facts about some body or bodies, does not entail that the body should be the same body in each case. It is a contingent fact that it is the same body. For it is possible to imagine the following case. There is a subject of visual experience, S, and there are three different relevant bodies: A, B and C. (1) Whether the eyelids of B and C are open or not is causally irrelevant to whether S sees; but S sees only if the eyelids of A are open. And if an operation is performed on the eyes of A, the result affects S's sight, but not if an operation is performed on the eyes of B and C. (2) Where A and B may be, however, is quite irrelevant to where S sees from, i.e. to what his possible field of vision is. This is determined only by where C is. So long as C is in the drawing-room and the curtains are drawn, S can see only what is in the drawing-room. (If one has any difficulty with this idea of "where one sees from," one may think of the way one tells, from looking at a photograph, where the camera was when it was taken. Just so S's perspective on the world is given by the position of C.) But (3) the direction in which the heads and eyeballs of A and C are turned is quite irrelevant to what S sees. Given the station of C, then which of all the views which are possible from this position is the view seen by S, depends on the direction in which the head and eyeballs of B are turned, wherever B may find himself. I have described now a situation in which the visual experience of S is dependent in three different ways on the state or position of each of the bodies, A, B and C. The dependence in each case will have certain repercussions on the way in which each of those bodies itself can be an object of visual experience to S. Thus S may never see A or B at all: but if S does see A or B, he can never see A with A's

eyelids closed and he can never see B's face, though he may sometimes catch a glimpse of B's profile "out of the corner of his eye" (as *we* say), and will perhaps become quite familiar with the view of the back of B's head. Whenever S is "looking in" a mirror, i.e. has a direct frontal view of a mirror, he will see the head of C; but he may get *any* view of the head, i.e. he will not necessarily see the face. Now, of course, our actual situation is not like this. Of course, in fact, for any subject of visual experience, S, there is just one body on the state and position of which the character of his visual experience is dependent in all three of these ways; and this triple dependence has its own familiar repercussions on the way in which that body itself becomes an object of visual experience for S. We have noted the contingency and the complexity of this dependence. If we turn to hearing and smell, the other "distance" senses, the dependence is less complicated, in that orientation is comparatively unimportant. But there is still the double dependence of the character of the experience on both the location and the state of certain organs of one and the same body. Again these could be imagined coming apart. We could e.g. give an independent definition of the point "from which" a sound is heard as follows: a sound α produced by a given source of sound β is *"heard from"* point P by subject S, if, given that no other changes take place except the movement of β, then α is heard more loudly by S when β is at P than when it is at any other point, and is heard by S with steadily diminishing loudness as β is moved in any direction away from P. Again, then, we might imagine "the point from which" sound is heard by a given hearer being dependent on the location of one body, while whether that hearer heard anything at all depended on the condition of the ears, the eardrums, &c. of another body. Equally obvious is the special position of one body in relation to all those experiences of a given subject which are assigned to the sense of touch. Countless material bodies may be observed by a given subject to be in, or to come into, contact with others; but there is only one body of which it is true that when that body is a party to such a situation of "establishing contact," then the subject normally has those experiences to which he alludes when he speaks of *feeling* some material body or other. The subject *feels* the dagger or the feather only when the dagger enters, or the feather lightly brushes, *this* body.

Such points illustrate some of the ways in which each person's body occupies a special position in relation to that person's perceptual experience. We may summarize such facts by saying that for each person there is one body which occupies a certain *causal* position in relation to that person's perceptual experience, a causal position which in various ways is unique in relation to each of the various kinds of perceptual experience he has; and— as a further consequence—that this body is also unique for him as an *object* of the various kinds of perceptual experience which he has. We also noted that this complex uniqueness of the single body appeared to be a contingent matter, or rather a cluster of contingent matters; for it seems that we can imagine many peculiar combinations of dependence and independence of aspects of our perceptual experience on facts about different bodies.

We reminded ourselves of the special position which a person's body occupies in his experience in the hope that it might help to provide an answer to two questions: viz: (1) Why are one's states of consciousness ascribed to anything at all? and (2) Why are they ascribed to the very same thing as certain corporeal characteristics, a certain physical situation &c.? But now I must say straight away that the facts I have been recalling do not seem to me to provide, by themselves, any answer to our questions at all. Of course, these facts explain something. They provide a good reason why a subject of experience should have a very special regard for just one body, why he should think of it as unique and perhaps more important than any other. They explain—if I may be permitted to put it so—why I feel pecularily attached to what in fact I call my own body; they even might be said to explain why, granted that I am

going to speak of one body as *mine*, I should speak of *this* body as mine. But they do not explain why I should have the concept of *myself* at all, why I should ascribe my thoughts and experiences to *anything*. Moreover, even if we were satisfied with some other explanation of why one's states of consciousness, thoughts and feelings and perceptions, were ascribed to *something*, and satisfied that the facts in question sufficed to explain why the "possession" of a particular body should be ascribed to the *same* thing (i.e. to explain why a particular body should be spoken of as standing in some special relation —called "being possessed by"—to that thing), yet the facts in question still do not explain why we should, as we do, ascribe certain corporeal characteristics not simply to the body standing in this special relation to the thing to which we ascribe thoughts and feelings, &c., but to the thing itself to which we ascribe those thoughts and feelings. For we say "*I* am bald" as well as "*I* am cold," "*I* am lying on the hearthrug" as well as "*I* see a spider on the ceiling." Briefly, the facts in question explain why a subject of experience should pick out one body from others, give it, perhaps, an honoured name and ascribe to it whatever characteristics it has; but they do not explain why the experiences should be ascribed to any subject at all; and they do not explain why, if the experiences are to be ascribed to something, they *and* the corporeal characteristics which might be truly ascribed to the favoured body should be ascribed to the same thing. So the facts in question do not explain the use that we make of the word "I," or how any word has the use that word has. They do not explain the concept we have of a person.

3. A possible reaction at this point is to say that the concept we have is wrong or confused, or, if we make it a rule not to say that the concepts we have are confused, that the usage we have, whereby we ascribe, or seem to ascribe, such different kinds of predicate to one and the same thing, is confusing, that it conceals the true nature of the concepts involved, or something of this sort. This reaction can be found in two very important

types of view about these matters. The first type of view is Cartesian, the view of Descartes and of others who think like him. Over the attribution of the second type of view I am more hesitant; but there is some evidence that it was held, at one period, by Wittgenstein and possibly also by Schlick. On both of these views, one of the questions we are considering—viz. "Why do we ascribe our states of consciousness to the very same thing as certain corporeal characteristics &c." —is a question which does not arise; for on both views it is only a linguistic illusion that both kinds of predicate are properly ascribed to one and the same thing, that there is a common owner, or subject, of both types of predicate. And on the second of these views, the other question we are considering—viz. "Why do we ascribe our states of consciousness to anything at all?"—is also a question which does not arise; for on this view, it is only a linguistic illusion that one ascribes one's states of consciousness at all, that there is any proper subject of these apparent ascriptions, that states of consciousness belong to, or are states of, anything.

That Descartes held the first of these views is well enough known.[1] When we speak of a person, we are really referring to one or both of two distinct substances, two substances of different types, each of which has its own appropriate type of states and properties; and none of the properties or states of either can be a property or state of the other. States of consciousness belong to one of these substances, and not to the other. I shall say no more about the Cartesian view at the moment —what I have to say about it will emerge later on—except to note again that while it escapes one of our questions, it does not escape, but indeed invites, the other: "Why are one's states of consciousness *ascribed* at all, to *any* subject?"

The second of these views I shall call the "no-ownership" or "no-subject" doctrine of the self. Whether or not anyone has explicitly held this view, it is worth reconstructing, or

constructing, in outline.[2] For the errors into which it falls are instructive. The "no-ownership" theorist may be presumed to start his explanations with facts of the sort which illustrate the unique causal position of a certain material body in a person's experience. The theorist maintains that the uniqueness of this body is sufficient to give rise to the idea that one's experiences can be ascribed to some particular, individual thing, can be said to be possessed by, or owned by, that thing. This idea, he thinks, though infelicitously and misleadingly expressed in terms of ownership, would have some validity, would make some sort of sense, so long as we thought of this individual thing, the possessor of the experiences, as the body itself. So long as we thought in this way, then to ascribe a particular state of consciousness to this body, this individual thing, would at least be to say something that might have been false; for

[1] Or at least widely enough supposed to justify our calling it the Cartesian view.

[2] The evidence that Wittgenstein at one time held such a view is to be found in the third of Moore's articles in *Mind* on "Wittgenstein's Lectures in 1930–33" (*Mind*, Vol. LXIV, especially pp. 13–14). He is reported to have held that the use of "I" was utterly different in the case of "I have a tooth-ache" or "I see a red patch" from its use in the case of "I've got a bad tooth" or "I've got a matchbox." He thought that there were two uses of "I" and that in one of them "I" was replaceable by "this body". So far the view might be Cartesian. But he also said that in the other use (the use exemplified by "I have a tooth-ache" as opposed to "I have a bad tooth"), the "I" *does not denote a possessor*, and that no ego is involved in thinking or in having tooth-ache; and referred with apparent approval to Lichtenberg's dictum that, instead of saying "I think," we (or Descartes!) ought to say "There is a thought" (i.e., "Es denkt").

The attribution of such a view to Schlick would have to rest on his article "Meaning and Verification" (see *Readings in Philosophical Analysis*, ed. Feigl and Sellars). Like Wittgenstein, Schlick quotes Lichtenberg, and then goes on to say: "Thus we see that unless we choose to call our body the owner or bearer of the data [the immediate data of experience]—which seems to be a rather misleading expression—we have to say that the data have no owner or bearer." The full import of Schlick's article is, however, obscure to me, and it is quite likely that a false impression is given by the quotation of a single sentence. I shall say merely that I have drawn on Schlick's article in constructing the case of my hypothetical "no-subject" theorist; but shall not claim to be representing his views.

Lichtenberg's anti-Cartesian dictum is, as the subsequent argument will show, one that I endorse, if properly used; but it seems to have been repeated, without being understood, by many of Descartes' critics. (I do not here refer to Wittgenstein and Schlick.)

the experience in question might have been causally dependent on the state of some other body; in the present admissible, though infelicitous, sense of the word, it might have "belonged" to some other individual thing. But now, the theorist suggests, one becomes confused: one slides from the admissible sense in which one's experiences may be said to belong to, or be possessed by, some particular thing, to a wholly inadmissible and empty sense of these expressions, in which the particular thing is not thought of as a body, but as something else, say an Ego, whose sole function is to provide an owner for experiences. Suppose we call the first type of possession, which is really a certain kind of causal dependence, "having₁," and the second type of possession "having₂"; and call the individual of the first type "B" and the supposed individual of the second type "E." Then the difference is that while it is genuinely a contingent matter that *all my experiences are had₁ by B,* it appears as a necessary truth that *all my experiences are had₂ by E.* But the belief in E and the belief in "having₂" is an illusion. Only those things whose ownership is logically transferable can be owned at all. So experiences are not owned by anything except in the dubious sense of being causally dependent on the state of a particular body; this is at least a genuine relationship to a thing, in that they might have stood in it to another thing. Since the whole function of E was to own experiences, in a logically nontransferable sense of "own," and since experiences are not owned by anything in this sense, for there is no such sense of "own," E must be eliminated from the picture altogether. It only came in because of a confusion.

I think it must be clear that this account of the matter, though it contains some of the facts, is not coherent. It is not coherent, in that one who holds it is forced to make use of that sense of possession of which he denies the existence, in presenting his case for the denial. When he tries to state the contingent fact, which he thinks gives rise to illusion of the "ego," he has to state it in some such form as "All *my* experiences are had₁ by (i.e. uniquely dependent on the state of) body B."

For any attempt to eliminate the *"my,"* or any expression with a similar possessive force, would yield something that was not a contingent fact at all. The proposition that *all* experiences are causally dependent on the state of a single body B, for example, is just false. The theorist means to speak of all the experiences *had by a certain person* being contingently so dependent. And the theorist cannot consistently argue that "all the experiences of person P" *means the same thing* as "all experiences contingently dependent on a certain body B"; for then his proposition would not be contingent, as his theory requires, but analytic. He must mean to be speaking of some class of experiences of the members of which it is in fact contingently true that they are all dependent on body B. The defining characteristic of this class is in fact that they are *"my* experiences" or "the experiences *of* some person," where the idea of possession expressed by "my" and "of" is the one he calls into question.

This internal incoherence is a serious matter when it is a question of denying what *prima facie* is the case: that is, that one does genuinely ascribe one's states of consciousness to something, viz. oneself, and that this kind of ascription is precisely such as the theorist finds unsatisfactory, i.e. is such that it does not seem to make sense to suggest, for example, that the identical pain which was in fact one's own might have been another's. We do not have to seek far in order to understand the place of this logically nontransferable kind of ownership in our general scheme of thought. For if we think, once more, of the requirements of identifying reference in speech to *particular* states of consciousness, or private experiences, we see that such particulars cannot be thus identifyingly referred to except as the states or experiences *of* some identified *person*. States, or experiences, one might say, *owe* their identity as particulars to the identity of the person whose states or experiences they are. From this it follows immediately that if they can be identified as particular states or experiences at all, they must be possessed or ascribable in just that way which the no-ownership theorist ridicules;

i.e. in such a way that it is logically impossible that a particular state or experience in fact possessed by someone should have been possessed by anyone else. The requirements of identity rule out logical transferability of ownership. So the theorist could maintain his position only by denying that we could ever refer to particular states or experiences at all; and *this* position is ridiculous.

We may notice, even now, a possible connection between the no-ownership doctrine and the Cartesian position. The latter is, straightforwardly enough, a dualism of two subjects, or two types of subject. The former could, a little paradoxically, be called a dualism too: a dualism of one subject—the body—and one non-subject. We might surmise that the second dualism, paradoxically so called, arises out of the first dualism, non-paradoxically so called; in other words, that if we try to think of that to which one's states of consciousness are ascribed as something utterly different from that to which certain corporeal characteristics are ascribed, then indeed it becomes difficult to see why states of consciousness should be ascribed, thought of as belonging to, anything at all. And when we think of this possibility, we may also think of another: viz. that both the Cartesian and the no-ownership theorist are profoundly wrong in holding, as each must, that there are two uses of "I," in one of which it denotes something which it does not denote in the other.

4. The no-ownership theorist fails to take account of all the facts. He takes account of some of them. He implies, correctly, that the unique position or role of a single body in one's experience is not a sufficient explanation of the fact that one's experiences, or states of consciousness, are ascribed to something which *has* them, with that peculiar non-transferable kind of possession which is here in question. It may be a necessary part of the explanation, but it is not, by itself, a sufficient explanation. The theorist, as we have seen, goes on to suggest that it is perhaps a sufficient explanation of something else: viz. of our confusedly and mistakenly *thinking* that states of consciousness are to

be ascribed to something in this special way. But this, as we have seen, is incoherent: for it involves the denial that someone's states of consciousness are anyone's. We avoid the incoherence of this denial, whilst agreeing that the special role of a single body in someone's experience does not suffice to explain why that experience should be ascribed to anyone. The fact that there is this special role does not, by itself, give a sufficient reason why what *we* think of as a subject of experience should have any use for the conception of himself as such a subject.

When I say that the no-ownership theorist's account fails through not reckoning with all the facts, I have in mind a very simple but, in this question, a very cental, thought: viz. that it is a necessary condition of one's ascribing states of consciousness, experiences, to oneself, in the way one does, that one should also ascribe them, or be prepared to ascribe them, to others who are not oneself.[3] This means not less than it says. It means, for example, that the ascribing phrases are used in just the same sense when the subject is another as when the subject is oneself.

---

[3] I can imagine an objection to the unqualified form of this statement, an objection which might be put as follows. Surely the idea of a uniquely applicable predicate, i.e. a predicate which belongs to only one individual, is not absurd. And, if it is not, then surely the most that can be claimed is that a necessary condition of one's ascribing predicates of a certain class to one individual, i.e. oneself, is that one should be prepared, or ready, on appropriate occasions, to ascribe them to other individuals, and hence that one should have a conception of what those appropriate occasions for ascribing them would be; but not, necessarily, that one should actually do so on any occasion.

The shortest way with the objection is to admit it, or at least to refrain from disputing it; for the lesser claim is all that the argument strictly requires, though it is slightly simpler to conduct it on the basis of the larger claim. But it is well to point out further that we are not speaking of a single predicate, or merely of some group or other of predicates, but of the whole of an enormous class of predicates such that the applicability of those predicates or their negations determines a major logical type or category of individuals. To insist at this level, on the distinction between the lesser and the larger claims is to carry the distinction over from a level at which it is clearly correct to a level at which it may well appear idle or, possibly, senseless.

The main point here is a purely logical one: the idea of a predicate is correlative with that of a *range* of distinguishable individuals of which the predicate can be significantly, though not necessarily truly, affirmed.

Of course the thought that this is so gives no trouble to the non-philosopher: the thought for example, that "in pain" means the same whether one says "I am in pain" or "He is in pain." The dictionaries do not give two sets of meanings for every expression which describes a state of consciousness: a first-person meaning and a second-and-third person meaning. But to the philosopher this thought has given trouble. How could the sense be the same when the method of verification was so different in the two cases —or, rather, when there *was* a method of verification in the one case (the case of others) and not, properly speaking, in the other case (the case of oneself)? Or, again —a more sophisticated scruple—how can it be right to talk of *ascribing* in the case of oneself? For surely there can be a question of ascribing only if there is or could be a question of identifying that to which the ascription is made: and though there may be a question of identifying the one who is in pain when that one is another, how can there be such a question when that one is oneself? But this query answers itself as soon as we remember that we *speak* primarily to others, for the information of others. In one sense, indeed, there is no question of my having to *tell who it is* who is in pain, when I am. In another sense, however, I may have to *tell who it is, i.e.* to let others know who it is.

What I have just said explains, perhaps, how one may properly be said to ascribe states of consciousness to oneself, given that one can ascribe them to others. But how is it that one can ascribe them to others? Now one thing here is certain: that *if* the things one ascribes states of consciousness to, in ascribing them to others, are thought of as a set of Cartesian egos to which only private experiences can, in correct logical grammar, be ascribed, *then* this question is unanswerable and this problem insoluble. If, in identifying the things to which states of consciousness are to be ascribed, private experiences are to be all one has to go on, then, just for the very same reason as that for which there is, from one's own point

of view, no question of telling that a private experience is one's own, there is also no question of telling that a private experience is another's. All private experiences, all states of consciousness, will be mine, i.e. no one's. To put it briefly. One can ascribe states of consciousness to oneself only if one can ascribe them to others. One can ascribe them to others only if one can identify other subjects of experience. And one cannot identify others if one can identify them *only* as subjects of experience, possessors of states of consciousness.

It might be objected that this way with Cartesianism is too short. After all, there is no difficulty in distinguishing bodies from one another, no difficulty in identifying bodies. Does not this give us an indirect way of identifying subjects of experience, while preserving the Cartesian mode? Can we not identify such a subject as, for example, "the subject that stands to that body in the same special relation as I stand in to this one," or, in other words, "the subject of those experiences which stand in the same unique causal relation to body N as *my* experiences stand in to body M?" But this suggestion is useless. It requires me to have noted that *my* experiences stand in a special relation to body M, when it is just the right to speak of *my* experiences at all that is in question. That is to say, it requires me to have noted that *my* experiences stand in a special relation to body M; but it requires me to have noted this as a condition of being able to identify other subjects of experiences, i.e. as a condition of my having the idea of myself as a subject of experience, i.e. as a condition of thinking of any experiences as *mine*. So long as we persist in talking, in the mode of this explanation, of experiences on the one hand, and bodies on the other, the most I may be allowed to have noted is that experiences, *all* experiences, stand in a special relation to body M, that body M is unique in just this way, that this is what makes body M unique among bodies. (This "most" is perhaps too much—because of the presence of the word "experiences.") The proffered explanation runs: "Another subject of experience is distinguished and identified as the subject of those experiences which stand in the same unique causal relationship to body N as *my* experiences stand in to body M." And the objection is: "But what is the word 'my' doing in this explanation?" It is not as though the explanation could get on without this word. There is a further objection, to which we will recur. It runs: "What right have we, in this explanation, to speak of *the* subject, implying uniqueness? Why should there not be any number of subjects of experience—perhaps qualitatively indistinguishable—each subject and each set of experiences standing in the same unique relation to body N (*or* to body M)? Uniqueness of the body does not guarantee uniqueness of the Cartesian soul."

What we have to acknowledge, in order to begin to free ourselves from these difficulties, is the primitiveness of the concept of a person. What I mean by the concept of a person is the concept of a type of entity such that *both* predicates ascribing states of consciousness *and* predicates ascribing corporeal characteristics, a physical situation &c. are equally applicable to a single individual of that single type. What I mean by saying that this concept is primitive can be put in a number of ways. One way is to return to those two questions I asked earlier: viz. (1) why are states of consciousness ascribed to anything at all? and (2) why are they ascribed to the very same thing as certain corporeal characteristics, a certain physical situation &c.? I remarked at the beginning that it was not to be supposed that the answers to these questions were independent of each other. Now I shall say that they are connected in this way: that a necessary condition of states of consciousness being ascribed at all is that they should be ascribed to the *very same things* as certain corporeal characteristics, a certain physical situation &c. That is to say, states of consciousness could not be ascribed at all, *unless* they were ascribed to persons, in the sense I have claimed for this word. We are tempted to think of a person as a sort of compound of two kinds of subject: a subject of experi-

ences (a pure consciousness, an ego) or the one hand, and a subject of corporeal attributes on the other. Many questions arise when we think in this way. But, in particular, when we ask ourselves how we come to frame, to get a use for, the concept of this compound of two subjects, the picture—if we are honest and careful—is apt to change from the picture of two subjects to the picture of one subject and one non-subject. For it becomes impossible to see how we could come by the idea of different, distinguishable identifiable subjects of experiences—different consciousnesses—*if this idea is thought of a logically primitive,* as a logical ingredient in the compound-idea of a person, the latter being composed of two subjects. For there could never be any question of assigning an experience, as such, to any subject other than oneself; and therefore never any question of assigning it to oneself either, never any question of ascribing it to a subject at all. So the concept of the pure individual consciousness—the pure ego—is a concept that cannot exist; or, at least, cannot exist as a primary concept in terms of which the concept of a person can be explained or analyzed. It can only exist, if at all, as a secondary, non-primitive concept, which itself is to be explained, analyzed, in terms of the concept of a person. It was the entity corresponding to this illusory primary concept of the pure consciousness, the ego-substance for which Hume was seeking, or ironically pretending to seek, when he looked into himself, and complained that he could never discover himself without a perception and could never discover anything but the perception. More seriously—and this time there was no irony, but a confusion, a Nemesis o confusion for Hume—it was this entity of which Hume vainly sought for the principle of unity, confessing himself perplexed and defeated; sought vainly because there is no principle of unity where there is no principle of differentiation. It was this, too, to which Kant, more perspicacious here than Hume accorded a purely formal ("analytic") unity the unity of the "I think" that accompanies all my perceptions and therefore might jus as well accompany none. Finally it is this, perhaps, of which Wittgenstein spoke when he said of the subject, first, that there is no such thing, and, second that it is not a part of the world, but its limit.

So, then, the word "I" never refers to this, the pure subject. But this does not mean, as the no-ownership theorist must think, that "I" in some cases does not refer at all. It refers, because I am a person among others; and the predicates which would, *per impossible,* belong to the pure subject if it could be referred to, belong properly to the person to which "I" does refer.

The concept of a person is logically prior to that of an individual consciousness. The concept of a person is not to be analyzed as that of an animated body or of an embodied anima. This is not to say that the concept of a pure individual consciousness might not have a logically secondary existence, if one thinks, or finds, it desirable. We speak of a dead person—a body—and in the same secondary way we might at least think of a disembodied person, retaining the logical benefit of individuality from having been a person.

5. It is important to realize the full extent of the acknowledgment one is making in acknowledging the logical primitiveness of the concept of a person. Let me rehearse briefly the stages of the argument. There would be no question of ascribing one's own states of consciousness, or experiences, to anything, unless one also ascribed, or were ready and able to ascribe, states of consciousness, or experiences, to other individual entities of the same logical type as that thing to which one ascribes one's own states of consciousness. The condition of reckoning oneself as a subject of such predicates is that one should also reckon others as subjects of such predicates. The condition, in turn, of this being possible, is that one should be able to distinguish from one another, to pick out or identify, different subjects of such predicates, i.e. different individuals of the type concerned. The condition, in turn, of this being possible is that the individuals

concerned, including oneself, should be of a certain unique type: of a type, namely, such that to each individual of that type there must be ascribed, or ascribable, *both* states of consciousness *and* corporeal characteristics. But this characterization of the type is still very opaque and does not at all clearly bring out what is involved. To bring this out, I must make a rough division, into two, of the kinds of predicates properly applied to individuals of this type. The first kind of predicate consists of those which are also properly applied to material bodies to which we would not dream of applying predicates ascribing states of consciousness. I will call this first kind M-predicates: and they include things like "weighs 10 stone," "is in the drawing-room" and so on. The second kind consists of all the other predicates we apply to persons. These I shall call P-predicates. P-predicates, of course, will be very various. They will include things like "is smiling," "is going for a walk," as well as things like "is in pain," "is thinking hard," "believes in God" and so on.

So far I have said that the concept of a person is to be understood as the concept of a type of entity such that *both* predicates ascribing states of consciousness *and* predicates ascribing corporeal characteristics, a physical situation &c. are equally applicable to an individual entity of that type. All I have said about the meaning of saying that this concept is primitive is that it is not to be analysed in a certain way or ways. We are not, for example, to think of it as a secondary kind of entity in relation to two primary kinds, viz. a particular consciousness and a particular human body. I implied also that the Cartesian error is just a special case of the more general error, present in a different form in theories of the no-ownership type, of thinking of the designations, or apparent designations, of persons as *not* denoting precisely the same thing or entity for all kinds of predicate ascribed to the entity designated. That is, if we are to avoid the general form of this error, we must *not* think of "I" or "Smith" as suffering from type-ambiguity. Indeed, if we want to locate type-ambiguity somewhere, we would do better to locate it in certain predicates like "is in the drawing-room" "was hit by a stone" &c., and say they mean one thing when applied to material objects and another when applied to persons.

This is all I have so far said or implied about the meaning of saying that the concept of a person is primitive. What has to be brought out further is what the implications of saying this are as regards the logical character of those predicates with which we ascribe states of consciousness. For this purpose we may well consider P-predicates in general. For though not all P-predicates are what we should call "predicates ascribing states of consciousness" (e.g. "going for a walk" is not), they may be said to have this in common, that they imply the possession of consciousness on the part of that to which they are ascribed.

What then are the consequences of the view as regards the character of P-predicates? I think they are these. Clearly there is no sense in talking of identifiable individuals of a special type, a type, namely, such that they possess both M-predicates and P-predicates, unless there is in principle some way of telling, with regard to any individual of that type, and any P-predicate, whether that individual possesses that P-predicate. And, in the case of at least some P-predicates, the ways of telling must constitute in some sense logically adequate kinds of criteria for the ascription of the P-predicate. For suppose in no case did these ways of telling constitute logically adequate kinds of criteria. Then we should have to think of the relation between the ways of telling and what the P-predicate ascribes, or a part of what it ascribes, always in the following way: we should have to think of the ways of telling as *signs* of the presence, in the individual concerned, of this different thing, viz. the state of consciousness. But then we could only know that the way of telling was a sign of the presence of the different thing ascribed by the P-predicate, by the observation of correlations between the two. But this observation we could each make only in one

case, viz. our own. And now we are back in the position of the defender of Cartesianism, who thought our way with it was too short. For what, now, does "our own case" mean? There is no sense in the idea of ascribing states of consciousness to oneself, or at all, unless the ascriber already knows how to ascribe at least some states of consciousness to others. So he cannot argue in general "from his own case" to conclusions about how to do this; for unless he already knows how to do this, he has no conception of *his own case,* or any *case,* i.e. any subject of experiences. Instead, he just has evidence that pain &c. may be expected when a certain body is affected in certain ways and not when others are. If he speculated to the contrary, his speculations would be immediately falsified.

The conclusion here is, of course, not new. What I have said is that one ascribes P-predicates to others on the strength of observation of their behavior; and that the behavior-criteria one goes on are not just signs of the presence of what is meant by the P-predicate, but are criteria of a logically adequate kind for the ascription of the P-predicate. On behalf of this conclusion, however, I am claiming that it follows from a consideration of the conditions necessary for any ascription of states of consciousness to anything. The point is not that we must accept this conclusion in order to avoid scepticism, but that we must accept it in order to explain the existence of the conceptual scheme in terms of which the sceptical problem is stated. But once the conclusion is accepted, the sceptical problem does not arise. So with the generality of sceptical problems: their statement involves the pretended acceptance of a conceptual scheme and at the same time the silent repudiation of one of the conditions of its existence. That is why they are, in the terms in which they are stated, insoluble.

But this is only half the picture about P-predicates. For of course it is true of some important classes of P-predicates, that when one ascribes them *to oneself,* one does not do so on the strength of observation of those behavior criteria on the strength of which one ascribes them to others. This is not true of all P-predicates. It is not, in general, true of those which carry assessments of character and capability: these, when self-ascribed, are in general ascribed on the same kind of basis as that on which they are ascribed to others. Even of those P-predicates of which it is true that one does not generally ascribe them to oneself on the basis of the criteria on the strength of which one ascribes them to others, there are many of which it is also true that their ascription is liable to correction by the self-ascriber on this basis. But there remain many cases in which one has an entirely adequate basis for ascribing a P-predicate to oneself, and yet in which this basis is quite distinct from those on which one ascribes the predicate to another. Thus one says, reporting a present state of mind or feeling: "I feel tired, am depressed, am in pain." How can this fact be reconciled with the doctrine that the criteria on the strength of which one ascribes P-predicates to others are criteria of a logically adequate kind for this ascription?

The apparent difficulty of bringing about this reconciliation may tempt us in many directions. It may tempt us, for example, to deny that these self-ascriptions are really ascriptions at all, to *assimilate* first-person ascriptions of states of consciousness to those other forms of behavior which constitute criteria on the basis of which one person ascribes P-predicates to another. This device seems to avoid the difficulty; it is not, in all cases, entirely inappropriate. But it obscures the facts, and is needless. It is merely a sophisticated form of failure to recognize the special character of P-predicates, or rather, of a crucial class of P-predicates. For just as there is not in general one primary process of learning, or teaching oneself, an inner private meaning for predicates of this class, then another process of learning to apply such predicates to others on the strength of a correlation, noted in one's own case, with certain forms of behavior, so— and equally—there is not in general one primary process of learning to apply such

predicates to others on the strength of behaviour criteria, and then another process of acquiring the secondary technique of exhibiting a new form of behaviour, viz. first-person P-utterances. Both these pictures are refusals to acknowledge the unique logical character of the predicates concerned. Suppose we write "Px" as the general form of propositional function of such a predicate. Then, according to the first picture, the expression which primarily replaces "x" in this form is "I," the first person singular pronoun: its uses with other replacements are secondary, derivative and shaky. According to the second pricture, on the other hand, the primary replacements of "x" in this form are "he," "that person," &c., and its use with "I" is secondary, peculiar, not a true ascriptive use. But it is essential to the character of these predicates that they have both first- and third-person ascriptive uses, that they are both self-ascribable otherwise than on the basis of observation of the behaviour of the subject of them, and other-ascribable on the basis of behaviour criteria. To learn their use is to learn both aspects of their use. In order to *have* this type of concept, one must be both a self-ascriber and an other-ascriber of such predicates, and must see every other as a self-ascriber. In order to *understand* this type of concept, one must acknowledge that there is a kind of predicate which is unambiguously and adequately ascribable *both* on the basis of observation of the subject of the predicate *and* not on this basis, i.e. independently of observation of the subject: the second case is the case where the ascriber is also the subject. If there were no concepts answering to the characterization I have just given, we should indeed have no philosophical problem about the soul; but equally we should not have our concept of a person.

To put the point—with a certain unavoidable crudity—in terms of one particular concept of this class, say, that of depression. We speak of behaving in a depressed way (of depressed behaviour) and we also speak of feeling depressed (of a feeling of depression). One is inclined to argue that feelings can be felt but not observed, and behaviour can be observed but not felt, and that therefore there must be room here to drive in a logical wedge. But the concept of depression spans the place where one wants to drive it in. We might say: in order for there to be such a concept as that of X's depression, the depression which X has, the concept must cover both what is felt, but not observed, by X and what may be observed, but not felt, by others than X (for all values of X). But it is perhaps better to say: X's depression *is* something, one and the same thing, which is felt, but not observed, by X, and observed, but not felt, by others than X. (Of course, what can be observed can also be faked or disguised). To refuse to accept this is to refuse to accept the *structure* of the language in which we talk about depression. That is, in a sense, all right. One might give up talking or devise, perhaps, a different structure in terms of which to soliloquize. What is not all right is simultaneously to pretend to accept that structure and to refuse to accept it; i.e. to couch one's rejection in the language of that structure.

It is in this light that we must see some of the familiar philosophical difficulties in the topic of the mind. For some of them spring from just such a failure to admit, or fully to appreciate, the character which I have been claiming for at least some P-predicates. It is not seen that these predicates could not have either aspect of their use, the self-ascriptive or the non-self-ascriptive, without having the other aspect. Instead, one aspect of their use is taken as self-sufficient, which it could not be, and then the other aspect appears as problematical. So we oscillate between philosophical scepticism and philosophical behaviourism. When we take the self-ascriptive aspect of the use of some P-predicates, say "depressed," as primary, then a logical gap seems to open between the criteria on the strength of which we say that another is depressed, and the actual state of being depressed. What we do not realize is that if this logical gap is allowed to open, then it swallows not only his depression, but our

depression as well. For if the logical gap exists, then depressed behaviour, however much there is of it, is no more than a sign of depression. But it can only become a sign of depression because of an observed correlation between it and depression. But whose depression? Only mine, one is tempted to say. But if *only* mine, then *not* mine at all. The sceptical position customarily represents the crossing of the logical gap as at best a shaky inference. But the point is that not even the syntax of the premises of the inference exists, if the gap exists.

If, on the other hand, we take the other-ascriptive uses of these predicates as primary or self-sufficient, we may come to think that all there is in the meaning of these predicates, as predicates, is the criteria on the strength of which we ascribe them to others. Does this not follow from the denial of the logical gap? It does not follow. To think that it does is to forget the self-ascriptive use of these predicates, to forget that we have to do with a class of predicates to the meaning of which it is essential that they should be both self-ascribable and other-ascribable to the same individual, when self-ascriptions are not made on the observational basis on which other-ascriptions are made, but on another basis. It is not that these predicates have two kinds of meaning. Rather, it is essential to the single kind of meaning that they do have, that both ways of ascribing them should be perfectly in order.

If one is playing a game of cards, the distinctive markings of a certain card constitute a logically adequate criterion for calling it, say, the Queen of Hearts; but, in calling it this, in the context of the game, one is also ascribing to it properties over and above the possession of those markings. The predicate gets its meaning from the whole structure of the game. So with the language in which we ascribe P-predicates. To say that the criteria on the strength of which we ascribe P-predicates to others are of a logically adequate kind for this ascription, is not to say that all there is to the ascriptive meaning of these predicates is these criteria. To say this is to forget that they are P-predicates, to forget the rest of the language-structure to which they belong.

6. Now our perplexities may take a different form, the form of the question: "But how can one ascribe to oneself, not on the basis of observation, the very same thing that others may have, on the basis of observation, reasons of a logically adequate kind for ascribing to one?" This question may be absorbed in a wider one, which might be phrased: "How are P-predicates possible?" or: "How is the concept of a person possible?" This is the question by which we replace those two earlier questions, viz.: "Why are states of consciousness ascribed at all, ascribed to anything?" and "Why are they ascribed to the very same thing as certain corporeal characteristics &c.?" For the answer to these two initial questions is to be found nowhere else but in the admission of the primitiveness of the concept of a person, and hence of the unique character of P-predicates. So residual perplexities have to frame themselves in this new way. For when we have acknowledged the primitiveness of the concept of a person and, with it, the unique character of P-predicates, we may still want to ask what it is in the natural facts that makes it intelligible that we should have this concept, and to ask this in the hope of a non-trivial answer, i.e. in the hope of an answer which does not *merely* say: "Well, there are people in the world." I do not pretend to be able to satisfy this demand at all fully. But I may mention two very different things which might count as beginnings or fragments of an answer.

First, I think a beginning can be made by moving a certain class of P-predicates to a central position in the picture. They are predicates, roughly, which involve doing something, which clearly imply intention or a state of mind or at least consciousness in general, and which indicate a characteristic pattern, or range of patterns, of bodily movement, while not indicating at all precisely any very definite sensation or experience. I mean such things as "going for a walk,"

"coiling a rope," "playing ball," "writing a letter." Such predicates have the interesting characteristic of many P-predicates that one does not, in general, ascribe them to oneself on the strength of observation, whereas one does ascribe them to others on the strength of observation. But, in the case of these predicates, one feels minimal reluctance to concede that what is ascribed in these two different ways is the same. This is because of the marked dominance of a fairly definite pattern of bodily movement in what they ascribe, and the marked absence of any distinctive experience. They release us from the idea that the only things we can know about without observation or inference, or both, are private experiences; we can know also, without telling by either of these means, about the present and future movements of a body. Yet bodily movements are certainly also things we can know about by observation and inference. Among the things that we observe, as opposed to the things we know without observation, are the movements of bodies similar to that about which we have knowledge not based on observation. It is important that we should understand such movements, for they bear on and condition our own; and in fact we understand them, we interpret them, only by seeing them as elements in just such plans or schemes of action as those of which we know the present course and future development without observation of the relevant present movements. But this is to say that we see such movements as *actions*, that we interpret them in terms of intention, that we see them as movements of individuals of a type to which also belongs that individual whose present and future movements we know about without observation; it is to say that we see others as self-ascribers, not on the basis of observation, of what we ascribe to them on this basis.

These remarks are not intended to suggest how the "problem of other minds" could be solved, or our beliefs about others given a general philosophical "justification." I have already argued that such a "solution" or "justification" is impossible, that the demand for it cannot be coherently stated. Nor are these remarks intended as *a priori* genetic psychology. They are simply intended to help to make it seem intelligible to us, at this stage, in the history of the philosophy of this subject, that we have the conceptual scheme we have. What I am suggesting is that it is easier to understand how we can see each other, and ourselves, as persons, if we think first of the fact that we act, and act on each other, and act in accordance with a common human nature. Now "to see each other as persons" is a lot of things, but not a lot of separate and unconnected things. The class of P-predicates that I have moved into the center of the picture are not unconnectedly there, detached from others irrelevant to them. On the contrary, they are inextricably bound up with the others, interwoven with them. The topic of the mind does not divide into unconnected subjects.

I spoke just now of a common human nature. But there is also a sense in which a condition of the existence of the conceptual scheme we have is that human nature should not be common—should not be, that is, a community nature. Philosophers used to discuss the question of whether there was, or could be, such a thing as a "group mind." For some the idea had a peculiar fascination, while to others it seemed utterly absurd and nonsensical and at the same time, curiously enough, pernicious. It is easy to see why these last found it pernicious: they found something horrible in the thought that people should cease to have to individual persons the kind of attitudes that they did have, and instead have attitudes in some way analogous towards groups; and that they might cease to decide individual courses of action for themselves and instead merely participate in corporate activities. But their finding it pernicious showed that they understood the idea they claimed to be absurd only too well. The fact that we find it natural to individuate as persons the members of a certain class of moving natural objects does not mean that such a conceptual scheme is inevitable for any class of beings not utterly unlike ourselves. A technique similar to that which I used in the last chapter to decide whether there was a place in the restricted auditory world for the concept of the self, is available to determine whether we might not construct the idea of a special kind of social world in which the concept of an individual person is replaced by that of a group. Think, to begin with, of certain aspects of actual human existence. Think, for example, of two groups of human beings engaged in some competitive, but corporate activity, such as battle, for which they have been exceedingly well trained. We may even suppose that orders are superfluous, though information is passed. It is easy to suppose that, while absorbed in such activity, the members of the groups make no references to individual persons at all, have no use for personal names or pronouns. They do, however, refer to the groups and apply to them predicates analogous to those predicates ascribing purposive activity which we normally apply to individual persons. They may *in fact* use in such circumstances the plural forms "we" and "they"; but these are not genuine plurals, they are plurals without a singular, such as occur in sentences like: "We have taken the citadel," "We have lost the game." They may also refer to elements in the group, to members of the group, but exclusively in terms which get their sense from the parts played by these elements in the corporate activity. Thus we sometimes refer to what are in fact persons as "stroke" or "square-leg."

When we think of such cases, we see that we ourselves, over a part of our social lives —not, happily, a very large part—do work with a set of ideas from which that of the individual person is excluded, in which its place is taken by that of the group. But might we not think of communities or groups such that this part of the lives of their members was the dominant part—or was not merely a part, but the whole? It sometimes happens, with groups of human beings, that, as *we* say, their members think, feel and act "as one." I suggest it is a condition for the existence of the concept of an individual person, that this should happen only sometimes.

It is quite useless to say, at this point: "But all the same, even if it happened all the time, every member of the group would *have* an individual consciousness, would embody an individual subject of experience." For, once more, there is no sense in speaking of the individual consciousness just as such, of the individual subject of experience just as such; there is no way of identifying such pure entities. It is true, of course, that, in suggesting the fantasy of total absorption in the group, I took our concept of an individual person as a starting point. It is this fact which makes the useless reaction a natural one. But suppose someone seriously advanced the following "hypothesis": that each part of the human body, each organ and each member, had an individual consciousness, was a separate centre of experiences. The "hypothesis" would be useless in the same way as the above remark, only more obviously so. Let us now suppose that there is a class of moving natural objects, divided into groups, each group exhibiting the same characteristic pattern of activity. Within each group there are certain differentiations of appearance accompanying differentiations of function, and in particular there is one member of each group with a distinctive appearance. Cannot one imagine different sets of observations which might lead us in one case to think of the particular member as the spokesman of the group, as its mouthpiece; and in the other case to think of him as its mouth, to think of the group as a single *scattered* body? The important point is that as soon as we adopt the latter way of thinking, then we abandon the former; we are no longer influenced by the human analogy in its first form, but only in its second; we are no longer tempted to say: Perhaps the members have consciousness. It is helpful here to remember the startling ambiguity of the phrase, "a body and its members."

7. Earlier, when I was discussing the concept of a pure individual consciousness, I said that though it could not exist as a primary concept to be used in the explanation of the concept of a person (so that there is no mind-body problem, as traditionally conceived), yet it might have a logically secondary existence. Thus, from within our actual conceptual scheme, each of us can quite intelligibly conceive of his or her individual survival of bodily death. The effort of imagination is not even great. One has simply to think of oneself as having thoughts and memories as at present, visual and auditory experiences largely as at present, even, perhaps—though this involves certain complications—some quasi-tactual and organic sensations as at present, whilst (*a*) having no perceptions of a body related to one's experience as one's own body is, and (*b*) having no power of initiating changes in the physical condition of the world, such as one at present does with one's hands, shoulders, feet and vocal chords. Condition (*a*) must be expanded by adding that no one else exhibits reactions indicating that he perceives a body at the point which one's body would be occupying if one were seeing and hearing in an embodied state from the point from which one is seeing and hearing is a disembodied state. One could, of course, imagine condition (*a*) being fulfilled, in both its parts, without condition (*b*) being fulfilled. This would be a rather vulgar fancy, in the class of the table-tapping spirits with familiar voices. But suppose we take disembodiment strictly in the sense that we imagine both (*a*) and (*b*) fulfilled. Then two consequences follow, one of which is commonly noted, the other of which is perhaps insufficiently attended to. The first is that the strictly disembodied individual is strictly solitary, and it must remain for him indeed an utterly empty, though not meaningless, speculation, as to whether there are any other members of his class. The other, and less commonly noticed point, is that in order to retain his idea of himself as an individual, he must always think of himself as *dis*embodied, as a *former* person. That is to say, he must contrive still to have the idea of himself as a member of a class or type of entities with whom, however, he is now

debarred from entering into any of those transactions the past fact of which was the condition of his having any idea of himself at all. Since then he has, as it were, no personal life of his own to lead, he must live much in the memories of the personal life he did lead; or he might, when this living in the past loses its appeal, achieve some kind of attenuated vicarious personal existence by taking a certain kind of interest in the human affairs of which he is a mute and invisible witness—much like that kind of spectator at a play who says to himself:

"That's what I should have done (or said)" of "If I were he, I should . . . ." In proportion as the memories fade, and this vicarious living palls, to that degree his concept of himself as an individual becomes attenuated. At the limit of attenuation there is, *from the point of view of his survival as an individual*, no difference between the continuance of experience and its cessation. Disembodied survival, on such terms as these, may well seem unattractive. No doubt it is for this reason that the orthodox have wisely insisted on the resurrection of the body.

SUGGESTED READINGS

Ayer, Alfred J. *The Problem of Knowledge*. Baltimore: Penguin Books, Inc., 1956. Chap. 5.

Blanshard, Brand. "The Nature of Mind," *Journal of Philosophy*, XXXVIII (1941), pp. 207–16.

Brightman, Edgar S. "The Person as the Key to Reality," *Person and Reality: An Introduction to Metaphysics*, ed. P. A. Bertocci, J. E. Newhall, and R. S. Brightman. New York: The Ronald Press Co., 1933, pp. 343–66.

Descartes, René. *Meditations*. New York: The Liberal Arts Press, 1951.

Ewing, Alfred C. "Professor Ryle's Attack on Dualism," *Preceedings of the Aristotelian Society*, LIII (1952–53).

Feigl, Herbert. "The Mind-Body Problem in the Development of Logical Empiricism," in Feigl and Broderick, *Readings in the Philosophy of Science*. New York: Appleton Century Crofts, 1953.

Hocking, William E. *The Self, Its Body and Freedom*. New Haven: The Yale University Press, 1928, Chap. 2.

Laird, John. *The Problems of the Self*. London: The Macmillan Co., 1917, Chaps. 7–10.

Lewis, Clarence I. *Mind and the World Order*. New York: Dover Publications, Inc., 1956.

Lovejoy, Arthur O. *The Revolt Against Dualism*. London: G. Allen & Unwin, Ltd., 1930, pp. 26–33; Chap. 8.

Maritain, Jacques. *The Person and the Common Good*. New York: Charles Scribner's Sons, 1947, Chap. III.

Pap, Arthur. "Semantic Analysis and Psycho-Physical Dualism," *Mind*, LXI-LXII (1952–53), pp. 209–21.

Pratt, James B. "The Nature of the Self," *Personal Realism*. New York: The Macmillan Co., 1922, pp. 297–317.

Spinoza, Benedict de. *Ethics*. New York: St. Martin's Press, 1956, Part II.

Stout, George F. "Final Treatment of the Psycho-Physical Problem," *Mind and Matter*. New York: The Macmillan Co., 1931, pp. 308–15.

PART V

THE WORLD, EMERGENCE, AND GOD

INTRODUCTION

The world is man's habitat. As a scientist he questions it. But its origin, order, and end have puzzled men since the earliest days of philosophical speculation; and speculation on these problems involves a bevy of extremely important questions. If the material world is all there is, then it seems it must always have been, and one must somehow explain its apparent organization and development. If it has not always been, then it seems one must explain its origin by some being who is eternal and capable of producing and ordering it. This being is generally called God. According to either hypothesis, the meaning, extension, and validity of the notion of causality is central, and one soon becomes involved in the question of teleology versus mechanism, in the nature of space and time, and in the relation of God and the world. This latter consideration leads, in turn, to questions of natural theology and to the philosophy of religion.

Plato (427–347 B.C.), an Athenian aristocrat, was greatly influenced by Socrates, the main character of his early dialogues. His metaphysical and political theories have had an enormous influence on the development of Western philosophy and remain important to this day. In his *Timaeus* (c. 350 B.C.), Plato devoted himself to cosmology and natural science. The theories he presented here dominated cosmological speculation for the greater part of the Middle Ages. Timaeus, the main character of the dialogue, argues that since the world is sensible, it must have been made by an intelligent designer according to an unchanging model. He explains the generation of the world soul, of time and the celestial motions, and of the human body and soul as a mixed result of Necessity and Reason, requiring a model, a copy, and a Receptacle of all Becoming (Space).

Whereas the Platonic and Aristotelian cosmologies were teleological, the rival cosmology, Democritus' Atomism, was materialistic and mechanistic. In modern times, mechanism was revitalized and modernized by Descartes and Newton, and the view of Nature as a machine dominated much of modern thought. In "Mechanism and Its Alternatives," C. D. Broad (see Introduction to Part IV) presents both the ideal and the limitations of Pure Mechanism. He then argues that teleology belongs to some things in the world—living organisms as well as machines—and goes on to analyze the relation of teleology and design, and Biological Mechanism and Deism. He concludes by tentatively evaluating the three possible theories of Substantial Vitalism, Emergent Vitalism, and Biological Mechanism.

Gottfried Wilhelm Leibniz (1646–1716), a rationalist philosopher born in Leipzig, invented the calculus independently of Newton. He is probably best known for his *Discourse on Metaphysics* (1686) and his *Monadology* (1720). In a short work entitled *Principles of Nature and Grace* (1714), he summarizes his philosophy. In the first half of the essay, he presents his theory of monads and of pre-established harmony. In the second half, he presents his statement of the principle of sufficient reason and argues from it to God and to his famous claim that this is the best of all possible worlds.

Arthur O. Lovejoy (1873–   ), Professor Emeritus at Johns Hopkins, Carus Lecturer (1927), and founder and first editor of the *Journal of the History of Ideas,* is the author of a number of important books, including *The Revolt Against Dualism* (1929) and *The Great Chain of Being* (1936). In his paper "The Meanings of 'Emergence' and Its Modes" (1927), he examines the meanings of emergence against the background of the preformationist assumption that there cannot be more in the effect than in the cause. After finding the case against general emergence unconvincing, he distinguishes five modes of possible emergence and defends a doctrine of existential emergence.

In his presidential address to the American Catholic Philosophical Association in 1955, James Collins (1917–   ), Professor of Philosophy at St. Louis University and author of *The Existentialists: A Critical Study* (1952), *The Mind of Kierkegaard* (1953), *A History of Modern European Philosophy* (1954), and *God in Modern Philosophy* (1959), examines three representative modern approaches to God in order to see how each affects the philosophical thought of the author concerned. Spinoza reduced God to a first deductive premise; Kant employed God as a postulate of moral harmony; and Hegel subordinated God to his dialectical absolutism. Collins briefly outlines the Thomistic answers to the difficulties each of these philosophers faced and concludes not that philosophers should refrain from studying about God, the truth of whose existence can be demonstrated, but that philosophers should refrain from making God a tool of their special views.

Alfred North Whitehead (see Introduction to Part I), in the concluding chapter of *Process and Reality,* discusses—without reference to existing religions—what the metaphysical principles of his system require as to the nature of God. For him, God is the chief exemplification of all metaphysical principles. Among other things, He is the principle of concretion, and is both primordial and consequent. "God and the World are the contrasted opposites in terms of which Creativity achieves its supreme task of transforming disjointed multiplicity, with its diversities in opposition, into concrescent unity, with its diversities in contrast."

Alfred Jules Ayer (1910–   ), Grote Professor of Mind and Logic at the

University of London, is a leading exponent of logical positivism and author of a number of works, including *The Foundations of Empirical Knowledge* (1940) and *The Problem of Knowledge* (1956). He presented a vigorous positivistic attack against metaphysics as a whole, in his book *Language, Truth and Logic* (1936), on the grounds that metaphysical statements were unverifiable and therefore meaningless. The attack extended also to religious knowledge and to all knowledge about God, His existence, and His attributes. Ayer's position has been modified somewhat since this early statement of his views, but the validity of such metaphysical knowledge remains a vital and disputed question at the present time.

PLATO

TIMAEUS*

CRITIAS. Consider now, Socrates, the order of the feast as we have arranged it. Seeing that Timaeus is our best astronomer and has made it his special task to learn about the nature of the Universe, it seemed good to us that he should speak first, beginning with the origin of the Cosmos and ending with the generation of mankind. After him I am to follow, taking over from him mankind, already as it were created by his speech, and taking over from you a select number of men superlatively well trained. Then, in accordance with the word and law of Solon, I am to bring these before ourselves, as before a court of judges, and make them citizens of this State of ours, regarding them as Athenians of that bygone age whose existence, so long forgotten, has been revealed to us by the record of the sacred writings; and thenceforward I am to proceed with my discourse as if I were speaking of men who already are citizens and men of Athens.

SOCRATES. Bounteous and magnificent, methinks, is the feast of speech with which I am to be requited. So then, Timaeus, it will be your task, it seems, to speak next,

when you have duly invoked the gods.

TIMAEUS. Nay, as to that, Socrates, all men who possess even a small share of good sense call upon God always at the outset of every undertaking, be it small or great; we therefore who are purposing to deliver a discourse concerning the Universe, how it was created or haply is uncreate, must needs invoke Gods and Goddesses (if so be that we are not utterly demented), praying that all we say may be approved by them in the first place, and secondly by ourselves. Grant, then, that we have thus duly invoked the deities; ourselves we must also invoke so to proceed, that you may most easily learn and I may most clearly expound my views regarding the subject before us.

Now first of all we must, in my judgment, make the following distinction. What is that which is Existent always and has no Becoming? And what is that which is Becoming always and never is Existent? Now the one of these is apprehensible by thought with the aid of reasoning, since it is ever uniformly existent; whereas the other is an object of opinion with the aid of unreasoning sensation, since it becomes and perishes and is never really existent. Again, everything which becomes must of necessity become owing to some Cause; for without a cause it is impossible for anything to attain becom-

---

* Sections 27A through 53B. Reprinted by permission of the publishers and The Loeb Classical Library, translated by R. G. Bury, PLATO: *Timaeus*, Cambridge, Mass.: Harvard University Press. The translator's footnotes have been omitted.

ing. But when the artificer of any object, in forming its shape and quality, keeps his gaze fixed on that which is uniform, using a model of this kind, that object, executed in this way, must of necessity be beautiful; but whenever he gazes at that which has come into existence and uses a created model, the object thus executed is not beautiful. Now the whole Heaven, or Cosmos, or if there is any other name which it specially prefers, by that let us call it,—so, be its name what it may, we must first investigate concerning it that primary question which has to be investigated at the outset in every case,—namely, whether it has existed always, having no beginning of generation, or whether it has come into existence, having begun from some beginning. It has come into existence; for it is visible and tangible and possessed of a body; and all such things are sensible, and things sensible, being apprehensible by opinion with the aid of sensation, come into existence, as we saw and are generated. And that which has come into existence must necessarily, as we say, have come into existence by reason of some Cause. Now to discover the Maker and Father of this Universe were a task indeed; and having discovered Him, to declare Him unto all men were a thing impossible. However, let us return and inquire further concerning the Cosmos,—after which of the Models did its Architect construct it? Was it after that which is self-identical and uniform, or after that which has come into existence? Now if so be that this Cosmos is beautiful and its Constructor good, it is plain that he fixed his gaze on the Eternal; but if otherwise (which is an impious supposition), his gaze was on that which has come into existence. But it is clear to everyone that his gaze was on the Eternal; for the Cosmos is the fairest of all that has come into existence, and He the best of all the Causes. So having in this wise come into existence, it has been constructed after the pattern of that which is apprehensible by reason and thought and is self-identical.

Again, if these premises be granted, it is wholly necessary that this Cosmos should be a Copy of something. Now in regard to every matter it is most important to begin at the natural beginning. Accordingly, in dealing with a copy and its model, we must affirm that the accounts given will themselves be akin to the diverse objects which they serve to explain; those which deal with what is abiding and firm and discernible by the aid of thought will be abiding and unshakable; and in so far as it is possible and fitting for statements to be irrefutable and invincible, they must in no wise fall short thereof; whereas the accounts of that which is copied after the likeness of that Model, and is itself a likeness, will be analogous thereto and possess likelihood; for as Being is to Becoming, so is Truth to Belief. Wherefore, Socrates, if in our treatment of a great host of matters regarding the Gods and the generation of the Universe we prove unable to give accounts that are always in all respects self-consistent and perfectly exact, be not thou surprised; rather we should be content if we can furnish accounts that are inferior to none in likelihood, remembering that both I who speak and you who judge are but human creatures, so that it becomes us to accept the likely account of these matters and forbear to search beyond it.

SOCRATES. Excellent, Timaeus! We must by all means accept it, as you suggest; and certainly we have most cordially accepted your prelude; so now, we beg of you, proceed straight on with the main theme.

TIMAEUS. Let us now state the Cause wherefor He that constructed it constructed Becoming and the All. He was good, and in him that is good no envy ariseth ever concerning anything; and being devoid of envy He desired that all should be, so far as possible, like unto Himself. This principle, then, we shall be wholly right in accepting from men of wisdom as being above all the supreme originating principle of Becoming and the Cosmos. For God desired that, so far as possible, all things should be good and nothing evil; wherefore, when He took over all that was visible, seeing that it was not in a state of rest but in a state of discordant and disorderly motion, He brought it into order out of disorder, deeming that the former state is in all ways better than the latter. For Him who is most good it neither was nor is permissible to perform any action save what is most fair. As he reflected, therefore, He perceived that of such creatures as are by nature visible, none that is irrational will be fairer, comparing wholes with wholes, than the rational; and further, that reason cannot possibly belong to any apart from Soul. So because of this reflexion He constructed reason within soul and soul within body as He fashioned the All, that so the work He was executing might be of its nature most fair and most good. Thus, then, is accordance with the likely account, we must declare that this Cosmos has verily come into existence as a Living Creature endowed with soul and reason owing to the providence of God.

This being established, we must declare that which comes next in order. In the semblance of which of the living Creatures did the Constructor of the Cosmos construct it? We shall not deign to accept any of those which belong by nature to the category of "parts"; for nothing that resembles the imperfect would ever become fair. But we shall affirm that the Cosmos, more than aught else, resembles most closely that Living Creature of which all other living creatures, severally and generically, are portions. For that Living Creature embraces and contains within itself all the intelligible Living Creatures, just as this Universe contains us and all the other visible living creatures that have been fashioned. For since God desired to make it resemble most closely that intelligible Creature which is fairest of all and in all ways most perfect, He constructed it as a Living Creature, one and visible, containing within itself all the living creatures which are by nature akin to itself.

Are we right, then, in describing the Heaven as one, or would it be more correct to speak of heavens as many or infinite in number? One it must be termed, if it is to be framed after its Pattern. For that which embraces all intelligible Living Creatures could never be second, with another beside it; for if so, there must needs exist yet another Living Creature, which should embrace them both, and of which they two would each be a part; in which case this Universe could no longer be rightly described as modelled on these two, but rather on that third Creature which contains them both. Wherefore, in order that this Creature might resemble the all-perfect Living Creature in respect of its uniqueness, for this reason its Maker made neither two Universes nor an infinite number, but there is and will continue to be this one generated Heaven, unique of its kind.

Now that which has come into existence must needs be of bodily form, visible and tangible; yet without fire nothing could ever become visible, nor tangible without some solidity, nor solid without earth. Hence, in beginning to construct the body of the All, God was making it of fire and earth. But it is not possible that two things alone should be conjoined without a third; for there must needs be some intermediary bond to connect the two. And the fairest of bonds is that which most perfectly unites into one both itself and the things which it binds together; and to effect this in the fairest manner is the natural property of proportion. For whenever the middle term of any three numbers, cubic or square, is such that as the first term is to it, so is it to the last term,—and again, conversely, as the last term is to the middle, so is the middle to the first,—then the middle term becomes in turn the first and the last, while the first and last become in turn middle terms, and the necessary consequence will be that all the terms are interchangeable, and being interchangeable they all form a unity. Now if the body of the All had had to come into existence as a plane surface, having no depth, one middle term would have sufficed to bind together both itself and its fellow-terms; but now it is otherwise: for it behoved it to be solid of shape, and what brings solids into unison is never one middle term alone but always two. Thus it was that in the midst between fire and earth God set water and air, and having bestowed upon them so far as possible a like ratio one towards another—air being to water as fire to air, and water being to earth as air to water,—he joined together and constructed a Heaven visible and tangible. For these reasons and out of these materials, such in kind and four in number, the body of the Cosmos was harmonized by proportion and brought into existence. These conditions secured for it Amity, so that being united in identity with itself it became indissoluble by any agent other than Him who had bound it together.

Now of the four elements the construction of the Cosmos had taken up the whole of every one. For its Constructor had constructed it of all the fire and water and air and earth that existed, leaving over, outside it, no single particle or potency of any one of these elements. And these were his intentions: first, that it might be, so far as possible, a Living Creature, perfect and whole, with all its parts perfect; and next, that it might be One, inasmuch as there was nothing left over out of which another like Creature might come into existence; and further, that it might be secure from age and ailment, since He perceived that when heat and cold, and all things which have violent potencies, surround a composite body from without and collide with it they dissolve it unduly and make it to waste away by bringing upon it ailments and age. Wherefore, because of this reasoning, He fashioned it to be One single Whole, compounded of all wholes, perfect and ageless and unailing. And he bestowed on it the shape which was befitting and akin. Now for that Living Creature which is designed to embrace within itself all living creatures the fitting shape will be that which comprises within itself all the shapes there are; wherefore He wrought it into a round, in the shape of a sphere, equidistant in all directions from the centre to the extremities, which of all shapes is the most perfect and the most self-similar, since He deemed that the similar is infinitely fairer than the dissimilar. And on the outside round about, it was all made smooth with great exactness, and that for

many reasons. For of eyes it had no need, since outside of it there was nothing visible left over; nor yet of hearing, since neither was there anything audible; nor was there any air surrounding it which called for respiration; nor, again did it need any organ whereby it might receive the food that entered and evacuate what remained undigested. For nothing went out from it or came into it from any side, since nothing existed; for it was so designed as to supply its own wastage as food for itself, and to experience by its own agency and within itself all actions and passions, since He that had constructed it deemed that it would be better if it were self-sufficing rather than in need of other things. Hands, too, He thought He ought not to attach unto it uselessly, seeing they were not required either for grasping or for repelling anyone; not yet feet, nor any instruments of locomotion whatsoever. For movement He assigned unto it that which is proper to its body, namely, that one of the seven motions which specially belongs to reason and intelligence; wherefore He spun it round uniformly in the same spot and within itself and made it move revolving in a circle; and all the other six motions He took away and fashioned it free from their aberrations. And seeing that for this revolving motion it had no need of feet, He begat it legless and footless.

Such, then, was the sum of the reasoning of the ever-existing God concerning the god which was one day to be existent, whereby He made it smooth and even and equal on all sides from the centre, a whole and perfect body compounded of perfect bodies. And in the midst thereof He set Soul, which He stretched throughout the whole of it, and therewith He enveloped also the exterior of its body; and as a Circle revolving in a circle He stablished one sole and solitary Heaven, able of itself because of its excellence to company with itself and needing none other beside, sufficing unto itself as acquaintance and friend. And because of all this He generated it to be a blessed God.

Now as regards the Soul, although we are

essaying to describe it after the body, God did not likewise plan it to be younger than the body; for, when uniting them, He would not have permitted the elder to be ruled by the younger; but as for us men, even as we ourselves partake largely of the accidental and casual, so also do our words. God, however, constructed Soul to be older than Body and prior in birth and excellence, since she was to be the mistress and ruler and it the ruled; and He made her of the materials and in the fashion which I shall now describe.

Midway between the Being which is indivisible and remains always the same and the Being which is transient and divisible in bodies, He blended a third form of Being compounded out of the twain, that is to say, out of the Same and the Other; and in like manner He compounded it midway between that one of them which is indivisible and that one which is divisible in bodies. And He took the three of them, and blent them all together into one form, by forcing the Other into union with the Same, in spite of its being naturally difficult to mix. And when with the aid of Being He had mixed them, and had made of them one out of three, straightway He began to distribute the whole thereof into so many portions as was meet; and each portion was a mixture of the Same, of the Other, and of Being. And He began making the division thus:

First He took one portion from the whole; then He took a portion double of this; then a third portion, half as much again as the second portion, that is, three times as much as the first; the fourth portion He took was twice as much as the second; the fifth three times as much as the third; the sixth eight times as much as the first; and the seventh twenty-seven times as much as the first.

After that He went on to fill up the intervals in the series of the powers of 2 and the intervals in the series of powers of 3 in the following manner:

He cut off yet further portions from the original mixture, and set them in between the portions above rehearsed, so as to place two Means in each interval,—one a Mean which exceeded its Extremes and was by them exceeded by the same *proportional part* or *fraction* of each of the Extremes respectively; the other a Mean which exceeded one Extreme by the same *number* or *integer* as it was exceeded by its other Extremes.

And whereas the insertion of these links formed fresh intervals in the former intervals, that is to say, intervals of 3:2 and 4:3 and 9:8, He went on to fill up the 4:3 intervals with 9:8 intervals. This still left over in each case a fraction, which is represented by the terms of the numerical ratio 256:243.

And thus the mixture, from which He had been cutting these portions off, was now all spent.

Next, He split all this that He had put together into two parts lengthwise; and then He laid the twain one against the other, the middle of one to the middle of the others, like a great cross +; and bent either of them into a circle, and joined them, each to itself and also to the other, at a point opposite to where they had first been laid together. And He compassed them about with the motion that revolves in the same spot continually, and He made the one circle outer and the other inner. And the outer motion He ordained to be the Motion of the Same, and the inner motion the Motion of the Other. And He made the Motion of the Same to be toward the right along the side, and the Motion of the Other to be towards the left along the diagonal; and He gave the sovranty to the Revolution of the Same and of the Uniform. For this alone He suffered to remain uncloven, whereas He split the inner Revolution in six places into seven unequal circles, according to each of intervals of the double and triple intervals, three double and three triple. These two circles then He appointed to go in contrary directions; and of the seven circles into which He split the inner circle, He appointed three to revolve at an equal speed, the other four to go at speeds equal neither with each other nor with the speed of the aforesaid three, yet moving at speeds the ratios of which one to another are those of natural integers.

And when the construction of the Soul had all been completed to the satisfaction of its constructor, then He fabricated within it all the Corporeal, and uniting them centre to centre He made them fit together. And the Soul, being woven throughout the Heaven every way from the centre to the extremity, and enveloping it in a circle from without, and herself revolving within herself, began a divine beginning of unceasing and intelligent life lasting throughout all time. And whereas the body of the Heaven is visible, the Soul is herself invisible but partakes in reasoning and in harmony, having come into existence by the agency of the best of things intelligible and ever-existing as the best of things generated. Inasmuch, then, as she is a compound, blended of the natures of the Same and the Other and Being, these three portions, and is proportionately divided and bound together, and revolves back upon herself, whenever she touches anything which has its substance dispersed or anything which has its substance undivided she is moved throughout her whole being and announces what the object is identical with and from what it is different, and in what relation, where and how and when, it comes about that each thing exists and is acted upon by others both in the sphere of the Becoming and in that of the ever-uniform. And her announcement, being identically true concerning both the Other and the same, is borne through the self-moved without speech or sound; and whenever it is concerned with the sensible, and the circle of the Other moving in straight course proclaims it to the whole of its Soul, opinions and beliefs arise which are firm and true; and again, when it is concerned with the rational, and the circle of the Same, spinning truly, declares the facts, reason and knowledge of necessity result. But should anyone assert that the substance in which

these two states arise is something other than Soul, his assertion will be anything rather than the truth.

And when the Father that engendered it perceived it in motion and alive, a thing of joy to the eternal gods, He too rejoiced; and being well-pleased He designed to make it resemble its Model still more closely. Accordingly, seeing that that Model is an eternal Living Creature, He set about making this Universe, so far as He could, of a like kind. But inasmuch as the nature of the Living Creature was eternal, this quality it was impossible to attach in its entirety to what is generated; wherefore He planned to make (a movable image of Eternity,) and, as He set in order the Heaven, of that Eternity which abides in unity He made an eternal image, moving according to number, even that which we have named Time. For simultaneously with the construction of the Heaven He contrived the production of days and nights and months and years, which existed not before the Heaven came into being. And these are all portions of Time; even as "Was" and "Shall be" are generated forms of Time, although we apply them wrongly, without noticing, to Eternal Being. For we say that it "is" or "was" or "will be," whereas, in truth of speech, "is" alone is the appropriate term; "was" and "will be," on the other hand, are terms properly applicable to the Becoming which proceeds in Time, since both of these are motions; but it belongs not to that which is ever changeless in its uniformity to become either older or younger through time, nor ever to have become so, nor to be so now, nor to be about to be so hereafter, nor in general to be subject to any of the conditions which Becoming has attached to the things which move in the world of Sense, these being generated forms of Time, which imitates Eternity and circles round according to number. And besides these we make use of the following expressions,—that what is become *is* become, and what is becoming *is* becoming, and what is about to become *is* about to become, and what is non-existent *is* non-existent; but none of these expressions is accurate. But the present is not, perhaps, a fitting occasion for an exact discussion of these matters.

Time, then, came into existence along with the Heaven, to the end that having been generated together they might also be dissolved together, if ever a dissolution of them should take place; and it was made after the pattern of the Eternal Nature, to the end that it might be as like thereto as possible; for whereas the pattern is existent through all eternity, the copy, on the other hand, is through all time, continually having existed, existing, and being about to exist. Wherefore, as a consequence of this reasoning and design on the part of God, with a view to the generation of Time, the sun and moon and five other stars, which bear the appellation of "planets," came into existence for the determining and preserving of the numbers of time. And when God had made the bodies of each of them He placed them in the orbits along which the revolution of the Other was moving, seven orbits for the seven bodies. The Moon He placed in the first circle around the Earth, the Sun in the second above the Earth; and the Morning Star and the Star called Sacred to Hermes He placed in those circles which move in an orbit equal to the Sun in velocity, but endowed with a power contrary thereto; whence it is that the Sun and the Star of Hermes and the Morning Star regularly overtake and are overtaken by one another. As to the rest of the stars, were one to describe in detail the positions in which He set them, and all the reasons therefore, the description, though but subsidiary, would prove a heavier task than the main argument which it subserves. Later on, perhaps, at our leisure these points may receive the attention they merit.

So when each of the bodies whose co-operation was required for the making of Time had arrived in its proper orbit; and when they had been generated as living creatures, having their bodies bound with living bonds, and had learnt their appointed duties; then they kept revolving around the circuit of the Other, which is transverse and passes through the circuit of the Same and is dominated thereby; and part of them moved in a greater, part in a smaller circle, those in the smaller moving more quickly and those in the greater more slowly. And because of the motion of the Same, the stars which revolved most quickly appeared to be overtaken by those which moved most slowly, although in truth they overtook them; for, because of their simultaneous progress in two opposite directions, the motion of the Same, which is the swiftest of all motions, twisted all their circles into spirals and thus caused the body which moves away from it most slowly to appear the nearest. And in order that there might be a clear measure of the relative speeds, slow and quick, with which they travelled round their eight orbits, in that circle which is second from the earth God kindled a light which now we call the Sun, to the end that it might shine, so far as possible, throughout the whole Heaven, and that all the living creatures entitled thereto might participate in number, learning it from the revolution of the Same and Similar. In this wise and for these reasons were generated Night and Day, which are the revolution of the one and most intelligent circuit; and Month, every time that the Moon having completed her own orbit overtakes the Sun; and Year, as often as the Sun has completed his own orbit. Of the other stars the revolutions have not been discovered by men (save for a few out of the many); wherefore they have no names for them, nor do they compute and compare their relative measurements, so that they are not aware, as a rule, that the "wanderings" of these bodies, which are hard to calculate and of wondrous complexity, constitute Time. Nevertheless, it is still quite possible to perceive that the complete number of Time fulfils the Complete Year when all the eight circuits, with their relative speeds, finish together and come to a head, when measured by the revolution of the Same and Similarly-moving. In this wise and for these reasons were generated all those stars which turn themselves about as they travel through Heaven, to the end that this Universe might be as similar as possible to the perfect and intelligible Living Creature in respect to its imitation of the Eternal Nature thereof.

Now in all other respects this World has already, with the birth of Time, been wrought in the similitude of that whereunto it was being likened, but inasmuch as it did not as yet contain generated within it the whole range of living creatures, therein it was still dissimilar. So this part of the work which was still undone He completed by moulding it after the nature of the Model. According, then, as Reason perceives Forms existing in the Absolute Living Creature, such and so many as exist therein did He deem that this World also should possess. And these Forms are four,—one the heavenly kind of gods; another the winged kind which traverses the air; thirdly, the class which inhabits the waters; and fourthly, that which goes on foot on dry land. The form of the divine class He wrought for the most part out of fire, that this kind might be as bright as possible to behold and as fair; and likening it to the All He made it truly spherical; and He placed it in the intelligence of the Supreme to follow therewith, distributing it round about over all the Heaven, to be unto it a veritable adornment cunningly traced over the whole. And each member of this class He endowed with two motions, whereof, the one is uniform motion in the same spot, whereby it conceives always identical thoughts about the same objects, and the other is a forward motion due to its being dominated by the revolution of the Same and Similar; but in respect of the other five motions they are at rest and move not, so that each of them may attain the greatest possible perfection. From this cause, then, came into existence all those unwandering stars which are living creatures divine and eternal and abide for ever revolving uniformly in the same spot; and those which keep swerving and wandering have been generated in the fashion previously described. And Earth, our nurse, which is globed around the pole that stretches through all,

He framed to be the wardress and fashioner of night and day, she being the first and eldest of all the gods which have come into existence within the Heaven. But the choric dances of these same stars and their crossings one of another, and the relative reversals and progressions of their orbits, and which of the gods meet in their conjunctions, and how many are in opposition, and behind which and at what times they severally pass before one another and are hidden from our view, and again re-appearing send upon men unable to calculate alarming portents of the things which shall come to pass hereafter,— to describe all this without an inspection of models of these movements would be labour in vain. Wherefore, let this account suffice us, and let our discourse concerning the nature of the visible and generated gods have an end.

Concerning the other divinities, to discover and declare their origin is too great a task for us, and we must trust to those who have declared it aforetime, they being, as they affirmed, descendants of gods and knowing well, no doubt, their own forefathers. It is, as I say, impossible to disbelieve the children of gods, even though their statements lack either probable or necessary demonstration; and inasmuch as they profess to speak of family matters, we must follow custom and believe them. Therefore let the generation of these gods be stated by us, following their account, in this wise: Of Gê and Uranus were born the children Oceanus and Tethys; and of these, Phorkys, Cronos, Rhea, and all that go with them; and of Cronos and Rhea were born Zeus and Hera and all those who are, as we know, called their brethren; and of these again, other descendants.

Now when all the gods, both those who revolve manifestly and those who manifest themselves so far as they choose, had come to birth, He that generated this All addressed them thus:

"Gods of gods, those works whereof I am framer and father are indissoluble save by my will. For though all that is bound may be dissolved, yet to will to dissolve that which is fairly joined together and in good case were the deed of a wicked one. Wherefore ye also, seeing that ye were generated, are not wholly immortal or indissoluble, yet in no wise shall ye be dissolved nor incur the doom of death, seeing that in my will ye possess a bond greater and more sovereign than the bonds wherewith, at your birth, ye were bound together. Now, therefore, what I manifest and declare unto you do ye learn. Three mortal kinds still remain ungenerated; but if these come not into being the Heaven will be imperfect; for it will not contain within itself the whole sum of the kinds of living creatures, yet contain them it must if it is to be fully perfect. But if by doing these creatures came into existence and partook of life, they would be made equal unto gods; in order, therefore, that they may be mortal and that this World-all may be truly All, do ye turn yourselves, as Nature directs, to the work of fashioning these living creatures, imitating the power showed by me in my generating of you. Now so much of them as it is proper to designate 'immortal,' the part we call divine which rules supreme in those who are fain to follow justice always and yourselves, that part I will deliver unto you when I have sown it and given it origin. For the rest, do ye weave together the mortal with the immortal, and thereby fashion and generate living creatures, and give them food that they may grow, and when they waste away receive them to yourselves again."

Thus He spake, and once more into the former bowl, wherein He had blended and mixed the Soul of the Universe, He poured the residue of the previous material, mixing it in somewhat the same manner, yet no longer with a uniform and invariable purity, but second and third in degree of purity. And when He had compounded the whole He divided it into souls equal in number to the stars, and each several soul He assigned to one star, and setting them each as it were in a chariot He showed them the nature of the Universe, and declared unto them the laws of destiny,—namely, how that the first birth should be one and the same ordained

for all, in order that none might be slighted by Him; and how it was needful that they, when sown each into his own proper organ of time, should grow into the most godfearing of living creatures; and that, since human nature is two-fold, the superior sex is that which, hereafter should be designated "man." And when, by virtue of Necessity, they should be implanted in bodies, and their bodies are subject to influx and efflux, these results would necessarily follow,—firstly, sensation that is innate and common to all proceeding from violent affections; secondly, desire mingled with pleasure and pain; and besides these, fear and anger and all such emotions as are naturally allied thereto, and all such as are of a different and opposite character. And if they shall master these they will live justly, but if they are mastered, unjustly. And he that has lived his appointed time well shall return again to his abode in his native star, and shall gain a life that is blessed and congenial; but whoso has failed therein shall be changed into woman's nature at the second birth; and if, in that shape, he still refraineth not from wickedness he shall be changed every time, according to the nature of his wickedness, into some bestial form after the similitude of his own nature; nor in his changings shall he cease from woes until he yields himself to the revolution of the Same and Similar that is within him, and dominating by force of reason that burdensome mass which afterwards adhered to him of fire and water and earth and air, a mass tumultuous and irrational, returns again to the semblance of his first and best state.

When He had fully declared unto them all these ordinances, to the end that He might be blameless in respect of the future wickedness of any one of them, He proceeded to sow them, some in the Earth, some in the Moon, others in the rest of the organs of Time. Following upon this sowing, He delivered over to the young gods the task of moulding mortal modies, and of framing and controlling all the rest of the human soul which it was still necessary to add, together with all that belonged thereto, and of governing this mortal creature in the fairest and best way possible, to the utmost of their power, except in so far as it might itself become the cause of its own evils.

So He, then, having given all these commands, was abiding in His own proper and wonted state. And as He thus abode, His children gave heed to their Father's command and obeyed it. They took the immortal principle of the mortal living creature, and imitating their own Maker, they borrowed from the Cosmos portions of fire and earth and water and air, as if meaning to pay them back, and the portions so taken they cemented together; but it was not with those indissoluble bonds wherewith they themselves were joined that they fastened together the portions but with numerous pegs, invisible for smallness; and thus they constructed out of them all each several body, and within bodies subject to inflow and outflow they bound the revolutions of the immortal Soul. The souls, then, being thus bound within a mighty river neither mastered it nor were mastered, but with violence they rolled along and were rolled along themselves, so that the whole of the living creature was moved, but in such a random way that its progress was disorderly and irrational, since it partook of all the six motions: for it progressed forwards and backwards, and again to right and to left, and upwards and downwards, wandering every way in all the six directions. For while the flood which foamed in and streamed out, as it supplied the food, was immense, still greater was the tumult produced within each creature as a result of the colliding bodies, when the body of a creature happened to meet and collide with alien fire from without, or with a solid lump of earth or liquid glidings of waters, or when it was overtaken by a tempest of winds driven by air, and when the motions due to all these causes rushing through the body impinged upon the Soul. And for these reasons all such motions were then termed "Sensations," and are still so termed to-day. Moreover, since at that time they were causing, for the moment, constant and widespread motion, joining with the

perpetually flowing stream in moving and violently shaking the revolutions of the Soul, they totally blocked the course of the Same by flowing contrary thereto and hindered it thereby in its ruling and its going; while, on the other hand, they so shook up the course of the Other that in the three several intervals of the double and the triple, and in the mean terms and binding links of the ³⁄₂, ⁴⁄₃, and ⁹⁄₈,—these being not wholly dissoluble save by Him who had bound them together,—they produced all manner of twistings, and caused in their circles fractures and disruptions of every possible kind, with the result that, as they barely held together one with another, they moved indeed but moved irrationally, being at one time reversed, at another oblique, and again upside down. Suppose, for example, that a man is in an upside down position, with his head resting on the earth and his feet touching something above, then, in this position of the man relative to that of the onlookers, his right will appear left to them, and his left right, and so will theirs to him. This, and such like, are just what the revolutions of the Soul experience with intensity; and every time they happen upon any external object, whether it be of the class of the Same or of the Other, they proclaim it to be the same as something or other than something contrary to the truth, and thereby prove themselves false and foolish, and devoid, at such times, of any revolution that rules and guides. And whenever external sensations in their movement collide with these revolutions and sweep along with them also the whole vessel of the Soul, then the revolutions, though actually mastered, appear to have the mastery. Hence it comes about that, because of all these affections, now as in the beginning, so often as the Soul is bound within a mortal body it becomes at the first irrational. But as soon as the stream of increase and nutriment enters in less volume, and the revolutions calm down and pursue their own path, becoming more stable as time proceeds, then at length, as the several circles move each according to its natural track, their revolutions are straightened out and they announce the Same and the Other aright, and thereby they render their possessor intelligent. And if so be that this state of his soul be reinforced by right educational training, the man becomes wholly sound and faultless, having escaped the worst of maladies; but if he has been wholly negligent therein, after passing a lame existence in life he returns again unperfected and unreasoning to Hades. These results, however, come about at a later time. Regarding the subjects now before us, we must give a more exact exposition; and also regarding the subjects anterior to these, namely, the generation of bodies in their several parts, and the causes and divine counsels whereby the Soul has come into existence, we must hold fast to the most probable account, and proceed accordingly, in the exposition now to be given.

The divine revolutions, which are two, they bound within a sphere-shaped body, in imitation of the spherical form of the All, which body we now call the "head," it being the most divine part and reigning over all the parts within us. To it the gods delivered over the whole of the body they had assembled to be its servant, having formed the notion that it should partake in all the motions which were to be. In order, then, that it should not go rolling upon the earth, which has all manner of heights and hollows, and be at a loss how to climb over the one and climb out of the other, they bestowed upon it the body as a vehicle and means of transport. And for this reason the body acquired length, and, by God's contriving, shot forth four limbs, extensible and flexible, to serve as instruments of transport, so that grasping with these and supported thereon it was enabled to travel through all places, bearing aloft the chamber of our most divine and holy part. In this wise and for these reasons were legs and hands attached to all men; and inasmuch as they demand the forepart superior to the hinder part in honour and dignity, the Gods gave us the most part of our going in this direction. Thus it was necessary that man should have the forepart of his body distinct and dissimilar. Wherefore, dealing first with the vessel of the head, they set the face in the front thereof and bound within it organs for all the forethought of the Soul; and they ordained that this, which is the natural front, should be the leading part. And of the organs they constructed first light-bearing eyes, and these they fixed in the face for the reason following. They contrived that all such fire as had the property not of burning but of giving a mild light should form a body akin to the light of every day. For they caused the pure fire within us which is akin to that of day, to flow through the eyes in a smooth and dense stream; and they compressed the whole substance, and especially the centre, of the eyes, so that they occluded all other fire that was coarser and allowed only this pure kind of fire to filter through. So whenever the stream of vision is surrounded by mid-day light, it flows out like unto like, and coalescing therewith it forms one kindred substance along the path of the eyes' vision, wheresoever the fire which streams from within collides with an obstructing object without. And this substance, having all become similar in its properties because of its similar nature, distributes the motions of every object it touches, or whereby it is touched, throughout all the body even unto the Soul, and brings about that sensation which we now term "seeing." But when the kindred fire vanishes into night, the inner fire is cut off; for when it issues forth into what is dissimilar it becomes altered in itself and is quenched, seeing that it is no longer of like nature with the adjoining air, since that air is devoid of fire. Wherefore it leaves off seeing, and becomes also an inducement to sleep. For the eyelids —whose structure the Gods devised as a safeguard for the vision,—when they are shut close, curb the power of the inner fire; which power dissipates and allays the inward motions, and upon their allaying quiet ensues; and when this quiet has become intense there falls upon us a sleep that is well-nigh dreamless; but when some greater motions are still left behind, according to their nature and the positions they occupy such and so great are the images they produce, which images are copied within and are remembered by the sleepers when they awake out of the dream.

And it is no longer difficult to perceive the truth about the formation of images in mirrors and in bright and smooth surfaces of every kind. It is from the combination with each other of the inner and the outer fires, every time that they unite on the smooth surface and are variously deflected, that all such reflections necessarily result, owing to the fire of the reflected face coalescing with the fire of the vision on the smooth and bright surface. And left appears as right, because contact takes place between opposite portions of the visual stream and opposite portions of the object, contrary to the regular mode of collision. Contrariwise, right appears as right and left as left whenever the fire changes sides on coalescing with the object wherewith it coalesces; and this occurs whenever the smooth surface of the mirrors, being elevated on this side and on that, repels the right portion of the visual stream to the left and the left to the right. And when this same mirror is turned lengthwise to the face it makes the whole face appear upside down, since it repels the bottom of the ray to the top, and conversely the top to the bottom.

Now all these are among the auxiliary Causes which God employs as his ministers in perfecting, so far as possible, the Form of the Most Good; but by the most of men they are supposed to be not auxiliary but primary causes of all things—cooling and heating, solidifying and dissolving, and producing all such effects. Yet they are incapable of possessing reason and thought for any purpose. For, as we must affirm, the one and only existing thing which has the property of acquiring thought is Soul; and Soul is invisible, whereas fire and water and earth and air are all visible bodies; and the lover of thought and knowledge must needs pursue first the causes which belong to the Intelligent Nature, and put second all such as are of the class of things which are moved by others, and themselves, in turn, move others because they cannot help it. And we also must act likewise. We must

declare both kinds of Causes, but keep distinct those which, with the aid of thought, are artificers of things fair and good, and all those which are devoid of intelligence and produce always accidental and irregular effects.

Now regarding the auxiliary causes which have helped the eyes to acquire the power which they now possess, let this statement suffice. Next we must declare the most important benefit effected by them, for the sake of which God bestowed them upon us. Vision, in my view, is the cause of the greatest benefit to us, inasmuch as none of the accounts now given concerning the Universe would ever have been given if men had not seen the stars or the sun or the heaven. But as it is, the vision of day and night and of months and circling years has created the art of number and has given us not only the notion of Time but also means of research into the nature of the Universe. From these we have procured Philosophy in all its range, than which no greater boon ever has come or will come, by divine bestowal, unto the race of mortals. This I affirm to be the greatest good of eyesight. As for all the lesser goods, why should we celebrate them? He that is no philosopher when deprived of the sight thereof may utter vain lamentations! But the cause and purpose of that best good, as we must maintain, is this,— that God devised and bestowed upon us vision to the end that we might behold the revolutions of Reason in the Heaven and use them for the revolvings of the reasoning that is within us, these being akin to those, the perturbable to the imperturbable; and that, through learning and sharing in calculations which are correct by their nature, by imitation of the absolutely unvarying revolutions of the God we might stabilize the variable revolutions within ourselves.

Concerning sound also and hearing, once more we make the same declaration, that they were bestowed by the Gods with the same object and for the same reasons; for it was for these same purposes that speech was ordained, and it makes the greatest contribution thereto; music too, in so far as it uses audible sound, was bestowed for the sake of harmony. And harmony, which has motions akin to the revolutions of the Soul within us, was given by the Muses to him who makes intelligent use of the Muses, not as an aid to irrational pleasure, as is now supposed, but as an auxiliary to the inner revolution of the Soul, when it has lost its harmony, to assist in restoring it to order and concord with itself. And because of the unmodulated condition, deficient in grace, which exists in most of us, Rhythm also was bestowed upon us to be our helper by the same deities and for the same ends.

The foregoing part of our discourse, save for a small portion, has been an exposition of the operations of Reason; but we must also furnish an account of what comes into existence through Necessity. For, in truth, this Cosmos in its origin was generated as a compound, from the combination of Necessity and Reason. And inasmuch as Reason was controlling Necessity by persuading her to conduct to the best end the most part of the things coming into existence, thus and thereby it came about, through Necessity yielding to intelligent persuasion, that this Universe of ours was being in this wise constructed at the beginning. Wherefore if one is to declare how it actually came into being on this wise, he must include also the form of the Errant Cause, in the way that it really acts. To this point, therefore, we must return, and taking once again a fresh starting-point suitable to the matter we must make a fresh start in dealing therewith, just as we did with our previous subjects. We must gain a view of the real nature of fire and water, air and earth, as it was before the birth of Heaven, and the properties they had before that time; for at present no one has as yet declared their generation, but we assume that men know what fire is, and each of these things, and we call them principles and presume that they are elements of the Universe, although in truth they do not so much as deserve to be likened with any likelihood, by the man who has even a grain of sense, to the class of syllables. For the present, however, let our procedure be as

follows. We shall not now expound the principle of all things—or their principles, or whatever term we use concerning them; and that solely for this reason, that it is difficult for us to explain our views while keeping to our present method of exposition. You, therefore, ought not to suppose that I should expound them, while as for me—I should never be able to convince myself that I should be right in attempting to undertake so great a task. Strictly adhering, then, to what we previously affirmed, the import of the "likely" account, I will essay (as I did before) to give as "likely" an exposition as any other (nay, more so), regarding both particular things and the totality of things from the very beginning. And as before, so now, at the commencement of our account, we must call upon God the Saviour to bring us safe through a novel and unwonted exposition to a conclusion based on likelihood, and thus begin our account once more.

We must, however, in beginning our fresh account of the Universe make more distinctions than we did before; for whereas then we distinguished two Forms, we must now declare another third kind. For our former exposition those two were sufficient, one of them being assumed as a Model Form, intelligible and ever uniformly existent, and the second as the model's Copy, subject to becoming and visible. A third kind we did not at that time distinguish, considering that those two were sufficient; but now the argument seems to compel us to try to reveal by words a Form that is baffling and obscure. What essential property, then, are we to conceive it to possess? This in particular,—that it should be the receptacle, and as it were the nurse, of all Becoming. Yet true though this statement is, we must needs describe it more plainly. That, however, is a difficult task, especially because it is necessary, for its sake, to discuss first the problem of fire and its fellow elements. For in regard to these it is hard to say which particular element we ought really to term water rather than fire, and which we ought to term any one element rather than each and all of them, while still employing a terminology that is reliable and stable. How, then, shall we handle this problem, and what likely solution can we offer? First of all, we see that which we now call "water" becoming by condensation, as we believe, stones and earth; and again, this same substance, by dissolving and dilating, becoming breath of air; and air through combustion becoming fire; and conversely, fire when contracted and quenched returning back to the form of air; and air once more uniting and condensing into cloud and mist; and issuing from these, when still further compressed, flowing water; and from water earth and stones again: thus we see the elements passing on to one another, as it would seem, in an unbroken circle the gift of birth. Accordingly, since no one of these ever remains identical in appearance, which of them shall a man definitely affirm to be any one particular element and no other without incurring ridicule? None such exists. On the contrary, by far the safest plan in treating of these elements is to proceed thus: Whatsoever object we perceive to be constantly changing from one state to another, like fire, that object, be it fire, we must never describe as "this" but as "suchlike," nor should we ever call water "this" but "suchlike"; nor should we describe any other element, as though it possessed stability, of all those which we indicate by using the terms "this" and "that" and suppose ourselves to refer to a definite object. For such an object shuns and eludes the names "this" and "that" and every name which indicates that they are stable. Thus we must not call the several elements "these," but in regard to each of them and all together we must apply the term "suchlike" to represent what is always circling round: thus we shall call that which is constantly "suchlike" by the name of fire, and so with everything else that is generated. But that "wherein" they are always, in appearance, coming severally into existence, and "wherefrom" in turn they perish, in describing that and that alone should we employ the terms "this" and "that"; whereas, in describing what is "suchlike"—hot, for instance, or white, or any of the opposite qualities, or any compounds thereof—we ought never to apply to it any of these terms.

But we must bestir ourselves to explain this matter again yet more clearly. Now imagine that a man were to model all possible figures out of gold, and were then to proceed without cessation to remodel each of these into every other,—then, if someone were to point to one of the figures and ask what it *is,* by far the safest reply, in point of truth, would be that it is gold; but as for the triangle and all the other figures which were formed in it, one should never describe them as "being" seeing that they change even while one is mentioning them; rather one should be content if the figure admits of even the title "suchlike" being applied to it with any safety. And of the substance which receives all bodies the same account must be given. It must be called always by the same name; for from its own proper quality it never departs at all; for while it is always receiving all things, nowhere and in no wise does it assume any shape similar to any of the things that enter into it. For it is laid down by nature as a moulding-stuff for everything, being moved and marked by the entering figures, and because of them it appears different at different times. And the figures that enter and depart are copies of those that are always existent, being stamped from them in a fashion marvelous and hard to describe, which we shall investigate hereafter.

For the present, then, we must conceive of three kinds,—the Becoming, that "Wherein" it becomes, and the source "Wherefrom" the Becoming is copied and produced. Moreover, it is proper to liken the Recipient to the Mother, the Source to the Father, and what is engendered between these two to the Offspring; and also to perceive that, if the stamped copy is to assume diverse appearances of all sorts, that substance wherein it is set and stamped could not possibly be suited to its purpose unless it were itself devoid of all those forms which it is about to receive from any quarter. For were it similar to any of the entering forms, on receiving forms of an opposite or wholly different kind, as they arrived, it would copy them badly, through obtruding its own visible shape. Wherefore it is right that the substance which is to receive within itself all the kinds should be void of all forms; just as with all fragrant ointments, men bring about this condition by artistic contrivance and make the liquids which are to receive the odours as odourless as possible; and all who essay to mould figures in any soft material utterly refuse to allow any previous figure to remain visible therein, and begin by making it even and as smooth as possible before they execute the work. So likewise it is right that the substance which is to be fitted to receive frequently over its whole extent the copies of all things intelligible and eternal should itself, of its own nature, be void of all the forms. Wherefore, let us not speak of her that is the Mother and Receptacle of this generated world, which is perceptible by sight and all the senses, by the name of earth or air or fire or water, or any aggregates or constituents thereof: rather, if we describe her as a Kind invisible and unshaped, all-receptive, and in some most perplexing and most baffling way partaking of the intelligible, we shall describe her truly.

In so far as it is possible to arrive at the nature of this kind from the foregoing account, one may state it most correctly in this way. That part of it which is made fiery appears each time as fire, that which has been liquefied as water; and it appears as earth and air in so far as it receives copies of these. But let us investigate the matter by more exact reasoning, and consider this question. Does there exist any self-subsisting fire or any of those other objects which we likewise term "self-subsisting realities"? Or is it only these things which we see, or otherwise perceive by means of bodily senses, that exist, possessed of sensible reality; beside which no other things exist anywhere or anyhow, and it is merely an idle assertion of ours that there always exists an intelligible Form of every object, whereas it is really nothing more than a verbal phrase? Now, on the one hand, it would be improper

to dismiss the question before us without a trial and a verdict, and simply to asseverate that the fact is so; while, on the other hand, we ought not to burden a lengthy discourse with another subsidiary argument. If, however, it were possible to disclose briefly some main determining principle, that would best serve our purpose.

This, then, is the view for which I, for my part, cast my vote. If Reason and True Opinion are two distinct Kinds, most certainly these self-subsisting Forms do exist, imperceptible by our senses, and objects of Reason only; whereas if, as appears to some, True Opinion differs in naught from Reason, then, on the contrary, all the things which we perceive by our bodily senses must be judged to be most stable. Now these two Kinds must be declared to be two, because they have come into existence separately and are unlike in condition. For the one of them arises in us by teaching, the other by persuasion; and the one is always in company with true reasoning, whereas the other is irrational; and the one is immovable by persuasion, whereas the other is alterable by persuasion; and of the one we must assert that every man partakes, but of Reason only the gods and but a small class of men. This being so, we must agree that One Kind is the self-identical Form, ungenerated and indestructible, neither receiving into itself any other from any quarter nor itself passing anywhither into another, invisible and in all ways imperceptible by sense, it being the object which it is the province of Reason to contemplate; and a second Kind is that which is named after the former and similar thereto, an object perceptible by sense, generated, ever carried about, becoming in a place and out of it again perishing, apprehensible by Opinion with the aid of Sensation; and a third Kind is ever-existing Place, which admits not of destruction, and provides room for all things that have birth, itself being apprehensible by a kind of bastard reasoning by the aid of non-sensation, barely an object of belief; for when we regard this we dimly dream and affirm that it is somehow necessary that all that exists should exist *in* some spot and occupying some *place,* and that that which is neither on earth nor anywhere in the Heaven is nothing. So because of all these and other kindred notions, we are unable also on waking up to distinguish clearly the unsleeping and truly subsisting substance, owing to our dreamy condition, or to state the truth—how that it belongs to a copy—seeing that it has not for its own even that substance for which it came into being, but fleets ever as a phantom of something else—to come into existence *in* some other thing, clinging to existence as best it may, on pain of being nothing at all; whereas to the aid of the really existent there comes the accurately true argument, that so long as one thing is one thing, and another something different, neither of the two will ever come to exist in the other so that the same thing becomes simultaneously both one and two.

Let this, then, be, according to my verdict, a reasoned account of the matter summarily stated,—that Being and Place and Becoming were existing, three distinct things, even before the Heaven came into existence; and that the Nurse of Becoming, being liquefied and ignified and receiving also the forms of earth and of air, and submitting to all the other affections which accompany these, exhibits every variety of appearance; but owing to being filled with potencies that are neither similar nor balanced, in no part of herself is she equally balanced, but sways unevenly in every part, and is herself shaken by these forms and shakes them in turn as she is moved. And the forms, as they are moved fly continually in various directions and are dissipated; just as the particles that are shaken and winnowed by the sieves and other instruments used for the cleansing of corn fall in one place if they are solid and heavy, but fly off and settle elsewhere if they are spongy and light. So it was also with the Four Kinds when shaken by the Recipient: her motion, like an instrument which causes shaking, was separating farthest from one another the dissimilar, and pushing most closely together the similar; wherefore also these Kinds occupied different places even before that the Universe was organized and generated out of them. Before that time, in truth, all these things were in a state devoid of reason or measure, but when the work of setting in order this Universe was being undertaken, fire and water and earth and air, although possessing some traces of their own nature, were yet so disposed as everything is likely to be in the absence of God; and inasmuch as this was then their natural condition, God began by first marking them out into shapes by means of forms and numbers. And that God constructed them, so far as He could, to be as fair and good as possible, whereas they had been otherwise,—this above all else must always be postulated in our account.

CHARLIE DUNBAR BROAD

MECHANISM AND ITS ALTERNATIVES*

The Ideal of Pure Mechanism

Let us first ask ourselves what would be the ideal of a mechanical view of the material

---

* From *The Mind and Its Place in Nature* by C. D. Broad, Chapter II. London: Routledge & Kegan Paul Ltd., 1925. Reprinted by permission of the publisher.

realm. I think, in the first place, that it would suppose that there is only one fundamental kind of stuff out of which every material object is made. Next, it would suppose that this stuff has only one intrinsic quality, over and above its purely spatioemporal and causal characteristics. The property ascribed to it might, *e.g.*, be inertial mass or electric charge. Thirdly, it would suppose that there is only one fundamental kind of change, viz., change in the relative positions of the particles of this stuff. Lastly, t would suppose that there is one fundamental law according to which one particle of this stuff affects the changes of another particle. It would suppose that this law connects particles by pairs, and that the action of any two aggregates of particles as wholes on each other is compounded in a simple and uniform way from the actions which the constituent particles taken by pairs would have on each other. Thus the essence of Pure Mechanism is (*a*) a single kind of stuff, all of whose parts are exactly alike except for differences of position and motion; (*b*) a single fundamental kind of change, viz., change of position. Imposed on this there may of course be changes of a higher order, *e.g.*, changes of velocity, of acceleration, and so on; (*c*) a single elementary causal law, according to which particles influence each other by pairs; and (*d*) a single and simple principle of composition, according to which the behaviour of any aggregate of particles, or the influence of any one aggregate on any other, follows in a uniform way from the mutual influences of the constituent particles taken by pairs.

A set of gravitating particles, on the classical theory of gravitation, is an almost perfect example of the ideal of Pure Mechanism. The single elementary law is the inverse-square law for any pair of particles. The single and simple principle of composition is the rule that the influence of any set of particles on a single particle is the vector-sum of the influences that each would exert taken by itself. An electronic theory of matter departs to some extent from this ideal. In the first place, it has to assume at present that there are two ultimately different kinds of particle, viz., protons and electrons. Secondly, the laws of electro-magnetics cannot, so far as we know, be reduced to central forces. Thirdly, gravitational phenomena do not at present fall within the scheme; and so it is necessary to

ascribe masses as well as charges to the ultimate particles, and to introduce other elementary forces beside those of electro-magnetics.

On a purely mechanical theory all the apparently different kinds of matter would be made of the same stuff. They would differ only in the number, arrangement and movements of their constituent particles. And their apparently different kinds of behaviour would not be ultimately different. For they would all be deducible by a single simple principle of composition from the mutual influences of the particles taken by pairs; and these mutual influences would all obey a single law which is quite independent of the configurations and surroundings in which the particles happen to find themselves. The ideal which we have been describing and illustrating may be called "Pure Mechanism."

When a biologist calls himself a "Mechanist" it may fairly be doubted whether he means to assert anything so rigid as this. Probably all that he wishes to assert is that a living body is composed only of constituents which do or might occur in non-living bodies, and that its characteristic behaviour is wholly deducible from its structure and components and from the chemical, physical and dynamical laws which these materials would obey if they were isolated or were in non-living combinations. Whether the apparently different kinds of chemical substance are really just so many different configurations of a single kind of particles, and whether the chemical and physical laws are just the compounded results of the action of a number of similar particles obeying a single elementary law and a single principle of composition, he is not compelled as a biologist to decide. I shall later on discuss this milder form of "Mechanism," which is all that is presupposed in the controversies between mechanistic and vitalistic biologists. In the meanwhile I want to consider how far the ideal of Pure Mechanism could possibly be an adequate account of the world as we know it.

Limitations of Pure Mechanism. No one of course pretends that a satisfactory account even of purely physical processes in terms of Pure Mechanism *has* ever been given; but the question for us is: How far, and in what sense, *could* such a theory be adequate to all the known facts? On the face of it external objects have plenty of other characteristics beside mass or electric charge, *e.g.*, colour, temperature, etc. And, on the face of it, many changes take place in the external world beside changes of position, velocity, etc. Now of course many different views have been held about the nature and status of such characteristics as colour; but the one thing which no adequate theory of the external world can do is to ignore them altogether. I will state here very roughly the alternative types of theory, and show that none of them is compatible with Pure Mechanism as a complete account of the facts.

1. There is the naïve view that we are in immediate cognitive contact with parts of the surfaces of external objects, and that the colours and temperatures which we perceive quite literally inhere in those surfaces independently of our minds and of our bodies. On this view Pure Mechanism breaks down at the first move, for certain parts of the external world would have various properties different from and irreducible to the one fundamental property which Pure Mechanism assumes. This would not mean that what scientists have discovered about the connexion between heat and molecular motion, or light and periodic motion of electrons would be wrong. It might be perfectly true, so far as it went; but it would certainly not be the whole truth about the external world. We should have to begin by distinguishing between "macroscopic" and "microscopic" properties, to use two very convenient terms adopted by Lorentz. Colours, temperatures, etc., would be macroscopic properties, *i.e.*, they would need a certain minimum area or volume (and perhaps, as Dr. Whitehead has suggested, a certain minimum duration) to inhere in. Other properties, such as mass or electric charge, might be able to inhere in volumes smaller than these minima and even in volumes and durations of any degree of smallness. Molecular and electronic theories of heat and light would then assert that a certain volume is pervaded by such and such

a temperature or such and such a colour i and only if it contains certain arrangement of particles moving in certain ways. What we should have would be laws connecting the macroscopic qualities which inhere in a vol ume with the number, arrangement, and motion of the microscopic particles which are contained in this volume.

On such a view how much would be lef of Pure Mechanism? (i) It would of course not be true of macroscopic properties. (ii) I might still be true of the microscopic particles in their interactions with each other. It might be that there is ultimately only one kind of particle, that it has only one non-spatio-temporal quality, that these particles affect each other by pairs according to a single law, and that their effects are compounded according to a single law. (iii) But, even if this were true of the microscopic particles in their relations *with each other,* it plainly could not be the *whole truth* about them. For there will also be laws connecting the presence of such and such a configuration of particles, moving in such and such ways, in a certain region, with the pervasion of this region by such and such a determinate value of a certain macroscopic quality, *e.g.*, a certain shade of red or a temperature of 57°C. These will be just as much laws of the external world as are the laws which connect the motions of one particle with those of another. And it is perfectly clear that the one kind of law cannot possibly be reduced to the other; since colour and temperature are irreducibly different characteristics from figure and motion, however close may be the causal connexion between the occurrence of the one kind of characteristic and that of the other. Moreover, there will have to be a number of different and irreducible laws connecting microscopic with macroscopic characteristics; for there are many different and irreducible determinable macroscopic characteristics, *e.g.*, colour, temperature, sound, etc. And each will need its own peculiar law.

2. A second conceivable view would be that in perception we are in direct cognitive contact with parts of the surfaces of external objects, and that, so long as we are looking

at them or feeling them, they do have the colours or temperatures which they then seem to us to have. But that the inherence of colours and temperatures in external bodies is dependent upon the presence of a suitable bodily organism, or a suitable mind, or of both, in a suitable relation to the external object.

On such a view it is plain that Pure Mechanism cannot be an adequate theory of the external world of matter. For colours and temperatures would belong to external objects on this view, though they would characterise an external object only when very special conditions are fulfilled. And evidently the laws according to which, *e.g.*, a certain shade of colour inheres in a certain external region when a suitable organism or mind is in suitable relations to that region cannot be of the mechanical type.

3. A third conceivable view is that physical objects can seem to have qualities which do not really belong to any physical object, *e.g.*, that a pillar-box can seem to have a certain shade of red although really no physical object has any colour at all. This type of theory divides into two forms. (*a*) It might be held that, when a physical object seems to have a certain shade of red, there really is *something* in the world which has this shade of red, although this something cannot be a physical object or literally a part of one. Some would say that there is a red mental state—a "sensation"—; others that the red colour belongs to something which is neither mental nor physical.[1] On either of these alternatives it would be conceivable that Pure Mechanism was the whole truth about matter considered in its relations with matter. But it would be certain that it is not the whole truth about matter when this limitation is removed. Granted that bits of matter only *seem* to be red or to be hot, we still claim to know a good deal about the conditions under which one bit of matter will seem to be red and another to be blue and about the conditions

under which one bit of matter will seem to be hot and another to be cold. This knowledge belongs partly to physics and partly to the physiology and anatomy of the brain and nervous system. We know little or nothing about the mental conditions which have to be fulfilled if an external object is to seem red or hot to a percipient; but we can say that this depends on an unknown mental factor x and on certain physical conditions a, b, c, etc., partly within and partly outside the percipient's body, about which we know a good deal. It is plain then that, on the present theory, physical events and objects do not merely interact mechanically with each other; they also play their part, along with a mental factor, in causing such and such an external object to seem to such and such an observer to have a certain quality which really no physical object has. In fact, for the present purpose, the difference between theories (2) and (3) is simply the following. On theory (2) certain events in the external object, in the observer's body, and possibly in his mind, cause a certain quality to inhere in the external object so long as they are going on. On theory (3) they cause the same quality to *seem* to inhere in the same object, so long as they are going on, though *actually* it does not inhere in any physical object. Theory (1), for the present purpose, differs from theory (2) only in taking the naïve view that the body and mind of the observer are irrelevant to the *occurrence* of the sensible quality in the external object, though of course it would admit that these factors are relevant to the *perception* of this quality by the observer. This last point is presumably common to all three theories.

I will now sum up the argument. The plain fact is that the external world, as perceived by us, seems not to have the homogeneity demanded by Pure Mechanism. If it *really* has the various irreducibly different sensible qualities which it *seems* to have, Pure Mechanism cannot be true of the whole of the external world and cannot be the whole truth about any part of it. The best that we can do for Pure Mechanism on this theory is to divide up the external world first on a macro-

---

[1] (*b*) It might be held that *nothing* in the world really has colour, though certain things *seem* to have certain colours. The relation of "seeming to have" is taken as ultimate.

scopic and then on a microscopic scale; to suppose that the macroscopic qualities which pervade any region are causally determined by the microscopic events and objects which exist within it; and to hope that the latter, in their interactions with *each other* at any rate, fulfil the conditions of Pure Mechanism. This result may remind the reader of the carefully qualified compliment which Mr. Gibbon pays to the morality of the Negroes in a foot-note which I forbear from quoting. We must remember, moreover, that there is no *a priori* reason why microscopic events and objects should answer the demands of Pure Mechanism even in their interactions with each other; that, so far as science can tell us at present, they do not; and that, in any case, the laws connecting them with the occurrence of macroscopic qualities *cannot* be mechanical in the sense defined.

If, on the other hand, we deny that physical objects have the various sensible qualities which they seem to us to have, we are still left with the fact that some things *seem* to be red, others to be blue, others to be hot, and so on. And a complete account of the world must include some explanation of such events as "seeming red to me," "seeming blue to you," etc. We can admit that the ultimate physical objects may all be exactly alike, may all have only one non-spatio-temporal and non-causal property, and may interact with each other in the way which Pure Mech-

anism requires. But we must admit that they are also cause-factors in determining the *appearance,* if not the *occurrence,* of the various sensible qualities at such and such places and times. And, in these transactions, the laws which they obey *cannot* be mechanical.

We may put the whole matter in a nutshell by saying that the appearance of a plurality of irreducible sensible qualities forces us, no matter what theory we adopt about their status, to distinguish two different kinds of law. One may be called "intra-physical" and the other "trans-physical." The intra-physical laws may be, though there seems no positive reason to suppose that they are, of the kind required by Pure Mechanism. If so, there is just one ultimate elementary intra-physical law and one ultimate principle of composition for intra-physical transactions. But the trans-physical laws cannot satisfy the demands of Pure Mechanism; and, so far as I can see, there must be at least as many irreducible trans-physical laws as there are irreducible determinable sense-qualities. The nature of the trans-physical laws will of course depend on the view that we take about the status of sensible qualities. It will be somewhat different for each of the three alternative types of theory which I have mentioned, and it will differ according to which form of the third theory we adopt. But it is not necessary for our present purpose to go into further detail on this point. . . .

Teleology, Mechanism, and Design

I have so far discussed Mechanism and its alternatives in a perfectly general way; and have said nothing in detail concerning those peculiar facts about living organisms which make it plausible to distinguish a "Vital Order" with "ultimate characteristics" of its own. Now the peculiarities of living organisms are often summed up in the phrase that organisms are "Teleological Systems." And there is thought to be some special connexion between Teleology and Design, and some special opposition between Teleology and

Mechanism. I shall end this chapter by trying to clear up these points.

Teleology is an observable characteristic which certainly belongs to some things in the world. Design is a particular cause which certainly produces teleology in some cases. I want to begin by defining "teleology" in such a way that there shall be no doubt of its existence and that the admission of this fact shall not presuppose the acceptance of any special theory. Suppose that a system is composed of such parts arranged in such ways as night have been expected *if* it had been constructed by an intelligent being to fulfil a certain purpose which he had in mind. And suppose that, when we investigate the system more carefully under the guidance of this hypothesis, we discover hitherto unnoticed parts or hitherto unnoticed relations between the parts, and that these are still found to accord with the hypothesis. Then I should call this system "teleological." It will be noticed that there are two clauses in the definition. The first is that our more or less superficial knowledge of the system suggests that it was designed for a special purpose which a rational mind might be likely to entertain. The second is that, if we use this hypothesis as a clue to more minute investigation, we continue to find that the system is constructed as if the hypothesis were true. I think that probably both factors are necessary. Of any system whatever we might suppose that it was designed to do what we actually find it doing. But in general we should not find that this gave us any clue to investigating its more minute structure or predicting its unobserved behaviour.

Now it seems to me perfectly certain that the world contains systems which are teleological, in this sense. The most obvious examples of such systems are machines, like watches, motor-cars, etc. In this case of course we start by knowing that they have in fact been designed by intelligent beings for a certain purpose, such as telling the time or conveying people quickly along roads. Knowing this we can explain, as we say, "what each part is for." Suppose now we were to meet with a certain machine for the first time and to know nothing about the purpose of its constructor. As we have met with plenty of other machines (though none exactly like this); as we know that all of these have been made by some human being for some purpose; and as we know of no machines which have arisen in any other way; we may legitimately infer that this one also was constructed by a human being for some purpose. By studying the action of the machine we may then be able to guess what the purpose probably was. We can then predict

how it will probably be constructed in detail, and how it will probably work under various circumstances. And, if our predictions are found to be true, it is likely that we have hit on the true purpose of the machine. I will call the kind of teleology which is shown by watches, motor-cars, and other artificial machines, "external teleology." By this I mean that the purpose for which such systems were constructed, and by which their minute structure can be anticipated, is not wholly or mainly to keep themselves going or to produce other machines like themselves. Their main function is to do something, such as telling the time, which is of interest not to themselves but to their makers or other men.

Now it seems to me equally clear that living organisms are teleological systems in the sense defined. The most superficial knowledge of organisms does make it look as if they were very complex systems designed to preserve themselves in face of varying and threatening external conditions and to reproduce their kind. And, on the whole, the more fully we investigate a living organism in detail the more fully does what we discover fit in with this hypothesis. One might mention, *e.g.,* the various small and apparently unimportant glands in the human body whose secretions are found to exercise a profound influence over its growth and well-being. Or again we might mention the production in the blood of antitoxins when the body is attacked by organisms likely to injure it. I will call this kind of teleology "internal teleology." Whatever be the right explanation of it, it is plainly a fact.

We have now to consider the relation between Teleology and Design. (i) The definition of "teleology" involves a hypothetical reference to design. The system is teleological provided it acts *as if* it were designed for a purpose. But it does not involve anything more than this. It remains a question of fact whether the system was actually the result of a design in someone's mind. (ii) So far as we know, the teleology of non-living machines is always due to design. They behave in the characteristic way in which they do behave simply because their parts are constructed and fitted together in certain special ways, and we have no reason to suppose that this special arrangement could arise spontaneously without the intervention of a mind which deliberately chose it. (iii) The real paradox about organisms is that they are teleological systems which seem nevertheless to arise without design. It is this last fact which we must now discuss.

Many organisms have minds connected with them. But we know that, if they were designed at all, the mind which designed them was certainly not the mind which animates them, unless this be extraordinarily different from what it appears to be both to itself and to others. The highest type of mind which we are acquainted with is that which animates a human body. If we designed our own organisms we are quite unaware of the fact. And the enterprise seems altogether beyond our powers. The most skilled physiologist does not know how to make a living body; but, if we say that his mind designed his own organism, we must suppose that it performed as an embryo a feat which it is totally incapable of performing in its developed state. We must say then that, if organisms are designed by minds, either (*a*) the designing mind is altogether different from an enormously wiser and more skilful than the animating mind; or (*b*) that the animating mind, as known to itself by introspection and to others by communication, is the merest fragment of the total animating mind, and that the part of it which does not appear to itself or to others is of superhuman wisdom and ingenuity. Of course it might be held that the designing mind, or the designing part of the animating mind, though extraordinarily clever at its own particular job, takes no interest in anything else; or that it works in a wholly different way from the minds which are known to us. But this will not help us. If the conception of design is to provide any explanation of the peculiarities of organisms we must mean by "design" something of the same nature as the only designs that we know anything about, viz., our own. Otherwise we are merely playing with words. Now we have designs only when we imagine a possible

state of affairs, apply our knowledge of the properties and laws of matter to discover how it might be brought about, and then use our technical skill to shape the material and to arrange it in those ways which we have seen to be necessary for our purpose. If the minds which design organisms act in this way they must have a superhuman knowledge of the laws and properties of matter, superhuman mathematical ability to work out the consequences of various possible combinations, and superhuman technical skill; and all analogy makes it most unlikely that a mind which took no interest in anything but the one job of manufacturing organisms would have these powers. If, on the other hand, the minds which design organisms act in some quite different and to us unknown way, then we have no right to call them "minds" or to call their mode of operation "design." We are merely assuming a wholly mysterious cause for the teleology of organisms, and tricking ourselves into the belief that it is an explanation by using the familiar words "mind" and "design." I conclude then that, if organisms be the result of design in any intelligible sense, their designers may fairly be called "gods"; and either we are gods in disguise or there are superhuman beings who make organisms.

These considerations remove one positive argument in favour of the theory of entelechies. I am sure that many people who look with a friendly eye on entelechies do so because of the teleological nature of organisms. They think of entelechies as little minds which design organisms and direct and control their growth and reactions. But they modestly regard entelechies as very inferior minds or as the inferior parts of the minds which animate organisms. Now, if I am right, this modesty is wholly out of place. If the hypothesis of an entelechy is to explain anything, we must suppose that an entelechy is a very superior mind or the very superior part of the mind which animates an organism. The theory insinuates itself into our confidence by pretending that the entelechy is so lowly a mind as scarcely to deserve the name; but it can explain the facts only if it supposes the entelechy to be so exalted a mind as to deserve the name of a "god."

I pass now to the relations between Teleology and Design, on the one hand, and Biological Mechanism* on the other. It is evident that, up to a point, there is no opposition between teleology and mechanism. Nothing can be more thoroughly teleological than a watch or a motor-car; yet these are machines, and their characteristic behaviour is wholly deducible from the special arrangement of their parts and from the general laws which these parts would equally obey in isolation or in other and non-teleological complexes. We may say then that, so long as we take a material system as a going concern and do not raise questions about its origin, there is no reason whatever why its characteristic behaviour should not be at once teleological and capable of complete mechanistic explanation. Now the mechanistic biologist regards organisms as very complex machines; and indeed if we were not very familiar with artificial self-acting and self-regulating machinery it would never have entered our heads to suggest a mechanistic theory of vital behaviour. So long as he confines his attention to a developed organism there is nothing preposterous in this theory. It is only when we consider the *origin* of teleological systems that a legitimate doubt arises whether teleology and mechanistic explanation are *ultimately* consistent with each other.

(i) Every system which is *certainly known* to be at once teleological and mechanistic is an artificial machine; and, if we follow its history far enough backwards, we always come to one or more *organisms,* which are teleological but not *certainly* mechanistic systems. It is true that many machines are themselves made by machines; but sooner or later in this chain we come to human bodies which made these machines and were not themselves made by machinery. Thus,

apart altogether from any question of minds and their designs, there is something dangerously like a vicious circle in professing to explain the teleology of organisms by analogy with artificial machines. For, the moment we begin to consider the *origin* of organisms in general or of any particular organism, we have to admit that *all* artificial machines were ultimately made by organisms whilst *no* organism is ever made by an artificial machine.

To this objection I think that the following answer might be made. It might be said: "Admittedly we must distinguish two kinds of machines, viz., natural and artificial. We can quite well admit the general principle that *all* machines are made by other machines. Natural machines (*i.e.,* organisms) are always made by other natural machines; artificial machines may be made proximately by other artificial machines, but in the long run in the history of any artificial machine we come to a natural machine. We admit then that natural machines are *causally* prior to artificial machines; but this involves no logical circle. We first derive the general notion of machinery and of a mechanistic explanation of teleological behavior from the specially simple and obvious case of artificial machines, at a time when we do not suspect that our bodies are themselves natural machines. Eventually we *apply* the notion thus derived to our bodies, and find that it fits them perfectly. There is no inconsistency between the facts (*a*) that the recognition of artificial machines is psychologically prior to the recognition of natural machines, and (*b*) that the existence of natural machines is causally prior to the existence of artificial machines." I think that this is a valid answer to the particular logical objection raised above. But it does not exhaust the difficulties of Biological Mechanism; and this brings us to our next point.

(ii) It is true, but it is not the whole truth, to say that in the history of every system which is positively known to be both teleological and mechanistic (*i.e.,* of every artificial machine) we come at length to an organism. We also come to the mind which animates this organism; to a design in this

---

* [Biological Mechanism asserts that "*in theory*, everything that is characteristic of the behavior of a living body could be deduced from an adequate knowledge of its structure, the chemical compounds which make it up, and the properties which these show in isolation or in non-living wholes." (Ed.)]

278 · The World, Emergence, and God

mind; and to the deliberate arrangement of matter in view of an end. And this seems to be essential for the production of a teleological system out of non-teleological materials. On a mechanistic theory the teleological behaviour of a system must be due wholly to the initial configuration of its parts; and, if matter has only the properties which physicists and chemists ascribe to it, it has no tendency by itself to fall into those extraordinarily special arrangements which alone can give rise to teleological behaviour. Now, if the analogy of organisms to artificial machines is to be used at all, it must be used fairly; we must not ignore one essential part of the facts about the origin of artificial machines. Let us then apply the whole analogy to organisms. It is certain that, when one organism produces another by ordinary processes of generation, the mind of the first does not design and construct the second, as it would if it were producing an artificial machine like a watch or a type-writer. This in itself need cause no trouble to the Mechanist. When one artificial machine produces another the mind of the first does not design the second, for artificial machines have no minds. The Biological Mechanist will therefore simply say that the generation of one organism by another is analogous to the production of one artificial machine by another. But, as we have seen, the latter series eventually brings us back to a mind with designs. Hence, if the Biological Mechanist is to apply his analogy fairly, there are only two courses open to him. The first is to say that there always have been organisms, and that organisms have never arisen from inorganic matter. On this alternative he has a series of natural machines going back to infinity. In that case of course every artificial machine will also have an infinite ancestry of other machines, since the production of an artificial machine eventually brings one back to a natural machine. Such a theory would be self-consistent; though it would still leave the awkward difference that design enters into the history of *every* artificial machine and of *no* natural machine. It is of course an alternative that most mechanists would be

very loath to take; for one of the advantages claimed for Biological Mechanism over Substantial Vitalism* is that the former does and the latter does not render the development of living from non-living matter conceivable.

The other possible alternative is to admit that organisms arose in the remote past out of non-living matter. This means, on the mechanistic view, that natural machines arose from matter which was not arranged in the form of a machine. And this can be consistently held *only* if the Biological Mechanist will postulate at that point the intervention of a mind which deliberately designed and arranged non-living matter in the form of a natural machine. For, as we have seen, the only systems which we positively *know* to be machines have all arisen in this way; and, if matter has no properties except those which chemists and physicists assign to it, there is not the least reason to suppose that it can spontaneously fall into the extremely special configuration which is needed if the resulting system is to behave teleologically. Thus the proper complement to a completely mechanistic theory about organisms is some form of the doctrine of Deism; a result which accords very well with that simple piety which is so characteristic of Biological Mechanists.

But, even if we are willing to go thus far with the Biological Mechanist, we cannot allow him to leave the matter there. Every system which is positively known to be a machine has been ultimately made, not by a pure spirit, but by a mind which animates an organism which it did not design or construct. This mind formed a design; in consequence of this the organism which it animates has moved in various ways; and it is thus and thus only that the design has been realised in foreign matter. Once more, if we are to use the analogy of machines at all, we must use it fairly and not ignore these parts of it which, so far as we can see, are essential but which are not convenient. The Biological Mechanist, having been brought will-

---

* [Substantial Vitalism "assumes that a necessary factor in explaining the characteristic behavior of living bodies is the presence in them of a particular component, often called an 'Entelechy'." (Ed.)]

ingly or unwillingly to Deism, must now take a further step and ascribe to God an organism which God's mind animates. And by all analogy we must suppose that God did not design or construct his own organism; since, so far as our experience goes *no* mind designs or constructs the organism which it animates. Thus, in the end, we shall be brought to one organism at least, viz., God's, which presumably has not arisen out of non-living matter either spontaneously or by design. This seems to be the final result of seriously and fairly applying the analogy between organisms and machines, when we cease to confine our attention to the organism as a going concern and try to account also for the origin of organisms, as Biological Mechanism would wish to do.

Tentative Decision between the Three Theories of Organisms

When we consider the teleological characteristics of organisms the three possible theories of Substantial Vitalism, Emergent Vitalism,* and Biological Mechanism cease to be on a level. In the first place, there seems to be nothing to be said for Substantial Vitalism, and a great deal to be said against it. We may therefore provisionally reject it, and confine our attention to Emergent Vitalism and Biological Mechanism. It seems to me that, so long as we merely consider the behaviour of the organism as a going concern, there is no strong argument for deciding between the two types of theory. For it is quite certain that a material system, once it is in being, can be teleological and at the same time mechanistic in its behaviour. Hence, even if we did not see our way to explain certain teleological characteristics of developed organisms mechanistically, the Biological Mechanist could always answer that this is merely because we do not yet know enough about the minute structure of the machine or about the more obscure physico-chemical properties of non-living matter. And this is what he *is* continually occupied in saying. But, when we come to consider the *origin* of organisms as well as their behaviour, the case is altered. We find that Biological Mechanism about the developed organism cannot consistently be held without an elaborate Deistic theory about the origin of organisms. This is because Biological Mechanism is admittedly a theory of the organism based on its analogy to self-acting and self-regulating machines. These, so far as we can see, neither do arise nor could have arisen without design and deliberate interference by someone with matter. And, in applying our analogy, we have no right whatever to ignore this side of it. I do not of course assert that this is a conclusive objection to Biological Mechanism. Deism has always seemed to me a much more sensible theory than most of its more pretentious successors. But I do wish to make it quite clear that Biological Mechanism is committed logically to a great deal more than is commonly supposed. If Emergent Vitalism could dispense with the need for all this Deistic supplementation it would *pro tanto* score over Biological Mechanism. But can it?

It might well be thought that in this matter Emergent Vitalism is no better off than Biological Mechanism. On both theories the peculiar behaviour of an organism is completely determined by its structure and its components and by nothing else. The only difference is that on the Emergent View the peculiar behaviour of such systems must be "seen to be believed," whilst on the Mechanistic View it could in theory have been foretold from the structure and the behaviour of the components in isolation or in non-living wholes. If you make it an objection to the Mechanistic Theory that the characteristic behaviour of the organism depends on the arrangement of its parts, and that this ar-

---

* [Emergent Vitalism claims that characteristic properties of the whole cannot be deduced from even the most complete knowledge of its constituents either in isolation or in another whole in which they are differently related. (Ed.)]

rangement could only have happened by design, does not the objection apply equally strongly to the Emergent Theory? This argument is plausible, but I do not think that it is sound. The Biological Mechanist points to the analogy between organisms and artificial machines, and asks us to believe on this ground that organisms are machines. To this we answered that matter has no natural tendency to arrange itself in the form of *machines* (*i.e.,* of teleological systems whose characteristic behaviour is *mechanistically* explicable); and that therefore, *if* organisms be of the nature of machines, there is no reason to suppose that they could have arisen spontaneously and without design. But it is perfectly consistent for a man to hold that matter has *no* tendency to fall spontaneously into the form of *machines* and that it *has* a natural tendency to fall into the form of *organisms;* provided he holds, as the Emergent Vitalist does, that organisms are not machines but are systems whose characteristic behaviour is emergent and not mechanistically explicable. Thus the real difference is that a possibility is open to the Emergent Vitalist, who recognises two fundamentally different kinds of teleological system, and that this possibility is closed to the Biological Mechanist, who recognises only one kind.

Of course this possibility, which is open to the Emergent Vitalist and not to the Biological Mechanist, is very vague and needs to be worked out in much greater detail. This would be the task of the empirical scientist rather than the critical philosopher. I will content myself with saying that the Emergent Vitalist should not rest with nothing better than the vague statement that matter has a natural tendency to fall into that kind of structure which has vital behaviour as its emergent characteristic. If Emergence be true at all there are probably many Orders below the Vital Order. What must be assumed is not a special tendency of matter to fall into the kind of arrangement which has vital characteristics, but a general tendency for complexes of one order to combine with each other under suitable conditions to form complexes of the next order. At each stage in this process we shall get things with new and irreducibly characteristic properties and new intra-ordinal laws, whilst there will probably remain certain complexes of all the lower orders. The universe would thus grow continually more varied, so long as the special conditions necessary for this combination of complexes of lower order to give complexes of higher order continued; and at every new stage new possibilities of further development would begin. It would be the business of the believer in Emergence to determine the precise condition under which the passage from one order to the next can take place; to state definitely what are the irreducibly characteristic features of each order; and to deduce those characteristic features which can be deduced.

It seems to me then that on the whole Emergent Vitalism is distinctly to be preferred to Biological Mechanism. It does not *necessitate* a complicated Deistic supplement, as Biological Mechanism does; and this seems to me to be an advantage. At the same time it is perfectly *consistent with* the view that there is a God who created and controls the material world; so that, if there should be any good reason to believe in such a Being, the Emergent Vitalist could meet the situation with a quiet mind.

GOTTFRIED WILHELM LEIBNIZ

THE PRINCIPLES OF NATURE AND OF GRACE, BASED ON REASON*

1. *Substance* is a being capable of action. It is simple or compound. *Simple substance* is that which has no parts. *Compound substance* is a collection of simple substances, or *monads*. *Monas* is a Greek word signifying unity or that which is one. Compounds, or bodies, are pluralities, and simple substances—lives, souls, and spirits—are unities. There must of necessity be simple substances everywhere, for without simple substances there would be no compounds. As a result, the whole of nature is full of life.

2. *Monads,* having no parts, can neither be formed nor unmade. They can neither begin nor end naturally, and therefore they last as long as the universe, which will change but will not be destroyed. They cannot have shapes, for then they would have parts. It follows that one monad by itself and at a single moment cannot be distinguished from another except by its internal qualities and actions, and these can only be its *perceptions*—that is to say, the representations of the compound, or of that which is without, in the simple—and its *appetitions* that is to say, its tendencies from one perception to another—which are the principles of change. For the simplicity of a substance does not prevent the plurality of modifications which must necessarily be found together in the same simple substance; and these modifications must consist of the variety of relations of correspondence which the substance has with things outside. In the same way there may be found, in one *center* or point, though it is perfectly simple, an infinity of angles formed by the lines which meet in it.

3. Everything is a plenum in nature. Everywhere there are simple substances actually separated from each other by their own actions, which continually change their relations. And each outstanding simple substance or monad which forms the center of a compound substance (such as an animal, for example), and is the principle of its uniqueness, is surrounded by a mass composed of an infinity of other monads which constitute the body belonging to this central monad, corresponding to the affections by which it represents, as in a kind of center, the things which are outside of it. This body is *organic* when it forms a kind of automaton or natural machine, which is a machine not only as a whole but also in its smallest observable parts. And since everything is connected because of the plenitude of the world, and each body acts on every other one more or less, depending on the distance, and is affected by its reaction, it follows that each monad is a living mirror, or a mirror endowed with an internal action, and that it represents the universe according to its point of view and is regulated as completely as is the universe itself. The perceptions in the monad arise from each other according to the laws of the appetites or of the *final causes of good and of evil,* which consist in observable perceptions, whether regulated or unregulated, in the same way that bodily changes and external phenomena arise from each other according to the laws of *efficient causality,* that is, of motions. Thus there is a perfect *harmony* between the perceptions of the monad and the motions of the body, pre-established from the beginning between

* Reprinted from *Philosophical Papers and Letters* by Gottfried Wilhelm Leibniz, translated and edited by Leroy E. Loemaker, by permission of the University of Chicago Press. ©1956 by the University of Chicago.

the system of efficient causes and that of final causes. It is in this that the accord and the physical union of soul and body consist, without either one being able to change the laws of the other.

4. Together with a particular body, each monad makes a living substance. Thus not only is there life, everywhere, joined to members or organs, but there are also infinite degrees of it in the monads, some of which dominate more or less over others. But when the monad has organs so adjusted that by means of them the impressions which are received, and consequently also the perceptions which represent these impressions, are heightened and distinguished (as, for example, when rays of light are concentrated by means of the shape of the humors of the eye and act with greater force), then this may amount to *sensation,* that is to say, to a perception accompanied by *memory*—a perception of which there remains a kind of echo for a long time, which makes itself heard on occasion. Such a living being is called an *animal,* as its monad is called a *soul.* When this soul is raised to the level of *reason,* it is something more sublime and is counted among the *spirits,* as will be explained presently.

It is true that animals are sometimes in the condition of simple living beings, and their souls in the condition of simple monads, namely, when their perceptions are not distinct enough so that they can be remembered. This happens in a deep sleep without dreams or in a swoon. But perceptions which have become completely confused must be developed again in animals, for reasons which I shall give below in Section 12. So it is well to make a distinction between perception, which is the inner state of the monad representing external things, and *apperception,* which is consciousness or the reflective knowledge of this inner state itself and which is not given to all souls or to any soul all the time. It is for lack of this distinction that the Cartesians have made the mistake of disregarding perceptions which are not themselves perceived, just as people commonly disregard imperceptible bodies. It is this too which has made these same Cartesians think that only spirits are monads and that there is no soul in beasts, still less other *principles of life.* And after having defied the everyday opinion of men too much in denying that beasts have feelings, they adjusted their views too far to popular prejudices, on the other hand, when they confused a *long stupor* coming from a great confusion of perceptions with *death* in the *rigorous* sense, in which all perception would cease. This has confirmed the poorly grounded opinion that certain souls are destroyed and has supported the pernicious view of certain so-called freethinkers who have denied the immortality of our souls.

5. There is a connection between the perceptions of animals which has some resemblance to reason, but it is grounded only on the memory of *facts* or effects and not on the knowledge of *causes.* Thus a dog runs away from the stick with which he has been beaten, because his memory represents to him the pain which the stick had caused him. Men too, insofar as they are empiricists, that is to say, in three-fourths of their actions, act only like beasts. For example, we expect day to dawn tomorrow because we have always experienced this to be so; only the astronomer predicts it with reason, and even his prediction will ultimately fail when the cause of daylight, which is by no means eternal, stops. But *reasoning* in the *true* sense depends on necessary or eternal truths, as are those of logic, number, and geometry, which make the connection of ideas indubitable and their conclusions infallible. Animals in which such consequences cannot be observed are called *beasts,* but those who know these necessary truths are the ones properly called *rational animals,* and their souls are called *spirits.* These souls are capable of performing acts of reflection and of considering what is called "I," "substance," "soul," "spirit"—in a word, things and truths which are immaterial. It is this which makes us capable of the sciences or of demonstrative knowledge.

6. The investigations of the moderns have taught us, and reason confirms them, that the living beings whose organs are known to us, that is, plants and animals, do not come from putrefaction or chaos, as the ancients believed, but from *preformed* seeds, and therefore from the transformation of living beings existing prior to them. There are little animals in the seeds of large animals, which assume a new vesture in conception, which they appropirate and which provides them with a method of nourishment and growth, so that they may emerge into a greater stage and propagate the large animal. It is true that the souls of human spermatic animals are not rational and become so only when conception determines them for human nature. Just as animals in general are not completely born in conception or *generation,* moreover, neither do they completely perish in what we call *death,* for it is reasonable that what has no natural beginning also has no end within the order of nature. Thus, abandoning their masks or their rags, they merely return, but to a finer stage, on which, however, they can be as sensitive and as well ordered as on the larger one. And what has been said about grosser animals takes place also in the generation and death of spermatic animals themselves, that is, they are the enlargements of other smaller spermatic animals, in proportion to which they may be considered large, for everything in nature proceeds to infinity.

Not only souls, therefore, but animals as well, cannot be generated or perish; they are only developed, enveloped, reclothed, stripped, transformed. Souls never leave the whole of their bodies and do not pass from one body to another entirely new to them. Thus there is no *metempsychosis,* though there is *metamorphosis.* Animals change, take on, and put off, only parts; in nutrition this takes place little by little and through minute, insensible particles, but continually, while in conception or in death, where much is acquired or lost all at once, it occurs suddenly and noticeably but infrequently.

7. So far we have been speaking simply as *natural scientists;* now we must rise to *metaphysics* and make use of the great, but not commonly used, *principle* that *nothing takes place without a sufficient reason;* in other words, that nothing occurs for which it would be impossible for someone who has enough knowledge of things to give a reason adequate to determine why the thing is as it is and not otherwise. This principle having been stated, the first question which we have a right to ask will be, "Why is there something rather than nothing?" For nothing is simpler and easier than something. Further, assuming that things must exist, it must be possible to give a reason *why they should exist as they do* and not otherwise.

8. Now this sufficient reason for the existence of the universe cannot be found in the series of contingent things, that is to say, of bodies and their representations in souls. For since matter is in itself indifferent to motion or rest, and to one motion rather than to another, one cannot find in it a reason for motion and still less for some particular motion. Although the present motion in matter arises from preceding motion, and that in turn from motion which preceded it, we do not get further however far we may go, for the same question always remains. The sufficient reason, therefore, which needs no further reason, must be outside of this series of contingent things and is found in a substance which is the cause of this series or which is a necessary being bearing the reason for its existence within itself; otherwise we should not yet have a sufficient reason with which to stop. This final reason for things is called *God.*

9. This simple primary substance must include eminently the perfections contained in the derivative substances which are its effects. Thus it will have perfect power, knowledge, and will; that is to say, it will have omnipotence, onmiscience, and sovereign goodness. And since justice, taken in its most general sense, is nothing but goodness conforming with wisdom, there is also necessarily a sovereign justice in God. The reason which has made things exist through

him has also made them depend on him for their existence and operation, and they are continually receiving from him that which causes them to have some perfection. But whatever imperfection remains with them come from the essential and original limitation of the created beings.

10. It follows from the supreme perfection of God that he has chosen the best possible plan in producing the universe, a plan which combines the greatest variety together with the greatest order; with situation, place, and time arranged in the best way possible; with the greatest effect produced by the simplest means; with the most power, the most knowledge, the greatest happiness and goodness in created things which the universe could allow. For as all possible things have a claim to existence in God's understanding in proportion to their perfections, the result of all these claims must be the most perfect actual world which is possible. Without this it would be impossible to give a reason why things have gone as they have rather than otherwise.

11. The supreme wisdom of God has made him choose especially those *laws of motion* which are best adjusted and most fitted to abstract or metaphysical reasons. There is conserved the same quantity of total and absolute force or of action, also the same quantity of relative force or of reaction, and, finally, the same quantity of directive force. Furthermore, action is always equal to reaction, and the entire effect is always equal to its full cause. It is surprising that no reason can be given for the laws of motion which have been discovered in our own time, and part of which I myself have discovered, by a consideration of *efficient causes* or of matter alone. For I have found that we must have recourse to *final causes* and that these laws do not depend upon the *principle of necessity,* as do the truths of logic, arithmetic, and geometry, but upon the *principle of fitness,* that is to say, upon the choice of wisdom. This is one of the most effective and obvious proofs of the existence of God for those who can probe into these matters thoroughly.

12. It follows also from the perfection of the supreme Author, not only that the order of the entire universe is the most perfect possible, but also that each living mirror which represents the universe according to its own point of view, that is, each *monad* or each substantial center, must have its perceptions and its appetites regulated in the best way compatible with all the rest. From this it also follows that souls, that is to say, the most dominant monads, or rather animals themselves, cannot fail to awake from the state of stupor into which death or some other accident may place them.

13. For everything has been regulated in things, once for all, with as much order and agreement as possible; the supreme wisdom and goodness cannot act except with perfect harmony. The present is great with the future; the future could be read in the past; the distant is expressed in the near. One could learn the beauty of the universe in each soul if one could unravel all that is rolled up in it, but that develops perceptibly only with time. But, since each distinct perception of the soul includes an infinity of confused perceptions which envelop the entire universe, the soul itself does not know the things which it perceives until it has perceptions which are distinct and heightened. And it has perfection in proportion to the distinctness of its perceptions.

Each soul knows the infinite, knows everything, but confusedly. Thus when I walk along the seashore and hear the great noise of the sea, I hear separate sounds of each wave but do not distinguish them; our confused perceptions are the result of the impressions made on us by the whole universe. It is the same with each monad. Only God has a distinct knowledge of everything, for he is the source of everything. It has been very well said that he is everywhere as a center but that his circumference is nowhere, since everything is immediately present to him without being withdrawn at all from this center.

14. As for the reasonable soul or *spirit,* there is something more in it than in monads or even in simple souls. It is not only a

mirror of the universe of creatures but also an image of divinity. The spirit not only has a perception of the works of God but is even capable of producing something which resembles them, though in miniature. For not to mention the wonders of dreams in which we invent, without effort but also without will, things which we should have to think a long time to discover when awake, our soul is architectonic also in its voluntary actions and in discovering the sciences according to which God has regulated things (by weight, measure, number, etc.). In its own realm and in the small world in which it is allowed to act, the soul imitates what God performs in the great world.

15. For this reason all spirits, whether of men of higher beings [*genies*], enter by virtue of reason and the eternal truths into a kind of society with God and are members of the City of God, that is to say, the most perfect state, formed and governed by the greatest and best of monarchs. Here there is no crime without punishment, no good action without a proportionate reward, and, finally, as much virtue and happiness as is possible. And this takes place, not by a dislocation of nature, as if what God has planned for souls could disturb the laws of bodies, but by the very order of natural things itself, by virtue of the harmony preestablished from all time between the realms of nature and of grace, between God as architect and God as monarch, in such a way that nature leads to grace, and grace perfects nature by using it.

16. Thus, though reason cannot teach us the details of the great future, these being reserved for revelation, we can be assured by this same reason that things are arranged in a way which surpasses our desires. God being also the most perfect, the happiest, and therefore the most lovable of substances, and *true pure love* consisting in the state which causes pleasure to be taken in the perfections and the felicity of the beloved, this love must give us the greatest pleasure of which one is capable, since God is its object.

17. And it is easy to love him as we

ought if we know him as I have said. For though God is not visible to our external senses, he is nonetheless most love-worthy and gives very great pleasure. We see how much pleasure honors give to men, although they do not consist of qualities which appear to the external senses. Martyrs and fanatics, though the affection of the latter is not well ordered, show what power the pleasure of the spirit has. What is more, even the pleasures of sense are reducible to intellectual pleasures, known confusedly. Music charms us, although its beauty consists only in the agreement of numbers and in the counting, which we do not perceive but which the soul nevertheless continues to carry out, of the beats or vibrations of sounding bodies which coincide at certain intervals. The pleasures which the eye finds in proportions are of the same nature, and those caused by other senses amount to something similar, although we may not be able to explain them so distinctly.

18. It may even be said that the love of God already gives us, here and now, a foretaste of future felicity. And, although it is disinterested, by itself it constitutes our greatest good and interest, even when we do not seek these in it and when we consider only the pleasure it gives and disregard the utility it produces. For it gives us a perfect confidence in the goodness of our Author and Master, and this produces a true tranquility of spirit, not such as the Stoics have who resolutely force themselves to be patient, but by a present contentment which itself assures us of future happiness. And, apart from the present pleasure, nothing could be more useful for the future, for the love of God also fulfils our hopes and leads us in the way of supreme happiness, since, by virtue of the perfect order established in the universe, everything is done in the best possible way, as much for the general good as for the greatest particular good of those who are convinced of it and are satisfied by the divine government. This cannot fail to be true of those who know how to love the source of all good. It is true that the supreme happiness (with whatever *beatific*

vision or knowledge of God it may be accompanied) cannot ever be full, because God, being infinite, cannot ever be known entirely. Thus our happiness will never consist, and ought never to consist, in complete joy, which leaves nothing to be desired and which would stupefy our spirit, but in a perpetual progress to new pleasures and new perfections.

ARTHUR O. LOVEJOY

THE MEANINGS OF "EMERGENCE" AND ITS MODES*

There is an old and persistent tendency in the human mind to conceive of the causal relation as rationally explantory, and, therefore, to assimilate it, vaguely or explicitly, to the logical relations of inclusion, implication, or equivalence. That "there cannot be more in the effect than there is in the cause" is one of the propositions that men have been readiest to accept as axiomatic; a cause, it has been supposed, does not "account for" its effect, unless the effect is a thing which the eye of reason could somehow discern *in* the cause, upon a sufficiently thorough analysis. This antipathy to the notion of an absolute epigenesis has left its mark deep and wide upon the history of thought; it appears, indeed, at the very outset of Western speculation in the struggles of the physiologers with the supposed difficulty of admitting qualitative change. Two of the later episodes in the history of what may be named the preformationist assumption about causality may pertinently be remembered here.

The first is the doctrine of most mediaeval European metaphysics that all the "perfections," or positive attributes, of the creatures must be possessed by the First Cause—even though it was found necessary to assert with equal emphasis that that Cause and its creatures have no attributes in common. In this theological form the preformationist principle implied an addition to the empirically known sum of reality; it left undiminished the abundance and diversity of nature and did not exclude quantitative and qualitative change from the natural order, but placed behind these a supersensible cause in which all this abundance and diversity were declared to be in some fashion antecedently or eternally contained. Since this way of construing the assumption meant no simplification of the universe for our understanding, it was not serviceable to natural science. But in the seventeenth century there began to develop a conception which, while it fulfilled the same assumption, did so in a significantly different way—the conception, namely, of natural events as combinations or rearrangements of relatively simple, pre-existent entities, of which the total number or quantity remains invariant, and of each of which the qualities and laws of action remain the same through all the combinations into which it may enter. By this mechanistic conception of causation there is nothing *substantive* in the consequent which was not in the antecedent, and the supposed paradox of epigenesis is thus avoided. But in this second form the preformationist assumption implied a program of reduction or simplification; it was in its essence a scheme for abating the difference of things. For if complexes contain nothing (except their patterns) not already in their simple components, *rerum cognoscere causas* means learning to see in the complex nothing but its beggarly elements—the meager qualities and limited re-

* From *Proceedings of the Sixth International Congress of Philosophy*, 1926, pp. 20–33. Reprinted by permission of the author.

pertoire of the simple, merely multiplied a certain number of times. Scientific explanation becomes equivalent to mathematical analysis; and if the method is universalized, all philosophy, in Hobbes's phrase, becomes "nothing but addition and subtraction." But many complex things have properties not convincingly describable as multiples of the properties of the simple things through the combination of which they arise; and thus the notion of observed causal processes as rearrangements of the unchanging, while formally denying that there is "more" in the effect than there is in the cause, nevertheless seemed to imply that there is less in the cause than is apprehended in the effect. The mechanistic conception escaped this paradox only through its conjunction with another feature of most seventeenth-century and subsequent philosophy; its plausibility at the outset and ever since has been wholly dependent upon its association with some form of psycho-physical dualism. By means of this all that considerable part of the data of experience, together with the phenomenon of experiencing itself, which seemed plainly irreconcilable with the principle of quantitative and qualitative constancy could conveniently be assigned to the side of the "merely subjective." The eventual triumphs of that principle in modern science were made possible through the restriction of its literal application to the physical order, after that order had first been carefully purged of the classes of facts most recalcitrant to such application.

I have recalled these historical commonplaces because they lead up to the first of a series of distinctions which I wish to propose. The phrasing of the question laid down for our discussion implies, and most judicious readers of recent English and American philosophy, I suspect, feel, that the now modish terms "emergence" and "emergent evolution" stand in some need of clarification. In current use their meanings are various and usually vague; and though it may be recognized that they point towards some real and important philosophical issues, the precise nature of those issues, their relations to one another, and the logical procedure suitable

for dealing with them have not yet, perhaps, been formulated quite so clearly and methodically as could be wished. It is, therefore, towards such preliminary definition, discrimination, and correlation of problems that I shall chiefly attempt to contribute. While some opinions on certain of the issues themselves will be expressed, it must be with the brevity that is indistinguishable from dogmatism; and the primary purpose of this paper is merely to offer some prolegomena to any future discussion of "emergence."

What is needed, however, is not an extreme narrowing of the signification of the general term. In this case, as often in philosophical terminology, it is better to leave to the generic term a meaning so broad as to appear vague, and to approach precise definitions and clear-cut issues by progressively distinguishing species within the genus. "Emergence," then (or "epigenesis," which would be a much more appropriate word), may be taken loosely to signify any augmentative or transmutative event, any process in which there appear effects that, in some one or more of several ways yet to be specified, fail to conform to the maxim that "there cannot be in the consequent anything more than, or different in nature from, that which was in the antecedent." And the first distinction which it is essential to make, in reducing this vague general notion to something more definite and discussable, is between what I shall call the theses of the possibility of general and the actuality of specific emergence, theses antithetic respectively to the first and second sorts of preformationism.[1] To affirm the possibility of general emergence is to reject the preformationist assumption formally and absolutely, and therefore to deny the validity of any argument from it to the existence of a metempirical cause or causes which somehow precontain "all that is in the effects." But to many this assumption apparently still has the

---

[1] The adjectives "general" and "specific" are not free from ambiguity; the former here means "predicable of the whole, but not necessarily of every part," the latter, "predicable of some part or parts, but not necessarily of the whole."

force of an axiom, and the argument in question, therefore, figures conspicuously in some recent discussions of our theme. Thus Taylor repeats the scholastic maxim: "The principle *e nihilo nihil fit,*" he writes, "is fundamental to all explanation"; and it is therefore "true that no cause can contribute to its effect what it has not to give. The full and ultimate cause of every effect in a process of evolution will have to be found not simply in the special character of its recognized antecedents but in the character of the eternal which is at the back of all development. And this must contain"—though "in a more eminent manner"—"all that it bestows, though it may contain much more." [2] Boodin has recently built a highly original superstructure upon the same ancient foundation; for the main argument of his interesting volume on *Cosmic Evolution* appears to be, in brief, that philosophy must "explain" the seeming emergence of novelty in the course of evolution, that "causality from behind cannot account for more than there is in the antecedents," and that therefore the higher forms of being which are progressively attained in terrestrial history must have preexisted in, and been communicated through ready-made "energy-patterns" from, some other part of the universe,—the "evolution of new levels" being "obviously" impossible, since it would be tantamount to "something coming from nothing." [3]

The issue here is not only the most fundamental one in our topic but one of the crucial issues in all philosophy. If we really know that an absolute or general emergence is impossible we know something very curious and important about the universe. But the proof of its impossibility usually offered I find unconvincing for numerous reasons, of which a few may be briefly indicated. The universal cause or set of causes in which all that is in the (temporal) effects is declared to be pre-contained must be one of three things: a temporal *prius*, or an eternal

which contains the temporal effects as its parts, or an eternal extraneous to those effects. If taken in the first of these senses, the assumption on which the argument rests cannot, of course, mean that the effects themselves are in the cause; it can only mean either (a) that the effects collectively do not *differ* either qualitatively or quantitatively from the *prius*—that is to say, that they are either mere repetitions of it, or else that they differ only in some relational property which is regarded as unimportant, such as the arrangement or distribution of the qualities and components present in the cause; or (b) that they are never of higher metaphysical rank or excellence than the cause. This latter is what the supposed axiom seems often to reduce to; the "lower" we are told, can come from the "higher," but not the "higher" from the "lower"; the stream of being cannot rise higher than its source. But—though this will seem to some a hard saying—neither of these forms of the preformationist assumption appears to be justified by anything better than a prejudice—an idol of the tribe, at best. The supposed axiom lacks self-evidence, and though there are some, there are no cogent, reasons for postulating it. Concerning the qualitative and quantitative relations of two existents of different dates we have no *a priori* knowledge. It is entirely conceivable that temporal reality as a whole is not only augmented, but attains higher levels, within any finite time which we may choose to consider; and there are some to whom this evidently seems the more satisfying thing to postulate. Certainly, if consistently carried out, metaphysical preformationism has less edifying and cheering implications that are sometimes attributed to it. If the sum of being and the sum of realized value are constant—and unless they are either constant or diminishing the pretended axiom is false, and there *is* at times an absolute emergence —then the whole movement and travail of the creation is but a barren shuffling-about of the same pieces; an increase or ascent in one region must be simultaneously compensated by an equivalent decrease or decline elsewhere; the more the universe changes, the

---

[2] A. E. Taylor, *Evolution in the Light of Modern Knowledge* (1925), p. 460.
[3] J. E. Boodin *op. cit.*, (1925), pp. 44, 67, 82, 96–98, 101 and *passim.*

more it is the same thing. If, however, the "Cause" is conceived as a supratemporal totality which contains the temporal effects, the impossibility of general emergence undeniably follows; an "eternal" cannot grow or improve. But such a conception implies the true inclusion of a real succession in a *totum simul;* and no ingenuity has ever succeeded in showing this to be other than a self-contradiction. This aside, since the temporal world is still admitted to be in some sense real, the whole of *that* world may in that same sense conceivably differ at different moments in the number of its elements or in their value. Finally, if the Cause by which "all that is in the effects" is said to be possessed is conceived as an eternal that does *not* contain those effects within its being— which I take to be the orthodox scholastic view—the same difficulties present themselves as in the first case, together with some additional ones. The notion of an existent which at once is alien to all succession or change, and yet is the efficient cause of a series of temporal changes, is, to say the least, elusive; and the supposition that that cause must "possess" all that is in the temporal effects seems not only gratuitous—the same venerable prejudice as before—but also self-contradictory. None of their *distinctive* qualities can be predicable of it, except in a sense so eminent as to be no sense at all. And even if the qualities were the same, their "communication" to the effects would mean the emergence of additional existence *instances* of those qualities, unless they were at the same time lost by the Cause. And in any case, there is nothing in this last form of the argument which would preclude emergence in the world in which alone, by hypothesis, change occurs at all.

There is, then, no valid *a priori* argument against the possibility of general (which, of course, does not necessarily mean perpetual) emergence to be drawn from the notion of causality. The subject is one on which we have no means of arriving at objective conclusions, unless it be through more or less probable inferences from experience. It may be suggested that reasons for regarding general emergence as impossible (or meaningless) are to be found in the experimental data upon which the special theory of relativity is based. An examination of the sufficiency of those data as grounds for such a conclusion cannot be attempted in the time at my disposal.

The thesis of specific emergence means denial of the second form of preformationism; it is the assertion on empirical grounds of the occurrence, among the phenomena investigable by science, of events which are not mere rearrangements of pre-existent natural entities in accordance with laws identical for all arrangements of those entities. It is to be observed that the reality of specific emergence is usually asserted by those who declare general or absolute emergence to be inconceivable. This combination of views is, at least on the face of it, logically possible, since the denial of qualitative and quantitative constancy in certain empirically observable changes does not of itself forbid the supposition of an ulterior general cause of whose relation to the entire series of changes the supposed axiom about causality would hold good; and the combination is natural, because there is a radical incompatibility of temper between the two types of preformationism. On the other hand, if such a compensatory general cause is excluded, any instance of specific emergence, however slight, would obviously imply also general emergence, an augmentation of the total sum of things. The opposition in certain scientific quarters to current doctrines of specific emergence seems to be due in no small part to the same feeling as is expressed in the scholastic principle—the feeling that there would be something queer and illogical about a universe in which substantive increments popped into existence. The chief significance of our problem is, then, that it raises definitely the question of the tenability of this historic assumption, common to and potent in both traditional theology and mechanistic science, in spite of their mutual antipathy.

Agreeing in what they deny, doctrines of specific emergence may differ in two respects in what they affirm: in their accounts, namely, of the occasions of emergence, and of the types of actual emergents. In the first regard we must first of all distinguish between indeterminist and determinist theories. The former declare that there are instances of emergence which are reducible to no causal law; no fixed occasions can be formulated upon which they invariably occur. The hypothesis of "undetermined evolution" to which Professor Driesch has referred is, I take it, a theory of this sort; but it is undesirable to define this as the only or the "strict" sense of "emergent evolution." The determinist kind of theory declares that whenever certain specific occasions appear a specific variety of emergent uniformly arises. The general nature of these occasions may be variously conceived. One abstractly possible sort would consist merely in intervals in the proper time of one or another physical system; but the most widely current hypothesis on the matter—the so-called theory of creative synthesis—finds the chief, if not the only, occasions of emergence to consist in the formation of special integrations of matter and (or) energy. The question what, in fact, these occasions are, must, of course, depend upon the character of the emergents which can be shown really to arise. Before raising this question of fact it is useful to consider what types of emergent there conceivably *may* be—what, in other words, are the ways in which it is possible to think of a consequent as differing positively, otherwise than in the rearrangement of the same elements, from its causally necessary antecedent. In distinguishing these modes of possible emergence I shall—in order to gain brevity by combining two definitions—put the enumeration in the form of a statement of the meaning of "emergent evolution," that term in general here signifying the occurrence as a feature of the evolutionary process of *any* of the modes of emergence. An "emergent evolution" may, then, be said to have taken place if, upon comparison of the present phase (called Ph.N), of earth-history (say that since the appearance of *homo sapiens*) with any prior phase (called Ph.A),

there can be shown to be present in Ph.N any one or more of the five following features lacking in Ph.A (1) Instances of some general type of change admittedly common to both phases (e.g., relative motion of particles), of which. instances the manner of conditions of occurrence could not be described in terms of, nor predicted from, the laws which would have been sufficient for the description and (given the requisite determination of the variables) the prediction of all changes of that type occurring in Ph.A. Of this evolutionary emergence of laws one, though not the only conceivable, occasion would be the production, in accordance with one set of laws, of new local integrations of matter, the motions of which, and therefore of their component particles, would thereupon conform to vector, i.e., directional, laws emergent in the sense defined. This first mode differs from the others in that it implies no quantitative variability of the prime or irreducible *existents* (other than relations) in the system under consideration. (2) New qualities and, especially, classes of qualities (e.g., the so-called secondary qualities) attachable as adjectives to entities already present, though without those accidents, in Ph.A. (3) Particular entities *not* possessing all the essential attributes characteristic of those found in Ph.A, and having distinctive types of attributes (not merely configurational) of their own. (4) Some type or types of event or process irreducibly different in kind from any occurring in Ph.A. (5) A greater quantity, or number of instances, not explicable by transfer from outside the system, of any one or more types of prime entity common to both phases.

In the enumeration of types of possible emergence included in this definition, the most significant point is the contrast between the first, which may be called functional, and the remaining four, which may be called existential, emergence. Several writers have recently declared that any attempt to prove the reality of the first mode is subject (for familiar reasons, inherent in the notion of a "law," which need not be recalled here) to an intrinsic logical limitation. Our inability, they remark, at any given time to discover, or even conceive of the general nature of, any single law or set of joint laws from which all the motions of manner in its differing integrations would be deducible, is not conclusive proof that. no such law is formulable; "within the physical realm it always remains logically possible," Broad has said, "that the appearance of emergent laws is due to our imperfect knowledge of microscopic structure or to mathematical incompetence." This *non possumus* does not seem to me to be itself conclusively established; but as there is no time to give reasons, I shall not here challenge it. Even supposing it true, it would not follow that the emergence of laws can be said to be improbable. Such emergence would, to be sure, imply the impossibility of a complete unification of science; and there is for this reason, we are often told, a decisive methodological presumption against it. But here we must distinguish between heuristic rules and propositions of fact. It is the business of the scientific investigator to look for identities of law in seemingly diverse phenomena, and to find as many of them as he can; it is not the business of the philosopher to assume *a priori* that nature must to an indefinite degree lend itself to the gratification of this ambition. Though rigorous and conclusive proof of the first mode of emergence be impossible, the hypothesis of its occurrence seems to me to be patently the more probable in the present state of our knowledge. But with these cursory dogmatizings I leave to others the question of functional emergence, in order to consider somewhat less summarily that of existential emergence.

Concerning this the first thing to remark is that. an attempt to prove it is not subject to the same general logical disability said to inhere in any argument for emergent laws. An existential emergent would be a quality, or a thing or event possessing distinctive non-configurational qualities, which was found in the subsequent and not in the prior phase of some causal process; and its presence in the one case and absence in the other

would be facts determinable either by observation or by inference from observed data. Where observation of both phases is possible the proof of existential emergence can be direct and virtually complete, as in the case of the qualitative changes (whether they be "objective" or "subjective") incident to chemical synthesis, which have long been recognized, under a different terminology, as examples of such emergence. This simplest instance—which, however, is not quite so simple logically as it looks—obvious and commonplace though it is, has a crucial importance which some writers on the subject do not appear to realize; for it alone suffices to show that there can be no general and decisive theoretical presumption against *other* hypotheses of existential emergence, that nature is assuredly no affair of mere rearrangements. In less simple but philosophically more consequential and controversial cases, the argument for existential emergence may involve somewhat complex and difficult reasonings, and therefore attain a less high degree of probability; but even in these cases, to which I shall shortly return, the difficulty is of a kind different from, and less fundamental than, that said to infect all reasonings concerning emergence of laws.

With the distinction between functional and existential emergents in mind we are also in a position to deal with the commonest general or antecedent objection brought against theories of specific emergence. The objection was raised, in differing terms, by several participants in the recent discussion of the subject by the English philosophical societies. To characterize an effect as "emergent," it is urged, is to give up the attempt to "explain" it; and since science cannot give up this attempt, the characterization can have, at best, no more than a provisional validity, as a way of admitting that certain things have not as yet been completely "explained." Now, what sort of explanation is it that these critics desiderate in theories of emergence? "Causal explanation" in the empirical sense—the assumption that every event follows upon some other *nach einer Regel,* the "determinism of the experimentalist"—is, as we have seen, entirely compatible with the belief in emergence. The sort of explanation which specific emergence, or emergent evolution, would exclude, is simply that demanded by the second form of preformationism—the conception of an event as *neither* (a) manifesting any law, or mode of uniform behavior *nor* (b) containing any existent, not found in the antecedent phase of the sequence to which it belongs. To maintain then, that everything is "explicable," in the sense incongruous with emergence, is to raise a definite, though by no means simple, question of fact; it is to imply, for example, that, barring mere summations or rearrangements, there is to be found in the present phase of terrestrial history no existence whatever—no quality, type of entity, or kind of process—which could not already have been discerned by a scientific angel observing the cold-gaseous-nebula stage of the development of our solar system. This proposition cannot be said to have a high degree of *prima facie* plausibility; and its truth cannot be assumed *a priori* merely because it is one of the two conceivable ways of satisfying the demand for a special type of so-called "explanation" which is not practically indispensable to science.

Wholesale attempts to rule out, *ab initio*, all specific hypotheses of existential emergence by *a priori* assumptions of this sort being excluded, both assertors and deniers of any such hypotheses must address themselves to the analysis of definite empirical data. The assertor must (if the question be that of emergent evolution) point out some type of observable entity, event, or quality— call it E—existent in Ph.N which does not appear to be adequately describable in the same terms as would describe any entity, event, etc., which we can with probability suppose to have existed in Ph.A. The denier must attempt to show that everything in E *is* describable in the same terms as some class of entities, events, or qualities in Ph.A; to this end he may employ either of two methods, which may be termed the reductive and the retrotensive; i.e., he may either (1) seek by analysis to reduce E to the same descriptive terms as are sufficient for certain events, etc., admittedly found in Ph.A; or (2) admitting that E has the characters attributed to it by the assertor of emergence, he may maintain that these characters were already present in the earlier phase—in other words, must be supposed to be present in all phases —of the process.

The general logical nature of the problem being thus formulated, we may consider a particular hypothesis of existential emergence, which I hold to be true. It is nowise original, being substantially the same as the theory to which Broad has given the name of "emergent materialism"—though that designation seems to me a veritable *lucus a non lucendo*. According to this hypothesis, both the third and fourth modes of emergence— i.e., emergence of new types of entities and of new kinds of event or process—have appeared in evolution, in the form, but only in the form, of what may be called "transphysical" emergence. By this I mean the production, as effects of the formation of certain complex and late-evolved integrations of living matter, when acted upon by certain forms of radiant energy, of psychical events and psychical objects. An example of a psychical event is an act of awareness. By psychical objects I mean individual entities empirically existent, having extension and certain other of the properties commonly called psychical, but differing from true physical objects in that they do not conform to the laws of physics, have individually only an ephemeral existence, have collectively no quantitative or numerical constancy, have no direct dynamical relations with one another, and are grouped into "private" sets, i.e., each is accessible only to an act of awareness of an individual organism. Examples of such entities are sensa and images, both delusive and veridical. In other words the "generative theory of sensa," recently defended by a number of writers, is a part of the hypothesis of existential emergent evolution I am presenting. The initial cases of transphysical emergence were followed by a further evolution of the same type, conditioned upon the formation of new and still more complex integration of matter and (or) energy, and the process thus far apparently culminates in the cognitive and affective functions of the human organism.

To the plain man, and to some men of science, these theses will, I dare say, seem rather obvious, and not much in need of defence. But in philosophy they manifestly raise numerous highly controversial issues. The existential emergence they assert is attacked chiefly from two sides, and by the two methods already defined: the reductive method is at present represented by behaviorism,[4] the retrotensive mainly by panphyschism, or the mind-stuff theory. The behavioristic argument I shall not here examine; the view that both the act and the content of awareness, when I apprehend an object distant in space or time, are adequately describable as present changes of the relative position of molecules under my skin, really seems to me to be itself adequately describable by Broad's epithet, "silly." There is, however, an important contemporary doctrine which would apply the reductive method to the immediate objects of awareness, but not to the act of awareness; the former, it declares, are simply parts of the physical world, and, if emergent at all, are at any rate not trans-physical emergents. This contention is assuredly deserving of serious discussion; but the reasons for rejecting it are too complex to be presented here. The attempts of pan-psychists to escape from the admission of trans-physical emergence seem plainly to be due, in part, to the influence of an attenuated, vestigial form of the ancient pseudo-axiom mentioned at the outset; while it is not necessarily maintained by them that specific emergence is impossible in principle or nonexistent in fact. They apparently feel that a causal antecedent cannot be so *very* different in nature from its effect as a physical event is from a mental one. Thus the author of a recent admirably lucid defence of the mind-stuff theory remarks that "discontinuity in evolution would be a baf-

fling and unintelligible phenomenon," and declared that the mind-stuff theory alone "gives us a universe without such unintelligible breaches." "If a mind is simply a brain regarded from the outside, . . . the gradual evolution of a brain *is* the gradual evolution of a mind"; thus "there is no need to postulate any discontinuity in evolution to account for the appearance upon the scene of minds, of consciousness, of qualities." Yet the same writer tells us that "the units" of mind-stuff "which make up our mental states" and also our brains "are not *aware* of anything—neither of anything else nor of themselves. They just *exist; . . .* the fact of their constituting a group of units that function together, or the fact of their being in such and such a position in space and time, is a fact about them, not an aspect of their psychic being." Nor do they possess any of (at least) the secondary qualities. It is only when, "as a product of organic evolution," brains are formed, that "awareness," and therewith qualities, make their appearance.[5] This, however, is to strain at an emergent gnat and swallow an emergent camel. The cognition of external objects and their relations, which is somehow achieved through the brain, is not the sum of the atomic, non-cognitive sentiencies supposed to inhere in its component particles; and it is therefore no more "accounted for" by the assumed sentiency of those particles than it is by their motion. It is as blankly different and discontinuous a new fact as anything could be. So little, at best, can be accomplished by the retrotensive method that it is not surprising to find in some recent pan-psychism a tendency to invoke the aid of the reductive, i.e., to describe the *higher* mental functions in somewhat vaguely behavioristic terms. But behaviorism does not, by becoming vaguer, become more convincing.

Another attempt to employ the retrotensive method for avoiding the admission of trans-physical emergence is to be seen in the parallelistic form of emergent evolu-

---

[4] A behaviorist might without inconsistency admit functional while denying existential emergence.

[5] Drake, *Mind and Its Place in Nature* (1926), pp. 97–100, 241–243.

tionism, the view that psycho-physical "duality of nature does not *arise* in the course of evolutionary advance, it is there *ab initio*," but that emergence occurs (in just what modes is not very clear) in the psychical as well as the physical sense, though in each independently. Such a view, however, appears to involve the general doctrine, at once confused and incredible, that physical events can have no causal relation to mental ones— which implies that sensations are not due to physical stimuli, and that if a man, after receiving a blow on the head, loses his memory, the blow is wholly irrelevant to the amnesia, which is causally explicable, if at all, solely by the thoughts he was thinking before he was hit. This doctrine does not appear to me to lie within the bounds of serious discussion. The retrotensive method, therefore, not only gratuitously extends to the whole of nature a concomitance for which there is probable evidence only in a special class of cases; it also either falls short of its objective or else implies impossible consequences.

We have, therefore, abundant reason to believe that in the history of our planet there have occurred genuine new births of time, a sheer increase and diversification and enrichment of the sum of things here. And no reason, except an arbitrary pseudo-axiom, can be given for assuming that this has been merely a cosmical game of beggar-my-neighbor. On the other hand, we have no empirical reason for asserting—and serious reasons for doubting—that a similar process is the general rule throughout the physical universe, or that the higher emergents occur at all frequently in space and time. Yet, even though no knowledge which we possess concerning evolution justifies that generalized or cosmic meliorism which now so widely does duty for a religion, there nevertheless lies before our terrestrial race in its own little corner of the world a future which, if dim with uncertainties and beset with perils, is not necessarily devoid of possibilities immeasurably transcending all that the past has brought forth. There perhaps yet remain to mankind, we are told, some thousand million years; if it be so, before this long day ends it is possible that, besides all that man's laboring reason may achieve, there may yet emerge out of the latent generative potencies of matter, as there quite certainly have emerged before our strange planetary history, new and richer forms of being, such as no prescience of ours could foresee and no contrivance of ours create.

JAMES COLLINS

GOD AS A FUNCTION IN MODERN SYSTEMS OF PHILOSOPHY*

From even a cursory study of the history of modern philosophy, there emerges a salient fact having special significance for us. Running throughout the entire course of modern speculation is a persistent and central interest in the problem of God. At the

* From *Proceedings of the American Catholic Philosophical Association*, Volume XXVIII (1954), pp. 1–17. Reprinted with permission of the publisher and of the author.

very outset, the ferment of Renaissance thought comes in large measure from a preoccupation with the questions of the relationship between God and the world and the extent of man's knowledge of the divine nature. The two extreme answers of Bruno's pantheism and Montaigne's skepticism set the stage for the grand enterprise of the seventeenth-century rationalist systems, in which the role of God is crucially important. And if the empiricists and Kant feel obliged to make a fundamental criticism of rationalism, they are compelled to do so largely because of the difficulties encountered in squaring the rationalist doctrine on God with the deliverances of the scientific method and the implications of the scientific way of knowing the material universe. The proximity of the problem of God to the heart of the modern philosophical development is clearly evident also in the systems of the nineteenth century. We cannot fully understand the basis of the conflict between idealism and positivism, unless we examine their conflicting views about God and about the ability of the human mind to gain knowledge of an infinite and immaterial reality. This same fundamental orientation of philosophy extends into our contemporary age, even when it displays itself only in a semantic interest in the use of the terms "God" and "gods."

There is nothing paradoxical, therefore, in maintaining that the great modern minds have been just as deeply challenged by the question of God's existence, nature and creative activity as were the great medieval minds. Now that the history of modern philosophy is being viewed in multiple dimension, rather than in a narrowly epistemological and methodological way, the bearing of natural theological questions upon the systematic developments in modern philosophy can be clearly discerned. The differences between the medieval theologians and the modern philosophers do not stem from any depreciation of the problem of God, on the part of the moderns. The fact *that* God, counts a good deal in determining the nature of one's outlook is universally admitted: oppositions arise in attempting to specify precisely *how* one's view of God is to be integrated with the rest of one's philosophical doctrines. It may be useful, then, to examine briefly a few representative modern approaches to God, in order to discover how this problem does affect in a radical way the spirit and structure of a philosophy.

For this purpose, we will interrogate three leading philosophers from as many centuries:

Spinoza from the seventeenth, Kant from the eighteenth, and Hegel from the nineteenth cenutry. In each instance, let us confine our inquiry to some one specific issue which is relevant to our main subject. Of Spinoza we will ask: what relation does God bear toward the starting point of philosophy? The question presented to Kant is this: what difference does one's conception of existence make in the demonstration of God's existence? And finally, Hegel will be invited to state the way in which he envisages the relationship between the God of religion and the Absolute of idealistic philosophy. From the answers which we may be able to extract from these key witnesses, it may be possible to ascertain at least a few of the functions of the doctrine on God in modern philosophical systems. The findings will have more than a purely historical import, however, since at the same time they define the actual speculative situation with which every theistic philosopher today must reckon, if his teaching is to become effective.

I

Our first question is a methodological one, dealing with God's role in the proper starting point of philosophy. This problem was one of the major ways in which seventeenth-century rationalists formulated their doctrine on method. In their preocupation with the starting point of speculation, they showed the effect of the late Renaissance and early modern development of skepticism. One of the key issues in the revival of Pyrrhonism was a concentrated attack upon the sources of knowledge. The underlying argument was that, if the fountainheads of human cognition can be shown to be polluted, then it can also be shown that the contagion is visited upon all the enterprises of science and philosophy. Although the specific lines of skeptical criticism were many, the most radical one focussed upon the relation between our rational and our sensuous powers. Reason is essentially dependent upon sense, and sensation is notoriously weak, subjective and illusory.

Hence all our human efforts at attaining speculative truth are vitiated by the unreliable nature of our primary source of cognition: sensation.

The Cartesian method of doubt was evoked as an extreme remedy against this Pyrrhonian contention. In effect, Descartes challenged the assumption that reason does stand in any kind of essential dependence upon the senses. Instead of attempting the delicate task of vindicating the senses in their general reliability, Descartes preferred to follow an easier and apparently more effective path. His strategy of methodic doubt removed the senses definitely from the role of primary sources of human knowledge. They were demoted to a secondary position, in a desperate move to meet the skeptics on their own ground.

Descartes elevated the pure intelligence (or reason, liberated from any essential reference to sensuous sources) into the position of the primary and sole fount of all genuine knowledge. A purely intellectual intuition of the thinking, existent self thus became the proper starting point in philosophy. But in man's case, even a purely intellectual power is subject to temporal conditions. Skepticism might easily enter again through the breach existing between my present intuition and my remembrance of past acts of intuiting and reasoning. And without perfect assurance about the reliability of memory and reasoning, no philosophical system can be constructed. Before reconstituting physics, ethics and the other branches of knowledge, Descartes had to silence the retrospective suspicion that perhaps, in times past, his pure intelligence was the victim of deceit and hence is now operating on spurious capital.

Since he had cut off the purely intellectual power from any immediate reference to sensibly existent things, Descartes could remove this surmise only by an appeal to God as the author of his mind. He could not proceed to a study of the physical world and human conduct until he had first established the existence of the perfect being, God. Although God is not the first step in the Cartesian course of meditation, His existence

and nature must be determined as the immediate implication of the existing, thinking self. The Cartesian doctrine on God as truthful, omnipotent, free and immutable had to be demonstrated almost at the outset of the reconstruction of knowledge, since it served an important instrumental function in establishing the subsequent system. Descartes needed a God who could close the gap between present intuition and remembrance of past cognitions, who could guarantee our ineradicable belief in a real external world, and who could secure the immutability of physical laws and the continuity of the temporal process. In modern philosophy, natural theology tends to disappear as a unified doctrine, precisely because God is not studied for His own sake but as a tool of various epistemological, metaphysical, physical and moral enterprises.

But is the Cartesian God capable of serving these farflung systematic ends? This was Spinoza's disturbing question. He answered in the negative, in view of the qualification that, for Descartes, the doctrine on God stands *almost* at the beginning of the search for wisdom. In Spinoza's eyes, this was a dangerous compromise which destroyed the rigor of methodic thinking. Either God operates as the unconditionally first principle in philosophy or else a systematic deduction of the body of truths is impossible. Such a deductive process is only as adequate as the leading idea from which it takes its rise. If the initial step in speculation is anything less than the infinitely powerful substance of God, the adequate germinal principle is lacking for the total derivation of a philosophical outlook. Consequently, Spinoza substituted God for the finite self as the methodic point of departure for his thought. Just as the order of being starts with the divine substance, so the best order of our speculation about being must start with the divine substance. In this way, the emanation of all demonstrative truths from the primal true idea of God is mathematically assured.

Descartes had proved God's existence by showing this truth to be a necessary implication of the thinking self. The favorite Cartesian proof was the so-called ontological argument, based on the idea of the infinitely perfect being, an idea which he likened to the workman's stamp upon his product. Spinoza now suggested that the human mind is much more intimately related to the divine substance than the simile of the artisan and his product suggests. For the human mind is an expression of God, in the pregnant sense of being a modal development under the divine attribute of thought. The probative force of the ontological argument derives precisely from viewing the human mind and its ideas as modal expressions of the affirmative power of the unique infinite substance. The specific sense in which the human self "implies" the existence of God was radically redefined by Spinoza. The thinking self is implicated as one finite stage in the pantheistic relationship between God and His modes. Methodology merely requires the philosopher to pattern the order of his ideas after the order of things: this means to begin philosophy with God, who is the purely immanent cause and substantial principle of the finite self.

There is a historical, as well as doctrinal, sense in which Spinoza regarded the Cartesian order of demonstration as a compromise. To begin philosophy with the existence of the self is to occupy an unstable halfway station between theistic realism and a pantheism of substance. Spinoza recognized three alternate starting points for philosophy: the sensible world, the intelligible finite self, and the infinite substance of God. He looked upon the medieval realists as sensual and deluded minds, because they accepted the sensible world as the real starting point of philosophizing and trusted the senses as indispensable and generally reliable sources of knowledge. In repudiating the sensuous basis of knowledge, Spinoza sided with Descartes against theistic realism. But he felt that the recession from the senses had not been carried through far enough. The thinking finite self is not sufficiently removed from the senses to withstand every skeptical doubt. Above all, the finite existent does not enjoy a sufficiently powerful ontological status, in

a theistic outlook, to provide the watershed for a metaphysical deduction of the real. For both these reasons, Spinoza was compelled to expand the Cartesian critique of the senses to include a critique of the finite self, taken as a distinct substantial being. There was nowhere else for Spinoza to make his philosophical beginning than with a pantheistically conceived God.

When Thomists encounter this Spinozistic position, they are reminded sharply of the intellectual sting behind certain remarks in St. Thomas which they may previously have treated as harmless commonplaces. St. Thomas has a clear-cut way of distinguishing between theological wisdom and philosophical wisdom or human philosophy (understanding the latter term simply as the perfection of natural reason, rather than as a counterposition to the Christian doctrine on creation and beatitude). From the standpoint of order, theological wisdom begins with a consideration of God and then proceeds to a study of creatures, insofar as they are related to God and bear the divine likeness. In philosophical wisdom or human philosophy, however, a start is made with sensible created things themselves, which are studied in their own proper causes, and only at the end of the investigation is God reached. St. Thomas' main interest is to show that the theological approach is superior, since it is similar to God's primary inspection of His own essence, in the knowledge of which He knows all other things. Yet St. Thomas adds that there is no basic conflict between these two orders of study, since the principles of both kinds of wisdom are derived from the unity of the divine truth. In our own day, we should not forget this positive Thomistic confidence in human philosophy.

One consequence of the modern rejection of realism was that the Thomistic description of the order of human philosophical wisdom no longer seemed to be indisputable. Descartes asked whether we should begin with sensible finite things or with a purely intelligible finite thing, the thinking self. Spinoza challenged the view that we should start with finite created things at all, whether they be sensible or purely intelligible. What St. Thomas held to be the characteristic order of theological wisdom became, in the Spinozistic perspective, the proper order of philosophical wisdom. Thereafter, this reversal became the watermark of all forms of rationalistic idealism. It was read into the very meaning of a philosophical system, since the idealists aimed to provide a strictly deductive type of speculation. To do so, they were obliged to transfer from sacred to human wisdom the prescription that one must take God as the starting point.

Another cognate distinction of St. Thomas underwent a similar transformation. The entire Aristotelian tradition had wavered between regarding metaphysics as the science of being as such and as the science of the first substance. Aquinas resolved this issue by maintaining that the proper subject of metaphysics is being considered as such or in respect to the act of existing, which is not confined to matter. God is studied by metaphysics or philosophical theology not as the subject of the science but only as the ultimate principle of the subject of this science, i.e. insofar as He is the causal source of being and substance, act and potency. But sacred theology does have God as its proper subject, and extends to the various material realizations of being and substance only in the degree that the latter help us to understand God. Once again, Spinoza unwittingly transferred the traits of Thomistic sacred theology to his own philosophy, in regard to its proper subject as well as its point of departure. He made God the proper subject of metaphysics, and studied the principles of being and the finite world only in reference to God. In order to maintain this conception of metaphysics, however, Spinoza had to provide a naturalistic counterpart for revelation. This he found in the claim that the human mind has an intuitive insight into the divine essence itself. And to back up this claim, in turn, he had to suppose a pantheistic merger of the human mind with the divine intellect, against the background of a monism of substance and its modes.

As a consequence of these fundamental changes, Spinoza claimed a good deal more for metaphysics than did Aquinas. In the Spinozistic metaphysics, there can be an a priori, ontological proof of God's existence, based on our intuitive knowledge of the divine essence. A deductive demonstration of the structure and existence of the finite world is also possible, in virtue of our wholly nonempirical knowledge of the unique divine substance. For Aquinas, on the contrary, the beginning is made with being precisely as grasped by the intellect in the things presented to the senses. Knowledge that God exists is the result of a posteriori demonstration only, and it leads to no intuition of the divine essence and act of existing in themselves. We are justified in affirming that God exists only because of the requirements of being and the condition of finite beings of our experience. Only at the end of the metaphysical quest can we conclude that the existence of an infinite, transcendent being is demanded by the experiential world, considered in respect to its principles of being. Metaphysics alone can attain to formal knowledge of the existence of the ultimate source of its proper subject. But this knowledge is terminal and does not serve as the premise for a metaphysical deduction of the finite world. Since the human mind is not a modal expression of the divine substance under the attribute of thought, it cannot construct a deductive and nonempirical metaphysics. But the metaphysical truths which it can indeed establish, respect the integrity of God's transcendent freedom and man's personal subsistence.

II

As a second problem we propose to inquire of Kant how his notion of existence affected his analysis of proofs of God's existence. That there was a definite connection in Kant's mind between these two problems, is clear from his early cosmological writings, where he accepted several current proofs of God's existence. But he soon noticed that even such antithetically related thinkers as Leibniz and Hume agreed upon one thing: the unique significance of existence. It was reflected in the Leibnizian distinction between necessary truths of essence and contingent truths of existence. On Hume's part, there was the parallel contrast between ideal relations and relations expressive of matter of fact or existence. In both cases, the distinction was intended to prevent any *direct* reduction of existential to essential propositions. The main difference between Leibniz and Hume on this score was that the former hoped to make at least an *indirect* reduction of existential to essential propositions, by means of the principle of perfection or the best, whereas the latter regarded these two types of propositions as being mutually irreducible in every respect.

Faced with this issue, Kant quite sensibly maintained that no resolution can be obtained, until the meaning of existence is settled. He phrased the question in this way: what is the "more" that existence adds, over and above the bare essence? He was not satisfied by the rationalist suggestion that existence is simply the consummatory act within the very line of essence. It does no good to define existence as the complement of possibility or essence, since this leaves fundamentally unclarified the precise nature of the existential contribution to the essence. Kant also rejected another rationalist contention, namely, that existence merely renders determinate certain traits of the essence which were left undetermined in the purely ideal or essential order. For, one can conceive of the essence in a fully determinate manner, even including some definite spatial and temporal traits, and yet have no assurance that there is any existing instance of this fully determinate essence. Existence does not merely remedy a defect within the essential sphere. It makes some kind of addition even to a perfectly constituted essence, and that addition is a perfection of a new sort.

But when Kant turned to Hume for some guidance about the exact nature of the existential perfection, he received a disappointing answer. From the standpoint of a radical phenomenalism, all that Hume could say was that existence is indistinguishable from the condition of being an object of perception. Every object of perception, whether it be an impression or an idea, would then seem to have a valid claim upon existence. This was very close to Berkeley's position, except that Hume did not have the comfort of invoking the Berkeleyan God as the underwriter of real existence. Hence Hume had to appeal to the purely immanent laws of association, in order to distinguish between real and imagined existence. Those perceptual objects which hang together in a coherent system, established through regular associative bonds, deserve to be called real things. As Kant perceived, however, the Humean explanation told nothing about existence as a perfection *of things* but only about certain conditions under which we can regard *our knowledge* as real. These conditions indicated that those propositions are rightly regarded as having existential import which can be synthesized with the total network of coherent and permanent relations among perceived objects.

The net result of Kant's consultation of these sources can be summed up in two propositions. (1) From his critical reading of Leibniz and his school, Kant drew the negative conclusion that existence is not a mere predicate or determination of the essence. It cannot be derived solely by analysis of the concept of the essence or logical subject, since even an exhaustive analytic knowledge of the essence leaves us ignorant of whether or not the essence actually exists. Essential analysis remains in the realm of possibility. It does not furnish any real grounds for making the transition to the actuality of the existent thing. (2) Hume told Kant that, as far as phenomenalism can ascertain, there is no distinctive real predicate of existence. This did not mean that existence is nothing distinctive but only that it does not have the same status as an essential predicate. Expressed in a more positive way, existence somehow signifies incorporation of the object in the actual order. Existence effects an absolute positing of the essence, along with all its predicates, in the field of actuality. The index of this existential incorporation is the establishment of some real connection between the object in question and the totality of our experience.

Kant recognized at once that these two conclusions had an important bearing upon the question of speculative proofs of God's existence. 1. God is no exception to the rule that analysis of the concept of the essence can never yield real knowledge of existence. Hence the ontological argument is invalid: it tries to draw out of the concept of the most perfect being something which is not contained therein as an analytic property or predicate. All that a purely a priori approach can do is to invoke the principle of contradiction. This may prove that there is no intrinsic incompatibility between the constituent notes of the essence, but it warrants no assertion about the thing's real existence. The ontological argument remains in the logical order and does not determine anything about God as an existent being.

2. Having eliminated the a priori approach in the light of this criticism of Leibniz, Kant then employed Hume's view of existence to undermine any a posteriori proof of God's existence. In an a posteriori inference, we must appeal to the principles of experience, in addition to the principle of contradiction. Now, Kant laid down three conditions for determining what is an object of experience or a warranted inference from experience. The presumed experiential object must be subject to temporal process; it must be finite and capable of representation under some pattern of imagination; finally, it must belong to the field of appearances proportioned to our apperceptive consciousness. Clearly enough, the reality signified by the idea of the most perfect being cannot fulfil any of these indispensable conditions. For God is eternal, infinite or beyond imaginative representation, and a thing-in-itself rather than an appearance. Kant concluded that therefore God can neither be a direct object of experience nor be inferred with speculative validity from what does belong to the realm

of experience. The a posteriori proof is just as lacking in existential content as is the a priori.

With some aspects of Kant's analysis, a philosophical realist can agree. One major point in common is the doctrinal connection between the problem of existence in general and that of God's existence. An inadequate conception of existence may lead to an invalid argument for God's existence. Furthermore, Kant and Thomistic realism concur in thier criticism of the rationalist theory of existence as the culminating predicate in the line of essence itself. This provides a solid reason for rejecting any proof which derives God's existence from some prior affirmation of the power of the divine essence. We cannot import self-causality into the divine essence without simultaneously threatening God's transcendence and freedom in creation. Spinoza's deterministic monism of substance is the pure position toward which every metaphysics based on the strict ontological argument and its presuppositions about existence inevitably gravitates.

Yet Kant's way of saving the divine transcendence and freedom involves the sacrifice of every speculative demonstration of God's existence. His position is not dictated by any direct examination of the realistic a posteriori proofs, however, but by his theory of existence. There are two major characteristics of the Kantian view of existence. First, it is not a doctrine on existence but on the conditions for a certain type of existential *knowledge*. Kant's chief instrument of inquiry is a theory of knowledge which is unregulated by a metaphysics of being in its ultimate act. Accepting Hume's account of the purely phenomenal character of the object of knowledge, he must deny that the human mind can gain any genuine knowledge of things in their own intrinsic principles of being. Hence the paradox that the Kantian doctrine on existence supplies no speculative insight into the act of existing on the part of the existent thing. This accounts for the remarkable divergence between the Thomistic a posteriori way of making the demonstration concerning God's existence and Kant's reformulation of the cosmological argument. Although both Aquinas and Kant agree that the divine essence cannot be the starting point of the argument, they disagree fundamentally concerning the proper starting point in the finite order. Aquinas begins with finite beings, known in their own essence and its distinct act of existing, whereas Kant's only possible point of departure is the contingency of objects of appearance, prescinding entirely from the essential nature and existential act of the thing-in-itself. Kant's criticism holds good only for a proof which accepts his own phenomenalistic starting point.

The second noteworthy feature of the Kantian teaching on existence is its *relational* or systemic basis. Once again, the paramount influence of Hume over Kant is unmistakable. Both men hold that what we know in an existential way is only the coherent and stable connectedness of phenomenal objects in the field of experience. Kant traces this system of phenomenal reality to the necessary and universal structure of consciousness, rather than to Hume's psychological laws of association. Nevertheless, Kant continues the Humean tradition of characterizing the knowable existent in terms of something else—its reference to the connected whole of appearances—rather than in terms of its intrinsic principles of being, which remain unknowable. Existential knowledge thus becomes a process of fitting a presumed object of perception into the set of relations constituting the system of possible experience. But such a relational or systemic conception of existence misses the very act in virtue of which a thing can be said to exist. Hence it provides no basis for demonstrative knowledge about God's act of existing. What prevents Kant from achieving this demonstration is not so much the transcendence of God to experience as the thoroughly nonexistential character of the Kantian doctrine on experience and the object of knowledge.

Furthermore, the purely contextual theory of existential knowledge is unavoidably univocal, since the three conditions of experience enumerated previously are themselves univocal, formal aspects of consciousness. Even before he inspects the a posteriori proofs for God's existence, Kant is committed to the position that existential inference can move only within the confines of the finite field of homogeneous appearances. That is why he presents the cosmological argument as though one must abandon the existential terrain entirely and make a purely ideal adjustment of the idea of necessity to the idea of the most perfect being. This procedure is certainly illegitimate, but it is a procedure required only by the relational notion of existential knowledge and its univocal conditions.

The very careful statement which St. Thomas makes about the nature of the demonstration in question serves for critical evaluation of both Leibniz and Kant. What we prove is not precisely God's existence but the truth of our proposition that God exists. The negative part of this statement is relevant for Leibniz, whereas the affirmative part bears upon Hume and Kant. Taken in itself, the divine act of existing is infinite and identical with the divine essence. Hence it transcends the intellect of man, in his temporal condition, so that God in His own being remains in some fashion an unknown God. There can be no question of a demonstration of His existence from a prior knowledge of His essence (or a simultaneous but separate knowledge), both because of the infinite perfection of the divine essence and because its infinite actuality is nothing other than the divine act of existing itself. Outside the imagination of the rationalist systematist, there is no privileged sort of pre-existential power of the divine essence which can be captured and domiciled by the human mind. The ontological argument is not a highway, leading to demonstration *of* God's act of existing, but a byway in which one forgets the majesty of God and the limits of human intelligence.

Nevertheless, we are not left without natural knowledge and even demonstration *concerning* God's existence. The human inquirer can establish the truth of the proposition

"God exists," and hence can have demonstrative knowledge that God does exist. In a preliminary way, however, he must make a far more radical renovation of existential inference than Kant made. Kant performed part of the common task by rescuing existential propositions from the dialectic of essences. But he failed to criticize Hume's theory of knowledge and existence with anything approaching the thoroughness of his critique of Leibniz and Wolff on this score. Having determined what existence is not, Kant failed to state its positive perfection. His is an existential epistemology without existence, precisely because of its divorce between the knowable object of experience and the existent thing. When realism reintroduces human intelligence to knowledge of existent beings, it bears a threefold fruit. First, it reincorporates epistemology within metaphysics, since existential knowledge is specified primarily by a grasp of the existent thing as existent. Second, it permits existential inference to ground itself in this grasp of the thing in its ultimate act of being, and thus to regulate itself by the distinctive deliverances and implications of the order of existent finite things. Finally, it enables existential demonstration to terminate in knowledge of the truth of our proposition about God's existence, even though an essential vision of the divine act of existing exceeds our ability here on earth. These three consequences of a realistic theory of existential demonstration render unnecessary the alternative of either inserting a special divine gnosis into philosophy or of relapsing into speculative agnosticism concerning the problem of God's existence.

III

Only the briefest mention can be made of our third main problem. The purpose of inquiring about the relation between God and the Hegelian Absolute is to underline the significance of the word "function," as applied to the modern treatment of God. Modern philosophers have taken a thoroughly functional approach to God, attempting to use the doctrine on God as a means of strengthening their own systems. Thus, Spinoza's God performs the systematic office of guaranteeing the objective truth of ideas, securing the continuity of deductive reasoning, and overcoming the inconveniences of Cartesian dualism. Kant's God has a negative role in the speculative order and a positive role in the practical. The idea of God is the supreme test case proving the impotence of pure speculative reason to determine existence in a nonempirical way and hence to construct a metaphysics. In the moral sphere, God does not provide the foundation of Kantian obligation but He does render obligation more meaningful, by making the finite, intelligible self free and immortal and by harmonizing nature and duty. It is in the Hegelian God, however, that the instrumentalist or systematist approach is brought to the climax of subordinating the God of realism and religion to something higher.

Hegel's early theological training introduced him to some unsatisfactory conceptions of God. He found it difficult to reconcile the theological tradition with Kant's glorification of duty for its own sake and with the Graeco-Romantic emphasis upon religious harmony with vital cosmic forces. The only way to synthesize all these currents was to find some position elevated above them all. This Archimedean point proved to be the doctrine on the absolute spirit or thought. In the notion of the absolute, Hegel found the all-inclusive whole by means of which he could criticize and transform other philosophies and traditions. He sometimes referred to his philosophy as the culmination of the Protestant movement, but it was that sort of culminating moment which devours whatever has gone before.

Hegel lauded religion for maintaining the universal actuality of the supreme being. But he deplored the fact that the religious apprehension of the supreme being was expressed under the imperfect form of faith and feeling. Relying upon a mere pictorial representation of the relation between man and God, religion prevented the empirical individual from asserting his dialectical identity with the supreme actuality. Hegel's own philosophy intervened at this point to dissolve the illusion that the finite mind and the divine spirit are irreducibly distinct. His philosophy became the final judge of the true import of religious convictions. The God of religious belief and theistic philosophy was sublated into the absolute of Hegel's idealism. Within the philosophy of the absolute, the finite individual was considered valuable only as being a dialectical aspect of the absolute spirit itself. Thus Hegel used the concept of God as a means of demonstrating the unconditioned truth of his doctrine on the absolute and hence the unquestionable primacy of his philosophy over every other philosophical and religious explanation of being.

From the time of Feuerbach onwards, it has been fashionable for secular humanism to protest against "the tyranny of the absolute." This protest is certainly well made, if it is meant as a criticism of Hegel's dialectical monism of the absolute spirit. But it is often expanded to include a rejection of God and theistic religion, in which extended usage the original protest loses its historical bearings. For secular humanism forgets that the Hegelian absolute is itself at odds with the religious view of God as the supreme personal being, who is the free creator of finite persons and respects their integrity of personal being and freedom. The tyranny of the Hegelian absolute is even more intolerable to the religious believer than to the secular humanist, since it subverts both real terms in the creator-creature relationship. That is why there is an ultimate convergence between religion and theistic metaphysics in the dual affirmation that we can gain some demonstrative knowledge about God's existence and that God's own being is irreducibly distinct from the world. The divine act of existing is reserved from our natural vision and can never properly serve an instrumental function in philosophy.

The negative character of this conclusion may throw some light upon one development in contemporary philosophy. We have seen that each of our representative thinkers misconceived the role of God in philosophy. Spinoza reduced God to a first deductive premise in a monistic determinism. Kant found no way to know God in the speculative order and hence employed Him as a postulate of moral harmony. And Hegel subordinated God to the exigencies of his dialectical absolutism. The unsatisfactory consequences of these typical approaches to God might suggest that the problem of God should be eliminated entirely from philosophy. This is precisely what Heidegger in Germany and Merleau-Ponty in France are now advocating. Their standpoint amounts to a philosophical neutralism, which refrains in principle from making any philosophical pronouncements about God. They claim that both theism and antitheism are non-philosophical doctrines, belonging solely to the theological sphere (in the sense of a revealed theology). They recognize no properly philosophical way of dealing with the question of God's existence, nature and governance of the universe.

But it does not seem to me that there are sufficient historical grounds for accepting this neutral, methodological "a-theism," which seeks •to prescind completely in philosophy from the conflict between theism and antitheism. From the experience of four centuries of modern speculation about God, it can only be concluded that many philosophers have exploited the concept of God unwarrantedly for their own systematic purposes. The trouble does not lie in the fact that they concerned themselves philosophically with the problem of God, but rather in the manner in which they posed this problem and regarded its position within the total system of their philosophy. Hence the historical evidence does not suggest that philosophers should refrain from studying about God but only that they should refrain from making God a mere tool of their own special view of things. More positively expressed, philosophers must come to recognize both that we can demonstrate the truth about God's existence and nature and also that God is the culmination of all our philosophical demonstrations and the goal of our practical strivings. Undoubtedly, this region of inquiry contains more than the average amount of doctrinal pitfalls. But to examine these historical difficulties patiently and illuminate the philosophical route to a sound knowledge of God is surely one of the major responsibilities laid upon those philosophers who are trying to cultivate the resources of St. Thomas within the given context of our age.

ALFRED NORTH WHITEHEAD

GOD AND THE WORLD*

Section I

So long as the temporal world is conceived as a self-sufficient completion of the creative act, explicable by its derivation from an ultimate principle which is at once eminently real and the unmoved mover, from this conclusion there is no escape: the best that we can say of the turmoil is, "For so he giveth his beloved—sleep." This is the message of religions of the Buddhistic type, and in some sense it is true. In this final discussion we have to ask, whether metaphysical principles impose the belief that it is the whole truth. The complexity of the world must be reflected in the answer. It is childish to enter upon thought with the simple-minded question, What is the world made of? The task of reason is to fathom the deeper depths of the many-sidedness of things. We must not expect simple answers to far-reaching questions. However far our gaze penetrates, there are always heights beyond which block our vision.

The notion of God as the "unmoved mover" is derived from Aristotle, at least so far as Western thought is concerned. The The notion of God as "eminently real" is a favourite doctrine of Christian theology. The combination of the two into the doctrine of an aboriginal, eminently real, transcendent creator, at whose fiat the world came into being, and whose imposed will it obeys, is the fallacy which has infused tragedy into the histories of Christianity and of Mahometanism.

When the Western world accepted Christianity, Caesar conquered; and the received text of Western theology was edited by his lawyers. The code of Justinian and the theology of Justinian are two volumes expressing one movement of the human spirit. The brief Galilean vision of humility flickered throughout the ages, uncertainly. In the official formulation of the religion it has assumed the trivial form of the mere attribution to the Jews that they cherished a misconception about their Messiah. But the deeper idolatry, of the fashioning of God in the image of the Egyptian, Persian, and Roman imperial rulers, was retained. The Church gave unto God the attributes which belonged exclusively to Caesar.

In the great formative period of theistic philosophy, which ended with the rise of Mahometanism, after a continuance coeval with civilization, three strains of thought emerge which, amid many variations in detail, respectively fashion God in the image of an imperial ruler, God in the image of a personification of moral energy, God in the image of an ultimate philosophical principle. Hume's *Dialogues* criticize unanswerably these modes of explaining the system of the world.

The three schools of thought can be asso-

* From *Process and Reality: An Essay in Cosmology* by Alfred North Whitehead. New York: The Macmillan Company, 1929. Part V, Chapter II. Reprinted by permission.

ciated respectively with the divine Caesars, the Hebrew prophets, and Aristotle. But Aristotle was antedated by Indian, and Buddhistic, thought; the Hebrew prophets can be paralleled in traces of earlier thought; Mahometanism and the divine Caesars merely represent the most natural, obvious, theistic idolatrous symbolism, at all epochs and places.

The history of theistic philosophy exhibits various stages of combination of these three diverse ways of entertaining the problem. There is, however, in the Galilean origin of Christianity yet another suggestion which does not fit very well with any of the three main strands of thought. It does not emphasize the ruling Caesar, or the ruthless moralist, or the unmoved mover. It dwells upon the tender elements in the world, which slowly and in quietness operate by love; and it finds purpose in the present immediacy of a kingdom not of this world. Love neither rules, nor is it unmoved; also it is a little oblivious as to morals. It does not look to the future; for it finds its own reward in the immediate present.

Section II

Apart from any reference to existing religions as they are, or as they ought to be, we must investigate dispassionately what the metaphysical principles, here developed, require on these points, as to the nature of God. There is nothing here in the nature of proof. There is merely the confrontation of the theoretic system with a certain rendering of the facts. But the unsystematized report upon the facts is itself highly controversial, and the system is confessedly inadequate. The deductions from it in this particular sphere of thought cannot be looked upon as more than suggestions as to how the problem is transformed in the light of that system. What follows is merely an attempt to add another speaker to that masterpiece, Hume's *Dialogues Concerning Natural Religion.* Any cogency of argument entirely depends upon elucidation of somewhat exceptional elements in our conscious experience—those elements which may roughly be classed together as religious and moral intuitions.

In the first place, God is not to be treated as an exception to all metaphysical principles, invoked to save their collapse. He is their chief exemplification.

Viewed as primordial, he is the unlimited conceptual realization of the absolute wealth of potentiality. In this aspect, he is not *before* all creation, but *with* all creation. But, as primordial, so far is he from "eminent reality," that in this abstraction he is "deficiently actual"—and this in two ways. His feelings are only conceptual and so lack the fulness of actuality. Secondly, conceptual feelings, apart from complex integration with physical feelings, are devoid of consciousness in their subjective forms.

Thus, when we make a distinction of reason, and consider God in the abstraction of a primordial actuality, we must ascribe to him neither fulness of feeling, nor consciousness. He is the unconditioned actuality of conceptual feeling at the base of things; so that, by reason of this primordial actuality, there is an order in the relevance of eternal objects to the process of creation. His unity of conceptual operations is a free creative act, untrammelled by reference to any particular course of things. It is deflected neither by love, nor by hatred, for what in fact comes to pass. The *particularities* of the actual world presuppose *it;* while *it* merely presupposes the *general* metaphysical character of creative advance, of which it is the primordial exemplification. The primordial nature of God is the acquirement by creativity of a primordial character.

His conceptual actuality at once exemplifies and establishes the categoreal conditions. The conceptual feelings, which compose his primordial nature, exemplify in their subjective forms their mutual sensitivity and their subjective unity of subjective aim. These subjective forms are valuations determining the relative relevance of eternal objects for each occasion of actuality.

He is the lure for feeling, the eternal urge of desire. His particular relevance to each creative act as it arises from its own conditioned standpoint in the world, constitutes him the initial "object of desire" establishing the initial phase of each subjective aim. A quotation from Aristotle's *Metaphysics*[1] expresses some analogies to, and some differences from, this line of thought: "And since that which is moved and mover is intermediate, there is a mover which moves without

being moved, being eternal, substance, and actuality. And the object of desire and the object of thought are the same. For the apparent good is the object of appetite, and the real good is the primary object of rational desire. But desire is consequent on opinion rather than opinion on desire; for the thinking is the starting point. And thought is moved by the object of thought, and one side of the list of opposites is in itself the object of thought; . . ." Aristotle had not made the distinction between conceptual feelings and the intellectual feelings which alone involve consciousness. But if "conceptual feeling," with its subjective form of valuation, be substituted for "thought," "thinking," and "opinion," in the above quotation, the agreement is exact.

[1] Cf. *Metaphysics* 1072, trans. by Professor W. D. Ross. My attention was called to the appositeness of this particular quotation by Mr. F. J. Carson.

Section III

There is another side to the nature of God which cannot be omitted. Throughout this exposition of the philosophy of organism we have been considering the primary action of God on the world. From this point of view, he is the principle of concretion—the principle whereby there is initiated a definite outcome from a situation otherwise riddled with ambiguity. Thus, so far, the primordial side of the nature of God has alone been relevant.

But God, as well as being primordial, is also consequent. He is the beginning and the end. He is not the beginning in the sense of being in the past of all members. He is the presupposed actuality of conceptual operation, in unison of becoming with every other creative act. Thus by reason of the relativity of all things, there is a reaction of the world on God. The completion of God's nature into a fulness of physical feeling is derived from the objectification of the world in God. He shares with every new creation its actual world; and the concrescent creature is objectified in God as a novel element in God's objectification of that actual world. This

prehension into God of each creature is directed with the subjective aim, and clothed with the subjective form, wholly derivative from his all-inclusive primordial valuation. God's conceptual nature is unchanged, by reason of its final completeness. But his derivative nature is consequent upon the creative advance of the world.

Thus, analogously to all actual entities, the nature of God is dipolar. He has a primordial nature and a consequent nature. The consequent nature of God is conscious; and it is the realization of the actual world in the unity of his nature, and through the transformation of his wisdom. The primordial nature is conceptual, the consequent nature is the weaving of God's physical feelings upon his primordial concepts.

One side of God's nature is constituted by his conceptual experience. This experience is the primordial fact in the world, limited by no actuality which it presupposes. It is therefore infinite, devoid of all negative prehensions. This side of his nature is free, complete, primordial, eternal, actually deficient, and unconscious. The other side originates with physical experience derived from the temporal world, and then acquires integration with the primordial side. It is determined, incomplete, consequent, "everlasting," fully actual, and conscious. His necessary goodness expresses the determination of his consequent nature.

Conceptual experience can be infinite, but it belongs to the nature of physical experience that it is finite. An actual entity in the temporal world is to be conceived as originated by physical experience with its process of completion motivated by consequent, conceptual experience initially derived from God. God is to be conceived as originated by conceptual experience with his process of completion motivated by consequent, physical experience, initially derived from the temporal world.

Section IV

The perfection of God's subjective aim, derived from the completeness of his primordial nature, issues into the character of his consequent nature. In it there is no loss, no obstruction. The world is felt in a unison of immediacy. The property of combining creative advance with the retention of mutual immediacy is what in the previous section is meant by the term "everlasting."

The wisdom of subjective aim prehends every actuality for what it can be in such a perfected system—its sufferings, its sorrows, its failures, its triumphs, its immediacies of joy—woven by rightness of feeling. into the harmony of the universal feeling, which is always immediate, always many, always one, always with novel advance, moving. onward and never perishing. The revolts of destructive evil, purely self-regarding, are dismissed into their triviality of merely individual facts; and yet the good they did achieve in individual joy, in individual sorrow, in the introduction of needed contrast, is yet saved by its relation to the completed whole. The image— and it is but an image—the image under which this operative growth of God's nature is best conceived, is that of a tender care that nothing be lost.

The consequent nature of God is his judgment on the world. He saves the world as it passes into the immediacy of his own life. It is the judgment of a tenderness which loses nothing that can be saved. It is also the judgment of a wisdom which uses what in the temporal world is mere wreckage.

Another image which is also required to understand his consequent nature, is that of his infinite patience. The universe includes a threefold creative act composed of (i) the one infinite conceptual realization, (ii) the multiple solidarity of free physical realizations in the temporal world, (iii) the ultimate unity of the multiplicity of actual fact with the primordial conceptual fact. If we conceive the first term and the last term in their unity over against the intermediate multiple freedom of physical realizations in the temporal world, we conceive of the patience of God, tenderly saving the turmoil of the intermediate world by the completion of his own nature. The sheer force of things lies in the intermediate physical process: this is the energy of physical production. God's rôle is not the combat of productive force with productive force, or destructive force with destructive force; it lies in the patient operation of the overpowering rationality of his conceptual harmonization. He does not create the world, he saves it: or, more accurately, he is the poet of the world, with tender patience leading it by his vision of truth, beauty, and goodness.

Section V

The vicious separation of the flux from the permanence leads to the concept of an entirely static God, with eminent reality, in relation to an entirely fluent world, with deficient reality. But if the opposites, static and fluent, have once been so explained as separately to characterize diverse actualities, the interplay between the thing which is static and the things which are fluent involves contradiction at every step in its explanation. Such philosophies must include the notion of "illusion" as a fundamental principle—the notion of *"mere* appearance." This is the final platonic problem.

Undoubtedly, the intuitions of Greek, Hebrew, and Christian thought have alike embodied the notions of a static God condescending to the world, and of a world *either* thoroughly fluent, *or* accidentaly static, but finally fluent—"heaven and earth shall pass away." In some schools of thought, the fluency of the world is mitigated by the assumption that selected components in the world are exempt from this final fluency, and achieve a static survival. Such components are not separated by any decisive line from analogous components for which the assumption is not made. Further, the survival is construed in terms of a final pair of opposites, happiness for some, torture for others.

Such systems have the common character of starting with a fundamental intuition which we do mean to express, and of entangling themselves in verbal expressions, which carry consequences at variance with the initial intuition of permanence in fluency and of fluency in permanence.

But civilized intuition has always, although obscurely, grasped the problem as double and not as single. There is not the mere problem of fluency *and* permanence. There is the double problem: actuality with permanence, requiring fluency as its completion; and actuality with fluency, requiring permanence as its completion. The first half of the problem concerns the completion of

God's primordial nature by the derivation of his consequent nature from the temporal world. The second half of the problem concerns the completion of each fluent actual occasion by its function of objective immortality, devoid of "perpetual perishing," that is to say, "everlasting."

This double problem cannot be separated into two distinct problems. Either side can only be explained in terms of the other. The consequent nature of God is the fluent world become "everlasting" by its objective immortality in God. Also the objective immortality of actual occasions requires the primordial permanence of God, whereby the creative advance ever re-establishes itself endowed with initial subjective aim derived from the relevance of God to the evolving world.

But objective immortality within the temporal world does not solve the problem set by the penetration of the finer religious intuition. "Everlastingness" has been lost; and "everlastingness" is the content of that vision upon which the finer religions are built—the "many" absorbed everlastingly in the final unity. The problems of the fluency of God and of the everlastingness of passing experience are solved by the same factor in the universe. This factor is the temporal world perfected by its reception and its reformation, as a fulfilment of the primordial appetition which is the basis of all order. In this way God is completed by the individual, fluent satisfactions of finite fact, and the temporal occasions are completed by their everlasting union with their transformed selves, purged into conformation with the eternal order which is the final absolute "wisdom." The final summary can only be expressed in terms of a group of antitheses, whose apparent self-contradiction depend on neglect of the diverse categories of existence. In each antithesis there is a shift of meaning which converts the opposition into a contrast.

It is as true to say that God is permanent

and the World fluent, as that the World is permanent and God is fluent.

It is as true to say that God is one and the World many, as that the World is one and God many.

It is as true to say that, in comparison with the World, God is actual eminently, as that, in comparison with God, the World is actual eminently.

It is as true to say that the World is immanent in God, as that God is immanent in the World.

It is as true to say that God transcends the World, as that the World transcends God.

It is as true to say that God creates the World, as that the World creates God.

God and the World are the contrasted opposites in terms of which Creativity achieves its supreme task of transforming disjoined multiplicity, with its diversities in opposition, into concrescent unity, with its diversities in contrast. In each actuality these are two concrescent poles of realization—"enjoyment" and "appetition," that is, the "physical" and the "conceptual." For God the conceptual is prior to the physical, for the World the physical poles are prior to the conceptual poles.

A physical pole is in its own nature exclusive, bounded by contradiction: a conceptual pole is in its own nature all-embracing, unbounded by contradiction. The former derives its share of infinity from the infinity of appetition; the latter derives its share of limitation from the exclusiveness of enjoyment. Thus, by reason of his priority of appetition, there can be but one primordial nature for God; and, by reason of their priority of enjoyment, there must be one history of many actualities in the physical world.

God and the World stand over against each other, expressing the final metaphysical truth that appetitive vision and physical enjoyment have equal claim to priority in creation. But no two actualities can be torn apart: each is all in all. Thus each temporal occasion embodies God, and is embodied in God. In God's nature, permanence is primordial and flux is derivative from the World: in the World's nature, flux is primordial and permanence is derivative from God. Also the World's nature is a primordial datum for God; and God's nature is a primordial datum for the World. Creation achieves the reconciliation of permanence and flux when it has reached its final term which is everlastingness—the Apotheosis of the World.

Opposed elements stand to each other in mutual requirement. In their unity, they inhibit or contrast. God and the World stand to each other in this opposed requirement. God is the infinite ground of all mentality, the unity of vision seeking physical multiplicity. The World is the multiplicity of finites, actualities seeking a perfected unity. Neither God, nor the World, reaches static completion. Both are in the grip of the ultimate metaphysical ground, the creative advance into novelty. Either of them, God and the World, is the instrument of novelty for the other.

In every respect God and the World move conversely to each other in respect to their process. God is primordially one, namely, he is the primordial unity of relevance of the many potential forms: in the process he acquires a consequent multiplicity, which the primordial character absorbs into its own unity. The World is primordially many, namely, the many actual occasions with their physical finitude; in the process it acquires a consequent unity, which is a novel occasion and is absorbed into the multiplicity of the primordial character. Thus God is to be conceived as one and as many in the converse sense in which the World is to be conceived as many and as one. The theme of Cosmology, which is the basis of all religions, is the story of the dynamic effort of the World passing into everlasting unity, and of the static majesty of God's vision, accomplishing its purpose of completion by absorption of the World's multiplicity of effort.

Section VI

The consequent nature of God is the fulfilment of his experience by his reception of the multiple freedom of actuality into the harmony of his own actualization. It is God as really actual, completing the deficiency of his mere conceptual actuality.

Every categoreal type of existence in the world presupposes the other types in terms of which it is explained. Thus the many eternal objects conceived in their bare isolated multiplicity lack any existent character. They require the transition to the conception of them as efficaciously existent by reason of God's conceptual realization of them.

But God's conceptual realization is nonsense if thought of under the guise of a barren, eternal hypothesis. It is God's conceptual realization performing an efficacious rôle in multiple unifications of the universe, which are free creations of actualities arising out of decided situations. Again this discordant multiplicity of actual things, requiring each other and neglecting each other, utilizing and discarding, perishing and yet claiming life as obstinate matter of fact, requires an enlargement of the understanding to the comprehension of another phase in the nature of things. In this later phase, the many actualities are one actuality, and the one actuality is many actualities. Each actuality has its present life and its immediate passage into novelty; but its passage is not its death. This final phase of passage in God's nature is ever enlarging itself. In it the complete adjustment of the immediacy of joy and suffering reaches the final end of creation. This end is existence in the perfect unity of adjustment as means, and in the perfect multiplicity of the attainment of individual types of self-existence. The function of being a means is not disjoined from the function of being an end. The sense of worth beyond itself is immediately enjoyed as an overpowering element in the individual self-attainment. It is in this way that the immediacy of sorrow and pain is transformed into an element of triumph. This is the notion of redemption through suffering, which haunts the world. It is the generalization of its very minor exemplification as the aesthetic value of discords in art.

Thus the universe is to be conceived as attaining the active self-expression of its own variety of opposites—of its own freedom and its own necessity, of its own multiplicity and its own unity, of its own imperfection and its own perfection. All the "opposites" are elements in the nature of things, and are incorrigibly there. The concept of "God" is the way in which we understand this incredible fact—that what cannot be, yet is.

Section VII

Thus the consequent nature of God is composed of a multiplicity of elements with individual self-realization. It is just as much a multiplicity as it is a unity; it is just as much one immediate fact as it is an unresting advance beyond itself. Thus the actuality of God must also be understood as a multiplicity of actual components in process of creation. This is God in his function of the kingdom of heaven.

Each actuality in the temporal world has its reception into God's nature. The corresponding element in God's nature is not temporal actuality, but is the transmutation of that temporal actuality into a living, ever-present fact. An enduring personality in the temporal world is a route of occasions in which the successors with some peculiar completeness sum up their predecessors. The correlate fact in God's nature is an even more complete unity of life in a chain of elements for which succession does not mean loss of immediate unison. This element in God's nature inherits from the temporal counterpart according to the same principle as in the temporal world the future inherits from the past. Thus in the sense in which the present occasion is the person *now,* and yet with his own past, so the counterpart in God is that person in God.

But the principle of universal relativity is not to be stopped at the consequent nature of God. This nature itself passes into the temporal world according to its gradation of relevance to the various concrescent occasions. There are thus four creative phases in which the universe accomplishes its actuality. There is first the phase of conceptual origination, deficient in actuality, but infinite in its adjustment of valuation. Secondly, there is the temporal phase of physical origination, with its multiplicity of actualities. In this phase full actuality is attained; but there is deficiency in the solidarity of individuals with each other. This phase derives its determinate conditions from the first phase. Thirdly, there is the phase of perfected actuality, in which the many are one everlastingly, without the qualification of any loss either of individual identity or of completeness of unity. In everlastingness, immediacy is reconciled with objective immortality. This phase derives the conditions of its being from the two antecedent phases. In the fourth phase, the creative action completes itself. For the perfected actuality passes back into the temporal world, and qualifies this world so that each temporal actuality includes it as an immediate fact of relevant experience. For the kingdom of heaven is with us today. The action of the fourth phase is the love of God for the world. It is the particular providence for particular occasions. What is done in the world is transformed into a reality in heaven, and the reality in heaven passes back into the world. By reason of this reciprocal relation, the love in the world passes into the love in heaven, and floods back again into the world. In this sense, God is the great companion— the fellow-sufferer who understands.

We find here the final application of the doctrine of objective immortality. Throughout the perishing occasions in the life of each temporal Creature, the inward source of distaste or of refreshment, the judge arising out of the very nature of things, redeemer or goddess of mischief, is the transformation of Itself, everlasting in the Being of God. In this way, the insistent craving is justified— the insistent craving that zest for existence be refreshed by the ever-present, unfading importance of our immediate actions, which perish and yet live for evermore.

ALFRED JULES AYER

CRITIQUE OF THEOLOGY*

It is now generally admitted, at any rate by philosophers, that the existence of a being having the attributes which define the god of any non-animistic religion cannot be demonstratively proved. To see that this is so, we have only to ask ourselves what are the premises from which the existence of such a god could be deduced. If the conclusion that a god exists is to be demonstratively certain, then these premises must be certain; for as the conclusion of a deductive argument is already contained in the premises, any uncertainty there may be about the truth of the premises is necessarily shared by it. But we know that no empirical prop-

* From *Language, Truth and Logic* by Alfred Jules Ayer, pp. 114–120. Reprinted through permission by Dover Publications, Inc., New York 14, New York.

osition can ever be anything more than prob-able. It is only *a priori* propositions that are logically certain. But we cannot deduce the existence of a god from an *a priori* proposi-tion. For we know that the reason why *a priori* propositions are certain is that they are tautologies. And from a set of tautologies nothing but a further tautology can be validly deduced. It follows that there is no possi-bility of demonstrating the existence of a god.

What is not so generally recognized is that there can be no way of proving that the existence of a god, such as the God of Christianity, is even probable. Yet this also is easily shown. For if the existence of such a god were probable, then the proposition that he existed would be an empirical hypoth-esis. And in that case it would be possible to deduce from it, and other empirical hy-potheses, certain experiential propositions which were not deducible from those other hypotheses alone. But in fact this is not possible. It is sometimes claimed, indeed, that the existence of a certain sort of regu-larity in nature constitutes sufficient evidence for the existence of a god. But if the sen-tence "God exists" entails no more than that certain types of phenomena occur in certain sequences, then to assert the existence of a god will be simply equivalent to asserting that there is the requisite regularity in nature; and no religious man would admit that this was all he intended to assert in asserting the existence of a god. He would say that in talking about God, he was talking about a transcendent being who might be known through certain empirical manifestations, but certainly could not be defined in terms of those manifestations. But in that case the term "god" is a metaphysical term. And if "god" is a metaphysical term, then it cannot be even probable that a god exists. For to say that "God exists" is to make a metaphys-ical utterance which cannot be either true or false. And by the same criterion, no sentence which purports to describe the nature of a transcendent god can possess any literal sig-nificance.

It is important not to confuse this view of religious assertions with the view that is adopted by atheists, or agnostics.[1] For it is characteristic of an agnostic to hold that the existence of a god is a possibility in which there is no good reason either to believe or disbelieve; and it is characteristic of an atheist to hold that it is at least probable that no god exists. And our view that all utterances about the nature of God are non-sensical, so far from being identical with, or even lending any support to, either of these familiar contentions, is actually incompatible with them. For if the assertion that there is a god is nonsensical, then the atheist's asser-tion that there is no god is equally non-sensical, since it is only a significant propo-sition that can be significantly contradicted. As for the agnostic, although he refrains from saying either that there is or that there is not a god, he does not deny that the ques-tion whether a transcendent god exists is a genuine question. He does not deny that the two sentences "There is a transcendent god" and "There is no transcendent god" express propositions one of which is actually true and the other false. All he says is that we have no means of telling which of them is true, and therefore ought not to commit our-selves to either. But we have seen that the sentences in question do not express propo-sitions at all. And this means that agnosti-cism also is ruled out.

Thus we offer the theist the same comfort as we gave to the moralist. His assertions cannot possibly be valid, but they cannot be invalid either. As he says nothing at all about the world, he cannot justly be accused of saying anything false, or anything for which he has insufficient grounds. It is only when the theist claims that in asserting the existence of a transcendent god he is express-ing a genuine proposition that we are entitled to disagree with him.

It is to be remarked that in cases where deities are identified with natural objects, assertions concerning them may be allowed to be significant. If, for example, a man tells me that the occurrence of thunder is

---

[1] This point was suggested to me by Professor H. H. Price.

alone both necessary and sufficient to establish the truth of the proposition that Jehovah is angry, I may conclude that, in his usage of words, the sentence "Jehovah is angry" is equivalent to "It is thundering." But in sophisticated religions, though they may be to some extent based on men's awe of natural process which they cannot sufficiently understand, the "person" who is supposed to control the empirical world is not himself located in it; he is held to be superior to the empirical world, and so outside it; and he is endowed with super-empirical attributes. But the notion of a person whose essential attributes are non-empirical is not an intelligible notion at all. We may have a word which is used as if it named this "person," but, unless the sentences in which it occurs express propositions which are empirically verifiable, it cannot be said to symbolize anything. And this is the case with regard to the word "god," in the usage in which it is intended to refer to a transcendent object. The mere existence of the noun is enough to foster the illusion that there is a real, or at any rate a possible entity corresponding to it. It is only when we enquire what God's attributes are that we discover that "God," in this usage, is not a genuine name.

It is common to find belief in a transcendent god conjoined with belief in an after-life. But, in the form which it usually takes, the content of this belief is not a genuine hypothesis. To say that men do not ever die, or that the state of death is merely a state of prolonged insensibility, is indeed to express a significant proposition, though all the available evidence goes to show that it is false. But to say that there is something imperceptible inside a man, which is his soul or his real self, that it goes on living after he is dead, is to make a metaphysical assertion which has no more factual content than the assertion that there is a transcendent god.

It is worth mentioning that, according to the account which we have given of religious assertions, there is no logical ground for antagonism between religion and natural science. As far as the question of truth or falsehood is concerned, there is no opposition between the natural scientist and the theist who believes in a transcendent god. For since the religious utterances of the theist are not genuine propositions at all, they cannot stand in any logical relation to the propositions of science. Such antagonism as there is between religion and science appears to consist in the fact that science takes away one of the motives which make men religious. For it is acknowledged that one of the ultimate sources of religious feeling lies in the inability of men to determine their own destiny; and science tends to destroy the feeling of awe with which men regard an alien world, by making them believe that they can understand and anticipate the course of natural phenomena, and even to some extent control it. The fact that it has recently become fashionable for physicists themselves to be sympathetic towards religion is a point in favour of this hypothesis. For this sympathy towards religion marks the physicists' own lack of confidence in the validity of their hypotheses, which is a reaction of their part from the anti-religious dogmatism of nineteenth-century scientists, and a natural outcome of the crisis through which physics has just passed.

It is not within the scope of this enquiry to enter more deeply into the causes of religious feeling, or to discuss the probability of the continuance of religious belief. We are concerned only to answer those questions which arise out of our discussion of the posibility of religious knowledge. The point which we wish to establish is that there cannot be any transcendent truths of religion. For the sentences which the theist uses to express such "truths" are not literally significant.

An interesting feature of this conclusion is that it accords with what many theists are accustomed to say themselves. For we are often told that the nature of God is a mystery which transcends the human understanding. But to say that something transcends the human understanding is to say that it is unintelligible. And what is unintelligible cannot significantly be described. Again, we are told that God is not an object of reason but an object of faith. This may be nothing more than an admission that the existence of god must be taken on trust, since it cannot be proved. But it may also be an assertion that God is the object of a purely mystical intuition, and cannot therefore be defined in terms which are intelligible to the reason. And I think there are many theists who would assert this. But if one allows that it is impossible to define God in intelligible terms, then one is allowing that it is impossible for a sentence both to be significant and and to be about God. If a mystic admits that the object of his vision is something which cannot be described, then he must also admit that he is bound to talk nonsense when he describes it.

For his part, the mystic may protest that his intuition does reveal truths to him, even though he cannot explain to others what these truths are; and that we who do not possess this faculty of intuition can have no ground for denying that it is a cognitive faculty. For we can hardly maintain *a priori* that there are no ways of discovering true propositions except those which we ourselves employ. The answer is that we set no limit to the number of ways in which one may come to formulate a true proposition. We do not in any way deny that a synthetic truth may be discovered by purely intuitive methods as well as by the rational method of induction. But we do say that every synthetic proposition, however it may have been arrived at, must be subject to the test of actual experience. We do not deny *a priori* that the mystic is able to discover truths by his own special methods. We wait to hear what are the propositions which embody his discoveries, in order to see whether they are verified or confuted by our empirical observations. But the mystic, so far from producing propositions which are empirically verified, is unable to produce any intelligible propositions at all. And therefore we say that his intuition has not revealed to him any facts. It is no use his saying that he has apprehended facts but is unable to express them. For we know that if he really had acquired any information, he would be able

to express it. He would be able to indicate in some way or other how the genuineness of his discovery might be empirically determined. The fact that he cannot reveal what he "knows," or even himself devise an empirical test to validate his "knowledge," shows that his state of mystical intuition is not a genuinely cognitive state. So that in describing his vision the mystic does not give us any information about the external world; he merely gives us indirect information about the condition of his own mind.

These considerations dispose of the argument from religious experience, which many philosophers still regard as a valid argument in favour of the existence of a god. They say that it is logically possible for men to be immediately acquainted with God, as they are immediately acquainted with a sense-content, and that there is no reason why one should be prepared to believe a man when he says that he is seeing a yellow patch, and refuse to believe him when he says that he is seeing God. The answer to this is that if the man who asserts that he is seeing God is merely asserting that he is experiencing a peculiar kind of sense-content, then we do not for a moment deny that his assertion may be true. But, ordinarily, the man who says that he is seeing God is saying not merely that he is experiencing a religious emotion, but also that there exists a transcendent being who is the object of this emotion; just as the man who says that he sees a yellow patch is ordinarily saying not merely that his visual sense-field contains a yellow sense-content, but also that there exists a yellow object to which the sense-content belongs. And it is not irrational to be prepared to believe a man when he asserts the existence of a yellow object, and to refuse to believe him when he asserts the existence of a transcendent god. For whereas the sentence "There exists here a yellow-coloured material thing" expresses a genuine synthetic proposition which could be empirically verified, the sentence "There exists a transcendent god" has, as we have seen, no literal significance.

We conclude, therefore, that the argument

from religious experience is altogether fallacious. The fact that people have religious experiences is interesting from the psychological point of view, but it does not in any way imply that there is such a thing as religious knowledge, any more than our having moral experiences implies that there is such a thing as moral knowledge. The theist, like the moralist, may believe that his experiences are cognitive experiences, but, unless he can formulate his "knowledge" in propositions that are empirically verifiable, we may be sure that he is deceiving himself. It follows that those philosophers who fill their books with assertions that they intuitively "know" this or that moral or religious "truth" are merely providing material for the psychoanalyst. For no act of intuition can be said to reveal a truth about any matter of fact unless it issues in verifiable propositions. And all such propositions are to be incorporated in the system of empirical propositions which constitutes science.

SUGGESTED READINGS

Alexander, Samuel. *Space, Time and Deity*. London: The Macmillan Co., 1920.

Anselm, Saint. *Proslogium,* I-IV; *Monologium*. La Salle, Illinois: The Open Court Publishing Co., 1954.

Aquinas, St. Thomas. *Summa Theologica,* Ia, ii; Ia, xliv–xlix in *The Basic Writings of St. Thomas Aquinas*. New York: Random House, 1954.

Aristotle. *Metaphysics*. New York: Columbia University Press, 1952, Book Lambda.

Bergson, Henri. *Creative Evolution*. New York: Henry Holt and Co., 1911.

Collins, James. "Towards a Realistic Philosophy of God," *God in Modern Philosophy*. Chicago: Henry Regnery Co., 1959.

Descartes, René. *Meditations*. New York: The Liberal Arts Press, 1951, III, V.

Hartshorne, Charles. "Whitehead's Idea of God," in *The Philosophy of Alfred North Whitehead*, ed. Paul Schlipp. New York: Tudor Publishing Co., 1951.

Hocking, William E. *The Meaning of God in Human Experience*. New Haven: Yale University Press, 1912.

Hume, David. *Dialogues Concerning Natural Religion*. New York: Hafner Publishing Co., 1955, Parts I, V, IX.

James, William. *The Varieties of Religious Experience*. New York: Random House, 1902.

Kant, Immanuel. *Critique of Pure Reason*. New York: St. Martin's Press, 1956, "Transcendental Dialectic," Bk. II, Chap. III.

Laird, John. *Theism and Cosmology*. London: G. Allen & Unwin, Ltd., 1940.

Locke, John. *Essay Concerning Human Understanding*. Chicago: Henry Regnery, 1956, Bk. IV, Chap. X.

Lucretius. *On The Nature of Things*. London: Oxford University Press, 1950.

Newton, Sir Isaac. *Sir Isaac Newton's Mathematical Principles of Natural Philosophy and his System of the World,* trans. Andrew Motte, ed. Florian Cajori. Berkeley, California: University of California Press, 1934, pp. 6–12, 543–47.

Spinoza, Benedict de. *Ethics*. New York: St. Martin's Press, 1956, Book I.

Stace, Walter T. *Time and Eternity*. Princeton, N.J.: Princeton University Press, 1952.

INDEX